THE PROPHET MUHAMMAD'S KNOWLEDGE *of* THE UNSEEN

صلی اللہ تعالیٰ علیہ وسلم

THE PROPHET MUHAMMAD'S KNOWLEDGE *of* THE UNSEEN

صلى الله تعالى عليه وسلم

by

QADI YUSUF AL-NABHANI

TRANSLATION & NOTES BY

GIBRIL FOUAD HADDAD

First published in the US by Institute for Spiritual & Cultural Advancement
17195 Silver Parkway #401, Fenton, MI 48430, USA
Tel: (888) 278-6624
Fax:(810) 815-0518
Email: info@sufilive.com
Web: http://www.sufilive.com
Purchase online at: http://www.isn1.net

Amended edition and translation of the chapter on
the Prophet's *'ilm al-ghayb* from the 1317/1899
Beirut edition of al-Nabhani's
ḤUJJATULLĀH 'ALĀ AL-'ĀLAMĪN FĪ MU'JIZĀT SAYYID AL-MURSALĪN
(*The Overwhelming Proof of Allah over the Worlds
in the Stunning Miracles of the Master of Prophets*)

ISBN: 978-1-938058-62-2

Cataloging-in-Publication Data

al-Nabhānī, Yūsuf ibn Ismā'īl, 1849 or 1850-1932.

The Prophet Muḥammad's knowledge of the unseen صلى الله عليه وسلم. Arabic edition and English translation and notes by Gibril Fouad Haddad.
lvi+469p. 23 cm. Index.

1. Muḥammad, Prophet, -632 -- Miracles. 2. Muḥammad, Prophet -- Prophecies. 3. Muḥammad, Prophet -- Companions -- Miracles. 4. Hadith -- texts. 5. Hadith -- Criticism, interpretation, etc. 6. Islam – Doctrines. I. Haddad, Gibril Fouad, 1960- . II. Title. III. Title: *Ḥujjat Allāh 'alā al-ālamīn fī mu'jizāt Sayyid al-Mursalīn* -- excerpts. English and Arabic.

Cover image: Cairo-made *sitāra* of the Ka'ba gifted by Sultan Ahmad I in 1015/1606. Nasser D. Khalili Collection of Hajj and the Arts of Pilgrimage © Nour Foundation.

بسم الله الرحمن الرحيم

This work is humbly dedicated to the memory of my dear Mother, to Mawlana al-Shaykh Nazim al-Haqqani who requested it, to Mawlana Shaykh Hisham Kabbani who made it possible, and to the original compiler, Shaykh Yusuf al-Nabhani, whose *madad* fills it. May Allah bless them and grant them the highest levels!

The translator wishes to thank Dr. Abd al-Malik Horler for his meticulous review of the English text from the beginning of the book to the chapter on al-Harith b. Suwayd during our years in Damascus.

﴿ وَلَوۡلَا فَضۡلُ ٱللَّهِ عَلَيۡكَ وَرَحۡمَتُهُۥ لَهَمَّت طَّآئِفَةٞ مِّنۡهُمۡ أَن
يُضِلُّوكَ وَمَا يُضِلُّونَ إِلَّآ أَنفُسَهُمۡۖ وَمَا يَضُرُّونَكَ مِن شَيۡءٖۚ وَأَنزَلَ
ٱللَّهُ عَلَيۡكَ ٱلۡكِتَٰبَ وَٱلۡحِكۡمَةَ وَعَلَّمَكَ مَا لَمۡ تَكُن تَعۡلَمُۚ وَكَانَ
فَضۡلُ ٱللَّهِ عَلَيۡكَ عَظِيمٗا ﴿١١٣﴾ ﴾ النساء

﴿ وَيَوۡمَ نَبۡعَثُ فِي كُلِّ أُمَّةٖ شَهِيدًا عَلَيۡهِم مِّنۡ أَنفُسِهِمۡۖ وَجِئۡنَا بِكَ
شَهِيدًا عَلَىٰ هَٰٓؤُلَآءِۚ وَنَزَّلۡنَا عَلَيۡكَ ٱلۡكِتَٰبَ تِبۡيَٰنٗا لِّكُلِّ شَيۡءٖ وَهُدٗى
وَرَحۡمَةٗ وَبُشۡرَىٰ لِلۡمُسۡلِمِينَ ﴿٨٩﴾ ﴾ النحل

﴿ عَٰلِمُ ٱلۡغَيۡبِ فَلَا يُظۡهِرُ عَلَىٰ غَيۡبِهِۦٓ أَحَدًا ﴿٢٦﴾ إِلَّا مَنِ ٱرۡتَضَىٰ مِن
رَّسُولٖ فَإِنَّهُۥ يَسۡلُكُ مِنۢ بَيۡنِ يَدَيۡهِ وَمِنۡ خَلۡفِهِۦ رَصَدٗا ﴿٢٧﴾ ﴾ الجن

﴿ مَّا كَانَ ٱللَّهُ لِيَذَرَ ٱلۡمُؤۡمِنِينَ عَلَىٰ مَآ أَنتُمۡ عَلَيۡهِ حَتَّىٰ يَمِيزَ ٱلۡخَبِيثَ مِنَ
ٱلطَّيِّبِۗ وَمَا كَانَ ٱللَّهُ لِيُطۡلِعَكُمۡ عَلَى ٱلۡغَيۡبِ وَلَٰكِنَّ ٱللَّهَ يَجۡتَبِي مِن رُّسُلِهِۦ مَن
يَشَآءُۖ فَـَٔامِنُواْ بِٱللَّهِ وَرُسُلِهِۦۚ وَإِن تُؤۡمِنُواْ وَتَتَّقُواْ فَلَكُمۡ أَجۡرٌ عَظِيمٞ ﴿١٧٩﴾ ﴾
آل عمران

﴿ وَمَا هُوَ عَلَى ٱلۡغَيۡبِ بِضَنِينٖ ﴿٢٤﴾ ﴾ التكوير

﴿ وَأُنَبِّئُكُم بِمَا تَأْكُلُونَ وَمَا تَدَّخِرُونَ فِي بُيُوتِكُمْ إِنَّ فِي ذَٰلِكَ لَآيَةً لَّكُمْ إِن كُنتُم مُّؤْمِنِينَ ﴿٤٩﴾ ﴾ آل عمران

« إِنِّي أَرَى مَا لَا تَرَوْنَ وَأَسْمَعُ مَا لَا تَسْمَعُونَ »

حم ت جه ك طب عن أبي ذر

« قَالَ نَعَمْ إِنِّي لَأُصَدِّقُهُ مَا هُوَ أَبْعَدُ مِنْ ذَلِكَ أُصَدِّقُهُ فِي خَبَرِ السَّمَاءِ فِي غَدْوَةٍ أَوْ رَوْحَةٍ فَلِذَلِكَ سُمِّيَ أَبَا بَكْرٍ الصِّدِّيقَ رَضِيَ اللهُ عَنْهُ »

ك قال صحيح ابن سعد طب وفي مسند الشاميين ابن أبي عاصم في الآحاد

The fact that "the knowledge of the Tablet and the Pen is but part of his sciences" consists in that his sciences are multifarious, including universals and particulars, hidden matters and minutiae, subtle wisdoms and arcane sciences pertaining to the Essence and the Attributes, whereas the science of the Tablet and the Pen are a mere few lines *(suṭūr)* out of the lines of his knowledge and a mere river from the seas of his knowledge. Then, in addition to this, it is from the blessing of his existence according to the report that was said to be transmitted: *The first thing Allah created is my light*, that is, He looked at it with a gaze of majesty, so it cleaved in two, and from its two halves were created the two worlds. This [light] is what is meant by the Pen, hence the transmitted report: *The first thing Allah created is the Pen,* so there is no contradiction. The upshot is: this world and the next are after-effects *(āthār)* of your existence and generosity, and whatever appeared out of the Pen and onto the Tablet is from the secrets of your wisdoms and the lights of your sciences.

Mullā ʿAlī al-Qārī, *al-Zubda fī Sharḥ al-Burda*.[1]

[1]From the ms. copy in the handwriting of the *musnid* Sayyid Muḥammad Ṣāliḥ al-Khaṭīb al-Dimashqī (also containing al-Qārī's two treatises on the *Mawlid*), folios 54b-55a.

"I heard my Shaykh the erudite Imam and Ḥadīth Master Abū al-Ḥajjāj al-Mizzī say—Allah engulf him in His immense mercy—that the first to speak on the subject [of the superiority of the evidentiary miracles of the Prophet Muḥammad ﷺ over those of all previous Prophets ﷺ] was the **Imam Abū ʿAbd Allāh Muḥammad b. Idris al-Shāfiʿī** ﷺ. The Ḥadīth Master Abū Bakr al-Bayhaqī—Allah have mercy on him—narrated in his book *Dalāʾil al-Nubuwwa* from his Shaykh Abū ʿAbd Allāh al-Ḥākim: Abū Aḥmad b. Abī al-Ḥasan told me: ʿAbd al-Raḥmān b. Abī Ḥātim al-Rāzī told us: from his father who said that ʿAmr b. Sawwād [b. al-Aswad b. ʿAmr al-ʿAmiri al-Baṣrī (d. 245)] said that al-Shāfiʿī said: 'All that Allah gave to the Prophets he also gave to Muḥammad ﷺ.' ʿAmr said: 'He granted ʿĪsā ﷺ [the power] to resurrect the dead.' Al-Shāfiʿī replied: 'He gave Muḥammad ﷺ the tree-stump beside which he used to address the people, and when a pulpit was built for him [and he moved away], the stump began to moan until its voice was heard by all: this is a greater miracle than that.' These were his very words."

Ibn Kathīr, *al-Bidāya wal-Nihāya*
(Turāth ed. 6:289=Maʿārif ed. 6:258).

O our Master, O Messenger of Allah!
You are the goal of existence
and the Master of every begetter and offspring.
You are the truly unique, unflawed jewel
around which revolve the totality of created things.
You are the light whose rising has filled the earths and heavens.
Your blessings cannot be numbered.
Your stunning miracles also elude count.
The stones and the trees greeted you.
Mute animals spoke before you.
Pure water gushed and ran from your fingers.
The tree-stump wept when you left it.
The salt well became sweet with one spit from your lips.
Through your blessed apostleship we were forever spared disfiguration into beasts,
being swallowed by the earth,
and eternal punishment.
And with your thorough mercy all kinds of kindness encompass us
until the veil becomes lifted.

Muḥammad al-Rawwās, *Bawāriq al-Ḥaqq* (p. 339).

I yearn to see the one whom Allah created
To be unique in creation!
No beloved one is purer nor more elevated than this one.
The Beloved of Allah is His servant, the Praised One
Whose name was cut out from the name
Of the Most Glorious One!
His are the attributes that no eloquence can express.
It is enough honor that for him the moon split in two.
What more do you ask than that Allah perfected his beauty?
And verily Allah endowed him with the best character.
And verily Allah created his light to be the greatest blessing,
and He called him "Beloved" before He created creation!
And because of his light the sun was clouded over,
Because of his overwhelming light filling the firmament!
The clouds showed a great miracle and moved
Like a wild herd,
And thunder clapped and rain poured
Upon his mere request.
What more do you want than the softening of the rock
When he walked upon it with his sandaled feet,
Although you did not see its marks
When he trod on the sand?
Allah has elevated him to His presence
Above the Angelic world.
Were it not for him, there would never be Paradise,
Nor heavens, and no earth!
What an honor Allah bestowed upon him when He gave
Ten salutations to those who would
Send to him only one!

al-Ḥāfiẓ Wajīh al-Dīn Ibn al-Dayba'ī (d. 944)

CONTENTS

Dedication v
Epigraphs vii
Remarks on Style xv
Abbreviations / الرموز xvii
Glossary xix
Hadith Sources and Gradings xxi
  Earliest *Sīra*s xxi
  al-Wāqidī xxii
  Sayf b. ʿUmar xxii
  The Hadiths cited herein xxiii
  Forgeries xxiv
  Nabhāni's respect for Hadith xxvi
Transmission chains; *duʿā'* xxvii
Life and Works of Nabhānī xxix
  His teachers xxx
  Descriptive bibliography xxxiii
  "I am the Prophet's slave" xlvi
  Nabhāni's grave in Beirut lv-lvi
Nabhānī's Preface 1
  Superiority of the Prophet ﷺ 2
  Sources 6
  Muʿjiza; supernatural wonders 7
The Unseen besides the Hour 25
Important note: this is a glimpse 35
Unseen of some Companions 36
Abū Bakr 36
Abū Bakr and ʿUmar 37
Abū Bakr, ʿUmar, ʿUthmān 38
Abū Bakr, ʿUmar, ʿAlī 45
Abū Bakr, ʿUmar, ʿUthmān, ʿAlī 46
The Four, Ṭalḥa and al-Zubayr 47
ʿUmar 47
ʿUthmān 51
ʿAlī 59
Fāṭima 76
al-Ḥasan b. ʿAlī 77
al-Ḥusayn b. Alī 78
ʿĀʾisha 84
Umm Salama 88
Zaynab 89
Maymūna 90
Rayḥāna 90
al-Zubayr b. al-ʿAwwām 91
Saʿd b. Abī Waqqāṣ 94
ʿAbd al-Raḥmān b. ʿAwf 96
Jaʿfar, Zayd, and Ibn Rawāḥa 97
al-ʿAbbās b. ʿAbd al-Muṭṭalib 111
His wife Umm al-Faḍl 113
ʿAbd Allāh b. ʿAbbās 115
Nawfal b. al-Ḥārith 118
ʿAbd Allāh b. Masʿūd 119
ʿAmmār b. Yāsir 120
ʿAyyāsh b. Abī Rabīʿa 124
Ṣuhayb 126
Abū Dharr 128
Abū al-Dardāʾ 137
Ḥāṭib b. Abī Baltaʿa 139
ʿAbd Allāh b. Salām 143
The Anṣār 144
Thābit b. Qays 147
Zayd b. Arqam 147
Muʿādh b. Jabal 148
al-Barāʾ b. Mālik 150
al-Nuʿmān b. Bashīr 151
ʿAbd Allāh b. Unays 153
ʿUmayr b. ʿAdī 156
Abū Qatāda 158
Rāfiʿ b. Khadīj 162
Abū Saʿīd al-Khudrī 163
Abū Khaythama 164
Khālid b. al-Walīd 165
ʿAmr b. Sālim al-Khuzāʿī 171
ʿUmayr b. Wahb al-Jumaḥī 176
ʿAmr b. al-ʿĀṣ 178
Abū Mūsā al-Ashʿarī 179
Abū Hurayra, Samura 181
ʿAttāb, Jubayr, Ḥakīm, Suhayl 187
Suhayl b. ʿAmr 188
Abū Sufyān b. Ḥarb 191
Muʿāwiya b. Abī Sufyān 199
ʿIkrima b. Abī Jahl 205
ʿUthmān b. Ṭalḥa 205
Shayba b. ʿUthmān b. Ṭalḥa 207
Tamīm al-Dārī 214
ʿAbd Allāh b. Busr 218
ʿUrwa b. Masʿūd al-Thaqafī 219
Jarīr b. ʿAbd Allāh al-Bajalī 223
Zayd al-Khayr 225
Wāʾil b. Ḥujr 226
Ṣurad b. ʿAbd Allāh al-Azdī 226
Ḥārith, Juwayriya's father 229
ʿAdī b. Ḥātim 230

ʿAmr b. al-Ghafwāʾ 235
al-Ḥārith b. Sawāʾ 237
Masʿūd b. al-Ḍaḥḥāk 238
Ḥabīb b. Maslama al-Fihrī 239
Surāqa b. Mālik 240
Qudad or Qudar b. ʿAmmār 241
Dhūl-Jawshan 242
Abū Ṣufra 244
Ḥārith b. ʿAbd Kulāl 245
Umm Waraqa 246
Wābisat al-Asadī 247
Qays b. Kharasha 250
Abū Rayḥāna 251
ʿAmr b. al-Ḥamiq 252
Aqraʿ b. Shufay al-ʿAkkī 253
al-Nuḍayr b. al-Ḥārith 254
Qabāth b. Ashyam 256
Muʿāwiya al-Laythī 258
ʿAwf b. Mālik al-Ashjaʿī 261
The ʿAbd al-Qays delegation 263
A desert Arab Companion 270
A hypocrite who repented 272
al-Ḥārith b. Suwayd 277
an Anṣārī and a Thaqafī 281
ʿUyayna b. Ḥiṣn al-Fazārī 283
Quraysh Badr defeat foretold 284
Worms eat Quraysh's charter 305
Conquest of nations and cities 315
Chosroes, Caesar, Persia, Rome 331
Ḥārith b. Abī Shimr al-Ghassānī 346
A pagan leader destroyed 348
Jazʾ b. Suhayl al-Sulamī 349
Persia and Rome continued 351
Mafrūq b. ʿAmr, Ibn Qubaysa 352
Khuraym b. Uways b. Ḥāritha 355
Persia and Rome continued 360
Prediction of Muslim empire 375
Prediction of caliphs and kings 382
Prediction of the Umayyads 392
Prediction of the Abbasids 408
Other unseen matters predicted 416

Bibliography 441
Hadith Index 447

Remarks on Style and the Arabic text

Text in square brackets [ ] marks out glosses, explanatory notes, or other types of additions that are not part of the original text. For example: “The Prophet ﷺ stood among us [speaking] for a long time and did not leave out one thing from that time until the rising of the Final Hour.” **Acute brackets** < > mark out variant wordings, completions, correctives, or other original segments omitted by al-Nabhānī. For example, “My beloved, the Messenger of Allah ﷺ, informed me that the rebellious faction shall kill me <and that my last meal on earth shall be a drink of diluted milk>.’” **Numbers in bold square brackets [ ]** mark out the page number in the original Beirut: al-Maṭba‘at al-Adabiyya 1316/1898 one-volume lithographic 900-page edition of al-Nabhānī’s work.

Dates in the main text and footnotes are usually Hijrī while publication dates in the bibliography are usually Gregorian.

The attribution of a report to “Jābir” in short refers, in ḥadīth convention, to Jābir b. ʿAbd Allāh b. ʿAmr al-Anṣārī ؓ among the thirty-odd Companions named Jābir. Qāḍī al-Nabhānī’s frequent reference to “Abū Nuʿaym” is to the major ḥadīth Master Abū Nuʿaym al-Aṣbahānī’s *Dalā’il al-Nubuwwa* which, unlike his masterpiece *Ḥilyat al-Awliyā’*, has not been published in full to date; the single volume published by Dār al-Nafā’is in Beirut under the title *Dalā’il al-Nubuwwa*, edited by Muḥammad Qalʿajī and ʿAbd al-Barr ʿAbbās, is in fact—by their own admission in the introduction—a digest known as the *Muntakhab min Dalā’il al-Nubuwwa*. The three-volume Mecca edition entitled *Dalā’il al-Nubuwwa* is also an incomplete version. Imam al-Suyūṭī apparently had access to the full *Dalā’il* and the Qāḍī relied wholly on his two-volume *al-Khaṣā’iṣ al-Nabawiyya al-Kubrā* for referencing to that work. The Qāḍī’s equally frequent unqualified reference to al-Bayhaqī is to his identically-titled six-volume masterpiece *Dalā’il al-Nubuwwa* (Dār al-Kutub al-ʿIlmiyya) also on the basis of al-Suyūṭī’s referencing in the *Khaṣā’iṣ*. As the Qāḍī said, “[*al-Khaṣā’iṣ*] is the largest and most valuable source of the present work and the most comprehensive of all the books that were compiled on this subject except for the present work.”

When the Qāḍī cites the weaker version of an authentic ḥadīth I point this out in the footnote and provide the Arabic text of the best version unless al-Nabhānī cites it elsewhere. An example of this is the ḥadith al-Nabhānī cites "from Abū al-Ashhab, from a man of Muzayna, that the Prophet ﷺ said, '‘Umar! wear new clothes, live a blameless life, and die a martyr!'" This is a weak *mursal* chain – Abū al-Ashhab never met the Companions – found in Ibn Sa‘d and Ibn Abī Shayba, while the established version has a *musnad* chain from Ibn ‘Umar narrated in Ibn Mājah, Aḥmad, and others. I cited the latter version in Arabic.[2] Similarly when he merely cites the paraphrase from the *Khaṣā'iṣ*, I usually cite the original text in fuller form.

[2]See hadīth at note 99.

Abbreviations

ʿAbd al-Razzāq = ʿAbd al-Razzāq's *Muṣannaf* in Ḥ. al-Aʿẓamī's 11-volume edition.
Abū Dāwūd = Abū Dāwūd's *Sunan.*
Abū Nuʿaym = Abū Nuʿaym's *Ḥilyat al-Awliyā'*. See also Remarks on Style.
Abū Yaʿlā = Abū Yaʿlā's *Musnad.*
Aḥmad = Aḥmad's *Musnad* in Shuʿayb al-Arna'ūṭ's 50-volume Mu'assasat al-Risāla ed.
Al-Bayhaqī, see Remarks on Style.
Al-Bazzār = al-Bazzār's *Musnad.*
Bidāya = Ibn Kathīr's *al-Bidāya wal-Nihāya* in the 14-volume Dār al-Maʿārif edition.
al-Bukhārī = al-Bukhārī's *Ṣaḥīḥ.*
al-Dārimī = al-Dārimī's *Musnad*, also known as his *Sunan.*
Fatḥ, Fatḥ al-Bārī = Ibn Ḥajar's work in the 13-volume 1959 ʿAbd al-Bāqī edition.
Fayḍ, Fayḍ al-Qadīr = al-Munāwī's work in the original Cairo 6-volume edition.
al-Ḥākim = al-Ḥākim's *Mustadrak* in the original 4-volume Hyderabad edition.
al-Haythamī = al-Haythamī's *Majmaʿ al-Zawā'id* in the 10-volume Cairo/Beirut edition.
Ibn Abī Shayba = Ibn Abī Shayba's *Muṣannaf* in Kamāl al-Ḥūt's 7-volume edition.
Ibn ʿAsākir = Ibn ʿAsākir's *Tārīkh Dimashq* in the 70-volume Dār al-Fikr edition.
Ibn Ḥibbān = *Ṣaḥīḥ Ibn Ḥibbān* in the 18-volume Risāla edition.
Ibn Hishām = Ibn Hishām's *Sīra* in the 6-volume Dār al-Jīl edition.
Ibn Isḥāq = Ibn Isḥāq's *Sīra* (also titled *al-Maghāzī*) in Ḥamīdullāh's edition.
Ibn Khuzayma = Ibn Khuzayma's *Ṣaḥīḥ* in M. al-Aʿẓamī's 4-volume edition.
Ibn Mājah = Ibn Mājah's *Sunan.*
Ibn Qāniʿ = Ibn Qāniʿ's *Muʿjam al-Ṣaḥāba.*
Ibn Saʿd = Ibn Saʿd's *al-Ṭabaqāt al-Kubrā* in the 8-volume Dār Ṣādir edition.
Iktifā' = al-Kilāʿī's *al-Iktifā' bimā Taḍammanahu min Maghāzī Rasūlillāh.*
Iṣāba = Ibn Ḥajar's *al-Iṣāba fī Tamyīz al-Ṣaḥāba* in the 8-volume Dār al-Jīl edition.
Istīʿāb = Ibn ʿAbd al-Barr's *al-Istīʿāb fī Maʿrifat al-Aṣḥāb* in the 8-volume Dār al-Jīl ed.
al-Jāmiʿ al-Saghīr = al-Suyūṭī's work in the standard 10,031-ḥadīth numbering.
Kāmil = Ibn ʿAdī's *al-Kāmil fī Ḍuʿafā' al-Rijāl* in the Dār al-Fikr 7-volume edition.
Kanz = al-Muttaqī al-Hindī's *Kanz al-ʿUmmāl.*
Khaṣā'iṣ = al-Suyūṭī's *al-Khaṣā'iṣ al-Kubrā.*
al-Khaṭīb = al-Khaṭīb al-Baghdādī's *Tārīkh Baghdād*
Mīzān = al-Dhahabī's *Mīzān al-Iʿtidāl*, mostly in the 8-volume ʿIlmiyya edition.
Yāqūt = Yāqūt al-Ḥamawī's *Muʿjam al-Buldān.*
Muslim = Muslim's *Ṣaḥīḥ.*
al-Nasā'ī = al-Nasā'ī's ("Minor") *Sunan* (*al-Mujtabā*).
Naṣb = al-Zaylaʿī's *Naṣb al-Rāya.*
Nayl = al-Shawkānī's *Nayl al-Awṭār.*
Rawḍ = al-Suhaylī's *al-Rawḍ al-Unuf.*
Ṣifat al-Ṣafwa = Ibn al-Jawzī's *Ṣifat al-Ṣafwa.*
Tarātīb = al-Kattānī's *al-Tarātīb al-Idāriyya* in the Dār al-Kitāb al-ʿArabī edition.
al-Tirmidhī = al-Tirmidhī's *Sunan.*
al-ʿUqaylī = al-ʿUqaylī's *al-Ḍuʿafā' min al-Ruwāt* in the 4-volume Qalʿajī edition.
al-Wāqidī = al-Wāqidī's *Maghāzī* in Marsden Jones' 3-volume edition.
Zād = Ibn al-Qayyim's *Zād al-Maʿād.*

الرموز

ت	سنن الترمذي
تهذيب	تهذيب الكمال للمزي
جه	سنن ابن ماجه
حم	مسند أحمد
خ	صحيح البخاري
خت	التاريخ الكبير للبخاري
خد	الأدب المفرد للبخاري
خز	صحيح ابن خزيمة
خصائص	الخصائص الكبرى للسيوطي
خط	تاريخ الخطيب
د	سنن أبي داود
ز	مسند البزار
ش	مصنف ابن أبي شيبة
ض	الأحاديث المختارة للضياء المقدسي
ط	مسند أبي داود الطيالسي
طأ	الموطأ
طب طس طص	المعجم الكبير والأوسط والصغير للطبراني
ع	مسند أبي يعلى
عد	الكامل في الضعفاء لإبن عدي
عق	مصنف عبد الرزاق
فتح	فح الباري للحافظ ابن حجر
ق	متفق عليه
قط	سنن الدارقطني
ك	مستدرك الحاكم
م	صحيح مسلم
مج	مجمع الزوائد للهيثمى
مى	سنن الدارمى
ميزان	ميزان الإعتدال في نقد الرجال للذهبي
ن	سنن النسائى الصغرى (المجتبى)
هب	شعب الإيمان للبيهقى
هق	السنن الكبرى للبيهقى

Glossary

mursal pl. ***marāsīl*** "Dispatched." Said of a type of broken-chained ḥadīth or its chain when it is missing the link of the Companion that narrated it from the Prophet ﷺ or the link of the Successor or both. By extension, any ḥadīth attributed to the Prophet ﷺ without its nearest links. Antonyms: *musnad*, *mawṣūl*, and *muttaṣil*.

musnad pl. ***masānīd*** "Supported." A narration backed by a continuous narrative chain going back to the Prophet ﷺ, unlike the ***mursal***. With a capital, a compilation of such narrations. In construct with the name of a Companion or later narrator(s), it denotes the collected set of the reports from that narrator or group.

mutawātir "Mass-narrated." Applies to sound ḥadīths which have, at each link of the transmission chain, a number of narrators such as would preclude collusion and collective fabrication on their part. The determination of that number varies among the Scholars of ḥadīth. Al-Suyūṭī considers they must be at least ten at each link of the chain but the determining factor is the conclusiveness of a high number rather than a specific count. See ***ṣaḥīḥ***.

ṣaḥīḥ pl. ***ṣiḥāḥ*** "Sound." The highest degree of authentication for a ḥadīth – second only to mass-transmitted *(mutawātir)* narrations – or of its chains of transmission. In rare cases, the chain alone can be sound but not the ḥadīth itself, or, less rarely, vice-versa, as a sound ḥadīth can also be narrated through a defective chain. With a capital, a compilation of such ḥadīths such as those of al-Bukhārī and Muslim, Abū 'Awāna's *Musnad*, Ibn Khuzayma, Ibn Ḥibbān, al-Ḥākim's *al-Mustadrak 'alā al-Ṣaḥīḥayn*, Ibn al-Sakan's *al-Aḥādīth al-Ṣiḥāḥ* (which Ibn Ḥazm placed third after the two *Saḥīḥ*s in terms of strength and reliability according to al-Dhahabī in *Tadhkirat al-Ḥuffāẓ*), Ibn al-Jārūd's *al-Muntaqā min al-Sunan al-Musnada*, and al-Ḍiyā' al-Maqdisī's *al-Aḥādīth al-Mukhtāra*. Also of that caliber of authenticity is Ibn al-Qaṭṭān al-Fāsīi's *Bayān al-Wahm wal-Īhām al-Wāqi'īna fī Kitāb al-Aḥkām*. The term *al-Ṣiḥāḥ al-Sitta* or "Six *Ṣaḥīḥ*s" is loosely applied to the whole formed by the first two together with the four major books of *Sunan* (al-Tirmidhī, Abū Dāwūd, al-Nasā'ī, and Ibn Mājah, the latter sometimes replaced by Mālik's *Muwaṭṭa'* or al-Dārimī's *Sunan*).

Note on Ḥadīth Sources and Gradings

Among the extant manuscripts of the numerous ḥadīth collections compiled in the earliest Hijrī centuries are ʿAbd Allāh b. ʿAmr b. al-ʿĀṣ' (d. 63) *al-Ṣaḥīfa al-Ṣādiqa*, originally containing about 1,000 ḥadīths of which 500 reached us, copied down by him directly from the Prophet ﷺ and transmitted to us by his great-grandson ʿAmr b. Shuʿayb (d. 118); Hammām b. Munabbih's (d. 101 or 131) *Ṣaḥīfa Ṣaḥīḥa* which has reached us complete in two manuscripts containing 138 ḥadīths narrated by Hammām from Abū Hurayra (d. 60) from the Prophet ﷺ; and the massive, partly-recovered second Hijrī century *Muṣannaf* of the Yemenite ḥadīth Master ʿAbd al-Razzāq b. Hammām b. Nāfiʿ al-Ṣanʿānī (d. 211), which includes the compendium of his teacher Maʿmar b. Rāshid al-Azdī (d. 151 or 154) – both principal sources of the Two Arch-Imams al-Bukhārī and Muslim in their *Ṣaḥīḥ*s – and is, with its 21,000+ narrations, the largest authentic early source of ḥadīth extant.

Earliest *Sīra*s

The earliest *Sīra*s or Prophetic biographies are the lost folios of Abān (d. 105), the son of ʿUthmān b. ʿAffān ؓ (d. 35), from whom Muḥammad b. Isḥāq b. Yasār al-Muṭṭalibī (80-150/152) narrated; the accomplished works of ʿUrwa (d. ~92-95) – the son of al-Zubayr b. al-ʿAwwām and Asmā' and nephew of ʿĀ'isha the learned daughters of Abū Bakr the Truthful ؓ – which he ordered burnt after a lifetime of teaching from them, during the sack of Madīna by the armies of Syro-Palestine under Yazīd b. Muʿāwiya in 63; the most reliable Muḥammad b. Shihāb al-Zuhrī's (d. 120) *Sīra*, from which Ibn Isḥāq borrowed much; ʿĀṣim b. ʿUmar b. Qatāda b. al-Nuʿmān al-Anṣārī's (d. 120 or 129) *Maghāzī* and *Manāqib al-Ṣaḥāba*, another principal *thiqa* source for Ibn Isḥāq and al-Wāqidī; ʿAbd Allāh b. Abī Bakr b. Muḥammad b. ʿAmr b. Ḥazm al-Anṣārī's (d. 135) tome, another main source for Ibn Isḥāq, al-Wāqidī, Ibn Saʿd, and al-Ṭabarī; the most reliable *Sīra* of the Madīnan Mūsā b. ʿUqba al-Asadī (d. 141), praised by Imam Mālik and used by Ibn Saʿd and al-Ṭabarī; Muḥammad b. Isḥāq's *Sīra*, praised by Imam al-Shāfiʿī, the oldest extant; Ibn ʿĀ'idh al-Azdī's

(d. 191) *Maghāzī*; Sayf b. ʿUmar al-Tamīmī's (d. 200) *al-Ridda wal-Futūḥ* and *al-Jamal* as per Ibn Ḥajar in *Tahdhīb al-Tahdhīb*.

al-Wāqidī

Imam Aḥmad said that Muḥammad b. ʿUmar b. Wāqid al-Aslamī al-Wāqidī (d. 207) was an "expert in the battles and campaigns" but "haphazard in assigning his chains of transmission." His rank as a ḥadīth narrator varies from "very weak" *(daʿīf jiddan)* to "fair" *(ḥasan)*. Ibn Taymiyya asserts, "No two people differ over the fact that Wāqidī is among the most knowledgeable of authorities in the details of military campaigns and among the best experts in all that pertains to them" while al-Dhahabī said, "There is no disagreement over the fact that he is weak, but he is honest and very valuable" and he is declared reliable by Ibn Sayyid al-Nās, al-ʿAynī, Ibn al-ʿArabī, Ibn Daqīq al-ʿĪd, Ibn al-Humām, and others.[3] A junior contemporary of Ibn Isḥāq, al-Wāqidī is Imam al-Ṭabarī's (d. 310) principal source in the latter's *Tārīkh* and his student and scribe Muḥammad b. Saʿd (d. 230) relied heavily on him in his *Ṭabaqāt*.

Sayf b. ʿUmar

Sayf b. ʿUmar is discarded (*matrūk*) in hadith but retained for history like al-Waqīdī, though not as strong. Al-Ṭabarī uses him but may be distancing himself from him when he says in his *Tārīkh*, "according to Sayf b. ʿUmar and his *riwāya*" (2:476 -477), "as for Sayf b. ʿUmar he says..." (2:511, 2:535), "according to what Sayf b. ʿUmar says" (2:608). Ibn Kathīr also relies on him very much in *al-Bidāya wal-Nihāya* as does Ibn Ḥajar in the *Iṣāba*. The latter said in the *Taqrīb* that Sayf was "weak in hadith but a pillar of reliance (*ʿumda*) in history." Dr. Nūr al-Din ʿItr in his notes on Ibn Rajab's *Sharh ʿIlal al-Tirmidhī* (2:554-555) includes him in the type of "Those that were declared weak in certain subjects and not others. This applies to those that devoted themselves to a certain discipline then went into other than it, such as,

[3]Cf. Abū Ghudda, *Thalāth Rasāʾil fī ʿIlm Mustalaḥ al-Ḥadīth* (p. 124-125 n.), marginalia on al-Ḥāzimī's *Shurūt al-Aʾimma*, and Ibn Taymiyya, *al-Sārim al-Maslūl* (p. 97).

in the *qirā'āt*, ʿĀṣim... or in history Ibn Isḥāq.... and Sayf." Al-Dhahabī calls him a "master chronicler" (*akhbarī ʿārif*). Ibn Ḥajar rejects Ibn Ḥibbān's report that Sayf was accused of heresy (*zandaqa*) and ʿItr points out in his notes on al-Dhahabī's *Mughnī* that Sayf's reports point to anything but *zandaqa*.

Authenticity of the hadiths cited in this book

The vast majority of the ḥadīths contained in this book are authentic. Care was taken to document every text attributed to the Prophet ﷺ as well as Companion-reports and later reports. The ḥadīths of the Two *Ṣaḥīḥ*s – by the Arch-Masters al-Bukhārī (194-256) and Muslim (204-261) – and the *Muwaṭṭa'* of Imam Mālik (93-179) are sound and need no further authentication. Next in reliability come the *Sunan* of the major Masters al-Tirmidhī (c.210-279), Abū Dāwūd (202-275), al-Nasā'ī (215-303), al-Dārimī (181-250), and Ibn Mājah (209-273) as well as the *Musnad* of Imam Aḥmad b. Ḥanbal (164-241). Next come the lesser collections of *Ṣaḥīḥ* narrations such as – in descending order of strength – the *Ṣaḥīḥ* of Ibn Khuzayma (223-311), three quarters of which are lost; that of his student Ibn Ḥibbān (d.354); al-Ḍiyā' al-Maqdisī's (567-643) *al-Aḥādīth al-Jiyād al-Mukhtāra*; Ibn al-Sakan's (294-353) *al-Sunan al-Ṣiḥāḥ*; Ibn al-Jārūd's (d. 307) *al-Muntaqā min al-Sunan al-Musnada*; Abū ʿAwāna's (d. 316) *Musnad*; and al-Ḥākim's (321-405) *Mustadrak*. Next come – in chronological order – the compilations of Abū Dāwūd al-Ṭayālisī (d. 204), Musaddad (150-228), Ibn Abī Shayba (d. 235), Ibn Abī al-Dunyā (208-281), Ibn Qutayba (213-276), Ibn Abī ʿĀṣim (d. 287), al-Ḥārith b. Abī Usāma (d. 282), al-Bazzār (215-292), Abū Yaʿlā (210-307), al-Ṭaḥāwī (229-321), the Narrator of the World al-Ṭabarānī (260-360), al-Dāraquṭnī (306-385), Abū Nuʿaym (336-430), al-Bayhaqī (384-458), Ibn ʿAbd al-Barr (368-463), al-Khaṭīb al-Baghdādī (392-463), al-Baghawī (d. 516), Ibn ʿAsākir (499-571), and others including the *Sīra* sources already mentioned.

For all those ḥadīths, the indications of the early and modern reliable authorities were scrupulously sought and cited wherever possible. I have used the verdicts of Imam Shihāb al-Dīn al-Būṣīrī on Ibn Mājah; those of the Imam of complete Mastership al-

Dhahabī on al-Ḥākim and others; those of the Imam Abū al-Faḍl Zayn al-Dīn al-'Irāqī's two foremost disciples, Imam Nūr al-Dīn al-Haythamī with his many books of *Zawā'id* on Aḥmad, Ṭabarānī, Abū Ya'lā, al-Bazzār and Ibn Ḥibbān, and the Shaykh al-Islām and Imam of Ḥadīth Mastership, the Commander of the Believers in Ḥadīth, Ibn Ḥajar al-'Asqalānī in his monumental *Fatḥ al-Bārī* and his books of *Amālī*. Among the modern scholars, Ḥusayn Salīm Asad on Abū Ya'lā and Ibn Ḥibbān; Shu'ayb al-Arna'ūṭ on Aḥmad, al-Ṭaḥāwī, al-Baghawī and Ibn Ḥibbān; 'Abd Allāh al-Luḥaydān on al-Ḥākim; and Khaldūn al-Aḥdab on al-Khaṭīb.

Forgeries

A negligible amount of forgeries were identified and flagged. By consensus it is forbidden to use or narrate forgeries as Prophetic reports. Knowledge of forgeries is an indispensable part of ḥadīth science. The peerless Imam of the Sunna, al-Bayhaqī, pledged that none of his works contained a single narration he knew was a forgery. The guideline in this is the verdict of the authorities in this science. The Prophet ﷺ said: **"Avoid relating my words except what you know for sure. Whoever lies about me willfully, let him take from now his seat in the Fire!"**[4] This terrible threat addresses not only wilful liars but also "well-intentioned" Muslims who, in the course of *da'wa*, are habitually lax in attributing to the Prophet ﷺ untraceable or unverified matters. To them, their good intentions are law over and above the emphatic command of the Holy Prophet ﷺ. We belong to Allah and to Him do we return!

عَنِ ابْنِ عَبَّاسٍ رَضِيَ اللهُ عَنْهُمَا عَنِ النَّبِيِّ ﷺ قَالَ اتَّقُوا الْحَدِيثَ عَنِّي إِلاَّ مَا عَلِمْتُمْ فَمَنْ كَذَبَ عَلَيَّ مُتَعَمِّدًا فَلْيَتَبَوَّأْ مَقْعَدَهُ مِنَ النَّارِ ت حسّنه حم وشطره الأخير متواتر متفق عليه

[4]Narrated from Ibn 'Abbās by Aḥmad with three chains, al-Tirmidhī *(ḥasan)*, and – with a sound chain – Ibn Abī Shayba. The second sentence is a mass-narrated *(mutawātir)* Prophetic ḥadīth from no less than 100 Companions per al-Kattānī, *Naẓm al-Mutanāthir*.

In all this the reliance is upon Allah ﷻ then upon the Prophet ﷺ who said: "When you hear a ḥadīth reported from me which your hearts recognize, at which your hair and skin become tender, and you feel it is near to you: know that I am the nearest of you to it. And when you hear a ḥadīth reported from me of which your hearts disapprove, from which your hair and skin recoil, and you feel it is far from you: know that I am the farthest among you from it."[5]

عَنْ أَبِي حُمَيْدٍ عَبْدِ الرَّحْمَنِ بْنِ سَعْدٍ وَعَنْ أَبِي أُسَيْدٍ مَالِكِ بْنِ رَبِيعَةَ السَّاعِدِيَّيْنِ الأَنْصَارِيَّيْنِ رَضِيَ اللهُ عَنْهُمَا أَنَّ النَّبِيَّ ﷺ قَالَ إِذَا سَمِعْتُمُ الْحَدِيثَ عَنِّي تَعْرِفُهُ قُلُوبُكُمْ وَتَلِينُ لَهُ أَشْعَارُكُمْ وَأَبْشَارُكُمْ وَتَرَوْنَ أَنَّهُ مِنْكُمْ قَرِيبٌ فَأَنَا أَوْلاَكُمْ بِهِ وَإِذَا سَمِعْتُمُ الْحَدِيثَ عَنِّي تُنْكِرُهُ قُلُوبُكُمْ وَتَنْفِرُ أَشْعَارُكُمْ وَأَبْشَارُكُمْ وَتَرَوْنَ أَنَّهُ مِنْكُمْ بَعِيدٌ فَأَنَا أَبْعَدُكُمْ مِنْهُ حم ز حب إسناده صحيح على شرط مسلم

Accordingly, the great *Tābi'ī* al-Rabī' b. Khuthaym said: "Truly, a ḥadīth [either] possesses a light light the light of day – those who know it recognize it – or it possesses darkness like the darkness of night, which makes it unrecognizable."[6]

قال الإمامان السيوطي والسخاوي رحمهما الله في تدريب الراوي وفتح المغيث

قَالَ الرَّبِيعُ بْنُ خُثَيْمٍ إِنَّ لِلْحَدِيثِ ضَوْءً كَضَوْءِ النَّهَارِ تَعْرِفُهُ وَظُلْمَةً كَظُلْمَةِ اللَّيْلِ تُنْكِرُهُ

[5]Narrated from Abū Ḥumayd al-Anṣārī and Abū Usayd al-Sā'idī by Aḥmad (al-Arna'ūt ed. 25:456 §16058 *isnād sahīh 'alā shart Muslim*), al-Bazzār (*Zawā'id* §187), Ibn Ḥibbān (1:263 §63) and others with a sound chain of *Sahīh* narrators cf. al-Haythamī (1:150) and Ibn Kathīr in his *Tafsīr* (1:473, 2:264).

[6]Cited by al-Suyūṭī in *Tadrīb al-Rāwī* and al-Sakhāwī in *Fath al-Mughīth*.

al-Nabhānī's Superlative Respect for Hadith

Imam Yūsuf b. Ismāʿīl al-Nabhānī was one of the *rabbānī* scholars whose type is all but extinguished in our time as they have been replaced by common scholars (*ʿawāmm al-ʿulamā'*) in accordance with the Prophetic predictions to that effect for the end of times. He possessed an extremely high sense of respect and *adab* for the Station of the Prophet ﷺ and as a result refrained from critiquing the grade of any hadith remotely attributed to him ﷺ together with a top hadith master's sense of propriety and justice, hence his general acceptance and good opinion of everything he includes in his books, most especially the hadiths devoted to the unfathomable honor and supernal status of the Seal of Messengers ﷺ, the extent of whose greatness is known truly to Allah alone. This is also our *madhhab* ﴾**and the outcome belongs to the Godwary**﴿. May Allah have mercy on him and grant him the Highest Paradise and Greatest Proximity.

Translator's Chains of Transmission and Invocation

Glory to Allah first and last. Blessings and salutations of peace upon His Messenger our Master Muḥammad ﷺ and upon his Family and Companions. The pauper in need of his Lord, Gibril Fouad Haddad received the honor of narrating al-Qāḍī Yūsuf al-Nabhānī's encyclopedic masterpiece on the miracles of the Holy Prophet Muḥammad ﷺ entitled *Ḥujjat Allāh 'alā al-'Ālamīn bi-Mu'jizāt Sayyid al-Mursalīn* from the Ulema of Mecca, Beirut, Damascus and Fes. I narrate Qāḍī al-Nabhānī's *Ḥujjat Allāh* from five teachers: Shaykh Muḥammad b. al-Sayyid 'Alawī al-Mālikī al-Makkī; Shaykh Ḥusayn 'Usayrān al-Shāfi'ī al-Naqshbandī al-Bayrūtī; Shaykh Abū al-Jūd Muḥammad Taysīr b. Tawfīq b. al-Makhzūmī al-Makkī al-Dimashqī al-Shāfi'ī; Shaykh 'Abd al-Raḥmān b. 'Abd al-Ḥayy al-Kattānī al-Fāsī; and Shaykh Abū al-Faḍl 'Abd Allāh b. Muḥammad al-Ṣiddīq al-Ghumārī, all of them from the Qāḍī himself—Allah have mercy on them, shower His greatest mercy on the Qāḍī Yūsuf al-Nabhānī, bless him with the Highest Company in Paradise, thank and reward him abundantly on behalf of the *Umma*.

Truly the benefit of his spiritual company, meticulous teaching, love for the Seal of Prophets ﷺ, and spirit of humility and truth is palpable to anyone that looks into his works. The Community of Islam have placed these pearls next to the legacies of other love-consumed, learned authorities of the past. To presume to render their works justice in any language, a fortiori the Divinely-inspired discourse of the Best of Creation, would be overreaching were it not for the Prophetic injunctions that **Deeds are only according to intentions** and that **One may carry knowledge to another who is more knowledgeable**. May Allah therefore benefit the reader with this book; forgive its mistakes; count it as a deed done for and by the honor of His Exalted, Noble Messenger; and convey its reward to the Qāḍī Yūsuf, to my Masters, Mawlana Shaykh Nazim al-Haqqani, Mawlana Shaykh Hisham Kabbani, and all my teachers, and to every sincere seeker of the most extraordinary being to walk the earth.

The Righteous Life and Blessed Works of the Poet of the Holy Prophet ﷺ the Pious Erudite Imam al-Qāḍī Yūsuf al-Nabhānī

(1265-1350/1849-1932)

Al-Nabhānī wrote of himself in his first published book, *al-Sharaf al-Mu'abbad li-Āli Muḥammad* ﷺ (1309/1891), in *Asbāb al-Ta'līf lil-'Abdi al-Ḍa'īf*, and in *Jāmi' Karāmāt al-Awliyā'* (both 1329/1911):

> I am the *faqīr* Yūsuf b. Ismā'īl b. Yūsuf b. Ismā'īl b. Muḥammad Nāṣir al-Dīn al-Nabhānī. We go back to the Banū Nabhān, an Arab desert folk who settled of old in the town of Ijzim[7] North of the Holy sites in the land of Palestine, presently part of the district *(qaḍā')* of Ḥaifa in 'Akka, province of Beirut. I was born in Ijzim in 1265/1849 approximately.
>
> I read the Qur'ān with my Master and father, the righteous Shaykh and meticulous memorizer of the Book of Allah, Shaykh Ismā'īl al-Nabhānī who is now [in 1891] past eighty, in full possession of his senses, of strong build and excellent health, and who spends most of his time in works of obedience.
>
> My father's daily devotion in every twenty-four hours was one third of the Qur'ān, then he would complete the Qur'ān three times every week. The praise for this belongs to Allah! ﴾**Say: In the bounty of Allah and in His mercy: therein let them rejoice. It is better than what they hoard**﴿ (10:58).
>
> Then he sent me – Allah save him and thank him on my behalf! – to Cairo for study. I entered the Mosque of al-Azhar the day of al-Sabt in early Muḥarram of the year 1283 [16 May 1866] and resided there until Rajab 1289 [October 1872]. During that time, I learnt all that Allah destined for me to learn of the sciences of the *Sharī'a* and its preparatory disciplines at the

[7] 28 kms. south of Ḥaifa, Palestine on the Southern edge of Mount Carmel, 100 meters above sea level.

hands of the accomplished teachers and major established masters of the time, any one of whom, if he were found in a place, would be the leader of its people to the gardens of Paradise and would meet their requirements in all of the sciences – the spoken and the rational.

One of them, or rather their peerless leader was the accomplished, erudite teacher, the refuge of meticulous understanding, the Shaykh of all Shaykhs, Teacher of all Teachers, *Sayyidī* al-Shaykh **Ibrāhīm al-Saqqā** al-Shāfiʻī who died in 1298 aged around ninety years. He spent his entire blessed long life reading lessons until most of the Ulema of our time became his students, either directly, or through an intermediary. I attended his classes – Allah have mercy on him! – for three years and read with him the two commentaries – *al-Taḥrīr* and *al-Manhaj* – of Shaykh al-Islam Zakariyyā al-Anṣārī together with their marginalia by al-Sharqāwī and al-Bujayrimī respectively.

Also among my teachers is the venerable erudite Scholar, *Sayyidī* al-Shaykh **al-Sayyid Muḥammad al-Damanhūrī** al-Shāfiʻī who died in 1286 aged around ninety years.

Also the erudite Scholar *Sayyidī* al-Shaykh **Ibrāhīm al-Zurrū al-Khalīlī** al-Shāfiʻī who died in 1287 aged around seventy.

Also the erudite Scholar *Sayyidī* al-Shaykh **Aḥmad al-Ajhūrī al-Ḍarīr** al-Shāfiʻī who died in 1293 aged around sixty.

Also the erudite Scholar *Sayyidī* al-Shaykh **Ḥasan al-ʻAdawī** al-Mālikī who died in 1298 aged around eighty.

Also the erudite Scholar *Sayyidī* al-Shaykh **al-Sayyid ʿAbd al-Hādī Najā al-Abyārī** who died in 1305 aged just over seventy years.

Also Shaykh **Shams al-Dīn Muḥammad al-Anbābī** al-Shāfiʻī the Master of al-Azhar Mosque, who died in 1313.

Also Shaykh **ʿAbd al-Raḥmān al-Sharbīnī** al-Shāfiʻī the Master of al-Azhar Mosque, who died in 1326.

Also Shaykh **ʿAbd al-Qādir al-Rāfiʿī** al-Ḥanafī al-Ṭarabulsī the Master of the Damascenes' Porch *(Ruwāq al-Shawāmm)* in al-Azhar Mosque, who died in 1323.

Also Shaykh **Yūsuf al-Barqāwī** al-Ḥanbalī the Master of the Ḥanbalīs' Porch in al-Azhar Mosque.[8]

[And many others, some of whom are named in *Hādī al-Murīd* and *Jāmiʿ Karāmāt al-Awliyāʾ*.]

[After I graduated and returned home to Ijzim] I began to hold a number of religious courses in ʿAkka and my home town of Ijzim. Then I travelled frequently to Beirut, then Damascus where I met the eminent Ulema. Chief among them was the Jurist of Damascus at the time, our Master the erudite Imam, **al-Sayyid al-Sharīf Maḥmūd Effendī Ḥamza** – Allah have mercy on him! – with whom I read the beginning of al-Bukhārī's *Ṣaḥīḥ*, after which he gave me a general certificate comprising the rest of the *Ṣaḥīḥ* as well as all his other narrations and his own works. He wrote this long certificate in his superb style and handsome handwriting.

Then I headed for Constantinople twice and worked there for several years. I edited the periodical *al-Jawāʾib* until it folded. I also proofread the Arabic books that came out of its press. My monthly salary there was ten Līras for editing and proofreading. I worked on this for about two or three hours [daily] and did it on the insistant request of the paper's owner, Aḥmad Effendī Fāris. He considered me his greatest blessing and showed great sadness at seeing me leave for my new position with the government [as a judge]. He offered me to work as his partner or a raise, but I refused.

I left Constantinople, the first time, for Iraq. I went to the district of Kawī Ṣanjaq in the province of Mosul. Then I returned to Constantinople. I left it a second time in 1300 when I was appointed head judge of al-Jaza' court in al-Lādhiqiyya on the Syro-Palestinian sea-shore. After living there for five years the *Dawla* – Allah grant her victory! – transferred me to

[8] *Al-Sharaf al-Muʾabbad li-Āli Muḥammad* ﷺ (p. 140-142).

the head judgeship of the court of al-Qudus al-Sharīf. This took place through those at whose hands Allah decreed goodness for me, without request nor prior knowledge on my part. Then, after less than a year – eight months to be precise – they promoted me, without request nor prior knowledge on my part, to the chief judgeship of the Beirut Court of Justice. This was in 1305/1888.[9]

After al-Nabhānī retired he turned entirely to writing and worshipping. He travelled to al-Madīna al-Munawwara and lived in the Noble Neighborhood for a while. Then he returned to Beirut where he passed on to the mercy of His Lord in the beginning of the month of Ramaḍān 1350/1932.

[9] *Asbāb al-Ta'līf* (p. 290, 332) and *Jāmi' Karāmāt al-Awliyā'* (2:52).

Bibliography of al-Nabhānī's Works

Afḍalu al-Ṣalawāt 'alā Sayyid al-Sādāt (The Choicest Invocations of Blessings on the Master of Masters) <1309>.

Aḥsan al-Wasā'il fī Naẓmi Asmā'i al-Nabiyyi al-Kāmil (The Best Means in Versifying the Names of the Perfect Prophet ﷺ), in three hundred verses, in print. The Qāḍī wrote a brief history of the compilations of the Prophetic Names in his introduction to his commentary on al-Jazūlī's *Dalā'il al-Khayrāt* titled *al-Dalālāt al-Wāḍiḥāt* in which he mentioned various recensions to date:

Al-Qāḍī 'Iyāḍ's superlative masterpiece *al-Shifā'*
Ibn Diḥya's *Nihāyat al-Sūl fī Khaṣā'iṣ al-Rasūl*
al-Fākihānī's *al-Fajr al-Munīr*
Abū 'Imrān al-Zanātī's compendium (201 names)
al-Jazūlī's devotional masterpiece *Dalā'il al-Khayrāt* in which he relied on al-Zanātī
al-Suyūṭī's *al-Ḥadā'iq fī Asmā'i Khayr al-Khalā'iq* (300+ names)
al-Suyūṭī's *al-Riyāḍ al-Anīqa fī Asmā'i Khayr al-Khalīqa* listing sources for the *Ḥadā'iq*
al-Suyūṭī's *al-Bahjat al-Saniyya* (500 names)
al-Sakhāwī's *al-Qawl al-Badī' fil-Ṣalāt 'alāl-Ḥabīb al-Shafī'* (450 names)
al-Qasṭallānī's *al-Mawāhib al-Ladunniyya* in which he relied on al-Sakhāwī
al-Zurqānī's *Sharḥ al-Mawāhib* (800+ names)
al-Nabhānī's *Aḥsan al-Wasā'il* in verse and *al-Asmā fīmā li-Rasūlillāhi ﷺ min al-Asmā* in prose (830 names)

A trilingual Arabic-English-Urdu recension was published by Shaykh Anīs Ludhianvī *raḥimahullāh* in the United Kingdom.

al-Aḥādīth al-Arba'īn fī Faḍā'il Sayyid al-Mursalīn (Forty Narrations on the Excellent Traits of the Master of Messengers ﷺ), in print.

al-Aḥādīth al-Arba'īn fī Faḍl al-Jihād wal-Mujāhidīn (Forty Narrations on the Excellence of Jihād and Mujāhidīn), in print.

al-Aḥādīth al-Arba'īn fī Wujūbi Ṭā'at Amīr al-Mu'minīn (Forty Narrations on the Obligatoriness of Obeying the Commander of the Believers), in print.

al-Aḥādīth al-Arba'īn min Amthāl Afṣaḥ al-Mursalīn (Forty Narrations Containing Similes Made by the Most Eloquent of All Messengers ﷺ), in print.

al-Anwār al-Muḥammadiyya (The Muḥammadan Lights), an abridgment of al-Qasṭallānī's *al-Mawāhib al-Ladunniyya* (The Otherworldly Bestowals) <1312> in 632 pages.

al-Arba'ūna Arba'īn min Aḥādīthi Sayyid al-Mursalīn (Forty Times Forty Narrations from the Master of Messengers) <1329 and 1372>, forty collections of forty ḥadīths, each collection on a different topic, and each from forty different books.

Arba'ūna Ḥadīthan fī Arba'īna Ṣīghatin fil-Ṣalāti 'alā al-Nabī (Forty Narrations on Forty Wordings of Invocations of Blessings on the Prophet ﷺ).

Arba'ūna Ḥadīthan fī Faḍā'ili Ahl al-Bayt (Forty Narrations on the High Merits of the People of the Prophetic House).

Arba'ūna Ḥadīthan fī Faḍli Abī Bakr (Forty Narrations on the Excellence of Abū Bakr).

Arba'ūna Ḥadīthan fī Faḍli Abī Bakrin wa-'Umar (Forty Narrations on the Excellence of Abū Bakr and 'Umar).

Arba'ūna Ḥadīthan fī Faḍli 'Alī (Forty Narrations on the Excellence of 'Alī).

Arba'ūna Ḥadīthan fī Faḍli Arba'īna Ṣaḥābiyyan (Forty Ḥadīths on the Hight Merits of Forty Prophetic Companions).

Arba'ūna Ḥadīthan fī Faḍli Lā Ilāha Illā Allāh (Forty Narrations on the Excellence of *Lā Ilāha Illā Allāh*).

Arba'ūna Ḥadīthan fī Faḍli 'Umar (Forty Narrations on the Excellence of 'Umar).

Arba'ūna Ḥadīthan fī Faḍli 'Uthmān (Forty Narrations on the Excellence of 'Uthmān).

Arba'ūna Ḥadīthan fī Madḥi al-Sunnati wa-Dhammi al-Bid'a (Forty Ḥadīths on the Praise of the Sunna and the Blame of Innovation). Al-Nabhānī selected narrations found for the most part in al-Suyūṭī's *al-Amru bil-Ittibā' wal-Nahī 'an al-Ibtidā'* then warned about "the three arch-innovators of the times": Jamāl al-Dīn al-Afghānī, Muḥammad 'Abduh al-Miṣrī, and Rashīd Riḍā the owner of the periodical *al-Manār*.

al-Asālīb al-Badī'a fī Faḍl al-Ṣaḥāba wa-Iqnā'i al-Shī'a (The Beautiful Methods in [Presenting] the High Merits of the Companions and Persuading the Shī'īs").

Asbāb al-Ta'līf min al-'Ājiz al-Ḍa'īf (The Reasons Why This Helpless Poorling Writes), appended to the *Jāmi' Karāmāt al-Awliyā'*.

al-Asmā fīmā li-Rasūlillāhi ﷺ *min al-Asmā* (The Apex in Knowledge of the Names of the Prophet ﷺ) in which the Qāḍī listed 830 to 860 names of the Prophet ﷺ in a 300-verse poem.

al-Bashā'ir al-Īmāniyya fīl-Mubashshirāt al-Manāmiyya (Faith-Informed Glad Tidings in the Mercy-Telling Dreams), in print.

al-Burhān al-Musaddad fī Ithbāti Nubuwwati Sayyidinā Muḥammad ﷺ (The Ironclad Demonstration of the Prophethood of our Master Muḥammad ﷺ), in print.

Dalīl al-Tujjār ilā Akhlāq al-Akhyār (The Guide of Traders in the High Manners of the Elect), in print.

al-Dalālāt al-Wāḍiḥāt Sharḥ Dalā'il al-Khayrāt, a commentary on Imam al-Jazūlī's manual of invocations of blessings on the Prophet ﷺ, the foremost manual of its kind. Shaykh Bassām 'Abd al-Wahhāb al-Jābī produced a good new edition of this work in 2001 printed with the fully vowelized *Dalā'il*.[10]

Al-Nabhānī's introduction to the *Dilālāt* is rich in historical and legal details on the etiquette of invoking blessings on the

[10]Cairo: al-Dār al-Ghannā', 2001.

Prophet ﷺ. In the introduction to this work the Qāḍī recapitulates his detailed examination – which he first presented in the introduction to *Sa'ādat al-Dārayn* – of the preferability of adding the title *Sayyidinā* ("our Master") to the name of the Prophet ﷺ in *tashahhud*. This is the position preferred by the late Shāfi'ī authorities in particular such as Ibn 'Abd al-Salām, al-Isnawī, al-Maḥallī, al-Suyūṭī, al-Fayrūzābādī, al-Ramlī, al-Sakhāwī, al-Haytamī, al-Nabhānī himself, and others. This is also the preferred position of some of the contemporary Ḥanafī Ulema of Syria such as the two ḥadīth Masters Nūr al-Dīn 'Itr and his teacher Shaykh 'Abd Allāh Sirāj al-Dīn, while al-Wānsharīsī relates two views from the Mālikīs.[11]

Shaykh Nūr al-Dīn 'Itr said:

> The Four Schools are in agreement over the permissibility of saying *Sayyidinā Muḥammad* inside prayer, a fortiori outside it. The difference of opinion is between the Ḥanafīs who said it is preferable not to say *Sayyidinā* in *tashahhud*, and the Shāfi'īs who consider it necessary out of respect. The Ḥanafīs have a rule: strict obedience is better than respect *(al-imtithāl khayrun min al-adab)*. The proof of the Shāfi'īs is that the Prophet ﷺ omitted it out of humbleness but he did say, "I am the Master of human beings on the Day of Resurrection and this is no vain boast.... Ādam and all those after him are nowhere but under my flag, and I will be the first one to rise from the earth – this is no vain boast!"[12] Therefore we stick to this proof! As for the statement that this is a *bid'a*: the statement itself is the *bid'a* as none of the past Imams of Islam ever said such a thing. Rather, the ḥadīth we just mentioned is firmly established as authentic. Our teacher, the ḥadīth Master of these lands, the *Muḥaddith* Shaykh 'Abd Allāh Sirāj al-Dīn – who follows the Ḥanafī *madhhab* – chose this position and declared it in one of his public classes before all of us. He said it is better to say

[11] Al-Wānsharīsī, *al-Mi'yār al-Mu'rib* (11:81).

[12] Narrated from Abū Sa'īd al-Khudrī by al-Tirmidhī *(ḥasan saḥīḥ)* and Aḥmad and from Ibn 'Abbās by Aḥmad.

Sayyidinā Muḥammad. He chose the Shāfi'ī *madhhab* in the matter, out of respect.[13]

Other proofs for giving precedence to respect *(adab)* over obedience *(ṭā'a)* in *tashahhud* are: [1] the refusal of Abū Bakr to pray as imām in front of the Prophet ﷺ although the latter ordered him. After the prayer, the Prophet ﷺ asked him: "Abū Bakr, what prevented you from standing firm when I ordered you to?" Abū Bakr excused himself with his famous statement: "*Mā kāna li-Ibni Abī Quḥāfata an yataqaddama bayna yaday Rasūlillāh* – It was not fitting for the son of Abū Quḥāfa to stand ahead of the Messenger of Allah." The Prophet ﷺ approved of him.[14] [2] The statement of Ibn Mas'ūd: "When you invoke blessings on your Prophet, invoke blessings in the best possible way *(idhā ṣallaytum fa-aḥsinū al-ṣalāta 'alā nabiyyikum)* for – you do not know – this might be shown to him. Therefore, say: 'O Allah! Grant your *ṣalāt*, mercy, and blessings upon the Master of Messengers *(sayyid al-Mursalīn)*, the Imam of the Godfearing, and the Seal of Prophets, Muḥammad your servant and Messenger, the Imam of goodness and leader of goodness and Messenger of Mercy! O Allah! Raise him to a glorious station for which the first and the last of creatures will yearn! O Allah! Grant mercy to Muḥammad and to the House of Muḥammad as You granted mercy to Ibrāhīm and to the House of Ibrāhīm! Truly, You are the Lord of glory and praise! O Allah! Bless Muḥammad and the House of Muḥammad as You blessed Ibrāhīm and the House of Ibrāhīm! Truly, You are the Lord of glory and praise!'"[15]

[13]'Itr, class on *I'lām al-Anām Sharḥ Bulūgh al-Marām*, Jāmi' al-Shamsiyya, Damascus, Ramaḍān 1422.

[14]Narrated from Sahl b. Sa'd al-Sā'idī by al-Bukhārī, Muslim, Mālik, Abū Dāwūd, al-Nasā'ī, and Aḥmad.

[15]Narrated from Ibn Mas'ūd by Ibn Mājah, Abū Ya'lā (9:175 §5267), al-Ṭabarānī in *al-Kabīr* (9:115 §8594), Abū Nu'aym (1985 ed. 4:271), and al-Bayhaqī in the *Shu'ab* (2:208 §1550), all through 'Abd al-Raḥmān b. 'Abd Allāh b. 'Utba al-Mas'ūdī who is weak although al-Mundhirī declared the chain fair in *al-Targhīb* (1997 ed. 2:329 §2588) cf. *Fatḥ* (11:158). Al-Būṣīrī in *Misbāḥ al-Zujāja* (1:111) said it is corroborated by an identical narration from Ibn 'Umar by Aḥmad b. Manī' in his *Musnad*. Al-Mas'ūdī is further corroborated by Abū Salama al-Mughīra b. al-Nu'mān in 'Abd al-Razzāq (2:213-214 §3109-3112) while al-Dāraquṭnī in his *'Ilal* (5:15 §682) cites yet two other chains to Ibn

The proofs for calling the Prophet ﷺ *sayyid* are in the verses ﴾**lordly** *(sayyidan)*, **chaste, a Prophet of the righteous**﴿ (3:39) and ﴾**and they met her lord and master** *(sayyidahā)* **at the door**﴿ (12:42) as well as the following Prophetic narrations: [1] "I am the Master *(sayyid)* of human beings";[16] [2] "This son of mine [al-Ḥasan] is a leader of men *(sayyid)*";[17] [3] "Get up to meet your chief *(qūmū ilā sayyidikum)* [Saʿd b. 'Ubāda]";[18] this ḥadīth is also narrated as *Qūmu li-sayyidikum* which means the same thing.[19] (It is noteworthy that the Prophet ﷺ specifically invoked the blessings and mercy of Allah upon the family of Saʿd b. 'Ubāda as well as Jābir b. ʿAbd Allāh and the family of Ibn Abī Awfā.) [4] Sahl b. Ḥunayf said "My liege-lord!" *(yā sayyidī)* when he asked the Prophet ﷺ a certain question.[20] [5] Mālik and Sufyān gave the fatwa that one should not say *Yā Sayyidī* in *du'ā'* but *Yā Rabbī*.[21]

al-Faḍā'il al-Muḥammadiyya (The Muḥammadan High Merits), in print.

Mas'ūd, raising the narration to a grade of *hasan* at the very least, or rather *sahīh in shā' Allāh*.

[16]Narrated from: Abū Hurayra by al-Bukhārī, Muslim, al-Tirmidhī *(hasan sahīh)*, Abū Dāwūd, Aḥmad, al-Nasā'ī in *al-Sunan al-Kubrā* (6:378), Ibn Abī Shayba (6:307, 6:317, 7:257), Ibn Saʿd (1:20), Ibn Ḥibbān (14:381), al-Bayhaqī in *al-Sunan al-Kubra* (9:4); Ḥudhayfa by al-Ḥākim (4:617) and al-Ṭabarānī in *al-Awsat* cf. al-Haythamī (10:377) and others; Abū Saʿīd al-Khudrī by al-Tirmidhī *(hasan sahīh)*, Ibn Mājah, and Aḥmad; by Aḥmad and al-Dārimī; Ibn ʿAbbās by Aḥmad; 'Ubāda b. al-Sāmit by al-Ḥākim (1990 ed. 1:83 *sahīh*); Ibn Mas'ūd by Ibn Ḥibbān (14:398); ʿAbd Allāh b. Salām by al-Ṭabarānī and Abū Yaʿlā cf. al-Haythamī (8:253) and al-Maqdisī's *al-Ahādīth al-Mukhtāra* (9:455); and Jābir b. ʿAbd Allāh by al-Ḥākim (1990 ed. 2:660 *sahīh al-isnād*) and al-Ṭabarānī in *al-Awsat* cf. al-Haythamī (10:376); etc.

[17]Narrated from Abū Bakrah by al-Bukhārī, al-Tirmidhī, al-Nasā'ī, Abū Dāwūd, and Aḥmad.

[18]Narrated from Abū Saʿīd al-Khudrī by al-Bukharī, Muslim, Abū Dāwūd, al-Nasā'ī, and Aḥmad.

[19]Cf. al-Ṭaḥāwī, *Mushkil al-Āthār* (2:38), Ibn Kathīr, *Bidāya* (4:122), and al-Zabīdī, *Ithāf al-Sādat al-Muttaqīn* (7:142).

[20]Narrated from Sahl b. Ḥunayf by Abū Dāwūd, Aḥmad, al-Nasā'ī in *al-Kubrā* (6:72 §10086, 6:256 §10873) and *'Amal al-Yawm wal-Layla* (p. 252 §257, p. 564 §1034), al-Ṭaḥāwī in *Sharh Ma'ānī al-Āthār* (4:329), al-Ṭabarānī in *al-Kabīr* (6:93 §5615), al-Ḥākim (1990 ed. 4:458 *isnād sahīh*),

[21]Cited by Ibn Rajab in his *Jāmi' al-'Ulum wal-Hikam* (Dār al-Maʿrifa ed. p. 107).

al-Fatḥ al-Kabīr fī Ḍamm al-Ziyādat ilāl-Jāmi' al-Ṣaghīr (The Great Divine Opening: [Al-Suyūṭī's] *al-Jāmi' al-Ṣaghīr* [edited together] With Its Addenda), in print.

Hādī al-Murīd ilā Ṭuruq al-Asānīd (Guide for the Seeker to the Paths of Transmission) <1317>, appended to *Ṣalawāt al-Thanā'* and detailing al-Nabhānī's *Thabat* or compendium of transmission chains in ḥadīth and other Islamic sources.

Ḥizb al-Awliyā' al-Arba'īn al-Mustaghīthīna bi-Sayyid al-Mursalīn ﷺ (The Devotion of the Forty Friends of Allah That Seek Help Through the Master of Messengers ﷺ), also known as *Ḥizb al-Istighāthāt bi-Sayyid al-Sādāt* ﷺ, in print.

Ḥusn al-Shir'ati fī Mashrū'iyyati Ṣalāt al-Ẓuhri Idhā Ta'addadat al-Jumu'a wa-Bayān Ḥukm al-Ta'addud 'alā al-Madhāhib al-Arba'a (The Beauty of the Law in Permitting *Ẓuhr* Prayer When More than One *Jumu'a* is Held [in one and the same region] and the Exposition of the Status of Multiple *Jumu'as* According to the Four Schools), published in Damascus in the sixties.

Irshād al-Ḥāyārā fī Taḥdhīr al-Muslimīn min Madāris al-Naṣārā (Guidance of the Perplexed: Warning the Muslims Against [Sending their Children to] the Christians Schools). Al-Nabhānī also wrote an abridgment titled *Mukhtaṣar Irshād al-Ḥāyārā*.

al-Istighāthat al-Kubrā bi-Asmā' Allāh al-Ḥusnā (The Great Invocation of Help Through the Beautiful Names of Allah), printed together with *Riyāḍ Ahl al-Janna*.

Itḥāf al-Muslim bi-Aḥādīth al-Targhīb wal-Tarhīb min al-Bukhārī wa-Muslim (A Gift for Every Muslim in the Narrations of Encouragement to Goodness and Deterrence from Evil from al-Bukhārī and Muslim) <1329>.

Jāmi' Karāmāt al-Awliyā' (Compendium of the Miraculous Gifts of the Friends of Allah) <1329> in two volumes (reprint Beirut: al-Maktaba al-Thaqāfiyya, 1991), an encyclopedia of the miracles of the Muslim saints in the introduction to which he includes a bibliography for his works which served for the present bibliography. In this introduction he also said (1:9-11): "I will mention the titles of some of the books from which I quoted material":

– al-Tibrīzī's *Mishkāt al-Maṣābīḥ* (The Niche of Lights c.737).
– al-Rāzī's (d. 606) *al-Tafsīr al-Kabīr*.
– Usāma b. Munqidh's *al-I'tibār* (The Book of Reflection) by the Emir Usāma b. Munqidh (d. 584).
– al-Qushayrī's (d. 465) *al-Risāla al-Qushayriyya* (Epistle to the Sufis).
– *Miṣbāḥ al-Ẓalām fil-Mustaghīthīna bi-Khayri al-Anām* (The Illumination of Darkness Concerning Those Who Seek Aid by Means of the Prophet ﷺ) by Abū ʿAbd Allāh b. al-Nuʿmān al-Marrākishī's (d. 683).
– *Rūḥ al-Qudus* (The Spirit of Holiness), *al-Futūḥāt al-Makkiyya* (The Meccan Disclosures), *Mawāqi' al-Nujūm* (The Orbits of the Stars), and *al-Muḥāḍarāt* (The Conferences) by the Greatest Shaykh, Sayyidī Muḥyī al-Dīn b. al-ʿArabī (d. 636).
– Imam al-Yafi'ī's (d. 768) *Rawḍ al-Rayyāḥīn* (The Grove of Sweet Scents) and *Nashr al-Maḥāsin* (The Proclamation of Perfections).
– *Tuffāḥ al-Arwāḥ* (The Apple of Spirits) by Kamāl al-Dīn Muḥammad b. Abī al-Ḥasan ʿAlī al-Sirāj al-Rifā'ī al-Qurashī al-Shāfi'ī who lived in the Eighth Century and was a contemporary of al-Subkī and Ibn Taymiyya.
– *Sharḥ al-Ḥikam al-'Aṭā'iyya* (Commentary on the Aphorisms of Ibn 'Aṭā' Allāh) by the Knower of Allah, Ibn 'Abbād (d. 792).
– *Tuḥfat al-Aḥbāb fīl-Khuṭaṭ wal-Mazārāt* (Gift to Loved Ones on Famous Graves) by Nūr al-Dīn ʿAlī b. Aḥmad al-Sakhāwī al-Ḥanafī (d. after 889).
– *Al-Ishārāt li-Amākin al-Ziyārāt fī Dimashq al-Shām* (Visitation Shrines in Damascus) by Ibn al-Ḥawrānī, 11th c.
– *Tuḥfat al-Anām fī Faḍā'il al-Shām* (The Gem of Creatures Concerning the Merits of al-Shām) by Shaykh Jalāl al-Dīn al-Baṣrī al-Dimashqī who composed it in 1002.
– *Ṭabaqāt al-Khawāṣṣ min Ahl al-Yaman* (Biography-Layers of the Elite of Yemen by Imam Zayn al-Dīn Aḥmad b. Aḥmad al-Sharjī al-Zubaydī (d. 893) the author of the abridged *Ṣaḥīḥ al-Bukhārī* [*al-Tajrīd al-Ṣarīḥ*].
– Qāḍī ʿAbd al-Raḥmān al-ʿAlīmī al-Ḥanbalī's (d. 927) *al-Uns al-Jalīl* (The Sublime Friendship).

– Ṭāsh Kubrā's (d. 893) *al-Shaqā'iq al-Nu'māniyya* (The Red Anemones), a biographical dictionary of the Ḥanafīs.
– Sayyidī al-Shaykh 'Alwān al-Ḥamawī's (d. 936) *Sharḥ Ta'iyyat Ibn Ḥabīb al-Ṣafadī* (Commentary on Ibn Ḥabīb's Poem Written with the Rhyme Tā') and *Nasamāt al-Asḥār fī Karāmāt al-Awliyā' al-Akhyār* (The Pre-Dawn Breezes: The Miraculous Gifts of the Friends of Allah).
– Shaykh Muḥammad b. Yaḥyā al-Tādhifī al-Ḥanbalī's (d. 963) *Qalā'id al-Jawāhir fī Manāqib al-Shaykh 'Abd al-Qādir* (The Necklaces of Diamonds Concerning the Great Merits of Shaykh 'Abd al-Qādir).
– Imam 'Abd al-Wahhāb al-Sha'rānī's (d. 973) *al-Minan al-Kubrā* (The Vast Grants), *al-Baḥr al-Mawrūd* (The Sea That Serves All), *al-Ajwibat al-Marḍiyya* (The Satisfying Replies), and *al-Ṭabaqāt al-Kubrā* (Major Biographical Layers).
– Imam al-Munāwī's (d. 1021) *Ṭabaqāt al-Kubrā and al-Ṣughrā* (Major and Minor Biography-Layers of the Sufis).
– Shaykh Aḥmad b. al-Mubārak's *al-Ibrīz fī Manāqib Sayyidī 'Abd al-'Azīz al-Dabbāgh* (The Pure Gold: The Great Merits of My Master 'Abd al-'Azīz al-Dabbāgh), composed from the year 1129.
– al-Sayyid Muḥammad b. Abī Bakr al-Shillī Bā 'Alawī's (d. 1093) *al-Mashra' al-Rāwī fī Manāqib Sādātinā Āl Bā 'Alawī* (The Quenching Watering-Station: The Great Merits of Our Masters of the Bā 'Alawī Shaykhs).
– Shaykh Muḥammad Najm al-Dīn al-Ghazzī's (d. 1061) *al-Kawākib al-Sā'ira fī A'yān al-Mi'at al-'Āshira* (The Revolving Stars: Eminent Persons of the 10th Century).
– al-Shihāb Aḥmad al-Muqrī's (d. 1041) *Nafḥ al-Ṭīb* (The Wafts of Sweet Scents).
– al-Muḥibbī's (d. 1111) *Khulāṣat al-Athar fī A'yān al-Qarn al-Ḥādī 'Ashar* (The Epitome of Reports: Eminent Persons of the Eleventh Century).
– al-Sayyid Muḥammad Khalīl al-Murādī's (d. 1206) *Silk al-Durar fi A'yān al-Qarn al-Thānī 'Ashar* (The Pearl String: Eminent Persons of the Twelfth Century).
– 'Abd al-Raḥmān b. Ḥasan al-Jabartī's (d. 1237) *Tārīkh Miṣr* (History of Egypt).

- *Sharḥ al-Ṭarīqat al-Muḥammadiyya* by my Master, the Knower, Shaykh ʿAbd al-Ghanī al-Nābulusī (d. 1144).
- *Sharḥ al-Burda* (Commentary on the Poem of the Mantle) by our teacher, Shaykh Ḥasan al-ʿAdawī al-Miṣrī (d. 1303).
- *al-Ḥadā'iq al-Wardiyya fi Ḥaqā'iq Ajillā' al-Ṭarīqat al-Naqshbandiyya* (The Fields of Roses Concerning the Spiritual Realities of the Naqshbandi Grandmasters) by Shaykh ʿAbd al-Majīd, the son of our teacher, the erudite scholar and spiritual guide Shaykh Muḥammad al-Khānī al-Naqshbandī (d. 1317).

Jāmiʿ al-Ṣalawāt (The Compendium of the Invocations of Blessings) <1318>.

Jāmiʿ al-Thanā'i ʿalā Allāh (The Compendium of the Glorification of Allah ﷻ), in print.

Jawāhir al-Biḥār fī Faḍā'il al-Nabī al-Mukhtār (Jewels of the Seas on the Elect Prophet's ﷺ Excellences) <1327> in four volumes [I-IV]. This work is a massive anthology of excerpts from the masterpieces of classical Islam centering on the greatness of the Holy Prophet Muḥammad ﷺ. The work shows al-Nabhānī's erudition and his devotion to this great topic. Among the books excerpted, in order of appearance in the *Jawāhir*:

[I] ʿIyāḍ, *al-Shifā'*
al-Ḥakīm al-Tirmidhī's *Nawādir*
Abū Nuʿaym's *Dalā'il*
al-Māwardī, *Aʿlām al-Nubuwwa*
Ibn ʿArabī's *Futūḥāt*
al-Rāzī's *Tafsīr*
Ibn al-Fāriḍ's *Tā'iyya*
Ibn ʿAbd al-Salām, *Bidāyat al-Sūl*
al-Nawawī's *Tahdhīb al-Asmā'*
al-Dīrīnī's *Ṭahārat al-Qulūb*
Ibn Sayyid al-Nās *Nūr al-ʿUyūn*
Ibn al-Ḥajj, *al-Madkhal ʿalā al-Mawlid*
ʿAbd al-Karīm al-Jīlī's works
Ibn al-Muqrī's *Rawḍ* and marginalia
al-Suyūṭī's *Khaṣā'iṣ*
al-Subkī's *al-Taʿẓīm wal-Minna*
Ibn al-Humām's *al-Musāyara*
al-Qārī's *Sharḥ al-Shifā'*
al-Qūnawī's *Sharḥ al-Arbaʿīn*

[II] Al-Qasṭallānī's *Mawāhib*
al-Shaʿrānī's various books
al-Haytamī on *al-Hamziyya* and *Fatāwā*
Ibn ʿAllān, *Taʿrīf* on the Prophet's omnipresence in full
al-Munāwī's *Sharḥ al-Jāmiʿ al-Ṣaghīr*

al-Sirhindī's *Maktūbāt*
al-Fāsī, *Sharḥ Dalā'il al-Khayrāt*
al-Khafājī's *Sharḥ al-Shifā'* and his *Ḥāshiyat Tafsīr al-Bayḍāwī*
Ismā'īl Ḥaqqī's *Rūḥ al-Bayān*
al-Dabbāgh's *al-Ibrīz*
al-Zurqānī's *Sharḥ al-Mawāhib*
al-Nābulusī's various works
Muṣṭafā al-Bakrī on Ibn Mashīsh and Nawawī's *Ḥizb*
al-'Aydarūs, commentary on al-Badawī
Jamal, *Sharḥ Dalā'il al-Khayrāt*
al-Zabīdī's *Sharḥ al-Iḥyā'*
al-Mīrghanī on Ibn Mashīsh
Muḥammad al-Bakrī on the Prophet's *wafāt*

[III] al-Ghazzālī's *Iḥyā'*
Ṣāwī's *Tafsīr* and commentaries
Aḥmad b. Idrīs *al-'Uqd al-Nafīs*
al-Tijānī's *Jawāhir al-Ma'ānī*
Abū al-'Abbās Ibn Qudāma, *Taḥqīq*
Ibn al-Jazzār's *al-Qawl al-Ḥaqq*
Badr al-Dīn b. Ḥabīb's *al-Najm al-Thāqib*
al-Muqrī's *Fatḥ al-Muta'āl fī Madḥ al-Ni'āl*
Ibn Taymiyya, *al-Ṣārim al-Maslūl*
'Abd al-Qādir Jazā'irī, *Mawāqif*
al-Muqrī's *Nafḥ al-Ṭīb*
Ibn Khallikān on the *Mawlid*
al-Nābulusī on the *Mawlid*
Muḥammad al-Maghribī on the *Mawlid*
al-Haytamī on the *Mawlid*
Aḥmad 'Ābidīn on al-Haytamī's *Mawlid*
al-Shāmī al-Ṣāliḥī's *al-Mi'rāj al-Kabīr*
al-Ajhūrī's *al-Nūr al-Wahhāj*
al-Nābulusī's *al-Radd al-Matīn*
al-Barzanjī's *Mawlid*
al-Dirdīr's *Mawlid*

[IV] al-Sammanūdī's *Khulāṣat al-Wafā*
Nābulusī, *al-Riḥla al-Ḥijāziyya*
al-Mīrghanī, *al-As'ila al-Nafīsa*
Raṣṣā', *Tadhkirat al-Muḥibbīn*
Ibn al-Zamalkānī, *'Ujālat al-Rākib*
al-Shihāb al-Ramlī's *Fatāwā*
al-Sammān on *tawajjuh* to the Prophet ﷺ
al-Armayūnī's *Arba'ūn fil-Ṣalāt 'alā al-Nabī* ﷺ
Abū al-Ḥasan al-Bakrī, *'Iqd al-Jawāhir*
'Alī Dede Būsnawī, *Muḥāḍarat al-Awā'il*
al-'Arḍī's *Madārij al-Wuṣūl*
al-Yāfi'ī's *Nashr al-Maḥāsin*
al-Silāwī's *Ta'ẓīm al-Ittifāq*
al-Suyūṭī, *al-Qawl al-Muḥarrar*
al-Jīlī's *al-Nāmūs al-A'ẓam*
'Abd Allāh Būsnawī, *Maṭāli' al-Nūr*
Aḥmad al-'Aṭṭās Bā 'Alawī's *Ijāza* & others

Khulāṣat al-Kalām fī Tarjīḥi Dīn al-Islām (The Summation Concerning the Preferability of the Religion of Islam), in print.

al-Khulāṣat al-Wafiyya fī Rijāl al-Majmū'at al-Nabhāniyya, in print, a concise biographical guide to the *Majmū'a Nabhāniyya*.

al-Majmū'atu al-Nabhāniyya fil-Madā'iḥ al-Nabawiyya (The Nabhān Collection of Prophetic Praises) <1320>, recently republished, with a marginal glossary.

Mithāl al-Na'l al-Sharīf (The Image of the Noble Sandals [of the Prophet ﷺ]), in print. The Indian Ḥanafī Scholar Ashraf 'Alī al-Tahānawī entitled a chapter *Nayl al-Shifā' bi-Na'l al-Muṣṭafā* (Obtaining Remedy through the Sandals of the Elect One ﷺ) in his book *Zād al-Sa'īd* (Provision for the Fortunate). The Shaykh of our *Shuyūkh* and *Muḥaddith* of India, Muḥammad Zakariyyā Kandihlawī, said in his English translation of Imam al-Tirmidhī's foundational work *al-Shamā'il al-Nabawiyya wal-Khaṣā'il al-Muṣṭafawiyya* (The Prophetic Traits and Muḥammadan Features):

> Mawlānā Ashraf 'Alī Thanwī Ṣāḥib has written in his book *Zādus-Sa'īd* a detailed treatise on the *barakāt* [blessings] and virtues of the shoes of Rasūlullāh *ṢallAllāhu 'alayhi wasallam*. Those interested in this should read that book [which is available in English]. In short, it may be said that it [the Prophet's ﷺ sandal] has countless qualities. The Ulema have experienced it many a time. One is blessed [through it] by seeing RasūlAllāh *ṣalla Allāhu 'alayhi wasallam* in one's dreams; one gains safety from oppressors and every heartfelt desire is attained. Every object is fulfilled by its *tawassul*. The method of the latter is also mentioned therein.

al-Mubashshirāt al-Manāmiyya, see *al-Bashā'ir al-Īmāniyya*.

Mufarrij al-Kurūb wa-Mufarriḥ al-Qulūb (The Remover of Difficulties and Cheer of Hearts), in print, a collection of Prophetic supplications for the removal of difficulties.

Mukhtaṣar Irshād al-Ḥāyārā, see *Irshād al-Ḥāyārā*.

Muntakhab al-Ṣaḥīḥayn (Anthology from the Two *Ṣaḥīḥ*s [of al-Bukhārī and Muslim]), in print, containing about 3,000 ḥadīths.

al-Muzdawijatu al-Gharrā fīl-Istighāthati bi-Asmā’ Allāh al-Ḥusnā (The Shining Verse and Prose of Seeking Help Through the Beautiful Divine Names).

al-Naẓm al-Badī‘ fī Mawlid al-Shafī‘ ﷺ (The Fine Poetry on the Birth of the Intercessor ﷺ) <1312>.

Nujūm al-Muhtadīn wa-Rujūm al-Mu‘tadīn fi Ithbāti Nubuwwati Sayyidinā Muḥammadin Sayyid al-Mursalīn wal-Raddu ‘alā A‘dā’ihi Ikhwāni al-Shayāṭīn (The Stars of the Well-Guided and the Missiles against the Attackers in Affirmation of the Prophethood of our Master Muḥammad ﷺ the Master of Messengers, and the Refutation of His Enemies the Brothers of Devils), a massive volume in print.

al-Qaṣīdat al-Rā’iyya al-Kubrā fī Waṣfi al-Ummat al-Islāmiyyati wal-Milal al-Ukhrā (The Major *Rā’*-Rhyming Poem Describing the Muslim Umma and the Other Groups), in print.

al-Qaṣīdat al-Rā’iyya al-Ṣughrā fī Dhamm al-Bid‘ati wa-Ahlihā wa-Madḥi al-Sunnati al-Gharrā’ (The Minor *Rā’*-Rhyming Poem on the Blame of Innovation and the Praise of the Radiant Sunna), in print.

al-Qawl al-Ḥaqq fī Madḥi Sayyid al-Khalq (The Word of Truth on the Praise of the Master of Creation), in print.

Qurrat al-‘Ayn min al-Bayḍāwī wal-Jalālayn (The Coolness of the Eyes from al-Bayḍāwī and al-Jalālayn), a combined epitome of the two foremost linguistic Qur’anic Commentaries, in print.

Raf‘ al-Ishtibāh fī Istiḥālati al-Jihati ‘alā Allāh (The Removal of Uncertainty Concerning the Impossibility of Direction for Allah ﷻ), published as part of *Shawāhid al-Ḥaqq*.

al-Raḥmat al-Muhdāt fī Faḍli al-Ṣalāt (The Bestowed Gift Concerning the Excellence of Prayer), in print.

Ryāḍ al-Janna fī Adhkār al-Kitābi wal-Sunna (The Groves of Paradise: Supplications from the Qur’ān and Sunna), in print.

Sa‘ādatu al-Anām bi-Ittibā‘i Dīni al-Islām (The Bliss of Creatures in Following the Religion of Islam), in print.

Saʿādatu al-Dārayni fīl-Ṣalāti ʿalā Sayyidi al-Kawnayn (The Bliss of the Two Abodes in the Invocation of Blessings on the Master of the Two Universes) <1318> in 720 pages, comprising a sequence of ten-verse poems with a rhyme scheme per the Arabic alphabet, beginning with the *hamza* in the following poem:

1. *Anā ʿabdun li-sayyidi al-anbiyāʾi wa-walāʾī lahu al-qadīmu walāʾī*

أَنَا عَبْدٌ لِسَيِّدِ الأَنْبِيَا   وَوَلَائِي لَهُ القَدِيمُ وَلَائِي

I am the slave of the Master of Prophets
And my fealty to him has no beginning.

2. *Anā ʿabdun li-ʿabdihi wa-li-ʿabdi al-ʿabdi ʿabdun kadhā bi-ghayri intihāʾi*

أَنَا عَبْدٌ لِعَبْدِه وَلِعَبْدِ العَبْدِ عَبْدٌ كَذَا بِغَيْرِ انْتِهَاءِ

I am slave to his slave, and to his slave's slave,
And so forth endlessly!

3. *Anā lā antahī ʿanil-qurbi min bābi riḍāhu fī jumlati al-dukhalāʾi*

أَنَا لَا أَنْتَهِي عَنِ القُرْبِ مِنْ بَا   بِ رِضَاهُ فِي جُمْلَةِ الدُّخَلَاءِ

I do not cease to approach the door
Of his good pleasure among the novices.

4. *Anshuru al-ʿilma fī maʿālīhi lil-nāsi wa-ashdū bihi maʿ al-shuʿarāʾi*

أَنْشُرُ العِلْمَ فِي مَعَالِيهِ لِلنَّا   سِ وَأَشْدُو بِهِ مَعَ الشُّعَرَاءِ

I proclaim to all the science of his high attributes,
And sing this science among the poets.

5. *Fa ʿasāhu yaqūlu lī anta Salmānu walāʾī Ḥassānu ḥusni thanāʾī*

فَعَسَاهُ يَقُولُ لِي أَنْتَ سَلْمَا   نُ وَلَائِي حَسَّانُ حُسْنِ ثَنَائِي

Perhaps he will tell me: "You are the Salmān
Of my allegiance, the Ḥassān of my excellent homage!"

6. *Wa-bi-rūḥī afdī turāba ḥimāhu wa-lahu al-faḍlu fī qabūli fidāʾī*

وَبِرُوحِي أَفْدِي تُرَابَ حِمَاهُ   وَلَهُ الفَضْلُ فِي قَبُولِ فِدَائِي

My very soul I sacrifice for the dust of his sanctuary!
His favor should be that he accept my sacrifice.

7. *Fāza man yantamī ilayhi wa-lā ḥājata fīhi bi-dhālika al-intimā'i*

فَإِنَّ مَنْ يَنْتَمِي إِلَيْهِ وَلَا حَاجَةَ فِيهِ لِذَلِكَ الِانْتِمَاءِ

He has triumphed who ascribes himself to him
— Not that he needs such following,

8. *Huwa fī ghunyatin 'ani al-khalqi ṭurran wa-humu al-kullu 'anhu dūna ghinā'i*

هُوَ فِي غُنْيَةٍ عَنِ الخَلْقِ طُرًّا   وَهُمُ الكُلُّ عَنْهُ دُونَ غَنَاءِ

For he is not in need of creation at all,
While they all need him without exception.

9. *Wa-huwa lil-Lāhi waḥdihi 'abduhu al-khāliṣu mujallā al-ṣifāti wal-asmā'i*

وَهُوَ لِلَّهِ وَحْدِهِ عَبْدُهُ الخَا‌لِصُ مُجَلَّى الصِّفَاتِ وَالأَسْمَاءِ

He belongs to Allah alone, Whose pure servant he is,
As his attributes and names have made manifest;

10. *Kullu faḍlin fīl-khalqi fa-huwa min Allāhi ilayhi wa-minhu lil-ashyā'i*

كُلُّ فَضْلٍ فِي الخَلْقِ فَهُوَ   مِنَ اللهِ إِلَيْهِ وَمِنْهُ لِلْأَشْيَاءِ

And every single favor in creation comes from Allah
To him, and from him to everything else.

Sa'ādat al-Ma'ād fī Muwāzanat Bānat Su'ād (The Bliss of the Return in Metrical Correspondence to [Ka'b b. Zuhayr's Poem] 'Su'ād Has Departed'), in print.

Sabīl al-Najāt fīl-Ḥubbi fil-Lāhi wal-Bughḍi fil-Lāh (The Path to Salvation in Loving for the sake of Allah and Hating for the Sake of Allah), in print.

al-Sābiqātu al-Jiyādu fī Madḥi Sayyid al-'Ibād ﷺ (The Excellent Enduring Good Deeds in the Praise of the Master of All Servants ﷺ), in print.

Ṣalawāt al-Akhyār 'alā al-Nabiyyi al-Mukhtār ﷺ (The Invocations of Blessings of the Chosen Ones on the Elect Prophet ﷺ).

al-Ṣalawāt al-Alfiyya fīl-Kamālāt al-Muḥammadiyya (The 1,000-Verse Invocations of Blessings on the Muḥammadan Perfections), an abridgment of his book *Salawāt al-Thanā' 'alā Sayyid al-Anbiyā'* (The Invocations of Laud and Praise on the Liege-lord of Prophets) to be carried on one's person and read in a single sitting. Among its patent and subtle benefits are the many names and attributes of the Holy Prophet ﷺ which it contains, some of them harder to come by in other compilations. Among the more outstanding Prophetic names and attributes:

al-Ladhī Infalaqat minhu al-Anwār ﷺ He from whom cleaved lights
al-Ladhī Khalaqtahu min Nūrika wa-Khalaqta minhu Jamī'a Makhlūqātika ﷺ He whom You created out of the light belonging to You and out of whom You created all Your creatures
Aṣl al-Bariyyāt ﷺ Principle of all creations
'Aynu Ḥayāt al-Dārayn ﷺ The wellspring of the life of this and the next abode
'Ayn al-Na'īm ﷺ The source of bliss / Bliss itself
Dhūl-Makānat al-Amīna ﷺ Possessor of the surest rank
Fātiḥat al-Mawjūdāt ﷺ Opening of all existent things
'Illat al-Sujūdi li-Ādama ﷺ The reason why they prostrated to Ādam upon them peace
Khalīfatuka al-Arḥam ﷺ The most merciful vicegerent of Allah Most High
Majlā al-Kamālāt al-Ilāhiyya al-A'ẓam ﷺ Greatest manifestation of the Divine Perfections
Man Ṭābat minhu al-Nujār ﷺ He because of whom his own ancestors are pure
Manba' al-Anwār ﷺ Wellspring of lights

Maẓhar Allāhi al-Tāmm ﷺ The complete manifestation of Allah Most High
Maẓhar al-Ṣifāt ﷺ The Manifestation of the Divine Attributes
Mir'āt al-Dhāt al-Qudsiyya ﷺ The Mirror of the Divine Essence
Nūr Allāhi al-Asbaq ﷺ The foremost Light of Allah
Al-Nūr al-Awwal ﷺ The primeval Light
Nūr Allāh al-Atamm ﷺ The all-complete Light of Allah
al-Qā'im bi-Ḥall al-Mushkilāt ﷺ In charge of solving difficulties
Rūḥ al-Arwāḥ wa-Abū al-Arwāḥ ﷺ The Spirit of spirits and father of souls
Rūḥu Jasad al-Kawnayn The soul in the body of this world and the next world
al-Sābiqu lil-Khalqi Nūruhu ﷺ He whose light precedes all creation
Ṣāḥib al-Rūḥ al-Kulliyya ﷺ Owner of the spirit that fills the universe
Ṣāḥib al-'Ulūm al-Nūrāniyya Owner of the sciences of light
Ṣāḥib al-'Ulūm al-Lādunniyya ﷺ Owner of the sciences from the Divine Presence
Sababu Wujūdi al-Akwān ﷺ The reason the created universes exist
Sababu Wujūdi al-Wujūd ﷺ Reason for the existence of existence
Shajarat al-Aṣl al-Nūrāniyya ﷺ The light-tree of the origin
Zakhkhāru al-Karami wal-Futuwwa ﷺ Of inexhaustible generosity and chivalry
Ẓillu Allāhi al-Wārif ﷺ The all-extended shadow of Allah Most High.

al-Ṣalawāt al-Arba'īn lil-Awliyā' al-Arba'īn (The Forty Invocations of Blessings by the Forty Friends of Allah).

Ṣalawāt al-Thanā' 'alā Sayyid al-Anbiyā' ﷺ (The Invocations of Blessings and Glory on the Master of Prophets) <1317>, followed by *Hādī al-Murīd.*

al-Sharaf al-Mu'abbad li-Āli Sayyidinā Muḥammad ﷺ (Everlasting Honor for Our Master Muḥammad's Family ﷺ) <1309>.

Shawāhid al-Ḥaqq fil-Istighātha bi Sayyid al-Khalq ﷺ (The Witnesses to Truth on the Obtainment of Aid through the Master of Creatures) <1323>, a summation of several hundred pages comprising several epistles in refutation of various heresies. Among them:

[1]On the affirmation of direction *(al-jiha)*: al-Nabhānī's magnificent epistle *Raf' al-Ishtibāh fī Istiḥālat al-Jiha 'alā*

Allāh (The Removal of Uncertainty Concerning the Impossibility of Direction for Allāh ﷻ)[22] (p. 210-240), a refutation of Aḥmad b. Taymiyya's notorious *Fatwā Ḥamawiyya* which had adduced the "verses of unapparent meaning" *(mutashābihāt)* to affirm direction and place for the Divinity. Other refutations include Imam Ibn Jahbal al-Kilābī's (d. 733) lengthy reply which Shaykh al-Islām Tāj al-Dīn Ibn al-Subkī reproduced in full in *Ṭabaqāt al-Shāfi'iyya al-Kubrā*;[23] Shaykh Muḥammad Sa'īd b. 'Abd al-Qādir al-Baghdādī al-Naqshbandī's (d. 1339) *al-Wajh fī Ibṭāl al-Jiha* in 36 folios as of yet unpublished;[24] and Imam Muḥammad Zāhid al-Kawtharī's *Khuṭūrat al-Qawli bil-Jiha* (The Gravity of the Doctrine that Attributes Direction to Allah ﷻ) in which he reports Imam al-Bayāḍī's explanation of Imam Abū Ḥanīfa's statement: Whoever says, 'I do not know whether my Lord is in the heaven or on earth' is a disbeliever and, similarly, whoever says, 'He is on the Throne and I do not know whether the Throne is in the heaven or on earth' is a disbeliever."[25] Al-Bayāḍī said in *Ishārāt al-Marām*:

> This is because he implies that the Creator has a direction and a boundary while anything possessing direction and boundary is necessarily created. So this statement explicitly attributes imperfection to Allah ﷻ. The believer in [Divine] corporeality and direction is someone who denies the existence of anything other than objects that can be pointed to with the senses. They deny the Essence of the Deity that is

[22]Recently published as a stand-alone monograph at Ghār Ḥirā' in Damascus.

[23]Ibn Jahbal wrote: "How can you say that Allah is literally *(ḥaqīqatan)* in *(fī)* the heaven, and literally above *(fawq)* the heaven, and literally in *(fī)* the Throne, and literally on *('alā)* the Throne?!" Ibn Jahbal, *Refutation of Ibn Taymiyya* §93 in Ibn al-Subkī, *Ṭabaqāt al-Shāfi'iyya al-Kubrā* (9:61).

[24]Cf. 'Imād 'Abd al-Salām Ra'ūf, *al-Āthār al-Khattiyya fī al-Maktabat al-Qādiriyya fī Baghdād* (2:493 ms. 642).

[25]In *al-Fiqh al-Absaṭ* ("The Greatest Wisdom"), the same work as the *Fiqh al-Akbar* but in catechetic form narrated from the Imam exclusively by Abū Muṭī' al-Ḥakam b. 'Abd Allāh b. Muslim al-Balkhī al-Khurāsānī through Abū 'Abd Allāh al-Ḥusayn b. 'Alī al-Alma'ī al-Kāshgharī (d. >484), both of them discarded as narrators.

transcendent beyond that. This makes them positively guilty of disbelief.[26]

Imam ʿAbd al-Qāhir al-Baghdādī in his *Uṣūl al-Dīn* cites, among those who consider the verse of *istiwā'* among the *mutashābihāt* or Qur'ānic ambiguities, Imam Mālik b. Anas, the seven jurists of Madīna and al-Aṣmā'ī.[27] Imam al-Pazdawī said of the attribute of corporeality in his *Uṣūl* that it is "known in principle but ambiguous in description *(maʿlūmun bi-aṣlihi mutashābihun bi-waṣfihi)*.[28] Al-Baghdādī's and al-Pazdawī's words show the fallacy of Ibn Taymiyya's claim in the epistle *al-Iklīl fīl-Mutashābih wal-Ta'wīl* that "I do not know any of the *Salaf* of the Community nor any of the Imams, neither Aḥmad b. Hanbal nor other than him, that considered these [the Divine Names and Attributes] as part of the *mutashābih*"![29] Al-Nabhānī (p. 251) points out that Ibn Taymiyya not only claimed to know the meaning of these verses, but also added categorical interpretive terms to their purported meanings such as "literally" *(ḥaqīqatan)* and "with His essence" *(bi dhātihi)*. He concludes, "If the meaning of such verses [of corporeality in relation to the Divine Attributes] were known, it could not be other than in the sense in which the attributes of created entites are known, as in *istiwā'* in the sense of sitting *(al-julūs)* which we know in relation to ourselves, and this applies to the rest of the ambiguous terms."

[2]On the proofs of the hearing of the Prophet ﷺ in his noble grave (p. 283-285) against the contrary assertions by modernist "Salafis" such as Nuʿmān al-Alūsī's *al-Āyāt al-Bayyināt fī ʿAdam Samāʿ al-Amwāt* (The Clear Signs that the Dead Cannot Hear) – whose editor went so far as to state: "I have found no evidence for the Prophet's ﷺ hearing of the salaam of those who greet him at his grave"![30]

[26]Al-Kawtharī, *Maqālāt* (p. 368-369).

[27]Cf. al-Khattābī in *Maʿālim al-Sunan* (Hims ed. 5:101) and al-Qārī in *al-Asrār al-Marfūʿa* (2nd ed. p. 209-210 §209; 1st ed. p. 126 §478).

[28]*Kashf al-Asrār* (1:55-60).

[29]*Majmūʿat al-Rasā'il* (13:294).

[30]Nāṣir al-Albānī, footnote to al-Alūsī's *al-Āyāt al-Bayyināt* (Maktab al-Islāmī ed. p. 80=

[3]On the proofs of *tawassul* or seeking the intermediary of the Prophet ﷺ: al-Nabhānī refutes in great detail those who deny the permissibility of *tawassul* adducing, among other texts, the proofs listed by the Mufti of Mecca, Shaykh al-Islam al-Sayyid Aḥmad Zaynī Daḥlān in his *Khulāṣat al-Kalām fī Bayān Umarā' al-Balad al-Ḥarām* (The Summation Concerning the Leaders of the Holy Land in full (p. 151-177). Daḥlān also authored *al-Durar al-Sunniyya fīl-Radd alā al-Wahhābiyya* (The Sunni Pearls in Refuting the Wahhābīs Cairo 1319, 1347), *Fitnat al-Wahhābiyya* (The Wahhābī Tribulation), all of these works detailing the development of the Wahhābī movement in Najd and the Hijāz. A number of the latter-day Scholars of *Ahl al-Sunna* in the Ḥijāz and its surroundings wrote book-length refutations along the same lines, notably Muḥammad b. ʿAbd al-Wahhāb's brother Sulaymān; the Yemeni scholar al-Sayyid 'Alawī b. al-Ḥabīb Aḥmad al-Ḥaddād Bā 'Alawī; the Ḥijāzī scholar Sayyid ʿAbd Allāh b. Ḥasan Bāshā Bā 'Alawī; Shaykh Ibrāhīm al-Samnūdī al-Manṣūrī (d. 1314); and the late erudite scholar Shaykh Salāmat al-'Azzāmī (d. 1376).[31]

[4]On the claimed impermissibility of travelling to visit the Prophet ﷺ: al-Nabhānī's counter-refutation (p. 241-247, 275-298) of Muḥammad b. ʿAbd al-Hādī's *al-Ṣārim al-Munkī fī Naḥr al-Subkī* (The Hurtful Blade in the Throat of al-Subkī [!]), a rabid attack on Shaykh al-Islam al-Taqī al-Subkī's masterpiece on the visitation of the Prophet ﷺ [*Shifā' al-*

Riyadh ed. p. 113) and *al-Silsila al-Ḍa'īfa* (§203).

[31]Cf. Sulaymān b. ʿAbd al-Wahhāb (d. 1210/1795), *Fasl al-Khitāb fī Madhhab Ibn ʿAbd al-Wahhāb*, also published as *al-Sawā'iq al-Ilāhiyya fī al-Radd 'alā al-Wahhābiyya*; 'Alawī b. Aḥmad al-Ḥaddād, *Misbāh al-Anām* (1216/1801) of which we published the introduction in full together with the translation of al-Sayyid Yūsuf al-Rifā'ī's *Advice to Our Brothers the Scholars of Najd* (1420/1999); Sayyid ʿAbd Allāh b. Ḥasan Bāshā Bā 'Alawī, *Sidq al-Khabar fī Khawārij al-Qarn al-Thānī 'Ashar* ("The Truthful News Concerning the Khawārij of the Twelve Century") (al-Lādhiqiyya, 1346/1928); Aḥmad Zaynī Daḥlān (d. 1304/1886), al-Samnūdī al-Manṣūrī, *Sa'ādat al-Dārayn fīl-Radd 'alāl-Firqatayn al-Wahhābiyya wal-Ẓāhiriyya* ("The Bliss of the Two Abodes in the Refutation of the Two Sects: Wahhābīs and Ẓāhirīs"), and Salāmat al-'Azzāmī, *al-Barāhīn al-Sāṭi'a fi Radd Ba'ḍ al-Bida' al-Shā'i'a* ("The Radiant Proofs in Refuting Some Widespread Innovations").

Siqām fī Ziyārati Khayr al-Anām ﷺ (The Healing of Hearts in Visiting the Best of Creatures)] in which Ibn ʿAbd al-Hādī "adopted the manner of fanatics and departed from the norms of ḥadīth Scholars" according to Shaykh ʿAbd al-ʿAzīz al-Ghumārī,[32] in defense of his teacher Ibn Taymiyya's aberrant fatwa that it was a sin to undertake travel with the intention of visiting the Prophet ﷺ. Ibn ʿAbd al-Hādī filled his book with unfounded accusations "in order to defend the innovations of his teacher.... It should have been titled *al-Shātim al-Ifkī* ('The Mendacious Abuser')."[33] He falsely accuses Imam al-Subkī of encouraging pilgrimage to the Prophet's ﷺ grave, prostration to it, circumambulating around it, and the belief that the Prophet ﷺ removes difficulty, grants ease, and causes whoever he wishes to enter into Paradise, all independently of Allah ﷻ! Nuʿmān al-Alūsī also wrote an attack on both Imams al-Haytamī and al-Subkī titled *Jalā' al-ʿAynayn fī Muḥākamat al-Aḥmadayn* which he dedicated to the Indian Wahhābī Ṣūfī, Ṣiddīq Ḥasan Khān al-Qinnawjī and in which, according to al-Nabhānī, he went even further than Ibn ʿAbd al-Hādī. Also among the counter-refutations of these two works: the Ḥāfiẓ of Ḥijāz in the 11th century Muḥammad ʿAlī b. ʿAllān al-Ṣiddīqī's *al-Mubrid al-Mubkī fī Radd al-Ṣārim al-Munkī*, al-Burhān Ibrāhīm b. ʿUthmān al-Samannūdī's *Nuṣrat al-Imām al-Subkī bi-Radd al-Ṣārim al-Munkī*, and a monograph by al-Akhnā'ī. Al-Nabhānī cites the poems of two other critics of al-Subkī – the Hanbalī Abūl-Muẓaffar Yūsuf b. Muḥammad b. Mas'ūd al-ʿUbadī al-ʿUqaylī al-Saramrī and Muḥammad b. Yūsuf al-Yumnī al-Yāfiʿī "who claimed to follow the Shāfiʿī school" – then proceeds to refute them as well as Ibn ʿAbd al-Hādī and Alūsī. Also rejecting Ibn Taymiyya's fatwa as invalid are Shaykh al-Islam Aḥmad Zaynī Daḥlān in his books, Abū ʿAbd Allāh b. al-Nuʿmān al-Maghribī al-Tilimsānī al-Mālikī in *Misbāh al-Anām fī al-Mustaghīthīn bi Khayr al-Anām*, Nūr al-Dīn Abū al-Ḥasan ʿAlī b. Burhān al-Dīn Ibrāhīm b. Aḥmad al-Ḥalabī

[32]In his *al-Tahānī fī al-Taʿqīb ʿalā Mawdūʿāt al-Sāghānī* (p. 49).

[33]Al-Nabhānī, *Shawāhid al-Haqq* (p. 275-276).

al-Qāhirī al-Shāfi'ī (975-1044/1567-1635)[34]–the author of the *Ṣīra Ḥalabiyya* (*Insān al-ʿUyūn fī Sīrat al-Nabī al-Ma'mūn*) and "one of the mountains of learning" (al-Muḥibbī) – in his *Bughyat al-Aḥlām* (both of them included in al-Nabhānī's *Ḥujjat Allāh 'alā al-'Ālamīn*), Imam al-Lacknawī's *Ibrāz al-Ghay fī Shifā' al-'Ay* (The Exposure of Deviation for the Healing of the Sick) and his three monographs on *ziyāra*, Shaykh Muhammad b. 'Alawī al-Mālikī's *Shifā' al-Fu'ād fī Ziyārati Khayr al-'Ibād*, the works of Sayyid Yūsuf al-Rifā'ī of Kuwait, those of Shaykh ʿĪsā al-Ḥimyarī of Dubai, etc.

Al-Nabhānī said of Ibn Taymiyya in *Shawāhid al-Ḥaqq*: "He refuted the Christians, the Shī'īs, the logicians, then the Ash'arīs and *Ahl al-Sunna*, in short, sparing no one whether Muslim or non-Muslim, Sunni or otherwise," all the while "clamoring a lot about following the *Salaf*" (p. 207). He also praised Ibn Taymiyya's "worthy book" (p. 275-276) *al-Ṣārim al-Maslūl 'alā Shātim al-Rasūl* (The Drawn Sword Against the Insulter of the Prophet ﷺ) and said that he saw in his dream that Ibn Taymiyya had been forgiven but that he was in a lower level of Paradise than Taqī al-Dīn al-Subkī. The Qāḍī never declared Ibn Taymiyya a disbeliever nor do any of the reliable Ulema of *Ahl al-Sunna*. May Allah forgive him and them, take us back to Him as Muslims, and join us with His righteous servants! *Āmīn.*

Among those who wrote a commendation *(taqrīẓ)* for this distinguished work is al-Nabhānī's student, the Mauritanian *ḥāfiẓ* Muḥammad Ḥabīb Allāh al-Shinqīṭī (1295-1362). Khayr al-Dīn al-Ziriklī, however, included in his entry on al-Nabhānī in *al-Aʿlām* ʿAbd al-Ḥafīẓ al-Fāsī's disrespectful remarks that "he authored many books in which he mixed together the precious and the worthless, and he mounted wild assaults against eminent personalities in Islam, such as Ibn Taymiyya and Ibn al-Qayyim."

[34]He narrates mainly from Shams al-Dīn al-Ramlī as well as Muḥammad al-Bakrī, al-Nūr al-Ziyādī, al-Shihāb Ibn Qāsim, Ibrāhīm al-ʿAlqamī, Ṣāliḥ al-Bulqīnī, Abū al-Nar al-Ṭabalāwī, ʿAbd Allāh al-Shanshūrī, Saʿ d al-Dīn al-Marḥūmī, Sālim al-Shabshīrī, ʿAbd al-Karīm al-Būlāqī, Muḥammad al-Khafājī, Abū bakr al-Shinwānī, Sālim al-Sanhūrī, and others. From him narrate al-Nūr al-Shabrāmallasī, al-Shams Muḥammad al-Wasīmī, al-Shams Muḥammad al-Naḥrīrī, and others. Al-Muḥibbī, *Khulāṣat al-Athar* (3:122-123).

al-Sihām al-Ṣā'iba li-Aṣḥāb al-Da'āwā al-Kādhiba (The Sure Missiles Against the Prevaricators) printed with *Shawāhid al-Ḥaqq*.

Tahdhīb al-Nufūs fī Tartīb al-Durūs (The Education of Souls in the Arrangement of the Lessons) <1329>, an abridgment of Imam al-Nawawī's *Riyāḍ al-Ṣāliḥīn*.

al-Taḥdhīr min Ittikhādh al-Ṣuwar wal-Taṣwīr (Warning against the Use of Photographs and Photography), in print.

Tanbīh al-Afkār ilā Ḥikmat Iqbāl al-Dunyā 'alā al-Kuffār (Awakening the Thoughts to the Wisdom Behind the World's Embrace of the Disbelievers).

Tarjīḥ Dīn al-Islām (The Preferability of the Religion of Islam), in print.

Ṭayyibat al-Gharrā' fī Madḥi Sayyid al-Anbiyā' ﷺ (The Radiant Ṭayyiba [Pure One, another name for Madīna] on the Praise of the Master of Prophets ﷺ), a poem with its glossary <1314>.

al-'Uqūd al-Lu'lu'iyya fīl-Madā'iḥ al-Nabawiyya (The Strings of Pearls: Prophetic Praises), in print.

Wasā'il al-Wuṣūl ilā Shamā'il al-Rasūl ﷺ (The Means of Arrival to the Characteristics of the Messenger ﷺ), a commentary on Imam al-Tirmidhī's *Shamā'il* (see above, *Mithāl al-Na'l al-Sharīf*). A supercommentary on the *Wasā'il* authored by the late Meccan Shaykh al-Lahjī was published in four large volumes, entitled *Nihāyat al-Sūl*.

al-Wird al-Shāfī (The Healing Spring), in print, an abridgment of Imam al-Jazarī's *al-Ḥiṣn al-Ḥaṣīn* (The Superfortress), a manual of supplications and invocations from the Sunna.

The writer of these lines was privileged to visit the light-bathed grave of Qāḍī Yūsuf al-Nabhānī—Allah have mercy on him!—in the Bāshūrā neighborhood of the Basṭa district of Beirut on the day of Jumu'a 24 Dhūl-Ḥijja 1423 / 8 March 2002, the tombstone of which—erected in 1371/1952 by the representative of the Rashīdiyya Dandarāwiyya Ṭarīqa in Beirut—reads "The Ḥassān [b. Thābit] of Aḥmad ﷺ, Yūsuf Ismā'īl al-Nabhānī."

The next day I was honored to meet one of the Qāḍī's students, the venerable Shaykh Ḥusayn ʿUsayrān al-Shāfiʿī al-Naqhsbandī (1329-1426/1911-2005)—Allah have mercy on him!—in the company of the Beirut educator and legal theorist from *Ahl al-Bayt* Dr. Bassim Itani and thanks to him. Shaykh Ḥusayn ʿUsayrān kindly granted me his chains of transmission to the Qāḍī, including that of the present work, among other prestigious chains in his possession. I also narrate the same from the other authorities already mentioned above, from Qāḍī al-Nabhānī. ﴾**This is of the bounty of my Lord**﴿, (27:40) ﴾**He selects for His mercy whom He will. Allah is of infinite bounty**﴿ (3:74). ﴾**And peace be unto the Messengers**﴿, especially the Master of Messengers, ﴾**and praise be to Allah, Lord of the Worlds!**﴿ (37:181-182).

Al-Nabhānī's Preface

All praise and thanks to Allah Who supported our Master Muḥammad with brilliant stunning miracles and open proofs ✻ and strengthened him with shining tokens and overwhelming signs, ✻ conveying them to us through sound chains of transmission and mass-reported narrations ✻ until their bright suns and clear full moons lit up the worlds.

I praise and thank Him – Exalted is He! – for making this noble Prophet the most perfect of all the Prophets in his Law, ✻ most abundant of them in miracles, ✻ greatest in proofs, ✻ clearest in signs, ✻ most handsome in physical frame, ✻ most accomplished in moral character, ✻ superior in essence, names, and attributes, ✻ of most elevated station in His Presence ✻ and the highest of them in degrees both in the world and the hereafter.

Indeed, the Prophets – the blessings of Allah be upon him and them! – are the liege lords of the Muḥammadan Community ✻ and the princes of his nation ✻ so that the peoples in relation to them are like vassals in relation to their sovereign ✻ or the tribe in relation to its chief. ✻ In reality, the Prophets and their communities are part of the Community of this noblest of Prophets ✻ and subjects of the realm of this greatest of Sultans ✻ – the blessings and peace of Allah Most High be upon him!

I bear witness that there is no God but Allah, the One lone, ✻ absolutely unique, everlasting, eternally-besought God ✻ Who neither begot nor was begotten ✻ and to Whom none compares; ✻ and I bear witness that our Master Muḥammad is His elect servant, ✻ chosen Messenger, ✻ and well-pleasing Beloved ✻ whom He preferred above all dwellers of the earth and heaven.

O Allah, our Lord! Bless him with the best and utmost blessing; ✻ a continuous, all-encompassing blessing; ✻ a blessing that equals all the blessings You have poured and shall ever pour on him since before time began until eternity and in between; ✻ a blessing that matches all past and future blessings invoked upon him by the generality of Your creatures—human beings, jinn, and angels; ✻ a blessing that passes reach and defies count so that words and numbers fail to attain reach and count; ✻ a blessing by which You will make me the happiest of Believers and grant me triumph in obtaining Your good pleasure and his good pleasure in this life and the next; ✻ and bless also his Family, wives, and relatives among the believers on all his sides; ✻ as well as his Companions, who were honored to behold his most noble person and witness his stunning miracles; ✻ and greet them all with Your salutation of peace!

[The Superiority of our Master Muḥammad ﷺ]

To begin: it is no secret to whoever has the least notion of the history of Prophets and Messengers – upon them blessings and peace! – that their foremost leader and the master of all God-created beings is Muḥammad ﷺ. He surpasses them in miracles and proofs, ✻ leads them in merits and qualities, ✻ and outshines them in excellent traits and attributes. ✻ He is the most renowned of them in the heavenly Books with regard to prophecies and tidings, ✻ the most truthful with regard to his corroborations by the ancients and those in latter days, ✻ the strongest in his demonstrations and clearest in his expository signs, ✻ the most exalted in station and noblest in states, ✻ and the best in all aspects of his characteristics.

The reason all this describes the Prophet ﷺ is only because he leads the largest of all the Communities of human beings, has the most inclusive mission *(da'wa)*, brought the most perfect legislation *(sharī'a)*, and is their seal in Prophethood and the last of them in Messengership. Thus, the entire world stands in greater need of his Message and of recording and verifying it than it does **[3]** of the Messages of all the other Prophets. For every Prophet was followed by another Prophet who would reaffirm or complete what his predecessor had brought or else bring a new Law, until Allah sent our Master Muḥammad ﷺ and, with him, forever sealed *(khatama)* the Prophethood of Prophets and the Messengership of Messengers – upon him and them blessings and peace! His canon abrogated those canons; his sea drowned out those streams; his sun eclipsed those stars.

It follows that he ﷺ is the Prophet of Prophets and Messengers ✻ and the Envoy to all creatures without exception; ✻ while his Law is the vast ocean with which nothing of the previous dispensations differs except it has once and for all superseded it with a new dispensation. ✻ Moreover, his Law has added [to all that came before] rulings, lights, and secrets in untold proportions which none knows but Allah and whoever Allah has taught. ✻ Hence, his stunning miracles and the proofs of his Prophethood ﷺ are more numerous and greater ✻ and more manifest and lasting ✻ than the miracles and Prophetic proofs of all other Prophets.

Rather, if all that took place at their hands was brought together and multiplied many times, it still would not match one stunning miracle of his ﷺ, namely, the Qur'ān. ✻ Likewise, if the totality of their immense merits, – upon him and them blessings and peace! – were to be collected, they would not match one merit of his, namely, the Ascent above the heavens and all that it brought him in the way of lights, secrets, love, and proximity in that blessed night.

Then what should we say when his miracles and merits – Allah bless and greet him! – cannot be counted, ✻ nor is the help *(madad)* of those miracles and merits ever cut off whether in his life or after his death. ✻ Nor did any stunning miracle take place for any of the Prophets – upon them blessings and peace! – except a greater one or the like of it took place for him ﷺ. Furthermore, all their miracles came to an end at some point or another, whereas he ﷺ has innumerable miracles that still remain current.

Among them, or rather the greatest such miracle, is the pre-eternal Divine Discourse ✻ and most noble Qur'ān ✻ that contains, among other things, many thousands of stunning miracles and proofs, ✻ perfections and merits, ✻ conclusive demonstrations, ✻ and glorious signs; ✻ and the suns of its signs are forever rising over all the firmaments ✻ with their dazzlings lights, ✻ brilliant to behold, ✻ and perpetually radiant.

Another still current miracle is what he ﷺ told in his lifetime to the effect that there shall befall countless new matters after his death, among them the conditions of the Final Hour and its signs. Many of the latter already took place in the previous centuries exactly as he ﷺ had predicted and continue to appear in every time and place so that there is no doubt that whatever did not yet take place so far shall take place at some future time – namely, the major signs of the Final Hour.

Now, if someone were to tell of one thousand occurrences, for example, then was shown to be truthful in nine hundred and ninety-nine of them: no one would doubt that the remaining report will also prove him truthful. This is only a hypothetical illustration for the stature of the Prophet ﷺ is beyond such a comparison and his truthfulness is established far beyond that of any hypothetical reporter in terms that defeat analogy. For there remains in the latter example a weak possibility of lying with regard to the last of the thousand reports. As for the Prophet ﷺ, in the light of his abundant tidings, before his existence, in the heavenly books and [the reports of] the rabbis, monks, jinns, and seers; his endless stunning miracles; tried truthfulness in all he said would take place both in his lifetime and after his death out of all kinds of things unseen and unknown at the time of their mention; the perfection of his personal attributes *(shamā'il)*; the wealth of his qualities; his fame both before **[4]** and after Prophethood, among his people, for truthfulness and honesty to the point they had named him The Trusted

One *(al-amīn)* – nor was any lie ever reported coming from him whether before or after Prophethood: in the light of all this, it is definitely impossible that his report be untruthful. Nor does anyone doubt his truthfulness except those made blind of hearts ✻ or those whom news of his miracles and tidings did not reach.

Also among his still current miracles are the miraculous gifts of the saints *(karāmāt al-awliyā')* of his Community – Allah bless and greet him! – for they all count among his stunning miracles and they are continuously taking place in every age and region of the world. Should we compute, for example, all of their occurrences from east to west for a single month, we would reach millions. Their news have spread incessantly in every corner of the world ✻ filling books and volumes ✻ but they are only a drop in the sea of the occurrences that were not recorded and went with the passage of time ✻ into oblivion as if they had never taken place. ✻ Few indeed are the Muslims who hold right belief in the Friends of Allah except they witness some of these miraculous gifts. Many of the latter are witnessed by some of those who deny the reality of these miracles or disbelieve in the sainthood *(wilāya)* of their authors just as many of the idolaters used to witness the stunning miracles of the Prophet ﷺ while disbelieving in him. So their miraculous gifts – Allah be well-pleased with them! – are offshoots *(furū')* of his stunning miracles ﷺ just as they themselves are also considered branches of him. Therefore, inevitably, they and their miraculous gifts must face something of what he ﷺ and his stunning miracles faced, such as the denials of doubters and the disdain of the obstinate.

[The Sources]

The Imams of the *Umma* of the Prophet ﷺ have transmitted his stunning miracles in every time and place from generation to generation, those that came later *(khalaf)* receiving them from those that came earlier *(salaf)*: the Successors narrated them from the Companions and then, in turn, the Ulema of the Community, giants of our Nation, and ḥadīth Masters *(al-ḥuffāẓ)* took them. ✻ This has been the practice both in the beginning and now. ✻ Out of these reports they compiled books and volumes ✻ which they disseminated in all the regions of Islam at all times. ✻ Among those works are all the books identically titled "The Proofs of Prophethood" *(Dalā'il al-Nubuwwa)* by the ḥadīth Masters Abū Bakr al-Bayhaqī (384-458), Abū Nuʿaym al-Aṣbahānī (336-430), Abū al-Shaykh al-Aṣbahānī (274-369), Abū al-Qāsim al-Ṭabarānī (260-360), Abū Zur'a al-Rāzī (190/ 200?-264/268), Abū Bakr Ibn Abī al-Dunyā (208-281), Abū Isḥāq al-Ḥarbī (198-285), Abū [Bakr] Ja'far al-Firyābī (207-301), and Abū ʿAbd Allāh [Aḥmad b. Mas'ūd al-Khayyāṭ] al-Maqdisī (d. 274) as well as *al-Wafā fī Faḍā'il al-Muṣṭafā* (The Fulfillment of the Pact in Describing the Qualities of the Chosen One) by the ḥadīth Master Abū al-Faraj Ibn al-Jawzī (510-597), and other works. All of the above mention their material together with its known chains and varied paths of transmission. All of these are large books, each one amounting to many volumes. *Sharaf al-Muṣṭafā* (The Loftiness of the Chosen One), for example, by the ḥadīth Master Abū Saʿd [ʿAbd al-Raḥman b. al-Ḥasan b. 'Aliyyak] al-Naysabūrī (d. 431), adds up to eight volumes. Also among the compilations specializing in this topic are *A'lām al-Nubuwwa* by the Imam Abū al-Ḥasan al-Māwardī (d. 450) and *al-Khaṣā'iṣ [al-Nabawiyya] al-Kubrā* (The Special Attributes of the Prophet ﷺ) by the last of the ḥadīth Masters Jalāl al-Dīn al-Suyūṭī (849-911). Among the works dedicated to the generality of his exalted states ﷺ are *al-Shifā bi-Ta'rīf Ḥuqūq al-Muṣṭafā* (The Healing in Knowing the Rights of the Chosen One) by the brilliant Imam, al-Qāḍī 'Iyāḍ (471-544); *al-Mawāhib al-Ladunniyya* (The Divine Bestowals) by the Imam Shams al-Dīn al-Qasṭallānī (851-923); *al-Sīra al-Nabawiyya* (The Prophetic Biography) by the erudite authority al-Sayyid Aḥmad

Daḥlān (d. 1304), which collates most of the books that were compiled over his biography ﷺ. The latter [five] works adduce their reports of his stunning miracles ﷺ without chains of transmission except, perhaps, for *al-Shifā*. [...]

There are also books compiled on a specific aspect of the proofs of his Prophethood ﷺ such as [*Khayr*] *al-Bishr* [*fī Khayr al-Bashar*] (The Greatest Joy Concerning the Best of Human Beings) by [Shams al-Dīn Abū ʿAbd Allāh Muḥammad b. Muḥammad] Ibn Ẓafar [al-Ṣaqallī al-Makkī] (d. 565); *Miṣbāḥ al-Ẓalām fī al-Mustaghīthīn bi Khayr al-Anām* [*fīl-Yaqaẓati wal-Manām*] (The Illumination of Darkness Concerning Those Who Seek Help through the Best of Creatures in a Wakeful State or in Dreams) by Abū ʿAbd Allāh [Shams al-Dīn Muḥammad b. Mūsā] Ibn al-Nuʿmān [al-Marrākishī al-Tilimsānī al-Mālikī] (d. 683); and *al-Ishāʿa li Ashrāṭ al-Sāʿa* (The News Concerning the Conditions of the Final Hour) by al-Sayyid Muḥammad al-Barzanjī (1040-1103).

The meaning of "stunning miracle" **(muʿjiza)** *and the difference between it and all other supernatural wonders*

The Imam and most prudent qāḍī Abu al-Ḥasan ʿAlī b. Muḥammad al-Māwardī said—Allah Most High have mercy on him—in his book *Aʿlām al-Nubuwwa* (The Marks of Prophethood):

If the conclusive proofs of the Prophets to their Nations is the feat that cannot possibly be imitated *(al-muʿjiz)* and indicates their truthfulness, then such a feat is whatever miraculously disrupts the customary laws known to human beings *(kharaqa ʿādat al-bashar)* – especially those aspects that cannot be breached except with Divine power – and indicates that Allah Most High has singled out that Prophet with those proofs as a confirmation of His singling him out with His Message. The feat that cannot possibly be imitated thus becomes a proof *(dalīl)* of his truthfulness in the claim of his Prophethood if it takes place at a time of legal duty *(al-taklīf)*. If it takes place at the Final Hour when the circumstances of legal duty no longer apply, among its portents there might be, on his part, miraculous disruptions of custom; however, they will not constitute an inimitable feat for the claimant of Prophethood. The breach of custom is relevant in the inimitable feat only because custom is shared by both the one that tells the truth and the liar, while the unusual typifies the truthful apart from the liar. If it is established that the inimitable feat is confined to what we said, namely, breach of natural custom, we might divide all that is out of the ordinary into ten categories:

- First, all that human beings are unable to do, such as creating bodies, changing the essences of things, and reviving the dead. All this, in whatever proportion, is an inimitable feat since both a little of it and much of it are beyond human ability.
- Second, acts whose genus *(jins)* lies within human power but whose proportion *(miqdār)* eludes it, such as crossing huge distances in a short time. Such are inimitable feats because they are breaches of custom, but the theologians *(mutakallimūn)* differ over the part that constitutes an inimitable feat. Some of them hold that it is only the particular aspect that lies beyond human ability because only that aspect is matchless, while others hold that it is an inimitable feat as a whole because it is inseparable from its various components.
- Third, displaying knowledge of something unknown to human beings, as when one tells of unseen events. There are two conditions for this knowledge to be an inimitable feat: repetition to the point that coincidence is precluded, and freedom of any cause or effect from which it might be inferred.
- Fourth, whatever variety *(naw')* lies beyond human power even if its genus lies **[9]** within it, such as the Qur'ān whose style is beyond the classifications of discourse. It is an inimitable feat because its variety lies beyond power and so it lies beyond it as a genus also. Inability to imitate it together with ability to use

its instrument *(āla)* – language – make it an even more imposing stunning miracle.

- Fifth, whatever is part of the acts of human beings but leads to that which lies beyond their power, such as the healing that occurs in the midst of disease and the sprouting that occurs in the midst of seeding. For the instant healing of a long-standing disease and the reaping of a crop that gives its yield before its time are inimitable feats that breach customary natural laws and lie beyond human power.
- Sixth, [predicting] inability to do something that one can normally do, such as the warning to a speaker that he will become unable to speak and informing a writer that he will become unable to write. This is an inimitable feat that concerns the one who is made unable exclusively of others, for only the latter is fully aware of his impotence while others are not fully aware of it.
- Seventh, endowing an animal with speech or an inanimate object with movement: if this occurs upon his summoning or a sign of his, then it is an inimitable feat by him; if this occurred without his summoning or sign then it is not an inimitable feat, even as a breach of custom, because the latter case is not related to him any more than anyone else but rather is one of the oddities of the times.
- Eighth, causing things to appear outside their [normal] time, such as summer fruit in winter and vice-versa. If their continued cultivation outside their time is possible then it is not an inimitable feat, and if it is not possible then it is an inimitable feat whether he caused the feat to appear or was asked for it.
- Ninth, the springing forth of water that was not there before or the drying up of water that had sprung forth provided such occurrences took place without causes extraneous to him: such are among his stunning miracles because they are breaches of natural custom.

- Tenth, sating a huge number of hungry people with a little food and/or quenching their thirst with a little water. This is an inimitable feat with regard to them exclusively of others for the reasons we already mentioned.

Those ten categories and whatever enters, as they do, into the definition of inimitable feats, all have the same probative force in establishing [the veracity of] the inimitable feat and confirming the one who caused its manifestation in his claim of Prophethood. This holds true even if [the level of] inimitability varies greatly among them, just as the proofs of pure monotheism *(dalā'il al-tawḥīd)* may differ in concealment or clarity although each and every one of them is a proof. As for deeds that human beings are able to attempt even if they are unable to actually do them like he does, performing such deeds is not an inimitable feat because their genus is performable and whatever is added is only superior proficiency. Nor do manufactured objects that differ in [the quality of] their manufacturers provide an inimitable feat for the most dexterous among them by which he might claim Prophethood.[35]

Sayyīdī the Imam and Knower of Allah, Shaykh ʿAbd al-Wahhāb al-Shaʿrānī ؓ said in the twenty-ninth topic of his book *al-Yawāqīt wal-Jawāhir [fī 'Aqā'id al-Akābir]* (The Gems and Jewels: Doctrines of the Authorities):

> Know that the Real – Most High and Exalted is He! – did not send the Messengers except to cause people to come out of darkness into light by permission of their Lord. This is shown by the fact that He did not send forth a Messenger except in a time of confusion and mental faltering between transcendence and anthropomorphism. Allah ﷻ therefore showed them His immense favor in elevating for them a person described as coming to them from Allah ﷻ with a Message by which he shall put an end to their confusion. So they looked into the matter in the full light of reason and saw that it was possible

[35] Al-Māwardī, *A'lām al-Nubuwwa* (p. 58-61).

and conceivable. Accordingly, they did not decide to deny it. But they did not see a sign pointing to his truthfulness so they stopped short of confirming him and, instead, asked him: "Did you bring any sign from Allah ﷻ by which we might know that it is true you were sent by Him? For nothing stands between us and you except such a sign." Whereupon he brought them an stunning miracle. Then some of the people believed and some of them disbelieved.

Nor did Allah ﷻ support **[10]** all His Messengers with resplendent stunning miracles except as a foundation for their nations to follow them, for human nature dictates that people never follow one another except after some demonstration has been made. The vast majority of the scholars of Islamic Principles *(al-uṣūliyyūn)* have defined the stunning miracle as a matter that disrupts natural custom *(amrun khāriqun lil-'āda)* together with a challenge and the absence of resistance on the part of those to whom the Messenger is sent, as such a breach cannot take place at their hands. What is meant by "challenge" *(al-taḥaddī)* is the challenge of the allegation of Messengership. What we have said shows that the latter accompanying condition is not in the sense of "a challenge to produce the like thereof," which is the literal meaning of challenge, but only in the sense that it meets the requirement of one's allegation of Messengership. In other words, everyone to whom it is said, "If you are truly a Messenger, then perform an stunning miracle for us," then Allah produces at his hands an unimitable feat: the manifestation of that feat at his hands is a proof that he is truthful and tantamount to his openly declaring a challenge.

I saw in *Sirāj al-'Uqūl* (The Light of Minds) by Shaykh Abū Ṭāhir al-Qazwīnī[36] – Allah have mercy on him! – the following: "Know that the categorical proof that establishes beyond doubt the Prophethood of Prophets is the stunning miracles. Those miracles are Divinely-created acts that breach natural custom at the hand of the asserter of Prophethood and confirm his claim.

[36]A commentary on al-Baydāwī's (d. 685) basic manual *Minhāj al-Wuṣūl ilā 'Ilm al-Uṣūl* by Abū Ṭāhir Muḥammad b. Ṭāhir al-Qazwīnī (d. ?) titled *Sirāj al-'Uqūl ilā Minhāj al-Wuṣūl*. Cf. *Kashf al-Ẓunūn*.

Such acts are tantamount to the explicit declaration by Allah Most High to him, 'You are My Envoy,' in confirmation of what he asserts. Similar to this is when a person stands in the midst of others before a strong king and says, 'O you who are present! I am the emissary of this king, and the sign by which you will know that I tell the truth is that the king shall stand and remove the crown from his head,' whereupon the king, on the spot, gets up and removes his crown immediately after the claimant made his claim. Is not this act of the king tantamount to his saying, 'You spoke truly and, indeed, you are my emissary'?"[37]

The difference between the miraculous gift *(karāma)* and the stunning miracle *(mu'jiza)* is that the latter take place together with a challenge, namely, the claim of Messengership; while the *walī* (saint) does not issue a challenge with the miraculous gift. And the reality of this is that when the *walī* claims that he is a *walī* through the performance of an act that disrupts natural custom, this in no way diminishes the Prophetic miracle, whereas if he were to claim, through the same act, that he was a Prophet, he would be lying in his claim; and a liar could not possible be a Friend of Allah Most High, so it is incorrect that anything of what takes place at the hands of Prophets and *awliyā* should ever take place at his hands.

The difference between miracles [on the one hand] and witchcraft *(siḥr)* and quackery *(sha'wadha)* [on the other] is that the miracle remains – together with its traces – for some time after the Prophet, while witchcraft quickly vanishes. Further, miracles are performed by a Prophet in the midst of witnesses and the most eminent persons of a region while quackery is foisted upon children, the simple-minded, and the ignorant.

The difference between miracles and oracles *(kahāna)* is that the miracle is an act that disrupts natural custom together with a challenge, all of which being tantamount to a verbatim Divine

[37]Al-Qazwīnī's example appears to be missing the two conditions stated by al-Māwardī in the third category of the acts that breach natural custom for them to qualify as stunning miracles, namely, "repetition to the point coincidence is precluded and freedom of any cause or effect from which it might be inferred."

confirmation of the truthfulness of His Prophet as we said; whereas oracles are expressions that come up in the discourse of a seer, some probably true and some probably false. The Prophet is never other than perfect in his physical frame and moral character, while the seer can be more or less demented and of deficient physique. Should the latter claim Prophethood through his oracles, another might make the same claim with no difference between the two whatsoever, contrary to Prophethood. Should a Prophet issue a challenge through an stunning miracle then a false claimant make the same claim, it is impermissible that a miracle should take place at his hands in the same way that it does at the hands of the one who tells the truth. The Scholars *(al-nās)* have spoken at length about the impossibility of an stunning miracle taking place at the hands of a liar and a near-consensus has formed around this verdict.

The author [al-Qazwīnī] spoke of this at length in his book *Sirāj al-'Uqūl* and the gist of it is that the conditions *sine qua non* of the stunning miracle are (a) that the act contravene natural custom because ordinary acts are shared equally by those who tell the truth and those who lie; (b) that the act take place at a time when individual and collective legal responsibility still applies, for the matters that take place on the Day of Resurrection – such as the cleaving of the heaven **[11]** and the overthrow of the sun – are disruptions of natural custom but not stunning miracles, and responsibility no longer applies in the hereafter; (c) that the act be accompanied by a challenge, meaning a claim of Messengership, for certain acts might take place at certain times – such as earthquakes and hurricanes – which are not stunning miracles because no challenge accompanies them; and (d) that the act be without precedent whatsoever, for if one were to receive a certain Sūra of the Qur'ān and then proceed to some faraway tribe that the call to Religion has not yet reached, announcing it to them, it would not form an stunning miracle. Ponder this discussion for it is valuable.[38]

The author of *al-Mawāhib al-Ladunniyya* [al-Qasṭallānī] said:

[38]Al-Sha'rānī, *al-Yawāqīt* (p. 281-291).

Know that the stunning miracle is a matter that disrupts natural custom together with a challenge that indicates the truthfulness of Prophets – upon them blessings and peace! It was named a "disabling act" *(mu'jiza)* because people are unable to come up with anything like it. Its [four] conditions are (i) that it breach natural custom – such as [1] the splitting of the moon[39] by the Chosen One ﷺ and [2] the gushing of water from his fingers.[40] (ii) That it be accompanied by a challenge – demanding a rebuttal and counter-response *(al-mu'āraḍa wal-muqābala)*. The verifying authorities defined the challenge as a summons to the Message. (iii) That none be able to perform, by way of counter-response, anything remotely comparable to what the challenger has done. [And (iv) "that it take place in accordance with the claim made by the one who produces it as a challenge," as mentioned further below.]

As for the breach of custom unaccompanied by a challenge it is only a miraculous gift; similarly, the breach that precedes the challenge, such as [3] the shading of the cloud[41] and [4] the splitting of the breast[42] that took place for our Prophet ﷺ before the announcement of the Message. These are not stunning miracles but only miraculous gifts *(karāmāt)* which may take place at the hands of the *awliyā*, and the Prophets before Pro-

[39]Ibn Kathīr in his *Tafsīr* and al-Kattānī in *Nazm al-Mutanāthir* (§264) include it among the mass-narrated narrations.

[40]Al-Kattānī includes it among the mass-narrated narrations in *Nazm al-Mutanāthir* (§267).

[41]Narration of the trip of Abū Ṭālib with his nephew to Buṣra then the latter ﷺ was young, narrated from Abū Mūsa al-Ash'arī by al-Tirmidhī *(ḥasan gharīb)*, Ibn Abī Shayba, al-Ḥākim *(saḥīḥ)*, Abū Nu'aym in *Dalā'il al-Nubuwwa* (p. 170-172 §109), and al-Bayhaqī in *Dala'il al-Nubuwwa* as cited in al-Suyūṭī's *al-Khaṣā'is al-Kubrā* (1:206), while Ibn Ḥajar said its chain was strong and its narrators trustworthy in *al-Iṣāba* (1:179) and *Fatḥ al-Bārī* (10:345). Also narrated with a similar wording in Ibn Sa'd (1:121), Ibn Hishām (1:180), Abu Nu'aym in *Dalā'il al-Nubuwwa* (p. 168-170 §108), and al-Bayhaqī in *Dalā'il al-Nubuwwa* as cited in al-Suyūṭī's *Khaṣā'is* (1:208).

[42]Once in childhood as narrated from Anas by Muslim and Aḥmad and another time before the Ascent over the heavens as narrated from Mālik b. Ṣa'ṣa'a and Anas b. Mālik by al-Bukhari and Muslim. Two other times are reported, one in childhood as well and one in the cave of Ḥirā' at the time of the first revelation. Al-Kattānī includes it among the mass-narrated reports in *Nazm al-Mutanāthir* (p. 123-134 §261) and Mūḥtāyin al-Fārisī lists twelve narrations to that effect in *al-Nūr al-Lāmi'* (p. 113-120).

phethood are, at the very least, *awliyā*. Therefore, the appearance of these miraculous gifts is permissible for them as a foundation for their Prophethood.

Furthermore, phenomena that take place a certain time after a challenge do not count as something comparable *(muqārana)* in the general acceptance of the term, such as the narrations of the utterance of the two testimonies of faith[43] by some of the dead after his death ﷺ and similar reports that have reached the rank of mass narrations. Also outside the definition of "something comparable" is witchcraft accompanied by a challenge, for it is possible for those addressed by the Message to counter witchcraft by producing something comparable.

There is a difference of opinion whether witchcraft actually alters objects and changes their nature or not. Some said yes to the point they hold it feasible for a sorcerer to change a human being into a donkey. Others said that no one can actually alter an object or change its nature except Allah Most High or His Prophets, while neither sorcerers nor the righteous *awliyā* can actually alter objects. They said:

> If we should hold feasible for the sorcerer what we hold feasible for a Prophet, then what difference do you still make between them? Should you invoke the erudite Qāḍī Abū Bakr al-Bāqillānī's position that "the difference consists only in the challenge," we reply that this is patently incorrect in many respects. First, positing challenge as a pre-condition has no basis whether from the Book or the Sunna or the statement of a Companion or Consensus. Whatever is devoid of demonstration is null and void.
>
> Second, most of his signs ﷺ and the most universal and far-reaching of them were free of challenge: endowing the pebbles with speech, the gushing of water, feeding two hundred people with half a liter of food, spitting into the [salt] spring

[43]*Ashhadu an lā ilāha illa-l-Lāh wa ashhadu anna Muḥammadan rasūlullāh*: "I bear witness that there is no God but Allāh and that Muḥammad is the Messenger of Allah," declaring which enters one into Islam.

[that turned sweet], 5 the uttering of the tree-stump,[44] the complaint of the camel, and so on with the rest of his major stunning miracles. It may be that he ﷺ did not issue a challenge with other than the Holy Qur'an. Shame, then, to whoever claims that "none of the miracles remain except these two[45]" while turning a blind eye to an ocean of miracles surging like waves! Truly, whoever says that the latter are neither stunning miracles nor signs is closer to unbelief *(kufr)* than to innovation *(bid'a)*.[46] And he ﷺ used to say upon instances [of a miraculous sign]: "I bear witness that I **[12]** am the Messenger of Allah."

[Examples: [1] Salama b. al-Awka' and Abū Hurayra narrated: "When the travel provision of the people decreased [in Tabūk] they thought of slaughtering their camels but 'Umar came to the Prophet ﷺ and said, 'How will they survive their camels?' The Prophet ﷺ said, 6 'Call to them to bring every remainder of their travel provisions.' A piece of leather was spread and they brought whatever they had. Then the a Messenger of Allah ﷺ stood and supplicated, then he blessed over the food and summoned them to being their bags. The people supplied themselves to the last one. Then the Messenger of Allah ﷺ said, b 'I bear witness that there is no god but Allah and that I am the Messenger of Allah!'"[47]

[2] Abū Hurayra narrated that the Prophet ﷺ declared one of the fighters of the Muslim army as being destined for the Fire although he had fought hard and had been mortally wounded. Some people were murmuring about this. During the night the ailing man, unable to bear with his pain, committed suicide. Upon hearing this, the Prophet ﷺ said, 7 "Allah is greatest! I bear witness that I am the

[44]Narrated from Sahl b. Sa'd by al-Bukhārī and Muslim; from Jābir and Ibn 'Umar by al-Bukhārī and Aḥmad; from Burayda and from Abū Sa'īd al-Khudrī by al-Dārimī; from Ibn 'Abbās by al-Dārimī, Aḥmad, and Ibn Mājah; from Anas by al-Tirmidhī *(ḥasan ṣaḥīḥ gharīb)*, Aḥmad, and Ibn Mājah; from Umm Salama by Bayhaqī in *Dalā'il al-Nubuwwa*; from Ubay b. Ka'b by al-Shāfi'ī, Aḥmad, al-Dārimī, Ibn Mājah, Abū Ya'lā, and Sa'īd b. Manṣūr. This incident took place in the year 8 cf. al-Dhahabī, *Tārīkh* (*Maghāzī* p. 621). The ḥadīth was declared mass-narrated *(mutawātir)* by 'Iyāḍ in *al-Shifā'* (chapter on the miracles of the Prophet ﷺ), Tāj al-Dīn al-Subkī in *Sharh Mukhtasar Ibn al-Ḥājib*, al-Suyūṭī in *al-Azhār al-Mutanāthira*, and al-Kattānī in *Nazm al-Mutanāthir* while 'Abd al-Ra'ūf al-Munāwī in his commentary on al-'Irāqī entitled *Sharh Alfiyyat al-Siyar* said it is mass-narrated in meaning *(mutawātir al-ma'nā)*, as also indicated by Bayhaqī in *Dalā'il al-Nubuwwa* and Ibn Ḥajar in *Fatḥ al-Bārī*. Cf. al-Ghumārī, *al-Ibtihāj* (p. 167-168).

[45]Presumably, the challenges to produce 10 sūras the like thereof (Q 11:13) or at least one (2:23, 10:38).

[46]Because many of the stunning miracles other than the Qur'ān are also mass-narrated *(mutawātir)*.

[47]From Salama b. al-Akwa' by al-Bukhārī and Muslim and from Abū Hurayra by Muslim and Aḥmad. See also Ibn Mardūyah's *Amālī* (p. 151).

servant of Allah and His Messenger!" Then he ordered Bilāl to summon the people and said, [a] "None enters Paradise except a submissive soul *(nafsun muslimatun)*" and that [b] "Allah supports this Religion even through the rebel!"[48]

[3] Jābir b. ʿAbd Allāh narrated: "There was a Jew in Madīna who would lend me money up to the date-harvest season. – Jābir had a piece of land which was on the way to Ruma. – One year the trees produced little, so repayment was delayed. The Jew came to me at the time of harvest but I could gather nothing from my land. I asked him to give me another year's respite but he refused. The news reached the Prophet ﷺ whereupon he said to his companions: [8] 'Let us go and ask the Jew for a respite for Jābir.' They all came to me in my garden and the Prophet ﷺ began to speak with the Jew but the latter kept saying, 'Abū al-Qāsim, I will not grant him respite!' When the Prophet saw this, he stood up and walked around the orchard then came back and talked to the Jew some more, but the latter kept refusing his request. I got up and brought some fresh ripe dates *(rutab)* and put them in front of the Prophet ﷺ. He ate then said to me, 'Where is your hut, Jābir?' I informed him and he said, 'Spread out a bed for me in it.' I spread out a bed and he entered and napped. When he woke up, I brought him some more dates and he ate again then got up and talked to the Jew once more but the latter again refused his request. Then the Prophet ﷺ took another walk amid the date-palms whose branches were now full of fruit! and said, 'Jābir! Harvest your dates and repay your debt.' The Jew stayed with me while I plucked the dates until I repaid him his debt in full and there remained with me the same amount of dates. I went out until I reached the Prophet ﷺ and told him of the good news, whereupon he said: [a] 'I bear witness that I am the Messenger of Allah.'"[49]

[4] ʿĀ'isha narrated the ḥadīth of *istisqā'* and the supplication for rain spoken by the Prophet ﷺ on the pulpit, after which rain poured heavily. When the Prophet ﷺ saw the people rushing for cover he smiled until his teeth showed and said: [9] "I bear witness that Allah is able over all things and that I am the servant of Allah and His Messenger!"[50]

[5] ʿUmar narrated: "The Messenger of Allah ﷺ went out one day with ʿUmar b. al-Khaṭṭāb. A woman came up to them and said to the Prophet ﷺ: 'Messenger of Allah, I am a respectable Muslima but I have a husband in my house who is like a woman.' He said: [10] 'Call your husband.' She called him – he was a cobbler – and the Prophet ﷺ said to him: 'What do you say about your wife, ʿAbd Allāh?' He replied: 'By the One Who honored you! I try my best with her. [lit.: My head has not remained dry away from her.]' His wife said: 'Hardly once a month!' The Prophet ﷺ said to her: 'Do you hate him?' She said Yes. The Prophet ﷺ said: 'Bring your heads close together.' He placed the woman's forehead against her husband's forehead and said: 'O Allah! Make harmony between them and make them love one another.' Later, the Prophet ﷺ was passing by the bedding market together with ʿUmar b. al-Khaṭṭāb, and the same woman was out carrying hides

[48]Narrated by al-Bukhārī, Muslim, and Aḥmad.

[49]Al-Bukhārī narrated it in his *Saḥīḥ*.

[50]Narrated by Abū Dāwūd who said its chain was good while the ḥadīth was graded *saḥīḥ* by all of Abū 'Awāna, Ibn al-Sakan, Ibn Ḥibbān, al-Ḥākim, and al-Nawawī cf. al-Tahānawī, *I'lā' al-Sunan* (8:188).

on top of her head. When she saw the Prophet ﷺ she threw them down, came over to him and kissed his feet. The Prophet ﷺ said: 'How are you with your husband?' She replied: 'By the One Who honored you! There is no new possession, no old inheritance and no child of mine dearer to me than him!' The Prophet ﷺ said: a 'I bear witness that I am the Messenger of Allah.' Whereupon 'Umar said: 'And I, too, bear witness that you are the Messenger of Allah.'"[51]]

Third – and this puts to rest the argument – Allah ﷻ said **﴾And they swear a solemn oath by Allah that if there come unto them a portent they will believe therein. Say: Portents are with Allah and (so is) that which tells you that if such came unto them they would not believe﴿** (6:109) and **﴾Naught hinders Us from sending portents save that the folk of old denied them﴿** (17:59). He has named "portents" those stunning miracles requested from the Prophets and did not impose, as a pre-condition, any challenge from anyone else. So it is correct to say that the pre-condition of a challenge is null and void! This is the gist of what Shaykh Abū Umāma Ibn al-Naqqāsh said in his *Tafsīr*.[52] It was answered that the pre-condition of [the miracle] being accompanied by a challenge does not mean the request to produce something similar as the literal meaning of challenge goes but only the affirmation of Messengership.

Fourth among the conditions of the stunning miracle is that it take place in conformity with the claim made by the one who produces it as a challenge. When any of these conditions does not exist or is not fulfilled, there is no stunning miracle.

If you ask what the best term is for what the Prophets brought: is it "the stunning miracle" *(mu'jiza)*, or "the sign" *(āya)* or "the proof" *(dalīl)*? The answer is that the great Imams of the past

[51]Al-Bayhaqī narrated it from 'Umar and Jābir through al-Tirmidhī and al-Bukhārī in *Dalā'il al-Nubuwwa* (6:228-229). Ibn Kathīr mentions it in *al-Bidāya wal-Nihāya.*

[52]The Cairene Abū Umāma Shams al-Dīn Muḥammad b. 'Alī b. 'Abd al-Wāhid al-Dakkālī, Ibn al-Naqqāsh (d. 763) authored a large Qur'anic commentary titled *al-Sābiq wal-Lāhiq* on the principle of not quoting anything from any other commentator as mentioned by al-Suyūṭī in *Tabaqāt al-Nuhāt*, Hajjī Khalīfa in *Kashf al-Zunūn* (2:973), and al-Adnahwī's (11th c.) *Tabaqāt al-Mufassirīn* (p. 339 §441).

named the stunning miracles of the Prophet ﷺ "the proofs *(dalā'il)* of Prophethood" and "the signs *(āyāt)* of Prophethood". The term *mu'jiza* does not appear in the Qur'ān nor even in the Sunna. Both only contain the terms "sign" *(āya)*, "evidence" *(bayyina)*, and "demonstration" *(burhān)*. Many of the theologians *(ahl al-kalām)* do not use the name of *mu'jiza* except for Prophets exclusively – upon them peace – while those who affirm disruptions of natural custom at the hands of the *awliyā* name them "miraculous gifts" *(karāmāt)*. The Predecessors *(Salaf)* used the term *mu'jiza* for both, such as Imam Aḥmad and others, as opposed to what is a sign and demonstration of a Prophet's Prophethood, in which case it must be restricted to him. They sometimes named the miraculous gifts "signs" because they indicated the Prophethood of the one followed by the wali at whose hand it took place.

Ibn Ḥajar [al-Haytamī] (909-973) said in his commentary on the *Hamziyya*:

> The truth is that "challenge" here is not in its original sense of requesting a countering and comparable action *(al-mu'āraḍa wal-muqābala)* but rather that of the claim of Messengership. All of the stunning miracles of the Prophet ﷺ are to that effect. Nor is this contradicted by the spectacular supernatural events that might appear at the hands of the endtimes Arch-Liar *(al-dajjāl)* because the latter does not claim Prophethood but Divinity and his mendacity is established by categorical proofs, on top of the fact that he only displays those feats to confuse and mislead people and for no other reason.[53]

[Abū al-Ṭayyib] al-Fāsī[54] (775-832) said in his commentary on *Dalā'il al-Khayrāt*:

[53]Al-Haytamī, *al-Minah al-Makkiyya* (1:232).

[54]The Imam, Ḥadīth Master, and historian Abū al-Ṭayyib Muḥammad b. Aḥmad b. ʿAlī al-Taqī al-Fāsī al-Ḥasanī al-Makkī al-Mālikī. He had five hundred *shuyūkh*, among them Ibn Ḥajar, al-Bulqīnī, al-ʿIrāqī, al-Haythamī, Fāṭima bint al-Ḥarrāzī in Madīna, Maryam bint al-Adhraʿī in Cairo, and Khadīja bint Ibn al-Sulṭān in Damascus. Sakhāwī, *al-Ḍaw' al-Lāmi'* (7:18-20). He authored a large commentary on the *Dalā'il* which is in print.

The name of the supernatural feat that takes place at the hands of the Messenger together with a challenge is "a stunning miracle" *(mu'jiza)*. This is the nomenclature of the theologians. As for what takes place at his hands without a challenge, they say it is only called a sign *(āya)* or a proof *(dalīl)*. However, the totality of the signs that pertain to Prophets constitute an stunning miracle because they are affiliated with them and because they are so numerous. This is why the Prophet ﷺ said: 11 "There is no Prophet among the Prophets except he was granted signs the like of which caused people to believe in him. What I was granted is a[n everlasting] revelation revealed to me [alone], so I hope to be the most numerous of them in followers on the Day of Resurrection."[55] As for those besides the theologians, the major Imams call these acts the marks *(dalā'il)* of Prophethood and the signs *(āyāt)* of Prophethood. Hence, they call their works compiled on this subject, *Dalā'il al-Nubuwwa* and *Dalā'il al-I'jāz*, and many of them have authored such works.[56]

The erudite Emir mentioned supernatural acts in his notes on ʿAbd al-Salām saying:

> Know that supernatural acts are of seven types: (i) the stunning miracle **[13]** accompanied by a challenge; (ii) the "groundwork" *(irhāṣ)* before Prophethood which is its foundation as we say "to do the groundwork for a wall"; (iii) the miraculous gift for a wali; (iv) spontaneous aid *(al-ma'ūna)* befalling a common person and saving him from catastrophe; (v) beguilement *(istidrāj)* for a brazen transgressor in proportion to his claim. This happens only to one who claims Divinity as opposed to one who claims Prophethood, as the proofs of the exclusion of any created attributes from Divinity are so obvious that there is no fear of confusion; (vi) humiliation for the brazen transgressor in flat contradiction of his claim; and (vii) witchcraft and quackery, although it was said that those are not among the

[55]Narrated from Abū Hurayra by al-Bukhāri, Muslim, and Aḥmad.

[56]Abū al-Ṭayyib al-Fāsī, *Maṭāli' al-Masarrāt* (Cairo: Maymaniyya 1309 ed. p. 152), commentary on the *Ḥizb al-thānī min yawm al-thulāthā'* of Jazūlī's *Dalā'il al-Khayrāt.*

supernatural acts as they are quite customary with respect to their practice.[57]

The teacher of our teachers, the erudite Shaykh Ibrāhīm al-Bājūrī (d. 1276) said in his marginalia on *Jawharat al-Tawḥīd* in commentary of the author's [al-Laqānī's] statement, [verse 68] "With stunning miracles they were granted support out of Divine munificence" *(bil-muʿjizāti uyyidū takarruman)*:

> Know that the [Arabic] word for the stunning miracle *(muʿjiza)* is derived lexically from the word "inability" *(ʿajz)* – the opposite of power – and denotes, by convention, a supernatural act accompanied by a challenge consisting in the claim of Messengership or Prophethood together with the lack of effective opposition. Al-Saʿd [al-Taftāzānī] (712-792) said: "It is something extraordinary that appears at the hands of the claimant to Prophethood at a time of challenge to the naysayers, which the latter can produce nothing that compares to it."[58]
>
> The verifying authorities consider it has eight integral aspects:
>
> (i) It must consist in a discourse or deed or something that fails to take place; for example, respectively: the Qur'ān, the gushing of water from between his fingers ﷺ, and the failure of the fire to burn our Master Ibrāhīm عليه السلام. The attributes of the non-created are excluded from this aspect as in the case he might say, "The sign that I am truthful is that the Deity is described as the Creator."
>
> (ii) That it be truly supernatural, *i.e.* a breach of what people are naturally accustomed to over a period of time. Ordinary events are therefore excluded, for example the statement, "The sign that I am truthful is that the sun

[57]Muḥammad b. Muḥammad b. Aḥmad b. ʿAbd al-Qādir al-Sinbāwī, *Ḥāshiyat Ibn al-Amīr ʿalā Itḥāf al-Murīd Sharḥ Jawharat al-Tawḥīd lil-Shaykh ʿAbd al-Salām b. Ibrāhīm al-Laqānī* (ed. Aḥmad Farīd al-Mazyadī, p. 227-228).

[58]Al-Taftāzānī, *Sharḥ al-ʿAqāʾid al-Nasafiyya* (Darwīsh 1411/1990 ed. p. 207-208) under *wa-ayyadahum bil-muʿjizāt al-nāqiḍāt lil-ʿādāt.*

shall rise where it usually rises and set where it usually sets."

(iii) It must take place at the hands of the claimant to Prophethood. This excludes the miraculous gift *(karāma)* which takes place at the hands of an evidently righteous and pious servant. This aspect also excludes spontaneous aid which takes place at the hands of common people, saving them from catastrophe; it excludes entrapment, which is whatever occurrence takes place at the hands of a corrupt person as [repayment for his] deceit and scheming; and it excludes debasement, which is what takes place at his hands to belie him, as happened with Musaylima the arch-liar when he spat into the blind eye of a one-eyed man to heal it but the good eye went out instead.

(iv) It must be paired with the assertion of Prophethood or Messengership literally *ḥaqīqatan)* or else in effect *(ḥukman)*, if it comes a little later. This excludes the groundwork *(al-irhāṣ)*, namely, whatever miracles take place before Prophethood or Messengership as a preliminary or foundation, such as the shading of the cloud for him ﷺ before his mission <or [12] the light that shone in the forehead of his father ʿAbd Allāh>[59].

(v) The miracle must take place in accordance with the claim being made as opposed to any discordant phenomenon, for example if one were to say: "The sign that I am truthful is that the sea shall part in two" then the mountain parts in two.

(vi) The miracle must not be tantamount to a disavowal of what is being claimed. For example, if one were to say: "The sign that I am truthful is that this object shall speak," then the object speaks and declares that he is a

[59]In al-Bājūrī only (p. 299-300) but omitted by al-Nabhānī. Narrated by Ibn Saʿd in his *Tabaqāt* (1:58), al-Suhaylī in *al-Rawd al-Unuf* (1:102), al-Nuwayrī in *Nihāyat al-Arab* (16:58-61, 16:77), al-Ṭabarī in his *Tārīkh* (2:174, 2:243), al-Bayhaqī in *Dalā'il al-Nubuwwa* (1:87), and Ibn al-Athīr's *Tārīkh* (2:4). Ibn al-Jawzi cites it in *al-Wafā'* (p. 82-83, ch. 16 of *Abwāb Bidāyati Nabiyyinā*) and Ibn Hisham narrates it in his *Sīra*.

liar. This is other than if he were to revive a dead person who then declared him a liar, because the object has no will and its disavowal is therefore considered a Divine order, while a human being has free choice and his disavowal is not conclusive since he might choose to disbelieve in a true claim.

(vii) It must be impossible to counter it. This condition excludes witchcraft and charlatanry *(sha'badha)*, which is a sleight of hand suggesting that something is taking place in reality when in fact it is not, as in the case of the snakes [of the magicians]. Some of the Ulema added that

(viii) it must not take place at a time when natural customs are abolished, for example when the sun rises from **[14]** the place it usually sets. This excludes the phenomena that take place at the hands of the Anti-Christ as when he orders the sky to rain then it rains, and he orders the earth to sprout and it sprouts.

Then he [al-Bājūrī] said, concerning the author's [al-Laqānī] statement, [verse 73] "And his stunning miracles are many and resplendent" *(wa mu'jizātuhu kathīratun ghurar)*:

> Know that whatever miracles of his are definitely known and mass-transmitted such as the Qur'ān, there is no doubt that whoever denies them commits disbelief. As for evidence below that level, if it is well-known – such as the gushing of water from his fingers ﷺ – then the one who denies it commits a grave sin *(fisq)*. If the evidence is not well-known or is not firmly established through a sound or fair chain of transmission then the one who denies it is reprimanded only.[60]

I also saw a similar explanation in *Hidāyat al-Murīd Sharḥ Jawharat al-Tawḥīd* by its original author, the erudite scholar Ibrāhīm al-Laqānī.

[60] Al-Bājūrī, *Sharh Jawharat al-Tawhīd* (p. 297-300, 312).

بِسْمِ اللهِ الرَّحْمٰنِ الرَّحِيمِ

The *Mu'jizāt* (Stunning Miracles) of the Master of Prophets ﷺ That Consist in Revealing the Unseen

His expositions of unseen matters taking place either before or after his telling about them except the conditions of the Final Hour, which belong with the stunning miracles that took place after his death ﷺ

Know, first of all, that knowledge of the unseen is the priviledge of Allah Most High, and that its appearance on the tongue of the Messenger of Allah ﷺ and others comes from **[468]** Allah ﷻ either through revelation or through inspiration. The Prophet ﷺ said in the ḥadīth: "I swear it by Allah! Truly [13] I know nothing except what my Lord taught me."[61]

عَنْ عُقْبَةَ بْنِ عَامِرٍ رَضِيَ اللهُ عَنْهُ قَالَ إِنَّ رَسُولَ اللهِ ﷺ قَالَ أَنَا عَبْدٌ لاَ أَعْلَمُ إِلاَّ مَا عَلَّمَنِي رَبِّي أبو الشيخ في العظمة في حديث طويل

وفي الباب عن محمود بن لبيد وعُمارة بن حزم الأنصاريين الحديث رقم ٢٩٤ و٢٩٥

[61]Narrated from 'Uqba b. 'Āmir by Abū al-Shaykh in *al-'Azama* (4:1468-1469 §96714) as part of a longer narration that includes: "I shall inform you of what you came here to ask me about before you tell me and, if you wish, you can speak first then I will answer you… You came to ask me about Dhū al-Qarnayn…." Also narrated from from the Ansārī Companions Mahmūd b. Labīd and 'Umāra b. Hazm as part of the narration of the hypocrite and the lost camel notes 396-397.

Therefore, everything that came to us from him ﷺ consisting in news of the unseen is nothing other than the Divine disclosure to him as a proof for the actuality of his Prophethood and its truth.

The Prophet's ﷺ familiarity with and knowledge of the unseen is a well-known and universally recognized fact ✻ to the point that one of them would say to the other, [14] "Hush! By Allah, even if there is none among us to tell him, the very stones and pebbles would tell him."[62]

ذَكَرَ ابْنُ هِشَامٍ أَنّ رَسُولَ اللهِ ﷺ دَخَلَ الْكَعْبَةَ عَامَ الْفَتْحِ وَمَعَهُ بِلاَلٌ فَأَمَرَهُ أَنْ يُؤَذّنَ وَأَبُو سُفْيَانَ بْنُ حَرْبٍ وَعَتّابُ بْنُ أَسِيدٍ وَالْحَارِثُ بْنُ هِشَامٍ جُلُوسٌ بِفِنَاءِ الْكَعْبَةِ ، فَقَالَ عَتّابُ بْنُ أَسِيدٍ : لَقَدْ أَكْرَمَ اللهُ أَسِيدًا أَلاَ يَكُونُ سَمِعَ هَذَا ، فَيَسْمَعُ مِنْهُ مَا يَغِيظُهُ . فَقَالَ الْحَارِثُ بْنُ هِشَامٍ : أَمَا وَاللهِ لَوْ أَعْلَمُ أَنّهُ مُحِقّ لاَتّبَعْته ، فَقَالَ أَبُو سُفْيَانَ لاَ أَقُولُ شَيْئًا : لَوْ تَكَلّمْت لأَخْبَرَتْ عَنّي هَذِهِ الْحَصَى ، فَخَرَجَ عَلَيْهِمْ النّبِيّ ﷺ فَقَالَ قَدْ عَلِمْت الّذِي قُلْتُمْ ثُمّ ذَكَرَ ذَلِكَ لَهُمْ فَقَالَ الْحَارِثُ وَعَتّابٌ نَشْهَدُ أَنّك رَسُولُ اللهِ وَاللهِ مَا اطّلَعَ عَلَى هَذَا أَحَدٌ كَانَ مَعَنَا ، فَنَقُولُ أَخْبَرَك . ابن هشام شفاء روض اكتفاء أعلام النبوة

[62]Spoken by Abū Sufyān b. Ḥarb to 'Attāb b. Usayd and al-Ḥārith b. Hishām outside the Ka'ba on the conquest of Mecca as the Prophet ﷺ was inside with Bilāl, all three of whom entered Islam after the Prophet ﷺ reported their own words back to them. Narrated by Ibn Hishām (5:76), 'Umar b. Shayba as per Ibn Ḥajar in *al-Iṣāba* (4:429), and Ibn Isḥāq as per Ibn Kathīr in his *Tafsīr* (2:73) cf. 'Iyāḍ, *Shifā'*, *Iktifā'* (2:230), *Rawḍ* (4:173), and al-Māwardī, *A'lām al-Nubuwwa* (p. 165).

Al-Ṭabarānī narrated from Ibn ʿUmar رضي الله عنهما that the Prophet ﷺ said: "Truly [15] Allah has brought up the whole world before my eyes and I can see it and all that shall exist in it until the Day of Resurrection as if I were looking at the palm of my hand – a complete disclosure from Allah Who disclosed it to His Prophet just as He disclosed it to the Prophets before him."[63]

عَن ابْنِ عُمَرَ رَضِيَ اللهُ عَنْهُمَا مَرْفُوعاً إِنَّ اللهَ قَدْ رَفَعَ لِي الدُّنْيَا
فَأَنَا أَنْظُرُ إِلَيْهَا وَإِلَى مَا هُوَ كَائِنٌ فِيهَا إِلَى يَوْمِ الْقِيَامَةِ كَأَنَّمَا
أَنْظُرُ إِلَى كَفِّي هَذِهِ جِلِّيَاناً مِنَ اللهِ جَلاَّهُ لِنَبِيِّهِ كَمَا جَلاَّهُ
لِلنَّبِيِّينَ مِنْ قَبْلِهِ حل نعيم في الفتن زيادة الجامع الصغير خصائص كنز وهو ضعيف
جداً لانفراد سعيد بن سنان به

ʿAbd Allāh b. Rawāḥa said رضي الله عنه:

> [16] Among us is the Messenger of Allah reciting His Book
> As the radiant light cleaves the true dawn's sky.
> He showed us guidance after blindness and our hearts
> Now firmly know that all he says will take place.[64]

عَنِ الْهَيْثَمِ بْنِ أَبِي سِنَانٍ أَنَّهُ سَمِعَ أَبَا هُرَيْرَةَ رَضِيَ اللهُ عَنْهُ وَهُوَ
يَقُصُّ فِي قَصَصِهِ وَهُوَ يَذْكُرُ رَسُولَ اللهِ ﷺ إِنَّ أَخًا لَكُمْ لاَ
يَقُولُ الرَّفَثَ يَعْنِي بِذَلِكَ عَبْدَ اللهِ بْنَ رَوَاحَةَ :

[63] A very weak report narrated from Ibn ʿUmar by Nuʿaym b. Ḥammād in the *Fitan* (1:27) and, through the latter, Abū Nuʿaym (1985 ed. 6:101) both through Abū Mahdī Saʿīd b. Sinān al-Kindī who is discarded as a narrator and accused of forgery cf. al-Haythamī (8:287, 2:189, 4:272). Cited by Suyūṭī in *Ziyādat al-Jāmiʿ al-Saghīr* (§1312) and the *Khaṣāʾis* (2:185) as well as Qasṭallānī in the *Mawāhib* (3:559) cf. *Kanz* (§31810, §31971). In addition, "Nuʿaym is disclaimed in his narrations *(munkar al-ḥadīth)* despite his standing as an Imam." Ibn Ḥajar, *al-Amālī al-Ḥalabiyya* (p. 40).

[64] Narrated from Abū Hurayra by al-Bukhārī and Aḥmad, also in *al-Tārīkh al-Saghīr* (1:23) and Ibn Abī ʿĀṣim in *al-Āḥād wal-Mathānī* (4:38) cf. al-Qurṭubī (14:100) and Ibn Kathīr (3:460) in their *Tafsīr*s.

28 • The Prophet's ﷺ Knowledge of the Unseen

وَفِينَا رَسُولُ اللهِ يَتْلُو كِتَابَـــهُ   إِذَا انْشَقَّ مَعْرُوفٌ مِنَ الْفَجْرِ سَاطِعُ
أَرَانَا الْهُدَى بَعْدَ الْعَمَى فَقُلُوبُنَا   بِهِ مُوقِنَاتٌ أَنَّ مَا قَالَ وَاقِعُ
يَبِيتُ يُجَافِي جَنْبَهُ عَنْ فِرَاشِـــهِ   إِذَا اسْتَثْقَلَتْ بِالْمُشْرِكِينَ الْمَضَاجِعُ

خ حم

Ḥassān b. Thābit said ؓ:

<u>17</u> A Prophet who sees what others around him do not
And recites the Book of Allah in every assembly!
If he tells on any given day of something yet unseen,
What he says is confirmed on the morrow or next day.[65]

نَبِيٌّ يَرَى مَا لاَ يَرَى النَّاسُ حَوْلَهُ   وَيَتْلُو كِتَابَ اللهِ فِي كُلِّ مَشْهَـــدِ
وَإِنْ قَالَ فِي يَوْمٍ مَقَالَةَ غَائِـــبٍ   فَتَصْدِيقُهَا فِي ضَحْوَةِ الْيَوْمِ أَوْ غَدِ

عن حبيش بن خالد من شعر حسان في قصة أم معبد رضي الله عنهما طب أبو نعيم والتيمي في الدلائل ك صححه استيعاب اللآلكائي الطبري في التفسير حب في السيرة روض اكتفاء ابن سعد مرسلا

[The two quatrains refute the claim of the author of *Taqwiyat al-Īmān* that the Prophet ﷺ did not know what would happen on the next day on the grounds that he said, <u>18</u> "Avoid saying this" to the slave-girl reciting poetry when she said, "Among us is a Prophet that knows what happens tomorrow."[66] The reason for this order is not because he did not know – since it is established that Allah ﷻ is ❝the knower of the Unseen, and He reveals unto none His secret save unto every messenger whom

---

[65]Narrated from Hubaysh b. Khālid by al-Ṭabarānī in *al-Kabīr* (4:48-50), Abū Nuʿaym (p. 340 §238) and al-Taymī (p. 59-60) in their *Dalāʾil*, al-Ḥākim (3:9-10 *isnād ṣaḥīḥ*), Ibn ʿAbd al-Barr, *Istīʿāb* (4:1958-1962), al-Lālikāʾī in his *Iʿtiqād Ahl al-Sunna* (4:780) cf. al-Ṭabarī, *Tafsīr* (1:447-448), Ibn Ḥibbān, *Thiqāt* (1:128), *Rawd* (2:326), *Iktifāʾ* (1:343). Also from Abū Maʿbad al-Khuzāʿī by Ibn Saʿd (1:230-232) but this is *mursal* and Abū Maʿbad – unlike Umm Maʿbad – is a *Tābiʿī* cf. *Iṣāba* (§10545).

[66]Narrated from al-Rubayyiʿ bint Muʿawwidh in al-Bukhārī, the *Sunan*, and Aḥmad.

He has chosen﴿ (72:26-27) and that He revealed to the Prophet ﷺ knowledge of the future until the Day of Judgment and the Hereafter as well – but because knowledge of the unseen was attributed to him ﷺ in absolute terms when only Allah knows the unseen in absolute terms (as stated by Ibn Hajar in his commentary of this narration in *Fath al-Bārī*). Coming from the mouth of a child not yet qualified to pray (as stated by Ibn al-Qayyim in his marginalia on Abū Dāwūd' *Sunan*), such an assertion was reminiscent of the popular belief unbecoming of a Prophet but typical of the false claims of seers, oracles, astrologers etc. that they could know the future of their own devices, to which Allah ﷻ said ﴾**No soul knows what it will earn tomorrow**﴿ (31:34). Hence, the Prophet ﷺ, in Ibn Mājah's version (with a fair chain), added by way of explanation, "Only Allah knows what happens tomorrow" i.e. independently of anyone and with an absolute knowledge.]

Al-Bukhārī narrated from Ibn ʿUmar رضي الله عنهما: 19 "We kept away from conversation and leisurely talk with our women lest some revelation should come down concerning us. After the Prophet ﷺ died, we spoke more freely."[67]

عَنْ ابْنِ عُمَرَ رَضِيَ اللهُ عَنْهُمَا قَالَ كُنَّا نَتَّقِي الْكَلاَمَ وَالِانْبِسَاطَ إِلَى نِسَائِنَا عَلَى عَهْدِ النَّبِيِّ ﷺ هَيْبَةَ أَنْ يَنْزِلَ فِينَا شَيْءٌ فَلَمَّا تُوُفِّيَ النَّبِيُّ ﷺ تَكَلَّمْنَا وَانْبَسَطْنَا خ جه حم

Al-Bayhaqī narrated from Sahl b. Saʿd al-Sāʿidī رضي الله عنه: "I swear by Allah that 20 some of us would refrain from approaching his wife as he and she lay together under the same sheet for fear some Qur'anic revelation should come down concerning them!"[68]

عَنْ سَهْلِ بْنِ سَعْدٍ رَضِيَ اللهُ عَنْهُ قَالَ لَقَدْ كَانَ أَحَدُنَا يَكُفُّ عَنِ الشَّيْءِ وَهُوَ وَهِيَ فِي ثَوْبٍ وَاحِدٍ تَخَوُّفاً أَنْ يُنَزَّلَ فِيهِ شَيْءٌ مِنَ الْقُرْآنِ طب رجاله رجال الصحيح مج

[67]Narrated from Ibn ʿUmar by al-Bukhārī, Ibn Mājah, and Aḥmad.

[68]Narrated by al-Ṭabarānī in *al-Kabīr* (6:196 §5985) through *Saḥīh* narrators per al-Haythamī (10:284).

The listing of the miracles in this chapter cannot be exhausted because of their large number and the fact that they took place at his hands ﷺ in most of his states, whether they asked him questions or not, whatever circumstances dictated. These are the most numerous of his stunning miracles ﷺ. Qāḍī 'Iyāḍ said in *al-Shifā'*:

> His ﷺ knowledge of the unseen counts among those miracles of his that are known categorically and decisively, reaching us through mass transmission with vast numbers of narrators and congruent meanings.[69]

Imām Aḥmad and al-Ṭabarānī narrated that Abū Dharr ؓ said: 21 "When the Messenger of Allah ﷺ left us there was not a bird that flies but he had informed us about it."[70]

عَنْ أَبِي ذَرٍّ رَضِيَ اللهُ عَنْهُ قَالَ لَقَدْ تَرَكَنَا رَسُولُ اللهِ ﷺ وَمَا يَتَقَلَّبُ فِي السَّمَاءِ طَائِرٌ إِلاَّ ذَكَّرَنَا مِنْهُ عِلْمًا حَدَّثَنَا حَجَّاجٌ حَدَّثَنَا فِطْرٌ عَنِ الْمُنْذِرِ عَنْ أَبِي ذَرٍّ الْمَعْنَى حم طب رجاله ثقات مج

ط حب ع ز

Muslim narrated that 'Amr b. Akhṭab [Abū Zayd] al-Anṣārī ؓ said: 22 "The Prophet ﷺ prayed *fajr* with us then climbed the pulpit and addressed us until the time came for *ẓuhr*, then he descended and prayed. Then he climbed the pulpit and addressed us until the time came for *'aṣr*, whereupon he descended and prayed. Then he climbed the pulpit and addressed us until the sun set. He informed us about all that was to happen until the Day of Resurrection. The most knowledgeable of us is he who has memorized the most."[71]

[69]'Iyāḍ, *al-Shifā'* (p. 413-414): "... and congruent meanings pointing to his familiarity with the unseen."

[70]Narrated by Ṭabarānī, *al-Kabīr* (2:155 §1647) with trustworthy narrators per Haythamī (8:263-264), Aḥmad, al-Ṭayālisī, Ibn Sa'd (2:354), al-Bazzār (9:341 §3897), Ṭabarī in his *Tafsīr* (7:189) Ibn 'Abd al-Barr in *al-Istī'āb* (4:1655), Ibn Ḥibbān (1:267 §65 *isnād ṣaḥīḥ*), and al-Dāraquṭnī in his *'Ilal* (6:290 §1148). Cf. al-Haythamī, *Mawārid al-Ẓam'ān* (p. 47). Also narrated from Abū al-Dardā' by Abū Ya'lā (9:46 §5109 *isnād ṣaḥīḥ*).

[71]Thus narrated by Muslim and Aḥmad.

عَنْ أَبِي زَيْدٍ يَعْنِي عَمْرَو بْنَ أَخْطَبَ رَضِيَ اللهُ عَنْهُ قَالَ صَلَّى بِنَا رَسُولُ اللهِ ﷺ الْفَجْرَ وَصَعِدَ الْمِنْبَرَ فَخَطَبَنَا حَتَّى حَضَرَتِ الظُّهْرُ فَنَزَلَ فَصَلَّى ثُمَّ صَعِدَ الْمِنْبَرَ فَخَطَبَنَا حَتَّى حَضَرَتِ الْعَصْرُ ثُمَّ نَزَلَ فَصَلَّى ثُمَّ صَعِدَ الْمِنْبَرَ فَخَطَبَنَا حَتَّى غَرَبَتِ الشَّمْسُ فَأَخْبَرَنَا بِمَا كَانَ وَبِمَا هُوَ كَائِنٌ فَأَعْلَمُنَا أَحْفَظُنَا م حم

Al-Bukhārī and Muslim narrated that Ḥudhayfa ؓ said: [23] "The Prophet ﷺ stood among us [speaking] for a long time and did not leave out one thing from that time until the rising of the Final Hour except he told us about it. Whoever remembers it remembers it and whoever forgot it forgot it. All those who are present know this. Some of it I might have [469] forgotten, then I see it [happen] and remember it just as someone would remember a man who had been away and then appears before him and he instantly recognizes him."[72]

عَنْ حُذَيْفَةَ رَضِيَ اللهُ عَنْهُ قَالَ قَامَ فِينَا رَسُولُ اللهِ ﷺ مَقَامًا مَا تَرَكَ شَيْئًا يَكُونُ فِي مَقَامِهِ ذَلِكَ إِلَى قِيَامِ السَّاعَةِ إِلاَّ حَدَّثَ بِهِ حَفِظَهُ مَنْ حَفِظَهُ وَنَسِيَهُ مَنْ نَسِيَهُ قَدْ عَلِمَهُ أَصْحَابِي هَؤُلَاءِ وَإِنَّهُ لَيَكُونُ مِنْهُ الشَّيْءُ قَدْ نَسِيتُهُ فَأَرَاهُ فَأَذْكُرُهُ كَمَا يَذْكُرُ الرَّجُلُ وَجْهَ الرَّجُلِ إِذَا غَابَ عَنْهُ ثُمَّ إِذَا رَآهُ عَرَفَهُ ق ومثله عن أبي سعيد وعمر رضي الله عنهما

---

[72] Narrated from Hudhayfa by al-Bukhārī, Muslim, Abū Dāwūd, and Ahmad; and from Abū Saʿīd al-Khudrī by al-Tirmidhī *(hasan sahīh)* and Ahmad. Al-Bukhārī narrated something similar from ʿUmar.

Muslim also narrated that Ḥudhayfa said: [24] "The Prophet ﷺ informed me of all that would happen until the Day of Resurrection and there was nothing of it except I asked him about it, save that I did not ask him what would bring the people of Madīna out of Madīna."[73]

عَنْ حُذَيْفَةَ رَضِيَ اللهُ عَنْهُ أَنَّهُ قَالَ أَخْبَرَنِي رَسُولُ اللهِ ﷺ بِمَا هُوَ
كَائِنٌ إِلَى أَنْ تَقُومَ السَّاعَةُ فَمَا مِنْهُ شَيْءٌ إِلاَّ قَدْ سَأَلْتُهُ إِلاَّ أَنِّي
لَمْ أَسْأَلْهُ مَا يُخْرِجُ أَهْلَ الْمَدِينَةِ مِنَ الْمَدِينَةِ م حم

Abū Dāwūd also narrated that Ḥudhayfa said: "By Allah! [25] I do not know whether my companions forgot or pretended to forget it,[74] but [a] the Messenger of Allah ﷺ did not omit a single instigator of sedition until the end of the world, each with a minimum of three hundred followers, except he mentioned each one of them for us by his own name, the name of his father, and the name of his tribe."[75]

عَنْ حُذَيْفَةَ بْنِ الْيَمَانِ رَضِيَ اللهُ عَنْهُ وَاللهِ مَا أَدْرِي أَنَسِيَ
أَصْحَابِي أَمْ تَنَاسَوْا وَاللهِ مَا تَرَكَ رَسُولُ اللهِ ﷺ مِنْ قَائِدِ فِتْنَةٍ
إِلَى أَنْ تَنْقَضِيَ الدُّنْيَا يَبْلُغُ مَنْ مَعَهُ ثَلاَثَ مِائَةٍ فَصَاعِدًا إِلاَّ قَدْ
سَمَّاهُ لَنَا بِاسْمِهِ وَاسْمِ أَبِيهِ وَاسْمِ قَبِيلَتِهِ د

[Another narration from Ḥudhayfa: "The Prophet ﷺ was among us [speaking]. For each prayer, he came down, prayed, and returned to his place. [26] He told us about all that would take place from that very moment until the Rising of the Hour. [a] There is no leader of one hundred people or more, whether misguided or guided, except the

[73]Narrated from Ḥudhayfa by Muslim and Aḥmad with the wording: "until the rising of the Hour."

[74]To prevent *fitna*. Al-Qārī said in his commentary of *al-Shifā'*: "to turn to what is more important."

[75]Narrated from Ḥudhayfa by Abū Dāwūd.

Messenger of Allah ﷺ named him for us. Whoever remembers, remembers, and whoever forgot, forgot."[76] The Prophet ﷺ also said: [27] "There are seventy-odd missionaries of hellfire in my Community; if you wished, I would inform you of their names and the names of their fathers."[77]]

Abū Yaʿlā also narrated with a sound chain that Anas ؓ said: "The Messenger of Allah ﷺ came out angry and addressed the people, saying: [28] 'Today you will ask me about nothing except I shall tell you about it,' and we saw that Jibrīl was with him. So ʿUmar said: 'Messenger of Allah, only recently were we in a time of ignorance. We beg you, do not expose our disgrace! [a] Forgive us and may Allah forgive you! *(faʿfu ʿannā ʿafā-l-Lāhu ʿank)*'"[78]

عَنْ أَنَسٍ رَضِيَ اللهُ عَنْهُ قَالَ خَرَجَ رَسُولُ اللهِ ﷺ وَهُوَ غَضْبَانُ فَخَطَبَ النَّاسَ فَقَالَ لاَ تَسْأَلُونِي عَنْ شَيْءٍ الْيَوْمَ إِلاَّ أَخْبَرْتُكُمْ بِهِ وَنَحْنُ نَرَى أَنَّ جِبْرِيلَ مَعَهُ فَقَامَ إِلَيْهِ رَجُلٌ فَقَالَ يَا رَسُولَ اللهِ إِنَّا كُنَّا حَدِيثِي عَهْدٍ بِجَاهِلِيَّةٍ مَنْ أَبِي قَالَ أَبُوكَ حُذَافَةُ لأَبِيهِ الَّذِي يَدَّعِي فَسَأَلَهُ عَنْ أَشْيَاءٍ فَقَامَ إِلَيْهِ عُمَرُ بْنُ الخَطَّابِ قَالَ يَا رَسُولَ اللهِ إِنَّا كُنَّا حَدِيثِي عَهْدٍ بِجَاهِلِيَّةٍ فَلاَ تُبْدِ عَلَيْنَا سَوْآتِنَا قَالَ أَتَفْضَحُنَا بِسَرَائِرِنَا عَفَا اللهُ عَنْكَ رَضِينَا بِاللهِ رَبّاً وَبِالإِسْلاَمِ دِيناً وَبِمُحَمَّدٍ رَسُولاً قَالَ فَسُرِّيَ عَنْهُ ثُمَّ نَظَرَ فَقَالَ مَا رَأَيْتُ

[76]Narrated by al-Bazzār in his *Musnad* (7:240 § 2816). See also the reports from Ḥudhayfa in al-Dānī, *al-Sunan al-Wārida fī al-Fitan* (1:180-181 §2, 1:232-233 §31, 2:503-504 §202, 5:1098-1112 §596).

[77]Narrated from Ibn ʿUmar by Abū Yaʿlā (10:65 §5701) cf. Haythamī (7:259) and from ʿAbd Allāh b. ʿAmr b. al-ʿĀṣ by al-Harawī al-Anṣārī in *Dhamm al-Kalām* (3:191 §635).

[78]Narrated from Anas by Abū Yaʿlā (6:360 §3689) through the narrators of Bukhārī and Muslim according to al-Haythamī (7:188). A longer version is narrated in the *Sahīhayn*.

كَاليَومِ فِي الخَيْرِ وَالشَّرِّ إِنهَّا عُرِضَتْ عَلَيَّ الجَنَّةُ وَالنَّارُ دُونَ الحَائِطِ فَمَا رَأَيْتُ أَكْثَرَ مُقَنَّعاً مِنْ يَوْمَئِذٍ ع ورجاله رجال الصحيح مج وأصله عندهما

[The Arabic address "May Allah forgive you" may express thanks or good wishes without presupposing any offense on the part of the addressee. This is established by the ḥadīth of ʿAbd Allāh b. Sarjis al-Muzanī: "I visited the Prophet ﷺ and ate with him some of the food he had prepared then said: 29 "May Allah forgive you, Messenger of Allah! *(ghafara Allāhu laka yā Rasūlallāh)* to which the Prophet ﷺ replied "And you" *(wa-lak)*[79]; and the ḥadīth of 'Imrān b. Ḥusayn relating the words of a relative of his to the Prophet ﷺ: 30 "Ask Allah forgiveness for me and may Allah forgive you *(istaghfir lī ghafara Allāhu lak)*."[80]]

Abū Yaʿlā also narrated with a passable chain from Ibn ʿUmar رضي الله عنهما who said: "I heard the Messenger of Allah ﷺ say: 31 'This particular clan *(ḥayy)* of the Quraysh shall remain safe until they turn away from their Religion into apostates.' A man stood up saying: 'Messenger of Allah! Will I be in Paradise or in Hellfire?' The Prophet ﷺ answered, 'In Paradise.' Another stood asking the same, whereupon the Prophet ﷺ answered, 'In Hellfire.' Then [he said], a 'Say nothing to me as long as I say nothing to you. b Were it not for fear that you would stop burying one another *(lawlā an lā tadāfanū)* c I could certainly tell you about a great number of those who will be in the Fire and you would know who they are. If I am ordered to do it I shall certainly do it!'"[81]

عَنْ ابْنِ عُمَرَ رَضِيَ اللهُ عَنْهُمَا قَالَ سَمِعْتُ رَسُولَ اللهِ ﷺ يَقُولُ لاَ يَزَالُ هَذَا الحَيُّ مِنْ قُرَيْشٍ آمِنِينَ حَتىَّ يَرُدُّوهُمْ عَنْ دِينِهِمْ كُفَّاراً قَالَ فَقَامَ إِلَيْهِ رَجُلٌ فَقَالَ يَا رَسُولَ اللهِ أَفِي الجَنَّةِ أَنَا أَمْ

[79]Narrated from ʿAbd Allāh b. Sarjis by Aḥmad, al-Tirmidhī, and Muslim.

[80]Narrated from 'Imrān b. Ḥuṣayn by Aḥmad with a chain containing an unnamed Baṣrian *Tābiʿī* or Companion.

[81]Narrated from Ibn ʿUmar by Abū Yaʿlā (10:66 §5702) cf, Ibn Abī Ḥātim, *ʿIlal* (2:256 §2262). About that specific clan of the Quraysh see hadīth at note 543.

فِي النَّارِ قَالَ فِي الجَنَّةِ ثُمَّ قَامَ إِلَيْهِ آخَرُ فَقَالَ أَفِي الجَنَّةِ أَمْ فِي النَّارِ قَالَ فِي النَّارِ ثُمَّ قَالَ اسْكُتُوا عَنِّي مَا سَكَتُّ عَنْكُمْ فَلَوْلا أَنْ لاَ تَدَافَنُوا لأَخْبَرْتُكُمْ بِمَلَئِكُمْ مِنْ أَهْلِ النَّارِ حَتَّ تُفَرِّقُوهُمْ عَنِ المَوْتِ وَلَوْ أُمِرْتُ أَنْ أَفْعَلَ لَفَعَلْتُ ع

Important Note

Know that the narrations in this chapter are extremely numerous and their number cannot be all listed because, most of the time, the Prophet ﷺ would speak about the unseen in various matters for many different reasons. The *muḥaddithūn* mentioned them in their books, each contenting himself with a certain number of them. Out of His favor, Allah facilitated it for me to collect a vast number of them which I gathered from the contents of those books and then arranged in a beautiful way. The result is like an original work most pleasing to the reader, although most of it I compiled from the ḥadīth Master al-Suyūṭī's *al-Khaṣā'iṣ al-Kubrā* after I researched them, putting into the appropriate chapter whatever qualified as an stunning miracle, or a lofty quality, or a proof [of Prophethood]. The latter work is the largest and most valuable source of the present one and the most comprehensive of all the books compiled on this subject except for the present work which is—praise belongs to Allah—even more comprehensive, better organized, and more complete in its details and chapter divisions. Nevertheless, the *Khaṣā'iṣ* remain the source without which my book could not have been described in such glowing terms. Therefore, may Allah have mercy on its author and resurrect me in his group, under the standard of the Master of Messengers ﷺ!

His ﷺ Telling of Unseen Matters Related to Some of His Companions رضي الله عنهم

Abū Bakr رضي الله عنه

The Two Masters [al-Bukhārī and Muslim] narrated from ʿĀ'isha رضي الله عنها that the Prophet ﷺ said to her: 32 "Call your father and brother [ʿAbd al-Raḥmān] here so I will put something down in writing, for truly I fear lest someone forward a claim or form some ambition, and Allah and the believers refuse anyone other than Abū Bakr."[82]

عَنْ عَائِشَةَ رَضِيَ اللهُ عَنْهَا قَالَتْ قَالَ لِي رَسُولُ اللهِ ﷺ فِي مَرَضِهِ
ادْعِي لِي أَبَا بَكْرٍ أَبَاكِ وَأَخَاكِ حَتَّى أَكْتُبَ كِتَابًا فَإِنِّي أَخَافُ أَنْ
يَتَمَنَّى مُتَمَنٍّ وَيَقُولُ قَائِلٌ أَنَا أَوْلَى وَيَأْبَى اللهُ وَالْمُؤْمِنُونَ إِلاَّ أَبَا
بَكْرٍ م د حم

Al-Ḥākim narrated – declaring it *ṣaḥīḥ* – from Ibn Masʿūd رضي الله عنه **[470]** who said the Prophet ﷺ said: 33 "A man from the dwellers of Paradise is about to come into your sight." Whereupon Abū Bakr came and sat among them. [Then the Prophet ﷺ said the same thing and ʿUmar came.][83] The Prophet ﷺ had already given him the glad tidings of Paradise before that occasion.

[82]Spoken in the last days of the Prophet ﷺ. Narrated from ʿĀ'isha by Muslim, Abū Dāwūd, and Aḥmad.

[83]Narrated from Ibn Masʿūd by al-Tirmidhī *(gharīb)*, al-Ḥākim (3:136=1990 ed. 3:146, "chain sound per Muslim's criterion"), and Aḥmad in *Faḍā'il al-Saḥāba* (1:104 §76). It is confirmed as authentic by identical narrations from Jābir by Aḥmad with four good chains, al-Ṭabarāni – cf. al-Haythamī (9:57-58; 9:116-117) – with several chains in *al-Awsat* (7:110 §7002; 8:41 §7897), *Musnad al-Shāmiyyīn* (1:375 §651), *al-Kabīr* (10:167 §10343), al-Ḥārith in his *Musnad* (2:889 §961), al-Ṭayālisī in his *Musnad* (p. 234 §1674), Ibn Abī ʿĀṣim in *al-Sunna* (2:624 §1453), Aḥmad in *Faḍā'il al-Saḥāba* (1:209 §233; 2:577 §977), and al-Muḥibb al-Ṭabarī in *al-Riyāḍ al-Nadira* (1:301 §146); and from Abū Masʿud by al-Ṭabarānī in *al-Kabīr* (17:250 §695). All versions other than Ibn Masʿūd's add ʿAlī third, and al-Ṭabarānī – in one narration – ʿUthmān instead. Other versions by al-

عَنْ عَبْدِ اللهِ بْنِ مَسْعُودٍ رَضِيَ اللهُ عَنْهُ أَنَّ النَّبِيَّ ﷺ قَالَ يَطَّلِعُ
عَلَيْكُمْ رَجُلٌ مِنْ أَهْلِ الْجَنَّةِ فَاطَّلَعَ أَبُو بَكْرٍ ثُمَّ قَالَ يَطَّلِعُ
عَلَيْكُمْ رَجُلٌ مِنْ أَهْلِ الْجَنَّةِ فَاطَّلَعَ عُمَرُ ت استغربه ك صححه على
شرط مسلم وعن جابر حم طب طس ط وعن أبي مسعود طب

[34 "Abū Bakr is in *Janna*, 'Umar is in *Janna*, 'Uthmān is in *Janna*, 'Alī is in *Janna*, Ṭalḥa is in *Janna*, al-Zubayr (b. al-'Awwām) is in *Janna*, 'Abd al-Raḥmān b. 'Awf is in *Janna*, Sa'd [b. Abī Waqqaṣ], Sa'īd (b. Zayd b. 'Amr) is in *Janna*, and Abū 'Ubayda b. al-Jarrāḥ is in *Janna*."][84]

Abū Bakr and 'Umar رضي الله عنهما

Ibn Mājah and al-Ḥākim narrated from Ḥudhayfa ﷺ that the Prophet ﷺ said, 35 "Take for your leaders the two that come after me: Abū Bakr and 'Umar."[85]

Ṭabarānī mention 'Alī alone: in *al-Kabīr* from Ibn Mas'ūd (10:166-167 §10342, §10344) and from Umm Marthad (24:301 §764) cf. Ibn Abī 'Āṣim, *al-Āḥād wal-Mathānī* (6:234 §3467) and Ibn 'Abd al-Barr, *al-Istī'āb* (4:1957 §4209); also from Jābir in Aḥmad's *Faḍā'il al-Ṣaḥāba* (2:608 §1038) while one version from Ibn 'Abbās in the latter (1:454 §732) mentions 'Uthmān alone, cf. *Kanz al-'Ummāl* (§36211).

[84]Narrated from 'Abd al-Raḥmān b. 'Awf and Sa'īd b. Zayd in the *Sunan* and Aḥmad. The Prophet ﷺ spoke similarly of 'Abd Allāh b. Salām; the Muslim combatants of Badr, some specifically such as 'Ammār b. Yāsir; the Pledgers of Ḥudaybiya; Ja'far al-Ṭayyār; Bilāl b. Abī Rabāḥ; conditionally, the Bedouin who swore never to add to nor subtract anything from the Five Pillars; the Anṣārī exempt of envy; al-Ḥusayn b. 'Alī and his brother al-Ḥasan; Thābit b. Qays; Mālik, Abū Sa'id al-Khudrī's father; al-Ghumaysā' bint Milḥān, Anas's mother; Mu'āwiya (in *al-Firdaws* 5:482 §8830 and *Mizān* 2:243, 4:359); Hilāl al-Ḥabashī (Mawlā al-Mughīra b. Shu'ba in *Iṣāba* 6:550 §8996 cf. *Nawādir al-Uṣūl* §123 and *Ḥilya* 1985 ed. 2:81, the latter also mentioning Uways al-Qaranī), Jarīr (*Nawādir* §128), Sharīk b. Khubāsha al-Numayrī (*Iṣāba* 3:384 §3987), and al-Ḍaḥḥāk b. Khalīfa al-Anṣārī (*ibid.* 3:475 §4166).

[85]Part of a longer ḥadīth narrated from Ḥudhayfa by al-Tirmidhī *(ḥasan gharīb)*, Aḥmad in the *Musnad* with a sound chain according to al-Zayn (16:611 §23279) and in *Faḍā'il al-Ṣaḥāba* (1:187), al-Ṭaḥāwī with several sound and fair chains according to al-Arna'ūṭ in *Sharḥ Mushkil al-Āthār* (3:256-257 §1224-1226, 3:259 §1233), Ibn Abī Shayba (12:11), al-Ḥākim (3:75-76=1990 ed. 3:79-80 with three sound chains confirmed by al-Dhahabī, al-Bayhaqī in *al-Sunan al-Kubrā* (8:153 §16352), *al-Madkhal* (p. 122), and *al-I'tiqād* (p. 340-341). Ibn Ḥajar in *Talkhīṣ al-Ḥabīr* (4:190) declared that the chains of the ḥadīth are good and firmly established as authentic.

عَنْ حُذَيْفَةَ رَضِيَ اللهُ عَنْهُ قَالَ قَالَ رَسُولُ اللهِ ﷺ اقْتَدُوا
بِاللَّذَيْنِ مِنْ بَعْدِي أَبِي بَكْرٍ وَعُمَرَ ت حم وحسنه الترمذي

Abū Bakr, ʿUmar, and ʿUthmān ؓ

Abū Nuʿaym, al-Bazzār, Abū Yaʿlā, and Ibn Abī Khaythama narrated that Anas ؓ said: "I was with the Prophet ﷺ inside an enclosed garden when someone came and knocked on the gate. He said, [36] 'Anas, let him in, give him the glad tidings of Paradise, and tell him he shall be my successor.' Behold! It was Abū Bakr. Then another man came and knocked on the gate whereupon the Prophet ﷺ said, 'Let him in, give him the glad tidings of Paradise, and [a] tell him he shall be my successor after Abū Bakr.' Behold! It was ʿUmar. Then another man came and knocked on the gate so the Prophet ﷺ said, 'Let him in, give him the glad tidings of Paradise, and [b] tell him he shall be my successor after ʿUmar – and that he shall be killed.' Behold! It was ʿUthmān."[86]

عَنْ أَنَسٍ رَضِيَ اللهُ عَنْهُ قَالَ جَاءَ النَّبِيُّ ﷺ فَدَخَلَ إِلَى بُسْتَانٍ
فَأَتَى آتٍ فَدَقَّ البَابَ فَقَالَ يَا أَنَسُ قُمْ فَافْتَحْ لَهُ البَابَ وَبَشِّرْهُ
بِالجَنَّةِ وَبَشِّرْهُ بِالخِلَافَةِ مِنْ بَعْدِي فَإِذَا أَبُو بَكْرٍ رَضِيَ اللهُ عَنْهُ ثُمَّ
جَاءَ آتٍ فَدَقَّ البَابَ فَقَالَ يَا أَنَسُ قُمْ فَافْتَحْ لَهُ البَابَ وَبَشِّرْهُ
بِالجَنَّةِ وَبَشِّرْهُ بِالخِلَافَةِ مِنْ بَعْدِ أَبِي بَكْرٍ فَخَرَجْتُ فَإِذَا عُمَرُ
رَضِيَ اللهُ عَنْهُ الحديث موضوع خط عد ز كر أبو يعلى في المعجم ابن أبي عاصم في
السنة جميعهم من طريق صقر بن عبد الرحمن متّهم

[86]A forgery narrated from Anas by Abū Yaʿlā in his *Muʿjam* (p. 178), Ibn Abī ʿĀṣim in *al-Sunna* (2:557), Ibn ʿAdī, *Kāmil* (4:91), Khaṭīb (9:339-340), Bazzār and Ibn ʿAsākir, all of them through Saqr b. ʿAbd al-Raḥmān and his father who are both described as liars cf. al-Haythamī (5:175) and al-Aḥdab (7:96-101).

Al-Ḥākim – declaring it sound – and al-Bayhaqī narrated that Safīna ﵁ said, "When the Prophet ﷺ built the Mosque, Abū Bakr brought a stone and put it down; then ʿUmar brought a stone and put it down; then ʿUthmān brought a stone and put it down. Whereupon the Prophet ﷺ said, [37] 'These are the ones that shall govern after me.'"[87] There is in this narration an allusion to their order of succession – Allah be well-pleased with them! Indeed, it was mentioned explicitly in some narrations that he ﷺ was asked about it and replied, "These are the successors after me" while another narration has, "These are the ones who shall govern after me." Imam Abū Zurʿa [al-ʿIrāqī] said, "Its chain is safe and al-Ḥākim narrated it in the *Mustadrak* and declared it sound."[88]

عَنْ سَفِينَةَ رَضِيَ اللهُ عَنْهُ قَالَ لَمَّا بَنَى ﷺ المَسْجِدَ وَضَعَ حَجَراً ثُمَّ قَالَ لِيَضَعْ أَبُو بَكْرٍ حَجَرَهُ إِلَى جَنْبِ حَجَرِي ثُمَّ قَالَ لِيَضَعْ عُمَرُ حَجَرَهُ إِلَى جَنْبِ حَجَرِ أَبِي بَكْرٍ ثُمَّ قَالَ لِيَضَعْ عُثْمَانُ حَجَرَهُ إِلَى جَنْبِ حَجَرِ عُمَرَ ثُمَّ قَالَ هَؤُلاءِ الخُلَفَاءُ مِنْ بَعْدِي

ع عد مسند الحارث ابن أبي عاصم في السنة كر ك بلفظ هَؤُلاءِ وُلاةُ الأَمْرِ مِنْ بَعْدِي نعيم في الفتن ابن الجوزي في العلل وفي الباب عن عائشة انفرد به ك قال الذهبي موضوع لكن قبله البوصيري في الإتحاف

[87]Narrated from Safīna by al-Ḥārith in his *Musnad* (2:621 §593), Abū Yaʿlā, Ibn Abī ʿĀṣim in *al-Sunna* (2:550), Ḥākim (3:13=1990 ed. 3:14 *isnād ṣaḥīḥ*! but he said elsewhere the ḥadīth is false), Nuʿaym b. Ḥammād in the *Fitan*, al-Bayhaqī in the *Dalā'il* as well as Ibn ʿAsākir (30:218, 39:116, 39:171) through weak chains cf. Ibn ʿAdī (7:256) and Ibn al-Jawzī, *ʿIlal* (1:210). Also from ʿĀ'isha by al-Ḥākim (3:96-97=1990 ed. 3:103, al-Dhahabī declaring it inauthentic) through Aḥmad b. ʿAbd al-Raḥmān b. Wahb who al-Dhahabī said is disclaimed *(munkar)* and Abū Yaʿlā (8:295 §4884 *isnād ḍaʿīf*), but the latter also narrates it through a different, stronger chain cf. al-Haythamī (5:176) and al-Būṣīrī, *Itḥāf* (5:11-13). Also *mursal* from ʿAmr Abū Zurʿa by Ibn ʿAsākir (30:219, 39:171-172).

[88]But al-Bukhārī declares this narration "disclaimed" *(munkar)* cf. Ibn ʿAdī in *al-Kāmil* (2:440) while al-Dhahabī in his marginalia on the *Mustadrak* (3:97) considers it false and Ibn Kathīr terms it "very anomalous" *(gharīb jiddan)* in *al-Bidāya* (3:218). The Prophet ﷺ only alluded to Abū Bakr's successorship on abundant occasions such as by ordering him to lead the prayer or ordering the people to obey him and ʿUmar among other proofs.

Al-Bayhaqī and Abū Nuʿaym narrated that ʿAbd Allāh b. ʿAmr b. al-ʿĀṣ رضي الله عنهما said: "I heard the Prophet ﷺ say: [38] 'There shall be among you twelve caliphs. Abū Bakr al-Ṣiddīq shall not tarry but little after me, while the Master of the Arabs shall live a blameless life and die a martyr.' Someone asked, 'Who is he, Messenger of Allah?' He replied, ''Umar b. al-Khaṭṭāb!' Then he turned to ʿUthmān and said, 'As for you, they shall ask you to cast off a shirt that Allah vested you with. By the One Who sent me with the truth! Truly, if you cast it off, you shall not enter Paradise till the camel passes through the eye of the needle.'"[89]

عَنْ عبد الله بْنِ عَمْرٍو رَضِيَ اللهُ عَنْهُمَا قَالَ سَمِعْتُ رَسُولَ اللهِ ﷺ يَقُولُ يَكُونُ بَعْدِي اثْنَا عَشَرَ خَلِيفَةً: أَبُو بَكْرٍ الصِّدِّيقُ لا يَلْبَثُ بَعْدِي إِلا قَلِيلاً. وَصاحِبُ رَحَى دَارَةِ الْعَرَبِ يَعِيشُ حَمِيداً وَيَمُوتُ شَهِيداً قِيلَ مَنْ هُوَ يَا رَسُولَ اللهِ قَالَ عُمَرُ بْنُ الخَطَّابِ رَضِيَ اللهُ عَنْهُ ثُمَّ الْتَفَتَ إِلى عُثْمَانَ فَقَالَ وَأَنْتَ سَيَسْأَلُكَ النَّاسُ أَنْ تَخْلَعَ قَمِيصاً كَسَاكَ اللهُ عَزَّ وَجَلَّ وَالَّذِي نَفْسِي بِيَدِهِ لَئِنْ خَلَعْتَهُ لاَ تَدْخُلِ الجَنَّةَ ﴿حَتَّىٰ يَلِجَ ٱلْجَمَلُ فِى سَمِّ ٱلْخِيَاطِ﴾ طب طس وأبو نعيم في المعرفة وفيه ربيعة بن سيف قال خ عنده مناكير وقال في الميزان والسِيَر الخبر باطل

[89] Narrated from ʿAbd Allāh b. ʿAmr b. al-ʿĀṣ by al-Ṭabarānī in *al-Awsat* (8:319 §8749) and *al-Kabīr* (1:54 §12, 1:90 §142) – cf. al-Haythamī (5:178) – through Rabīʿa b. Sayf whom al-Bukhārī questioned; and Ibn Abī ʿĀṣim with a different chain and without mention of ʿUthmān in in *al-Āḥād wal-Mathānī* (1:96 §67) and *al-Sunna* (2:558); as well as the segment "Abū Bakr al-Siddīq shall not tarry but little after me" in *al-Āḥād wal-Mathānī* (1:73-74 §13), cf. *al-Sunna* (2:548), Ibn al-Jawzī in *Ṣifat al-Ṣafwa* (1:235-236) and – from him – al-Muḥibb al-Ṭabarī *mursal* from al-Zuhrī in *al-Riyāḍ al-Naḍira* (1:408 §329). Al-Dhahabī declared it "completely defective" *(wāhin)* in the *Siyar* (9:133=al-Arna'ūṭ ed. 10:411) and "false" *(bāṭil)* in his *Mīzān* (4:443), cf. Ibn ʿAdī's *Kāmil* (4:207), Ibn Ḥibbān's *al-Majrūḥīn* (2:42), and Ibn al-Qaysarānī, *Tadhkirat al-Mawḍūʿāt* (§1032).

[The established wording of this narration is: [39] "'Uthmān! Allah may vest you with a shirt. If the hypocrites demand that you remove it, do not remove it!" He said it thrice.][90]

Ibn 'Asākir narrated that Anas ؓ said: "The delegation of Banū al-Muṣṭaliq instructed me to ask the Messenger of Allah ﷺ, 'If we come next year and do not find you, to whom should we remit our [obligatory] *ṣadaqāt*?' I conveyed the question to him and he replied, [40] 'Remit them to Abū Bakr.' I told them his answer but they said, 'What if we do not find Abū Bakr?' I conveyed the question and he replied, 'Remit them to 'Umar.' They asked again, 'What if we do not find 'Umar?' He said, 'Tell them, remit them to 'Uthmān – and [a] may you perish the day 'Uthmān is killed!'"[91]

عَنْ أَنَسٍ رَضِيَ اللهُ عَنْهُ قَالَ وَجَّهَنِي وَفْدُ بَنِي المُصْطَلِقِ إِلَى
رَسُولِ اللهِ ﷺ فَقَالُوا سَلْهُ إِنْ جِئْنَا فِي العَامِ المُقْبِلِ فَلَمْ نَجِدْكَ
إِلَى مَنْ نَدْفَعُ صَدَقَاتِنَا؟ فَقُلْتُ لَهُ فَقَالَ قُلْ لَهُمْ يَدْفَعُوهَا إِلَى
أَبِي بَكْرٍ فَقَالُوا قُلْ لَهُ فَإِنْ لَمْ نَجِدْ أَبَا بَكْرٍ؟ فَقُلْتُ لَهُ فَقَالَ قُلْ
لَهُمْ يَدْفَعُوهَا إِلَى عُمَرَ فَقُلْتُ لَهُمْ فَقَالُوا قُلْ لَهُ فَإِنْ لَمْ نَجِدْ عُمَرَ؟
فَقُلْتُ لَهُ فَقَالَ قُلْ لَهُمْ يَدْفَعُوهَا إِلَى عُثْمَانَ وَتَبّاً لَكُمْ يَوْمَ يُقْتَلُ
عُثْمَانُ حل كر نعيم في الفتن كنز

Abū Ya'lā narrated with a sound chain from Sahl ؓ that [Mount] Uḥud trembled while the Messenger of Allah ﷺ, Abū Bakr, 'Umar, and 'Uthmān were on it, whereupon the Messenger of Allah ﷺ said: [41] "Keep firm *(uthbut)*, Uḥud! There is none on

[90]Narrated from 'Ā'isha with sound chains by al-Tirmidhī *(ḥasan gharīb)*, Ibn Hibbān, Aḥmad, Ibn Mājah, and al-Ḥākim.

[91]Narrated from Anas by Abū Nu'aym, *Hilya* (1985 ed. 8:358), Ibn 'Asākir (39:177), and Nu'aym in the *Fitan* (1:107-108 §260, 1:125 §295) cf. *Kanz* (§36333).

top of you but a Prophet, a *Ṣiddīq*, and two martyrs."[92] After that, ʿUmar and ʿUthmān were killed as martyrs and Abū Bakr died ؓ.

عَنْ أَنَسِ بْنِ مَالِكٍ رَضِيَ اللهُ عَنْهُ حَدَّثَهُمْ أَنَّ النَّبِيَّ ﷺ صَعِدَ أُحُدًا وَأَبُو بَكْرٍ وَعُمَرُ وَعُثْمَانُ فَرَجَفَ بِهِمْ فَقَالَ اثْبُتْ أُحُدُ فَإِنَّمَا عَلَيْكَ نَبِيٌّ وَصِدِّيقٌ وَشَهِيدَانِ خ ت د ن حم

Al-Ṭabarānī narrated from Ibn ʿUmar رضي الله عنهما that the Prophet ﷺ **[471]** was inside an enclosed garden when Abū Bakr sought permission to enter. He said, 42 "Give him permission and give him the glad tidings of Paradise." Then ʿUmar sought permission and he said, "Give him permission and give him the glad tidings of Paradise and martyrdom!" Then ʿUthmān sought permission and he said, "Give him permission and give him the glad tidings of Paradise and martyrdom."[93]

عَنْ عَبْدِ اللهِ بْنِ عُمَرَ رَضِيَ اللهُ عَنْهُمَا أَنَّ النَّبِيَّ ﷺ كَانَ فِي حَائِطٍ فَاسْتَأْذَنَ أَبُو بَكْرٍ فَقَالَ ائْذَنْ لَهُ وَبَشِّرْهُ بِالجَنَّةِ ثُمَّ اسْتَأْذَنَ عُمَرُ فَقَالَ ائْذَنْ لَهُ وَبَشِّرْهُ بِالجَنَّةِ وَبِالشَّهَادَةِ ثُمَّ اسْتَأْذَنَ عُثْمَانُ فَقَالَ ائْذَنْ لَهُ وَبَشِّرْهُ بِالجَنَّةِ وَبِالشَّهَادَةِ

The Two Masters narrated from Abū Mūsā al-Ashʿarī ؓ that the Prophet ﷺ was inside [the garden of] the well of Arīs one day and sat on the stone promontory of the well, in the middle, baring his shanks. "I [Abū Mūsā] said to myself: 'Today I shall be the Prophet's doorkeeper.' Then Abū Bakr came so I told him, 'Wait,' and went to tell the Prophet ﷺ, 'This is Abū Bakr asking per-

[92]Narrated from Anas by al-Bukhārī, al-Tirmidhī *(ḥasan ṣaḥīḥ)*, Abū Dāwūd, al-Nasāʾī, and Aḥmad.

[93]Narrated from Ibn ʿUmar by al-Ṭabarānī in *al-Kabīr* (12:327) cf. al-Haythamī (9:73).

mission to enter.' He replied, 43 'Give him permission and give him the glad tidings of Paradise.' Whereupon he entered and sat next to the Prophet ﷺ on the edge, dangling his legs. Then 'Umar came and I said, 'This is 'Umar asking permission to enter.' He replied, 'Give him permission and give him the glad tidings of Paradise.' Whereupon he entered and sat next to the Prophet ﷺ on his left, dangling his legs. Then 'Uthmān came and I said, this is 'Uthmān asking permission to enter.' He replied, 'Give him permission and give him the glad tidings of Paradise after a trial that will befall him.' He entered but found no room to sit on the edge of the well, so he sat opposite them on the other side of the well and dangled his legs." Sa'īd Ibn al-Musayyib said: "I saw in this an allusion to their graves."[94]

عَنْ أَبِي مُوسَى رَضِيَ اللّٰهُ عَنْهُ قَالَ كُنْتُ مَعَ النَّبِيِّ ﷺ فِي حَائِطٍ مِنْ حِيطَانِ الْمَدِينَةِ (وفي رواية سمّى الحائط بِئْرَ أَرِيسٍ وزاد في رواية وَهُوَ مُتَّكِئٌ يَرْكُزُ بِعُودٍ مَعَهُ بَيْنَ الْمَاءِ وَالطِّينِ) فَجَاءَ رَجُلٌ فَاسْتَفْتَحَ فَقَالَ النَّبِيُّ ﷺ افْتَحْ لَهُ وَبَشِّرْهُ بِالْجَنَّةِ فَفَتَحْتُ لَهُ فَإِذَا أَبُو بَكْرٍ فَبَشَّرْتُهُ بِمَا قَالَ النَّبِيُّ ﷺ فَحَمِدَ اللّٰهَ ثُمَّ جَاءَ رَجُلٌ فَاسْتَفْتَحَ فَقَالَ النَّبِيُّ ﷺ افْتَحْ لَهُ وَبَشِّرْهُ بِالْجَنَّةِ فَفَتَحْتُ لَهُ فَإِذَا هُوَ عُمَرُ فَأَخْبَرْتُهُ بِمَا قَالَ النَّبِيُّ ﷺ فَحَمِدَ اللّٰهَ ثُمَّ اسْتَفْتَحَ رَجُلٌ فَقَالَ لِي (وفي رواية فَسَكَتَ هُنَيْهَةً ثُمَّ قَالَ) افْتَحْ لَهُ وَبَشِّرْهُ بِالْجَنَّةِ عَلَى بَلْوَى تُصِيبُهُ فَإِذَا عُثْمَانُ فَأَخْبَرْتُهُ بِمَا قَالَ رَسُولُ اللّٰهِ ﷺ فَحَمِدَ

[94]Narrated by al-Bukhārī and Muslim as well as (without Ibn al-Musayyib's comment) al-Tirmidhī and Aḥmad. In one of Aḥmad's versions 'Uthmān walks to his seat saying, all the while, *Allāhumma sabran.*

اللهَ ثُمَّ قَالَ اللهُ الْمُسْتَعَانُ (وفي رواية فَقَالَ اللهُمَّ صَبْرًا أَوْ اللهُ
الْمُسْتَعَانُ وفي رواية أَنَّ النَّبِيَّ ﷺ كَانَ قَاعِدًا فِي مَكَانٍ فِيهِ مَاءٌ
قَدْ انْكَشَفَ عَنْ رُكْبَتَيْهِ أَوْ رُكْبَتِهِ فَلَمَّا دَخَلَ عُثْمَانُ غَطَّاهَا)
فَدَخَلَ (أي عثمان رَضِيَ اللهُ عَنْهُ) فَوَجَدَ الْقُفَّ قَدْ مُلِئَ
فَجَلَسَ وِجَاهَهُ مِنْ الشَّقِّ الْآخَرِ قَالَ شَرِيكُ بْنُ عَبْدِ اللهِ قَالَ
سَعِيدُ بْنُ المسَيِّبِ فَأَوَّلْتُهَا قُبُورَهُمْ ق ت حم

Al-Ṭabarānī and al-Bayhaqī narrated that Zayd b. Arqam ؓ said: "The Prophet ﷺ sent me out, saying, [44] 'Go and see Abū Bakr. You will find him sitting inside his house wrapped up in his cloth with his legs drawn up *(muḥtabyan)*. Give him the glad tidings of Paradise. Then go to the mountain until you find ʿUmar riding a donkey and his tall frame looming in the distance. Give him the glad tidings of Paradise. Then go to ʿUthmān; you will find him in the market selling and buying, and give him the glad tidings of Paradise after a harrowing ordeal.' I went and found them as the Messenger of Allah ﷺ had said, and I told them."[95]

عَنْ زَيْدِ بْنِ أَرْقَمَ رَضِيَ اللهُ عَنْهُ قَالَ بَعَثَنِي رَسُولُ اللهِ ﷺ فَقَالَ
انْطَلِقْ حَتَّى تَأْتِيَ أَبَا بَكْرٍ فَتَجِدَهُ فِي دَارِهِ جَالِساً مُحْتَبِيًا فَقُلْ لَهُ
إِنَّ رَسُولَ اللهِ ﷺ يَقْرَأُ عَلَيكَ السَّلامَ وَيقُولُ أَبْشِرْ بِالجَنَّةِ ثُمَّ
انْطَلِقْ حَتَّى تَأْتِيَ الثَّنِيَّةَ فَتَلْقَى عُمَرَ فِيهَا عَلَى حِمَارٍ تَلُوحُ صَلْعَتُهُ

[95]Part of a longer ḥadīth narrated from Zayd b. Arqam by al-Ṭabarānī in *al-Awsat* (1:266-267 §868), al-Bayhaqī in the *Dalā'il*, and al-Dhahabī in the *Siyar*, both indicating its weakness. If true, the events possibly preceded those of the narration of Abū Mūsā at Arīs. Cf. al-Haythamī (9:55-56) and Ibn Kathīr, *al-Bidāya*, section on *Dalā'il al-Nubuwwa*, chapter on "His ﷺ telling of unseen future matters."

فَقُلْ لَهُ إِنَّ رَسُولَ اللهِ ﷺ يَقْرَأُ عَلَيكَ السَّلامَ وَيقُولُ أَبْشِرْ بِالجَنَّةِ
ثُمَّ انْطَلِقْ حَتَّىٰ تَأْتِيَ السُّوقَ فَتَلْقَى عُثْمَانَ فِيهَا يَبِيعُ وَيَبْتَاعُ فَقُلْ
لَهُ إِنَّ رَسُولَ اللهِ ﷺ يَقْرَأُ عَلَيكَ السَّلامَ وَيقُولُ أَبْشِرْ بِالجَنَّةِ بَعْدَ
بَلاءٍ شَدِيدٍ طس وضعّفه هق والذهبي

Abū Bakr, ʿUmar, and ʿAlī رضي الله عنهم

Al-Ḥākim narrated – declaring it sound – from Jābir رضي الله عنه who said: "I walked with the Prophet ﷺ to [the house of] a woman who slaughtered a sheep for us. At that time he ﷺ said: 'Behold! [45] A man from the people of Paradise is about to enter.' Whereupon Abū Bakr came in. Then he said: 'Behold! A man from the people of Paradise is about to enter.' Whereupon ʿUmar came in. Then he said: 'Behold! A man from the people of Paradise is about to enter. O Allah, if You wish, let it be ʿAlī.' Whereupon ʿAlī entered."[96]

عَنْ جَابِرٍ رَضِيَ اللهُ عَنْهُ أَنَّ النَّبِيَّ ﷺ قَالَ لَيَدْخُلَنَّ رَجُلٌ مِنْ
أَهْلِ الجَنَّةِ فَدَخَلَ أَبُو بَكْرٍ رَضِيَ اللهُ عَنْهُ ثُمَّ قَالَ لَيَدْخُلَنَّ رَجُلٌ
مِنْ أَهْلِ الجَنَّةِ فَدَخَلَ عُمَرُ رَضِيَ اللهُ عَنْهُ ثُمَّ قَالَ لَيَدْخُلَنَّ رَجُلٌ
مِنْ أَهْلِ الجَنَّةِ اللهُمَّ إِنْ شِئْتَ فَاجْعَلْهُ عَلِيّاً قَالَ فَدَخَلَ عَلِيُّ
بْنُ أَبِي طَالِبٍ حم ك صححه وقد مر عن ابن مسعود بدون ذكر سيّدنا علي كرّم
الله وجهه

[96] See n. 83.

Abū Bakr, ʿUmar, ʿUthmān, and ʿAlī ﵃

Ahmad, al-Bazzār, and al-Ṭabarānī in *al-Awsaṭ* narrated that Jābir b. ʿAbd Allāh ﵄ said: "The Prophet ﷺ went out to visit [the widowed wife of] Saʿd b. al-Rabīʿ [who died at Uḥud]. He sat down and we sat down with him. Then he said, [46] 'A man from the dwellers of Paradise is about to come into your sight.' Whereupon Abū Bakr came. Then he said, 'A man from the dwellers of Paradise is about to come into your sight.' Whereupon ʿUmar came. Then he said, 'A man from the dwellers of Paradise is about to come into your sight.' Whereupon ʿUthmān came. Then he said, 'A man from the dwellers of Paradise is about to come into your sight. [a] O Allah! If You wish, let it be ʿAlī.' Whereupon ʿAlī came."[97]

عَنْ جَابِرِ بْنِ عَبْدِ اللهِ رَضِيَ اللهُ عَنْهُ قَالَ كُنَّا مَعَ رَسُولِ اللهِ ﷺ فَقَالَ يَطْلُعُ عَلَيْكُمْ رَجُلٌ أَوْ قَالَ يَدْخُلُ عَلَيْكُمْ رَجُلٌ يُرِيدُ رَجُلٌ مِنْ أَهْلِ الْجَنَّةِ فَجَاءَ أَبُو بَكْرٍ رَضِيَ اللهُ عَنْهُ ثُمَّ قَالَ يَطْلُعُ عَلَيْكُمْ أَوْ يَدْخُلُ عَلَيْكُمْ شَابٌّ يُرِيدُ رَجُلٌ مِنْ أَهْلِ الْجَنَّةِ قَالَ فَجَاءَ عُمَرُ رَضِيَ اللهُ عَنْهُ ثُمَّ قَالَ يَطْلُعُ عَلَيْكُمْ رَجُلٌ مِنْ أَهْلِ الْجَنَّةِ اللهُمَّ اجْعَلْهُ عَلِيًّا اللهُمَّ اجْعَلْهُ عَلِيًّا قَالَ فَجَاءَ عَلِيٌّ رَضِيَ اللهُ عَنْهُ حم الحارث في مسنده طب في مسند الشاميين

Abū Bakr, ʿUmar, ʿUthmān, ʿAlī, Ṭalḥa, and al-Zubayr ﵃

Muslim narrated from Abū Hurayra ﵁ that the Messenger of Allah ﷺ was on Mount Ḥirāʾ together with Abū Bakr, **[472]**

[97]Narrated from Jābir by al-Ḥārith in his *Musnad* (2:889 §961), Aḥmad, and Ṭabarānī in *Musnad al-Shāmiyyīn* (1:375 §651), all without mention of ʿUthmān. See also n. 83.

ʿUmar, ʿUthmān, ʿAlī, Ṭalḥa, and al-Zubayr when the rock moved, whereupon the Prophet ﷺ said: [47] "Be still [Ḥirā']! There is none on top of you but a Prophet, a *Ṣiddīq*, or a martyr."[98] ✱ Indeed, they all were killed as martyrs except Abū Bakr al-Ṣiddīq – Allah be well-pleased with all of them! The shuddering of the mountain took place again when he ﷺ was on top of it with some of his other Companions as we previously mentioned, in the fifth chapter.

عَنْ أَبِي هُرَيْرَةَ رَضِيَ اللهُ عَنْهُ أَنَّ رَسُولَ اللهِ ﷺ كَانَ عَلَى حِرَاءٍ هُوَ وَأَبُو بَكْرٍ وَعُمَرُ وَعُثْمَانُ وَعَلِيٌّ وَطَلْحَةُ وَالزُّبَيْرُ فَتَحَرَّكَتْ الصَّخْرَةُ فَقَالَ رَسُولُ اللهِ ﷺ اهْدَأْ فَمَا عَلَيْكَ إِلاَّ نَبِيٌّ أَوْ صِدِّيقٌ أَوْ شَهِيدٌ م ت حم

ʿUmar رضي الله عنه

Ibn Saʿd and Ibn Abī Shayba narrated from Abū al-Ashhab, from a man from Muzayna [near Madīna], that the Prophet ﷺ saw ʿUmar wearing a certain shirt whereupon he asked him, [48] "Is it new or has it been washed already?" ʿUmar replied, "It has been washed already." The Prophet ﷺ said, "ʿUmar! wear new clothes, live a blameless life, and die a martyr!" This is a *mursal* report.[99]

[98] Narrated from Abū Hurayra by Muslim, al-Tirmidhī *(saḥīḥ)*, and Aḥmad.

[99] Narrated with a weak *mursal* chain – as Abū al-Ashhab Jaʿfar b. Ḥayyān al-ʿUṭāridī did not meet the *Saḥāba* – by Ibn Abī Shayba (8:453, 10:402) and Ibn Saʿd (3:329) and al-Dūlābī (1:109) but with a *muttasil* chain of trustworthy narrators through al-Zuhrī as stated by al-Būṣirī in *Misbāḥ al-Zujāja* (4:82), all of them used by al-Bukhārī and Muslim as stated by al-Haythamī (9:73-74), from Ibn ʿUmar by Aḥmad in his *Musnad* (Arna'ūt ed. 9:440-442 §5620) and *Faḍā'il al-Saḥāba* (1:255 §322-323), Ibn Mājah, Ibn Ḥibbān (Arna'ūt ed. 15:320-322 §6897), al-Bazzār (*Zawā'id* §2504), Abū Yaʿlā (§5545), al-Ṭabarānī in *al-Kabīr* (12:283 §13127) and *al-Duʿā'* (p. 143 §399), Ibn al-Sunnī and al-Nasā'ī in their *ʿAmal al-Yawm wal-Layla* (respectively §269 and 1:275 §311), Abū Nuʿaym in *Akhbār Asbahān* (1:139), al-Azdī in his *Jāmiʿ* (11:223), ʿAbd b. Ḥumayd in his *Musnad* (p. 238 §723), Ibn ʿAbd al-Barr in *al-Istīʿāb* (3:1157), al-Baghawī in *Sharh al-Sunna* (12:50 §3112), and al-Bayhaqī in the *Shuʿab*, all through ʿAbd al-Razzāq (§20382) whom some of the Imams considered erroneous in his narration of this ḥadīth through al-Zuhrī as explained by Ibn Rajab in *Sharh ʿIlal al-Tirmidhī* (2:585). Con-

عَنِ ابْنِ عُمَرَ رَضِيَ اللهُ عَنْهُمَا قَالَ رَأَى النَّبِيُّ ﷺ عَلَى عُمَرَ ثَوْبًا أَبْيَضَ فَقَالَ أَجَدِيدٌ ثَوْبُكَ أَمْ غَسِيلٌ فَقَالَ فَلاَ أَدْرِي مَا رَدَّ عَلَيْهِ فَقَالَ النَّبِيُّ ﷺ الْبَسْ جَدِيدًا وَعِشْ حَمِيدًا وَمُتْ شَهِيدًا أَظُنُّهُ قَالَ وَيَرْزُقُكَ اللهُ قُرَّةَ عَيْنٍ فِي الدُّنْيَا وَالْآخِرَةِ جه حم وهذا لفظه ز ع حب طب هب وغيرهم وحسّنه الحافظ في نتائج الأفكار

The Two Masters narrate that ʿUmar b. al-Khaṭṭāb ﷺ asked one day: "Which of you remembers what the Messenger of Allah ﷺ said of the [49] dissension that shall surge like the waves of the sea?" Ḥudhayfa ﷺ said: "You need not worry about it, Commander of the Believers! For between you and it there is a gate closed shut." ʿUmar said: "Will the gate be opened or broken?" Ḥudhayfa said: "Broken." ʿUmar replied: "That is more appropriate than that it be let open." Later, Ḥudhayfa was asked who that gate was and he said: "That gate was ʿUmar." They asked him, "Did ʿUmar know that?" He replied, "Yes, as surely as night precedes day, and I spoke to him unambiguously!"[100]

عَنْ حُذَيْفَةَ رَضِيَ اللهُ عَنْهُ قَالَ قَالَ عُمَرُ رَضِيَ اللهُ عَنْهُ أَيُّكُمْ يَحْفَظُ حَدِيثَ رَسُولِ اللهِ ﷺ عَنِ الْفِتْنَةِ الَّتِي تَمُوجُ كَمَوْجِ الْبَحْرِ قَالَ قُلْتُ لَيْسَ عَلَيْكَ بِهَا يَا أَمِيرَ الْمُؤْمِنِينَ بَأْسٌ بَيْنَكَ وَبَيْنَهَا

sequently it was declared inauthentic by al-Bukhārī *("lā shay'")* in al-Tirmidhī's *ʿIlal* (p. 373), Ibn ʿAdī *("munkar")* in *al-Kāmil* (5:1948), al-Nasā'ī in *ʿAmal al-Yawm wal-Layla* quoting Yaḥyā b. Saʿīd al-Qaṭṭān – cf. al-Bayhaqī in *al-Sunan al-Kubrā* (6:85 §10143) – and Ibn Abī Ḥātim *("bāṭil")* in *al-ʿIlal* (1:490). Al-Ṭabarānī narrates it through another chain through al-Thawrī instead of al-Zuhrī in *al-Duʿā'* (§400) – cf. al-Haythamī, *Mawārid al-Zam'ān* (1:536 §2381) and al-Bazzār also narrates it from Jābir with a weak chain in his *Musnad* (*Zawā'id* §2503). In sum, Ibn Ḥibbān considers it authentic and Ibn Ḥajar in his *Natā'ij al-Afkār* (1:137-138) concludes it is at the very least "fair" *(ḥasan)* as does al-Arna'ūṭ in his edition of Ibn Ḥibbān.

[100]Narrated from Abū Wā'il Shaqīq b. Salama by al-Bukhārī and Muslim.

بَابٌ مُغْلَقٌ قَالَ فَيُكْسَرُ الْبَابُ أَوْ يُفْتَحُ قَالَ قُلْتُ لَا بَلْ يُكْسَرُ قَالَ فَإِنَّهُ إِذَا كُسِرَ لَمْ يُغْلَقْ أَبَدًا قَالَ قُلْتُ أَجَلْ فَهِبْنَا أَنْ نَسْأَلَهُ مَنْ الْبَابُ فَقُلْنَا لِمَسْرُوقٍ سَلْهُ قَالَ فَسَأَلَهُ فَقَالَ عُمَرُ رَضِيَ اللَّهُ عَنْهُ قَالَ قُلْنَا فَعَلِمَ عُمَرُ مَنْ تَعْنِي قَالَ نَعَمْ كَمَا أَنَّ دُونَ غَدٍ لَيْلَةً وَذَلِكَ أَنِّي حَدَّثْتُهُ حَدِيثًا لَيْسَ بِالْأَغَالِيطِ ق

Al-Bazzār, al-Ṭabarānī, and Abū Nuʿaym narrated that ʿUthmān b. Maẓʿūn ﷺ said: "I heard the Messenger of Allah ﷺ say of ʿUmar: 50 'This is the bolt of dissension *(ghalqu al-fitna)*! There shall not cease to stand between you and dissension a strongly shut gate as long as this man lives among you.'"[101]

عَنْ عُثْمَانَ بْنِ مَظْعُونَ قَالَ لِعُمَرَ بْنِ الْخَطَّابِ رَضِيَ اللَّهُ عَنْهُمَا مَرَرْتَ بِنَا يَوْماً وَنَحْنُ جُلُوسٌ مَعَ رَسُولِ اللَّهِ ﷺ فَقَالَ هَذَا غَلْقُ الْفِتْنَةِ وَأَشَارَ بِيَدِهِ لَا يَزَالُ بَيْنَكُمْ وَبَيْنَ الْفِتْنَةِ بَابٌ شَدِيدُ الْغَلْقِ مَا عَاشَ هَذَا بَيْنَ ظَهْرَانِيكُمْ طب ز فر تاريخ واسط معجم الصحابة لابن قانع ويقوّيه الذي بعده

Al-Ṭabarānī also narrated from Abū Dharr that the Prophet ﷺ said: 51 "No dissension can reach you as long as this man is among you," meaning ʿUmar.[102]

---

[101]Narrated by al-Ṭabarānī in *al-Kabīr* (9:38 §8321), al-Bazzār, al-Wāsiṭī in *Tārīkh Wāsit* (p. 244-245), and Ibn Qāniʿ in *Muʿjam al-Ṣaḥāba* (2:258 §774) with a weak chain, cf. al-Haythamī (9:72), but the report is confirmed by the next narration. The same is also narrated from Ibn ʿAbbās by al-Daylamī in *al-Firdaws* (1:438 §1785).

[102]Narrated by al-Ṭabarānī in *al-Awsaṭ* (2:267-268 §1945) with a chain of trustworthy narrators according to Ibn Hajar in *Fath al-Bārī* (1959 ed. 6:606) except that al-Haythamī (9:73) suspects a missing link between al-Hasan al-Baṣrī and Abū Dharr. The full narration states that Abū Dharr called ʿUmar "the padlock of dissension" *(qufl al-fitna)*.

عَنْ أَبِي ذَرٍّ قَالَ لِعُمَرَ بْنِ الخَطَّابِ رَضِيَ اللهُ عَنْهُمَا جِئْتُ رَسُولَ اللهِ ﷺ ذَاتَ يَوْمٍ وَرَسُولُ اللهِ ﷺ جَالِسٌ وَقَدِ اجْتَمَعَ عَلَيْهِ النَّاسُ فَجَلَسْتُ فِي آخِرِهِمْ فَقَالَ رَسُولُ اللهِ ﷺ لا تُصِيبُكُمْ فِتْنَةٌ مَا دَامَ هَذَا بَيْنَ ظَهْرَانِيكُمْ طس إسناده ثقات فتح لكنه منقطع مج

Khālid b. al-Walīd ؓ addressed the people in al-Shām one day and a man said to him: "The dissensions have appeared!" Khālid replied: [52] "Not as long as Ibn al-Khaṭṭāb is alive! That shall only happen after his time."[103] Khālid would not say such a thing of his own opinion, so it appears he heard it from the Prophet ﷺ or from whoever heard it from him.

عَنْ خَالِدِ بنِ الْوَلِيدِ رَضِيَ اللهُ عَنْهُ قَالَ كَتَبَ إِلَيَّ أَمِيرُ الْمُؤْمِنِينَ حِينَ أَلْقَى الشَّامُ بَوَانِيَةً بَثْنِيَّةً – أي خير الشام وما فيها من السعة والنعمة – وَعَسَلًا وَشَكَّ عَفَّانُ مَرَّةً قَالَ حِينَ أَلْقَى الشَّامُ كَذَا وَكَذَا فَأَمَرَنِي أَنْ أَسِيرَ إِلَى الْهِنْدِ وَالْهِنْدُ فِي أَنْفُسِنَا يَوْمَئِذٍ الْبَصْرَةُ قَالَ وَأَنَا لِذَلِكَ كَارِهٌ قَالَ فَقَامَ رَجُلٌ فَقَالَ لِي يَا أَبَا سُلَيْمَانَ اتَّقِ اللهَ فَإِنَّ الْفِتَنَ قَدْ ظَهَرَتْ قَالَ فَقَالَ وَابْنُ الْخَطَّابِ حَيٌّ؟ إِنَّمَا تَكُونُ بَعْدَهُ وَالنَّاسُ بِذِي بِلِّيَانَ وَذِي بِلِّيَانَ بِمَكَانِ كَذَا وَكَذَا فَيَنْظُرُ

[103]Narrated by Aḥmad, al-Ṭabarānī in *al-Kabīr* (4:116 §3841), Nuʿaym b. Ḥammād in *al-Fitan* (1:45, 1:281 §819), all with a chain containing an unknown narrator – Qays b. Khālid al-Bajalī – but the undiscredited *Tābiʿī* is an acceptable narrator, hence Ibn Ḥajar in *Fatḥ al-Bārī* (1959 ed. 13:15) declared the chain "fair" *(ḥasan)*. Cf. al-Haythamī (7:307-308) and al-Mubārakfūrī in *Tuḥfat al-Aḥwadhī* (6:368).

الرَّجُلُ فَيَتَفَكَّرُ هَلْ يَجِدُ مَكَانًا لَمْ يَنْزِلْ بِهِ مِثْلُ مَا نَزَلَ بِمَكَانِهِ الَّذِي هُوَ فِيهِ مِنْ الْفِتْنَةِ وَالشَّرِّ فَلاَ يَجِدُهُ قَالَ وَتِلْكَ الأَيَّامُ الَّتِي ذَكَرَ رَسُولُ اللهِ ﷺ بَيْنَ يَدَيْ السَّاعَةِ أَيَّامُ الْهَرْجِ فَنَعُوذُ بِاللهِ أَنْ تُدْرِكَنَا وَإِيَّاكُمْ تِلْكَ الأَيَّامُ   حم طب حماد في الفتن وحسّنه في الفتح مج

ʿUthmān ☺

Al-Ṭabarānī narrated that Zayd b. Thābit ☺ said that he heard the Prophet ﷺ say: [53] "'ʿUthmān passed by me while one of the angels was with me and the latter said, 'This is a martyr, his people will kill him. Truly we feel indeed shy before him.'"[104]

عَنْ زَيْدِ بْنِ ثَابِتٍ رَضِيَ اللهُ عَنْهُ قَالَ سَمِعْتُ رَسُولَ اللهِ ﷺ يَقُولُ مَرَّ بِي عُثْمَانُ وَعِنْدِي مَلَكٌ مِنَ الْمَلاَئِكَةِ فَقَالَ شَهِيدٌ يَقْتُلُهُ قَوْمُهُ إِنَّا لَنَسْتَحْيِي مِنْهُ   طب وفيه محمد بن إسماعيل الوساوسي متهم مج

Al-Ḥākim – he declared it sound – and al-Bayhaqī narrated that Abū Hurayra ☺ said at the time ʿUthmān was besieged: "I heard the Messenger of Allah ﷺ say: [54] 'A dissension and a strife shall take place.' We said, 'Messenger of Allah! What do you order us to do then?' He replied, 'Stay with the leader and his friends,' pointing to ʿUthmān."[105]

---

[104]Narrated from Zayd b. Thābit by Ṭabarānī, *al-Kabīr* (5:159) with a chain al-Haythamī (9:82) said contained "Muḥammad b. Ismāʿīl al-Wasāwisī who used to forge ḥadīths."
[105]Narrated from Abū Hurayra by al-Ḥākim (3:99=1990 ed. 3:105; 4:434=4:480 al-Dhahabī confirming it as sound); Ibn Abī Shayba (10:363 §32049); al-Ṭabarānī in *al-Awsaṭ* (9:175 §9457); Ibn Abī ʿĀṣim in *al-Sunna* (2:587 §1278); and al-Bayhaqī in *al-Iʿtiqād* (p. 368).

عَنْ أَبِي هُرَيْرَةَ رَضِيَ اللهُ عَنْهُ سَمِعْتُ رَسُولَ اللهِ ﷺ يَقُولُ إِنَّهَا سَتَكُونُ فِتْنَةٌ وَاخْتِلافٌ أَوِ اخْتِلافٌ وَفِتْنَةٌ قَالَ قُلْنَا يَا رَسُولَ اللهِ فَمَا تَأْمُرُنَا قَالَ عَلَيْكُمْ بِالأَمِيرِ وَأَصْحَابِهِ وَأَشَارَ إِلَى عُثْمَانَ

ش طس ك صححه

Ibn Mājah, al-Ḥākim – declaring it sound –, al-Bayhaqī, and Abū Nuʿaym narrated from ʿĀ'isha (رضي الله عنها): "The Messenger of Allah ﷺ summoned ʿUthmān and spoke to him confidentially whereupon the face of the latter changed. The Day of the House [when he was besieged] we told him, 'Will you not put up a fight?' He said, 'No! [55] The Messenger of Allah ﷺ took a covenant from me [not to fight at the time of my martyrdom] and I will fulfill it."[106]

عَنْ أَبِي سَهْلَةَ مَوْلَى عُثْمَانَ قَالَ قَالَ عُثْمَانُ رَضِيَ اللهُ عَنْهُ يَوْمَ الدَّارِ إِنَّ رَسُولَ اللهِ ﷺ قَدْ عَهِدَ إِلَيَّ عَهْدًا فَأَنَا صَابِرٌ عَلَيْهِ ت

قال حَسَنٌ صَحِيحٌ غَرِيبٌ جه حم حب ك ع ز ابن سعد

Ibn ʿAdī and Ibn ʿAsākir narrated that Anas ﵁ said: "The Messenger of Allah ﷺ said: [56] ''Uthmān! You will be given the caliphate after me but the hypocrites will want you to renounce it. Do not renounce it but fast on that day so that you will break your fast with me.'"[107]

[106]Narrated from Abū Sahla, ʿUthmān's freedman, by al-Tirmidhī *(hasan sahīh gharīb)*, Aḥmad in the *Musnad* and *Faḍā'il al-Saḥāba* (1:494), Ibn Mājah, Ibn Hibbān, al-Ḥākim (1990 ed. 3:106), Ibn Saʿd (3:66), Abū Yaʿlā (8:234), and al-Bazzār (2:60) with sound chains.

[107]Narrated from Anas by Ibn ʿAsākir (39:290), Ibn ʿAdī in *al-Kāmil* (3:27) and al-Dhahabī in his *Mīzān* (2:424) with a chain containing Abū al-Rahhāl Khālid b. Muḥammad al-Anṣārī who is weak and is the only one to report it but see above, note 90, for the sound form of this hadīth.

عَنْ أَنَسٍ رَضِيَ اللهُ عَنْهُ مَرْفُوعاً يَا عُثْمَانُ إِنَّكَ سَتَلِي الخِلافَةَ مِنْ بَعْدِي وَسَيُرِيدُكَ المنَافِقُونَ عَلَى خَلْعِهَا فَلا تَخْلَعْهَا وَصُمْ ذَلِكَ اليَوْمَ تَفْطُرُ عِنْدِي كر كامل ميزان عن أبي الرّحّال خالد بن محمد الأنصاري وقد روى الوجه المحفوظ عن عائشة مرفوعاً يَا عُثْمَانُ إِنَّهُ لَعَلَّ اللهَ يُقَمِّصُكَ قَمِيصًا فَإِنْ أَرَادُوكَ عَلَى خَلْعِهِ فَلاَ تَخْلَعْهُ لَهُمْ ت قال حسن غريب جه حم حب ك

Al-Ḥākim – declaring it sound – and Ibn Mājah narrated that Murra b. Ka'b **[473]** ﷺ said: "I heard the Messenger of Allah ﷺ mention a trial, at which time a man cloaked in his garment passed by. He said: [57] 'This man, at that time, shall follow right guidance.' I went to see him and it was 'Uthmān."[108]

عَنْ أَبِي الأَشْعَثِ الصَّنْعَانِيِّ أَنَّ خُطَبَاءَ قَامَتْ بِالشَّامِ وَفِيهِمْ رِجَالٌ مِنْ أَصْحَابِ رَسُولِ اللهِ ﷺ فَقَامَ آخِرُهُمْ رَجُلٌ يُقَالُ لَهُ مُرَّةُ بْنُ كَعْبٍ فَقَالَ لَوْلاَ حَدِيثٌ سَمِعْتُهُ مِنْ رَسُولِ اللهِ ﷺ مَا قُمْتُ وَذَكَرَ الْفِتَنَ فَقَرَّبَهَا فَمَرَّ رَجُلٌ مُقَنَّعٌ فِي ثَوْبٍ فَقَالَ هَذَا يَوْمَئِذٍ عَلَى الْهُدَى فَقُمْتُ إِلَيْهِ فَإِذَا هُوَ عُثْمَانُ بْنُ عَفَّانَ قَالَ فَأَقْبَلْتُ عَلَيْهِ بِوَجْهِهِ فَقُلْتُ هَذَا قَالَ نَعَمْ ت قال حسن صحيح جه حم ش طب ك نعيم في الفتن

[108]Narrated from Ka'b b. Murra al-Bahzī by al-Tirmidhī *(hasan sahīh)*, Ibn Mājah with a weak chain, Ahmad with several fair chains in his *Musnad* and *Fadā'il al-Sahāba* (1:450), al-Ḥākim (1990 ed. 3:109, 4:479 *sahīh*), Ibn Abī Shayba (6:360 §32025-32026, 7:442 §37090) with three chains, al-Ṭabarānī in *al-Kabīr* (19:161-162 §359, §362, 20:315 §750), and Nu'aym b. Hammād in *al-Fitan* (1:174 §461).

Al-Ḥākim narrated that Ibn ʿAbbās رضي الله عنهما said that the Prophet ﷺ told them that 58 drops from the blood of ʿUthmān shall fall on the verse ﴿**and Allah will suffice you (for defense) against them**﴾ (2:137); and this is what took place.

[The rest of the narration states: "And you will intercede on the Day of Resurrection for as many people as the population of Rabīʿa and Muḍar."][109]

عَنِ ابْنِ عَبَّاسٍ رَضِيَ اللهُ عَنْهُمَا قَالَ كُنْتُ قَاعِداً ثَمَّ النَّبِيِّ ﷺ إِذْ أَقْبَلَ عُثْمَانُ بْنُ عَفَّانٍ رَضِيَ اللهُ عَنْهُ فَلَمَّا دَنَا مِنْهُ قَالَ يَا عُثْمَانُ تُقْتَلُ وَأَنْتَ تَقْرَأُ سُورَةَ الْبَقَرَةِ فَتَقَعُ مِنْ دَمِكَ عَلَى ﴿فَسَيَكْفِيكَهُمُ ٱللَّهُ وَهُوَ ٱلسَّمِيعُ ٱلْعَلِيمُ﴾ البقرة وَتُبْعَثُ يَوْمَ الْقِيَامَةِ أَمِيراً عَلَى كُلِّ مَخْذُولٍ يَغْبِطُكَ أَهْلُ الْمَشْرِقِ وَالْمَغْرِبِ وَتَشْفَعُ فِي عَدَدِ رَبِيعَةَ وَمُضَرَ ك الطبري في التاريخ الجرح والتعديل قال الذهبي في التلخيص كذب بحت اهـ وجاء في المسند بأسانيد رجالها ثقات وطب عَنْ أَبِي أُمَامَةَ رَضِيَ اللهُ عَنْهُ أَنَّهُ سَمِعَ رَسُولَ اللهِ ﷺ يَقُولُ لَيَدْخُلَنَّ الْجَنَّةَ بِشَفَاعَةِ رَجُلٍ لَيْسَ بِنَبِيٍّ مِثْلُ الْحَيَّيْنِ أَوْ مِثْلُ أَحَدِ الْحَيَّيْنِ رَبِيعَةَ وَمُضَرَ وفي الترمذي حَدَّثَنَا أَبُو هِشَامٍ الرِّفَاعِيُّ الْكُوفِيُّ قَالَ حَدَّثَنَا يَحْيَى بْنُ الْيَمَانِ عَنْ جِسْرٍ أَبِي جَعْفَرٍ عَنْ الْحَسَنِ الْبَصْرِيِّ قَالَ قَالَ رَسُولُ اللهِ ﷺ يَشْفَعُ

[109] A forgery as stated by al-Haytamī in *al-Minaḥ al-Makkiyya* (1:494), narrated from Ibn ʿAbbās by al-Ḥākim (3:103=1990 ed. 3:110, al-Dhahabī: "an unadulterated lie"), from the grandmother of al-Zubayr b. ʿAbd Allāh by al-Ṭabarī in his *Tārīkh* (2:671), from 'Umra bint ʿAbd al-Rahmān by Ibn Abī Ḥātim in *al-Jarḥ* (4:179 §780), and from Waththāb by Ibn Saʿd (3:72) but the latter part is narrated by Aḥmad – without naming ʿUthmān – and al-Ṭabarānī while al-Tirmidhī, ʿAbd Allāh b. Aḥmad in *Faḍā'il al-Saḥāba*, and al-Ājurrī do name him but through a weak *mursal* chain.

عُثْمَانُ بْنُ عَفَّانَ رَضِيَ اللهُ عَنْهُ يَوْمَ الْقِيَامَةِ بِمِثْلِ رَبِيعَةَ وَمُضَرَ

ت عبدالله بن أحمد في فضائل الصحابة والمالقي من طريق الآجري في كتاب مقتل الشهيد عثمان جميعهم مرسلا

The ḥadīth Master al-Silafī narrated that Ḥudhayfa ﷺ said: [59] "The beginning of dissensions is the murder of ʿUthmān and the last of them is the coming out of the Anti-Christ.[110] By the One in Whose Hand is my soul! [a] None shall die with a mustard seed's worth of love for the killers of ʿUthmān except he shall follow the Anti-Christ if the latter comes in his lifetime and, if not, he shall believe in him in his grave." It is evident that Ḥudhayfa ﷺ heard this from the Prophet ﷺ for it is not something that can be said on the basis of opinion.

عَنْ حُذَيْفَةَ رَضِيَ اللهُ عَنْهُ قَالَ أَرَأَيْتُمْ يَوْمَ الدَّارِ كَانَتْ فِتْنَةٌ يَعْنِي قَتْلَ عُثْمَانَ فَإِنَّهَا أَوَّلُ الْفِتَنِ وَآخِرُهَا الدَّجَّالُ ش

Al-Ṭabarānī narrated with a sound chain from [Abū] Masʿūd ﷺ: "We were with the Prophet ﷺ in some campaign at which time distress befell the people. I saw in their faces the signs of dejection while I saw happiness in those of the hypocrites. Seeing this, the Messenger of Allah ﷺ said: [60] 'I swear by Allah that the sun shall not set before Allah first brings you some sustenance.' ʿUthmān understood that Allah and His Prophet ﷺ would most certainly be confirmed, so he bought fourteen mounts loaded with food and conveyed [seven] of them to the Prophet ﷺ. The signs of joy could be seen on the faces of the Muslims and those of sadness on the faces of the hypocrites. [a] I saw the Prophet ﷺ raising his hands until one could see the whiteness of his arm-pits, supplicating on behalf of ʿUthmān with a supplication I never heard him say for anyone before him."[111]

---

[110] Narrated to here from Hudhayfa by Ibn Abī Shayba (7:264 §35920).
[111] Narrated not from Ibn Masʿūd but Abū Masʿūd by Aḥmad in *Faḍāʾil al-Ṣaḥāba* (1:234 §287) and al-Ṭabarānī in *al-Kabīr* (17:249-250 §694) and *al-Awsaṭ* (7:195-196

عَنْ عُقْبَةَ بْنِ عَمْرٍو أَبِي مَسْعُودٍ رَضِيَ اللهُ عَنْهُ كُنْتُ مَعَ رَسُولِ
اللهِ ﷺ وَنَحْنُ غُزَاةٌ قَدْ أَصَابَ المسْلِمِينَ جَهْدٌ شَدِيدٌ حَتَّىٰ
عُرِفَتِ الكَآبَةُ فِي وُجُوهِ المسْلِمِينَ وَالْفَرَحُ فِي وُجُوهِ المُنَافِقِينَ
فَلَمَّا رَأَى ذَلِكَ رَسُولُ اللهِ ﷺ قَالَ وَاللهِ لاَ تَغِيبُ الشَّمْسُ حَتَّىٰ
يَأْتِيَكُمُ اللهُ بِرِزْقٍ فَعَلِمَ عُثْمَانُ أَنَّ اللهَ وَرَسُولَهُ سَيُصَدَّقَانِ فَوَجَّهَ
رَاحِلَتَهُ فَإِذَا هُوَ بِأَرْبَعِ عَشْرَةَ رَاحِلَةً فَاشْتَرَاهَا وَمَا عَلَيْهَا مِنْ
طَعَامٍ فَوَجَّهَ مِنْهَا سَبْعاً إِلَى رَسُولِ اللهِ ﷺ وَوَجَّهَ بِسَبْعٍ إِلَى أَهْلِهِ
فَلَمَّا رَأَى المسْلِمُونَ العِيرَ قَدْ جَاءَتْ فَعُرِفَ الفَرَحُ فِي وُجُوهِ
المؤْمِنِينَ وَالْكَآبَةِ فِي وُجُوهِ المنَافِقِينَ فَقَالَ رَسُولُ اللهِ ﷺ مَا هَذَا
قَالُوا أَرْسَلَ بِهَا عُثْمَانُ هَدِيَّةً لَكَ قَالَ فَرَأَيْتُهُ رَافِعاً يَدَيْهِ يَدْعُو
لِعُثْمَانَ مَا سَمِعْتُهُ يَدْعُو لِأَحَدٍ قَبْلَهُ وَلا بَعْدَهُ اللهُمَّ أَعْطِ عُثْمَانَ
وَافْعَلْ بِعُثْمَانَ رَافِعاً يَدَيْهِ حَتَّىٰ رَأَيْتُ بَيَاضَ إِبْطَيْهِ عبدالله بن أحمد
في فضائل الصحابة طب طس وحسّن إسناده مج

Al-Bayhaqī narrated from ʿUrwa that when the Prophet ﷺ alighted at Ḥudaybiya he sent ʿUthmān to the Quraysh saying, 61 "Tell them we have not come to fight but only for the Minor Pilgrimage and invite them to Islam." He also ordered him to visit all the male and female believers of Mecca and give them the glad tidings of impending victory and to tell them of the near appearance of his Religion in Mecca, if Allah wills so that the faith

§7255) through Saʿīd b. Muḥammad al-Warrāq who is weak although al-Haythamī (9:85-96=9:113-115 §14523, §14560) graded its chain fair.

should no longer be derided there. He went to see the Quraysh and told them this but they refused and declared that they would fight. Then the Messenger of Allah ﷺ summoned people to pledge their loyalty, whereupon someone called out: "Lo! Truly the Holy Spirit has descended upon the Messenger of Allah." Then the Muslims pledged to him that they would never desert him. Allah frightened the idolaters with this event so they released all the Muslims they had previously held and asked for a truce and treaty.[112] The Muslims said, while at Ḥudaybiya and before ʿUthmān got back, that the latter had reached the Kaʿba and circumambulated it. The Prophet ﷺ said: a "I do not think he circumambulated it while we are under siege!" When ʿUthmān returned they told him, "You circumambulated the House." He replied, "Perish your thought! By the One in Whose Hand is my soul, even if I had taken up residence there for one year with the Messenger of Allah ﷺ at Ḥudaybiya, I would not have circumambulated it until the Messenger of Allah ﷺ did. The Quraysh invited me to circumambulate it but I refused." The Muslims said, "The Messenger of Allah ﷺ is truly the most knowing of Allah among us and the one with the best opinion."[113]

قَالَ الوَاقِدِي فِي المغَازِي دَعَا رَسُولُ اللهِ ﷺ عُثْمَانَ رضي الله عنه فَقَالَ اذْهَبْ إِلَى قُرَيْشٍ فَخَبِّرْهُمْ أَنَّا لَمْ نَأْتِ لِقِتَالِ أَحَدٍ وَإِنَّمَا جِئْنَا مُعْتَمِرِينَ فَخَرَجَ عُثْمَانُ فَدَخَلَ عُثْمَانُ مَكَّةَ فَأَتَى أَشْرَافَهُمْ رَجُلًا رَجُلًا أَبَا سُفْيَانَ بْنَ حَرْبٍ وَصَفْوَانَ بْنَ أُمَيَّةَ وَغَيْرَهُمْ مِنْهُمْ مَنْ لَقِيَ بِبَلْدَحٍ وَمِنْهُمْ مَنْ لَقِيَ بِمَكَّةَ فَجَعَلُوا يَرُدُّونَ عَلَيْهِ إِنَّ مُحَمَّدًا لَا يَدْخُلُهَا عَلَيْنَا أَبَدًا قَالَ عُثْمَانُ رَضِيَ اللهُ عَنْهُ ثُمَّ كُنْت أَدْخُلُ

[112]Narrated to here from the Companion al-Miswar b. Makhrama and the *Tābiʿī* Marwān b. al-Ḥakam by al-Bukhārī, Muslim, Aḥmad and others.

[113]Narrated *mursal* from ʿUrwa b. al-Zubayr by Ibn ʿAsākir (39:76-78), al-Bayhaqī in *al-Sunan* (9:219, 9:221) and the *Dalāʾil*, and al-Ḥākim in *al-Iklīl*. Also al-Wāqidī and Ibn Saʿd (2:95-97) without chain. Cf. *Khaṣāʾiṣ* (1:408), Ibn Kathīr's *Tafsīr* (4:187), *Kanz* (§30152), and *ʿAwn al-Maʿbūd* (7:289).

عَلَى قَوْمٍ مُؤْمِنِينَ مِنْ رِجَالٍ وَنِسَاءٍ مُسْتَضْعَفِينَ فَأَقُولُ إنّ رَسُولَ اللهِ يُبَشّرُكُمْ بِالْفَتْحِ وَيَقُولُ أُظِلّكُمْ حَتّى لاَ يَسْتَخْفِي بِمَكّةَ الإِيمَانُ ثُمّ قَالَ إنّ اللهَ أَمَرَنِي بِالْبَيْعَةِ فَأَقْبَلَ النّاسُ يُبَايِعُونَهُ فَلَمّا نَظَرَتْ قُرَيْشٌ إلَى مَا رَأَتْ مِنْ سُرْعَةِ النّاسِ إلَى الْبَيْعَةِ وَتَشْمِيرِهِمْ إلَى الْحَرْبِ اشْتَدّ رُعْبُهُمْ وَخَوْفُهُمْ وَأَسْرَعُوا إلَى الْقَضِيّةِ وَقَالَ الْمُسْلِمُونَ يَا رَسُولَ اللهِ وَصَلَ عُثْمَانُ إلَى الْبَيْتِ فَطَافَ فَقَالَ رَسُولُ اللهِ ﷺ مَا أَظُنّ عُثْمَانَ يَطُوفُ بِالْبَيْتِ وَنَحْنُ مَحْصُورُونَ قَالُوا يَا رَسُولَ اللهِ وَمَا يَمْنَعُهُ وَقَدْ وَصَلَ إلَى الْبَيْتِ ؟ فَقَالَ النّبِيّ ﷺ ظَنّي بِهْ أَلّا يَطُوفَ حَتّى نَطُوفَ فَلَمّا رَجَعَ عُثْمَانُ رَضِيَ اللهُ عَنْهُ إلَى النّبِيّ ﷺ قَالُوا اشْتَفَيْت مِنْ الْبَيْتِ يَا عَبْدَ اللهِ قَالَ عُثْمَانُ بِئْسَ مَا ظَنَنْتُمْ بِي لَوْ كُنْتُ بِهَا سَنَةً وَالنّبِيّ مُقِيمٌ بِالْحُدَيْبِيَةِ مَا طُفْتُ وَلَقَدْ دَعَتْنِي قُرَيْشٌ إلَى أَنْ أَطُوفَ فَأَبَيْت ذَلِكَ عَلَيْهَا فَقَالَ الْمُسْلِمُونَ لِرَسُولِ اللهِ كَانَ أَعْلَمَنَا بِاللهِ تَعَالَى وَأَحْسَنِنَا ظَنّا كر ك في الإكليل ق في الدلائل جميعه مرسلاً خصائص وأصله في الصحيحين

ʿAlī رضي الله عنه

Al-Ṭabarānī narrated that Salmā the wife of Abū Rāfiʿ رضي الله عنها said: "I can still see myself with the Messenger of Allah ﷺ when he said: 62 'A man from Paradise is about to come into your presence.' Lo and behold! I heard the sound of footsteps and there was ʿAlī b. Abī Ṭālib **[474]** ؓ."[114]

عَنْ مُحَمَّدِ بْنِ الفَضْلِ الرَّافِعِي عَنْ جَدَّتِهِ سَلْمَى أَنَّهَا قَالَتْ إِنِّي لَمَعَ النَّبِيِّ ﷺ بِالأَسْوَاقِ فَقَالَ لَيَطْلَعَنَّ عَلَيْكُمْ رَجُلٌ مِنْ أَهْلِ الْجَنَّةِ إِذْ سَمِعْتُ الخَشْفَةَ فَإِذَا عَلِيُّ بْنُ أَبِي طَالِبٍ ؓ طب

Al-Ḥākim and al-Bayhaqī narrated that Abū Saʿīd al-Khudrī ؓ said: "We were with the Messenger of Allah ﷺ one time when his sandal strings broke, so ʿAlī stayed behind, mending them, after which the Prophet ﷺ walked a little and said: 'In truth 63 there will be, among you, one who will fight over the interpretation *(ta'wīl)* of the Qur'ān just as I fought over its revelation *(tanzīl)*.' Abū Bakr asked, 'Am I he?' The Prophet ﷺ said no. ʿUmar asked: 'Am I he?' The Prophet ﷺ said: a 'No, it is the sandal repairman *(khāṣif al-naʿl)*.'"[115]

عَنْ أَبِي سَعِيدٍ الْخُدْرِيِّ رَضِيَ اللهُ عَنْهُ كُنَّا جُلُوسًا نَنْتَظِرُ رَسُولَ اللهِ ﷺ فَخَرَجَ عَلَيْنَا مِنْ بَعْضِ بُيُوتِ نِسَائِهِ قَالَ فَقُمْنَا مَعَهُ فَانْقَطَعَتْ نَعْلُهُ فَتَخَلَّفَ عَلَيْهَا عَلِيٌّ يَخْصِفُهَا فَمَضَى رَسُولُ اللهِ ﷺ وَمَضَيْنَا مَعَهُ ثُمَّ قَامَ يَنْتَظِرُهُ وَقُمْنَا مَعَهُ فَقَالَ إِنَّ مِنْكُمْ

[114]Narrated from Salmā the wife of Abū Rāfiʿ in *al-Kabīr* (24:301) cf. al-Haythamī (9:156-157 §14693).

[115]Narrated from Abū Saʿīd al-Khudrī and ʿAlī by al-Tirmidhī *(ḥasan saḥīḥ gharīb)*, Aḥmad with a sound chain cf. al-Haythamī (9:133), al-Nasā'ī in *al-Sunan al-Kubrā* (5:115 §8416), Ibn Ḥibbān (15:385 §6937 *isnād ṣaḥīḥ*), al-Ḥākim (1990 ed. 2:149 and 4:443 *saḥīḥ* per Muslim's criterion; 3:122 *saḥīḥ* per the criterion of al-Bukhārī and Muslim), al-Baghawī in *Sharḥ al-Sunna* (10:233), Abū Yaʿla (§1086), Saʿīd b. Manṣūr in his *Sunan*, Ibn Abī Shayba (12:64), Abū Nuʿaym in *al-Ḥilya*, and al-Bayhaqī in the *Sunan* (9:229 §18618), *Dalā'il al-Nubuwwa* (6:435) and *Shuʿab al-Īmān*.

مَنْ يُقَاتِلُ عَلَى تَأْوِيلِ هَذَا الْقُرْآنِ كَمَا قَاتَلْتُ عَلَى تَنْزِيلِهِ فَاسْتَشْرَفْنَا وَفِينَا أَبُو بَكْرٍ وَعُمَرُ فَقَالَ لاَ وَلَكِنَّهُ خَاصِفُ النَّعْلِ قَالَ فَجِئْنَا نُبَشِّرُهُ قَالَ وَكَأَنَّهُ قَدْ سَمِعَهُ حم وفي الباب عن رِبْعِيِّ بْنِ حِرَاشٍ حَدَّثَنَا عَلِيُّ بْنُ أَبِي طَالِبٍ رَضِيَ اللهُ عَنْهُ بِالرَّحَبِيَّةِ قَالَ لَمَّا كَانَ يَوْمُ الْحُدَيْبِيَةِ خَرَجَ إِلَيْنَا نَاسٌ مِنَ الْمُشْرِكِينَ فِيهِمْ سُهَيْلُ بْنُ عَمْرٍو وَأُنَاسٌ مِنْ رُؤَسَاءِ الْمُشْرِكِينَ فَقَالُوا يَا رَسُولَ اللهِ خَرَجَ إِلَيْكَ نَاسٌ مِنْ أَبْنَائِنَا وَإِخْوَانِنَا وَأَرِقَّائِنَا وَلَيْسَ لَهُمْ فِقْهٌ فِي الدِّينِ وَإِنَّمَا خَرَجُوا فِرَارًا مِنْ أَمْوَالِنَا وَضِيَاعِنَا فَارْدُدْهُمْ إِلَيْنَا قَالَ فَإِنْ لَمْ يَكُنْ لَهُمْ فِقْهٌ فِي الدِّينِ سَنُفَقِّهُهُمْ فَقَالَ النَّبِيُّ ﷺ يَا مَعْشَرَ قُرَيْشٍ لَتَنْتَهُنَّ أَوْ لَيَبْعَثَنَّ اللهُ عَلَيْكُمْ مَنْ يَضْرِبُ رِقَابَكُمْ بِالسَّيْفِ عَلَى الدِّينِ قَدْ امْتَحَنَ اللهُ قَلْبَهُ عَلَى الإِيمَانِ قَالُوا مَنْ هُوَ يَا رَسُولَ اللهِ فَقَالَ لَهُ أَبُو بَكْرٍ مَنْ هُوَ يَا رَسُولَ اللهِ وَقَالَ عُمَرُ مَنْ هُوَ يَا رَسُولَ اللهِ قَالَ هُوَ خَاصِفُ النَّعْلِ وَكَانَ أَعْطَى عَلِيًّا نَعْلَهُ يَخْصِفُهَا ثُمَّ الْتَفَتَ إِلَيْنَا عَلِيٌّ فَقَالَ إِنَّ رَسُولَ اللهِ ﷺ قَالَ مَنْ كَذَبَ عَلَيَّ مُتَعَمِّدًا فَلْيَتَبَوَّأْ مَقْعَدَهُ مِنَ النَّارِ ت قَالَ حَسَنٌ صَحِيحٌ غَرِيبٌ ك قال صحيح على شرط مسلم

Abū Yaʿlā and al-Ḥākim – who graded it a sound report – narrated from Ibn ʿAbbās رضي الله عنهما that the Prophet ﷺ said to ʿAlī:

"In truth, [64] you shall certainly experience great hardship after me." He asked: "With my Religion safe?" The Prophet ﷺ said yes.[116]

عَنِ بْنِ عَبَّاسٍ رَضِيَ اللهُ عَنْهُمَا قَالَ قَالَ النَّبِيُّ ﷺ لِعَلِيٍّ أَمَا إِنَّكَ سَتَلْقَى بَعْدِي جَهْداً قَالَ بِالإِجْمَاعِ مِنْ دِينِي ؟ قَالَ بِالإِجْمَاعِ مِنْ دِينِكَ ك قال صحيح على شرط الشيخين

Al-Ṭabarānī narrated that ʿAlī ؓ said: [65] "The Prophet ﷺ took my pledge that I must fight traitors, outlaws, and renegades *(al-nākithīn wal-qāsiṭīn wal-māriqīn)*."[117]

قَوْلُ عَلِيِّ بْنِ أَبِي طَالِبٍ رَضِيَ اللهُ عَنْهُ عَهِدَ إِلَيَّ النَّبِيُّ ﷺ أَنْ أُقَاتِلَ النَّاكِثِينَ وَالْقَاسِطِينَ وَالْمَارِقِينَ ز ع أُمِرْتُ بِقِتَالِ النَّاكِثِينَ

[116]Narrated from Ibn ʿAbbās by al-Ḥākim (3:140=1990 ed. 3:151 *saḥīh* per al-Bukhārī and Muslim's criterion) and – *mursal* – Ibn Abī Shayba (6:372 §32117).

[117]Narrated from Abū Ayyūb al-Ansārī by al-Ḥākim (1990 ed. 3:150) with a "thoroughly obscure chain" according to al-Dhahabī in the *Mīzān* ('Attāb b. Thaʿlaba); from Ibn Mas'ūd by al-Shāshī in his *Musnad* (1:342 §322) and al-Ṭarabānī in *al-Awsat* (9:165) and *al-Kabīr* (10:91 §10053-10054) cf. al-Haythamī (6:235); from 'Alqama from ʿAlī by Ibn Abī ʿĀsim in *al-Sunna* (2:439) cf. al-Dāraquṭnī, *ʿIlal* (5:148 §780); from Khulayd al-'Asarī by al-Khaṭīb (8:340); and from ʿAlī b. Rabīʿa from ʿAlī by al-Bazzār (2:215 §604, 3:27 §774), Abū Yaʿlā (1:397 §519), al-Ṭabarānī in *al-Awsat* (8:213) cf. al-Haythamī (5:186, 7:238), and al-Zubayr b. Bakkār in *al-Muwaffaqiyyāt* (see below, section "His ﷺ Foretelling the Status of the Banū al-ʿAbbās") cf. *Khaṣāʾis* (2:203-204) with a chain containing al-Rabīʿ b. Sahl who is weak cf. Ibn Ḥajar in *Lisān al-Mīzān* (2:446 §1827) but the latter considers the meaning true although al-Dhahabī said *al-matnu munkar* in the *Mīzān* ('Attāb b. Thaʿlaba) cf. al-ʿUqaylī (3:480 *lā yathbutu fī hādhā al-bābi shay'*). Al-Aḥdab considers it *ṣaḥīḥ li-ghayrih* (*Zawāʾid* 6:401-405 §1261). Also related as a saying of ʿAmmār b. Yāsir by Abū Yaʿlā (3:194 §1623) and of Abū Ayyūb by Ṭabarānī, *al-Kabīr* (4:172 §4049) and al-Khaṭīb (13:186) cf. al-Haythamī (6:235, 7:238), Ibn al-Jawzī, *ʿIlal* (1:247), and al-Dhahabī, *Siyar* (Risāla ed. 2:410 *khabar wāhin*) and *Mīzān* (Aṣbagh b. Nabāta). Ibn al-Athīr said in *al-Nihāya* (cf. Ibn Ḥajar, *Talkhīs al-Ḥabīr* 4:44): "The traitors are the people of the Camel because they betrayed their pledge to him [ʿAlī], the outlaws are the people of Syro-Palestine because they ran away from truth and right, and the heretics are the people of Nahrawān [the *Khawārij*]." Al-Khaṭīb actually narrates this explanation from ʿAlī himself in *Muwaḍḍiḥ Awhām al-Jamʿ wal-Tafrīq* (1:393).

وَالْقَاسِطِينَ وَالمَارِقِينَ ك قال الذهبي إسناده مظلم ومتنه منكر مسند الشاشي طب طس ابن أبي عاصم في السنّة خط بلفظ أَمَرَنِي رَسُولُ اللهِ ﷺ ويروى موقوفاً على عمّار بن ياسر وأبي أيّوب الأنصاري وعن أبي سعيد عن علي قبيل صفّين فَالنَّاكِثِينَ الَّذِينَ فَرَغْنَا مِنْهُمْ - أي أهل الجمل - وَالْقَاسِطِينَ الَّذِينَ نَسِيرُ إِلَيْهِمْ -أي أهل الشام- وَالمَارِقِينَ لَمْ نَرَهُمْ بَعْدُ قَالَ وَكَانُوا أَهْلُ النَّهْرِ أي الخوارج خط في الجمع والتفريق نهاية تلخيص الحبير ولعله ثابت بمجموع طرقه وشواهده ورواه الزبير بن بكار مطولاً سيأتي في باب أخبار بني العباس والله أعلم

Al-Ḥumaydī, al-Ḥākim, and others narrated that Abū al-Aswad [al-Du'alī] said: "'Abd Allāh b. Salām came and said to ʿAlī as the latter had his foot in the stirrups: [66] 'Do not go to the people of Iraq! If you do, the sword blades shall fall on you there.' ʿAlī replied: 'I swear by Allah that the Messenger of Allah ﷺ told me the same before you did!'"[118]

عَنْ عَلِيِّ بْنِ أَبِي طَالِبٍ رَضِيَ اللهُ عَنْهُ قَالَ قَالَ لِي عَبْدُ اللهِ بْنُ سَلامٍ وَقَدْ وَضَعْتُ رِجْلِي فِي الغَرْزِ وَأَنَا أُرِيدُ العِرَاقَ لا تَأْتِ أَهلَ العِرَاقِ فَإِنَّكَ إِنْ أَتَيْتَهُمْ أَصَابَكَ ذُبَابُ السَّيْفِ بِهِ قَالَ عَلِيٌّ وَايْمُ اللهِ لَقَدْ قَالَهَا لِي رَسُولُ اللهِ ﷺ مسند الحميدي ز ع ابن أبي عاصم في السنّة حب ك ض

[118]Narrated from Abu al-Aswad, from ʿAlī by al-Ḥumaydī in his *Musnad* (1:30 §53), al-Bazzār (2:295-296 §718), Abū Yaʿlā (1:381 §491), Ibn Abī ʿĀṣim in *al-Āḥād* (1:144 §172), Ibn Ḥibbān (15:127 §6733), and al-Ḥākim (3:140=1990 ed. 3:151) all with chains containing the Shīʿī ʿAbd al-Malik b. Aʿyan and thus weakened by al-Dhahabī although considered strong by al-Haythamī (9:138) and fair by al-Arna'ūṭ while al-Ḍyā' al-Maqdisī retains it among the sound hadīths in *al-Mukhtāra* (2:128-129 §498).

The Prophet's ﷺ Knowledge of the Unseen • 63

Abū Nuʿaym narrated that ʿAlī ؓ said: "The Messenger of Allah ﷺ told me: 67 'There shall be dissensions and your people shall dispute with you.' I said, 'What do you order me to do?' He replied: 'Rule by the Book.'"[119]

عَنْ عَلِيٍّ رَضِيَ اللهُ عَنْهُ قَالَ قَالَ لِي رَسُولُ اللهِ ﷺ سَتَكُونُ فِتَنٌ وَسَتُحَاجُّ قَوْمَكَ قُلْتُ يَا رَسُولَ اللهِ فَمَا تَأْمُرُنِي قَالَ احْكُمْ بِالْكِتَابِ طس طص

Al-Bayhaqī narrated that ʿAlī ؓ said: "Fāṭima's hand was asked in marriage from the Messenger of Allah ﷺ [but he refused], so a freedwoman that belonged to me at the time said to me: 'Did you hear that Fāṭima's hand was asked in marriage? Then what prevents you from going to see the Messenger of Allah ﷺ about it?' I went to see him. 68 We held the Messenger of Allah ﷺ in great awe and reverence, so when I stood before him I became tongue-tied. I could not say a word! The Messenger of Allah ﷺ said: a 'What brings you?' I stayed silent. He said: b 'Perhaps you came to ask Fāṭima's hand?' I said yes!" [Then the Prophet ﷺ married him to Fāṭima with his Ḥaṭim-made metal shield for dowry.][120]

عَنْ عَلِيٍّ رَضِيَ اللهُ عَنْهُ قَالَ لَقَدْ خَطَبْتُ فَاطِمَةَ بِنْتَ النَّبِيِّ ﷺ فَقَالَتْ لِي مَوْلَاةٌ هَلْ عَلِمْتَ أَنَّ فَاطِمَةَ تُخْطَبُ قُلْتُ لَا أَوْ نَعَمْ قَالَتْ فَاخْطُبْهَا إِلَيْهِ قَالَ قُلْتُ وَهَلْ عِنْدِي شَيْءٌ أَخْطُبُهَا

---

[119] Narrated from the weak Shīʿī al-Ḥārith b. ʿAbd Allāh al-Aʿwar from ʿAlī by al-Ṭabarānī in *al-Awsaṭ* (2:29-30 §1132) and *al-Saghīr* (2:174 §978) with a chain also containing ʿAṭāʾ b. Muslim al-Khaffāf who is weak cf. al-ʿUqaylī in *al-Duʿafāʾ* (3:405 §1143).

[120] Narrated broken-chained from ʿAlī by al-Bayhaqī, *Sunan* (7:234 §14129) and al-Dūlābī, *al-Dhurriyya al-Ṭāhira* (p. 64) while the dowry segment is narrated from ʿAlī by Abū Yaʿlā (1:388 §503), al-Bayhaqī (7:234 §14128), and Aḥmad cf. al-Dyāʾ al-Maqdisī, *Mukhtāra* (2:339 §716).

عَلَيْهِ؟ قَالَ فَوَاللهِ مَا زَالَتْ تَرْجِينِي حَتَّى دَخَلْتُ عَلَيْهِ وَكُنَّا نُجِلُّهُ
وَنُعَظِّمُهُ فَلَمَّا جَلَسْتُ بَيْنَ يَدَيْهِ أُلْجِمْتُ حَتَّى مَا اسْتَطَعْتُ
الكَلامَ قَالَ هَلْ لَكَ مِنْ حَاجَةٍ فَسَكَتُّ قَالَهَا ثَلاثَ مَرَّاتٍ قَالَ
لَعَلَّكَ جِئْتَ تَخْطُبُ فَاطِمَةَ ؟ قُلْتُ نَعَمْ يَا رَسُولَ اللهِ قَالَ هَلْ
عِنْدَكَ مِنْ شَيْءٍ تَسْتَحِلُّهَا بِهِ؟ قَالَ قُلْتُ لا وَاللهِ يَا رَسُولَ اللهِ
قَالَ فَمَا فَعَلْتَ بِالدِّرْعِ الَّتِي كُنْتُ سَلَّحْتُكَهَا ؟ قَالَ عَلِيٌّ وَاللهِ
إِنَّهَا لَدِرْعٌ حَطِمِيَّةٌ مَا ثَمَنُهَا إِلاَّ أَرْبَعُمِائَةِ دِرْهَمٍ قَالَ اذْهَبْ فَقَدْ
زَوَّجْتُكَهَا وَابْعَثْ بِهَا إِلَيْهَا فَاسْتَحِلَّهَا بِهِ هق الدولابي في الذرّية الطاهرة
وروى شطره الأخير ع رجاله ثقات إلا أنه منقطع مج ض ورواه حم بإسناد ضعيف

Al-Ḥākim – he declared it sound – and Abū Nuʿaym narrated from ʿAmmār b. Yāsir رضي الله عنه that the Prophet ﷺ said to ʿAlī: 69
"The most criminal of all people is he that shall strike you here" – indicating his temple – "until blood soaks this" – indicating his beard.[121] Abū Nuʿaym narrated something like it from Jābir b. Samura and Ṣuhayb.

[121]Narrated from **(1)** ʿAmmār b. Yāsir with a fair to sound chain cf. al-Suyūṭī in *Tārīkh al-Khulafā'* (p. 173) by Aḥmad (30:256-267 §18321, §18326 *ḥasan lighayrih*) and in *Faḍā'il al-Ṣaḥāba* (2:687), al-Nasā'ī in *al-Sunan al-Kubrā* (5:153 §8538), al-Bazzār (4:254 §1417, §1424), Abū Nuʿaym in the *Dalā'il* (p. 552-553 §490), *Ḥilya* (1:141), and *Maʿrifat al-Ṣaḥāba* (§675), al-Ḥākim (3:140-141=1990 ed. 3:151 *ṣaḥīḥ* per Muslim's criterion, incorrectly), Ibn Hishām (3:144), al-Bukhārī in *al-Tārīkh al-Saghīr* (1:71), al-Ṭaḥāwī in *Sharḥ Mushkil al-Āthār* (§811), al-Dūlābī in *al-Asmā' wal-Kunā* (2:163), al-Ṭabarī in his *Tārīkh* (2:14), al-Bayhaqī in the *Dalā'il* (3:12-13), and others cf. al-Haythamī (9:136), and *mursal* from ʿUbayd Allāh b. Abī Bakr b. Anas b. Mālik by Ibn Saʿd (3:35); **(2)** Jābir b. Samura by Abū Nuʿaym in the *Dalā'il* (p. 553 §491), cf. *Khaṣā'iṣ* (2:420); **(3)** the Shīʿī Thaʿlaba b. Yazīd al-Ḥimmānī, from ʿAlī by Ibn Saʿd (3:34), Ibn Abī Ḥātim, Abū Nuʿaym in the *Dalā'il* (p. 552 §489), Ibn ʿAbd al-Barr in *al-Istīʿāb* (3:60), and al-Nuwayrī in *Nihāyat al-Arab* (20:211); **(4)** Suhayb, from ʿAlī by al-Ṭabarānī in *al-Kabīr* (8:38-39 §7311), Ibn ʿAbd al-Barr in *al-Istīʿāb* (3:1125), Ibn ʿAsākir, al-Rūyānī, Ibn Mardūyah, and Abū Yaʿlā (1:377 §485) cf. *Kanz* (§36563, §36577-8, §36587), Ibn al-

عَنْ عَمَّارِ بْنِ يَاسِرٍ قَالَ كُنْتُ أَنَا وَعَلِيٌّ رَفِيقَيْنِ فِي غَزْوَةِ ذَاتِ الْعُشَيْرَةِ إلى أن قال قَالَ رَسُولُ اللهِ ﷺ أَلاَ أُحَدِّثُكُمَا بِأَشْقَى النَّاسِ رَجُلَيْنِ قُلْنَا بَلَى يَا رَسُولَ اللهِ قَالَ أُحَيْمِرُ ثَمُودَ الَّذِي عَقَرَ النَّاقَةَ وَالَّذِي يَضْرِبُكَ يَا عَلِيُّ عَلَى هَذِهِ يَعْنِي قَرْنَهُ حَتَّى تُبَلَّ مِنْهُ هَذِهِ يَعْنِي لِحْيَتَهُ حم ن في الكبرى أبو نعيم في الدلائل ك صححه وفي الباب عن جابر بن سمرة وعلي وسيأتي مطولا

Al-Ḥākim narrated that Anas ؓ said: "I went in with the Prophet ﷺ to see ʿAlī who lay sick while Abū Bakr and ʿUmar were visiting him. One of them said to the other, 'I do not think that he will survive,' whereupon the Messenger of Allah ﷺ said: 'In truth, [70] he shall not die other than murdered and he shall not die until he is filled with bitterness.'"[122]

عَنْ أَنَسِ بْنِ مَالِكٍ رَضِيَ اللهُ عَنْهُ قَالَ دَخَلْتُ مَعَ النَّبِيِّ ﷺ عَلَى عَلِيِّ بْنِ أَبِي طَالِبٍ رَضِيَ اللهُ عَنْهُ يَعُودُهُ وَهُوَ مَرِيضٌ وَعِنْدَهُ أَبُو بَكْرٍ وَعُمَرُ رَضِيَ اللهُ عَنْهُمَا فَتَحَوَّلاَ حَتَّىٰ جَلَسَ رَسُولُ اللهِ ﷺ فَقَالَ أَحَدُهُمَا لِصَاحِبِهِ إِلاَّ هَالِكٌ فَقَالَ رَسُولُ

Jawzī's *Sifat al-Safwa* (1:332), and al-Haythamī (9:136); **(5)** Ḥayyān al-Asadī, from ʿAlī by al-Ḥākim (3:142-143 *sahīh*); and **(6)** Zayd b. Wahb, *mawqūf* from ʿAlī by al-Ḥākim (3:143) and Ibn Abī Asim in *al-Zuhd* (p. 132). Al-Talīdī overlooked this authentic narration in his *Tahdhīb al-Khasāʾis*!

[122] Narrated by al-Ḥākim (3:139=1990 ed. 3:150) with a "completely defective" *(wāhin)* chain (al-Dhahabī).

اللهِ ﷺ إِنَّهُ لَنْ يَمُوتَ إِلاّ مَقْتُولاً وَلَنْ يَمُوتَ حَتَّى يُمْلَأَ غَيْظاً ك

قال الذهبي إسناده واه

Al-Ḥākim narrated that Thawr b. Mijzā'a said: "I passed by Ṭalḥa on the Day of the Camel as he was [lying on the ground and] about to expire. He said to me: 'Which side are you on?' I replied, 'With the friends of the Commander of the Believers.' He said, 'Stretch out your hand so that I may pledge my loyalty to you.' I stretched my hand and he pledged his loyalty to me. Then his spirit came out. I went back to ʿAlī and told him. He said, 'Allah is greatest! The Messenger of Allah ﷺ said the truth: 71 Allah would not have Ṭalḥa enter Paradise except firmly bound by his pledge of loyalty to me.'"[123]

عَنْ ثَوْرِ بْنِ مَجْزَأَةَ قَالَ مَرَرْتُ بِطَلْحَةَ بْنِ عُبَيْدِ اللهِ يَوْمَ الجَمَلِ وَهُوَ صَرِيعٌ فِي آخِرِ رَمَقٍ فَوَقَفْتُ عَلَيْهِ فَرَفَعَ رَأْسَهُ فَقَالَ إِنِي لأَرَى وَجْهَ رَجُلٍ كَأَنَّهُ القَمَرُ مِمَّنْ أَنْتَ فَقُلْتُ مِنْ أَصْحَابِ أَمِيرِ المُؤْمِنِينَ عَلِيٍّ فَقَالَ أَبْسُطْ يَدَكَ أُبَايِعُكَ فَبَسَطْتُ يَدِي وَبَايَعَنِي فَفَاضَتْ نَفْسُهُ فَأَتَيْتُ عَلِيّاً فَأَخْبَرْتُهُ بِقَوْلِ طَلْحَةَ فَقَالَ اللهُ أَكْبَرُ اللهُ أَكْبَرُ صَدَقَ رَسُولُ اللهِ ﷺ أَبَى اللهُ أَنْ يَدْخُلَ طَلْحَةُ الجَنَّةَ إِلا وَبَيْعَتِي فِي عُنُقِهِ ك قال صاحب الكنز قال ابن حجر في الأطراف سنده ضعيف جدا اه أي أطراف الكتب العشرة وقال في الرسالة المستطرفة هي الموطأ

[123]Narrated by al-Ḥākim (1990 ed. 3:421) with "an extremely weak chain" according to Ibn Ḥajar in *al-Aṭrāf* [=*Itḥāf al-Mahara bi-Aṭrāf al-ʿAshara*, known as *Aṭrāf al-Kutub al-ʿAshara* in eight volumes, an alphabetical index to the ḥadīths comprised in the *Muwatta', Musnad al-Shāfiʿī, Musnad Aḥmad, Musnad al-Dārimī, Ṣaḥīḥ Ibn Khuzayma, Muntaqā Ibn al-Jārūd, Ṣaḥīḥ Ibn Ḥibbān, Mustadrak al-Ḥākim, Mustakhraj Abī ʿAwāna, Sharḥ Maʿānī al-Āthār,* and *Sunan al-Dāraquṭnī*] cf. *Kanz* (§31646).

ومسند الشافعي ومسند أحمد ومسند الدارمي وصحيح ابن خزيمة ومنتقى ابن الجارود وصحيح ابن حبان ومستدرك الحاكم ومستخرج أبي عوانة وشرح معاني الآثار وسنن الدارقطني وإنما زاد العدد واحدا لأن صحيح ابن خزيمة لم يوجد منه سوى قدر ربعه هكذا في لحظ الألحاظ ذيل تذكرة الحفاظ اهـ

Al-Bayhaqī narrated that Ibn Isḥāq said: "Yazīd b. Sufyān narrated to me from Muḥammad b. Ka'b that the scribe of the Messenger of Allah ﷺ at that truce – al-Ḥudaybiya – was ʿAlī b. Abī Ṭālib, at which time the Messenger of Allah ﷺ told him: 'Write: These are the terms of the truce between Muḥammad b. ʿAbd Allāh and Suhayl b. ʿAmr.' ʿAlī stalled and would not write anything less than 'Muḥammad the Messenger of Allah.' Whereupon the Messenger of Allah ﷺ said: 72 'Write it [in their terms]. Truly **[475]** you will suffer something similar and be forced.'"[124] This is what took place after the battle of Ṣiffīn when the pact of arbitration was drawn between him and Muʿāwiya – Allah be well-pleased with both of them and with the rest of the Companions of the Messenger of Allah ﷺ.

عَنْ عَلِيٍّ رَضِيَ اللهُ عَنْهُ قَالَ إِنِي كُنْتُ كَاتِبَ رَسُولِ اللهِ ﷺ يَوْمَ الحُدَيْبِيَةِ فَكَتَبَ هَذَا مَا صَالَحَ عَلَيْهِ مُحَمَّدٌ رَسُولُ اللهِ وَسُهَيْلُ بْنُ عَمْرٍو فَقَالَ سُهَيْلٌ لَوْ عَلِمْنَا أَنَّهُ رَسُولُ اللهِ مَا قَاتَلْنَاهُ امْحُهَا فَقُلْتُ هُوَ وَاللهِ رَسُولُ اللهِ وَإِنْ رَغِمَ أَنْفُكَ لا وَاللهِ لا أَمْحُهَا فَقَالَ رَسُولُ اللهِ ﷺ أَرِنِي مَكَانَهَا فَأَرَيْتُهُ فَمَحَاهَا وَقَالَ أَمَا إِنَّ

[124]Narrated from Muḥammad b. Ka'b, from 'Alqama b. Qays by al-Nasā'ī in *al-Sunan al-Kubrā* (5:167 §8756) cf. *Fath* (7:503) and *mursal* from Ibn Ka'b by al-Bayhaqī in the *Dalā'il*, both through Ibn Isḥāq cf. al-Suyūṭī, *Khasā'is* (1:409), *Sīra Ḥalabiyya* (2:707), and al-Khuzāʿī, *Takhrīj al-Dilālāt* (1995 ed. p. 178= 1985 ed. p. 188).

لَكَ مِثْلَهَا وَأَنْتَ مُضْطَرٌّ ن في الكبرى هق في الدلائل خصائص حلبية تخريج الدلالات

'Abd Allāh b. Aḥmad narrated in the appendices to the *Musnad*, as well as al-Bazzār, Abū Ya'lā, and al-Ḥākim, that 'Alī ﷺ said: "The Messenger of Allah ﷺ told me: 73 'There is in you a similarity to 'Īsā ﷺ: the Jews hated him to the point that they defamed his mother, and the Christians loved him to the point that they gave him the rank which is not his!'"[125] Then 'Alī said: 74 "Two types of people shall perish concerning me: a hater who forges lies about me, and a lover who over-praises me."[126] [Another version adds: "Truly, a I am not a Prophet nor do I receive revelation! But I put into practice the Book of Allah and the Sunna of His Prophet ﷺ as much as I can. Therefore, b as long as I order you to obey Allah, it is incumbent upon you to obey me whether you like it or not!"[127]

عَنْ عَلِيٍّ رَضِيَ اللهُ عَنْهُ قَالَ قَالَ لِي النَّبِيُّ ﷺ فِيكَ مَثَلٌ مِنْ عِيسَى أَبْغَضَتْهُ الْيَهُودُ حَتَّى بَهَتُوا أُمَّهُ وَأَحَبَّتْهُ النَّصَارَى حَتَّى أَنْزَلُوهُ بِالْمَنْزِلَةِ الَّتِي لَيْسَ بِهِ ثُمَّ قَالَ يَهْلِكُ فِيَّ رَجُلَانِ مُحِبٌّ مُفْرِطٌ يُقَرِّظُنِي بِمَا لَيْسَ فِيَّ وَمُبْغِضٌ يَحْمِلُهُ شَنَآنِي عَلَى أَنْ

[125]Narrated to here from Abū Maryam and either Abū al-Bakhtarī or 'Abd Allāh b. Salama by 'Abd Allāh b. Aḥmad in *al-Sunna* (p. 233-234 §1266-1268), al-Ḥārith b. 'Abd Allāh by Ibn 'Abd al-Barr in *al-Istī'āb* (3:37), al-Nuwayrī in *Nihāyat al-Arab* (20:5) and in Ibn Abī al-Ḥadīd's *Sharḥ Nahj al-Balāgha* (1:372).

[126]Narrated from 'Alī by Abū Ya'la (1:406 §534) and Aḥmad (Shākir ed. 2:167-168 §1377-1378 *isnād ḥasan*=Arna'ūṭ ed. 2:468-469 §1376-1377 *isnād ḍa'īf*); al-Ḥākim (3:123=1990 ed. 3:132 *isnād ṣaḥīḥ* but al-Dhahabī indicated its weakness due to al-Ḥakam b. 'Abd al-Mālik cf. *Taqrīb* as did Ibn al-Jawzī in *al-'Ilal al-Mutanāhiya* (1:227 §357) cf. al-Haythamī (9:133). Also narrated by al-Bayhaqī in *al-Sunan al-Kubrā* (5:137 §8488) and Aḥmad in *Faḍā'il al-Ṣaḥāba* (2:639 §1087, 2:713 §1221, 2:713 §1222).

[127]Narrated by Aḥmad with the same weak chain as the preceding version.

يَبْهَتَنِي حم ع ك وجاء بزيادة أَلاَ إِنِّي لَسْتُ بِنَبِيٍّ وَلاَ يُوحَى إِلَيَّ وَلَكِنِّي أَعْمَلُ بِكِتَابِ اللهِ وَسُنَّةِ نَبِيِّهِ ﷺ مَا اسْتَطَعْتُ فَمَا أَمَرْتُكُمْ مِنْ طَاعَةِ اللهِ فَحَقٌّ عَلَيْكُمْ طَاعَتِي فِيمَا أَحْبَبْتُمْ وَكَرِهْتُمْ

حم وضعّفهما ابن الجوزي في العلل والذهبي في التلخيص

Al-Ṭabarānī and Abū Nuʿaym narrated that Jābir b. Samura رضي الله عنهما said, "The Messenger of Allah ﷺ said to ʿAlī: [75] 'You will be given leadership and caliphate; and truly, this will be dyed red with this,' meaning his beard with [the blood from] his head."[128]

عَنْ جَابِرِ بْنِ سَمُرَةَ رَضِيَ اللهُ عَنْهُمَا قَالَ قَالَ رَسُولُ اللهِ ﷺ لِعَلِيٍّ رَضِيَ اللهُ عَنْهُ إِنَّكَ امْرُؤٌ مُسْتَخْلَفٌ وَإِنَّكَ مَقْتُولٌ وَهَذِهِ مَخْضُوبَةٌ مِنْ هَذِهِ لِحْيَتُهُ مِنْ رَأْسِهِ طب طس إسناده ضعيف جدا مج

The Two Masters [al-Bukhārī and Muslim] narrated that Salama [b. ʿAmr] b. al-Akwaʿ رضي الله عنه said: "'ʿAlī stayed behind because of ophthalmia when the Messenger of Allah ﷺ was in Khaybar. He said: 'How can I stay behind and not go with the Messenger of Allah ﷺ?' So he went out and caught up with him. On the eve of the victory granted by Allah the Messenger of Allah ﷺ said: 'I swear that [76] tomorrow I shall give the flag to a man whom both Allah and His Messenger love, through whom Allah woll grant victory.' Then, lo and behold! There was ʿAlī among us unexpectedly. They said, 'Here is ʿAlī!' so he gave him the flag and Allah granted victory through him."[129]

[128] Narrated with a very weak chain from Jābir b. Samura by al-Ṭabarānī in *al-Kabīr* (2:247 §2038) and *al-Awsat* (7:218 §7318) cf. al-Haythamī (9:136) but the prediction of the sword-blow is true cf. n. 121.

[129] Narrated from Salama b. al-Akwaʿ by al-Bukhārī, Muslim, and Aḥmad. The incident is also related from Sahl b. Saʿd, Burayda, Abū Hurayra, and others.

عَنْ سَلَمَةَ بْنِ الأَكْوَعِ رَضِيَ اللهُ عَنْهُ قَالَ كَانَ عَلِيٌّ رَضِيَ اللهُ عَنْهُ تَخَلَّفَ عَنْ النَّبِيِّ ﷺ فِي خَيْبَرَ وَكَانَ بِهِ رَمَدٌ فَقَالَ أَنَا أَتَخَلَّفُ عَنْ رَسُولِ اللهِ ﷺ فَخَرَجَ عَلِيٌّ فَلَحِقَ بِالنَّبِيِّ ﷺ فَلَمَّا كَانَ مَسَاءُ اللَّيْلَةِ الَّتِي فَتَحَهَا فِي صَبَاحِهَا فَقَالَ رَسُولُ اللهِ ﷺ لَأُعْطِيَنَّ الرَّايَةَ أَوْ قَالَ لَيَأْخُذَنَّ غَدًا رَجُلٌ يُحِبُّهُ اللهُ وَرَسُولُهُ أَوْ قَالَ يُحِبُّ اللهَ وَرَسُولَهُ يَفْتَحُ اللهُ عَلَيْهِ فَإِذَا نَحْنُ بِعَلِيٍّ وَمَا نَرْجُوهُ فَقَالُوا هَذَا عَلِيٌّ فَأَعْطَاهُ رَسُولُ اللهِ ﷺ فَفَتَحَ اللهُ عَلَيْهِ ق

Muslim also narrated it with a different wording from Salama b. al-Akwaʿ adding to the above: "Then [a] he spat into his eyes and he was cured. <He gave him the flag. Marḥab [a fighter from Khaybar] came out and declaimed: *'Khaybar knows my name is Marḥab, / In full armor a tried champion. / When wars come to me they blaze!'* ʿAlī said: [b] *'I am the one whose mother called the Lion / Like the beast of the jungles, awesome to see! I pay my enemies in full – an ample measure!'* He struck Marḥab's head and slew him. Victory followed at his hands.">[130]

عَنْ سَلَمَةَ رَضِيَ اللهُ عَنْهُ أَرْسَلَنِي رَسُولُ اللهِ ﷺ إِلَى عَلِيٍّ وَهُوَ أَرْمَدُ فَقَالَ لَأُعْطِيَنَّ الرَّايَةَ رَجُلًا يُحِبُّ اللهَ وَرَسُولَهُ أَوْ يُحِبُّهُ اللهُ وَرَسُولُهُ قَالَ فَأَتَيْتُ عَلِيًّا فَجِئْتُ بِهِ أَقُودُهُ وَهُوَ أَرْمَدُ حَتَّى أَتَيْتُ بِهِ رَسُولَ اللهِ ﷺ فَبَسَقَ فِي عَيْنَيْهِ فَبَرَأَ وَأَعْطَاهُ الرَّايَةَ وَخَرَجَ مَرْحَبٌ فَقَالَ

[130] Narrated from Salama b. al-Akwaʿ by Muslim. Nabhānī omitted the bracketed segment.

قَدْ عَلِمَتْ خَيْبَرُ أَنِّي مَرْحَبُ شَاكِي السِّلَاحِ بَطَلٌ مُجَرَّبُ
إِذَا الْحُرُوبُ أَقْبَلَتْ تَلَهَّبُ

فَقَالَ عَلِيٌّ

أَنَا الَّذِي سَمَّتْنِي أُمِّي حَيْدَرَهْ كَلَيْثِ غَابَاتٍ كَرِيهِ الْمَنْظَرَهْ
أُوفِيهِمُ بِالصَّاعِ كَيْلَ السَّنْدَرَهْ

قَالَ فَضَرَبَ رَأْسَ مَرْحَبٍ فَقَتَلَهُ ثُمَّ كَانَ الْفَتْحُ عَلَى يَدَيْهِ م

Al-Ḥārith and Abū Nuʿaym narrated it with yet another wording from Salama adding: "Then ʿAlī took it [the flag] and planted it right under their fort, whereupon one of the Jews looked down at him from the top of the fort and said: 'Who are you?' He replied: 'ʿAlī' The Jew said: 'You shall overcome, by the [Book] revealed to Mūsā!' ʿAlī did not return before Allah granted victory at his hands."[131] Abū Nuʿaym said: "There is in it a sign of the advanced knowledge of the Jews, thanks to their books, as to who is sent to fight against them and shall be granted victory." The account was also narrated from Ibn ʿUmar, Ibn ʿAbbās, Saʿd b. Abī Waqqāṣ, Abū Hurayra, Abū Saʿīd al-Khudrī, 'Imrān b. Ḥuṣayn, Jābir, and Abū Laylā al-Anṣārī. Abū Nuʿaym narrated all of them, and they all contain the account of the spitting into the eyes and their healing.

عَنْ سَلَمَةَ ﷺ فَخَرَجَ عَلِيٌّ وَاللهِ بِهَا يَأْنِحُ يُهَرْوِلُ هَرْوَلَةً وَإِنَّا خَلْفَهُ نَتْبَعُ أَثَرَهُ حَتَّى رَكَزَ رَايَتَهُ فِي رَضْمٍ مِنْ حِجَارَةٍ تَحْتَ الْحِصْنِ فَاطَّلَعَ إِلَيْهِ يَهُودِيٌّ مِنْ رَأْسِ الْحِصْنِ فَقَالَ مَنْ أَنْتَ ؟

[131]Narrated from Salama by Ibn Hishām in the *Sīra* (4:305-306), al-Ṭabarānī in *al-Kabīr* (7:35 §6303), and Ibn Ḥibbān in *al-Thiqāt* (2:13) cf. *Rawḍ* (4:76), *Zād* (3:285).

قَالَ أَنَا عَلِيّ بْنُ أَبِي طَالِبٍ قَالَ يَقُولُ الْيَهُودِيّ عَلَوْتُمْ وَمَا أُنْزِلَ
عَلَى مُوسَى أَوْ كَمَا قَالَ قَالَ فَمَا رَجَعَ حَتّى فَتَحَ اللهُ عَلَى يَدَيْهِ

سيرة ابن هشام طب

Al-Bayhaqī and Abū Nuʿaym narrated from Burayda رضي الله عنه that the Messenger of Allah ﷺ said: [77] "Tomorrow I will give the flag to a man <whom Allah and His Messenger love and> who loves Allah and His Messenger, and who will take it by force" at a time ʿAlī was not there yet. The Quraysh competed for it then ʿAlī arrived on his camel, eyes inflamed with ophthalmia. The Prophet ﷺ said: [a] "Come near" then he spat into his eyes – they were never sore again until he died – and gave him the flag.[132]

عَنْ بُرَيْدَةَ رضي الله عنه قَالَ حَاصَرْنا خَيْبَرَ فَأَخَذَ اللِّوَاءَ أَبُو بَكْرٍ فَانْصَرَفَ
وَلَمْ يُفْتَحْ لَهُ وَأَخَذَهُ مِنَ الغَدِ عُمَرُ وَلَمْ يُفْتَحْ لَهُ فَقَالَ رَسُولُ اللهِ
ﷺ إِنِي دَافِعٌ لِوَائِي غَداً إِلَى رَجُلٍ يُحِبُّهُ اللهُ وَرَسُولُهُ وَيُحِبُّ اللهَ
وَرَسُولَهُ لا يَرْجِعُ حَتىَّ يُفْتَحَ لَهُ وَبِتْنَا طَيِّبَةٌ أَنْفُسُنَا أَنَّ الفَتْحَ
غَداً فَلَمَّا أَصْبَحَ رَسُولُ اللهِ ﷺ صَلَّى الغَدَاةَ ثُمَّ قَامَ قَائِماً وَدَعَا
بِاللِّوَاءِ وَالنَّاسُ عَلَى مَصَافِّهِمْ فَمَا مِنَّا إِنْسَانٌ لَهُ مَنْزِلَةٌ ثُمَّ رَسُولِ
اللهِ ﷺ إِلا وَهُوَ يَرْجُو أَنْ يَكُونَ صَاحِبَ اللِّوَاءِ فَدَعَا عَلِيَّ بْنَ
أَبِي طَالِبٍ وَهُوَ أَرْمَدُ فَتَفَلَ فِي عَيْنَيْهِ وَمَسَحَ عَنْهُ وَدَفَعَ إِلَيْهِ
اللِّوَاءَ فَفَتَحَ اللهُ لَهُ ن في الكبرى بسند رجاله ثقات

[132]Narrated from Burayda by al-Nasāʾī in *al-Sunan al-Kubrā* (5:179 §8601), al-Ṭabarī in his *Tārīkh* (2:137).

Aḥmad, Abū Yaʿlā, al-Bayhaqī, and Abū Nuʿaym narrated that ʿAlī ؓ said: 78 "My eyes were never sore nor inflamed again after the Messenger of Allah spat into my eyes on the day of Khaybar."[133]

عَنْ عَلِيٍّ رَضِيَ اللهُ عَنْهُ قَالَ مَا رَمِدْتُ مُنْذُ تَفَلَ النَّبِيُّ ﷺ فِي عَيْنِي حم ع ط ض

[Another version states that Abū Laylā asked ʿAlī why he wore summer clothes in winter and winter clothes in summer to which he replied: "The day of Khaybar the Prophet ﷺ summoned me when my eyes were sore. I said to him: 'Messenger of Allah! I have ophthalmia.' He blew on my eyes and said: 79 'O Allah! remove from him hot and cold.' I never felt hot nor cold after that day."][134]

Ibn Isḥāq narrated that ʿAmmār b. Yāsir رضي الله عنهما said: "I and ʿAlī b. Abī Ṭālib teamed up in the expedition of al-ʿUshayra. When the Messenger of Allah ﷺ alighted there, we saw people from the Banū Mudlij working near one of their springs and in a date orchard. ʿAlī b. Abī Ṭālib said, 'Abū al-Yaqẓān, what if we went to see those people and look at them working?' I said, 'If you like.' So we went to them and looked at them work for a while. Then we became sleepy so I and ʿAlī went away until we found a low-lying sand-dune where we lay down. **[476]** There we slept. By Allah! Nothing woke us except the Messenger of Allah ﷺ himself, moving us with his foot, and we were all covered in sand from the spot where we had slept. That day, the Messenger of Allah ﷺ said to ʿAlī b. Abī Ṭālib: 80 'Abū Turāb! (Sand-Man)' – for he saw him covered in sand – then he said: 'Shall I not tell you of the two wickedest people ever?' We said, 'Do, Messenger of Allah!' He replied: 'The whitish man of Thamūd who hamstrung the she-camel and the man who shall strike you on this, ʿAlī' – he placed his hand on ʿAlī's temple – 'until this gets soaked from it' – he touched ʿAlī's beard."[135] Later, what the Prophet ﷺ had said took place and Allah

[133]Narrated by Aḥmad, Abū Yaʿlā (1:445 §593), and al-Ṭayālisī (p. 26 §189) with strong narrators cf. al-Haythamī (9:122), *Mukhtāra* (2:422-423 §810-811).

[134]Narrated from ʿAbd Allāh b. Abī Laylā by Aḥmad and Ibn Mājah with weak chains.

[135]This is the same as the hadīth in note 121.

Most High ordained the killing of ʿAlī رضي الله عنه in the exact way mentioned by the Messenger of Allah ﷺ at the hand of the most wretched of latter-day men, ʿAbd al-Raḥmān b. Muljam al-Murādī.

عَنْ عَمَّارِ بْنِ يَاسِرٍ رَضِيَ اللهُ عَنْهُ قَالَ كُنْتُ أَنَا وَعَلِيٌّ رَفِيقَيْنِ فِي غَزْوَةِ ذَاتِ الْعُشَيْرَةِ فَلَمَّا نَزَلَهَا رَسُولُ اللهِ ﷺ وَأَقَامَ بِهَا رَأَيْنَا أُنَاسًا مِنْ بَنِي مُدْلِجٍ يَعْمَلُونَ فِي عَيْنٍ لَهُمْ فِي نَخْلٍ فَقَالَ لِي عَلِيٌّ يَا أَبَا الْيَقْظَانِ هَلْ لَكَ أَنْ تَأْتِيَ هَؤُلَاءِ فَنَنْظُرَ كَيْفَ يَعْمَلُونَ فَجِئْنَاهُمْ فَنَظَرْنَا إِلَى عَمَلِهِمْ سَاعَةً ثُمَّ غَشِيَنَا النَّوْمُ فَانْطَلَقْتُ أَنَا وَعَلِيٌّ فَاضْطَجَعْنَا فِي صَوْرٍ مِنَ النَّخْلِ فِي دَقْعَاءَ مِنَ التُّرَابِ فَنِمْنَا فَوَاللهِ مَا أَهَبَّنَا إِلاَّ رَسُولُ اللهِ ﷺ يُحَرِّكُنَا بِرِجْلِهِ وَقَدْ تَتَرَّبْنَا مِنْ تِلْكَ الدَّقْعَاءِ فَيَوْمَئِذٍ قَالَ رَسُولُ اللهِ ﷺ لِعَلِيٍّ يَا أَبَا تُرَابٍ لِمَا يُرَى عَلَيْهِ مِنَ التُّرَابِ قَالَ أَلاَ أُحَدِّثُكُمَا بِأَشْقَى النَّاسِ رَجُلَيْنِ قُلْنَا بَلَى يَا رَسُولَ اللهِ قَالَ أُحَيْمِرُ ثَمُودَ الَّذِي عَقَرَ النَّاقَةَ وَالَّذِي يَضْرِبُكَ يَا عَلِيُّ عَلَى هَذِهِ يَعْنِي قَرْنَهُ حَتَّى تُبَلَّ مِنْهُ هَذِهِ يَعْنِي لِحْيَتَهُ سبق تخريجه في الباب نفسه

Al-Bayhaqī narrated that ʿAlī رضي الله عنه said: "The Prophet ﷺ said: 81 'A boy will be born to you after me whom I am giving my name and cognomen *(kunya)*'" – meaning Muḥammad b. al-Ḥanafiyya.[136]

[136]*I.e.* Muḥammad b. ʿAlī b. Abī Ṭālib. Narrated by ʿAbd Allāh b. Aḥmad in *Faḍā'il al-Ṣaḥāba* (2:676 §1155), Ibn ʿAsākir (38:308, 54:327, 54:330) with several chains, al-Khaṭīb (11:218), al-Ḥākim in *Maʿrifat ʿUlūm al-Ḥadīth* (*Kunā*) and al-Bayhaqī in the *Dalā'il* cf. Ibn al-Jawzī, *ʿIlal* (1:247) and *mursal* from al-Mundhir b. Yaʿlā al-Thawrī by Ibn Saʿd (5:91-92) cf. *Kanz* (§3429-34332, §37854, §37858). Also narrated by al-Tirmidhī *(ḥasan*

عَنْ عَلِيٍّ رَضِيَ اللهُ عَنْهُ قَالَ قَالَ لِي النَّبِيُّ ﷺ يُولَدُ لَكَ إِبْنٌ قَدْ نَحَلْتُهُ إِسْمِي وَكُنْيَتِي عبدالله بن أحمد في فضائل الصحابة خط كر ابن سعد ك في باب معرفة الكنى من علوم الحديث هق في الدلائل ابن الجوزي في العلل كنز وقواه الذهبي في السير لكن مرسلاً وقد ثبت الاسترخاص مسنداً عَنْ عَلِيِّ بْنِ أَبِي طَالِبٍ أَنَّهُ قَالَ يَا رَسُولَ اللهِ أَرَأَيْتَ إِنْ وُلِدَ لِي بَعْدَكَ أُسَمِّيهِ مُحَمَّدًا وَأُكَنِّيهِ بِكُنْيَتِكَ قَالَ نَعَمْ قَالَ فَكَانَتْ رُخْصَةً لِي ت قال حَسَنٌ صَحِيحٌ د حم وَعَنْ عَلِيٍّ رَضِيَ اللهُ عَنْهُ قَالَ قَالَ رَسُولُ اللهِ ﷺ إِنْ وُلِدَ لَكَ وَلَدٌ فَانْحَلْهُ إِسْمِي وَكُنْيَتِي ز

Fāṭima رضي الله عنها

It was mentioned in the *Sīra*, as narrated that Ibn ʿAbbās رضي الله عنهما said: "When the Sūra ﴾**When comes the Help of Allah, and Victory**﴿ (110) was revealed, the Messenger of Allah ﷺ summoned Fāṭima and said, 82 'My funeral has just been announced,' whereupon she wept. Then he said to her, a 'Do not weep for you shall be the first to follow me,' whereupon she laughed. Some of the wives of the Prophet ﷺ saw her and asked her, 'Fāṭima, we saw you cry then laugh?' She replied, 'He told me that his funeral had just been announced, so I cried. Then he said to me, Do not weep for you shall be the first to follow me, so I laughed.'"[137] Fāṭima رضي الله عنها lived

sahīh), Abū Dāwūd, Aḥmad and Ibn Saʿd (same page) with a chain of trustworthy narrators per al-Bukhārī's criterion but a different wording in which ʿAlī asks permission to use the name if a boy is born.

[137]Narrated with good chains from Ibn ʿAbbās and ʿĀ'isha by al-Dārimī, Ibn Saʿd (2:193), al-Ṭabarānī in *al-Kabīr* (22:415, 22:420) and *al-Awsat* (1:271 §883) cf. *Siyar* (Risāla ed. 2:131-132), al-Haythamī (9:23); and, in part, al-Bukhārī and Aḥmad. The explanation of the verse is narrated from Ibn ʿAbbās by al-Bukhārī and from Ibn ʿUmar by al-Bazzār and al-Bayhaqī cf. Ibn Kathīr, *Tafsīr* (4:562).

on for six months after the Prophet ﷺ according to the most authentic reports.

عَنْ ابْنِ عَبَّاسٍ رَضِيَ اللهُ عَنْهُمَا قَالَ لَمَّا نَزَلَتْ إِذَا جَاءَ نَصْرُ اللهِ وَالْفَتْحُ دَعَا رَسُولُ اللهِ ﷺ فَاطِمَةَ فَقَالَ قَدْ نُعِيَتْ إِلَيَّ نَفْسِي فَبَكَتْ فَقَالَ لاَ تَبْكِي فَإِنَّكِ أَوَّلُ أَهْلِي لِحَاقًا بِي فَضَحِكَتْ فَرَآهَا بَعْضُ أَزْوَاجِ النَّبِيِّ ﷺ فَقُلْنَ يَا فَاطِمَةُ رَأَيْنَاكِ بَكَيْتِ ثُمَّ ضَحِكْتِ قَالَتْ إِنَّهُ أَخْبَرَنِي أَنَّهُ قَدْ نُعِيَتْ إِلَيْهِ نَفْسُهُ فَبَكَيْتُ فَقَالَ لِي لاَ تَبْكِي فَإِنَّكِ أَوَّلُ أَهْلِي لاَحِقٌ بِي فَضَحِكْتُ مي ابن سعد طب طس بإسنادين أحدهما عن عائشة رضي الله عنها

وعَنْ عَبْدِ اللهِ بْنِ مَسْعُودٍ رَضِيَ اللهُ عَنْهُ قَالَ كُنْتُ مَعَ النَّبِيِّ ﷺ لَيْلَةَ وَفْدِ الْجِنِّ فَلَمَّا انْصَرَفَ تَنَفَّسَ فَقُلْتُ مَا شَأْنُكَ فَقَالَ نُعِيَتْ إِلَيَّ نَفْسِي يَا ابْنَ مَسْعُودٍ حم إسناده ضعيف جداً وفي الباب تفسير ابن عبّاس في الصحيح وابن عمر للآية

Al-Ḥasan b. ʿAlī رضي الله عنهما

Al-Bukhārī narrated that Abū Bakrah ؓ said: "The Messenger of Allah ﷺ said of al-Ḥasan: 83 'This son of mine is a leader of men *(sayyid)* and Allah may use him to reconcile two great factions of the Muslims.'"[138]

[138]Part of the famous narration of al-Hasan jumping on the Prophet's ﷺ back when the latter prostrated. Narrated from Abū Bakrah by Bukhārī with four chains, Tirmidhī *(hasan sahīh)*, al-Nasā'ī, Abū Dāwūd, and Ahmad with four chains, one of them (34:98-99 §20448 *hadīth sahīh*) with the wording "Allāh *will* use him" and others with al-Hasan al-Basrī's addendum: "By Allah, by Allah! Under his rule not a thimbleful of blood was shed."

عَنْ أَبِي بَكْرَةَ رَضِيَ اللهُ عَنْهُ قَالَ رَأَيْتُ رَسُولَ اللهِ ﷺ عَلَى الْمِنْبَرِ وَالْحَسَنُ بْنُ عَلِيٍّ إِلَى جَنْبِهِ وَهُوَ يُقْبِلُ عَلَى النَّاسِ مَرَّةً وَعَلَيْهِ أُخْرَى وَيَقُولُ إِنَّ ابْنِي هَذَا سَيِّدٌ وَلَعَلَّ اللهَ أَنْ يُصْلِحَ بِهِ بَيْنَ فِئَتَيْنِ عَظِيمَتَيْنِ مِنَ الْمُسْلِمِينَ خ ت ن د حم

This took place exactly as foretold. When ʿAlī ؓ was killed, people pledged their loyalty to al-Ḥasan ؓ to the death. Their number was more than forty thousand and they were more obedient to him than they had been to his father ﴿رضي الله عنه﴾. He remained caliph for about seven months in Iraq, Khurasān, and Transoxiana, after which Muʿāwiya marched against him. When the two armies met near al-Anbār, al-Ḥasan realized that eventual fighting would wipe out a great number of the Muslims and so did Muʿāwiya. A group of people sued for peace among the two and they reached an agreement. Thus did Allah stem the blood of the Muslims and thus did Allah bring to pass the saying of His Prophet ﷺ: "This son of mine is a leader of men and Allah shall use him to reconcile etc.," another wording stating [as above]: "and Allah may use him to reconcile two great factions of the Muslims."

[When the Rāfidī Abū ʿĀmir Sufyān b. al-Layl al-Kūfī and others jeered al-Ḥasan, calling him "blackener of the Believers' faces," "shame of the Believers" and "abaser of the Believers" for making peace he replied: 84 "Better shame than the Fire" and 85 "I did not abase them but hated to shed their blood in the pursuit of kingship."][139]

Al-Ḥusayn b. ʿAlī ﴿رضي الله عنهما﴾

Al-Ḥākim and al-Bayhaqī narrated that Umm al-Faḍl bint al-Ḥārith ﴿رضي الله عنها﴾ said: "I went in to see the Prophet ﷺ one day, carrying al-Ḥusayn, whom I placed in his lap. Then when I turned to look at him again, lo! I saw the eyes of the Messenger of Allah ﷺ

---

[139]Narrated from Abū al-Gharīf ʿUbayd Allāh b. Khalīfa by Ibn Abī Shayba (7:476 §37357), al-Ḥākim (1990 ed. 3:192), al-Khaṭīb (10:305), Ibn ʿAbd al-Barr in *al-Istīʿāb* (1:386-387), and al-Dhahabī in the *Siyar* (Risāla ed. 3:272 and 3:145) cf. *Fatḥ* (13:65) and *Sīra Ḥalabiyya* (3:359).

brimming with tears. He said: 86 'Jibrīl just came and told me that my Community would kill this son of mine, and he brought me a handful of his resting-ground – red earth.'"[140]

عَنْ أُمِّ الفَضْلِ بِنْتِ الحَارِثِ رَضِيَ اللهُ عَنْهَا دَخَلْتُ يَوْماً إِلى رَسُولِ اللهِ ﷺ فَإِذَا عَيْنَاهُ تُهَرِيقَانِ مِنَ الدُّمُوعِ قَالَتْ فَقُلْتُ يَا نَبِيَّ اللهِ بِأَبِي أَنْتَ وَأُمِّي مَالَكَ قَالَ أَتَانِي جِبْرِيلُ عَلَيْهِ السَّلامُ فَأَخْبَرَنِي أَنَّ أُمَّتِي سَتَقْتُلُ إِبْنِي هَذَا فَقُلْتُ هَذَا فَقَالَ نَعَمْ وَأَتَانِي بِتُرْبَةٍ مِنْ تُرْبَتِهِ حَمْرَاءَ ك قال صحيح على شرط الشيخين قال الذهبي بل منقطع ضعيف وله شاهد عن أم سلمة حسّنه في السير

Ibn Rāhūyah, al-Bayhaqī, and Abū Nuʿaym narrated from Umm Salama رضي الله عنها that the Messenger of Allah ﷺ **[477]** lay down one day and woke up sluggish, holding a handful of red earth in his hand and turning it this way and that. I said: "What is this earth, Messenger of Allah?" He replied: 87 "Jibrīl informed me that this one – meaning al-Ḥusayn – would be killed in the land of Iraq, and this is his resting-ground."[141]

عَنْ أُمِّ سَلَمَةَ رضي الله عنها أنَّ رسولَ الله ﷺ اِضْطَجَعَ ذَاتَ لَيْلَةٍ لِلنَّوْمِ فَاسْتَيْقَظَ وَهُوَ حَائِرٌ ثُمَّ اضْطَجَعَ فَرَقَدَ ثُمَّ اسْتَيْقَظَ

[140]Narrated from Umm al-Fadl by al-Hākim (3:176-177=1990 ed. 3:194) who said it is sound by the criteria of al-Bukhārī and Muslim but al-Dhahabī said: "No, it is *daʿīf munqatiʿ*, Shaddād did not meet Umm al-Fadl and Muhammad b. Musʿab [al-Qirqisānī] is weak." However, he cites the next report from Umm Salama in the *Siyar* (Risāla ed. 3:289) and said its chain was fair. Umm Salama is its correct narrator.

[141]Narrated from Umm Salama by Ibn Abī ʿĀṣim in *al-Āḥād wal-Mathānī* (1:310 §429), al-Ṭabarānī in *al-Kabīr* (3:109, 23:308), and al-Hākim (1990 ed. 4:440) with a fair chain cf. *Siyar* (Risāla ed. 3:289); and from ʿĀ'isha by al-Ṭabarānī in *al-Kabīr* (3:107 §2815). Also narrated from "ʿĀ'isha or Umm Salama" by Ahmad in the *Musnad* and *Fadā'il al-Sahāba* but with a very weak chain.

وَهُوَ حَائِرٌ دُونَ مَا رَأَيْتُ بِهِ الْمَرَّةَ الأُولَى ثُمَّ اضْطَجَعَ فَاسْتَيْقَظَ وَفِي يَدِهِ تُرْبَةٌ حَمْرَاءُ يُقَلِّبُهَا فَقُلْتُ مَا هَذِهِ التُّرْبَةُ يَا رَسُولَ اللهِ قَالَ أَخْبَرَنِي جِبْرِيلُ عَلَيْهِ السَّلامُ أَنَّ هَذَا يُقْتَلُ بِأَرْضِ الْعِرَاقِ لِلْحُسَيْنِ فَقُلْتُ لِجِبْرِيلَ أَرِنِي تُرْبَةَ الأَرْضِ الَّتِي يُقْتَلُ بِهَا فَهَذِهِ تُرْبَتُهَا كر ق في الدلائل ولفظ ك يُقَبِّلُهَا وحسّن إسناده الذهبي في النبلاء

Abū Nu'aym narrated that Umm Salama رضي الله عنها said: "Al-Ḥasan and al-Ḥusayn were playing in my house when Jibrīl descended and said, 'Muḥammad! Your Community will kill this son of yours,' signaling to al-Ḥusayn and bringing him [some of] his resting-ground; he smelled it and said, [88] 'It smells of hardship *(karb)* and affliction *(balā')*.' Then he said, [a] 'When this soil turns to blood, know that my son has been killed.'" So she kept it in a jar and she would look at it every day and say: "Truly [b] the day that you turn to blood will be a terrible day!"[142]

عَنْ أُمِّ سَلَمَةَ قَالَتْ كَانَ الْحَسَنُ وَالْحُسَيْنُ رَضِيَ اللهُ تَعَالَى عَنْهُمَا يَلْعَبَانِ بَيْنَ يَدَيِ النَّبِيِّ ﷺ فِي بَيْتِي فَنَزَلَ جِبْرِيلُ عَلَيْهِ السَّلَامُ فَقَالَ يَا مُحَمَّدُ إِنَّ أُمَّتَكَ تَقْتُلُ ابْنَكَ هَذَا مِنْ بَعْدِكَ فَأَوْمَأَ بِيَدِهِ إِلَى الْحُسَيْنِ فَبَكَى رَسُولُ اللهِ ﷺ وَضَمَّهُ إِلَى صَدْرِهِ ثُمَّ قَالَ رَسُولُ اللهِ ﷺ وَدِيعَةٌ عِنْدَكِ هَذِهِ التُّرْبَةُ فَشَمَّهَا رَسُولُ

[142]Narrated by Ṭabarānī in *al-Kabīr* (3:108 §2817), Abū Nu'aym, Ibn 'Asākir, al-Mizzī in *Tahdhīb al-Kamāl* (6:409), and Ibn Ḥajar in *Tahdhīb al-Tahdhīb* (2:300-301) through the *Rāfiḍī* 'Amr b. Thābit b. Hurmuz al-Bakrī who is weak or discarded cf. al-Haythamī (9:189), but Abū al-Shaykh also narrates it in *al-Fitan* with a different chain according to Ibn Nāṣir al-Dīn, *al-Lafẓ al-Mukarram bi-Faḍli 'Āshūrā' al-Muḥarram* in his *Rasā'il* (p. 89).

اللهِ ﷺ وَقَالَ وَيْحٌ كَرْبٌ وَبَلاَءٌ قَالَتْ وَقَالَ رَسُولُ اللهِ ﷺ يَا أُمَّ سَلَمَةَ إِذَا تَحَوَّلَتْ هَذِهِ التُّرْبَةُ دَماً فَاعْلَمِي أَنَّ ابْنِيَ قَدْ قُتِلَ قَالَ فَجَعَلَتْهَا أُمُّ سَلَمَةَ فِي قَارُورَةٍ ثُمَّ جَعَلَتْ تَنْظُرُ إِلَيْهَا كُلَّ يَوْمٍ وَتَقُولُ إِنَّ يَوْماً تَحَوَّلِينَ دَماً لَيَوْمٌ عَظِيمٌ طب كر أبو نعيم في الدلائل

رجاله كلهم ثقات غير عمرو بن ثابت وهو رافضي متروك قال ابن حبان كان يروي الموضوعات لكن رواه أبو الشيخ من وجه آخر

Ibn ʿAsākir narrated that Muḥammad b. ʿAmr[143] b. Ḥasan said: "We were with al-Ḥusayn ﷺ at the river of Karbalā' when he looked at Shimr b. Dhī al-Jawshan and said, 'Allah and His Messenger were right! The Messenger of Allah ﷺ said: 89 "I can see a spotted dog drooling over the blood of the people of my House."' Shimr was a leper."[144]

عَنْ مُحَمَّدِ بْنِ عَمْرِو بْنِ حَسَنٍ قَالَ كُنَّا مَعَ الْحُسَيْنِ بِنَهْرِ كَرْبَلاَءَ فَنَظَرَ إِلَى شِمْرِ بْنِ ذِي الْجَوْشَنِ فَقَالَ صَدَقَ اللهُ وَرَسُولُهُ قَالَ رَسُولُ اللهِ ﷺ كَأَنِّي أَنْظُرُ إِلَى كَلْبٍ أَبْقَعَ يَلِغُ فِي دِمَاءِ أَهْلِ بَيْتِي وَكَانَ شِمْرٌ أَبْرَصَ كر

Ibn al-Sakan, al-Baghawī, and Abū Nuʿaym narrated that Anas b. al-Ḥārith ﷺ said, "I heard the Messenger of Allah ﷺ say: 'Truly 90 this son of mine' – meaning al-Ḥusayn – shall be killed in a land

[143] ʿUmar in al-Nabhānī's text, corrected from *Tārīkh Dimashq* and *Kanz al-ʿUmmāl*.

[144] Narrated by Ibn ʿAsākir, *Tārīkh* (23:190, 55:16) cf. *Kanz* (§37717). Karbalā' is 24 miles northwest of Kūfa.

called Karbalā'. Whoever among you is present then, help him!' Hence, Anas b. al-Ḥārith went to Karbalā' and was killed there with al-Ḥusayn."[145]

عَنْ أَنَسِ بْنِ الْحَارِثِ رَضِيَ اللهُ عَنْهُ قال سَمِعْتُ رَسُولَ اللهِ ﷺ
يَقُولُ إِنَّ ابْنِي هَذَا يُقْتَلُ بِأَرْضٍ يُقَالُ لَهَا كَرْبَلاءُ فَمَنْ شَهِدَ
ذَلِكَ فَلْيَنْصُرْهُ قَالَ فَخَرَجَ أَنَسُ بْنُ الْحَارِثِ إِلَى كَرْبَلاءَ فَقُتِلَ مَعَ
الْحُسَيْنِ رَضِيَ اللهُ تَعَالَى عَنْهُمْ أَجْمَعِينَ كر ورواه أبو الفتح الأزدي في
المخزون في أفراد الصحابة ابن السكن والبغوي وأبو نعيم في الصحابة والدلائل

Al-Ṭabarānī narrated from ʿĀ'isha رضي الله عنها that the Prophet ﷺ said: 91 "Jibrīl told me that my son, al-Ḥusayn, would be killed after me in the land of al-Ṭaff [between Syria and Iraq], and he brought me this earth and told me that in it would be his resting-place."[146]

عَنْ عَائِشَةَ رَضِيَ اللهُ عَنْهَا مرفوعاً أَخْبَرَنِي جِبْرِيلُ أَنَّ ابْنِي
الْحُسَيْنَ يُقْتَلُ بَعْدِي بِأَرْضِ الطَّفِّ وجاءَنِي بِهَذِهِ التُّرْبَةِ وأَخْبَرَنِي
أَنَّ فِيهَا مَضْجَعَهُ ابن سعد طب طس

[145]Narrated from Suhaym, from Anas b. Mālik by Abū Nuʿaym in the *Dalā'il* (p. 554 §493) and *Maʿrifat al-Ṣaḥāba* (1:243 §97), al-Baghawī in *Muʿjam al-Ṣaḥāba* (1:63-64 §46), and Ibn al-Sakan in his Companion-compendium. Cf. Ibn Ḥajar, *Iṣāba* (1:121); al-Bukhārī, *al-Tārīkh al-Kabīr* (2:30 §1583); *al-Istīʿāb* (1:112); *al-Khaṣā'iṣ al-Kubrā* (2:451).

[146]Narrated from ʿĀ'isha by al-Ṭabarānī in *al-Kabīr* (3:107 §2814) and *al-Awsaṭ* (6:249 §6316) with weak chains per al-Haythamī (8:288, 9:188), cf. al-Suyūṭī, *Ziyādat al-Jāmiʿ al-Saghīr* (§147) and *Kanz* (§34299). It is overall fair since it and Umm Salama's narration are mutually reinforced.

Ahmad and Ibn Sa'd narrated it from 'Alī ؓ with the wording: 92 "We feel he will be killed on the shore of the Euphrates."[147]

عَنْ عَلِيٍّ رَضِيَ اللهُ عَنْهُ - مَرْفُوعاً - أَخْبَرَنِي جِبْرِيلُ أَنَّ حُسَيْنًا يُقْتَلُ بِشَاطِئِ الْفُرَاتِ حم ع طب ابن سعد كر آحاد ابن أبي عاصم

Al-Baghawī narrated in his *Mu'jam* as reported from Anas b. Mālik ؓ: 93 "The Angel of the region asked permission of his Lord to visit the Prophet ﷺ and he obtained it. He came to visit him during the day he usually spent with Umm Salama. The Prophet ﷺ said: a "Umm Salama, keep the door closed and let no one disturb us." As she reached the door, al-Ḥusayn darted in and ran to the Prophet ﷺ who began to hug him and kiss him. The angel said to him, "Do you love him?" He said yes. The angel continued: "Truly, your Community will kill him and, if you wish, I shall show you the place where he will be killed." He showed it to him and brought him some reddish earth [from it], which Umm Salama took and put in her robe. Thābit al-Bunānī – the narrator from Anas – said: "We considered that it was Karbalā'."[148]

[147]Narrated from 'Alī by Aḥmad (Risāla ed. 2:77-78 §648), Abū Ya'lā (§363), Ibn Abī 'Āṣim in *al-Āḥād wal-Mathānī* (1:308 §427), Ibn Abī Shayba (7:487 §37367), al-Bazzār (3:101 §884), al-Ṭabarānī in *al-Kabīr* (3:105 §2811), Ibn Abī 'Āṣim in *al-Āḥād wal-Mathānī* (§427), Ibn 'Asākir (14:188-189), Ibn Nāṣir al-Dīn, *Rasā'il* (p. 87), al-Mizzī in *Tahdhīb al-Kamāl* (6:407), and Ibn Ḥajar in *Tahdhīb al-Tahdhīb* (2:300), all with a passable to weak chain because of 'Abd Allāh b. Nujay al-Ḥadramī and his father cf. al-Arna'ūṭ in the *Musnad* and al-Munāwī, *Fayd* (1:204-205) as opposed to al-Haythamī (9:187) and al-Maqdisī in *al-Mukhtāra* (2:375 §758) while al-Dhahabī adduces a second weak chain that reinforces the first. This report contains 'Alī's call to his son *in absentia*, "*Sabran* Abā 'Abd Allāh!" Cf. Ibn Taymiyya, *Minhāj* (Qurṭuba ed. 3:367-368), Dhahabī, *Siyar* (Risala ed. 3:288=Fikr ed. 4:407-408).

[148]Narrated from Anas by Aḥmad, Abū Ya'lā (6:129 §3402), al-Bazzār (§2642), al-Ṭabarānī in *al-Kabīr* (3:106 §2813), Ibn Ḥibbān (15:142 §6742 *ḥadīth ḥasan*), Abū Nu'aym in the *Dalā'il* (p. 553 §492) and *Ma'rifat al-Sahāba* (§1782), al-Bayhaqī in the *Dalā'il* (6:469), Ibn 'Asākir (14:189-190), Ibn Nāṣir al-Dīn, *Rasā'il* (p. 88), and al-Mizzī in *Tahdhīb al-Kamāl* (6:408) cf. *Kanz* (§37672), al-Haythamī (9:187-190), al-Dhahabī, *Siyar* (3:288-289=Fikr ed. 4:408), and al-Suyūṭī's *Khasā'is* (2:450).

عَنْ أَنَسِ بْنِ مَالِكٍ قَالَ اسْتَأْذَنَ مَلَكُ الْقَطْرِ رَبَّهُ أَنْ يَزُورَ النَّبِيَّ ﷺ فَأَذِنَ لَهُ وَكَانَ فِي يَوْمِ أُمِّ سَلَمَةَ رَضِيَ اللهُ عَنْهَا فَقَالَ النَّبِيُّ ﷺ يَا أُمَّ سَلَمَةَ احْفَظِي عَلَيْنَا الْبَابَ لا يَدْخُلْ عَلَيْنَا أَحَدٌ قَالَ فَبَيْنَمَا هِيَ عَلَى الْبَابِ إِذْ جَاءَ الْحُسَيْنُ بْنُ عَلِيٍّ فَاقْتَحَمَ فَفَتَحَ الْبَابَ فَدَخَلَ فَجَعَلَ النَّبِيُّ ﷺ يَلْتَزِمُهُ وَيُقَبِّلُهُ فَقَالَ الْمَلَكُ أَتُحِبُّهُ؟ قَالَ نَعَمْ قَالَ إِنَّ أُمَّتَكَ سَتَقْتُلُهُ إِنْ شِئْتَ أَرَيْتُكَ الْمَكَانَ الَّذِي تَقْتُلُهُ فِيهِ قَالَ نَعَمْ قَالَ فَقَبَضَ قَبْضَةً مِنَ الْمَكَانِ الَّذِي قُتِلَ بِهِ فَأَرَاهُ فَجَاءَ سَهْلَةٌ أَوْ تُرَابٌ أَحْمَرُ فَأَخَذَتْهُ أُمُّ سَلَمَةَ فَجَعَلَتْهُ فِي ثَوْبِهَا قَالَ ثَابِتٌ فَكُنَّا نَقُولُ إِنَّهَا كَرْبَلاءُ

حم ع ز طب حب هق في الدلائل أبو نعيم في معرفة الصحابة والدلائل

In the narration of Mullā al-Mawṣilī, Umm Salama says, [94] "The Prophet ﷺ handed me a handful of red earth, saying: [a] 'This is from the ground on which he [al-Ḥusayn] shall be killed. When it turns to blood, know that he has been killed.'" Umm Salama said that she placed it "in a jar I had, and I used to apprehend the terrible day when it would turn to blood."[149] Al-Ḥusayn was martyred as he ﷺ had said, in Karbalā', in Iraq, near al-Kūfa, in a place also known as al-Ṭaff. This ḥadīth contains another stunning miracle of his ﷺ, namely, the disclosure that Umm Salama would live beyond the time when al-Ḥusayn would be killed.

[149]See n. 142.

ʿĀ'isha the Mother of the Believers رضي الله عنها

Al-Ḥākim – he declared it sound – and al-Bayhaqī narrated that Umm Salama رضي الله عنها said: "The Prophet ﷺ mentioned that one of the Mothers of the Believers would go to war, hearing which ʿĀ'isha laughed, whereupon he said: 95 'Wait, **[478]** fair little one *(ḥumayrā')*, lest it be you!' Then he turned to ʿAlī, saying: 'If you have her in your power, treat her gently!'"[150]

عَنْ أُمِّ سَلَمَةَ رَضِيَ اللهُ عَنْهَا قَالَتْ ذَكَرَ النَّبِيُّ ﷺ خُرُوجَ بَعْضِ أُمَّهَاتِ المؤْمِنِينَ وَضَحِكَتْ عَائِشَةُ فَقَالَ لَهَا انْظُرِي يَا حُمَيْرَاءَ أَنْ لاَ تَكُونِي أَنْتِ ثُمَّ الْتَفَتَ إِلَى عَلِيٍّ وَقَالَ يَا عَلِيُّ إِنْ وُلِّيْتَ مِنْ أَمْرِهَا شَيْئاً فَارْفِقْ بِهَا ك صححه وحسنه الحافظ ابن عساكر في الأربعين في مناقب أمهات المؤمنين

[This is one of a few accepted narrations containing the expression *yā ḥumayrā'*, others being: 96 "Fair little one! Do you wish to watch them [i.e. the Abyssinians at play]?";[151] 97 "Kissing neither annuls ablution nor cancels the fast. Fair little one! There is leeway in our Religion," spoken after kissing without renewing ablution;[152] and the report of the long prostration in the night of mid-Shaʿbān, after which the Prophet ﷺ said: 98 "Fair little one, did you think that the Prophet had broken his agreement with you?"[153] And Allah knows best.]

Aḥmad and others narrated from Abū Rāfiʿ رضي الله عنه that the Messenger

[150]Narrated from Umm Salama by al-Ḥākim (3:119=1990 ed. 3:129) with a strong chain cf. al-Suyūṭī *et al.*, *Sharḥ Sunan Ibn Mājah* (1:178). Abū Manṣūr Ibn ʿAsākir declared it fair in his *Arbaʿīn fī Manāqib Ummahāt al-Mu'minīn* (p. 71) and Ibn Kathīr declared it authentic it as narrated from him by al-Zarkashī in the 25th of the *khaṣā'iṣ* of ʿĀ'isha in his masterpiece *al-Ijāba*.

[151]Narrated from ʿĀ'isha by al-Nasā'ī in *al-Sunan al-Kubrā* (5:307 §8951) – a *saḥīḥ* narration as stated by Ibn Ḥajar in *Fatḥ al-Bārī* (2:444).

[152]Narrated from ʿĀ'isha by Ibn Rāhūyah in his *Musnad* (2:172) as per Ibn Ḥajar in *al-Dirāya* (1:45) and al-Zaylaʿī in *Nasb al-Rāya* (1:73). Weak per al-Bayhaqī, *Khilāfiyyāt*.

[153]Narrated from ʿĀ'isha by al-Bayhaqī in *Shuʿab al-Īmān* (3:382 §3835), grading it *mursal jayyid*.

of Allah ﷺ said to ʿAlī رضي الله عنه: 99 "There will be a conflict between you and ʿĀ'isha." He said: "Me, Messenger of Allah?" The Prophet ﷺ said yes. He replied, "Then I am the worst of them, Messenger of Allah!" The Prophet ﷺ said, "No, but when this happens, send her back to her safe haven."[154]

عَنْ أَبِي رَافِعٍ أَنَّ رَسُولَ اللهِ ﷺ قَالَ لِعَلِيٍّ إِنَّهُ سَيَكُونُ بَيْنَكَ وَبَيْنَ عَائِشَةَ أَمْرٌ قَالَ يَا رَسُولَ اللهِ أَنَا مِنْ بَيْنِ أَصْحَابِي قَالَ نَعَمْ قَالَ فَأَنَا أَشْقَاهُمْ قَالَ لاَ وَلَكِنْ إِذَا كَانَ ذَلِكَ فَارْدُدْهَا إِلَى مَأْمَنِهَا حم ز طب رجاله ثقات مج

Al-Bazzār and Abū Nuʿaym narrated that Ibn ʿAbbās رضي الله عنهما said the Messenger of Allah ﷺ said: 100 "One of you [women][155] will come out riding a heavy-maned *(adbab)* red camel, and the dogs of Haw'ab [between Mecca and Baṣra] will bark at her. Many will be killed to her right and her left. She will escape after near death."[156]

عَنِ ابْنِ عَبَّاسٍ رَضِيَ اللهُ عَنْهُمَا أَنَّ رَسُولَ اللهِ ﷺ قَالَ لِنِسَائِهِ أَيَّتُكُنَّ صَاحِبَةُ الْجَمَلِ الأَدْبَبِ تَخْرُجُ حَتَّى تَنْبَحَهَا كِلاَبُ

[154]Narrated from Abū Rāfiʿ by Aḥmad, al-Bazzār (9:326 §3881), al-Ṭabarānī in *al-Kabīr* (1:332 §995), all with a fair (cf. *Fatḥ* 13:55, al-Zayn 18:468 §27076) to weak chain (cf. Ibn al-Jawzī, *al-ʿIlal* 2:848-849 §1419), contrary to al-Haythamī's (7:234) claim that "all its narrators are trustworthy."

[155]Ibn Ḥajar said in *al-Iṣāba* (7:708), entry of "Salmā bint Mālik b. Ḥudhayfa b. Badr al-Fazāriyya, Umm Qarafa al-Sughrā, the paternal cousin of ʿUyayna b. Ḥiṣn": "After she [Umm Qarafa] had been captured and enslaved, ʿĀ'isha freed her, and the Prophet ﷺ visited the latter while Salmā was with her then he said, 'One of you shall be barked at by the dogs of Ḥaw'ab.' They said that there were fifty swords hanging in Umm Qarafa's house, belonging to fifty men that were all her unmarriageable kin."

[156]Narrated from Ibn ʿAbbās by al-Bazzār with a chain of trustworthy narrators, cf. al-Haythamī (7:234).

الْحَوْأَبِ يُقْتَلُ عَنْ يَمِينِهَا وَعَنْ يَسَارِهَا قَتْلَى كَثِيرٌ ثُمَّ تَنْجُو بَعْدَ مَا كَادَتْ ز رجاله ثقات مج فتح

Imām Aḥmad and others narrated that Qays[157] رضي الله عنه said that when ʿĀ'isha رضي الله عنها [while riding to battle] reached certain houses of the Banū ʿĀmir, some dogs began to bark at her. She asked, "What place is this?" They replied, al-Ḥaw'ab. She said, "I think I will turn back!" Al-Zubayr said, "Not before you go forward a little so that the people might see you and Allah reconcile them." She repeated, "I will turn back! I heard the Messenger of Allah ﷺ say, [101] 'What will one of you women do when the dogs of Ḥaw'ab bark at her?'"[158]

عَنْ قَيْسٍ قَالَ لَمَّا أَقْبَلَتْ عَائِشَةُ بَلَغَتْ مِيَاهَ بَنِي عَامِرٍ لَيْلًا نَبَحَتْ الْكِلَابُ قَالَتْ أَيُّ مَاءٍ هَذَا قَالُوا مَاءُ الْحَوْأَبِ قَالَتْ مَا أَظُنُّنِي إِلَّا أَنِّي رَاجِعَةٌ فَقَالَ بَعْضُ مَنْ كَانَ مَعَهَا بَلْ تَقْدَمِينَ فَيَرَاكِ الْمُسْلِمُونَ فَيُصْلِحُ اللهُ عَزَّ وَجَلَّ ذَاتَ بَيْنِهِمْ قَالَتْ إِنَّ رَسُولَ اللهِ ﷺ قَالَ لَنَا ذَاتَ يَوْمٍ كَيْفَ بِإِحْدَاكُنَّ تَنْبَحُ عَلَيْهَا كِلَابُ الْحَوْأَبِ حم ع ز ش حب ك صححه الحافظ والذهبي وابن كثير

[157]The senior *Tābiʿī* Qays b. Abī Ḥāzim al-Bajalī accepted Islam in the lifetime of the Prophet ﷺ.

[158]A sound ḥadīth as per Ibn Ḥajar in *Fatḥ al-Bārī* (13:55) and al-Dhahabī in the *Siyar* (Risala ed. 11:53) narrated from ʿĀ'isha by Ibn Abī Shayba (7:536 §37771=15:259-260), Abū Yaʿlā (8:282 §4868), al-Bazzār (§3275), Aḥmad with two chains of *Ṣaḥīḥ* narrators as per al-Haythamī (7:234), Ibn Rāhūyah in his *Musnad* (3:891 §1569), Ibn Ḥibbān (15:126-127 §6732 *ṣaḥīḥ al-isnād*), al-Ḥākim (3:120=1990 ed. 3:129), al-Bayhaqī in the *Dalā'il* (6:410), and with a sound *mursal* chain by al-Azdī in his *Jāmiʿ* (11:365). Also al-Ṭabarī's *Tārīkh* (3:11, 3:18) and Muḥibb al-Dīn al-Ṭabarī's *al-Samṭ al-Thamīn* (p. 93).

Al-Khaṭīb and Ibn ʿAsākir narrated from ʿĀ'isha رضي الله عنها that the Prophet ﷺ sent her to a woman he was proposing to so that she may take a look at her. [When she came back] she said, "I saw nothing to talk about." He replied: 102 "You saw a mole on her cheek that made every little hair of yours stand on end!" She said, "There is nothing secret to you! Who can hide anything from you?"[159]

عَنْ عَائِشَةَ أَنَّ رَسُولَ اللهِ ﷺ أَرْسَلَهَا إِلَى امْرَأَةٍ فَقَالَتْ مَا رَأَيْتُ طَائِلاً فقال لَقَدْ رَأَيْتِ خَالاً بِخَدِّهَا اقْشَعَرَّتْ مِنْهُ ذَوَائِبُكِ فَقُلْتُ مَا دُونَكَ سِرٌّ وَمَنْ يَسْتَطِيعُ أَنْ يَكْتُمَكَ كر ابن سعد خط أبو نعيم في تاريخ أصبهان

Umm Salama [the Mother of the Believers] رضي الله عنها

Al-Bayhaqī and Abū Nuʿaym narrated that Umm Salama رضي الله عنها said, "A parcel of meat was offered to me so I told the servant to prepare it for the Messenger of Allah ﷺ. A beggar came to the door and said, 'Give charity and may Allah bless you' but we replied, 'May Allah bless you.' The beggar left and then the Prophet ﷺ came. I told the servant to serve him the meat but when she went to fetch it, lo and behold, it had become a stone as hard as flint! The

[159]Narrated from (1) Ibn Abī Mulayka, from ʿĀ'isha by al-Ṭabarānī and Abū Nuʿaym as cited by Ibn Hajar in *al-Iṣāba* (7:726 *s.v.* Sharāf) from Abū Mūsā al-Aṣbahānī's *Dhayl Asmā' al-Sahāba* and (2) ʿAbd al-Raḥmān b. Sābit, from ʿĀ'isha by Ibn Saʿd (8:160) through al-Wāqidī (cf. p. xvii), Abū Nuʿaym in *Tārīkh Asbahān* (2:188), al-Khaṭīb (1:301 §165) from the latter, and Ibn ʿAsākir (51:36) from the latter, all through Jābir b. Yazīd al-Juʿfī who is weak. Cf. Aḥmad, *al-ʿIlal* (2:570 §3695), *Kanz* (§35460), al-Ahdab, *Zawā'id* (1:318-320 §77), and al-Haythamī (9:254). ʿĀ'isha's very last phrase ("Who…") is only in Abū Nuʿaym, al-Khaṭīb, and Ibn ʿAsākir. The Prophet ﷺ would send women to gather information on a potential spouse to "smell her breath and body odor (*aʿṭāf, ʿawāriḍ*) and look at her ankles (*ʿurqūbayhā, ʿarāqībihā*)." Narrated from Anas by Aḥmad, ʿAbd b. Ḥumayd, Ibn Abī Shayba, al-Ṭabarānī in *al-Awsaṭ*, al-Ḥākim, al-Bayhaqī, and Abū Dāwūd in his *Marāsīl*; Ibn al-Mulaqqin said in *al-Badr al-Munīr* (5:507-509) it is a sound hadith.

Prophet ﷺ said: 103 'Today a beggar came to you and you turned him away.' I said yes. He said: 'Tit for tat.'" It remained a stone – used as an anvil – in a corner of her house until she died.[160]

عَنْ أُمِّ سَلَمَةَ رَضِيَ اللهُ عَنْهَا قَالَتْ أُهْدِيَ إِلَيَّ بَضْعَةٌ مِنْ لَحْمٍ
فَقُلْتُ لِلْخَادِمِ ارْفَعِيهَا إِلَى رَسُولِ اللهِ ﷺ وَجَاءَ سَائِلٌ فَقَامَ
عَلَى الْبَابِ فَقَالَ تَصَدَّقُوا بَارَكَ اللهُ فِيكُمْ وَذَهَبَ السَّائِلُ وَجَاءَ
النَّبِيُّ ﷺ فَقُلْتُ لِلْخَادِمِ قَرِّبِي إِلَيْهِ اللَّحْمَ فَجَاءَتْ بِهَا فَإِذَا هِيَ
قَدْ صَارَتْ مَرْوَةَ حَجَرٍ فَقَالَ النَّبِيُّ ﷺ أَتَاكُمُ الْيَوْمَ سَائِلٌ
فَرَدَدْتُمُوهُ قُلْتُ نَعَمْ قَالَ فَإِنَّ ذَاكَ لِذَاكَ فَمَا زَالَتْ حَجَراً فِي
نَاحِيَةِ بَيْتِهَا تَدُقُّ عَلَيْهَا حَتَّى مَاتَتْ أبو نعيم في ذكر أخبار أصبهان

Zaynab the Mother of the Believers رضي الله عنها

Muslim narrated that ʿĀ'isha رضي الله عنها said that the Messenger of Allah ﷺ said: 104 "The fastest of you women in catching up with me [after death] is the one with the 'longest arm.' Therefore, be open-handed [in generosity]." After this, Zaynab [bint Jaḥsh] was the most open-handed because she used to work with her own hands and then perform charity."[161]

[160]Thus cited and referenced in the *Khaṣā'is* (2:178-179). Narrated with the ending, "Do not turn away the beggar without at least [giving him] a sip of water" by the Ḥanbalī Ḥadīth Master of Aṣbahān Abū Saʿīd al-Naqqāsh al-Ḥanbalī (331?-414) in his *Funūn al-ʿAjā'ib* (in *Majmūʿat Ajzā' Ḥadīthiyya* 1:113-114 §54) and Najm al-Dīn al-Nasafī (d. 527) in *al-Qand fī Tārīkh Samarqand* (p. 28 §15) with a very weak chain which is somewhat strengthened by Abū Nuʿaym's narration in *Akhbār Aṣbahān* (1:137) and al-Daylamī in *al-Firdaws* (§7345), with another very weak chain.

[161]Narrated from ʿĀ'isha by Muslim, al-Nasā'ī, al-Bazzār, and Ibn Hibbān (8:108 §3314). Zaynab spun.

عَنْ عَائِشَةَ أُمِّ الْمُؤْمِنِينَ قَالَتْ قَالَ رَسُولُ اللهِ ﷺ أَسْرَعُكُنَّ لِحَاقاً بِي أَطْوَلُكُنَّ يَداً قَالَتْ فَكُنَّ يَتَطَاوَلْنَ أَيَّتُهُنَّ أَطْوَلُ يَداً قَالَتْ فَكَانَتْ أَطْوَلَنَا يَداً زَيْنَبُ لِأَنَّهَا كَانَتْ تَعْمَلُ بِيَدِهَا وَتَصَدَّقُ م ن ز حب هق في الدلائل

Al-Bayhaqī narrated that al-Sha'bī said: "The women said, 'Messenger of Allah, which one of us shall be the fastest in catching up with you?' He said: 105 'The one with the longest arm.' Afterwards the women compared arms to see who had the longest but when Zaynab died they all realized that she had the longest arm in doing good and performing charity."[162]

عَنْ عَامِرٍ الشَّعْبِيِّ قَالَ قُلْنَ النِّسْوَةُ لِرَسُولِ اللهِ ﷺ أَيَّتُنَا أَسْرَعُ لُحُوقاً بِكَ قَالَ أَطْوَلُكُنَّ يَداً فَأَخَذْنَ يَتَذَارَعْنَ أَيَّتُهُنَّ أَطْوَلُ يَداً فَلَمَّا تُوُفِّيَتْ زَيْنَبُ عَلِمْنَ أَنَّهَا كَانَتْ أَطْوَلَهُنَّ يَداً فِي الْخَيْرِ وَالصَّدَقَةِ ابن سعد هق دلائل ابن منده في معجم الصحابة ابن الأثير في أسد الغابة

Maymūna the Mother of the Believers رضي الله عنها

Ibn Abī Shayba and al-Bayhaqī narrated that Yazīd b. al-Asamm said that Maymūna felt near her end in Mecca whereupon she said: "Take me out of Mecca. Truly I shall not die in it! Truly, 106 the Messenger of Allah ﷺ told me that I would not die in Mecca." So they carried her until they brought her to Sarif, to the tree under

[162]Narrated by Ibn Sa'd (8:108), al-Bayhaqī in the *Dalā'il*, Ibn Mandah in *Mu'jam al-Ṣaḥāba* (2:955-956), and Ibn al-Athīr in *Usd al-Ghāba*.

which <was set the tent in which> the Prophet ﷺ first cohabited with her, and she died there.[163]

عَنْ يَزِيدَ بْنِ الأَصَمِّ قَالَ ثَقُلَتْ مَيْمُونَةُ بِمَكَّةَ وَلَيْسَ عِنْدَهَا مِنْ
بَنِي أُخْتِهَا أَحَدٌ ، فَقَالَتْ أَخْرِجُونِي مِنْ مَكَّةَ فَإِنِّي لاَ أَمُوتُ بِهَا
أَخْبَرَنِي رَسُولُ اللهِ ﷺ أَنِّي لاَ أَمُوتُ بِهَا حَتَّى أَتَوْا بِهَا سَرِفَ إِلَى
الشَّجَرَةِ الَّتِي بَنَى بِهَا رَسُولُ اللهِ ﷺ تَحْتَهَا فِي مَوْضِعِ الْقُبَّةِ
فَمَاتَتْ ع رجاله رجال الصحيح مج خت هق في الدلائل

Rayḥāna رضي الله عنها

Al-Bayhaqī narrated that Ibn Isḥāq **[479]** said: ʿAbd Allāh b. Abī Bakr b. Muḥammad b. ʿAmr b. Ḥazm narrated to me that the Prophet ﷺ chose for himself, among the women of the Banū Qurayẓa, Rayḥāna bint [Shamʿūn b. Zayd b.] ʿAmr [as a concubine] but she refused to accept Islam so he left her alone but felt disappointed. As he was sitting among his Companions he heard the clatter of sandals behind him and said: 107 "These are the sandals of [Thaʿlaba] Ibn Saʿya[164] coming to announce to me Rayḥāna's *islām*!"[165]

[163]Narrated from Yazīd b. al-Asamm by Abū Yaʿlā (13:27 §7110) with a chain of *Sahīh* narrators cf. al-Haythamī (9:249), al-Bukhārī in *al-Tārīkh al-Kabīr* (5:127 §379) with a second chain cf. Ibn Kathīr in *al-Bidāya*, and al-Bayhaqī in the *Dalā'il*, all with the bracketed addition, omitted by al-Nabhānī. Sarif is a place about ten miles from Mecca where the Prophet ﷺ married Maymūna cf. Ibn al-Athīr, *al-Nihāya.*

[164]Spelt Saʿna in Nabhānī's text according to a variant spelling, cf. *al-Isāba* (1:79 §177).

[165]Narrated from Ayyūb b. Bashīr al-Muʿāwī by al-Wāqidī (2:518-520), Ibn Saʿd (8:131), Ibn Hishām (4:205-206), and Ibn ʿAsākir (3:239) cf. al-Ṭabarī's *Tārīkh* (2:103), Ibn Ḥajar's *al-Isāba* (7:658 §11197), and *al-Bidāya*, chapter on concubines.

عَنْ عَبْدِ اللهِ بْنِ أَبِي بَكْرِ بْنِ مُحَمَّدِ بْنِ عَمْرِو بْنِ حَزْمٍ أَنَّ النَّبِيَّ
ﷺ اِصْطَفَى لِنَفْسِهِ مِنْ نِسَاءِ بَنِي قُرَيْظَةَ رَيْحَانَةَ بِنْتَ عَمْرٍو
فَأَبَتْ أَنْ تُسْلِمَ فَعَزَلَهَا رَسُولُ اللهِ ﷺ وَوَجَدَ فِي نَفْسِهِ لِذَلِكَ
مِنْ أَمْرِهَا فَبَيْنَا هُوَ مَعَ أَصْحَابِهِ إِذْ سَمِعَ وَقْعَ نَعْلَيْنِ خَلْفَهُ فَقَالَ
إِنَّ هَذَا لَثَعْلَبَةُ بْنُ سَعْيَةَ يُبَشِّرُنِي بِإِسْلَامِ رَيْحَانَةَ ابن سعد ابن هشام
مغازي الواقدي تاريخ الطبري هق في الدلائل كر

Al-Zubayr b. al-ʿAwwām ؓ

Al-Hākim narrated that Qays ؓ said that ʿAlī said to al-Zubayr [at the Battle of the Camel]: "Do you not remember the day when you and I were together and the Messenger of Allah ﷺ asked you: [108] 'Do you [al-Zubayr] love him [ʿAlī]?' and you replied, 'Why not?' Then he ﷺ said: 'Lo! [a] You shall rebel against him and fight him unjustly.'" Hearing this, al-Zubayr retreated.[166]

عَنْ قَيْسِ بْنِ أَبِي حَازِمٍ قَالَ قَالَ عَلِيٌّ لِلزُّبَيْرِ أَمَا تَذْكُرُ يَوْمَ
كُنْتَ أَنَا وَأَنْتَ فِي سَقِيفَةِ قَوْمٍ مِنَ الأَنْصَارِ فَقَالَ لَكَ رَسُولُ
اللهِ ﷺ أَتُحِبُّهُ فَقُلْتُ مَا يَمْنَعُنِي قَالَ أَمَا إِنَّكَ سَتَخْرُجُ عَلَيْهِ

[166]Narrated from Qays b. Abī Ḥāzim and others by Ḥākim (3:366-367=1990 3:412-414), Ibn Abī Shayba (10:283 §19673), Ibn ʿAsākir (18:410), al-Bayhaqī through Muḥammad b. Sulaymān al-ʿĀbid who is unknown: Ibn Kathīr, *Bidāya* (6:213), Ibn al-Jawzī's *ʿIlal* (2:848), *Kanz* (§31202), al-Dhahabī, *Siyar* (Risala ed. 1:59), *Mīzān* (4:180, 4:411), al-ʿUqaylī's *Duʿafāʾ* [ʿAbd al-Malik b. Muslim], al-Haythamī (7:235). Al-Dāraquṭnī in his *ʿIlal* (4:245-246, 4:102-103) avers that it is not narrated by Qays but by Ismāʿīl al-Aḥmasī who is unknown, *mursal* from al-Zubayr whom he never met. However, it is also narrated through other weak chains cf. (i) al-Bayhaqī, *Dalāʾil* (6:415); (ii) *ditto* (4:414-415); (iii) Ibn Abī Shayba (15:283-284 §19674). See their extensive documentation in Ibn al-Mulaqqin's *Mukhtaṣar Istidrāk al-Dhahabī* (4:-2070-2077 §719).

وَتُقَاتِلُهُ وَأَنْتَ ظَالِمٌ قَالَ فَرَجَعَ الزُّبَيْرُ ك ش كر هق في الدلائل من طرق ضعيفة راجع مختصر إستدراك الذهبي لابن الملقن

Ibn Isḥāq said: "Ibn Shihāb, ʿĀṣim b. ʿUmar b. Qatāda, Muḥammad b. Yaḥyā b. Ḥayyān and others narrated to me from our Ulema that a man among the idolaters came out on his camel the day of Uḥud and issued a challenge to duel. The people kept back three times. Then al-Zubayr ﷺ went to fight him and jumped so he was with him on the camel. They fought on top of the camel. The Prophet ﷺ said: 109 'The one bottom-side is a dead man.' Then the idolater fell and al-Zubayr ﷺ fell on top of him and slew him."[167]

عَنْ ابْنِ إِسْحَاقَ أَنَّ رَجُلاً مِنَ الْمُشْرِكِينَ خَرَجَ يَوْمَ أُحُدٍ فَدَعَا إِلَى الْبِرَازِ فَأَحْجَمَ النَّاسُ عَنْهُ حَتَّى دَعَا ثَلاَثاً وَهُوَ عَلَى جَمَلٍ فَقَامَ إِلَيهِ الزُّبَيْرُ فَوَثَبَ إِلَيهِ وَهُوَ عَلَى بَعِيرِهِ فَاسْتَوَى مَعَهُ عَلَى رَحْلِهِ ثُمَّ عَانَقَهُ فَاقْتَتَلاَ فَوْقَ الْبَعِيرِ جَمِيعاً فَقَالَ رَسُولُ اللهِ ﷺ الَّذِي يَلِي حَضِيضَ الأَرْضِ مَقْتُولٌ فَوَقَعَ الْمُشْرِكُ وَوَقَعَ الزُّبَيْرُ عَلَيْهِ فَذَبَحَهُ هق في الدلائل

The Prophet ﷺ praised him and said: 110 "Every Prophet ﷺ has a close disciple *(ḥawārī)* and my close disciple is al-Zubayr."[168] Al-Bayhaqī narrated it in similar terms.

[167]Narrated by al-Bayhaqī in his *Dalā'il* (3:227), al-Dhahabī, *Tārīkh al-Islām* (*Maghāzī* p. 172-173) and al-Ṣāliḥī, *Subul al-Hudā* (4:287). Al-Zubayr was upset because the Prophet ﷺ had given a sword to Abū Dujāna al-Anṣārī instead of him – his ﷺ cousin.

[168]Narrated from Jābir by al-Bukhāri, Muslim, al-Tirmidhī, Ibn Mājah, and Aḥmad; ʿAlī by al-Tirmidhī *(ḥasan ṣaḥīḥ)* and Aḥmad; and ʿAbd Allāh b. al-Zubayr by Aḥmad with the words "my paternal cousin."

عَنْ جَابِرِ بْنِ عَبْدِ اللهِ رَضِيَ اللهُ عَنْهُمَا قَالَ قَالَ النَّبِيُّ ﷺ لِكُلِّ نَبِيٍّ حَوَارِيٌّ وَحَوَارِيَّ الزُّبَيْرُ ق وفي الباب عن سيدنا علي وسيدنا الزبير رضي الله عنهما

The Messenger of Allah ﷺ also said: 111 "Give the tidings of Hellfire to the killer of the son of Ṣafiyya."[169] Ibn Jurmūz ambushed and killed al-Zubayr after the latter had withdrawn from the Battle of the Camel.

عَنْ زِرِّ بْنِ حُبَيْشٍ قَالَ اسْتَأْذَنَ ابْنُ جُرْمُوزٍ عَلَى عَلِيٍّ رَضِيَ اللهُ عَنْهُ وَأَنَا عِنْدَهُ فَقَالَ عَلِيٌّ رَضِيَ اللهُ عَنْهُ بَشِّرْ قَاتِلَ ابْنِ صَفِيَّةَ بِالنَّارِ ثُمَّ قَالَ عَلِيٌّ رَضِيَ اللهُ عَنْهُ سَمِعْتُ رَسُولَ اللهِ ﷺ يَقُولُ إِنَّ لِكُلِّ نَبِيٍّ حَوَارِيًّا وَحَوَارِيَّ الزُّبَيْرُ سَمِعْت سُفْيَانَ يَقُولُ الْحَوَارِيُّ النَّاصِرُ حم بلإسناد صحيح فتح وفضائل الصحابة طب ابن سعد كر عَنْ مُصْعَبِ بْنِ عَبْدِ اللهِ الزُّبَيْرِيِّ قَالَ تَوَجَّهَ الزُّبَيْرُ إِلَى المدِينَةِ فَتَبِعَهُ عَمْرُو بْنُ جُرْمُوزٍ وَهُوَ مُتَوَجِّهٌ نَحْوَ الْمَدِينَةِ فَقَتَلَهُ غِيلَةً بِوَادِي السِّبَاعِ ك

[169] Narrated from ʿAlī by Aḥmad (Arna'ūṭ 2:98-99 *ḥasan*) and others with a sound chain as per Ibn Ḥajar in *Fatḥ al-Bārī* (6:229) but *mawqūf* as clarified by al-Khaṭīb in *al-Fasl lil-Wasl al-Mudraj* (1:146).

Saʿd b. Abī Waqqāṣ ﵁

Aḥmad narrated from ʿAmr b. al-ʿĀṣ ﵁ that the Prophet ﷺ said: [112] "The first to come in through this door is a man from among the dwellers of Paradise." Then Saʿd b. Abī Waqqāṣ entered.[170] Al-Bayhaqī narrated something similar from ʿUmar b. al-Khaṭṭāb ﵁. So did al-Bazzār, also from ʿUmar with the addition: "He ﷺ said this for three days and every day Saʿd entered."[171]

عَنْ عَبْدِ اللهِ بْنِ عَمْرِو بْنِ الْعَاصِ رَضِيَ اللهُ عَنْهُمَا أَنَّ النَّبِيَّ ﷺ قَالَ أَوَّلُ مَنْ يَدْخُلُ مِنْ هَذَا الْبَابِ رَجُلٌ مِنْ أَهْلِ الْجَنَّةِ فَدَخَلَ سَعْدُ بْنُ أَبِي وَقَّاصٍ حم بإسناد حسن مج وفي الباب عن سيدنا عمر بن الخطاب عد وابنه حب ز الأخير بزيادة قَالَ ذَلِكَ فِي ثَلاَثَةِ أَيَّامٍ كُلَّ ذَلِكَ يَدْخُلُ سَعْدٌ وأنس كر

The Two Masters narrated from Saʿd b. Abī Waqqāṣ ﵁ that the Messenger of Allah ﷺ said to him: [113] "It may be that you will live on so that people will benefit from you and others will be harmed by you."[172] This was said as Saʿd lay ill in Mecca and hated to die in the land from which he had emigrated. His illness grew worse until he was on the brink of death, whereupon the Prophet ﷺ visited him. Saʿd had no children but for one daughter so he said: "Messenger of Allah, shall I give away all my possessions as charity?" The Prophet ﷺ said no. And so forth until the Prophet ﷺ said: [a] "Give away one third, and one third is a lot." This is a famous narration. Then he ﷺ said to him: "It may be that you will live on so

[170] Narrated from ʿAbd Allāh b. ʿAmr b. al-ʿĀṣ by Aḥmad, from ʿUmar by Ibn ʿAdī, from Ibn ʿUmar by Ibn Ḥibbān (15:451), and from Anas by Ibn ʿAsākir.

[171] Narrated by al-Bazzār (2:244 §5835) with a weak chain because of ʿAbd Allāh b. Qays al-Raqāshī cf. al-Haythamī (8:151).

[172] Narrated as part of a longer narration from Saʿd by al-Bukhārī and Muslim.

that people will benefit from you and others will be harmed by you." Subsequently, Allah cured him of that illness, conquered Iraq at his hands, guided through him the throngs who entered Islam at his hands and shared in the spoils, harming through him the throngs of the idolaters against whom he fought, killing some and capturing others. He lived on after that illness for fifty years [and raised many sons]! Al-Nawawī said this ḥadīth was among the stunning miracles and that what he ﷺ said came true.[173]

عَنْ سَعْدِ بْنِ أَبِي وَقَّاصٍ رَضِيَ اللهُ عَنْهُ عَادَنِي رَسُولُ اللهِ ﷺ فِي حَجَّةِ الْوَدَاعِ مِنْ وَجَعٍ أَشْفَيْتُ مِنْهُ عَلَى الْمَوْتِ فَقُلْتُ يَا رَسُولَ اللهِ بَلَغَنِي مَا تَرَى مِنَ الْوَجَعِ وَأَنَا ذُو مَالٍ وَلاَ يَرِثُنِي إِلاَّ ابْنَةٌ لِي وَاحِدَةٌ أَفَأَتَصَدَّقُ بِثُلُثَيْ مَالِي قَالَ لاَ قَالَ قُلْتُ أَفَأَتَصَدَّقُ بِشَطْرِهِ قَالَ لاَ الثُّلُثُ وَالثُّلُثُ كَثِيرٌ إِنَّكَ أَنْ تَذَرَ وَرَثَتَكَ أَغْنِيَاءَ خَيْرٌ مِنْ أَنْ تَذَرَهُمْ عَالَةً يَتَكَفَّفُونَ النَّاسَ وَلَسْتَ تُنْفِقُ نَفَقَةً تَبْتَغِي بِهَا وَجْهَ اللهِ إِلاَّ أُجِرْتَ بِهَا حَتَّى اللُّقْمَةُ تَجْعَلُهَا فِي فِي امْرَأَتِكَ قَالَ قُلْتُ يَا رَسُولَ اللهِ أُخَلَّفُ بَعْدَ أَصْحَابِي قَالَ إِنَّكَ لَنْ تُخَلَّفَ فَتَعْمَلَ عَمَلاً تَبْتَغِي بِهِ وَجْهَ اللهِ إِلاَّ ازْدَدْتَ بِهِ دَرَجَةً وَرِفْعَةً وَلَعَلَّكَ تُخَلَّفُ حَتَّى يُنْفَعَ بِكَ أَقْوَامٌ وَيُضَرَّ بِكَ آخَرُونَ ق طأ سنن قال الإمام النووي في شرح مسلم هذا الحديث من المعجزات، فإن سعداً رضي الله عنه عاش حتى فتح العراق وغيره وانتفع به أقوام في دينهم ودنياهم وتضرر به الكفار في دينهم ودنياهم فإنهم قتلوا وصاروا إلى جهنم وسبيت

[173] Al-Nawawī, *Sharh Sahīh Muslim* (11:77-78).

نساؤهم وأولادهم وغنمت أموالهم وديارهم وولي العراق فاهتدى على يديه خلائق وتضرر
به خلائق بإقامته الحق فيهم من الكفار ونحوهم

ʿAbd al-Raḥmān b. ʿAwf ؓ

Al-Wāqidī and al-Zubayr b. **[480]** Bakkār narrated from ʿAbd al-ʿAzīz al-Zuhrī, from his paternal uncles Mūsā, ʿImrān, and Ismāʿīl who said that the Messenger of Allah ﷺ sent out ʿAbd al-Raḥmān b. ʿAwf in an expedition against Kalb in Dūma[174] and said: 114 "It may be Allah will grant victory at your hands and, if He does, marry the daughter of their king." He marched until he arrived then stood his ground for three days, inviting them to Islam, after which Aṣbagh b. ʿAmr al-Kalbī accepted Islam – he was a Christian – and, since he was their leader, a large throng of his people accepted Islam after him while he imposed the non-Muslim duty *(jizya)* on the rest. Then ʿAbd al-Raḥmān married Tumāḍir[175] bint al-Aṣbagh and brought her to al-Madīna.[176]

أَخْرَجَ ابْنُ سَعْدٍ مِنْ طَرِيقِ الْوَاقِدِي عَنْ شُيُوخِهِ قَالَ أَرْسَلَ رَسُولُ اللهِ ﷺ عَبْدَ الرَّحْمَنِ بْنَ عَوْفٍ فِي سَرِيَّةٍ إِلَى كَلْبٍ بِدُومَةِ الْجَنْدَلِ وَقَالَ إِنِ اسْتَجَابُوا لَكَ فَتَزَوَّجْ اِبْنَةَ مَلِكِهِمْ فَسَارَ حَتَّى قَدِمَ فَمَكَثَ ثَلاثَةَ أَيَّامٍ يَدْعُوهُمْ إِلَى الإِسْلامِ فَأَسْلَمَ أَصْبَغُ بْنُ عَمرٍو الْكَلْبِيُّ وَكَانَ نَصْرَانِيّاً وَكَانَ رَأْسَهُمْ وَأَسْلَمَ مَعَهُ نَاسٌ كَثِيرٌ

[174]The nearest city of al-Shām to Madīna, not far from Tabūk.

[175]Misspelt Tammām in al-Nabhānī's text.

[176]Narrated by al-Wāqidī in *al-Maghāzī*, Ibn Saʿd (2:89), Ibn Hishām (4:242), and al-Tabarī in his *Tārīkh* (3:158), cf. al-Nuwayrī in *Nihāyat al-Arab* (17:209-210), al-Sālihī, *Subul al-Hudā* (6:150), al-Nawawī, *Tahdhīb al-Asmā'* (1:280), al-Dhahabī, *Tārīkh* (*Maghāzī* p. 355-356), Ibn Kathīr, *Bidāya* (4:179) as well as al-Dāraqutnī in *al-Afrād* cited by Ibn Hajar in *al-Isāba* under al-Asbagh and Tumāḍir bint al-Asbagh.

مِنْ قَوْمِهِ وَأَقَامَ مَنْ أَقَامَ عَلَى إِعْطَاءِ الْجِزْيَةِ وَتَزَوَّجَ عَبْدُ الرَّحْمَنِ
تُمَاضِرَ بِنْتَ الأَصْبَغِ وَقَدِمَ بِهَا الْمَدِينَةَ وَأَخْرَجَهُ ابْنُ عَسَاكِرَ مِنْ
طَرِيقِ الْوَاقِدِيِّ حَدَّثَنِي عَبْدُ اللهِ بْنُ جَعْفَرٍ عَنْ ابْنِ أَبِي عَوْنٍ عَنْ
صَالِحِ بْنِ إِبْرَاهِيمَ بِهِ وَأَخْرَجَهُ مِنْ طَرِيقِ الزُّبَيْرِ بْنِ بَكَّارٍ حَدَّثَنِي
عَبْدُ الرَّحْمَنِ بْنُ عَبْدِ اللهِ بْنِ عَبْدِ الْعَزِيزِ الزُّهْرِيُّ عَنْ عُمُومَتِهِ
مُوسَى وَعِمْرَانَ وَلإِسْمَاعِيلَ نَحْوَهُ وَزَادَ فِيهِ وَأَكْثِرْ مِنْ ذِكْرِي
عَسَى اللهُ أَنْ يَفْتَحَ عَلَى يَدَيْكَ فَإِنْ فَتَحَ عَلَى يَدَيْكَ فَتَزَوَّجْ
اِبْنَةَ مَلِكِهِمْ وَاللهُ أَعْلَمُ السيوطي في الخصائص الكبرى

Ja'far, Zayd, and Ibn Rawāḥa

Al-Bukhārī narrated from Anas that the Messenger of Allah ﷺ sent out Zayd, Ja'far, and ['Abd Allāh] Ibn Rawāḥa and he gave Zayd the flag to carry. They all fell in combat <and the Messenger of Allah ﷺ described their death to the people before news of it came>. He told them: 115 "Zayd carried the flag and was struck down; then Ja'far seized it and was struck down; then 'Abd Allāh b. Rawāḥa seized it and was struck down. Then, Khālid b. al-Walīd seized it on his own initiative and victory was granted at his hands."[177] The Prophet ﷺ said this the day of the expedition of Mu'ta[178] in the land of al-Balqā'.

[177]Narrated from Anas by al-Bukhārī, Aḥmad, and al-Nasā'ī; 'Ā'isha by Abū Dāwūd; and 'Abd Allāh b. Ja'far in a longer narration by Ahmad (3:278-279 §1750 *isnād sahīh*). The bracketed segment is also narrated with the addition "eyes brimming with tears" from Anas by Abū Nu'aym, *Dalā'il* (p. 530 §458) and others.

[178]In present-day Jordan near Iraq. The most thorough description of this campaign is in the 46th chapter of al-Ṣāliḥī's *Subul al-Hudā* (6:228-261). See also Abū Shuhba, *al-Sīra al-Nabawiyya* (2:426-431).

عَنْ أَنَسِ بْنِ مَالِكٍ رضي الله عنه أَنَّ رَسُولَ اللهِ ﷺ بَعَثَ زَيْدًا وَجَعْفَرًا وَعَبْدَ اللهِ بْنَ رَوَاحَةَ وَدَفَعَ الرَّايَةَ إِلَى زَيْدٍ فَأُصِيبُوا جَمِيعًا قَالَ أَنَسٌ فَنَعَاهُمْ رَسُولُ اللهِ ﷺ إِلَى النَّاسِ قَبْلَ أَنْ يَجِيءَ الْخَبَرُ قَالَ أَخَذَ الرَّايَةَ زَيْدٌ فَأُصِيبَ ثُمَّ أَخَذَ جَعْفَرٌ فَأُصِيبَ ثُمَّ أَخَذَ عَبْدُ اللهِ بْنُ رَوَاحَةَ فَأُصِيبَ ثُمَّ أَخَذَ الرَّايَةَ بَعْدُ سَيْفٌ مِنْ سُيُوفِ اللهِ خَالِدُ بْنُ الْوَلِيدِ ع بإسناد صحيح مج هق وفي الدلائل كر وأصله ق

Al-Bukhārī narrated from Ibn ʿUmar رضي الله عنهما that [116] the Prophet ﷺ gave command to Zayd b. Ḥāritha over the Mu'ta expedition and said if Zayd is killed then let Ja'far take command and, if Ja'far is killed, Ibn Rawāḥa.[179]

عَنْ عَبْدِ اللهِ بْنِ عُمَرَ رَضِيَ اللهُ عَنْهُمَا قَالَ أَمَّرَ رَسُولُ اللهِ ﷺ فِي غَزْوَةِ مُؤْتَةَ زَيْدَ بْنَ حَارِثَةَ فَقَالَ رَسُولُ اللهِ ﷺ إِنْ قُتِلَ زَيْدٌ فَجَعْفَرٌ وَإِنْ قُتِلَ جَعْفَرٌ فَعَبْدُ اللهِ بْنُ رَوَاحَةَ خ وفي الباب عن ابن عباس حم

Al-Wāqidī said that Rabīʿa b. ʿUthmān narrated to him, from ʿUmar b. al-Ḥakīm, from his father: "Al-Nuʿmān b. Mahṣ the Jew came and stood near the Messenger of Allah ﷺ with the rest of the people. Then the Messenger of Allah ﷺ said: [117] 'Zayd b. Ḥāritha is in command of the troops;[180] if Zayd is killed, then

[179]Narrated from Ibn ʿUmar by al-Bukhārī and from ʿAbd Allāh b. Ja'far by Ahmad cf. n. 177 above.

[180]They were 3,000 and fought for seven days, cf. Sālihī, *Subul al-Hudā* (6:229, 6:238).

Ja'far b. Abī Ṭālib; if Ja'far is killed, then ʿAbd Allāh b. Rawāḥa. And if ʿAbd Allāh is killed, then let the Muslims choose one of their men and put him in command.' Al-Nuʿmān said: 'Abū al-Qāsim, if you are truly a Prophet, then whoever you name, whether few or many, shall all be struck down. Truly, if the Prophets of the Israelites who put a man in command of the people said, If So-and-so is struck down then So-and-so is in command, even if they were to name a hundred men, all of them would be struck down.' Then the Jew began to say to Zayd, 'Be warned that you shall never return to Muḥammad if he is truly a Prophet.' Zayd said: 'I bear witness that he is truthful and faithful!'"[181] Al-Bayhaqī and Abū Nuʿaym narrated it.

عَنْ عُمَرَ بْنِ الْحَكَمِ عَنْ أَبِيهِ رَضِيَ اللهُ عَنْهُ قَالَ جَاءَ النُّعْمَانُ
بْنُ فُنْحُصٍ الْيَهُودِيُّ فَوَقَفَ عَلَى رَسُولِ اللهِ ﷺ مَعَ النَّاسِ
فَقَالَ رَسُولُ اللهِ ﷺ زَيْدُ بْنُ حَارِثَةَ أَمِيرُ النَّاسِ فَإِنْ قُتِلَ زَيْدٌ
فَجَعْفَرُ بْنُ أَبِي طَالِبٍ فَإِنْ قُتِلَ جَعْفَرٌ فَعَبْدُ اللهِ بْنُ رَوَاحَةَ فَإِنْ
قُتِلَ عَبْدُ الرَّحْمَنِ بْنُ رَوَاحَةَ فَلْيَرْتَضِي الْمُسْلِمُونَ بَيْنَهُمْ رَجُلاً
فَلْيَجْعَلُوهُ عَلَيْهِمْ فَقَالَ النُّعْمَانُ أَبَا الْقَاسِمِ إِنْ كُنْتَ نَبِيّاً
فَسَمَّيْتَ مَنْ سَمَّيْتَ قَلِيلاً أَوْ كَثِيراً أُصِيبُوا جَمِيعاً إِنَّ الأَنْبِيَاءَ مِنْ
بَنِي إِسْرَائِيلَ كَانُوا إِذَا اسْتَعْمَلُوا الرَّجُلَ عَلَى الْقَوْمِ فَقَالُوا إِنْ
أُصِيبَ فُلاَنٌ فَفُلاَنٌ فَلَوْ سَمَّوْا مِائَةً أُصِيبُوا جَمِيعاً ثُمَّ جَعَلَ

[181]Narrated by al-Wāqidī (1:756), Ibn Hishām (3:427), Abū Nuʿaym in the *Dalā'il* (p. 528-529 §457), al-Bayhaqī in his (4:360-361), Ibn ʿAsākir, al-Suyūṭī in *al-Khasā'is* (2:70-72 where the Jew is identified as al-Nuʿmān b. Rihṭī), and al-Sāliḥī in *Subul al-Hudā* (6:228) through various chains.

الْيَهُودِيُّ يَقُولُ لِزَيْدٍ أَعْهِدْ فَلاَ تَرْجِعُ إِلَى مُحَمَّدٍ أَبَداً إِنْ كَانَ
مُحَمَّدٌ نَبِيّاً قَالَ زَيْدٌ فَأَشْهَدُ أَنَّهُ نَبِيٌّ صَادِقٌ بَارٌّ الواقدي في المغازي
وعنه هق في الدلائل كر الذهبي في التاريخ

Al-Wāqidī and al-Bayhaqī narrated that Abū Hurayra ؓ said: "I was present at Mu'ta and <when the enemy approached us> I saw an unprecedented, innumerable quantity of men, arms, livestock, silk, and gold. I was in a daze. Thābit b. Aqram said to me, 'Well, Abū Hurayra? It seems you are seeing a huge host!' I said yes. He replied, 118 'You did not witness Badr with us. Truly, we did not vanquish through numbers!'"[182]

عَنْ أَبِي هريرة رَضِيَ اللهُ عَنْهُ قَالَ شَهِدْتُ مُؤْتَةَ فَلَمَّا رَآنَا
الْمُشْرِكُونَ رَأَيْنَا مَا لاَ قِبَلَ لِأَحَدٍ بِهِ مِنَ الْعِدَّةِ وَالسِّلاَحِ
وَالْكُرَاعِ وَالدِّيبَاجِ وَالْحَرِيرِ وَالذَّهَبِ فَبَرِقَ بَصَرِي فَقَالَ لِي ثَابِتُ
بْنُ أَقْرَمُ مَا لَكَ يَا أَبَا هُرَيْرَةَ كَأَنَّكَ تَرَى جُمُوعاً كَثِيرَةً قُلْتُ نَعَمْ
قَالَ تَشْهَدُ مَعَنَا بَدْراً إِنَّا لَمْ نُنْصَرْ بِالْكَثْرَةِ الواقدي ومن طريقه هق في
الدلائل

Al-Bayhaqī and Abū Nuʿaym narrated from Mūsā b. ʿUqba that Ibn Shihāb said: "They said that the Messenger of Allah ﷺ said: 119 'Ja'far b. Abī Ṭālib went past me in a group of angels, flying just as they flew, and he had two wings.' They also said that Yaʿlā b. Munya came to the Messenger of Allah ﷺ bringing the

[182]Narrated by al-Wāqidī (2:760) and, through him, al-Bayhaqī in the *Dalā'il* (4:362) cf. al-Sālihī, *Subul al-Hudā* (6:235). Al-Nabhānī omits the bracketed segment.

news of the combatants of Mu'ta, whereupon the Messenger of Allah ﷺ said to him: [120] 'If you wish, tell me the news and, if you wish, I shall tell you the news.' He replied, 'You tell me, Messenger of Allah.' The Messenger of Allah ﷺ then told him the news of what had happened to them and described it from beginning to end. **[481]** Yaʿlā said: 'By the One Who sent you with the Truth, you did not leave out one iota from what happened to them. It is exactly as you said.' He ﷺ said: [a] 'Allah removed distances for me so that I could see their battle.'"[183]

عَنْ مُوسَى بْنِ عُقْبَةَ قَالَ زَعَمُوا أَنَّ رَسُولَ اللهِ ﷺ قَالَ مَرَّ عَلَيَّ جَعْفَرُ بْنُ أَبِي طَالِبٍ فِي الْمَلَائِكَةِ يَطِيرُ كَمَا يَطِيرُونَ وَلَهُ جَنَاحَانِ وَزَعَمُوا أَنَّ يَعْلَى بْنَ مُنْيَةَ قَدِمَ عَلَى رَسُولِ اللهِ ﷺ بِخَبَرِ أَهْلِ مُؤْتَةَ فَقَالَ لَهُ رَسُولُ اللهِ ﷺ إِنْ شِئْتَ فَأَخْبِرْنِي وَإِنْ شِئْتَ أَخْبَرْتُكَ قَالَ أَخْبِرْنِي يَا رَسُولَ اللهِ فَأَخْبَرَهُ رَسُولُ اللهِ ﷺ خَبَرَهُمْ كُلِّهِمْ وَوَصَفَهُ لَهُمْ فَقَالَ وَالَّذِي بَعَثَكَ بِالْحَقِّ مَا تَرَكْتَ مِنْ حَدِيثِهِ حَرْفاً لَمْ تَذْكُرْهُ وَإِنَّ أَمْرَهُمْ لَكَمَا ذَكَرْتَ فَقَالَ إِنَّ اللهَ رَفَعَ لِيَ الأَرْضَ حَتَّى رَأَيْتُ مُعْتَرَكَهُمْ المغازي لموسى بن عقبة وعنه هق في الدلائل كر

Al-Bayhaqī narrated that [Abū] Qatāda ﷺ said that the Messenger of Allah ﷺ sent out the "army of the commanders," saying: [121] "Your commander is Zayd b. Ḥāritha; if Zayd is struck down, then Jaʿfar; if Jaʿfar is struck down, then ʿAbd Allāh b. Rawāḥa."

[183] Narrated chainless by Mūsā b. ʿUqba in his *Maghāzī* (p. 264-265) and through him al-Bayhaqī in the *Dalā'il* (4:364-365) as cited by al-Ṣāliḥī in *Subul al-Hudā* (6:242), and Ibn ʿAsākir.

Then they departed and were away for as long as Allah wished. Then, [one day,] the Messenger of Allah ﷺ climbed the pulpit and ordered that people be summoned to congregational prayer. The people gathered then he said to them: [a] "I shall tell you what happened to your army. They marched forth and met the enemy. Zayd was killed as a martyr. Then Ja'far seized the flag and fought the enemy hard until he was killed as a martyr. Then ʿAbd Allāh b. Rawāḥa took the flag and stood his ground firmly until he was killed as a martyr. Then Khālid b. al-Walīd took the flag and assumed command of his own initiative." Then the Messenger of Allah ﷺ said: [b] "Truly he is one of Your drawn swords and You grant him victory!" That day Khālid was named Sayfullāh.[184]

عَنْ أَبِي قَتَادَةَ فَارِسُ رَسُولِ اللهِ ﷺ قَالَ بَعَثَ رَسُولُ اللهِ ﷺ
جَيْشَ الأُمَرَاءِ وَقَالَ عَلَيْكُمْ زَيْدُ بْنُ حَارِثَةَ فَإِنْ أُصِيبَ زَيْدٌ
فجَعْفَرٌ فَإِنْ أُصِيبَ جَعْفَرٌ فعَبْدُ اللهِ بْنُ رَوَاحَةَ الأَنْصَارِيُّ فَوَثَبَ
جَعْفَرٌ فَقَالَ بِأَبِي أَنْتَ يَا نَبِيَّ اللهِ وَأُمِّي مَا كُنْتُ أَرْهَبُ أَنْ
تَسْتَعْمِلَ عَلَيَّ زَيْدًا قَالَ امْضُوا فَإِنَّكَ لا تَدْرِي أَيُّ ذَلِكَ خَيْرٌ
قَالَ فَانْطَلَقَ الْجَيْشُ فَلَبِثُوا مَا شَاءَ اللهُ ثُمَّ إِنَّ رَسُولَ اللهِ ﷺ
صَعِدَ الْمِنْبَرَ وَأَمَرَ أَنْ يُنَادَى الصَّلاةُ جَامِعَةٌ فَقَالَ رَسُولُ اللهِ
ﷺ نَابَ خَيْرٌ أَوْ ثَابَ خَيْرٌ شَكَّ عَبْدُ الرَّحْمَنِ أَلاَ أُخْبِرُكُمْ عَنْ

[184]Narrated from Abū Qatāda al-Ḥārith b. Rib'ī al-Salamī al-Anṣārī by Aḥmad with a chain of trustworthy narrators (Haythamī 6:156); Ibn Saʿd (2:129-130); Nasā'ī, *Kubrā* (5:48 §8159, 5:76 §8282) and *Faḍā'il* (p. 18 §56, p. 53 §177), Ibn Abī Shayba (7:412 §36966), Tabarī, *Tārīkh* (2:151), Ibn Ḥibbān (15:522 §7048 *isnād sahīh*), al-Ṭaḥāwī in the *Mushkil* (13:166-167 §5170 *isnād ṣaḥīḥ*), and Bayhaqī, *Dalā'il* (4:367-368). The title "Sword of Allah" for Khālid b. al-Walīd is narrated from Anas, Abū Hurayra, Abū Bakr, ʿAbd Allāh b. Ja'far, and Abū Saʿīd al-Khudrī in al-Bukhārī, al-Tirmidhī, Aḥmad, and Ḥākim.

جَيْشِكُمْ هَذَا الْغَازِي إِنَّهُمْ انْطَلَقُوا حَتَّى لَقُوا الْعَدُوَّ فَأُصِيبَ زَيْدٌ شَهِيدًا فَاسْتَغْفِرُوا لَهُ فَاسْتَغْفَرَ لَهُ النَّاسُ ثُمَّ أَخَذَ اللِّوَاءَ جَعْفَرُ بْنُ أَبِي طَالِبٍ فَشَدَّ عَلَى الْقَوْمِ حَتَّى قُتِلَ شَهِيدًا أَشْهَدُ لَهُ بِالشَّهَادَةِ فَاسْتَغْفِرُوا لَهُ ثُمَّ أَخَذَ اللِّوَاءَ عَبْدُ اللهِ بْنُ رَوَاحَةَ فَأَثْبَتَ قَدَمَيْهِ حَتَّى أُصِيبَ شَهِيدًا فَاسْتَغْفِرُوا لَهُ ثُمَّ أَخَذَ اللِّوَاءَ خَالِدُ بْنُ الْوَلِيدِ وَلَمْ يَكُنْ مِنَ الأُمَرَاءِ هُوَ أَمَّرَ نَفْسَهُ فَرَفَعَ رَسُولُ اللهِ ﷺ أُصْبُعَيْهِ وَقَالَ اللهُمَّ هُوَ سَيْفٌ مِنْ سُيُوفِكَ فَانْصُرْهُ وَقَالَ عَبْدُ الرَّحْمَنِ مَرَّةً فَانْتَصِرْ بِهِ فَيَوْمَئِذٍ سُمِّيَ خَالِدٌ سَيْفَ اللهِ حم ن في الكبرى ش ابن سعد حب مشكل الآثار

Al-Wāqidī said: "Muḥammad b. Ṣāliḥ al-Tammār narrated to me from ʿĀṣim b. ʿUmar b. Qatāda; likewise, ʿAbd al-Jabbār b. 'Umāra b. Ghaziyya narrated to me from ʿAbd Allāh b. Abī Bakr b. Ḥazm, both saying that [122] when the armies met at Mu'ta the Messenger of Allah ﷺ sat on the *minbar* and the distance that stood between him and al-Shām was folded up so that he beheld their battle directly. The Messenger of Allah ﷺ said: [a] 'Zayd took the flag, whereupon the devil came to him and made him long for life and hate death, and he made him long for the world. Zayd said: "Now that belief dominates in the hearts of the believers, you make me long for the world?" Then he marched and fought until he was martyred. [a] He entered Paradise marching. After him, Ja'far took the flag, whereupon the devil came to him and made him long for life and hate death, and he made him long for the world. Ja'far said: "Now that belief dominates in the hearts of the believers, you make me long for the world?" Then he marched and fought until he was martyred. [b] He entered Paradise flying with two wings of ruby and going wherever he wished. Then ʿAbd Allāh b. Rawāḥa took the flag and was martyred. [c] He entered Paradise having turned sideways *(muʿtariḍan).*' When they heard this, the Anṣār were pained. Someone asked, 'Messenger of Allah ﷺ, why had he turned sideways?' He replied: d 'When he was wounded he flinched, so he rebuked himself and braced up, then he was martyred and entered Paradise.' Hearing this, the people were happy again."[185] Al-Bayhaqī narrated it.

الواقدي في المغازي: حَدَّثَني مُحَمَّدُ بْنُ صَالِحٍ عَنْ عَاصِمِ بْنِ عُمَرَ بْنِ قَتَادَةَ وَحَدَّثَني عَبْدُ الجَبَّارِ بْنُ عُمَارَةَ بْنِ عَبْدِ اللهِ بْنِ أَبِي بَكْرٍ زَادَ أَحَدُهُمَا عَلَى صَاحِبِهِ فِي الحَدِيثِ قَالَا لَمَّا التَقَى النَّاسُ بِمُؤْتَةَ جَلَسَ رَسُولُ اللهِ ﷺ عَلَى المِنْبَرِ وَكُشِفَ لَهُ مَا بَيْنَهُ وَبَيْنَ الشَّامِ فَهُوَ يَنْظُرُ إِلَى مُعْتَرَكِهِمْ فَقَالَ ﷺ أَخَذَ الرَّايَةَ زَيْدُ بْنُ حَارِثَةَ فَجَاءَهُ الشَّيْطَانُ فَحَبَّبَ إِلَيْهِ الحَيَاةَ وَكَرَّهَ إِلَيْهِ المَوْتَ وَحَبَّبَ إِلَيْهِ الدُّنْيَا فَقَالَ الآنَ حِينَ اُسْتُحْكِمَ الإِيمَانُ فِي قُلُوبِ المُؤْمِنِينَ تُحَبَّبُ إِلَيَّ الدُّنْيَا فَمَضَى قِدْمًا حَتَّى اُسْتُشْهِدَ فَصَلَّى عَلَيْهِ رَسُولُ اللهِ ﷺ وَقَالَ اسْتَغْفِرُوا لَهُ فَقَدْ دَخَلَ الجَنَّةَ وَهُوَ يَسْعَى ثُمَّ أَخَذَ الرَّايَةَ جَعْفَرُ بْنُ أَبِي طَالِبٍ فَجَاءَهُ الشَّيْطَانُ فَمَنَّاهُ الحَيَاةَ وَكَرَّهَ إِلَيْهِ المَوْتَ وَمَنَّاهُ الدُّنْيَا فَقَالَ الآنَ حِينَ اُسْتُحْكِمَ الإِيمَانُ فِي قُلُوبِ المُؤْمِنِينَ تُمَنِّينِي الدُّنْيَا ثُمَّ مَضَى قِدْمًا حَتَّى اُسْتُشْهِدَ فَصَلَّى عَلَيْهِ رَسُولُ اللهِ ﷺ وَدَعَا لَهُ ثُمَّ قَالَ

---

[185] Narrated *mursal* from ʿAbd Allāh b. Abī Bakr by Wāqidī (2:761-762), Ibn Saʿd (4:37), Bayhaqī, Abū Nuʿaym, *Dalāʾil* (p. 528-529 §457), Ibn ʿAsākir cf. Ibn Hishām (5:28), Ibn Kathīr, *Bidāya* (Muʾta), *Nasb* (2:284), chapters on al-Najāshī's funeral prayer in absentia.

اسْتَغْفِرُوا لِأَخِيكُمْ فَإِنَّهُ شَهِيدٌ دَخَلَ الْجَنَّةَ فَهُوَ يَطِيرُ فِي الْجَنَّةِ بِجَنَاحَيْنِ مِنْ يَاقُوتٍ حَيْثُ يُشَاءُ مِنْ الْجَنَّةِ ثُمَّ أَخَذَ الرَّايَةَ بَعْدَهُ عَبْدُ اللهِ بْنُ رَوَاحَةَ فَاسْتُشْهِدَ وَدَخَلَ الْجَنَّةَ مُعْتَرِضًا فَشَقَّ ذَلِكَ عَلَى الأَنْصَارِ فَقَالَ رَسُولُ اللهِ ﷺ أَصَابَهُ الْجِرَاحُ قِيلَ يَا رَسُولَ اللهِ مَا اعْتِرَاضُهُ قَالَ لَمَّا أَصَابَتْهُ الْجِرَاحُ نَكَلَ فَعَاتَبَ نَفْسَهُ فَشَجُعَ فَاسْتُشْهِدَ فَدَخَلَ الْجَنَّةَ فَسُرِّيَ عَنْ قَوْمِهِ الواقدي وعنه ابن سعد هق أبو نعيم كلاهما في الدلائل كر

Al-Wāqidī also narrated from his authorities: 123 "The earth was folded up for the Messenger of Allah ﷺ so that he could see the folk in the field of battle. When Khālid b. al-Walīd took up the flag, the Messenger of Allah ﷺ said: a "Now blazes the furnace!"[186]

ابن سعد في الطبقات الكبرى من طريق الواقدي عن شيوخه قالوا رُفِعَتِ الأَرْضُ لِرَسُولِ اللهِ ﷺ حَتَّى نَظَرَ إِلَى مُعْتَرَكِ الْقَوْمِ فَلَمَّا أَخَذَ خَالِدُ ابْنُ الْوَلِيدِ اللِّوَاءَ قَالَ رَسُولُ اللهِ ﷺ وَالآنَ حَمِيَ الْوَطِيسُ ابن عائذ في المغازي الواقدي ابن سعد كر

[186] *Al-āna ḥamya al-waṭīs*. Narrated by Ibn ʿĀ'idh al-Azdī (d. 191) in his *Maghāzī*, al-Wāqidī (2:764), Ibn Saʿd (2:129), and Ibn ʿAsākir. Cf. *Kanz* (§29917) and al-Ṣāliḥī, *Subul al-Hudā* (6:238). The Prophet ﷺ also said this in the battle of Ḥunayn as in Muslim. Al-Jāḥiẓ in *al-Bayān wal-Tabyīn* ("Eloquence and Rhetoric") (2:15) said no one in the history of literature preceded him ﷺ in using this expression and it became a proverb.

Ibn Sa'd narrated through Sālim b. Abī al-Ja'd, from Abū al-Yusr, from the Companion Abū 'Āmir, that the Prophet ﷺ – when news of Ja'far and his friends reached him – remained sad for a time then smiled. Asked why, he said: 124 "My Companions were killed, but later, I saw them ﴾**as brethren, face to face, resting on couches raised**﴿ (15:47). I saw in one of them reluctance, as if he loathed the sword. I saw Ja'far as an angel with two wings smeared with blood, his top quills dyed red!"[187]

عَنْ أَبِي عَامِرٍ الصَّحَابِيِّ أَنَّ النَّبِيَّ ﷺ لَمَّا جَاءَهُ خَبَرُ جَعْفَرٍ وَأَصْحَابِهِ مَكَثَ حَزِيناً ثُمَّ تَبَسَّمَ فَقِيلَ لَهُ فَقَالَ إِنَّهُ أَحْزَنَنِي قَتْلُ أَصْحَابِي حَتَّى رَأَيْتُهُمْ فِي الجَنَّةِ ﴿إِخْوَانًا عَلَى سُرُرٍ مُّتَقَـٰبِلِينَ﴾ وَرَأَيْتُ فِي بَعْضِهِمْ إِعْرَاضاً كَأَنَّهُ كَرِهَ السَّيْفَ وَرَأَيْتُ جَعْفَراً مَلَكاً ذَا جَنَاحَيْنِ مُضَرَّجاً بِالدِّمَاءِ مَصْبُوغَ الْقَوَادِمِ ابن سعد ورواه مختصرا ش طب ابن أبي عاصم كر وهذا لفظ الخصائص

Al-Ḥākim narrated that Ibn 'Abbās رضي الله عنهما said that as the Prophet ﷺ was sitting and Asmā' bint 'Umays [Ja'far's wife] was not far from him, lo and behold! he returned someone's greeting then said: 125 "Asmā'! Here is Ja'far with Jibrīl, Mīkā'īl, and Isrāfīl, all greeting us, so return their salaam! **[482]** He had already informed me that he met the idolaters on such-and-such a day, three or four days ago. At that time he said: 'I met the idolaters and was stabbed in my body, from my top quills down, in seventy-three places with lance, dagger, and sword. Then I took the flag with my right hand

187 Narrated from Abū 'Āmir by Ibn Sa'd (2:129-130) and *mursal*, in shorter form, by Ibn Abī Shayba (6:381 §32200, 7:415 §36975) cf. al-Ṣāliḥī, *Subul* (6:242-243) and *Kanz* (§30244), and – last sentence alone – by al-Ṭabarānī in *al-Kabīr* (2:107 §1468). Another narration from Abū 'Āmir in the latter (2:108 §1472), Ibn Abī Shayba (4:209), and Ibn Abī 'Āṣim's *al-Āḥād wal-Mathānī* (1:276 §361) states that the Prophet ﷺ was informed in his sleep (cf. *al-Kabīr* 19:167 and Ibn Abī 'Āṣim's *al-Jihād* 2:552-553 §218). Henceforth Ibn 'Umar greeted Ja'far's son as "Ibn Dhī al-Janāḥayn": al-Bukhārī, *Saḥīḥ*.

and it was cut off. Then I took it with the left and it was cut off. Allah compensated me for my hands with two wings with which I fly with Jibrīl and Mīkā'īl, and I alight in whatever part of Paradise I wish and eat from its fruit wherever and whenever I wish.'"[188]

عَنِ ابْنِ عَبَّاسٍ رَضِيَ اللهُ عَنْهُمَا قَالَ بَيْنَمَا رَسُولُ اللهِ ﷺ جَالِسٌ وَأَسْمَاءُ بِنْتُ عُمَيْسٍ قَرِيبَةٌ مِنْهُ إِذْ رَدَّ السَّلَامَ ثُمَّ قَالَ يَا أَسْمَاءُ هَذَا جَعْفَرُ بْنُ أَبِي طَالِبٍ مَعَ جِبْرِيلَ وَمِيكَائِيلَ وَإِسْرَافِيلَ سَلَّمُوا عَلَيْنَا فَرُدِّي عَلَيْهِمُ السَّلَامَ وَقَدْ أَخْبَرَنِي أَنَّهُ لَقِيَ الْمُشْرِكِينَ يَوْمَ كَذَا وَكَذَا قَبْلَ مَمَرِّهِ عَلَى رَسُولِ اللهِ ﷺ بِثَلَاثٍ أَوْ أَرْبَعٍ فَقَالَ لَقِيتُ الْمُشْرِكِينَ فَأُصِبْتُ فِي جَسَدِي مِنْ مَقَادِيمِي ثَلَاثاً وَسَبْعِينَ بَيْنَ رَمْيَةٍ وَطَعْنَةٍ وَضَرْبَةٍ ثُمَّ أَخَذْتُ اللِّوَاءَ بِيَدِي الْيُمْنَى فَقُطِعَتْ ثُمَّ أَخَذْتُ بِيَدِي الْيُسْرَى فَقُطِعَتْ فَعَوَّضَنِي اللهُ مِنْ يَدَيَّ جَنَاحَيْنِ أَطِيرُ بِهِمَا مَعَ جِبْرِيلَ وَمِيكَائِيلَ أَنْزِلُ مِنَ الْجَنَّةِ حَيْثُ شِئْتُ وَآكُلُ مِنْ ثِمَارِهَا مَا شِئْتُ ك طب طس كر وفي الباب مختصرا عن البراء وعلي ت ك حب ابن سعد

---

[188]Narrated in full and in brief from Ibn ʿAbbās by al-Ṭabarānī in *al-Kabīr* (2:107 §1466-1467, 11:396 §12112) and *al-Awsaṭ* (7:88 §6936), al-Ḥākim (3:210, 212=1990 ed. 3:232, 234) with a good chain per Ibn Ḥajar in the *Fatḥ* (7:67) cf. Ibn Hishām (5:28), al-Dhahabī, *Siyar* (Fikr ed. 3:134=Risala ed. 1:211), al-Haythamī (6:161, 9:272-273), al-Mundhirī in *al-Targhīb* (1997 ed. 2:106 §2117), and Ibn Ḥajar in *al-Iṣāba* (1:487). Narrated in brief form from Abū Hurayra by al-Tirmidhī *(ḥasan gharīb)*, Ibn Ḥibbān (15:521 §7047 *ṣaḥīḥ*), and al-Ḥākim (3:212 *ṣaḥīḥ*), from al-Barā' b. ʿĀzib by al-Ḥākim (1990 ed. 3:42) cf. *Kāmil*, *Mīzān*, and *Lisān* (s.v. ʿAmr b. ʿAbd al-Ghaffār al-Fuqaymī), from ʿAlī by Ibn Saʿd (4:39), and from al-Zubayr by Ibn ʿAbd al-Barr in *al-Istīʿāb* (1:242-243) cf. *Fayḍ al-Qadīr* (4:8-9 §4383) and *Talkhīṣ al-Ḥabīr* (3:214).

Ibn Isḥāq, Ibn Sa'd, al-Bayhaqī, and Abū Nu'aym narrated that Asmā' bint 'Umays [رضي الله عنها] said: "The Messenger of Allah ﷺ came in to see me and said: 126 'Bring me Ja'far's children.' When I brought them he smelled them[189] and his eyes filled with tears. I said, 'Messenger of Allah, what makes you weep? Have you heard something about Ja'far and his friends?' He said: 'Yes, they were struck down today.'"[190]

عَنْ أَسْمَاءَ بِنْتِ عُمَيْسٍ قَالَتْ لَمَّا أُصِيبَ جَعْفَرٌ وَأَصْحَابُهُ دَخَلْتُ عَلَى رَسُولِ اللهِ ﷺ وَقَدْ دَبَغْتُ أَرْبَعِينَ مَنِيئَةً وَعَجَنْتُ عَجِينِي وَغَسَّلْتُ بَنِيَّ وَدَهَنْتُهُمْ وَنَظَّفْتُهُمْ فَقَالَ رَسُولُ اللهِ ﷺ ائْتِينِي بِبَنِي جَعْفَرٍ قَالَتْ فَأَتَيْتُهُ بِهِمْ فَشَمَّهُمْ وَذَرَفَتْ عَيْنَاهُ فَقُلْتُ يَا رَسُولَ اللهِ بِأَبِي أَنْتَ وَأُمِّي مَا يُبْكِيكَ أَبَلَغَكَ عَنْ جَعْفَرٍ وَأَصْحَابِهِ شَيْءٌ قَالَ نَعَمْ أُصِيبُوا هَذَا الْيَوْمَ قَالَتْ فَقُمْتُ أَصِيحُ وَاجْتَمَعَ إِلَيَّ النِّسَاءُ وَخَرَجَ رَسُولُ اللهِ ﷺ إِلَى أَهْلِهِ فَقَالَ لَا تُغْفِلُوا آلَ جَعْفَرٍ مِنْ أَنْ تَصْنَعُوا لَهُمْ طَعَامًا فَإِنَّهُمْ قَدْ شُغِلُوا بِأَمْرِ صَاحِبِهِمْ حم مسند إسحاق بن راهويه طب هق في الدلائل أبو نعيم كذلك

[189]The traditional way of kissing.

[190]Narrated from Asmā' by Ibn Isḥāq as mentioned by Ibn Hishām (Tadmurī ed. 4:22), Aḥmad and Ibn Rāhūyah in their *Musnad*s, al-Ṭabarānī in *al-Kabīr* (24:143 §380), Abū Nu'aym in his *Dal'ā'il* (p. 530 §459) and al-Bayhaqī in his, cf. al-Haythamī (6:161). The narration continues: "Make food for the family of Ja'far, for they are preoccupied to distraction," a segment also narrated from 'Abd Allāh b. Ja'far by al-Tirmidhī *(hasan sahīh)*, Abū Dāwūd, and Ibn Mājah.

Al-Wāqidī, al-Bayhaqī and Ibn ʿAsākir narrated that ʿAbd Allāh b. Jaʿfar رضي الله عنهما said: "I remember precisely when the Messenger of Allah ﷺ came in to see my mother and announced to us the death of my father. He said: 'Lo! [127] I am giving you glad tidings that Allah gave Jaʿfar two wings with which he is flying in Paradise.' Another time, the Messenger of Allah ﷺ came to us as I was haggling over the price of a sheep with one of my brothers so he said: [a] 'O Allah! Grant him blessing in his transaction.' I have not sold or bought anything since but I have been blessed with it."[191]

عَنْ عَبْدِ اللهِ بْنِ جَعْفَرٍ قَالَ أَنَا أَحْفَظُ حِينَ دَخَلَ رَسُولُ اللهِ ﷺ عَلَى أُمِّي فَنَعَى لَهَا أَبِي وَقَالَ أَلاَ أُبَشِّرُكِ إِنَّ اللهَ جَعَلَ لِجَعْفَرٍ جَنَاحَيْنِ يَطِيرُ بِهِمَا فِي الْجَنَّةِ وَأَتَانَا رَسُولُ اللهِ ﷺ وَأَنَا أُسَاوِمُ شَاةَ أَخٍ لِي فَقَالَ اللهُمَّ بَارِكْ لَهُ فِي صَفَقَتِهِ فَمَا بِعْتُ شَيْئاً وَلاَ اشْتَرَيْتُ شَيْئاً إِلاَّ بُورِكَ لِي فِيهِ الواقدي هق في الدلائل كر

[One version ends with the words of the Prophet ﷺ to Asmā' concerning her children: [128] "Do you fear destitution for them when I am their guardian *(waliyyuhum)* in the world and hereafter?"][192]

Al-Ḥākim narrated that Ibn ʿAbbās رضي الله عنهما said: "The Messenger of Allah ﷺ said: [129] 'I entered Paradise and gazed. Lo and behold! There was Jaʿfar flying with the angels, and there was Ḥamza reclining on an elevated couch.'"[193]

[191]Narrated from ʿAbd Allāh b. Jaʿfar by al-Wāqidī (2:767), al-Bayhaqī in the *Dalā'il* (4:371), and Ibn ʿAsākir. The first segment is narrated from ʿAbd Allāh b. Jaʿfar and ʿAmr b. Ḥurayth by Ibn Saʿd (4:36-37), Abū Yaʿlā (3:47 §1467) with a chain of trustworthy narrators as per al-Haythamī (9:286), Ibn Abī ʿĀṣim in *al-Āḥād* (2:37 §714), al-Nasā'ī in *al-Sunan al-Kubrā* (5:48§8160), al-Ṭaḥāwī in *Sharḥ Mushkil al-Āthār* (13:164-165 §5169 *isnād saḥīḥ*, 14:458-459 §5756), Ibn Qāniʿ in *Muʿjam al-Ṣaḥāba* (2:203 §702), and al-Baghawī cf. *Tahdhīb al-Kamāl* (8:325 §1724) and *Iṣāba* (4:41).

[192]Narrated from ʿAbd Allāh b. Jaʿfar by Aḥmad (3:278-279 §1750 *isnād saḥīḥ*), Ibn Saʿd (4:36-37) and Ṭaḥāwī in *Sharḥ Mushkil al-Āthār* (13:164-165 §5169 *isnād saḥīḥ*).

[193]Narrated from Ibn ʿAbbās by al-Ṭabarānī in *al-Kabīr* (2:107 §1466), al-Ḥākim (3:196,

عَنْ ابْنِ عَبَّاسٍ رَضِيَ اللهُ عَنْهُمَا مَرْفُوعاً دَخَلْتُ الجَنَّةَ البَارِحَةَ فَنَظَرْتُ فِيهَا فَإِذَا جَعْفَرٌ يَطِيرُ مَعَ المَلائِكَةِ وَإِذَا حَمْزَةُ مُتَّكِىءٌ عَلَى سَرِيرٍ   طب ك وفي الباب عن أبي أيوب طص وعن علي عد بسند واه

Al-Dāraquṭnī narrated that Ibn ʿUmar رضي الله عنهما said: "We were with the Messenger of Allah ﷺ when he raised his head to the sky and said: [130] 'And upon you be peace and the mercy of Allah!' At this, the people said, 'Messenger of Allah, what does this mean?' He replied: [a] 'Ja'far b. Abī Ṭālib passed by with a throng of angels and greeted me.'"[194]

عَنْ ابْنِ عُمَرَ رَضِيَ اللهُ عَنْهُمَا قَالَ كُنَّا مَعَ رَسُولِ اللهِ ﷺ فَرَفَعَ رَأْسَهُ إِلَى السَّمَاءِ فَقَالَ وَعَلَيْكُمُ السَّلامُ وَرَحْمَةُ اللهِ فَقَالَ النَّاسُ يَا رَسُولَ اللهِ مَا هَذَا قَالَ مَرَّ بِي جَعْفَرُ بْنُ أَبِي طَالِبٍ فِي مَلأٍ مِنَ الْمَلاَئِكَةِ فَسَلَّمَ عَلَيَّ   قط في غرائب مالك كذا في الخصائص والإصابة

Ibn Saʿd narrated that Muḥammad b. ʿUmar b. ʿAlī [b. Abī Ṭālib] رضي الله عنه said the Messenger of Allah ﷺ said: [131] "I saw Ja'far as an angel flying in Paradise, the top of his two wings bloodied, and I saw Zayd below him. I said, [a] 'I did not think that Zayd was below Ja'far in

3:209=1990 ed. 3:217, 3:231) who declared it sound as did al-Suyūṭī in *al-Jāmiʿ al-Saghīr* (§4184) while al-Dhahabī objected as its chain contains Salama b. Wahrām whom Abū Dāwūd declared weak. But Salama is "truthful" *(sadūq)* cf. Ibn Ḥajar, *Taqrīb* (§2515) and al-Arna'ūṭ's *Taḥrīr* (2:61 §2515) when he does not narrate to Zamʿat b. Ṣāliḥ which is the case in one of al-Ḥākim's two chains. The report is further confirmed by a similar narration from Abū Ayyūb al-Anṣārī by Ṭabarānī in *al-Saghīr* (1:75 §94) with a passable chain cf. al-Haythamī (9:166).

[194]Narrated by al-Dāraquṭnī in *Gharā'ib Mālik* with a weak chain as per Ibn Ḥajar in *al-Iṣāba* (1:487) and al-Suyūṭī in the *Khaṣā'iṣ*; also from Ibn ʿAbbās as already mentioned.

rank.' Then Jibrīl came to me and told me, 'Zayd is not below Ja'far in rank but we gave Ja'far preference due to his blood kinship to you.'"[195] Ḥākim narrated something similar from Ibn ʿAbbās رضي الله عنهما.

عَنْ مُحَمّدِ بْنِ عُمَرَ بْنِ عَلِيٍّ مُرْسَلاً قَالَ رَسُولُ اللهِ ﷺ رَأَيْتُ
جَعْفَرًا مَلِكًا يَطِيرُ فِي الْجَنّةِ تَدْمَى قَادِمَتَاهُ وَرَأَيْتُ زَيْدًا دُونَ
ذَلِكَ فَقُلْت مَا كُنْتُ أَظُنُّ أَنَّ زَيْدًا دُونَ جَعْفَرٍ فَأَتَى جِبْرِيلُ
عَلَيْهِ السّلاَمُ فَقَالَ إِنَّ زَيْدًا لَيْسَ بِدُونِ جَعْفَرٍ وَلَكِنَّا فَضَّلْنَا
جَعْفَرًا لِقَرَابَتِهِ مِنْكَ الواقدي ابن سعد كر وفي الباب عن ابن عباس ك بسند واه

Al-ʿAbbās رضي الله عنه

Abū Nuʿaym narrated with a sound chain from Ibn ʿAbbās رضي الله عنهما that when the Messenger of Allah ﷺ took a ransom from al-ʿAbbās [in exchange for his release when he was captured] after the battle of Badr, the latter said, "You have made me the poor man of Quraysh for the rest of my life!" The Prophet ﷺ replied: 132 "How can you be the poor man of Quraysh when you deposited gold nuggets with Umm al-Faḍl and told her, 'If I am killed, I have left you rich for the rest of your life'?" Hearing this, he said, "I bear witness that what you said is exactly what happened and none saw it except Allah!"[196]

[195]Narrated *mursal* from Muḥammad b. ʿUmar b. ʿAlī by Ibn Saʿd (4:38) cf. *Kanz* (§33213) and from Ibn ʿAbbās by al-Ḥākim (3:210=1990 ed. 3:232) but al-Dhahabi said: "Disclaimed, and its chain [in al-Ḥākim] is pitch-dark" *(munkar wa-isnāduhu muzlim)*.

[196]Narrated from Ibn ʿAbbās by Abū Nuʿaym in the *Dalā'il* (p. 476-477 §409-410) with two good chains cf. Ibn Ḥajar, *Fatḥ* (7:322) with the wording: "I bear witness that none but she and I know this, and truly I know that you are the Messenger of Allah!" In the other narration al-ʿAbbās recites the *kalima*.

عَنْ ابْن عَبَّاس رَضِيَ اللهُ عَنْهُمَا قَالَ لما كَانَ يَوْم بَدْرٍ أُسِرَ سَبْعُونَ فَجَعَلَ عَلَيْهِم رَسُولُ اللهِ ﷺ أَرْبَعِينَ أُوقِيَّةً ذَهَباً وَجَعَلَ عَلَى عَمِّه الْعَبَّاسِ مِائَةَ أُوقِيَّةٍ وَعَلَى عقيل ثَمَانِينَ فَقَالَ الْعَبَّاس لِلْقَرَابَةِ صَنَعْتَ هَذَا وَالَّذِي يَحْلِفُ بِهِ الْعَبَّاسُ لَقَدْ تَرَكْتَنِي فَقِيرَ قُرَيْشٍ مَا بَقِيْتُ قَالَ كَيفَ تَكُونُ فَقِيرَ قُرَيْشٍ وَقَدِ اسْتَوْدَعْتَ أُمَّ الْفَضْلِ بَنَادِقَ الذَّهَبِ فَقَالَ أَشْهَدُ أَنْ لاَ إِلَهَ إِلاَّ اللهُ وَأَنَّكَ رَسُولُ اللهِ وَاللهِ مَا أَخْبَرَكَ بِهَذَا إِلاَّ اللهُ فَأَنْزَلَ اللهُ ﴿ يَٰٓأَيُّهَا ٱلنَّبِيُّ قُل لِّمَن فِىٓ أَيْدِيكُم مِّنَ ٱلْأَسْرَىٰٓ إِن يَعْلَمِ ٱللَّهُ فِى قُلُوبِكُمْ خَيْرًا يُؤْتِكُمْ خَيْرًا مِّمَّآ أُخِذَ مِنكُمْ وَيَغْفِرْ لَكُمْ ۗ وَٱللَّهُ غَفُورٌ رَّحِيمٌ ﴿٧٠﴾ ﴾ الأنفال أبو نعيم في الدلائل بإسناد حسن فتح

Ibn Isḥāq and al-Bayhaqī narrated from al-Zuhrī and a number of other narrators that al-ʿAbbās said to the Messenger of Allah ﷺ: "I do not have enough to pay my ransom." The Prophet ﷺ replied: 133 "Then where is the money you and Umm al-Faḍl buried before you told her, 'If anything happens to me during my trip, use this money for my sons al-Faḍl, [ʿAbd Allāh,] and Qutham'?" Al-ʿAbbās said: "By Allah, I swear I know you are the Messenger of Allah! None knows this other than myself and Umm al-Faḍl."[197]

عَنِ الزُّهْرِيِّ وَجَمَاعَةٍ أَنَّ الْعَبَّاسَ رضي الله عنه قَالَ لِرَسُولِ اللهِ ﷺ مَا عِنْدِي مَا أَفْدِي بِهِ قَالَ فَأَيْنَ الْمَالُ الَّذِي دَفَنْتَهُ أَنْتَ وَأُمُّ

[197]Narrated by al-Bayhaqī in the *Dalā'il* (3:142). Cited by Ibn Kathīr in his *Tafsīr* (2:328) Sūrat 8:70 and *al-Bidāya*, chapter on the prisoners of Badr.

الْفَضْلِ فَقُلْتُ لَهَا إِنْ أُصِبْتُ فِي سَفَرِي هَذَا فَهَذَا الْمَالُ لِبَنِيِّ الْفَضْلِ وَعَبْدِ اللهِ وَقُثَمٍ فَقَالَ وَاللهِ إِنِّي لَأَعْلَمُ أَنَّكَ رَسُولُ اللهِ ﷺ وَاللهِ إِنَّ هَذَا لَشَيْءٌ مَا عَلِمَهُ أَحَدٌ غَيْرِي وَغَيْرُ أُمِّ الْفَضْلِ

ابن إسحاق هق في الدلائل وهذا لفظ الخصائص قال وأخرجه عن ابن عباس حم ابن سعد أبو نعيم وهق في الدلائل وعن عائشة ك صححه على شرط مسلم والله أعلم

Umm al-Faḍl the wife of al-ʿAbbās رضي الله عنها

Abū Nuʿaym narrated that Ibn ʿAbbās رضي الله عنهما said: "Umm al-Faḍl – his mother – narrated to me that as she passed by the Prophet ﷺ while he was sitting in the Chamber *(al-Ḥijr)* **[483]** he said to her: [134] 'You are pregnant with a boy. When you give birth, bring him to me.' <She said, 'How could that be when the Quraysh swore they will stay away from women?' He replied, 'It will be as I told you.'> When she gave birth she brought her child to him and he raised the call to prayer in his right ear and the start of prayer in his left. Then he blew some moist air into his mouth *(alba'ahu min rīqih)* and named him ʿAbd Allāh. Then he said: [a] 'Take the Father of Caliphs *(Abū al-Khulafā')* with you.' She went back and told al-ʿAbbās who came to the Prophet ﷺ asking for confirmation. The latter said: [b] 'Just as she said, this is the Father of Caliphs, <and the Caliphate will be yours, ʿAbbās, after 132,> until al-Saffāḥ comes out from them, <then al-Manṣūr,> to the time when al-Mahdī comes out from them, to the time those that shall pray behind 'Īsā b. Maryam [عليهما السلام] come out from them.'"[198]

[198]Narrated from Ibn ʿAbbās by Ṭabarānī in *al-Kabīr* (10:289-290 §10580), Abū Nuʿaym in the *Dalā'il* (p. 550-551 §487), Khaṭīb (1:63), and – the only version with the bracketed segments – by Ṭabarānī, *Awsat* (9:102 §9250), "a feebly worded, spurious report fabricated ignorantly by Aḥmad b. Rāshid b. Khuthaym" cf. al-Dhahabī, *Mīzān* (*s.v.* Aḥmad b. Rāshid al-Hilālī), al-Zayla'ī, *Naṣb al-Rāya* (1:347), Ibn Ḥajar, *Lisān* (1:171 §548), al-Haythamī (5:187), Ibn al-Jawzī, *'Ilal* (1:291-292), and al-Aḥdab, *Zawā'id* (1:169-172 §28) despite Ibn Ḥibbān's entry, *Thiqāt* (8:40 §12153). "Every ḥadīth mentioning the caliphate being among the offspring of al-ʿAbbās is a lie, as is every ḥadīth blaming al-Walīd and al-Marwān b. al-Ḥakam." Ibn al-Qayyim, *al-Manār al-Munīf* (p. 117).

عَنْ أُمِّ الْفَضْلِ رَضِيَ اللهُ عَنْهَا قَالَتْ مَرَرْتُ بِرَسُولِ اللهِ ﷺ وَهُوَ جَالِسٌ بِالحِجْرِ فَقَالَ يَا أُمَّ الْفَضْلِ قُلْتُ لَبَّيْكَ يَا رَسُولَ اللهِ قَالَ إِنَّكِ حَامِلٌ بِغُلاَمٍ قُلْتُ كَيْفَ وَقَدْ تَحَالَفَتْ قُرَيْشٌ أَنْ لاَ يَأْتُوا النِّسَاءَ قَالَ هُوَ مَا أَقُولُ فَإِذَا وَضَعْتِيْهِ فَأْتِينِي بِهِ قَالَتْ فَلَمَّا وَضَعْتُهُ أَتَيْتُ بِهِ النَّبِيَّ ﷺ فَأَذَّنَ فِي أُذُنِهِ الْيُمْنَى وَأَقَامَ فِي أُذُنِهِ الْيُسْرَى وَأَلْبَأَهُ مِنْ رِيقِهِ وَسَمَّاهُ عَبْدَ اللهِ ثُمَّ قَالَ اذْهَبِي بِأَبِي الخُلَفَاءِ قَالَتْ فَأَتَيْتُ الْعَبَّاسَ فَأَعْلَمْتُهُ ثُمَّ أَتَى النَّبِيَّ ﷺ فَقَالَ يَا رَسُولَ اللهِ قَالَتْ أُمُّ الْفَضْلِ كَذَا وَكَذَا قَالَ هِيَ يَا عَبَّاسُ بَعْدَ ثِنْتَيْنِ وَثَلاثِينَ وَمِائَةٍ ثُمَّ مِنْكُمُ السَّفَّاحُ وَالمَنْصُورُ وَالمَهْدِيُّ وَهِيَ فِي أَوْلاَدِهِمْ حَتَّ يَكُونَ آخِرُهُمُ الَّذِي يُصَلِّي بِالمَسِيحِ عِيسَى ابْنِ مَرْيَمَ طب طس أبو نعيم في الدلائل خط تفرد به أحمد بن راشد الهلالي وهو المتّهم به مج ميزان

[A Prophetic narration states: 135 "The Mahdī and the [last] *Khilāfa* will most definitely be from the Quraysh but he shall have an origin and lineage from Yemen."][199]

[199]Narrated by al-Khaṭīb (5:391) with a *maqṭū'* chain from Ka'b al-Aḥbār through Nu'aym b. Ḥammād (cf. his *Fitan* 1:375 §1115, 1:394-396 §1185-1190) cf. al-Dānī, *al-Sunan al-Wārida fī al-Fitan* (5:1097) and from 'Abd Allāh b. 'Amr by Nu'aym in the *Fitan* (1:400 §1204-1205); Taqī al-Dīn Manṣūr b. Fallāḥ al-Yamanī (d. 680) in *al-Mughnī fī al-Naḥū* as cited by al-Suyūṭī in *'Uqūd al-Zabarjad* (3:282 §1718), ḥadīth: "He [the Mahdī] is Qurashī, Yamānī…" See also the authentic narrations naming the Mahdī as al-Qaḥṭānī cf. *Fatḥ* (13:214).

ʿAbd Allāh b. ʿAbbās رضي الله عنهما

Al-Bayhaqī and Abū Nuʿaym narrated from al-ʿAbbās b. ʿAbd al-Muṭṭalib رضي الله عنه that he sent his son ʿAbd Allāh to the Messenger of Allah ﷺ for a certain need but the latter found a man with him and returned without addressing him because he was not alone. Afterwards, the Messenger of Allah ﷺ found al-ʿAbbās and the latter told him, "I sent my son to you but he found you had company and was unable to speak to you, so he returned." The Prophet ﷺ said: [136] "Yes, this was Jibrīl, and he [ʿAbd Allāh] shall not die before first losing his sight, and he shall be granted knowledge."[200]

عَنِ الْعَبَّاسِ بْنِ عَبْدِ المطَّلِبِ رَضِيَ اللهُ عَنْهُ أَنَّهُ بَعَثَ ابْنَهُ عَبْدَ اللهِ إِلَى رَسُولِ اللهِ ﷺ فِي حَاجَةٍ فَوَجَدَ عِنْدَهُ رَجُلاً فَرَجَعَ وَلَمْ يُكَلِّمْهُ مِنْ أَجْلِ مَكَانِ الرَّجُلِ مَعَهُ فَلَقِيَ رَسُولُ اللهِ ﷺ الْعَبَّاسَ بَعْدَ ذَلِكَ فَقَالَ الْعَبَّاسُ أَرْسَلْتُ إِلَيْكَ إِبْنِي فَوَجَدَ عِنْدَكَ رَجُلاً فَلَمْ يَسْتَطِعْ أَنْ يُكَلِّمَكَ فَرَجَعَ قَالَ وَرَآهُ قَالَ نَعَمْ قَالَ أَتَدْرِي مَنْ ذَلِكَ الرَّجُلُ ذَلِكَ جِبْرِيلُ عَلَيْهِ السَّلَامُ وَلَنْ يَمُوتَ حَتَّى يَذْهَبَ بَصَرُهُ وَيُؤْتَى عِلْماً طس إسناده ثقات مج هق في الدلائل زوائد فضائل الصحابة ورواه حم مختصرا بإسناد صحيح على شرط مسلم

Abū Nuʿaym narrated that Ibn ʿAbbās رضي الله عنهما said: "I passed by the Messenger of Allah ﷺ as I was wearing white clothes and he

[200]Narrated by al-Ṭabarānī in *al-Awsat* (4:142 §3821) with a chain of trustworthy narrators as per al-Haythamī (9:277) and al-Bayhaqī in the *Dalāʾil*. Al-Dhahabī in the *Siyar* (Fikr ed. 4:443-445=Risala ed. 3:339-341) cites it together with several similar narrations, one of them by Aḥmad with three sound chains in the *Musnad* (Arnaʾūṭ ed. 4:417 §2679, 5:45-46 §2847 *ʿalā shart Muslim*) cf. his son in *Faḍāʾil al-Saḥāba* (2:974 §1917-1918).

was discussing in private with Diḥya. I was unaware that this was, in fact, Jibrīl. I passed by without giving salaam. Jibrīl said: 'How white his clothes are! His offspring will be leaders. If he had greeted me I would have replied to him.' On my way back, the Prophet ﷺ said to me: [137] 'What prevented you from giving salaam?' [I said:] 'I saw you discussing in private with Diḥyat al-Kalbī and loathed to interrupt you both.' He said: 'You saw him?' I said yes. He said: [a] 'It was Jibrīl and lo! your sight shall fade and return to you only at the time of your death.'" <'Ikrima said that when Ibn ʿAbbās died and was placed on his bier, a very white bird came and disappeared into his shroud. 'Ikrima said: "This was the glad tidings of the Messenger of Allah ﷺ that he had given him." When he was placed into his lateral niche *(laḥd)* he was prompted with a phrase heard by all at the graveside: ﴾**O soul at peace! Return unto your Lord, content in His good pleasure! Enter you among My bondmen and enter you My Garden!**﴿ (89:27-30).>[201]

عَنِ ابْنِ عَبَّاسٍ رَضِيَ اللهُ عَنْهُمَا قَالَ مَرَرْتُ بِرَسُولِ اللهِ ﷺ
وَعَلَيَّ ثِيَابٌ بِيضٌ وَهُوَ يُنَاجِي دِحْيَةَ بْنَ خَلِيفَةَ الْكَلْبِيَّ وَهُوَ
جِبْرِيلُ عَلَيْهِ السَّلامُ وَأَنَا لاَ أَعْلَمُ فَلَمْ أُسَلِّمْ فَقَالَ جِبْرِيلُ يَا
مُحَمَّدُ مَنْ هَذَا قَالَ هَذَا ابْنُ عَمِّي هَذَا ابْنُ عَبَّاسٍ قَالَ مَا أَشَدَّ
وَضْحَ ثِيَابِهِ أَمَا إِنَّ ذُرِّيَّتَهُ سَتَسُودُ بَعْدَهُ لَوْ سَلَّمَ عَلَيْنَا رَدَدْنَا
عَلَيْهِ فَلَمَّا رَجَعْتُ قَالَ لِي رَسُولُ اللهِ ﷺ يَا ابْنَ عَبَّاسٍ مَا

[201]Narrated from Maymūn b. Mahrān by Abū Nuʿaym (1985 ed. 1:329) and al-Ṭabarānī in *al-Kabīr* (10:237 §10586) with a chain containing unknowns cf. *Siyar* (*op. cit.*), al-Haythamī (9:276), and *Khasā'is* (2:202). The bracketed segment is narrated without mention of 'Ikrima through two chains from Abū al-Zubayr and Saʿīd b. Jubayr by al-Ḥākim (3:543-544), Abū Nuʿaym in *Maʿrifat al-Ṣaḥāba* (2: 1704 §4269), and al-Balādhurī in *Ansāb al-Ashrāf* (3:54); from Saʿīd b. Jubayr, ʿAbd Allāh b. Yāmīn's father, and Maymūn b. Mahrān by al-Ṭabarānī in *al-Kabīr* (10:236-237 §10581-10586) and Abū Nuʿaym in the *Maʿrifa* (2:1703-1704 §4268); and from Bujayr b. Abī ʿUbayd by al-Dhahabī in *Tārīkh al-Islām* (Years 61-80 p. 161) and *Siyar* (Fikr ed. 4:456) where he said the account of the white bird is *mutawātir*.

مَنَعَكَ أَنْ تُسَلِّمَ قُلْتُ بِأَبِي أَنْتَ وَأُمِّي رَأَيْتُكَ تُنَاجِي دِحْيَةَ بْنَ خَلِيفَةَ فَكَرِهْتُ أَنْ تَنْقَطِعَ عَلَيْكُمَا مُنَاجَاتُكُمَا قَالَ وَقَدْ رَأَيْتَهُ قُلْتُ نَعَمْ قَالَ أَمَا إِنَّهُ سَيَذْهَبُ بَصَرُكَ وَيُرَدُّ عَلَيْكَ فِي مَوْتِكَ قَالَ عِكْرِمَةُ فَلَمَّا قُبِضَ ابْنُ عَبَّاسٍ وَوُضِعَ عَلَى سَرِيرِهِ جَاءَ طَائِرٌ شَدِيدُ الْوَهَجِ فَدَخَلَ فِي أَكْفَانِهِ فَأَرَادُوا نَشْرَ أَكْفَانِهِ فَقَالَ عِكْرِمَةُ مَا تَصْنَعُونَ هَذِهِ بُشْرَى رَسُولِ اللهِ ﷺ الَّتِي قَالَ لَهُ فَلَمَّا وُضِعَ فِي لَحْدِهِ تُلُقِّيَ بِكَلِمَةٍ فَسَمِعَهَا مَنْ عَلَى شَفِيرِ قَبْرِهِ ﴿يَٰٓأَيَّتُهَا ٱلنَّفْسُ ٱلْمُطْمَئِنَّةُ ﴿٢٧﴾ ٱرْجِعِىٓ إِلَىٰ رَبِّكِ رَاضِيَةً مَّرْضِيَّةً ﴿٢٨﴾ فَٱدْخُلِى فِى عِبَٰدِى ﴿٢٩﴾ وَٱدْخُلِى جَنَّتِى ﴿٣٠﴾﴾ الفجر طب حل كر ورواه ك مختصرا وقال الذهبي في السير حكاية الطير متواترة اهـ. وجاء بلفظ أَمَا إِنَّهُ شَدِيدُ وَضَحِ الثِّيَابِ وَلَيَلْبَسَنَّ ذُرِّيَّتُهُ مِنْ بَعْدِهِ السَّوَادَ كر

Abū Nuʿaym narrated that Ibn ʿAbbās رضي الله عنهما said: 138 "The Messenger of Allah ﷺ told me that my sight would fade and it did. He told me that I would drown and I did drown in the lake of [al-]Ṭabariyya once. And he told me I would undertake emigration one day, after a civil strife. O Allah! You are my witness that my emigration today is to Muḥammad b. ʿAlī b. Abī Ṭālib."[202]

[202]I.e. Muḥammad b. al-Ḥanafiyya, whose mother was Khawla bint Jaʿfar b. Qays. Cited by Suyūṭī in his *Khasā'is* (2:248) where he says it is related by Abū Nuʿaym. After al-Ḥusayn died, Ibn ʿAbbās joined Ibn al-Hanafiyya and the latter lead the funeral prayer when Ibn ʿAbbās died cf. Abū Nuʿaym, *Maʿrifat al-Ṣaḥāba* (2:1700). Ibn al-Ḥanafiyya's *wasiyya* for the Caliphate was to Ibn ʿAbbās's grandson, Muḥammad b. ʿAlī cf. Ibn ʿAsākir (54:338-340, 28:203-204, 31:55, 32:271) and al-Dhahabī, *Siyar* (Fikr ed. 4:454).

عَنِ ابْنِ عَبَّاسٍ رَضِيَ اللهُ عَنْهُمَا قَالَ إِنَّ رَسُولَ اللهِ ﷺ حَدَّثَنِي أَنَّهُ سَيَذْهَبُ بَصَرِي فَقَدْ ذَهَبَ وَحَدَّثَنِي إِنِّي سَأَغْرَقُ وَقَدْ غَرِقْتُ فِي بُحَيْرَةِ الطَّبَرِيَّةِ وَحَدَّثَنِي أَنِّي سَأُهَاجِرُ مِنْ بَعْدِ فِتْنَةٍ اللهُمَّ إِنِّي أُشْهِدُكَ أَنَّ هِجْرَتِي الْيَوْمَ إِلَى مُحَمَّدِ بْنِ عَلِيِّ بْنِ أَبِي طَالِبٍ رَضِيَ اللهُ عَنْهُمَا قال في الخصائص رواه أبو نعيم اه ويرويه الشيعة في أسفارهم مطولا

Nawfal b. al-Ḥārith ﷺ

Ibn Saʿd and al-Bayhaqī narrated that ʿAbd Allāh b. al-Ḥārith b. Nawfal said that when Nawfal b. al-Ḥārith was captured at Badr, the Messenger of Allah ﷺ said to him: 139 "Ransom yourself, Nawfal!" He replied: "I have nothing with which to ransom myself." The Prophet ﷺ said: "Ransom yourself with your property in Jeddah." Nawfal said: "I bear witness you are the Messenger of Allah!" Then he ransomed himself with it.[203]

عَنْ عَبْدِ اللهِ بْنِ الحَارِثِ بْنِ نَوْفَلٍ قَالَ لَمَّا أُسِرَ نَوْفَلُ بْنُ الحَارِثِ بِبَدْرٍ قَالَ لَهُ رَسُولُ اللهِ ﷺ أَفْدِ نَفْسَكَ يَا نَوْفَلُ قَالَ مَا لِي شَيْءٌ أَفْدِي بِهِ نَفْسِي قَالَ أَفْدِ نَفْسَكَ مِنْ مَالِكَ الَّذِي بِجَدَّةَ قَالَ أَشْهَدُ أَنَّكَ رَسُولُ اللهِ فَفَدَى نَفْسَهُ بِهَا ابن سعد ك استيعاب

[203]Narrated by Ibn Saʿd (4:46), al-Ḥākim (3:246=1990 ed. 3:274), Ibn ʿAbd al-Barr, *al-Istīʿāb* (4:1512 §2642), and Ibn Ḥajar, *al-Iṣāba* (6:479). The property consisted of spears and the ransom was 1,000 of them.

ʿAbd Allāh b. Masʿūd ؓ

Al-Bayhaqī narrated that Ibn Masʿūd ؓ said: "When the Messenger of Allah ﷺ was returning from al-Ḥudaybiya we alighted in the late night to sleep and he said: [140] 'Who will guard us?' I said, 'I will.' But he replied: [a] 'You will fall asleep!' Then he said again: 'Who will guard us?' I said, 'I will' and guarded them until the dawn was about to rise, at which time the saying of the Messenger of Allah ﷺ reached me – 'You will fall asleep!' – so I fell asleep and did not wake up until the sun was high. When we woke up, the Messenger of Allah ﷺ said: **[484]** [b] 'If Allah had not wished that you sleep through it [the prayer], you would not have slept through it. However, He wished for this to take place for the benefit of those after you.' Then he did what he usually did and said: [c] 'Let whoever oversleeps of my Community do the same.' Then the people went searching for their mounts and they came back, each with his mount, except for that of the Messenger of Allah ﷺ. Whereupon he said: 'Go there.' I went to where he had directed me and found her with her reins entangled in a tree, and brought her. I said: 'Messenger of Allah, I found her reins entangled in a tree, they could not have come disentangled except by hand.'"[204]

عَنْ عَبْدِ اللهِ بْنُ مَسْعُودٍ رَضِيَ اللهُ عَنْهُ قَالَ لَمَّا انْصَرَفْنَا مِنْ
غَزْوَةِ الْحُدَيْبِيَةِ، قَالَ رَسُولُ اللهِ ﷺ مَنْ يَحْرُسُنَا اللَّيْلَةَ قَالَ عَبْدُ
اللهِ فَقُلْتُ أَنَا فقال إنك تنام ثم أعاد مَنْ يَحْرُسُنَا اللَّيْلَةَ قُلْتُ
أَنَا حَتَّى عَادَ مِرَارًا قُلْتُ أَنَا يَا رَسُولَ اللهِ قَالَ فَأَنْتَ إِذًا قَالَ

[204]Narrated from Ibn Masʿūd by Aḥmad (al-Arnaʾūṭ 6:243-244 §3710 *isnād daʿīf* cf. 6:333 §4307 *isnād ḥasan*), Abū Dāwūd al-Ṭayālisī in his *Musnad*, and others; another authentic version states that Bilāl was the guard that slept through, the rest of the narration being identical as narrated by Aḥmad (6:170-171 §3657, 7:426-428 §4421 both *isnād ḥasan*) and others, as confirmed by the briefer narrations from Abū Qatāda and Abū Hurayra by al-Bukhārī and Muslim. The Prophet's ﷺ camel was similarly lost and found on two other occasions during the expeditions of Banū Muṣṭaliq and Tabūk, cf. below, section "A Hypocrite Who Then Accepted Islam."

فَحَرَسْتُهُمْ حَتَّى إِذَا كَانَ وَجْهُ الصُّبْحِ أَدْرَكَنِي قَوْلُ رَسُولِ اللهِ ﷺ إِنَّكَ تَنَامُ فَنِمْتُ فَمَا أَيْقَظَنَا إِلاَّ حَرُّ الشَّمْسِ فِي ظُهُورِنَا فَقَامَ رَسُولُ اللهِ ﷺ وَصَنَعَ كَمَا كَانَ يَصْنَعُ مِنَ الْوُضُوءِ فِي رَكْعَتَيِ الْفَجْرِ ثُمَّ صَلَّى بِنَا الصُّبْحَ فَلَمَّا انْصَرَفَ قَالَ إِنَّ اللهَ عَزَّ وَجَلَّ لَوْ أَرَادَ أَنْ لاَ تَنَامُوا لَمْ تَنَامُوا وَلَكِنْ أَرَادَ أَنْ تَكُونُوا لِمَنْ بَعْدَكُمْ فَهَكَذَا لِمَنْ نَامَ أَوْ نَسِيَ قَالَ ثُمَّ إِنَّ نَاقَةَ رَسُولِ اللهِ ﷺ وَإِبِلَ الْقَوْمِ تَفَرَّقَتْ فَخَرَجَ النَّاسُ فِي طَلَبِهَا فَجَاءُوا بِإِبِلِهِمْ إِلاَّ نَاقَةَ رَسُولِ اللهِ ﷺ فَقَالَ عَبْدُ اللهِ قَالَ لِي رَسُولُ اللهِ ﷺ خُذْ هَهُنَا فَأَخَذْتُ حَيْثُ قَالَ لِي فَوَجَدْتُ زِمَامَهَا قَدِ الْتَوَى عَلَى شَجَرَةٍ مَا كَانَتْ لِتَحُلَّهَا إِلاَّ يَدٌ حم ط ع ن في الكبرى طب هق وفي الدلائل بألفاظ مختلفة متقاربة وقد تكررت الواقعة في غزوتي بني مصطلق وتبوك كما سيأتي

ʿAmmār b. Yāsir رضي الله عنهما

The Two Masters [al-Bukhārī and Muslim] narrated from Abū Saʿīd ؓ and Muslim from Umm Salama and Qatāda رضي الله عنهما that the Messenger of Allah ﷺ said to ʿAmmār: [141] "The rebellious faction shall kill you."[205] The ḥadīth Master al-Suyūṭī said: "This narration is mass-transmitted from over twenty Companions as I showed in *al-[Azhār al-Mutanāthira fīl-]Aḥādīth al-Mutawātira*."

[205]Narrated from Abū Saʿīd al-Khudrī by al-Bukhārī, Muslim, and Aḥmad; Umm Salama and Abū Qatāda by Muslim; Abū Hurayra by al-Tirmidhī *(ḥasan sahīh gharīb)*, ʿAbd Allāh b. ʿAmr b. al-ʿĀṣ, his father 'Amr, Khuzayma b. Thābit, and Abū Qatāda by Aḥmad, a mass-transmitted *(mutawātir)* narration as per Ibn ʿAbd al-Barr and al-Suyūṭī, from thirty-one authorities (see Arabic text) cf. al-Kattānī, *Nazm* (§237).

عَنْ أَبِي سَعِيدٍ خ وأُمِّ سَلَمَةَ م وَأَبِي هُرَيْرَةَ ت رَضِيَ اللهُ عَنْهُمْ أَنَّ رَسُولَ اللهِ ﷺ قَالَ لِعَمَّارٍ تَقْتُلُكَ الْفِئَةُ الْبَاغِيَةُ ق قال الحافظ محمد بن جعفر الكتاني في نظم المتناثر من الحديث المتواتر ما نصه أورده السيوطي في الأزهار من حديث (١) أبي سعيد (٢) وأبي قتادة (٣) وأم سلمة (٤) وحذيفة (٥) وابن مسعود (٦) وعمار بن ياسر (٧) وعمرو بن العاص (٨) وابنه عبد الله (٩) وعمرو بن حزم (١٠) وخزيمة بن ثابت (١١) وعثمان بن عفان (١٢) وأنس (١٣) وأبي هريرة (١٤) وأبي رافع (١٥) وجابر بن عبد الله (١٦) ومعاوية بن أبي سفيان (١٧) وعبد الله بن عباس (١٨) وزيد بن أبي أوفى الأسلمي (١٩) وجابر بن سمرة (٢٠) وأبي اليسر السلمي كعب بن عمرو (٢١) وزياد بن الفرد (٢٢) وكعب ابن مالك (٢٣) وأبي أمامة الباهلي (٢٤) وعائشة أربعة وعشرين نفساً قلت أي الكتاني ورد أيضاً من حديث (٢٥) ابن عمر (٢٦) وأبي أيوب (٢٧) وقتادة بن العمان (٢٨) وزيد بن ثابت (٢٩) وعمرو بن ميمون قال ابن عساكر وقد أدرك النبي ﷺ ولم يره (٣٠) وعمر (٣١) ومولاةٍ لعمار ابن ياسر وممن صرح بتواتره السيوطي في خصائصه الكبرى وقال الحافظ ابن حجر في تخريج أحاديث الرافعي قال ابن عبد البر تواترت الأخبار بذلك وهو من أصح الحديث وقال ابن دحية لا مطعن في صحته ولو كان غير صحيح لرده معاوية وأنكره ونقل ابن الجوزي عن الخلال في العلل أنه حكى عن أحمد قال قد روى هذا الحديث من ثمانية وعشرين طريقاً ليس فيها طريق صحيح وحكى أيضاً عن أحمد وابن معين وأبي خيثمة أنهم قالوا لم يصح ونص ابن عبد البر في الاستيعاب في ترجمة عمار وتواترت الآثار عن النبي صلى الله عليه وسلم أنه قال تقتل عماراً الفئة الباغية وهذا من أخباره بالغيب وإعلام نبوته صلى الله عليه وسلم وهو من أصح الأحاديث اهـ

Al-Bayhaqī and Abū Nuʿaym narrate that a freedwoman of ʿAmmār's said: "ʿAmmār suffered an accident and was unconscious then recovered as we were weeping all around him. He said: 'Do you fear that I shall die in my bed? [142] My beloved, the Messenger of Allah ﷺ, informed me that the rebellious faction shall kill me <and that my last meal on earth shall be a drink of diluted milk>.'"[206]

عَنْ مَوْلَاةٍ لِعَمَّارِ بْنِ يَاسِرٍ قَالَتْ اِشْتَكَى عَمَّارُ شَكْوَى ثَقُلَ مِنْهَا فَغُشِيَ عَلَيْهِ فَأَفَاقَ وَنَحْنُ نَبْكِي حَوْلَهُ فَقَالَ مَا يُبْكِيكُمْ أَتَخْشَوْنَ أَنِّي أَمُوتُ عَلَى فِرَاشِي أَخْبَرَنِي حَبِيبِي ﷺ أَنَّهُ تَقْتُلُنِي الْفِئَةُ الْبَاغِيَةُ وَأَنَّ آخِرَ زَادِي مَذْقَةٌ مِنْ لَبَنٍ ع ز بإسناد حسن مج هق في الدلائل كر

Al-Ḥākim narrated – declaring it sound – and others that ʿAmmār b. Yāsir was brought a cup of milk the day of Ṣiffīn, whereupon he smiled. Asked why, he replied, "Truly, the Messenger of Allah ﷺ said: [143] 'His last drink in the world shall be milk.'" Then he marched forth and was killed.[207]

عَنْ عَنْ أَبِي الْبَخْتَرِيِّ أَنَّ عَمَّارًا أُتِيَ بِشَرْبَةٍ مِنْ لَبَنٍ فَضَحِكَ فَقِيلَ لَهُ مَا يُضْحِكُكَ قَالَ إِنَّ النَّبِيَّ ﷺ قَالَ إِنَّ آخِرَ شَرَابٍ تَشْرَبُهُ لَبَنٌ حِينَ تَمُوتُ حم ع ابن سعد ك هق في الدلائل والبلاذري في أنساب الأشراف وفيهما أيضا أُتِيَ يَومَ صِفِّينَ وزادوا في آخره ثُمَّ تَقَدَّمَ فَقُتِلَ حم ش ابن أبي عاصم في الآحاد ابن سعد كر

[206]Narrated by Abū Yaʿlā (3:189 §1614) and al-Bazzār with a fair chain per al-Haythamī (9:295, 298) as well as al-Bayhaqī, *Dalā'il* (6:421) as cited in *al-Bidāya*. The bracketed segment is similarly narrated by Ibn Saʿd (3:257), Aḥmad (31:172-173 §18880 *ṣaḥīḥ*), Abū Yaʿlā (3:196 §1626), Ibn Abī Shayba (15:302), Ibn Abī ʿĀṣim (§272), Abū Nuʿaym (1:141), al-Ṭabarānī in *al-Awsaṭ* (6:301 §6471), al-Ḥākim (3:385, 389 =1990 ed. 3:435, 439), and al-Bayhaqī in the *Dalā'il* (2:552), with a sound chain according to al-Arna'ūṭ.

[207]Narrated by Ibn Saʿd (3:257), Aḥmad (31:178 §18883 *ṣaḥīḥ*), al-Ḥākim (3:389=1990 ed. 3:439) all without the last phrase, which is in Ibn Saʿd (3:258), Ibn Abī ʿĀṣim's *Āḥād* (1:208 §272) and elsewhere.

Ibn Saʿd narrated that Hudhayl ﵁ said: "They came to the Prophet ﷺ telling him that a wall had collapsed on top of ʿAmmār and that he had died, whereupon he said: 144 "ʿAmmār has not died.'"[208]

عَنْ هُذَيْلٍ قَالَ أَتَى النَّبِيُّ ﷺ فَقِيلَ لَهُ إِنَّ عَمَّاراً وَقَعَ عَلَيْهِ حَائِطٌ فَمَاتَ قَالَ مَا مَاتَ عَمَّارٌ ابن سعد ش حم في فضائل الصحابة كر

Imām Aḥmad, al-Ṭabarānī, and al-Ḥākim narrated from ʿAmr b. al-ʿĀṣ ﵁: 145 "The Quraysh are restless against ʿAmmār.[209] a The killer of ʿAmmār and his plunderer are in the Fire!"[210]

عَنْ عَبْدِ اللهِ بْنِ عُمَرَ رَضِيَ اللهُ عَنْهُمَا قَالَ أَتَى عَمْرَو بْنَ الْعَاصِ رَجُلاَنِ يَخْتَصِمَانِ فِي دَمِ عَمَّارٍ وَسَلَبِهِ قَالَ عَمْرٌو خَلِّيَا عَنْهُ وَاتْرُكَاهُ فَإِنِّي سَمِعْتُ رَسُولَ اللهِ ﷺ يَقُولُ اللهُمَّ أُولِعَتْ قُرَيْشٌ بِعَمَّارٍ قَاتِلُ عَمَّارٍ وَسَالِبُهُ فِي النَّارِ ع ك قال صحيح على شرط الشيخين ابن أبي عاصم في الآحاد ورواه مختصراً حم كر ورواه ابن سعد مطولا

[The killer of ʿAmmār was Abū al-Ghādiya Yasār b. Sabuʿ al-Juhanī al-Shāmī at Ṣiffīn although Imam Aḥmad relates from him the *mutawātir* sayings of the Prophet ﷺ from his Farewell Pilgrimage ḥadīth: 146 "Do not return to being disbelievers or astray after me, striking one another's neck"[211] and 147 "People! Truly, your lives

[208]Narrated from Hudhayl by Ibn Saʿd (3:254), Ibn Abī Shayba (6:386 §32250), Ibn ʿAsākir (43:416, 436).

[209]ʿAmmār and both his parents were tortured by the Quraysh before the Hijra: Aḥmad (1:492-493 §439), Ibn Saʿd (3:248, 4:136), al-Ḥākim (3:388-389), al-Haythamī (9:293), and Ibn Ḥajar, *Iṣāba* (3:610-611).

[210]Narrated from ʿAmr b. al-ʿĀṣ by al-Ḥākim (3:387=1990 ed. 3:437), Ibn Abī ʿĀṣim in *al-Āḥād* (2:102 §803), and Ibn ʿAsākir in his *Tārīkh* (43:426, 43:474). Ibn Kathīr cites it in *al-Bidāya*, Year 37.

[211]Narrated from Abū al-Ghādiya by Aḥmad in his *Musnad* and – from others – in the *Siḥāh* and *Sunan*.

and properties are sacred to one another until you meet your Lord just as the sanctity of this Day of yours ('Arafa), in this country of yours, in this month of yours! Lo! Have I conveyed the Message?"[212]]

ʿAmmār was killed at the battle of Ṣiffīn on the side of the rightful Imam, our Master ʿAlī ؓ. The rebellious faction killed him, that is, the faction of Muʿāwiya ؓ.

'Ayyāsh b. Abī Rabīʿat al-Makhzūmī ؓ

Ibn Saʿd narrated that al-Zuhrī said that the Messenger of Allah ﷺ wrote to al-Ḥārith, Masrūḥ, and Nuʿaym Banī ʿAbd Kulāl of the Ḥimyar, sending the letter with 'Ayyāsh b. Abī Rabīʿa al-Makhzūmī and saying: [148] "When you get to their country, do not enter it by night but wait until it is morning. Then wash and purify yourself in the best way you can, pray two *rak'a*s, ask Allah for success and acceptance, seek refuge in Allah, take my letter in your right hand, and deliver it to their right hand for they shall accept it. [a] Recite to them ﴾**Those who disbelieve among the People of the Scripture and the idolaters could not have left off (erring) till the clear proof came unto them, a messenger from Allah, reading purified pages containing correct scriptures. Nor were the People of the Scripture divided until after the clear proof came unto them. And they are ordered naught else than to serve Allah, keeping religion pure for Him, as men by nature upright, and to establish worship and to pay the poor due. That is true religion. Lo! those who disbelieve, among the People of the Scripture and the idolaters, will abide in the fire of hell. They are the worst of created beings. (And) lo! those who believe and do good works are the best of created beings. Their reward is with their Lord: Gardens of Eden underneath which rivers flow, wherein they dwell for ever. Allah has pleasure in them and they have pleasure in Him. This is (in store) for him who fears his Lord**﴿ (98:1-8). When you have finished, [b] say: 'Muḥammad believes, and I am the first of the believers.' After

[212] *Ibid.*, *Iṣāba* and Ibn ʿAsākir (26:174) who also (15:367) names Ḥuwayy b. Māti' b. Zur'a as the killer.

this, no argument will be raised against you except you shall shatter it, nor fancy book except their light shall fade even as they read it. c When they resort to jargon *(raṭinū)*, say: 'Translate it!' and say: 'Allah is sufficient for me! ﴾**I believe in whatever Scripture Allah has sent down, and I am commanded to be just among you. Allah is our Lord and your Lord. Unto us our works and unto you your works; no argument between us and you. Allah will bring us together, and unto Him is the journeying**﴿ (42:15). When they submit, request of them their three rods to which they usually prostrate whenever they see them. These rods are made of tamarisk wood, **[485]** one rod varnished white and yellow, one with knobs that looks like bamboo, one jet-black that looks like ebony. Take them and burn them in their market-place." 'Ayyāsh said: "I went out and did what the Messenger of Allah ﷺ told me. I went out to them and told them I was the messenger of the Messenger of Allah then I did what he told me. They accepted it and all took place just as he had said.[213]

عَنِ الزُّهْرِيِّ قَالَ كَتَبَ رَسُولُ اللهِ ﷺ إِلَى الحَارِثِ وَمَسْرُوحٍ وَنُعَيْمِ بْنِ عَبْدِ كُلَالٍ مِنْ حِمْيَرٍ وَبَعَثَ بِالْكِتَابِ مَعَ عَيَّاشِ بْنِ أَبِي رَبِيعَةَ المخْزُومِيِّ وَقَالَ إِذَا جِئْتَ أَرْضَهُمْ فَلاَ تَدْخُلَنَّ لَيْلاً حَتَّى تُصْبِحَ ثُمَّ تَطَهَّرْ فَأَحْسِنْ طُهُورَكَ وَصَلِّ رَكْعَتَيْنِ وَسَلِ اللهَ النَّجَاحَ وَالْقَبُولَ وَاسْتَعِذْ بِاللهِ وَخُذْ كِتَابِي بِيَمِينِكَ وَادْفَعْهُ بِيَمِينِكَ فِي أَيْمَانِهِمْ فَإِنَّهُمْ قَابِلُونَ وَاقْرَأْ عَلَيْهِمْ ﴿لَمْ يَكُنِ ٱلَّذِينَ كَفَرُوا۟ مِنْ أَهْلِ ٱلْكِتَٰبِ وَٱلْمُشْرِكِينَ مُنفَكِّينَ حَتَّىٰ تَأْتِيَهُمُ ٱلْبَيِّنَةُ ١﴾ فَإِذَا فَرَغْتَ مِنْهَا فَقُلْ آمَنَ مُحَمَّدٌ وَأَنَا أَوَّلُ الْمُؤْمِنِينَ فَلَنْ تَأْتِيَكَ

[213]Narrated *mursal* from al-Zuhrī by Ibn Sa'd (1:282-283) and Ibn 'Asākir in his *Tārīkh* (47:246-247).

حُجَّةٌ إِلاَّ دُحِضَتْ وَلاَ كِتَابٌ زُخْرِفَ إِلاَّ ذَهَبَ نُورُهُ وَهُمْ
قَارِئُونَ عَلَيْكَ فَإِذَا رَطِنُوا فَقُلْ تَرْجِمُوا وَقُلْ حَسْبِيَ اللهُ ﴿ءَامَنتُ
بِمَآ أَنزَلَ ٱللَّهُ مِن كِتَٰبٍۖ وَأُمِرْتُ لِأَعْدِلَ بَيْنَكُمُۖ ٱللَّهُ رَبُّنَا وَرَبُّكُمْۖ لَنَآ
أَعْمَٰلُنَا وَلَكُمْ أَعْمَٰلُكُمْۖ لَا حُجَّةَ بَيْنَنَا وَبَيْنَكُمُۖ ٱللَّهُ يَجْمَعُ بَيْنَنَاۖ
وَإِلَيْهِ ٱلْمَصِيرُ﴾ من سورة الشورى فَإِذَا أَسْلَمُوا فَسَلْهُمْ قُضُبَهُمْ
الثَّلاَثَةَ الَّتِي إِذَا حَضَرُوا بِهَا سَجَدُوا وَهِيَ مِنَ الأَثْلِ قَضِيبٌ
مُلَمَّعٌ بِبَيَاضٍ وَصُفْرَةٍ وَقَضِيبٌ ذُو عُجَرٍ كَأَنَّهُ خَيْزَرَانٌ وَالأَسْوَدُ
الْبَهِيمُ كَأَنَّهُ مِنْ سَاسَمٍ ثُمَّ أَخْرِجْهَا فَحَرِّقْهَا بِسُوقِهِمْ قَالَ عياش
فَخَرَجْتُ أَفْعَلُ مَا أَمَرَنِي رَسُولُ اللهِ ﷺ حَتَّى إِذَا دَخَلْتُ إِذَا
النَّاسُ قَدْ لَبِسُوا زِينَتَهُمْ قَالَ فَمَرَرْتُ لأَنْظُرَ إِلَيْهِمْ حَتَّى انْتَهَيْتُ
إِلَى سُتُورٍ عِظَامٍ عَلَى أَبْوَابِ دُورٍ ثَلاثَةٍ فَكَشَفْتُ السِّتْرَ
وَدَخَلْتُ الْبَابَ الأَوْسَطَ فَانْتَهَيْتُ إِلَى قَوْمٍ فِي قَاعَةِ الدَّارِ
فَقُلْتُ أَنَا رُسُولُ رَسُولِ اللهِ وَفَعَلْتُ مَا أَمَرَنِي فَقَبِلُوا وَكَانَ كَمَا
قَالَ ﷺ ابن سعد كر

Ṣuhayb ﵁

Al-Ḥākim and al-Bayhaqī narrated that Ṣuhayb ﵁ said the Messenger of Allah ﷺ said: [149] "It was shown to me that the abode of your emigration was a saline land in the middle of a stony area – Hajar or Yathrib." Ṣuhayb continued: "The Messenger of

Allah ﷺ then went out to al-Madīna and Abū Bakr went with him. I wanted to go out with him but was prevented by some Quraysh riders. That night I kept on my feet and did not sit down until they said: 'Allah relieved you by ailing him with his stomach!' But I was fine. They slept and I slipped out but some of them caught up with me and wanted to take me back. I told them, 'What if I gave you a few ounces of gold in exchange for my freedom?' They let go of me and I took them to Mecca and told them: 'Dig under that door-step and you will find the ounces under it.' Then I left and joined up with the Prophet ﷺ in Qubā' as he was about to leave it. When he saw me, he said: 'Abū Yaḥyā! Your sale has gained threefold.' I replied, 'Messenger of Allah, none was faster than me in reaching you and none but Jibrīl ﷺ told you!'"[214]

عَنْ صُهَيْبٍ رَضِيَ اللهُ عَنْهُ قَالَ قَالَ رَسُولُ اللهِ ﷺ أُرِيتُ دَارَ هِجْرَتِكُمْ سَبْخَةً بَيْنَ ظَهْرَانَيْ حَرَّةٍ فَإِمَّا أَنْ تَكُونَ هَجَرَ وَإِمَّا أَنْ تَكُونَ يَثْرِبَ فَخَرَجَ رَسُولُ اللهِ ﷺ إِلَى الْمَدِينَةِ وَخَرَجَ مَعَهُ أَبُو بَكْرٍ وَكُنْتُ قَدْ هَمَمْتُ بِالْخُرُوجِ مَعَهُ وَصَدَّنِي فِتْيَانٌ مِنْ قُرَيْشٍ فَجَعَلْتُ لَيْلَتِي تِلْكَ أَقُومُ وَلاَ أَقْعُدُ فَقَالُوا قَدْ شَغَلَهُ اللهُ عَنْكُمْ بِبَطْنِهِ وَلَمْ أَكُنْ سَاكِناً فَنَامُوا فَخَرَجْتُ فَلَحِقَنِي مِنْهُمْ نَاسٌ بَعْدَ مَا سِرْتُ يُرِيدُونَ رَدِّي فَقُلْتُ لَهُمْ هَلْ لَكُمْ أَنْ أُعْطِيَكُمْ أَوَاقٍ مِنْ ذَهَبٍ وَحِلَّةً سِيَرَاءَ بِمَكَّةَ وَتُخَلُّونَ سَبِيلِي فَفَعَلُوا فَتَبِعْتُهُمْ إِلَى

[214]Suhayb also offered them two silk mantles. Narrated from Ṣuhayb by al-Ḥākim (3:400=1990 ed. 3:452 *ṣaḥīḥ*), al-Bayhaqī in the *Dalā'il* (2:522-523), al-Bazzār (§2085), and al-Ṭabarānī in *al-Kabīr* (8:31 §7296) cf. al-Haythamī (6:60) and *Fath* (7:228). The first part (without the capture and ransom) is narrated from 'Ā'isha by al-Bukhārī, Aḥmad and others as part of a longer narration with the wording: "I was shown the abode of your emigration. I saw a saline land planted with date palms between two rocks – meaning two rocky fields. Hearing this, many emigrated to Madīna including some of those who had gone to Abyssinia." On "Hajar" see Yāqūt (5:393).

مَكَّةَ فَقُلْتُ احْفُرُوا تَحْتَ أُسْكُفَّةِ الْبَابِ فَإِنَّ تَحْتَهَا الأَوَاقِيَ وَاذْهَبُوا إِلَى فُلَانَهْ بِآيَةِ كَذَا وَكَذَا فَخُذُوا الحِلَّتَيْنِ وَخَرَجْتُ حَتَّى قَدِمْتُ عَلَى رَسُولِ اللهِ ﷺ قَبْلَ أَنْ يَتَحَوَّلَ مِنْهَا فَلَمَّا رَآنِي قَالَ يَا أَبَا يَحْيَى رَبِحَ الْبَيْعُ ثَلَاثاً فَقُلْتُ يَا رَسُولَ اللهِ مَا سَبَقَنِي إِلَيْكَ أَحَدٌ وَمَا أَخْبَرَكَ إِلَّا جِبْرِيلُ ﷺ طب ز ك هق في الدلائل قال الهيثمي فيه جماعة لم أعرفهم مج وأصله عند خ حم دون قصة صهيب رضي الله عنه

Abū Dharr ؓ

Al-Ḥākim – who declared it sound – and al-Bayhaqī narrated that Umm Dharr ؓ said: "I swear by Allah that it is not ʿUthmān that banished Abū Dharr but rather the Messenger of Allah ﷺ who said [to Abū Dharr]: 150 'When the houses reach Salʿ, exit from here.' When the houses reached Salʿ and beyond, Abū Dharr left for al-Shām.[215]

عَنْ عَبْدِ اللهِ بْنِ الصَّامِتِ قَالَ قَالَتْ أُمُّ ذَرٍّ وَاللهِ مَا سَيَّرَ عُثْمَانُ أَبَا ذَرٍّ وَلَكِنْ رَسُولَ اللهِ ﷺ قَالَ إِذَا بَلَغَ الْبُنْيَانُ سَلْعاً – جبل في المدينة – فَاخْرُجْ مِنْهَا قَالَ أَبُو ذَرٍّ فَلَمَّا بَلَغَ الْبُنْيَانُ سَلْعاً وَجَاوَزَ خَرَجَ أَبُو ذَرٍّ إِلَى الشَّامِ ك قال صحيح على شرط الشيخين ابن سعد كر الخلال في السنة وذكره الحافظ في الفتح والسمعاني في فضائل الشام

---

[215] Narrated by Ibn ʿAsākir (66:202) and al-Ḥākim (1990 ed. 3:387 ṣaḥīḥ per the criteria of al-Bukhārī and Muslim), cf. Ibn Saʿd (4:226), al-Khallāl in *al-Sunna* (1:107), Ibn ʿAsākir (1:91, 66:191-192, 66:198), *Fatḥ* (3:274), *al-Iṣāba* (7:16), and *Siyar* (Fikr ed. 3:389=Risāla 2:63).

Salʿ is a mountain in Madīna. They differed as to Abū Dharr's actual name and the correct finding is that his name is Jundub [b. Junāda b. Sakan] رضي الله عنه.

[Abū Dharr first went to al-Shām as narrated in al-Bukhārī, then Muʿāwiya wrote to ʿUthmān complaining that he was declaring asceticism obligatory, whereupon ʿUthmān recalled him to al-Madīna, after which Abū Dharr asked permission to retire to al-Rabadha.[216] [151] The Prophet ﷺ once nicknamed Abū Dharr "Junaydib."][217]

Al-Ḥākim and Abū Nuʿaym narrated that Umm Dharr رضي الله عنها said that when Abū Dharr was about to breathe his last, he said, "I heard the Messenger of Allah ﷺ say to a group that included me: [152] 'Lo! A man from among you shall die in a desert land attended by a troop of the Muslims.' None of that group survives today and each of them died in his village or town, among his people. I am that man, so check the road [for that troop]. "I [Umm Dharr] said: 'How can that be, when the Ḥajj party has already gone and the road is completely deserted?' As I was saying this to him, lo and behold, some riders came within sight of me! I motioned to them with my cloak and they rushed over and came up to me. Then they attended him and stayed with him until they buried him."[218] Among them was Ibn Masʿūd رضي الله عنه.[219] Abū Dharr was in al-Rabadha, a land in between Yanbuʿ and al-Madīna al-Munawwara.

عَنْ أُمِّ ذَرٍّ رَضِيَ اللهُ عَنْهَا قَالَتْ لَمَّا حَضَرَتْ أَبَا ذَرٍّ الْوَفَاةُ قَالَ سَمِعْتُ رَسُولَ اللهِ ﷺ يَقُولُ لِنَفَرٍ أَنَا فِيهِمْ لَيَمُوتَنَّ رَجُلٌ مِنْكُمْ بِفَلَاةٍ مِنَ الْأَرْضِ يَشْهَدُهُ عِصَابَةٌ مِنَ الْمُؤْمِنِينَ وَلَيْسَ مِنْ أُولَئِكَ

[216]Narrated from Zayd b. Wahb by al-Bukhārī and from ʿAbd Allāh b. al-Sāmit by Ibn Saʿd (4:232) with a sound chain according to al-Arna'ūṭ cf. Ibn Ḥibbān (15:54-55).

[217]Narrated from Abū Dharr by Ibn Mājah.

[218]Narrated with good chains from Umm Dharr by al-Ḥākim (3:344-346=1990 ed. 3:388), al-Bayhaqī in the *Dalā'il* (6:401-402), Abū Nuʿaym (1:169-170), Ibn Ḥibbān (15:57-61 §6670-6671 *qawī*), Ibn ʿAbd al-Barr in *al-Istīʿāb* (1:215-217=1:253-254), Ibn al-Athīr in *Usd al-Ghāba* (1:358), cf. Ibn Saʿd (4:232-233), Ibn Abī ʿĀṣim in *al-Āḥād* (2:229 §984), Aḥmad and al-Bazzār (9:447-448 §4060).

[219]Cf. Ibn Saʿd (4:233-234).

النَّفَرِ أَحَدٌ إِلاَّ وَقَدْ مَاتَ فِي قَرْيَةٍ وَجَمَاعَةٍ فَأَنَا ذَلِكَ الرَّجُلُ
فَأَبْصِرِي الطَّرِيقَ فَقُلْتُ أَنَّى وَقَدْ ذَهَبَ الحَاجُّ وَتَقَطَّعَتِ الطَّرِيقُ
فَبَيْنَمَا أَنَا وَهُوَ كَذَلِكَ إِذَا أَنَا بِرِجَالٍ عَلَى رِحَالِهِمْ فَأَلَحْتُ بِثَوْبِي
فَأَسْرَعُوا إِلَيَّ حَتَّى وَقَفُوا عَلَيَّ فَحَضَرُوهُ وَقَامُوا عَلَيْهِ حَتَّى دَفَنُوهُ
حم ز حب ابن سعد ك هق في الدلائل حل وفي المعرفة ابن أبي عاصم في الآحاد
كر قال الهيثمى رواه أحمد من طريقين ورجال الطريق الأولى رجال الصحيح ورواه
البزار بنحوه باختصار وهذا اللفظ للسيوطي في الخصائص اختصره ورواه بالمعنى
وَفِيهِم ابْنُ مَسْعودٍ رَضِيَ اللهُ عَنْهُ وَكَانَ بِالرَّبَذَةِ وَهِيَ أَرْضٌ بَينَ
يَنْبُعَ وَالْمَدِينَةِ الْمُنَوَّرَةِ ك هق في الدلائل كر سيرة ابن هشام والمدائني في التاريخ

Ibn Abī Shayba narrated that Abū Dharr ﷺ said: "The Messenger of Allah ﷺ said <to me>: 153 'Woe to you when I am gone!' I wept and said, 'Messenger of Allah! Am I really going to survive you?' He said: 'Yes. When you see construction on Mount Salʿ, go and live with the Bedouins in the land of Quḍāʿa. <It is as near as one bow's length or two, or one spear's length or two.>'"[220]

عَنْ أَبِي ذَرٍّ رَضِيَ اللهُ عَنْهُ قَالَ رَسُولُ اللهِ ﷺ وَيْحَكَ بَعْدِي
فَبَكَيْتُ فَقُلْتُ يَا رَسُولَ اللهِ وَإِنِّي لَبَاقٍ بَعْدَكَ قَالَ نَعَمْ فَإِذَا
رَأَيْتَ الْبِنَاءَ عَلَى جَبَلِ سَلْعٍ فَالْحَقْ بِالْغَرْبِ من أَرْضِ قُضَاعَةَ

[220]Narrated by Ibn al-Aʿrābī in his *Muʿjam* (1:75 §109), Ibn Abī Shayba with a weak chain according to Ibn ʿAsākir (66:200), al-Dāraquṭnī in his *ʿIlal* (6:236 §1097), and al-Dhahabī in the *Siyar* (Fikr ed. 3:394=Risala ed. 2:70). Al-Būṣīrī in *Itḥāf al-Khiyara al-Mahara* (8:68 §7493) refers it to "Ibn Abī Shayba through Ṭalḥa b. ʿAmr who is weak." Al-Nabhānī omitted the bracketed segments.

فَإِنَّهُ سَيَأْتِي يَوْمٌ قَابَ قَوْسٍ أَوْ قَوْسَيْنِ أَوْ رُمْحٍ أَوْ رُمْحَيْنِ معجم
ابن الأعرابي قط في العلل كر وعزاه البوصيري إلى ابن أبي شيبة في إتحاف الخيرة المهرة

Ibn Sa'd narrated that Abū Dharr ﷺ said: "The Prophet ﷺ said: 154 'Abū Dharr! What will you do when you see leaders inclined to [hoard up] booty?' I replied: 'I shall strike with my sword.' He said: 'Shall I not show you a better way? a Bear with it until you meet me.'"[221]

عَنْ أَبِي ذَرٍّ رَضِيَ اللهُ عَنْهُ قَالَ رَسُولُ اللهِ ﷺ يَا أَبَا ذَرٍّ كَيْفَ أَنْتَ إِذَا كَانَتْ عَلَيْكَ أُمَرَاءُ يَسْتَأْثِرُونَ بِالْفَيْءِ قُلْتُ إِذَنْ أَضْرِبُ بِسَيْفِي قَالَ أَفَلَا أَدُلُّكَ عَلَى مَا هُوَ خَيْرٌ مِنْ ذَلِكَ إِصْبِرْ حَتَّى تَلْقَانِي ابن سعد الدولابي في الكنى

Abū Nu'aym and Ibn 'Asākir narrated that Abū Dharr ﷺ said: 155 "The Messenger of Allah ﷺ informed me that they would not be empowered to kill me nor would they seduce me from my

[221]Narrated from Abū Dharr by Ibn Sa'd (4:622) and Dūlābī in *al-Kunā wal-Asmā'* (1:285 §1015). Something similar is narrated by Aḥmad through seven chains graded weak by al-Arna'ūt (cf. 35:217-444 §21291, §21382, §21551, §21558-21559) but see al-Talīdī, *Itḥāf Ahl al-Wafā* (p. 289 n.5 *sanaduhu ṣaḥīḥ* from Asmā' bint Yazīd through Shahr b. Ḥawshab); al-Ṭabarānī in *al-Awsaṭ* (3:59 §2474); Ibn Abī 'Āṣim in *al-Sunna* (§1104-1105); Ibn Ḥibbān (15:52-56 §6668-6669); Bazzār (§4057); and Ibn 'Asākir (1:147-148) cf. al-Haythamī (5:223) and, with good confirmatory chains, Abū Dāwūd and Ibn Mājah. Shahr is reliable according to Bukhārī, Tirmidhī, Aḥmad, Ibn Ma'īn, Abū Zur'a, Ya'qūb b. Sufyān, Ṣāliḥ Jazra, and al-'Ijlī; also Ibn al-Ṣalāḥ in *Ṣiyānat Ṣaḥīḥ Muslim* (p. 122), Ibn Daqīq al-'Īd in *al-Imām* (in *Naṣb* 1:18), Ibn al-Jawzī in *al-Taḥqīq*, al-Nawawī in the introduction to *Sharḥ Ṣaḥīḥ Muslim* (1:92-93), al-Dhahabī in the *Siyar* (Risala ed. 4:378), Ibn Hajar in the *Fath* (1989 ed. 3:65) and *Natā'ij al-Afkār* (1:361), and Ibn 'Abd al-Hādī in *al-Muḥarrar* (p. 105), cf. Mamdūḥ, *al-Ta'rīf* (2:178) and 'Itr, *al-Imām al-Tirmidhī* (p. 221). In one version in Abū Dāwūd the Prophet ﷺ instructs Abū Dharr not to leave his home and, should an intruder try to kill him, cover himself with a sheet rather than fight back. In Aḥmad with a sound chain: the Prophet ﷺ keeps repeating to Abū Dharr the verse ﴾**And for those who fear Allāh He prepares a way out and He provides for them from a source they never expected**﴿ (65:2-3) until the latter became drowsy.

Religion. <[a] He informed me that I entered Islam alone and would die alone and be risen on the Day of Resurrection alone>."[222] **[486]**

عَنْ أَبِي ذَرٍّ رَضِيَ اللهُ عَنْهُ قَالَ أَخْبَرَنِي رَسُولُ اللهِ ﷺ أَنَّهُمْ لَنْ يُسَلَّطُوا عَلَى قَتْلِي وَلَنْ يَفْتِنُونِي عَنْ دِينِي وَأَخْبَرَنِي أَنِّي أَسْلَمْتُ فَرْداً وَأَمُوتُ فَرْداً وَأُبْعَثُ يَوْمَ الْقِيَامَةِ فَرْداً كر خط في رواية الصحابة عن التابعين

Abū Nu'aym also narrated from Asmā' bint Yazīd رضى الله عنها that the Prophet ﷺ found Abū Dharr sleeping in the Mosque and said to him: [156] "Do I see you sleeping in the Mosque?" He replied, "Where can I sleep when I have no other house?" The Prophet ﷺ said: "What will you do when they expel you from it?" "I shall go to *al-Shām* <for verily *al-Shām* is the land of emigration, the land of the Final Gathering, and the land of Prophets. So I shall be one of its dwellers>." "What will you do when they expel you from al-Shām?" "I shall return here." "What if they expel you a second time?" "Then I shall take up my sword and fight until I die!" The Prophet ﷺ said: [a] "I shall show you a better way. Let yourself be led wherever they lead you and let them steer you wherever they steer you until you meet me in that very state."[223]

عَنْ أَسْمَاءَ بِنْتِ يَزِيدَ أَنَّ أَبَا ذَرٍّ الْغِفَارِيَّ كَانَ يَخْدُمُ النَّبِيَّ ﷺ فَإِذَا فَرَغَ مِنْ خِدْمَتِهِ آوَى إِلَى الْمَسْجِدِ فَكَانَ هُوَ بَيْتُهُ يَضْطَجِعُ فِيهِ فَدَخَلَ رَسُولُ اللهِ ﷺ الْمَسْجِدَ لَيْلَةً فَوَجَدَ أَبَا ذَرٍّ

[222]Narrated by Ibn 'Asākir (66:194) and al-Khaṭīb in his *Riwāyat a-Ṣaḥāba 'an al-Tābi'īn* as epitomized by Ibn Ḥajar in his *Nuzhat al-Sāmi'īn*. See further below for the bracketed segment.

[223]Narrated by Aḥmad through two chains, one of them through Shahr b. Ḥawshab as documented in the next to previous note. Al-Nabhānī skipped the bracketed segment.

نَائِمًا مُنْجَدِلاً فِي الْمَسْجِدِ فَنَكَتَهُ رَسُولُ اللهِ ﷺ بِرِجْلِهِ حَتَّى اسْتَوَى جَالِسًا فَقَالَ لَهُ رَسُولُ اللهِ ﷺ أَلاَ أَرَاكَ نَائِمًا قَالَ أَبُو ذَرٍّ يَا رَسُولَ اللهِ فَأَيْنَ أَنَامُ وهَلْ لِي مِنْ بَيْتٍ غَيْرُهُ فَجَلَسَ إِلَيْهِ رَسُولُ اللهِ ﷺ فَقَالَ لَهُ كَيْفَ أَنْتَ إِذَا أَخْرَجُوكَ مِنْهُ قَالَ إِذَنْ أَلْحَقَ بِالشَّامِ فَإِنَّ الشَّامَ أَرْضُ الْهِجْرَةِ وَأَرْضُ الْمَحْشَرِ وَأَرْضُ الأَنْبِيَاءِ فَأَكُونُ رَجُلاً مِنْ أَهْلِهَا قَالَ لَهُ كَيْفَ أَنْتَ إِذَا أَخْرَجُوكَ مِنَ الشَّامِ قَالَ إِذَنْ أَرْجِعَ إِلَيْهِ فَيَكُونَ هُوَ بَيْتِي وَمَنْزِلِي قَالَ لَهُ كَيْفَ أَنْتَ إِذَا أَخْرَجُوكَ مِنْهُ الثَّانِيَةَ قَالَ إِذَنْ آخُذَ سَيْفِي فَأُقَاتِلَ عَنِّي حَتَّى أَمُوتَ قَالَ فَكَشَّرَ إِلَيْهِ رَسُولُ اللهِ ﷺ فَأَثْبَتَهُ بِيَدِهِ قَالَ أَدُلُّكَ عَلَى خَيْرٍ مِنْ ذَلِكَ قَالَ بَلَى بِأَبِي أَنْتَ وَأُمِّي يَا نَبِيَّ اللهِ قَالَ رَسُولُ اللهِ ﷺ تَنْقَادُ لَهُمْ حَيْثُ قَادُوكَ وَتَنْسَاقُ لَهُمْ حَيْثُ سَاقُوكَ حَتَّى تَلْقَانِي وَأَنْتَ عَلَى ذَلِكَ حم د جه ز طب حب ابن أبي عاصم في السنة وأورده الحافظ ابن عبد الهادي في فضائل الشام

Al-Hārith b. Usāma narrated from Abū al-Muthannā al-Mulaykī that the Messenger of Allah ﷺ would say to his Companions when he came to them: 157 "'Uwaymir is the wise man of my Community and Jundub is the fugitive of my Community, he shall live alone and die alone, and Allah shall raise him alone."[224]

[224]Narrated by al-Hārith *mursal* through trustworthy narrators in his *Musnad* (2:925) cf. Ibn Hajar, *al-Matālib al-'Āliya* (§4112), al-Suyūtī, *al-Jāmi' al-Saghīr* (§5645), *Fayd* (4:368), and *Kanz* (§33132). Narrated without mention of Jundub by Ibn 'Asākir and al-

'Uwaymir is Abū al-Dardā' [ʿĀmir b. Mālik] and Jundub is Abū Dharr رضي الله عنهما.

عَنْ أَبِي الْمُثَنَّى الْمُلَيْكِيِّ مُرْسَلاً قَالَ إِنَّ رَسُولَ اللهِ ﷺ كَانَ إِذَا خَرَجَ إِلَى أَصْحَابِهِ قَالَ عُوَيْمِرٌ حَكِيمُ أُمَّتِي وَجُنْدَبٌ طريدُ أُمَّتِي يَعِيشُ وَحْدَهُ وَيَمُوتُ وَحْدَهُ وَاللهُ يَبْعَثُهُ وَحْدَهُ مسند الحارث بسند مرسل صحيح قال المناوي في فيض القدير لعل صوابه الأملوكي بفتح الهمزة وسكون الميم وضم اللام وآخره كاف نسبة إلى أملوك بطن من ردمان قبيلة من رعين

Ibn Saʿd narrated that Muḥammad b. Sīrīn said that the Messenger of Allah ﷺ said to Abū Dharr: [158] "When construction reaches Salʿ, depart from here," – he motioned with his hand towards al-Shām – "and it does not seem to me your rulers shall call you back." He replied: "Messenger of Allah, should I not fight whoever comes between me and your orders?" The Prophet ﷺ said: "No! [a] Hear and obey, even an Abyssinian slave." When this took place, he went out to al-Shām. Then Muʿāwiya wrote to ʿUthmān that Abū Dharr was corrupting the people in Shām, so ʿUthmān sent for him, whereupon he came back then went back out to al-Rabadha. He arrived there as the prayer had been raised and the imām was an Abyssinian slave employed by ʿUthmān. He stood back but Abū Dharr told him, "Step forward and lead the prayer, for I was commanded to hear and obey, even an Abyssinian slave – meaning you."[225] Al-Rabadha is a land in between Yanbuʿ and al-Madīna al-Munawwara.

Tabarānī in *al-Awsat* and *Musnad al-Shāmiyyīn* (2:88 §967) on the occasion of Abū al-Dardā's single-handed dislodging of the *Kuffār* from a position overlooking the Prophet ﷺ in the battle of Uḥud cf. Ibn ʿAbd al-Barr, *al-Istīʿāb* (4:1646), Ibn Kathīr in his *Tafsīr* (1:426 for Q 3:153), *Siyar* (Fikr ed. 4:15=Risala ed. 2:339), *al-Iṣāba* (4:747), *al-Jāmiʿ al-Saghīr* (§3752), *Fayd* (3:396), and *Kanz* (§33508). Narrated also without mention of 'Uwaymir cf. n. 226. Abū al-Muthannā is the *Tābiʿī* Damdam al-Ḥimṣī al-Umlūkī.

[225] See also n. 215.

عَنْ مُحَمَّدِ بْنِ سِيرِينَ عَنْ أَبِي ذَرٍّ رَضِيَ اللهُ عَنْهُ أَنَّ رَسُولَ اللهِ ﷺ قَالَ لَهُ يَا أَبَا ذَرٍّ إِذَا بَلَغَ الْبِنَاءُ سَلْعًا فَاخْرُجْ وَقَالَ بِيَدِهِ ضَرَبَ بِهِ نَحْوَ الشَّامِ وَقَالَ وَلاَ أَرَى أُمَرَاءَكُمْ إِلاَّ سَيُحُولُونَ بَيْنَكَ وَبَيْنَ ذَلِكَ قُلْتُ يَحُولُونَ بَيْنِي وَبَيْنَ أَمْرِكَ الَّذِي أَمَرْتَنِي بِهِ قَالَ نَعَمْ قَالَ أَبُو ذَرٍّ يَا رَسُولَ اللهِ أَفَلاَ آخُذُ سَيْفِي فَأَضْرِبُ بِهِ مَنْ يَحُولُ بَيْنِي وَبَيْنَ أَمْرِكَ الَّذِي تَأْمُرُنِي بِهِ قَالَ وَلَكِنْ تَسْمَعُ وَتُطِيعُ وَلَوْ لِعَبْدٍ حَبَشِيٍّ فَلَمَّا بَلَغَ الْبِنَاءُ سَلْعًا وَذَلِكَ فِي إِمْرَةِ عُثْمَانَ بْنِ عَفَّانَ خَرَجَ أَبُو ذَرٍّ إِلَى الشَّامِ فَمَالَ إِلَيْهِ أَهْلُ الشَّامِ وَكَتَبَ مُعَاوِيَةُ إِلَى عُثْمَانَ إِنْ كَانَتْ لَكَ فِي الشَّامِ حَاجَةٌ فَأَرْسِلْ إِلَى أَبِي ذَرٍّ فَكَتَبَ إِلَيْهِ عُثْمَانُ أَنْ أَقْبِلْ فَلَمَّا قَرَأَ الْكِتَابَ أَقْبَلَ وَقَالَ سَمْعٌ وَطَاعَةٌ قَالَ فَجَعَلَ يَمُرُّ فِي مَرْدُودٍ وَمَرْدُودٌ فِيهِ فُلُوسٍ فَقَالُوا انْظُرُوا إِلَى رِقَابِكُمْ هَذَا يَزْهَدُ فِي الدُّنْيَا وَهَذِهِ الدَّنَانِيرُ مَعَهُ فَلَمَّا نَظَرُوا إِلَى فُلُوسٍ فَارْتَحَلَ بِأَهْلِهِ حَتَّى أَتَى الْمَدِينَةَ فَأَتَى عُثْمَانَ فَسَلَّمَ عَلَيْهِ فَقَالَ عِنْدِي يَا أَبَا ذَرٍّ هَاهُنَا تَغْدُو عَلَيْكَ اللَّقَاحُ وَتَرُوحُ قَالَ الدُّنْيَا لاَ حَاجَةَ لِي فِيهَا ائْذَنْ لِي فَأَخْرُجُ إِلَى الْمَدِينَةِ قَالَ قَدْ أَذِنْتُ لَكَ قَالَ فَخَرَجَ أَبُو ذَرٍّ لِلصَّلاَةِ فَقَالَ مَنْ عَامِلُ هَذَا الْمَاءِ قَالُوا هَذَا فَإِذَا هُوَ عَبْدٌ حَبَشِيٌّ فَقَالَ اللهُ

أَكْبَرُ صَدَقَ اللهُ عَزَّ وَجَلَّ وَرَسُولُهُ أُمِرْتُ أَنْ أَسْمَعَ وَأُطِيعَ وَلَوْ لِعَبْدٍ حَبَشِيٍّ فَتَقَدَّمْ ابن سعد كر والخلال في السنة وذكره الحافظ في الفتح والسمعاني في الفضائل

Ibn Isḥāq and al-Bayhaqī narrated that Ibn Mas'ūd ﷺ said that when the Messenger of Allah ﷺ marched to Tabūk certain men stayed behind, after which Abū Dharr went out after him. One of the Muslim sentries sighted him and said, "Messenger of Allah, there is a man walking on the road [behind]." The Messenger of Allah ﷺ said: 159 "Be Abū Dharr!" The people kept watch then said, "Messenger of Allah, it is – by Allah – Abū Dharr!" Hearing this, he said: a "Allah have mercy on Abū Dharr! He walks alone, he shall die alone, and he shall be resurrected alone." Then time did whatever work it did and Abū Dharr was banished to al-Rabadha to die there, in the sole company of his wife and son. He was placed on the roadside when a riding party passed by, among them 'Abd Allāh b. Mas'ūd. He enquired what this was and they said this was body of Abū Dharr. Ibn Mas'ūd said, "The Messenger of Allah ﷺ spoke the truth! He said: "Allah have mercy on Abū Dharr! He walks alone, he shall die alone, and he shall be resurrected alone." Then he dismounted and attended to him in person.[226]

عَنِ ابْنِ مَسْعُودٍ رَضِيَ اللهُ عَنْهُ قَالَ لَمَّا سَارَ رَسُولُ اللهِ ﷺ إِلَى تَبُوكٍ تَخَلَّفَ رِجَالٌ ثُمَّ لَحِقَهُ أَبُو ذَرٍّ فَنَظَرَ نَاظِرٌ مِنَ الْمُسْلِمِينَ فَقَالَ يَا رَسُولَ اللهِ إِنَّ هَذَا الرَّجُلَ يَمْشِي عَلَى الطَّرِيقِ وَحْدَهُ فَقَالَ رَسُولُ اللهِ ﷺ كُنْ أَبَا ذَرٍّ فَلَمَّا تَأَمَّلَهُ الْقَوْمُ قَالُوا يَا رَسُولَ

226Narrated from Ibn Mas'ūd by al-Ḥākim (3:50-51=1990 ed. 3:52) with a very weak *mursal* chain through Yazīd b. Sufyān who is discarded and Ibn Isḥāq cf. Ibn Ḥibbān's *Thiqāt* (2:94), *Iṣāba* (7:129), and *Siyar* (Fikr ed. 3:384-385=Risala ed. 2:56-57); and al-Bayhaqī in the *Dalā'il*.

The Prophet's ﷺ Knowledge of the Unseen • **137**

اللهِ هُوَ وَاللهِ أَبُو ذَرٍّ! فَقَالَ رَسُولُ اللهِ ﷺ رَحِمَ اللهُ أَبَا ذَرٍّ يَمْشِي وَحْدَهُ وَيَمُوتُ وَحْدَهُ وَيُبْعَثُ وَحْدَهُ فَضَرَبَ الدَّهْرَ مِنْ ضَرْبِهِ وَسُيِّرَ أَبُو ذَرٍّ إِلَى الرَّبَذَةِ فَلَمَّا حَضَرَهُ الْمَوْتُ أَوْصَى امْرَأَتَهُ وَغُلَامَهُ إِذَا مُتُّ فَاغْسِلَانِي وَكَفِّنَانِي ثُمَّ احْمِلَانِي فَضَعَانِي عَلَى قَارِعَةِ الطَّرِيقِ فَأَوَّلُ رَكْبٍ يَمُرُّونَ بِكُمْ فَقُولُوا هَذَا أَبُو ذَرٍّ فَلَمَّا مَاتَ فَعَلُوا بِهِ كَذَلِكَ فَاطَّلَعَ رَكْبٌ فَمَا عَلِمُوا بِهِ حَتَّى كَادَتْ رَكَائِبُهُمْ تَطَأُ سَرِيرَهُ فَإِذَا ابْنُ مَسْعُودٍ فِي رَهْطٍ مِنْ أَهْلِ الْكُوفَةِ فَقَالُوا مَا هَذَا فَقِيلَ جِنَازَةُ أَبِي ذَرٍّ فَاسْتَهَلَّ ابْنُ مَسْعُودٍ رَضِيَ اللهُ عَنْهُ يَبْكِي فَقَالَ صَدَقَ رَسُولُ اللهِ ﷺ يَرْحَمُ اللهُ أَبَا ذَرٍّ يَمْشِي وَحْدَهُ وَيَمُوتُ وَحْدَهُ وَيُبْعَثُ وَحْدَهُ فَنَزَلَ فَوَلِيَهُ بِنَفْسِهِ حَتَّى أَجَنَّهُ ك عن ابن إسحاق وصححه قال الذهبي فيه إرسال هق في الدلائل

[Abū Hurayra ؓ similarly decried the governor of Madīna Marwān b. al-Hakam, warned of a terrible disaster about to befall the Arabs, kept to himself many of the Prophetic narrations touching on the *fitan*, and prayed for death before the year 60, the year Yazīd b. Muʿāwiya came to power.]

Abū al-Dardāʼ ؓ

Al-Bayhaqī and Abū Nuʿaym narrated from Abū al-Dardāʼ ؓ: "I said, Messenger of Allah, I have heard that you said that many people shall renege after their belief." He said: 160 "Yes, but you are not of them." <Abū al-Dardāʼ died before ʿUthmān was killed.>[227]

---

[227]Narrated by al-Bukhārī in *al-Tārīkh al-Saghīr* (1:60 §226), al-Tabarānī in *al-Kabīr* (1:89 §137) and *Musnad al-Shāmiyyīn* (1:167 §280), Ibn Abī ʿĀsim in *al-Āḥād* (1:129

عَنْ أَبِي الدَّرْدَاءِ رَضِيَ اللهُ عَنْهُ قَالَ قُلْتُ يَا رَسُولَ اللهِ بَلَغَنِي أَنَّكَ تَقُولُ لَيَرْتَدَنَّ أَقْوَامٌ بَعْدَ إِيمَانِهِمْ قَالَ أَجَلْ وَلَسْتَ مِنْهُمْ فَتُوُفِّيَ أَبُو الدَّرْدَاءِ قَبْلَ أَنْ يُقْتَلَ عُثْمَانُ رَضِيَ اللهُ عَنْهُ هق في الدلائل كر ويروى بإسناد صحيح بلفظ لَيَكْفُرَنَّ خ في التاريخ الأوسط طب ورجاله رجال الصحيح غير أبي عبدالله الاشعري وهو ثقة ومسند الشاميين ابن أبي عاصم في الآحاد والديات أبو نعيم في المعرفة الفريابي في صفة المنافق كر

Al-Ṭayālisī narrated from Yazīd b. Abī Ḥabīb that two men appeared before Abū al-Dardā' quarelling over ownership of a span *(shibr)* of earth. Abū al-Dardā' said, "I heard the Messenger of Allah ﷺ say: 161 'When you are in a certain land and hear two men quarrelling over ownership of a span of earth, depart from that land.'" Abū al-Dardā' departed for al-Shām.[228]

عَنْ يَزِيدَ بْنِ أَبِي حَبِيبٍ أَنَّ رَجُلَيْنِ اخْتَصَمَا إِلَى أَبِي الدَّرْدَاءِ رَضِيَ اللهُ عَنْهُ فِي شِبْرٍ مِنَ الأَرْضِ فَقَالَ أَبُو الدَّرْدَاءِ إِنِّي سَمِعْتُ رَسُولَ اللهِ ﷺ يَقُولُ ثُمَّ إِذَا كُنْتَ فِي أَرْضٍ فَسَمِعْتَ رَجُلَيْنِ يَخْتَصِمَانِ فِي شِبْرِ أَرْضٍ فَاخْرُجْ مِنْهَا فَخَرَجَ أَبُو الدَّرْدَاءِ فَأَتَى الشَّامَ ط طب بإسناد رجاله ثقات لكنه مرسل مج

§141 and 4:81 §2037), and others with chains of trustworthy narrators cf. – without the bracketed segment – al-Haythamī (9:367), al-Dhahabī, *Siyar* (Fikr ed. 10:6=Risala ed. 11:518), and al-Firyābī, *Sifat al-Munāfiq* (p. 79).

[228]Narrated by al-Ṭayālisī in his *Musnad* (1:132 §983) and al-Ṭabarānī in *al-Kabīr* both with a strong *mursal* chain missing the link to Abū al-Dardā' cf. al-Haythamī (4:174). Cf. hadith from Abū Dharr, "You will conquer a land where the *qīrāṭ* is mentioned..." see below, section "His ﷺ Foretelling the Killing of Certain People and Conquest of Cities."

Al-Bayhaqī and Abū Nu'aym narrated that Jubayr b. Nufayr ؓ said that Abū al-Dardā' used to worship an idol and that 'Abd Allāh b. Rawāḥa, Muḥammad b. Maslama entered his house and broke his idol. When Abū al-Dardā' returned and saw this he said [to himself]: "Woe to you! Should you not defend **[487]** yourself?" Then he went to the Prophet ﷺ. When Ibn Rawāḥa saw him coming, he said: "Here comes Abū al-Dardā' and I do not think he comes except to pick a fight." But the Prophet ﷺ said: [162] "No, he only comes to submit, for my Lord has promised me Abū al-Dardā' would submit." Then he came over and accepted Islam.[229]

عَنْ جُبَيْرِ بْنِ نُفَيْرٍ قَالَ كَانَ أَبُو الدَّرْدَاءِ يَعْبُدُ صَنَماً وَأَنَّ عَبْدَ
اللهِ بْنَ رَوَاحَةَ وَمُحَمَّدَ بْنَ مَسْلَمَةَ دَخَلاَ بَيْتَهُ فَكَسَرَا صَنَمَهُ
فَرَجَعَ أَبُو الدَّرْدَاءِ فَرَآهُ فَقَالَ وَيْحَكَ هَلاَّ دَفَعْتَ عَنْ نَفْسِكَ ثُمَّ
ذَهَبَ إِلَى النَّبِيِّ ﷺ فَنَظَرَ إِلَيْهِ ابْنُ رَوَاحَةَ مُقْبِلاً فَقَالَ هَذَا أَبُو
الدَّرْدَاءِ وَمَا أُرَى جَاءَ إِلاَّ فِي طَلَبِنَا فَقَالَ النَّبِيُّ ﷺ لاَ إِنَّمَا جَاءَ
لِيُسْلِمَ فَإِنَّ رَبِّي وَعَدَنِي بِأَبِي الدَّرْدَاءِ أَنْ يُسْلِمَ ابن سعد ك هق كر

Ḥāṭib b. Abī Balta'a ؓ

The Two Masters [al-Bukhārī and Muslim] narrated that 'Alī ؓ said: "The Messenger of Allah ﷺ sent me out with al-Zubayr and al-Miqdād, saying: [163] 'Ride out until you reach the meadow of Khākh. There, you will find a woman travelling with a letter. Seize the letter from her.' We set out on horseback at top speed until we reached the meadow. Lo and behold, there was the woman. We said to her: 'Hand over the letter.' She replied, 'I do not have any letter!' We said, 'You will either hand over the letter

[229]Narrated by Ibn Sa'd in the chapter on Abū al-Dardā', al-Ḥākim (3:336-337), al-Bayhaqī in the *Dalā'il* (6:301), and Ibn 'Asākir (47:106) cf. *Siyar* (Fikr ed. 4:16=2:340).

or take off your clothes.' She took it out of her braids. We brought the letter to the Messenger of Allah ﷺ and it contained a message from Ḥāṭib b. Abī Balta'a to some of the pagans in Mecca informing them of some of the activities of the Messenger of Allah ﷺ. The Messenger of Allah said: 'Ḥāṭib! What is this?' Ḥāṭib replied, "Messenger of Allah, do not hasten to condemn me. I was intimate with the Quraysh' – meaning, an ally of theirs – 'but did not originate from them, while the other emigrants with you had relatives in Mecca protecting their dependents and property there. Since I laxked relatives among them I desired to oblige them with a favor for which they might protect my family. I never did this out of reneging nor in preference of disbelief after Islam!' The Messenger of Allah ﷺ said: 'Lo! [a] Ḥāṭib has told you the truth.' 'Umar said, 'Messenger of Allah, allow me to cut off the head of this hypocrite.' The Messenger of Allah ﷺ said: 'Ḥāṭib took part in Badr. Who knows? [b] Perhaps Allah has already looked at those who fought at Badr and said, Do what you like, I have forgiven you!' Then Allah revealed the Sūra [beginning] ﴿**O you who believe! Choose not My enemy and your enemy for friends. Do you give them friendship when they disbelieve in that truth which has come unto you, driving out the messenger and you because you believe in Allah, your Lord? If you have come forth to strive in My way and seeking My good pleasure, (show them not friendship). Do you show friendship unto them in secret, when I am best Aware of what you hide and what you proclaim? And whosoever does it among you, he verily has strayed from the right way**﴾ (60:1)."[230]

عَنْ عَلِيٍّ رَضِيَ اللهُ عَنْهُ بَعَثَنِي رَسُولُ اللهِ ﷺ أَنَا وَالزُّبَيْرَ
وَالْمِقْدَادَ بْنَ الأَسْوَدِ قَالَ انْطَلِقُوا حَتَّى تَأْتُوا رَوْضَةَ خَاخٍ فَإِنَّ
بِهَا ظَعِينَةً وَمَعَهَا كِتَابٌ فَخُذُوهُ مِنْهَا فَانْطَلَقْنَا تَعَادَى بِنَا خَيْلُنَا

[230]Narrated in the *Sahīhayn*, *Sunan*, and *Musnad*, some without the Qur'anic verse. Khākh lies between Mecca and Madīna. Some commentators mentioned that Ḥāṭib was from Yemen.

حَتَّى انْتَهَيْنَا إِلَى الرَّوْضَةِ فَإِذَا نَحْنُ بِالظَّعِينَةِ فَقُلْنَا أَخْرِجِي الْكِتَابَ فَقَالَتْ مَا مَعِي مِنْ كِتَابٍ فَقُلْنَا لَتُخْرِجِنَّ الْكِتَابَ أَوْ لَنُلْقِيَنَّ الثِّيَابَ فَأَخْرَجَتْهُ مِنْ عِقَاصِهَا فَأَتَيْنَا بِهِ رَسُولَ اللَّهِ ﷺ فَإِذَا فِيهِ مِنْ حَاطِبِ بْنِ أَبِي بَلْتَعَةَ إِلَى أُنَاسٍ مِنَ الْمُشْرِكِينَ مِنْ أَهْلِ مَكَّةَ يُخْبِرُهُمْ بِبَعْضِ أَمْرِ رَسُولِ اللَّهِ ﷺ فَقَالَ رَسُولُ اللَّهِ ﷺ يَا حَاطِبُ مَا هَذَا قَالَ يَا رَسُولَ اللَّهِ لاَ تَعْجَلْ عَلَيَّ إِنِّي كُنْتُ امْرَأً مُلْصَقًا فِي قُرَيْشٍ وَلَمْ أَكُنْ مِنْ أَنْفُسِهَا وَكَانَ مَنْ مَعَكَ مِنَ الْمُهَاجِرِينَ لَهُمْ قَرَابَاتٌ بِمَكَّةَ يَحْمُونَ بِهَا أَهْلِيهِمْ وَأَمْوَالَهُمْ فَأَحْبَبْتُ إِذْ فَاتَنِي ذَلِكَ مِنَ النَّسَبِ فِيهِمْ أَنْ أَتَّخِذَ عِنْدَهُمْ يَدًا يَحْمُونَ بِهَا قَرَابَتِي وَمَا فَعَلْتُ كُفْرًا وَلاَ ارْتِدَادًا وَلاَ رِضًا بِالْكُفْرِ بَعْدَ الإِسْلاَمِ فَقَالَ رَسُولُ اللَّهِ ﷺ لَقَدْ صَدَقَكُمْ قَالَ عُمَرُ يَا رَسُولَ اللَّهِ دَعْنِي أَضْرِبْ عُنُقَ هَذَا الْمُنَافِقِ قَالَ إِنَّهُ قَدْ شَهِدَ بَدْرًا وَمَا يُدْرِيكَ لَعَلَّ اللَّهَ أَنْ يَكُونَ قَدِ اطَّلَعَ عَلَى أَهْلِ بَدْرٍ فَقَالَ اعْمَلُوا مَا شِئْتُمْ فَقَدْ غَفَرْتُ لَكُمْ فَأَنْزَلَ اللَّهُ السُّورَةَ ﴿يَٰٓأَيُّهَا ٱلَّذِينَ ءَامَنُوا۟ لَا تَتَّخِذُوا۟ عَدُوِّى وَعَدُوَّكُمْ أَوْلِيَآءَ تُلْقُونَ إِلَيْهِم بِٱلْمَوَدَّةِ وَقَدْ كَفَرُوا۟ بِمَا جَآءَكُم مِّنَ ٱلْحَقِّ يُخْرِجُونَ ٱلرَّسُولَ وَإِيَّاكُمْ ۙ أَن تُؤْمِنُوا۟ بِٱللَّهِ رَبِّكُمْ إِن كُنتُمْ خَرَجْتُمْ جِهَٰدًا فِى سَبِيلِى وَٱبْتِغَآءَ مَرْضَاتِى ۚ تُسِرُّونَ إِلَيْهِم بِٱلْمَوَدَّةِ

وَأَنَا۠ أَعْلَمُ بِمَآ أَخْفَيْتُمْ وَمَآ أَعْلَنتُمْ ۚ وَمَن يَفْعَلْهُ مِنكُمْ فَقَدْ ضَلَّ سَوَآءَ ٱلسَّبِيلِ

﴿١﴾ المتحنة ق ت د حم

Ibn Isḥāq and al-Bayhaqī narrated that ʿUrwa said: "When the Messenger of Allah ﷺ decided to march on Mecca, Ḥāṭib b. Abī Baltaʿa wrote to the Quraysh informing them of his decision then gave the message to a woman of Muzayna together with a sum of money in exchange for her conveying it to the Quraysh. She put the message inside her headdress then entwined her braids over it and went out with it. Then news of what Ḥāṭib had done came to the Messenger of Allah ﷺ from heaven so he sent ʿAlī b. Abī Ṭālib and al-Zubayr b. al-ʿAwwām, saying: [164] 'Find a woman with whom Ḥāṭib sent a letter to the Quraysh warning them.'"[231]

عَنْ عُرْوَةَ بْنِ الزُّبَيْرِ وَغَيْرِهِ قَالُوا لَمَّا أَجْمَعَ رَسُولُ اللهِ ﷺ الْمَسِيرَ إِلَى مَكَّةَ، كَتَبَ حَاطِبُ بْنُ أَبِي بَلْتَعَةَ كِتَابًا إِلَى قُرَيْشٍ يُخْبِرُهُمْ بِالَّذِي أَجْمَعَ عَلَيْهِ رَسُولُ اللهِ ﷺ مِنْ الأَمْرِ فِي السَّيْرِ إِلَيْهِمْ ثُمَّ أَعْطَاهُ امْرَأَةً زَعَمَ مُحَمَّدُ بْنُ جَعْفَرٍ أَنَّهَا مِنْ مُزَيْنَةَ وَزَعَمَ لِي غَيْرُهُ أَنَّهَا سَارَةُ مَوْلَاةٌ لِبَعْضِ بَنِي عَبْدِ الْمُطَّلِبِ وَجَعَلَ لَهَا جُعْلاً عَلَى أَنْ تُبَلِّغَهُ قُرَيْشًا فَجَعَلَتْهُ فِي رَأْسِهَا ثُمَّ فَتَلَتْ عَلَيْهِ قُرُونَهَا ثُمَّ خَرَجَتْ بِهِ وَأَتَى رَسُولَ اللهِ ﷺ الْخَبَرُ مِنَ السَّمَاءِ بِمَا صَنَعَ

[231]Narrated from ʿUrwa by Ibn Hishām, al-Wāqidī (2:797-798), al-Bayhaqī in the *Dalā'il* (4:16) and, through Ibn Isḥāq, by al-Ṭabarī in his *Tafsīr* (28:59-60) and *Tārīkh* (2:155), cf. Ibn Ḥibbān, *al-Thiqāt* (2:40-41) and Ibn Kathīr's *Tafsīr* (4:347) and *Bidāya*.

The Prophet's ﷺ Knowledge of the Unseen • *143*

حَاطِبٌ فَبَعَثَ عَلِيَّ بْنَ أَبِي طَالِبٍ وَالزُّبَيْرَ بْنَ الْعَوَّامِ رَضِيَ اللهُ عَنْهُمَا فَقَالَ أَدْرِكَا امْرَأَةً قَدْ كَتَبَ مَعَهَا حَاطِبُ بْنُ أَبِي بَلْتَعَةَ بِكِتَابٍ إِلَى قُرَيْشٍ يُحَذِّرُهُمْ سيرة ابن إسحاق مغازي الواقدي هق في الدلائل

ʿAbd Allāh b. Salām ؓ

The Two Masters [al-Bukhārī and Muslim] narrated from ʿAbd Allāh b. Salām ؓ that the Prophet ﷺ told him: 165 "You shall remain steadfast in Islam to your death."[232] ✲ Al-Bayhaqī also narrated from him ؓ that the Prophet ﷺ told him: 166 "That is the dwelling of martyrs but you shall not be granted it."[233]

عَنْ عَبْدِ اللهِ بْنِ سَلَامٍ قَالَ لَهُ رَسُولُ اللهِ ﷺ أَنْتَ عَلَى الْإِسْلَامِ حَتَّى تَمُوتَ ق حم وجاء في تعبير رؤياه مرفوعاً وَأَمَّا الْجَبَلُ فَهُوَ مَنْزِلُ الشُّهَدَاءِ وَلَنْ تَنَالَهُ م هق في الدلائل

Ibn Saʿd and al-Ḥākim narrated from Saʿd ؓ [488] that the Prophet ﷺ was given a bowl of food from which he ate. Part of it was left untouched and he said: 167 "A man shall enter from this gate from the dwellers of Paradise and eat this remnant." Then ʿAbd Allāh b. Salām came and ate it.[234]

---

[232]Narrated from ʿAbd Allāh b. Salām by al-Bukhārī, Muslim, and Aḥmad.
[233]Narrated from ʿAbd Allāh b. Salām by Muslim in the Prophet's ﷺ interpretation of his dream.
[234]Narrated from Saʿd by Aḥmad through ʿĀsim b. Bahdala (3:63 §1458, 3:150-151 §1591-1592 *isnād ḥasan*), ʿAbd b. Ḥumayd (§152), Abū Yaʿlā (2:75 §721, 2:98 §754), and al-Bazzār (§1156) in their *Musnad*s, Ibn Ḥibbān (16:121 §7164), and al-Ḥākim (3:416) who graded its chain sound, cf. *Mukhtāra* (3:260-261 §1066), *Iṣāba* (4:725 *sanad ḥasan*), al-Haythamī (9:326).

عَنْ سَعْدِ بْنِ أَبِي وَقَّاصٍ أَنَّ النَّبِيَّ ﷺ أُتِيَ بِقَصْعَةٍ فَأَكَلَ مِنْهَا فَفَضَلَتْ فَضْلَةٌ فَقَالَ رَسُولُ اللهِ ﷺ يَجِيءُ رَجُلٌ مِنْ هَذَا الْفَجِّ مِنْ أَهْلِ الْجَنَّةِ يَأْكُلُ هَذِهِ الْفَضْلَةَ قَالَ سَعْدٌ وَكُنْتُ تَرَكْتُ أَخِي عُمَيْراً يَتَوَضَّأُ قَالَ فَقُلْتُ هُوَ عُمَيْرٌ فَجَاءَ عَبْدُ اللهِ بْنُ سَلاَمٍ فَأَكَلَهَا حم ع ز حب ك وحسّن إسناده الحافظ في الإصابة

The Anṣār ﷺ

Al-Ḥākim and Abū Nuʿaym narrated from Anas ﷺ that the Messenger of Allah ﷺ said to the Anṣār: 168 "You shall experience, after I am gone, favoritism in shares and authority. Bear with it until you meet me at the Pond."[235]

عَنْ أَنَسِ بْنِ مَالِكٍ عَنْ أُسَيْدِ بْنِ حُضَيْرٍ رَضِيَ اللهُ عَنْهُمْ أَنَّ رَجُلاً مِنَ الأَنْصَارِ قَالَ يَا رَسُولَ اللهِ أَلاَ تَسْتَعْمِلُنِي كَمَا اسْتَعْمَلْتَ فُلاَنًا قَالَ سَتَلْقَوْنَ بَعْدِي أَثَرَةً فَاصْبِرُوا حَتَّى تَلْقَوْنِي عَلَى الْحَوْضِ ق طأ حم ت ن

Al-Ḥākim narrated from Miqsam that Abū Ayyūb al-Anṣārī came to Muʿāwiya asking some need of him but the latter disdained him and did not look his way. Abū Ayyūb said: 169

[235]Narrated from Anas and Usayd b. Ḥudayr by al-Bukhārī, Muslim, and Aḥmad; from ʿAbd Allāh b. Zayd by Muslim and Aḥmad; from Usayd by al-Tirmidhī *(ḥasan ṣaḥīḥ)* and al-Nasāʾī; from Abū Saʿīd al-Khudrī and al-Barāʾ b. ʿĀzib by Aḥmad; and in the *Muwaṭṭaʾ*.

"Indeed! The Messenger of Allah ﷺ did inform us that, after he is gone, we would be the victims of favoritism." Muʿāwiya said, "What did he order you to do?" Abū Ayyūb replied, "To bear with it until we drink from the Pond." Muʿāwiya said, "Then bear with it!" Abū Ayyūb was angered and swore that he would never speak to him again.[236]

عَنْ مِقْسَمٍ أَنَّ أَبَا أَيُّوبَ أَتَى مُعَاوِيَةَ فَذَكَرَ حَاجَةً لَهُ فَجَفَاهُ وَلَمْ يَرْفَعْ بِهِ رَأْساً فَقَالَ أَبُو أَيُّوبَ أَمَا أَنَّ رَسُولَ اللهِ ﷺ قَدْ أَخْبَرَنَا أَنَّهُ سَيُصِيبُنَا بَعْدَهُ أَثَرَةٌ قَالَ فَبِمَ أَمَرَكُمْ قَالَ أَمَرَنَا أَنْ نَصْبِرَ حَتَّى نَرِدَ عَلَيْهِ الْحَوْضُ قَالَ فَاصْبِرُوا إِذاً فَغَضِبَ أَبُو أَيُّوبَ وَحَلَفَ أَنَّهُ لاَ يُكَلِّمُهُ أَبَداً ك قال صحيح الإسناد وفي الباب عن ابن عباس ك طب مسند الروياني كر وأبي أيوب الأزدي المكي مرسلا ك وغيرهما

Muslim, al-Ṭayālisī, and al-Bayhaqī narrated that Abū Hurayra ؓ said: "On the day Mecca was conquered, the Anṣār said, 'Truly, a man longs to see his own town and return to the warmth of his kinsmen!' Then revelation came and, whenever revelation

[236]Narrated from Miqsam b. Bujra the freedman of Ibn ʿAbbās (also said to be that of ʿAbd Allāh b. al-Ḥārith) by al-Ḥākim (3:459-460=1990 ed. 3:520 *isnād ṣaḥīḥ*); from Ibn ʿAbbās by al-Ḥākim (3:461-462=1990 ed. 3:522); from Ibn ʿAbbās with a sound *mursal* chain by al-Ṭabarānī in *al-Kabīr* (4:125-126 §3876-3877), al-Rūyānī, and Ibn ʿAsākir cf. al-Haythamī (9:323) and *Kanz* (§37573); from Abū Ayyūb al-Azdī al-Makkī with a *mursal* chain by al-Ḥākim (1990 ed. 3:525) cf. *Iṣāba* (7:33); and – without mention of Abū Ayyūb – from Abū Saʿīd al-Khudrī by Aḥmad, Abū Yaʿlā (2:509-510 §1358), and Ibn al-Jaʿd (1:299-300 §2033) in their *Musnad*s with a strong chain; from Abū Qatāda by Aḥmad, al-Bayhaqī in *Shuʿab al-Īmān* (6:56-57 §7488), and Ibn ʿAbd al-Barr in *al-Istīʿāb* (3:1421) with a passable chain through ʿAbd Allāh b. Muḥammad b. ʿAqīl; from ʿUbāda b. al-Ṣāmit by al-Ṭabarānī with a weak chain; and from Anas by al-Ṭabarānī (4:122 §3861) with a passable chain cf. al-Haythamī (10:38). Only Miqsam's narration includes the last sentence al-Nabhānī cites. On favoritism see also the ḥadīth of Ibn Masʿūd in the section "His ﷺ Foretelling the Caliphs after Him Then the Kings."

came, it never remained hidden from us. As soon as it came, none of us would dare raise his eyes to the Messenger of Allah ﷺ until it was over. When revelation was over, he said: 170 'Assembly of the *Anṣār*! You said that a man longs to see his own town and return to the warmth of his kinsmen. Never! Then what would become of my name? Never! Truly, I am the servant of Allah and his Messenger. The living is with you and the dying is with you.' Hearing this, they came weeping and said, 'By Allah! We only said this because of our jealousy over Allah and His Prophet! (*al-ḍinn bil-Lāh wa-bi-Rasūlih*)' He said: a 'Truly, Allah and His Messenger believe you and excuse you.'"[237]

عَنْ أَبِي هُرَيْرَةَ قَالَ قَالَتِ الأَنْصَارُ يَوْمَ فَتْحِ مَكَّةَ أَمَّا الرَّجُلُ فَأَدْرَكَتْهُ رَغْبَةٌ فِي قَرْيَتِهِ وَرَأْفَةٌ بِعَشِيرَتِهِ قَالَ أَبُو هُرَيْرَةَ وَجَاءَ الْوَحْيُ وَكَانَ إِذَا جَاءَ الْوَحْيُ لاَ يَخْفَى عَلَيْنَا فَإِذَا جَاءَ فَلَيْسَ أَحَدٌ يَرْفَعُ طَرْفَهُ إِلَى رَسُولِ اللهِ ﷺ حَتَّى يَنْقَضِيَ الْوَحْيُ فَلَمَّا انْقَضَى الْوَحْيُ قَالَ رَسُولُ اللهِ ﷺ يَا مَعْشَرَ الأَنْصَارِ قُلْتُمْ أَمَّا الرَّجُلُ فَأَدْرَكَتْهُ رَغْبَةٌ فِي قَرْيَتِهِ كَلاَّ إِنِّي عَبْدُ اللهِ وَرَسُولُهُ هَاجَرْتُ إِلَى اللهِ وَإِلَيْكُمْ وَالْمَحْيَا مَحْيَاكُمْ وَالْمَمَاتُ مَمَاتُكُمْ فَأَقْبَلُوا إِلَيْهِ يَبْكُونَ وَيَقُولُونَ وَاللهِ مَا قُلْنَا الَّذِي قُلْنَا إِلاَّ الضِّنَّ بِاللهِ وَبِرَسُولِهِ فَقَالَ رَسُولُ اللهِ ﷺ إِنَّ اللهَ وَرَسُولَهُ يُصَدِّقَانِكُمْ وَيَعْذِرَانِكُمْ م

حم ن في الكبرى ش ط حب هق وفي الدلائل كر

[237]Narrated from Abū Hurayra by Muslim, Aḥmad, al-Nasā'ī in *al-Kubrā* (6:382), Ibn Abī Shayba (6:401, 7:397), Ibn Ḥibbān (11:73-76), al-Ṭayālisī (1:320 §2424), al-Bayhaqī in *al-Sunan al-Kubrā* (9:117) and the *Dalā'il*, and others.

Thābit b. Qays ؓ

Al-Ḥākim – he declares it sound –, al-Bayhaqī, and Abū Nuʿaym narrated through al-Zuhrī, from Ismāʿīl b. Muḥammad b. Thābit al-Anṣārī, from his father ؓ, that the Prophet ﷺ said to Thābit b. Qays b. Shammās ؓ: [171] "Thābit! Would you not be happy to live a blameless life, die a martyr, and enter Paradise?"[238] He said, "Yes!" He lived a blameless life and died a martyr the day Musaylima the arch-liar got killed.[239]

عَنْ إِسْمَاعِيلَ بْنِ مُحَمَّدِ بْنِ ثَابِتِ بْنِ شَمَّاسٍ عَنْ أَبِيهِ قَالَ رَسُولُ اللهِ ﷺ يَا ثَابِتُ أَلاَ تَرْضَى أَنْ تَعِيشَ حَمِيدًا وَتُقْتَلَ شَهِيدًا وَتَدْخُلَ الْجَنَّةَ فَعَاشَ حَمِيداً وَقُتِلَ شَهِيداً يَوْمَ مُسَيْلِمَةَ الْكَذَّابِ

ابن المبارك في الجهاد طأ المعرفة والتاريخ للفسوي ابن سعد البغوى ابن قانع طب طس رجاله ثقات مج مسند الشاميين حب أبو نعيم في المعرفة والدلائل ك هق في الدلائل وجاء مطولا عق ع ابن المبارك ابن أبي عاصم في الآحاد مسانيد الأوزاعي وابن منيع والروياني طب طس ك قال الذهبي ثبت أنه قتل يوم اليمامة

Zayd b. Arqam ؓ

Al-Bayhaqī narrated from Zayd b. Arqam ؓ that the Prophet ﷺ visited him to wish him well as he lay sick and told him: [172] "No harm shall come to you from your sickness. But how will you fare if, after I am gone, you grow old and become blind?" He said, "Then, I shall expect recompense *(aḥtasib)* and bear with it." The Prophet ﷺ said: "If you do, you shall enter Paradise without

[238] Narrated to here by Mālik in the *Muwaṭṭa'*.

[239] Narrated in this form and as part of a longer version by Ibn al-Mubārak in *al-Jihād*, al-Ṭabarānī in the *Kabīr*, *Awsaṭ* and *Musnad al-Shāmiyyīn*, al-Fasawī in *al-Maʿrifa wal-Tārīkh*, ʿAbd al-Razzāq and others.

reckoning." He lost his sight after the Prophet ﷺ died, then Allah returned his sight to him, then he died.[240]

عَنْ أُنَيْسَةَ ابْنَةِ زَيْدِ بْنِ أَرْقَمَ عَنْ أَبِيهَا أَنَّ النَّبِيَّ ﷺ دَخَلَ عَلَى زَيْدٍ يَعُودُهُ مِنْ مَرَضٍ كَانَ بِهِ فَقَالَ لَيْسَ عَلَيْكَ مِنْ مَرَضِكَ هَذَا بَأْسٌ وَلَكِنَّهُ كَيْفَ بِكَ إِذَا عَمَّرْتَ بَعْدِي فَعَمِيتَ قَالَ إِذًا أَحْتَسِبُ وَأَصْبِرُ قَالَ إِذًا تَدْخُلُ الْجَنَّةَ بِغَيْرِ حِسَابٍ قَالَ فَعَمِيَ بَعْدَ مَا مَاتَ النَّبِيُّ ﷺ ثُمَّ رَدَّ اللهُ عَلَيْهِ بَصَرَهُ ثُمَّ مَاتَ ع ز طب

هق في الدلائل كر وروى طرفا منه حم د خد هب

Mu'ādh b. Jabal رضي الله عنه

Aḥmad and al-Bayhaqī narrated from ʿĀṣim b. Ḥumayd al-Sakūnī that the Prophet ﷺ sent Mu'ādh b. Jabal to Yemen so he went out with him some distance to give him his last recommendations. When he finished he said: [173] "Mu'ādh! It may well be that *('asā an)* you shall not meet me again after this year in which I find myself. You might *(la 'allaka)* pass by my mosque here, and my grave [*i.e.* to visit me]." Mu'ādh wept. ✻ Aḥmad narrated it in a variant wording from ʿĀṣim b. [Ḥumayd][241] with a complete chain.

[The narration continues: Then the Prophet ﷺ turned and, facing Madīna, said: [a] "The people of my House there believe that they are the closest of all people to me but, in fact, the closest of people to me are those who guard themselves from Allah *(al-muttaqūn)*, whoever they are and wherever they are. O Allah! [b] I do not allow them at all to corrupt what I have reformed. I swear by Allah! [c] They shall turn my

[240]Narrated from Zayd by al-Ṭabarānī in *al-Kabīr* (5:211 §5126) cf. al-Haythamī (2:309 cf. Ibn Mākūlā's *Ikmāl* 1:361) and – without the phrase "after I am gone you grow old" – by al-Bukhārī in *al-Adab al-Mufrad* (p. 188 §532), Aḥmad (32:93-94 §1948 *isnād ḥasan*), al-Ṭabarānī in *al-Kabīr* (5:190 §5052, 5:204 §5098), and al-Bayhaqī in the *Shuʿab* (§9191). Other fair narrations from Zayd in Abū Dāwūd and al-Ḥākim (1:342) specify that his ailment was in his eyes and that it was ophtalmia.

[241]"ʿĀṣim b. Mu'ādh" in al-Nabhānī's text.

Community away from her Religion just as a cup is turned upside down in the riverbed!" Another version adds: d "Do not weep, Muʿādh! Weeping is from Shayṭān."²⁴²
By the people of his House here, the Prophet ﷺ means his paternal relatives: 174
"My father's relatives are not my patrons and friends *(awliyāʾ)*. My only Patron and Friend is Allah as well as the righteous among the believers."²⁴³]

عَنْ مُعَاذِ بْنِ جَبَلٍ قَالَ لَمَّا بَعَثَهُ رَسُولُ اللهِ ﷺ إِلَى الْيَمَنِ خَرَجَ مَعَهُ رَسُولُ اللهِ ﷺ يُوصِيهِ وَمُعَاذٌ رَاكِبٌ وَرَسُولُ اللهِ ﷺ تَحْتَ رَاحِلَتِهِ فَلَمَّا فَرَغَ قَالَ يَا مُعَاذُ إِنَّكَ عَسَى أَنْ لَا تَلْقَانِي بَعْدَ عَامِي هَذَا وَلَعَلَّكَ أَنْ تَمُرَّ بِمَسْجِدِي وَقَبْرِي فَبَكَى مُعَاذٌ جَشَعًا لِفِرَاقِ رَسُولِ اللهِ ﷺ ثُمَّ الْتَفَتَ فَأَقْبَلَ بِوَجْهِهِ نَحْوَ الْمَدِينَةِ فَقَالَ إِنَّ أَوْلَى النَّاسِ بِي الْمُتَّقُونَ مَنْ كَانُوا وَحَيْثُ كَانُوا حم ع ز ابن أبي عاصم في الآحاد طب حب هق وفي الدلائل أبو نعيم المعرفة كر

A l-Bayhaqī narrated through al-Zuhrī from Kaʿb b. Mālik ؓ: 175 "After the Prophet ﷺ accomplished the pilgrimage he sent out Muʿādh to Yemen. Then the Prophet ﷺ died.²⁴⁴

عَنِ ابْنِ كَعْبِ بْنِ مَالِكٍ ؓ قَالَ لَمَّا حَجَّ النَّبِيُّ ﷺ بَعَثَ مُعَاذاً إِلَى الْيَمَنِ فَقَدِمَ عَلَى أَبِي بَكْرٍ مِنَ الْيَمَنِ وَقَدْ تُوُفِّيَ رَسُولُ اللهِ ﷺ طأ طس حل هق في الدلائل كر

---

²⁴²Both versions narrated by Ahmad with two chains, al-Bazzār (7:91-92 §2647), and al-Tabarānī in *al-Kabīr* (20:121 §242) and *Musnad al-Shāmiyyīn* (2:102 §991), all with trustworthy narrators and a good chain cf. al-Haythamī (3:16, 9:22, 10:231-232), Ibn Abī ʿĀṣim in *al-Āḥād* (3:420 §1837), Ibn Ḥibbān (2:414-415 §647 *isnād qawī*), al-Bayhaqī in *al-Sunan al-Kubrā* (10:86). Muʿādh was mounted while the Messenger of Allah ﷺ was walking by Muʿādh's mount. This ḥadīth is proof that the Prophet ﷺ was granted knowledge of the place of his death.

²⁴³Narrated from ʿAmr b. al-ʿĀs by al-Bukhārī, Muslim, and Ahmad.

²⁴⁴Narrated from Ṭāwus al-Yamānī in the *Muwaṭṭaʾ* (*zakāt*) cf. *Nasb* (2:114) and others.

Al-Barā' b. Mālik ﵁

Al-Tirmidhī, al-Ḥākim – he declares it sound – and al-Bayhaqī narrated that Anas ﵁ said: "The Messenger of Allah ﷺ said: 176 'How many a weak, belittled servant **[489]** wearing two tattered garments *(ṭimrayn)*, if he calls upon Allah, Allah will surely fulfill his request! Among them is al-Barā' b. Mālik.'"[245]

عَنْ أَنَسِ بْنِ مَالِكٍ رَضِيَ اللهُ عَنْهُ قَالَ قَالَ رَسُولُ اللهِ ﷺ كَمْ مِنْ ضَعِيفٍ مُتَضَعَّفٍ ذِي طِمْرَيْنِ لَوْ أَقْسَمَ عَلَى اللهِ لأَبَرَّهُ مِنْهُمْ الْبَرَاءُ بْنُ مَالِكٍ ع ك هق في الدلائل حل وجاء بلفظ كَمْ مِنْ أَشْعَثَ أَغْبَرَ ذِي طِمْرَيْنِ لاَ يُؤْبَهُ لَهُ لَوْ أَقْسَمَ عَلَى اللهِ لأَبَرَّهُ مِنْهُمْ الْبَرَاءُ بْنُ مَالِكٍ ت وحسّنه حم وفي الباب عن معاذ جه طب وحذيفة حم وأبي هريرة م طس حب ك وابن مسعود وثوبان طب مج وقتادة عق

Al-Barā' encountered an enemy army at Tustar. When the Muslim ranks began to break they said to him: "Barā', the Prophet ﷺ said that if you called upon Allah He would prove you true, so call upon your Lord." He said: 177 "I call upon You, my Lord, to grant us victory over them." They were victorious. Then the two armies met again at Qanṭarat al-Sūs and the Muslims were being routed so they said: "Call upon your Lord, Barā'!" He said: "I call upon You, my Lord, to grant us victory over them and to join me up with Your Prophet." Then they charged and routed the cavalry. Al-Barā' was killed as a martyr.[246]

[245]Narrated from Anas by al-Tirmidhī *(ḥasan gharīb)*, Aḥmad, al-Ḥākim (3:292=1990 ed. 3:331 *saḥīḥ*), and others. Also narrated from Mu'ādh by Ibn Mājah, Ḥudhayfa by Aḥmad, Abū Hurayra by Ibn Ḥibbān (14:403 §6483) and al-Ḥākim (1990 ed. 4:364), Ibn Mas'ūd and Thawbān by al-Ṭabarānī cf. al-Haythamī (10:264), and Qatāda by 'Abd al-Razzāq (11:306 §20612).

[246]Narrated from Anas by al-Ḥākim (3:292=1990 ed. 3:331 *saḥīḥ*) and al-Lālikā'ī in *Karāmāt al-Awliyā'* (p. 148).

ثُمَّ قَالَ أنَسٌ فَإِنَّ الْبَرَاءَ لَقِيَ زَحْفاً مِنَ المشْرِكِينَ وَقَدْ أَوْجَعَ المشْرِكُونَ فِي المسْلِمِينَ فَقَالُوا يَا بَرَاءُ إِنَّ رَسُولَ اللهِ ﷺ قَالَ إِنَّكَ لَوْ أَقْسَمْتَ عَلَى اللهِ لأَبَرَّكَ فَأَقْسِمْ عَلَى رَبِّكَ فَقَالَ أَقْسَمْتُ عَلَيْكَ يَا رَبِّ لَمَا مَنَحْتَنَا أَكْتَافَهُمْ ثُمَّ الْتَقَوا عَلَى قَنْطَرَةِ السُّوسِ فَأَوْجَعُوا فِي المسْلِمِينَ فَقَالُوا لَهُ يَا بَرَاءُ أَقْسِمْ عَلَى رَبِّكَ فَقَالَ أَقْسَمْتُ عَلَيْكَ يَا رَبِّ لَمَا مَنَحْتَنَا أَكْتَافَهُمْ وَأَلْحَقْتَنِي بِنَبِيِّكَ ﷺ فَمُنِحُوا أَكْتَافَهُمْ وَقُتِلَ الْبَرَاءُ شَهِيداً ك هب وفي الدلائل حب في المشاهير والثقات حل اللالكائي في كرامات الأولياء

Al-Nuʿmān b. Bashīr رضي الله عنهما

Ibn Saʿd narrated that ʿĀṣim b. ʿUmar b. Qatāda said: "ʿAmra bint Rawāḥa came carrying her son al-Nuʿmān b. Bashīr in swathes to the Messenger of Allah ﷺ, saying 'Messenger of Allah, supplicate Allah that He make abundant his property and offspring!' He replied: [178] 'Will you not be happy that he live as his maternal uncle lived? He lived a blameless life, was killed as a martyr, and entered Paradise.'"[247]

عَنْ عَاصِمِ بْنِ عُمَرَ بْنِ قَتَادَةَ قَالَ جَاءَتْ عَمْرَةُ بِنْتُ رَوَاحَةَ تَحْمِلُ ابْنَهَا النُّعْمَانَ بْنَ بَشِيرٍ فِي لِيفَةٍ إِلَى رَسُولِ اللهِ ﷺ فَقَالَتْ يَا رَسُولَ اللهِ أُدْعُ اللهَ أَنْ يُكْثِرَ مَالَهُ وَوَلَدَهُ فَقَالَ أَوَمَا

[247] Narrated by Ibn Asakir (62:120) cf. Ibn Kathīr, *al-Bidāya* (Year 64). The maternal uncle is ʿAbd Allāh b. Rawāḥa.

تَرْضِينَ أَنْ يَعِيشَ كَمَا عَاشَ خَالُهُ حَمِيداً وَقُتِلَ شَهِيداً وَدَخَلَ الجَنَّةَ كر

Ibn Saʿd narrated from ʿAbd al-Malik b. ʿUmayr that Bashīr b. Saʿd brought al-Nuʿmān b. Bashīr to the Prophet ﷺ and said, "Messenger of Allah, supplicate Allah for my son!" He replied: 179 "Are you not happy that he should reach your age then go to al-Shām, where one of the hypocrites of *Ahl al-Shām* shall kill him?"[248]

عَنْ عَبْدِ المَلِكِ بْنِ عُمَيْرٍ أَنَّ بَشِيرَ بْنَ سَعْدٍ جَاءَ بِالنُّعْمَانِ بْنِ بَشِيرٍ إِلَى النَّبِيِّ ﷺ فَقَالَ يَا رَسُولَ اللهِ أُدْعُ لِابْنِي هَذَا فَقَالَ لَهُ رَسُولُ اللهِ ﷺ أَمَا تَرْضَى أَنْ يَبْلُغَ مَا بَلَغْتَ ثُمَّ يَأْتِيَ الشَّامَ فَيَقْتُلَهُ مُنَافِقٌ مِنْ أَهْلِ الشَّامِ كر

He also narrated that Maslama b. Muḥārib and others said: "When al-Ḍaḥḥāk b. Qays was killed in the meadow of Rāhiṭ in the caliphate of Marwān b. al-Ḥakam, al-Nuʿmān b. Bashīr desired to flee from Homs, of which he was governor, but he changed his mind and supplicated Allah for Ibn al-Zubayr. So the people of Ḥimṣ killed him and beheaded him.[249]

عَنْ مَسْلَمَةَ بْنِ مُحَارِبٍ وَغَيْرِهِ لَمَّا قُتِلَ الضَّحَّاكُ بْنُ قَيْسٍ بِمَرْجِ رَاهِطٍ وَكَانَ لِلنِّصْفِ مِنْ ذِي الحِجَّةِ سَنَةَ أَرْبَعٍ وَسِتِّينَ فِي

[248]Narrated by Ibn Asakir (62:120) cf. al-Mizzī in *Tahdhīb al-Kamāl* (29:416).

[249]Narrated by Ibn Saʿd (6:53), al-Ḥākim (3:531), and Ibn ʿAsākir cf. al-Mizzī and Ibn Ḥajar, *op. cit.*

خِلَافَةِ مَرْوَانَ بْنِ الحَكَمِ فَأَرَادَ النُّعْمَانُ بْنُ بَشِيرٍ أَنْ يَهْرُبَ مِنْ
حِمْصَ وَكَانَ عَامِلاً عَلَيْهَا فَخَافَ وَدَعَا لِابْنِ الزُّبَيْرِ فَطَلَبَهُ أَهْلُ
حِمْصَ فَقَتَلُوهُ وَاحْتَزُّوا رَأْسَهُ ك ابن سعد كر

ʿAbd Allāh b. Unays ؓ

Al-Bayhaqī and Abū Nuʿaym narrated that ʿAbd Allāh b. Unays ؓ said, "The Messenger of Allah ﷺ summoned me and said: 180 'I received news that [Khālid b. Sufyān] Ibn Nubayḥ al-Hudhalī is mobilizing people to raid me and he is in Nakhla or 'Urana. Go to him and kill him.' I said, Messenger of Allah, describe him to me so that I may recognize him.' He said: a 'The sign by which you shall know it is he, is that when you see him, you will get goose flesh.' I travelled until I reached him and when I saw him, I found the exact sign the Messenger of Allah ﷺ had described to me – goose flesh. I walked with him for a while until I saw my opportunity and I pounced on him with my sword and killed him. When I came back to the Messenger of Allah ﷺ he said: b 'Bless that face!' *(aflaḥa al-wajh.)* I said, 'I have killed him, Messenger of Allah!' He said, 'Spoken truly,' and he gave me a staff, adding: 'Keep this with you.' I said, 'Messenger of Allah, why have you given me this staff?' He said: c 'As a sign between you and me on the Day of Resurrection. Those that carry a staff will be very rare on that Day!'" ʿAbd Allāh paired it with his sword until the day he died, at which time – as he had instructed – it was placed with him in his shroud.[250]

[250]Narrated from ʿAbd Allāh b. Unays by Ibn Hishām (6:30-31), Aḥmad (25:440-442 §16047), Ibn Khuzayma (2:91 §982), Ibn Ḥibbān (16:114-116 §7160), al-Ṭabarī in his *Tārīkh* (2:208), Abū Yaʿlā (2:201-202 §905), al-Bayhaqī in the *Dalā'il* (4:24) and *Sunan* (3:255-256), Abū Nuʿaym in the *Dalā'il* (p. 517-519 §445), and Abū Dāwūd in part, all with a fair chain as per Ibn Ḥajar in the *Fath* (2:437) cf. al-Haythamī (6:203), al-Suyūṭī in the *Khaṣā'is* (2:12). Also Ibn Saʿd (2:50) without chain and, *mursal*, in the *Maghāzī* of Mūsā b. ʿUqba and ʿUrwa b. al-Zubayr cf. Talīdī, *Tahdhīb al-Khaṣā'is* (p. 175-176 §200).

عَنِ ابْنِ عَبْدِ اللهِ بْنِ أُنَيْسٍ عَنِ أَبِيهِ رَضِيَ اللهُ عَنْهُ قَالَ دَعَانِي رَسُولُ اللهِ ﷺ فَقَالَ إِنَّهُ قَدْ بَلَغَنِي أَنَّ خَالِدَ بْنَ سُفْيَانَ بْنِ نُبَيْحٍ يَجْمَعُ لِي النَّاسَ لِيَغْزُوَنِي وَهُوَ بِعُرَنَةَ فَأْتِهِ فَاقْتُلْهُ قَالَ قُلْتُ يَا رَسُولَ اللهِ انْعَتْهُ لِي حَتَّى أَعْرِفَهُ قَالَ إِذَا رَأَيْتَهُ وَجَدْتَ لَهُ أُقْشَعْرِيرَةً قَالَ فَخَرَجْتُ مُتَوَشِّحًا بِسَيْفِي حَتَّى وَقَعْتُ عَلَيْهِ وَهُوَ بِعُرَنَةَ مَعَ ظُعُنٍ يَرْتَادُ لَهُنَّ مَنْزِلًا وَحِينَ كَانَ وَقْتُ الْعَصْرِ فَلَمَّا رَأَيْتُهُ وَجَدْتُ مَا وَصَفَ لِي رَسُولُ اللهِ ﷺ مِنْ الْأُقْشَعْرِيرَةِ فَأَقْبَلْتُ نَحْوَهُ وَخَشِيتُ أَنْ يَكُونَ بَيْنِي وَبَيْنَهُ مُحَاوَلَةٌ تَشْغَلُنِي عَنْ الصَّلَاةِ فَصَلَّيْتُ وَأَنَا أَمْشِي نَحْوَهُ أُومِئُ بِرَأْسِي الرُّكُوعَ وَالسُّجُودَ فَلَمَّا انْتَهَيْتُ إِلَيْهِ قَالَ مَنْ الرَّجُلُ قُلْتُ رَجُلٌ مِنْ الْعَرَبِ سَمِعَ بِكَ وَبِجَمْعِكَ لِهَذَا الرَّجُلِ فَجَاءَكَ لِهَذَا قَالَ أَجَلْ أَنَا فِي ذَلِكَ قَالَ فَمَشَيْتُ مَعَهُ شَيْئًا حَتَّى إِذَا أَمْكَنَنِي حَمَلْتُ عَلَيْهِ السَّيْفَ حَتَّى قَتَلْتُهُ ثُمَّ خَرَجْتُ وَتَرَكْتُ ظَعَائِنَهُ مُكِبَّاتٍ عَلَيْهِ فَلَمَّا قَدِمْتُ عَلَى رَسُولِ اللهِ ﷺ فَرَآنِي فَقَالَ أَفْلَحَ الْوَجْهُ قَالَ قُلْتُ قَتَلْتُهُ يَا رَسُولَ اللهِ قَالَ صَدَقْتَ قَالَ ثُمَّ قَامَ مَعِي رَسُولُ اللهِ ﷺ فَدَخَلَ فِي بَيْتِهِ فَأَعْطَانِي عَصًا فَقَالَ أَمْسِكْ هَذِهِ عِنْدَكَ يَا عَبْدَ اللهِ بْنَ أُنَيْسٍ قَالَ فَخَرَجْتُ بِهَا عَلَى النَّاسِ فَقَالُوا مَا هَذِهِ الْعَصَا قَالَ قُلْتُ أَعْطَانِيهَا رَسُولُ اللهِ ﷺ وَأَمَرَنِي أَنْ أَمْسِكَهَا قَالُوا أَوَلَا تَرْجِعُ إِلَى رَسُولِ اللهِ ﷺ فَتَسْأَلَهُ عَنْ ذَلِكَ قَالَ فَرَجَعْتُ إِلَى رَسُولِ اللهِ ﷺ فَقُلْتُ يَا رَسُولَ اللهِ لِمَ أَعْطَيْتَنِي هَذِهِ الْعَصَا قَالَ آيَةٌ

بَيْنِي وَبَيْنَكَ يَوْمَ الْقِيَامَةِ إِنَّ أَقَلَّ النَّاسِ الْمُتَخَصِّرُونَ يَوْمَئِذٍ يَوْمَ الْقِيَامَةِ فَقَرَنَهَا عَبْدُ اللهِ بِسَيْفِهِ فَلَمْ تَزَلْ مَعَهُ حَتَّى إِذَا مَاتَ أَمَرَ بِهَا فَصُبَّتْ مَعَهُ فِي كَفَنِهِ ثُمَّ دُفِنَا جَمِيعًا حم ع خز حب هق في الدلائل وحسّن إسناده الحافظ وروى بعضه د

Al-Bayhaqī and Abū Nuʿaym narrated something similar from Mūsā b. ʿUqba, from Ibn Shihāb and from ʿUrwa. In that narration [Ibn Unays relates], "the Messenger of Allah ﷺ said: [181] 'When you see him you will be awed and feel afraid of him.' And I had never been afraid of anything. Indeed, when I saw him, I was awed and felt afraid of him. I said to myself: 'Allah and His Messenger spoke the truth.' I lay in wait for him until the people became quiet. Then I ambushed him and killed him." They say that the Messenger of Allah ﷺ told of his killing before ʿAbd Allāh b. Unays came.

Ibn Saʿd narrated something similar through al-Wāqidī, from his sources. That narration has: "'When you see him you will be awed and feel afraid of him, and you will think of Satan.' And I used to fear no man. Indeed, when I saw him, I was awed by him and said to myself: 'Allah and His Messenger ﷺ spoke the truth.'"

وَعَنْ موسى بن عقبة نحوه وفيه إِذَا رَأَيْتَهُ هِبْتَهُ وَفَرِقْتَ مِنْهُ قَالَ عَبْدُ اللهِ فَمَا فَرِقْتُ مِنْ شَيْءٍ قَطُّ فَلَمَّا رَأَيْتُهُ هِبْتُهُ وَفَرِقْتُ مِنْهُ فَقُلْتُ صَدَقَ اللهُ وَرَسُولُهُ ثُمَّ كَمِنْتُ لَهُ حَتَّى إِذَا هَدَأَ النَّاسُ اغْتَرَرْتُهُ وفي تاريخ المدينة لابن شبّة اعْتَوَرْتُهُ فَقَتَلْتُهُ فَيَزْعُمُونَ أَنَّ رَسُولَ اللهِ ﷺ أَخْبَرَ بِقَتْلِهِ قَبْلَ قُدُومِ عَبْدِ اللهِ بْنِ أُنَيْسٍ ابن سعد هق في الدلائل ورواه الواقدي بلفظ إِذَا رَأَيْته هِبْته وَفَرِقْت مِنْهُ وَذَكَرْت

الشَّيْطَانَ وَكُنْت لا أَهَابُ الرِّجَالَ إلى أن قال فَلَمَّا رَأَيْتُهُ هِبْتُهُ
فَقُلْتُ صَدَقَ اللهُ وَرَسُولُهُ

ʿUmayr [490] b. ʿAdī al-Khaṭmī ﷺ

The *Sīra* compilers narrated from ʿAbd Allāh b. al-Ḥārith b. al-Fuḍayl that his father said that 'Aṣmā' bint Marwān was the wife of a man from the Banū Khaṭma named Yazīd b. Zayd, and she used to revile Islam and Muslims and would exhort the unbelievers against the Prophet ﷺ. When news of this reached him, the Messenger of Allah ﷺ said: 182 "Who will defend me against the daughter of Marwān?" ʿUmayr b. ʿAdī al-Khaṭmī heard this when he was with the Messenger of Allah ﷺ. That night, he travelled to her house and killed her. Then he was with the Messenger of Allah again the next morning and said: "Messenger of Allah, I have killed her." The Prophet ﷺ replied: a "You have helped Allah and His Prophet, O ʿUmayr." He said: "Must I incur anything concerning her, Messenger of Allah?" He replied: b "No two goats will butt heads over her."[251] ʿUmayr returned to his people and the Banū Khaṭma were numerous in those days. He found them discussing the matter of Marwān's daughter. She had five grown sons. When ʿUmayr b. ʿAdī came to them, having just seen the Messenger of Allah ﷺ, he said, "O Banū Khaṭma, I am the one who killed Marwān's daughter. Scheme all you will against me, then you will have no respite!" Not the least harm came his way for his having killed her and, as the Prophet ﷺ had said, no two goats butted heads over her.[252]

[251]This expression became a proverb to refer to something to which no one objects in the least.

[252]Narrated by al-Wāqidī (1:172-173) cf. al-Quḍā'ī in *Musnad al-Shihāb* (2:48 §858), Ibn al-Sakan in *Mu'jam al-Saḥāba*, al-'Askarī in *al-Amthāl*, ʿIyāḍ in *al-Shifā*, and Ibn Kathīr, *Bidāya* (5:221, Year 11). Also, without full chains, by Ibn Hishām (6:49-50), Ibn Saʿd (2:27), and al-Ṣāliḥī in *Subul al-Hudā* (6:36-37). Something similar is narrated – with a very weak chain and without naming 'Umayr – from Ibn ʿAbbās by al-Quḍā'ī (2:46-47 §856-857), Ibn ʿAsākir, and al-Khaṭīb (13:99). Ibn Taymiyya in *al-Ṣārim al-Maslūl* (p. 95-104) considers al-Wāqidī's report authentic and discusses its probative

عَنْ عَبْدِ اللهِ بْنِ الحَارِثِ بْنِ الْفُضَيْلِ عَنْ أَبِيهِ قَالَ كَانَتْ عَصْمَاءُ بِنْتُ مَرْوَانَ تَحْتَ رَجُلٍ مِنْ بَنِي خَطْمَةَ يُقَالُ لَهُ يَزِيدُ بْنُ زَيْدٍ وَكَانَتْ تَعِيبُ الإِسْلامَ وَأَهْلَهُ وَتُحَرِّضُ الْكُفَّارَ عَلَى النَّبِيِّ ﷺ فَقَالَ رَسُولُ اللهِ ﷺ حِينَ بَلَغَهُ ذَلِكَ أَلاَ آخِذٌ لِي مِنْ ابْنَةِ مَرْوَانَ فَسَمِعَ ذَلِكَ مِنْ قَوْلِ رَسُولِ اللهِ ﷺ عُمَيْرُ بْنُ عَدِيٍّ الْخَطْمِيُّ وَهُوَ عِنْدَهُ فَلَمَّا أَمْسَى مِنْ تِلْكَ اللَّيْلَةِ سَرَى عَلَيْهَا فِي بَيْتِهَا فَقَتَلَهَا ثُمَّ أَصْبَحَ مَعَ رَسُولِ اللهِ ﷺ فَقَالَ يَا رَسُولَ اللهِ إِنِّي قَدْ قَتَلْتُهَا فَقَالَ نَصَرْتَ اللهَ وَرَسُولَهُ يَا عُمَيْرُ فَقَالَ هَلْ عَلَيَّ شَيْءٌ مِنْ شَأْنِهَا يَا رَسُولَ اللهِ فَقَالَ لاَ يَنْتَطِحُ فِيهَا عَنْزَانِ

الواقدي ابن سعد ابن هشام حب في السيرة مسند الشهاب وقال ابن الجوزي في العلل موضوع لكن صححه أحمد بن تيمية في رسالته الصارم المسلول وقال البخاري في الصحابة عمير بن عدي الأعمى قارئ بني خطمة وإمامهم

force at length. Ibn Ḥibbān in *al-Thiqāt* (1:208) narrates that 'Umayr had vowed to kill her if the Prophet ﷺ returned safe from Badr. Note that he was a blind man cf. *Iṣāba* (4:721) and al-Aḥdab, *Zawā'id Tārīkh Baghdād* (9:98-103 §1977). Ibn al-Jawzī considers it a forgery in his *'Ilal al-Mutanāhiya*. All of the above reports come through Muḥammad b. al-Ḥajjāj al-Lakhmī who is accused of forging it while his student Muḥammad b. Ibrāhīm b. al-ʿÀlā' al-Shāmī is also accused of lying cf. al-Ghumārī, *Fatḥ al-Wahhāb* (2:89-90). A sound report from Ibn 'Abbās mentions that a blind man killed his beloved female slave because she used to insult the Prophet ﷺ after which the latter declared non-liability *(hadar)* on her blood: narrated by Abū Dāwūd, al-Nasā'ī, al-Daraquṭnī in his *Sunan* (4:216-217), and al-Ṭabarānī in *al-Kabīr* (11:351 §11984), cf. Ibn Ḥajar, *Bulūgh al-Marām* (p. 255).

Abū Qatāda رضي الله عنه

Al-Bayhaqī narrated through ʿAbd Allāh b. Abī Qatāda that Abū Qatāda bought a horse from a market that had come to al-Madīna when Masʿadat al-Fazārī met him and said, "Abū Qatāda! What is this horse?" Abū Qatāda said, "A horse I want to use for jihād with the Messenger of Allah ﷺ. The other said, "How easy it will be to kill you all, how burning your pain!" Abū Qatāda said, "I, truly, am asking Allāh to let me meet you while I am riding it [in battle]." He replied, "*Āmīn*." One day, as Abū Qatāda was feeding his horse some dates in the fold of his garment, the horse raised its head and pricked up its ears. He said, "I swear by Allah that it can smell other horses." His mother said, "By Allah, my son! No one dared target us (*mā kunnā nurāmu*) in the Time of Ignorance; how then, when Allah brought Muḥammad ﷺ?" Then the horse raised its head and pricked up its ears a second time. Abū Qatāda said, "I swear by Allah that it can smell other horses." He saddled it and took his weapons then mounted his horse. A man came and said, "The milch camels were seized [by the Banū Fazāra]" – meaning, the milch camels of the Prophet ﷺ, in the raid of Dhū Qurad known as the Battle of the Woods *(ghazwat al-ghāba)* – "and the Prophet ﷺ has gone with his Companions to get them back!" Abū Qatāda went to see the Prophet ﷺ and the latter told him: 183 "Go, Abū Qatāda! May Allah accompany you." He said: "I went out and there were the camels being led by singing. I charged the armed guards. An arrow struck me in the forehead. I removed its shaft, thinking that I had taken out the blade. A rider came up to me, wearing a helmet, face hidden, and said, 'Allah has finally made me meet you, Abū Qatāda!' He uncovered his face and it was Masʿadat al-Fazārī. He said, 'Which would you like best? Swords? Spears? Or shall we dismount and fight?' I said, 'It is up to you.' He said, 'Dismount and fight.' We both dismounted and pounced on each other. I got on top of his chest and grabbed his sword. When he saw his sword in my hand, he said, 'Abū Qatāda! Spare me.' I said, 'No, by Allah!' He said, 'Then who will take care of my lads?' I said, 'The Fire.' Then I killed him, covered him with my garment, and wore his clothes. I took his weapons and sat on his horse. My horse had fled at the time we duelled. It went back to the camp, so they hamstrung it. **[491]** I went off and, further down, found his brother's son with seventeen riders. I speared his brother's son with a stab that shattered his spine. Those that were with him dispersed. I controlled the milch-camels with my spear. The Prophet ﷺ then came with his Companions. As they rode up to the camp site, they saw Abū Qatāda's horse, hamstrung. A man said, 'Messenger of Allah, Abū Qatāda's horse was hamstrung!' The Messenger of Allah ﷺ said: [a] 'Woe to your mother! Many [a horse] turn away from you in war!' He said it twice. Then the Prophet ﷺ and his Companions rode on until they reached the spot where we duelled. There, they spotted a man decked in Abū Qatāda's clothes. Someone said, ''Messenger of Allah, Abū Qatāda was martyred.' The Messenger of Allah ﷺ said: [b] 'Allah have mercy on Abū Qatāda! By the One Who bestowed on me the honor He did, I swear that Abū Qatāda is on their tracks, taunting them with *rajaz* rhymes!'[253] 'Umar b. al-Khaṭṭāb and Abū Bakr went to lift the garment and, seing Mas'ada's face, said, '*Allāhu akbar!* Allah and his Messenger spoke the truth!' Then I came into sight, herding the milch camels. The Prophet ﷺ said: [c] 'Bless that face, Abū Qatāda, Master of horsemen! [d] May Allah bless you, your children, and your children's children! What is this in your face?' I said, 'An arrow hit me.' He said: 'Come near me.' Then he removed the arrowhead gently, spat in the wound, and placed his palm over it. By the One Who honored him with Prophethood! I never suffered one blow nor even a scratch after that.''[254]

عَنْ عَبْدِ اللهِ بْنِ أَبِي قَتَادَةَ أَنَّ أَبَا قَتَادَةَ اشْتَرَى فَرَساً مِنْ دَوَابٍّ
دَخَلَتِ المدِينَةَ فَلَقِيَهُ مَسْعَدَةُ الْفَزَارِيُّ فَقَالَ يَا أَبَا قَتَادَةَ مَا هَذَا
الْفَرَسُ فَقَالَ أَبُو قَتَادَةَ فَرَسٌ أَرَدْتُ أَنْ أَرْبُطَهَا [زاد النبهاني

[253] *Yartajiz*. This may also mean "thundering" figuratively: al-Zamakhsharī, *Asās al-Balāgha* (p. 221-222).

[254] Narrated by al-Bayhaqī in the *Dalā'il* (4:191-193), also al-Wāqidī, Ibn Mandah in *Ma'rifat al-Sahāba*, and al-Ṭabarānī in *al-Saghīr* cf. Ibn Ḥajar, *Isāba* (7:329), and partly by Ibn 'Abd al-Barr in *al-Istī'āb* (2:584; 4:1731-1732). Cited by al-Suyūṭi in the *Khasā'is* (1:414-416). The Prophet's ﷺ praise of Abū Qatāda as the most skilled horseman is in Muslim. Cf. also al-Khuzā'ī, *Takhrīj al-Dilālāt* (1995 ed. p. 740-741=1985 ed. p. 727-728). One narration says he killed Mas'ada the day of Uḥud: *Isāba* (3:48).

لِلْجِهَادِ] مَعَ رَسُولِ اللهِ ﷺ فَقَالَ مَا أَهْوَنَ قَتْلَكُمْ وَأَشَدَّ جُرْأَتَكُمْ [وعند الصالحي حَرْبَكُمْ وفي الخصائص الكبرى حَرَّكُمْ] فَقَالَ أَبُو قَتَادَةَ أَمَا إِنِّي أَسْأَلُ اللهَ عَزَّ وَجَلَّ أَنْ أَلْقِيَنَّكَ وَأَنَا عَلَيْهَا قَالَ آمِين فَبَيْنَا أَبُو قَتَادَةَ ذَاتَ يَوْمٍ يُعْلِفُ فَرَسَهُ تَمْراً فِي طَرَفِ بُرْدَتِهِ إِذْ رَفَعَتْ رَأْسَهَا وَصَرَّتْ أُذُنَهَا فَقَالَ أَحْلِفُ بِاللهِ لَقَدْ حَسَّتْ بِرِيحِ خَيْلٍ فَقَالَتْ لَهُ أُمُّهُ وَاللهِ يَا بُنَيَّ مَا كُنَّا نُرَامُ فِي الجَاهِلِيَّةِ فَكَيْفَ حِينَ جَاءَ اللهُ بِمُحَمَّدٍ ﷺ ثُمَّ رَفَعَتِ الْفَرَسُ أَيْضاً رَأْسَهَا وَصَرَّتْ أُذُنَيْهَا فَقَالَ أَحْلِفُ بِاللهِ لَقَدْ حَسَّتْ بِرِيحِ خَيْلٍ فَأَسْرَجَهَا وَأَخَذَ سِلاَحَهُ ثُمَّ نَهَضَ فَلَقِيَهُ رَجُلٌ مِنَ الصَّحَابَةِ فَقَالَ لَهُ أُخِذَتْ اللِّقَاحُ [زاد النبهاني أي لِقَاحُ النَّبِيِّ ﷺ فِي غَزْوَةِ قُرَدٍ وَتُسَمَّى غَزْوَةَ الْغَابَةِ] وَقَدْ ذَهَبَ النَّبِيُّ ﷺ فِي طَلَبِهَا وَأَصْحَابُهُ فَلَقِيَ النَّبِيَّ ﷺ فَقَالَ لَهُ إِمْضِ يَا أَبَا قَتَادَةَ صَحِبَكَ اللهُ قَالَ أَبُو قَتَادَةَ هذا لفظ البيهقي وبقيته من الخصائص الكبرى فَخَرَجْتُ فَإِذَا بِالنِّيَاقِ تُحَادَى وَهَجَمْتُ عَلَى الْعَسْكَرِ فَرُمِيتُ بِسَهْمِهِمْ فِي جَبْهَتِي فَنَزَعْتُ قِدْحَهُ وَأَنَا أَظُنُّ أَنِّي نَزَعْتُ الْحَدِيدَةَ فَطَلَعَ عَلَيَّ فَارِسٌ فَارِهٌ عَلَى وَجْهِهِ مِغْفَرٌ فَقَالَ لَقَدْ لَقَّانِيَكَ اللهُ يَا أَبَا قَتَادَةَ وَكَشَفَ عَنْ وَجْهِهِ فَإِذَا مَسْعَدَةُ الْفَزَارِيُّ فَقَالَ أَيُّمَا أَحَبُّ إِلَيكَ مُجَالَدَةٌ أَوْ مُطَاعَنَةٌ أَوْ مُصَارَعَةٌ فَقُلْتُ ذَاكَ إِلَيْكَ فَقَالَ

صِرَاعٌ فَنَزَلَ عَنْ دَابَّتِهِ وَنَزَلْتُ عَنْ دَابَّتِي ثُمَّ تَوَاثَبْنَا فَإِذَا أَنَا عَلَى صَدْرِهِ فَضَرَبْتُ بِيَدِي إِلَى سَيْفِهِ فَلَمَّا رَأَى أَنَّ السَّيْفَ قَدْ وَقَعَ بِيَدِي قَالَ يَا أَبَا قَتَادَةَ إِسْتَحْيِنِي قُلْتُ لاَ وَاللهِ قَالَ فَمَنْ لِلصِّبْيَةِ قُلْتُ النَّارُ ثُمَّ قَتَلْتُهُ وَأَدْرَجْتُهُ فِي بُرْدِي ثُمَّ أَخَذْتُ ثِيَابَهُ فَلَبِسْتُهَا وَأَخَذْتُ سِلاَحَهُ ثُمَّ اسْتَوَيْتُ عَلَى فَرَسِهِ وَكَانَتْ فَرَسِي نَفَرَتْ حِينَ تَعَالَجْنَا فَرَجَعَتْ رَاجِعَةً إِلَى الْعَسْكَرِ فَعَرَفُوهَا ثُمَّ مَضَيْتُ فَأَشْرَفْتُ عَلَى ابْنِ أَخِيهِ وَهُوَ فِي سَبْعَةَ عَشَرَ فَارِساً فَطَعَنْتُ ابْنَ أَخِيهِ طَعْنَةً دَقَقْتُ صُلْبَهُ فَانْكَشَفَ مَنْ مَعَهُ وَحَبَسْتُ اللِّقَاحَ بِرُمْحِي وَأَقْبَلَ النَّبِيُّ ﷺ وَأَصْحَابُهُ فَلَمَّا انْتَهَوا إِلَى مَوْضِعِ الْعَسْكَرِ إِذَا بِفَرَسِ أَبِي قَتَادَةَ وَقَدْ عُرْقِبَتْ فَقَالَ رَجُلٌ يَا رَسُولَ اللهِ عُرْقِبَتْ فَرَسُ أَبِي قَتَادَةَ فَقَالَ رَسُولُ اللهِ ﷺ وَيْحُ أُمِّكَ رُبَّ عَدُوٍّ لَكَ فِي الْحَرْبِ مَرَّتَينِ ثُمَّ أَقْبَلَ رَسُولُ اللهِ ﷺ وَأَصْحَابُهُ حَتَّى انْتَهَوا إِلَى الْمَوْضِعِ الَّذِي تَعَالَجْنَا فِيهِ إِذَا هُمْ بِرَجُلٍ مُسَجًّى فِي ثِيَابِ أَبِي قَتَادَةَ فَقَالَ رَجُلٌ يَا رَسُولَ اللهِ اسْتُشْهِدَ أَبُو قَتَادَةَ فَقَالَ رَسُولُ اللهِ ﷺ رَحِمَ اللهُ أَبَا قَتَادَةَ وَالَّذِي أَكْرَمَنِي بِمَا أَكْرَمَنِي بِهِ إِنَّ أَبَا قَتَادَةَ عَلَى آثَارِ الْقَوْمِ يَرْتَجِزُ فَخَرَجَ عُمَرُ بْنُ الْخَطَّابِ وَأَبُو بَكْرٍ الصِّدِّيقُ يَسْعَى حَتَّى كَشَفَ الثَّوبَ فَإِذَا وَجْهُ مَسْعَدَةَ فَقَالَ اللهُ أَكْبَرُ صَدَقَ اللهُ وَرَسُولُهُ

وَأَطْلَعْتُ أَحُوشُ اللِّقَاحَ فَقَالَ النَّبِيُّ ﷺ أَفْلَحَ وَجْهُكَ أَبَا قَتَادَةَ سَيِّدَ الْفُرْسَانِ بَارَكَ اللهُ فِيكَ وَفِي وَلَدِكَ وَفِي وَلَدِ وَلَدِكَ مَا هَذَا بِوَجْهِكَ قُلْتُ سَهْمٌ أَصَابَنِي فَقَالَ ادْنُ مِنِّي فَنَزَعَ النَّصْلَ نَزْعاً رَفِيقاً ثُمَّ بَزَقَ فِيهِ وَوَضَعَ رَاحَتَهُ عَلَيْهِ فَوَالَّذِي أَكْرَمَهُ بِالنُّبُوَّةِ مَا ضُرِبَ عَلَيَّ سَاعَةً قَطُّ وَلاَ قُرِحَ عَلَيَّ   هق في الدلائل

[The Prophet ﷺ declaimed *rajaz* at least twice, when his finger was cut in battle and he said: 184 "What are you but a finger that bled in the way of Allah?"[255] and in the heat of combat at Ḥunayn:

    185 *I am the Prophet, this is no fib!*
          I am the son of 'Abd al-Muṭṭalib![256]]

Rāfiʿ b. Khadīj ☀

Al-Ṭayālisī, Ibn Saʿd, and al-Bayhaqī narrated through Yaḥyā b. ʿAbd al-Ḥamīr b. Rāfiʿ: "My grandmother told me that Rāfiʿ in the battle of Uḥud or Ḥunayn was hit by an arrow in his *thunduwa* so he came to see the Prophet ﷺ saying, 'Messenger of Allah, remove the arrow." He said: 186 "Rāfiʿ, if you wish, I shall remove both the arrow and the *qiṭba*; or, if you wish, I shall remove the arrow and leave the arrowhead and I shall bear witness for you on the Day of Resurrection that you are a martyr." He answered, "Messenger of Allah, remove the arrow and leave the arrowhead, and bear witness for me on the Day of Resurrection that I am a martyr!" <He lived long after that until, in the caliphate of Muʿāwiya, the wound reopened and he died.> [257] The *thanduwa* [or *thundu'a*]

---

[255] Narrated from Jundub b. Sufyān by al-Bukhārī, Muslim, al-Tirmidhī, and Aḥmad.

[256] Narrated from al-Barā' b. ʿĀzib by al-Bukhārī, Muslim, and Aḥmad.

[257] Narrated by Ṭabarānī, *Kabīr* (4:239 §4242) and Aḥmad, the latter without the bracketed segment, both with a chain of sound narrators cf. Haythamī (6:185, 9:346), Rāfiʿ's wife, Umm ʿAbd al-Ḥamīd, being a *ṣaḥābiyya* according to the *Iṣāba* (8:254). Narrated in full by al-Ḥākim (1990 ed. 3:648) from al-Wāqidī and, in part, by al-Ṭayālisī (p. 129 §962). Cited in the *Khaṣā'is* (2:221). Ibn Kathīr in *al-Bidāya* (6:227) said he lived until 73 or 74 (Muʿāwiya died in 60). Cf. *Iṣāba* (2:436) and Qārī in *Sharḥ Musnad Abī Ḥanīfa*.

for the man is the same as the breast for the woman, and the *qiṭba* is the arrowhead.

عَنِ امْرَأَةِ رَافِعِ بْنِ خَدِيجٍ أَنَّ رَافِعًا رَمَى مَعَ رَسُولِ اللهِ ﷺ يَوْمَ
أُحُدٍ وَيَوْمَ خَيْبَرَ قَالَ أَنَا أَشُكُّ بِسَهْمٍ فِي ثَنْدُوَتِهِ فَأَتَى النَّبِيَّ ﷺ
فَقَالَ يَا رَسُولَ اللهِ انْزِعِ السَّهْمَ قَالَ يَا رَافِعُ إِنْ شِئْتَ نَزَعْتُ
السَّهْمَ وَالْقُطْبَةَ جَمِيعًا وَإِنْ شِئْتَ نَزَعْتُ السَّهْمَ وَتَرَكْتُ الْقُطْبَةَ
وَشَهِدْتُ لَكَ يَوْمَ الْقِيَامَةِ أَنَّكَ شَهِيدٌ قَالَ يَا رَسُولَ اللهِ بَلْ
انْزِعِ السَّهْمَ وَاتْرُكِ الْقُطْبَةَ وَاشْهَدْ لِي يَوْمَ الْقِيَامَةِ أَنِّي شَهِيدٌ قَالَ
فَنَزَعَ رَسُولُ اللهِ ﷺ السَّهْمَ وَتَرَكَ الْقُطْبَةَ حم وجاء بزيادة فَعَاشَ
بِهَا حَتَّى كَانَ فِي خِلَافَةِ مُعَاوِيَةَ فَانْتَقَضَ بِهِ الْجُرْحُ فَمَاتَ بَعْدَ
الْعَصْرِ ط طب مسند أحمد بن منيع ك هق في الدلائل أبو نعيم في المعرفة

Abū Sa'īd al-Khudrī ﵁

Al-Bayhaqī narrated that Abū Sa'īd al-Khudrī ﵁ said, "We suffered hunger in a way we had never suffered before, so my sister said to me, 'Go to the Messenger of Allah and ask him for something.' I came as he was addressing the people, and he said: 187 <'Whoever abstains [from illicit things], Allah shall forgive him, and whoever does without [his needs], Allah shall enrich him.'> I said to myself, it is as if he means me by this! I must not ask him anything. I went back to my sister and told her. She said, 'You did well.' The next morning, by Allah! I toiled and harrowed myself heaving bricks and got some pay from a Jew. With it we bought food and ate. Later, the world poured in. Today, not one house of the *Anṣār* is wealthier than us." [258]

[258] Narrated by Abū Ya'lā (2:263), al-Ṭabarī in *Tahdhīb al-Āthār*, al-Bayhaqī in the

عَنْ أَبِي سَعِيدٍ الخُدْرِيِّ رَضِيَ اللهُ عَنْهُ قَالَ أَصَابَنَا جُوعٌ مَا أَصَابَنَا مِثْلُهُ قَطُّ فَقَالَتْ لِي أُخْتِي إِذْهَبْ إِلَى رَسُولِ اللهِ ﷺ فَاسْأَلْهُ فَذَهَبْتُ فَإِذَا هُوَ يَخْطُبُ فَقَالَ مَنْ يَسْتَعْفِفْ يُعِفَّهُ اللهُ وَمَنْ يَسْتَغْنِ يُغْنِهِ اللهُ فَقُلْتُ فِي نَفْسِي وَاللهِ لَكَأَنَّمَا أُرِدْتَ بِهَذَا لاَ جَرَمَ لاَ أَسْأَلُهُ شَيْئاً فَرَجَعْتُ إِلَى أُخْتِي فَأَخْبَرْتُهَا فَقَالَتْ أَحْسَنْتَ فَلَمَّا كَانَ مِنَ الْغَدِ فَإِنِّي وَاللهِ لأُتْعِبُ نَفْسِي تَحْتَ الآجِرِ إِذْ وَجَدْتُ مِنْ دَرَاهِمِ يَهُودَ فَابْتَعْنَا بِهِ وَأَكَلْنَا مِنْهُ وَجَاءَتِ الدُّنْيَا فَمَا مِنْ أَهْلِ بَيْتٍ مِنَ الأَنْصَارِ أَكْثَرُ أَمْوَالاً مِنَّا

ع الطبري في تهذيب الآثار هق في الدلائل وجاء دون ذكر الكلام النفسي حم ط ش مسند ابن الجعد ابن أبي الدنيا في القناعة والتعفف حب هق في الدلائل والشعب وأصله في الكتب التسعة هكذا وبلفظ يَسْتَعِفَّ وجاء أيضا وَمَنْ اِسْتَعَفَّ يُعِفَّهُ اللهُ حل وفي الباب عن حكيم بن حزام

Abū Khaythama ﷺ

Al-Bayhaqī narrated through Ibn Isḥāq who said that ʿAbd Allāh b. Abī Bakr b. Ḥazm narrated to him that Abū Khaythama went out after the Prophet ﷺ and caught up with him in Tabūk at the time he alighted there. The people said, "Here is a rider coming on the way." The Prophet ﷺ said: [188] "Be Abū Khaythama!" They said, "It is, by Allah! Abū Khaythama."[259]

Dalā'il (6:291), and without mention of the self-discourse by Ibn al-Jaʿd in his *Musnad* (p. 195 §1281) and Abū Nuʿaym (7:203). The bracketed segment is narrated from Ḥakīm b. Ḥizām and Abū Saʿīd by al-Bukhārī and Aḥmad; Abū Saʿīd from Muslim, Mālik, al-Tirmidhī, al-Nasā'ī, Abū Dāwūd, and Aḥmad.

[259]Narrated in this exact wording by al-Bayhaqī in the *Dalā'il* (5:223) and as part of a

عَنْ عَبْدِ اللهِ بْنِ أَبِي بَكْرِ بْنِ مُحَمَّدِ بْنِ عَمْرِو بْنِ حَزْمٍ أَنَّ أَبَا خَيْثَمَةَ لَحِقَ النَّبِيَّ ﷺ فَأَدْرَكَهُ بِتَبُوكٍ حِينَ نَزَلَهَا فَقَالَ النَّاسُ هَذَا رَاكِبٌ عَلَى الطَّرِيقِ مُقْبِلٌ فَقَالَ رَسُولُ اللهِ ﷺ كُنْ أَبَا خَيْثَمَةَ فَقَالُوا يَا رَسُولَ اللهِ هُوَ وَاللهِ أَبُو خَيْثَمَةَ م حم عق طب حب هق في الدلائل وهذا لفظه

Khālid b. al-Walīd ﵁

Al-Bayhaqī and Ibn Mandah narrated through Ibn Isḥāq that Yazīd b. Rūmān narrated to him **[492]** as well as ʿAbd Allāh b. Abī Bakr, that the Messenger of Allah ﷺ sent Khālid b. al-Walīd to Ukaydir, a man of Kinda who was king of Dūma [near Tabūk], a Christian. The Prophet ﷺ said: 189 "You will find him hunting oxen." Khālid marched until he sighted his fort on a clear, moonlit night. Ukaydir was on one of the rooftops with his wife when the ox came horning the gate of the palace. His wife said to him, "Have you ever seen anything like this?" He said, "No, by Allah!" She said, "Who would miss such an opportunity?" He said, "No one!" Then he came down, called for his horse to be readied, and rode out with a group of his relatives. They went out in pursuit and the cavalry of the Messenger of Allah ﷺ met them and captured him. A man from Ṭayyi' named Bujayr b. Bajra said the following on this occasion:

May the ox-driver be blessed for my
Sighting Allah guiding every guide!
Who, then, can turn away from the place near Tabūk?
Truly, we were commanded jihad.

Whereupon the Prophet ﷺ said to him: a "May Allah bless your mouth!" After this, he lived ninety years and did not lose a single tooth.[260]

longer ḥadīth from Kaʿb b. Mālik by Muslim, Aḥmad and others.

[260]Narrated *mursal* from ʿAbd Allāh b. Abī Bakr b. Ḥazm by al-Bayhaqī in *al-Sunan al-*

عَنْ يَزِيدَ بْنِ رُومَانَ وَعَبْدِ اللهِ بْنِ أَبِي بَكْرٍ أَنَّ رَسُولَ اللهِ ﷺ بَعَثَ خَالِدَ بْنَ الْوَلِيدِ إِلَى أُكَيْدِرِ بْنِ عَبْدِ الْمَلِكِ رَجُلٌ مِنْ كِنْدَةَ كَانَ مَلِكًا عَلَى دُومَةَ وَكَانَ نَصْرَانِيًّا فَقَالَ رَسُولُ اللهِ ﷺ لِخَالِدٍ إِنَّكَ سَتَجِدُهُ يَصِيدُ الْبَقَرَ فَخَرَجَ خَالِدٌ حَتَّى إِذَا كَانَ مِنْ حِصْنِهِ مَنْظَرَ الْعَيْنِ وَفِي لَيْلَةٍ مُقْمِرَةٍ صَافِيَةٍ وَهُوَ عَلَى سَطْحٍ وَمَعَهُ امْرَأَتُهُ فَأَتَتِ الْبَقَرُ تَحُكُّ بِقُرُونِهَا بَابَ الْقَصْرِ فَقَالَتْ لَهُ امْرَأَتُهُ هَلْ رَأَيْتَ مِثْلَ هَذَا قَطُّ قَالَ لاَ وَاللهِ قَالَتْ فَمَنْ يَتْرُكُ مِثْلَ هَذَا قَالَ لاَ أَحَدٌ فَنَزَلَ فَأَمَرَ بِفَرَسِهِ فَأُسْرِجَ وَرَكِبَ مَعَهُ نَفَرٌ مِنْ أَهْلِ بَيْتِهِ فِيهِمْ أَخٌ لَهُ يُقَالُ لَهُ حَسَّانُ فَخَرَجُوا مَعَهُ بِمَطَارِدِهِمْ فَتَلَقَّتْهُمْ خَيْلُ رَسُولِ اللهِ ﷺ فَأَخَذَتْهُ هق أصله في د هق في الدلائل بزيادة فَقَالَ رَجُلٌ مِنْ طَيِّئٍ يُقَالُ لَهُ بُجَيْرُ بْنُ بَجَرَةَ يَذْكُرُ قَوْلَ رَسُولِ اللهِ ﷺ لِخَالِدٍ إِنَّكَ سَتَجِدُهُ يَصِيدُ الْبَقَرَ وَمَا كَانَتْ صُنْعَةُ الْبَقَرَةِ تِلْكَ اللَّيْلَةَ حَتَّى اسْتَخْرَجَتْهُ لِقَوْلِ رَسُولِ اللهِ ﷺ

تَبَارَكَ سَائِقُ الْبَقَرَاتِ إِنِّي   رَأَيْتُ اللهَ يَهْدِي كُلَّ هَادٍ

Kubrā (9:187) and *musnad* from (1) Anas by al-Nasā'ī in *al-Sunan al-Kubrā* (5:259 §8836) and Ibn Abī Ḥātim in his *ʿIlal* (1:323-324 §967), (2) Ibn ʿAbbās by al-Wāqidī and Ibn ʿAsākir, (3) Bujayr b. Bajra (cf. next note), and Ḥudhayfa by al-Ḥākim (1990 ed. 4:565). Cf. al-Taymī, *Dalā'il*, (p. 137 §149), Ibn Hishām (5:206-207), al-Ṭabarī, *Tārīkh* (2:185), al-Ṣanʿānī, *Subul al-Salām* (4:66), *Iṣāba* (1:244), and *Kanz* (§30276-30277, §30280). The Prophet's ﷺ expression means, "How well you spoke!"

فَمَنْ يَكُ حَائِداً عَنْ ذِي تَبُوكٍ   فَإِنَّا قَدْ أُمِرْنَا بِالجِهَادِ

الواقدي أبو نعيم في الدلائل والمعرفة كر قال هق في الدلائل زاد فيه غيره وليس في روايتنا

فَقَالَ لَهُ النَّبِيُّ ﷺ لاَ يَفْضُضِ اللهُ فَاكَ فَأَتَى عَلَيْهِ تِسْعُونَ سَنَةً

فَمَا تَحَرَّكَ لَهُ ضِرْسٌ وَلاَ سِنٌّ   ابن إسحاق حسبما ذكر ابن كثير في السيرة

Ibn Mandah, Ibn al-Sakan, and Abū Nuʿaym narrated through Abū al-Mu'ārik al-Shammākh b. Mu'ārik b. Murra b. Sakhr b. Bujayr b. Bajrat al-Ṭā'ī who said that his father narrated to him from his grandfather, from his father Bujayr b. Bajra, "I was in the army of Khālid b. al-Walīd when the Prophet ﷺ sent him to Ukaydir of Dūma and said to him: 190 "You will find him hunting oxen." We came face-to-face with him on a moonlit night as he had gone out just as the Prophet ﷺ had described, and we took him. When we came back to the Prophet ﷺ, I declaimed poems to him, among them, *May the driver of the oxen be blessed*."[261]

عَنْ بُجَيْرِ بْنُ بَجْرَةَ قَالَ كُنْتُ فِي جَيْشِ خَالِدِ بْنِ الْوَلِيدِ حِينَ بَعَثَهُ النَّبِيُّ ﷺ إِلَى أُكَيْدِرِ دُومَةَ فَقَالَ لَهُ إِنَّكَ تَجِدُهُ يَصِيدُ الْبَقَرَ فَوَافَقْنَاهُ فِي لَيْلَةٍ مُقْمِرَةٍ وَقَدْ خَرَجَ كَمَا نَعَتَهُ رَسُولُ اللهِ ﷺ فَأَخَذْنَاهُ فَلَمَّا أَتَيْنَا النَّبِيَّ ﷺ أَنْشَدْتُهُ أَبْيَاتَ مِنْهَا

تَبَارَكَ سَائِقُ الْبَقَرَاتِ إِنِّي   رَأَيْتُ اللهَ يَهْدِي كُلَّ هَادِ

[261] Narrated from Bujayr: *mursal* by Ibn Isḥāq as cited in Ibn Hishām (2:526) and, through him, Abū Nuʿaym in the *Dalā'il* (p. 526-527 §455), al-Taymī in the *Dalā'il* (p. 144 §157), Ibn Mandah in *Maʿrifat al-Ṣaḥāba* (1:293-294) and al-Bayhaqī in the *Dalā'il*; and *musnad* by Ibn Ḥajar in the *Iṣāba* (1:268). The latter also narrates it from Ùrwa.

فَقَالَ النَّبِيُّ ﷺ لاَ يَفْضُضِ اللهُ فَاكَ فَأَتَتْ عَلَيْهِ تِسْعُونَ سَنَةً
وَمَا تَحَرَّكَ لَهُ سِنٌّ التيمي أبو نعيم هق في الدلائل والمعرفة لابن منده

Al-Bayhaqī also narrated that ʿUrwa said that when the Messenger of Allah ﷺ made for Madīna from Tabūk in a convoy, he sent Khālid b. al-Walīd with a force of four hundred and twenty riders to Ukaydir of Dūmat al-Jandal. Khālid said, "Messenger of Allah, what can we do in Dūmat al-Jandal when Ukaydir is there, and we only have a small unit of Muslims?" He replied: [191] "Perhaps Allah shall let you meet Ukaydir while he is hunting and you shall seize the key and capture him, so that Allah opens Dūma for you." Khālid marched until, approaching it, he alighted behind it, in keeping with the saying of the Messenger of Allah ﷺ that he might find him hunting. As Khālid and his troops were in their camp that night, the oxen came and started to rub against the gate of the fort while Ukaydir was drinking and carousing in his fort between his two wives. One of his wives looked out and saw the oxen rubbing against the gate. She said, "I have never seen as much meat as tonight!" He said, "What is it?" She said, "These oxen are rubbing against the gate and the wall!" He mounted his horse together with his pages and relatives [and rode out] until they passed by Khālid and his troops. They captured him and his company and put them in fetters. Khālid told him what the Messenger of Allah had said. Ukaydir replied, "By Allah, I never saw them – he meant the oxen – coming near us before, until recently. I used to lie in wait for them when I wanted to catch them, and ride after them for one or two days!"[262]

عَنْ عُرْوَةَ قَالَ لَمَّا تَوَجَّهَ رَسُولُ اللهِ ﷺ قَافِلاً إِلَى المَدِينَةِ بَعَثَ
خَالِدَ بْنَ الْوَلِيدِ فِي أَرْبَعَمِائَةٍ وَعِشْرِينَ فَارِساً إِلَى أُكَيْدِرِ دُومَةِ

[262]Narrated by al-Bayhaqī in the *Dalā'il* (5:251) and Ibn ʿAsākir (9:200) with a strong chain through Ibn Lahīʿa from Abū al-Aswad al-Du'alī cf. al-Dhahabī, *Tārīkh al-Islām* (2:646) and *Isāba* (1:244).

الْجَنْدَلِ فَلَمَّا عَهِدَ إِلَيْهِ عَهْدَهُ قَالَ خَالِدٌ يَا رَسُولَ اللهِ كَيْفَ بِدُومَةِ الْجَنْدَلِ وَفِيهَا أُكَيْدِرُ وَإِنَّمَا نَأْتِيهَا فِي عِصَابَةٍ مِنَ الْمُسْلِمِينَ فَقَالَ رَسُولُ اللهِ ﷺ لَعَلَّ اللهَ عَزَّ وَجَلَّ يُلْقِيكَ أُكَيْدِرَ أَحْسَبُهُ قَالَ يَقْتَنِصُ فَتَقْتَنِصُ الْمِفْتَاحَ وَتَأْخُذُهُ فَيَفْتَحُ اللهُ لَكَ دُومَةَ فَسَارَ خَالِدُ بْنُ الْوَلِيدِ حَتَّى إِذَا دَنَا مِنْهَا نَزَلَ فِي أَدْبَارِهَا لِذِكْرِ رَسُولِ اللهِ ﷺ لَعَلَّكَ تَلْقَاهُ يَصْطَادُ فَبَيْنَمَا خَالِدٌ وَأَصْحَابُهُ فِي مَنْزِلِهِمْ لَيلاً إِذْ أَقْبَلَتِ الْبَقَرُ حَتَّى جَعَلَتْ تَحْتَكُّ بِبَابِ الْحِصْنِ وَأُكَيْدِرُ يَشْرَبُ وَيَتَغَنَّى فِي حِصْنِهِ بَيْنَ امْرَأَتَيْهِ فَاطَّلَعَتْ إِحْدَى امْرَأَتَيْهِ فَرَأَتْ الْبَقَرَ تَحْتَكُّ بِالْبَابِ وَالْحَائِطِ فَقَالَتِ امْرَأَتُهُ لَمْ أَرَ كَاللَّيْلَةِ فِي اللَّحْمِ قَالَ وَمَا ذَاكَ فَقَالَتْ هَذِهِ الْبَقَرَةُ تَحْتَكُّ بِالْبَابِ وَالْحَائِطِ فَلَمَّا رَأَى ذَلِكَ أُكَيْدِرُ ثَارَ فَرَكِبَ عَلَى فَرَسٍ لَهُ مُعَدَّةٍ وَرَكِبَ عَلَمَتُهُ وَأَهْلُهُ فَطَلَبَهَا حَتَّى مَرَّ بِخَالِدٍ وَأَصْحَابِهِ فَأَخَذُوهُ وَمَنْ كَانَ مَعَهُ فَأَوْثَقُوهُمْ وَذَكَرَ خَالِدٌ قَولَ رَسُولِ اللهِ ﷺ وَقَالَ خَالِدٌ لأُكَيدِرَ أَرَأَيْتَكَ إِنْ أَجَرْتُكَ تَفْتَحُ لِي دُومَةَ قَالَ نَعَم فَانْطَلَقَ حَتَّى دَنَا مِنْهَا فَثَارَ أَهْلُهَا وَأَرَادُوا أَنْ يَفْتَحُوا لَهُ فَأَبَى عَلَيْهِمْ أَخُوهُ فَلَمَّا رَأَى ذَلِكَ قَالَ لِخَالِدٍ أَيُّهَا الرَّجُلُ خَلِّنِي فَلَكَ اللهَ لأَفْتَحَنَّهَا لَكَ إِنْ أَخِي لاَ يَفْتَحُهَا لِي مَا عَلِمَ أَنِّي فِي وَثَاقِكَ فَأَرْسَلَهُ خَالِدٌ فَفَتَحَهَا لَهُ فَلَمَّا دَخَلَ أَوْثَقَ

أَخَاهُ وَفَتَحَهَا لِخَالِدٍ ثُمَّ قَالَ اصْنَعْ مَا شِئْتَ فَدَخَلَ خَالِدٌ وَأَصْحَابُهُ فَذَكَرَ خَالِدٌ رَضِيَ اللهُ عَنْهُ لَهُ قَولَ رَسُولِ اللهِ ﷺ وَالَّذِي أَمَرَهُ فَقَالَ لَهُ أُكَيدِرُ وَاللهِ مَا رَأَيْتُهَا قَطُّ جَاءَتْنَا إِلاَّ الْبَارِحَةَ يُرِيدُ الْبَقَرَ وَلَقَدْ كُنْتُ أُضْمِرُ لَهَا إِذَا أَرَدْتُ أَخْذَهَا فَأَرْكَبُ لَهَا الْيَوْمَ وَالْيَومَيْنِ هق في الدلائل كر

Al-Bayhaqī also narrated that Bilāl b. Yaḥyā said that the Messenger of Allah ﷺ sent out Abū Bakr in command of the *Muhājirūn* to Dūmat al-Jandal and he sent with him Khālid b. al-Walīd in command of the Bedouins. He said to them: 192 "Go, and you shall find **[493]** Ukaydir of Dūma hunting wild beasts. Make a clean catch of him and send him to me." They went off and found him exactly as he ﷺ had said. They captured him and sent him.

عَنْ بِلاَلِ بْنِ يَحْيَى قَالَ بَعَثَ رَسُولُ اللهِ ﷺ أَبَا بَكْرٍ رَضِيَ اللهُ عَنْهُ عَلَى المهَاجِرِينَ إِلَى دُومَةَ الْجَنْدَلِ وَبَعَثَ خَالِدَ بْنَ الْوَلِيدِ رَضِيَ اللهُ عَنْهُ عَلَى الأَعْرَابِ مَعَهُ وَقَالَ انْطَلِقُوا فَإِنَّكُمْ سَتَجِدُونَ أُكَيْدِرَ دُومَةَ الْجَنْدَلِ يَقْتَنِصُ الْوَحْشَ فَخُذُوهُ أَخْذاً فَابْعَثُوا بِهِ إِلَيَّ وَلاَ تَقْتُلُوهُ وَحاصِرُوا أَهْلَهَا فَانْطَلَقُوا فَوَجَدُوا أُكَيدِرَ دُومَةَ كَمَا قَالَ رَسُولُ اللهِ ﷺ فَأَخَذُوهُ فَبَعَثُوا بِهِ إِلَى رَسُولِ اللهِ ﷺ هق في الدلائل كر

Ibn Saʿd narrated from al-ʿAbbās b. ʿAbd Allāh b. Maʿbad that Khālid b. al-Walīd wanted to go to Mecca and asked permission of the Prophet ﷺ for a man from the Banū Bakr to accompany him. The Messenger of Allah ﷺ said to him: [193] "Go with him <but [a] do not trust even your own firstborn brother>." Khālid rode out in his company. [One night,] he woke up as the other man had drawn his sword and was about to kill him, so Khālid killed him. [263]

قَالَ فِي الْخَصَائِصِ الْكُبْرَى وَأَخْرَجَ ابْنُ سَعْدٍ عَنِ الْعَبَّاسِ بْنِ عَبْدِ اللهِ بْنِ مَعْبَدٍ أَنَّ خَالِدَ بْنَ الْوَلِيدِ أَرَادَ الْخُرُوجَ إِلَى مَكَّةَ وَأَنَّهُ اسْتَأْذَنَ النَّبِيَّ ﷺ فِي رَجُلٍ مِنْ بَنِي بَكْرٍ يُرِيدُ أَنْ يَصْحَبَهُ فَقَالَ لَهُ رَسُولُ اللهِ ﷺ اُخْرُجْ بِهِ وَأَخُوكَ الْبَكْرِيُّ فَلاَ تَأْمَنْهُ فَخَرَجَ بِهِ فَاسْتَيْقَظَ خَالِدٌ وَقَدْ سَلَّ السَّيْفَ يُرِيدُ أَنْ يَقْتُلَهُ بِهِ فَقَتَلَهُ خَالِدٌ

لم أجده ويشبه أن يكون اختلط بخبر عمرو بن غفواء الآتي

ʿAmr b. Sālim al-Khuzāʿī ﷺ

Al-Ṭabarānī narrated that Maymūna the Mother of the believers said: "The Messenger of Allah ﷺ was sleeping with me one night and he got up to make ablution and pray. I heard him say during his ablution in the dead of night: [194] *"Labbayka labbayka labbayka"* – [like this,] three times – then *"nuṣirta nuṣirta nuṣirta"* [like this,] three times. When he came out, I asked him, "Messenger of Allah, I heard you say, during your ablution, 'In your service!' three times, and 'To your defense!' three times, as if you were addressing someone. Was there anyone with you?" He replied: [a] "This was the poetry champion *(rājiz)* of the Banū Kaʿb" – one of the sub-tribes of the Khuzāʿa – "invoking my aid *(yastaṣrikhunī)*[264] and

---

[263] I could not find it other than in the *Khaṣāʾiṣ*. Something similar is narrated from ʿAmr b. al-Ghafwāʾ al-Khuzāʿī (see his section further down) with ʿAmr instead of Khālid.

[264] Ibn Ḥajar, *Iṣāba* (4:631) has another wording: "invoking my mercy *(yastarḥimunī)*."

asserting that the Quraysh had helped the Banū Bakr against them." The latter had allied themselves with Quraysh the day of the Ḥudaybiya truce while the Khuzāʿa had allied themselves with the Prophet ﷺ and he became duty-bound to defend them. The support of the Quraysh for the Banū Bakr against the Khuzāʿa was therefore a violation of their truce with the Messenger of Allah ﷺ. This incident was the catalyst for the conquest of Mecca and, immediately afterwards, he prepared himself to enter it and conquered it.[265]

عَنْ مَيْمُونَةَ بِنْتِ الْحَارِثِ زَوجِ النَّبِيِّ ﷺ وَآلِهِ أَنَّ رَسُولَ اللهِ ﷺ بَاتَ عِنْدَهَا فِي لَيْلَتِهَا ثُمَّ قَامَ فَتَوَضَّأَ لِلصَّلاَةِ فَسَمِعَتْهُ وَهُوَ يَقُولُ لَبَّيْكَ لَبَّيْكَ لَبَّيْكَ ثَلاَثاً أَوْ نُصِرْتَ نُصِرْتَ نُصِرْتَ ثَلاَثاً قَالَتْ فَلَمَّا خَرَجَ مِنْ مُتَوَضَّئِهِ قُلْتُ يَا رَسُولَ اللهِ ﷺ بِأَبِي أَنْتَ وَأُمِّي سَمِعْتُكَ تُكَلِّمُ إِنْسَاناً فَهَلْ كَانَ مَعَكَ أَحَدٌ قَالَ هَذَا رَاجِزُ بَنِي كَعْبٍ يَسْتَصْرِخُنِي وَيَزْعُمُ أَنَّ قُرَيْشاً أَعَانَتْ عَلَيْهِمْ بَنِي بَكْرٍ

طب أبو نعيم في الدلائل وستأتي تتمته

Ibn Isḥāq said – as found in Ibn Hishām's *Sīra* – that when the Banū Bakr and Quraysh defeated the Khuzāʿa and looted them, violating the terms of the solemn pact to which they had agreed with the Messenger of Allah ﷺ by warring with the Khuzāʿa, his formal allies, ʿAmr b. Sālim al-Khuzāʿī, one of the Banū Kaʿb there, rode out until he came to see the Messenger of Allah ﷺ in al-

[265]Narrated from Maymūna by al-Ṭabarānī in the *Kabīr* (23:433-434 §1052) and *Saghīr* (2:167-169 §968) and al-Taymī in his *Dalā'il* (p. 73-74 §59), both with a slightly weak chain because of Yaḥyā b. Sulaymān b. Naḍla al-Madīnī cf. al-Haythamī (6:163-164) although Ibn ʿAdī in *al-Kāmil* (7:255 §2156) said "he narrated reports from Mālik and the Madinans, most of which are valid." Ibn Ḥibbān included him in his *Thiqāt* (9:269). Cf. *Isāba* (4:631), *Fath* (7:520), *Sīra Halabiyya* (3:5), and Dahlān's *Sīra* (2:76-77).

Madīna. His coming gave the impetus for the conquest of Mecca.[266] He stood before the Prophet ﷺ as the latter sat in the Mosque, in full sight of the people, and declaimed:

Lord! I am appealing to Muḥammad
by the time-honored pact of both our fathers.[267]
We were ever a son and you[268] *a father;*
then we entered Islam and remained loyal.
Help us, and may Allah help you always!
Summon His servants, they shall come in arms,
Among them, the Prophet, mobilized–
if he is wronged, his face glowers.
In his legion he marches, a sea, foaming.
Quraysh broke its treaty with you!
They violated the truce they pledged you,
made me as good as dead and buried![269]
They claimed I could not call on anyone
although they are meaner and less by far!
They snared us at Watīr during our vigils and
slew us as we bowed and prostrated.[270]

The Prophet ﷺ said: 195 "In your defense, ʿAmr b. Sālim!" <Then the Prophet ﷺ glimpsed a cloud in the sky and said: a "Truly this cloud is initiating the victory of the Banū Ka'b."> Then he ﷺ geared up **[494]** for the conquest of Mecca and took it.[271]

[266]Cf. Ibn ʿUmar's narration in Ibn Ḥibbān (13:140 §5996) and Ibn Ḥajar, *Talkhīṣ al-Ḥabīr* (4:131 §1929).

[267]*Allāhumma innī nāshidu Muḥammadā / ḥilfa abīnā wa'abīhi al-atladā.*

[268]*I.e.* the Banū Hāshim and Banū ʿAbd al-Muṭṭalib with a rhetorical trope of apostrophe *(iltifāt)* away from the third person singular to the second person plural.

[269]*Wa-ja'alū lī fī kadā'in raṣadā*, misspelt in Nabhānī as *wa-ja'alū lī fīka dā'in raṣadā.*

[270]Ibn ʿAsākir (43:519) narrated from Ibn al-Musayyib: "There is not one homebound woman of Banū Khuzāʿa except she memorized the verses of ʿAmr b. Sālim al-Khuzāʿī to the Messenger of Allah ﷺ."

[271]Narrated (1) through al-Zuhrī from ʿUrwa b. al-Zubayr from the Companion al-Miswar b. Makhrama and the *Tābiʿī* Marwān b. al-Ḥakam by Ibn Isḥāq in the *Maghāzī* (cf. Ibn Hishām 5:48, al-Ṭaḥāwī, *Sharḥ Maʿānī al-Āthār* 3:315-316, *Iṣāba* 4:630-631, and *Bidāya* 4:278), al-Ṭabarī in his *Tārīkh* (2:152-153), Ibn ʿAsākir in his *Tārīkh* (43:519-520), and al-Bayhaqī in the *Sunan al-Kubrā* (9:233), *Ṣughrā*, and *Dalāʾil*; (2) from Ibn ʿAbbās by Ibn Mandah and Abū Nuʿaym in *Maʿrifat al-Ṣaḥāba* as well as Ibn al-Athīr in *Usd al-Ghāba*

عَنْ ابْنِ إِسْحَاقَ حَدَّثَنِي الزُّهْرِيُّ عَنْ عُرْوَةَ بْنِ الزُّبَيْرِ عَنْ مَرْوَانَ بْنِ الْحَكَمِ وَالْمِسْوَرِ بْنِ مَخْرَمَةَ أنهما حدثاه جميعا قَالاَ كَانَ فِي صُلْحِ رَسُولِ اللهِ ﷺ يَوْمَ الْحُدَيْبِيَةِ بَيْنَهُ وَبَيْنَ قُرَيْشٍ أَنَّهُ مَنْ شَاءَ أَنْ يَدْخُلَ فِي عَقْدِ مُحَمَّدٍ وَعَهْدِهِ دَخَلَ وَمَنْ شَاءَ أَنْ يَدْخُلَ فِي عَقْدِ قُرَيْشٍ وَعَهْدِهِمْ دَخَلَ فَتَوَاثَبَتْ خُزَاعَةُ وَقَالُوا نَحْنُ نَدْخُلُ فِي عَقْدِ مُحَمَّدٍ ﷺ وَعَهْدِهِ وَتَواثَبَتْ بَنُو بَكْرٍ فَقَالُوا نَحْنُ نَدْخُلُ فِي عَقْدِ قُرَيْشٍ وَعَهْدِهِمْ فَمَكَثُوا فِي تِلْكَ الْهُدْنَةِ نَحْوَ السَّبْعَةِ أَوِ الثَّمَانِيَةَ عَشَرَ شَهْرًا ثُمَّ إِنَّ بَنِي بَكْرٍ الَّذِينَ كَانُوا دَخَلُوا فِي عَقْدِ قُرَيْشٍ وَعَهْدِهِمْ وَثَبُوا عَلَى خُزَاعَةَ الَّذِينَ كَانُوا دَخَلُوا فِي عَهْدِ رَسُولِ اللهِ ﷺ وَعَقْدِهِ لَيْلا بِمَاءٍ لَهُمْ يُقَالُ لَهُ الْوَتِيرُ قَرِيبٌ مِنْ مَكَّةَ فَقَالَتْ قُرَيْشٌ مَا يَعْلَمُ بِنَا مُحَمَّدٌ وَهَذَا اللَّيْلُ وَمَا يَرَانَا أَحَدٌ فَأَعَانُوهُمْ عَلَيْهِمْ بِالْكُرَاعِ وَالسِّلاحِ فَقَاتَلُوهَا مَعَهُمْ لِلضِّغْنِ عَلَى

(4:225-226 cf. *Isāba* 5:285); (3) from Abū Hurayra by al-Bazzār and al-Bayhaqī (cf. *Bidāya* 4:281) with a fair chain according to Ibn Ḥajar in the *Fatḥ* (7:520) and al-Haythamī (6:162); (4) from the *Tābi'ūn* Abū Salama and Yaḥyā b. ʿAbd al-Raḥmān b. Ḥāṭib by Ibn Abī Shayba (7:398 §36900) and (5) also *mursal* from 'Ikrima by Ibn Abī Shayba (7:400-401 §36902) and al-Ṭaḥāwī in *Sharḥ Ma'ānī al-Āthār* (3:291, 3 :312-313). The bracketed segment is narrated only through al-Zuhrī. Cf. *Iktifā'* (2:215); al-Fākihī, *Akhbār Makka* (5:103); *Istī'āb* (3:1175-1176); Ibn al-Qayyim, *Zād* (3:348-349); *Sīra Ḥalabiyya* (3:5-6); Ibn Taymiyya, *al-Sārim al-Maslūl* (2:214); *Isāba* (1:122), *Fatḥ* (7:519-520), *Talkhīs al-Ḥabīr* (4:131-132 §1929), Ibn al-Athīr, *Kāmil* (2:162), al-Suhaylī, *Rawd* (2:265), and *Kanz* (§14422, §30166, §30195, §30204). Al-Watīr or Watīn is a Khuzāʿa watering-point in the lowest area of Mecca cf. Yāqūt and *al-Nihāya*. Ibn Isḥāq and al-Wāqidī said 'Amr was accompanied by forty riders of the Banū Khuzāʿa when he arrived in Madīna. Another report by al-Bārūdī with a weak *munqati'* chain attributes those verses to Budayl b. Kulthūm b. Sālim al-Khuzāʿī cf. *Isāba* (1:274).

رَسُولِ اللهِ ﷺ وَأَنَّ عَمْرَو بْنَ سَالِمٍ رَكِبَ إِلَى رَسُولِ اللهِ ﷺ عِنْدَمَا كَانَ مِنْ أَمْرِ خُزَاعَةَ وَبَنِي بَكْرٍ بِالْوَتِيرِ حَتَّى قَدِمَ الْمَدِينَةِ إِلَى رَسُولِ اللهِ ﷺ يُخْبِرُهُ الْخَبَرَ وَقَدْ قَالَ أَبْيَاتٍ مِنَ الشِّعْرِ فَلَمَّا قَدِمَ عَلَى رَسُولِ اللهِ ﷺ أَنْشَدَهُ إِيَّاهَا:

اللهُمَّ إِنِّي نَاشِدٌ مُحَمَّدَا حِلْفَ أَبِينَا وَأَبِيهِ الأَتْلَدَا
كُنَّا وَلَدًا وَكُنْتَ وَالِدَا ثُمَّتَ أَسْلَمْنَا وَلَمْ نَنْزِعَ يَدَا
فَانْصُرْ رَسُولَ اللهِ نَصْرًا أَعْتَدَا وَادْعُ عِبَادَ اللهِ يَأْتُوا مَدَدَا
فِيهِمْ رَسُولُ اللهِ قَدْ تَجَرَّدَا إِنْ سِيمَ خَسْفًا وَجْهُهُ تَرَبَّدَا
فِي فَيْلَقٍ كَالْبَحْرِ يَجْرِي مُزْبِدَا إِنَّ قُرَيْشًا أَخْلَفُوكَ الْمَوْعِدَا
وَنَقَضُوا مِيثَاقَكَ الْمُؤَكَّدَا وَجَعَلُوا لِي بِكِدَاءٍ رَصَدًا
وَزَعَمُوا أَنْ لَسْتُ أَرْجُو أَحَدَا فَهُمْ أَذَلُّ وَأَقَلُّ عَدَدَا
هُمْ بَيَّتُونَا بِالْوَتِيرِ هُجَّدَا فَقَتَلُونَا رُكَّعًا وَسُجَّدَا

فَقَالَ رَسُولُ اللهِ ﷺ نُصِرْتَ يَا عَمْرُو بْنَ سَالِمٍ فَمَا بَرِحَ رَسُولُ اللهِ ﷺ مَرَّتْ عَنَانَةٌ فِي السَّمَاءِ فَقَالَ رَسُولُ اللهِ ﷺ إِنَّ هَذِهِ السَّحَابَةَ لَتَسْتَهِلُّ بِنَصْرِ بَنِي كَعْبٍ وَأَمَرَ رَسُولُ اللهِ ﷺ النَّاسَ بِالْجِهَازِ وَكَتَمَهُمْ مَخْرَجَهُ وَسَأَلَ اللهَ أَنْ يُعَمِّيَ عَلَى قُرَيْشٍ خَبَرَهُ حَتَّى يَبْغَتَهُمْ فِي بِلَادِهِمْ أبن إسحاق ز الطحاوفي في شرح المعاني ش هق أبو نعيم في المعرفة وهذا لفظ السنن الصغرى للبيهقي

ʿUmayr b. Wahb al-Jumaḥī رضي الله عنه

Al-Bayhaqī, al-Ṭabarānī, and Abū Nuʿaym narrated that Mūsā b. ʿUqba and ʿUrwa b. al-Zubayr both said that when the disgruntled pagans returned to Mecca after the encounter at Badr, ʿUmayr b. Wahb al-Jumaḥī went over and sat by Ṣafwān b. Umayya in the Chamber *(al-hijr)* [of Ismāʿīl عليه السلام by the Kaʿba]. Ṣafwān said, "It is ignominy to survive those that died at Badr." ʿUmayr replied, "Yes, by Allah! Life holds no good after them. Were it not for a debt I cannot repay and dependents for whom I have nothing to leave, I would go to Muḥammad and kill him! Nothing would please me so much; and I have a good excuse to approach him: I can say, 'I came for my son whom you captured.'" Ṣafwān rejoiced at his words and said, "I shall repay your debt! Your dependents and mine are as one in my expenditure! Nothing I can afford shall be kept from them!" Ṣafwān commissioned him, equipped him, and ordered ʿUmayr's sword brought and had it burnished and coated with poison. ʿUmayr said to Ṣafwān, "Keep my plan secret for a few days." Then ʿUmayr went out until he reached al-Madīna. He alighted at the door of the Mosque, tied his mount, took his sword, and proceeded to [search for] the Messenger of Allah ﷺ. The latter entered together with ʿUmar b. al-Khaṭṭāb. The Messenger of Allah ﷺ instructed ʿUmar to stay behind then said:
[196] "What brings you, ʿUmayr?" He replied, "I came for my captive that you are holding." The Prophet ﷺ said: [a] "Tell me the truth. What brings you?" He replied, "I only came for my captive!" The Prophet ﷺ said: "Then what did you contract to do with Ṣafwān b. Umayya in the Chamber?" ʿUmayr was startled and asked, "What did I contract with him?" "You let him commission you with killing me in exchange for taking charge of your dependents and paying off your debt, but Allah put an obstacle between you and your plan!" ʿUmayr said: "I bear witness that you are the Messenger of Allah! This conversation was between me and Ṣafwān in the Chamber and no one is aware of it except him and me – and Allah informed you of it. I believe in Allah and His Messenger." Then he

returned to Mecca and began to call the people to Islam and many of them entered Islam at his hands.[272]

عَنْ مُوسَى بْنِ عُقْبَةَ وَعَنْ عُرْوَةَ بْنِ الزُّبَيْرِ قَالاَ لَمَّا رَجَعَ وَفْدُ الْمُشْرِكِينَ إِلَى مَكَّةَ أَقْبَلَ عُمَيرُ بْنُ وَهْبٍ الْجُمَحِيُّ حَتَّى جَلَسَ إِلَى صَفْوَانَ بْنِ أُمَيَّةَ فِي الْحِجْرِ فَقَالَ صَفْوَانُ قَبُحَ لَكَ الْعَيْشُ بَعْدَ قَتْلَى بَدْرٍ قَالَ أَجَل وَاللهِ مَا فِي الْعَيْشِ خَيْرٌ بَعْدَهُمْ وَلَوْلاَ دَيْنٌ عَلَيَّ لاَ أَجِدُ لَهُ قَضَاءً وَعِيَالٌ لاَ أَدَعُ لَهُمْ شَيْئًا لَرَحَلْتُ إِلَى مُحَمَّدٍ فَقَتَلْتُهُ إِنْ مَلاَتُ عَيْنِي مِنْهُ فَإِنَّ لِي عِنْدَهُ عِلَّةً أَعْتَلُّ بِهَا أَقُولُ قَدِمْتُ عَلَى ابْنِي هَذَا الأَسِيرِ فَفَرِحَ صَفْوَانُ بِقَوْلِهِ وَقَالَ عَلَيَّ دَيْنُكَ وَعِيَالُكَ أُسْوَةُ عِيَالِي فِي النَّفَقَةِ لاَ يَسَعُنِي شَيْءٌ وَيُعْجِزُ عَنْهُمْ فَحَمَلَهُ صَفْوَانُ وَجَهَّزَهُ وَأَمَرَ بِسَيْفِ عُمَيرٍ فَصُقِلَ وَسُمَّ وَقَالَ عُمَيرٌ لِصَفْوانَ اكْتُمْنِي أَيَّاماً فَأَقْبَلَ عُمَيْرٌ حَتَّى قَدِمَ الْمَدِينَةَ فَنَزَلَ بَابَ الْمَسْجِدِ وَعَقَلَ رَاحِلَتَهُ وَأَخَذَ السَّيفَ فَعَمَدَ

[272]Narrated *mursal* through **(1)** Mūsā b. ʿUqba (in his *Maghāzī*) from al-Zuhrī by al-Ṭabarānī in *al-Kabīr* (17:59-60), al-Taymī in *Dalā'il al-Nubuwwa* (p. 140-141 §153), al-Bayhaqī in the *Dalā'il* (3:147), and Abū Nuʿaym in the *Maʿrifa* (4:2093-2095 §2189); **(2)** Abū al-Aswad from ʿUrwa (in his *Maghāzī*) also in *al-Kabīr* (17:56-57) and in Ibn Hishām (3:212-215) cf. al-Dhahabī, *Tārīkh* (*Maghāzī* p. 71-73); and **(3)** Ibn Isḥāq (in his *Sīra*) from Muḥammad b. Ja'far b. al-Zubayr by Abū Nuʿaym in the *Dalā'il* (p. 479-482 §413), also in *al-Kabīr* (17:58). Ibn Ḥajar cites all three chains in *al-Iṣāba* (4:726) then says: "It came to us through another, *muttaṣil* chain narrated by Ibn Mandah through Ibn al-Azhar, from ʿAbd al-Razzāq, from Ja'far b. Sulaymān, from Abū 'Imrān al-Jawnī [ʿAbd al-Malik b. Ḥabīb], from Anas or another. [Cf. al-Dhahabī, *Tārīkh* (*Maghāzī* p. 99-100).] Ibn Mandah said, 'This is a single-chained report *(gharīb)*, we do not know it to be from Abū 'Imrān except this way.' Ṭabarānī narrated it from ʿAbd al-Razzāq and said, 'I do not know it to be narrated except from Anas b. Mālik.'" Cf. Ibn Sayyid al-Nās, *'Uyūn al-Athar* (1:270).

إِلَى رَسُولِ اللهِ ﷺ فَدَخَلَ هُوَ وَعُمَرُ بْنُ الْخَطَّابِ رَضِيَ اللهُ عَنْهُ فَقَالَ رَسُولُ اللهِ ﷺ لِعُمَرَ تَأَخَّرْ ثُمَّ قَالَ مَا أَقْدَمَكَ يَا عُمَيْرُ قَالَ قَدِمْتُ عَلَى أَسِيرِي عِنْدَكُمْ قَالَ أَصْدِقْنِي مَا أَقْدَمَكَ قَالَ مَا قَدِمْتُ إِلاَّ فِي أَسِيرِي قَالَ فَمَاذَا شَرَطْتَ لِصَفْوَانَ بْنِ أُمَيَّةَ فِي الْحِجْرِ فَفَزِعَ عُمَيْرٌ وَقَالَ مَاذَا شَرَطْتُ لَهُ قَالَ تَحَمَّلْتَ لَهُ بِقَتْلِي عَلَى أَنْ يَعُولَ بَنِيكَ وَيَقْضِيَ دَيْنَكَ وَاللهُ حَائِلٌ بَيْنَكَ وَبَيْنَ ذَلِكَ قَالَ عُمَيْرٌ أَشْهَدُ أَنَّكَ رَسُولُ اللهِ إِنَّ هَذَا الْحَدِيثَ كَانَ بَيْنِي وَبَيْنَ صَفْوَانَ فِي الْحِجْرِ لَمْ يَطَّلِعْ عَلَيْهِ أَحَدٌ غَيْرِي وَغَيْرُهُ فَأَخْبَرَكَ اللهُ بِهِ فَآمَنْتُ بِاللهِ وَرَسُولِهِ ثُمَّ رَجَعَ إِلَى مَكَّةَ فَدَعَا إِلَى الإِسْلاَمِ فَأَسْلَمَ عَلَى يَدِهِ بَشَرٌ كَثِيرٌ مغازي موسى بن عقبة طب التيمي هق كلاهما في الدلائل أبو نعيم في المعرفة ذكره السيوطي في الخصائص ثم قال أخرجه البيهقي والطبراني من طريق ابن اسحاق حدثني محمد بن جعفر بن الزبير فذكره نحوه وأخرجه ابو نعيم عن الزهري نحوه وأخرجه ابن سعد وأبو نعيم عن عكرمة فهذه طرق مرسلة وأخرجه الطبراني وأبو نعيم من طريق أبي عمران الجوني عن أنس بن مالك موصولا بسند صحيح اهـ.

ʿAmr b. al-ʿĀṣ ﷺ

Al-Khaṭīb al-Baghdādī narrated that the Prophet ﷺ said one day to his Companions: 197 "Tonight a man of wisdom shall come to you." Then ʿAmr b. al-ʿĀṣ came as a *Muhājir*.[273]

[273]Narrated *mursal* from ʿAmr b. Dīnār by Ibn Abī Khaythama in his *Tārīkh*, al-Khaṭīb in *Muwaḍḍiḥ Awhām al-Jamʿ wal-Tafrīq* (Qalʿajī ed. 1:47=ʿUthmāniyya ed. 1:39), and

عَنْ عَمْرِو بْنِ دِينَارٍ قَالَ رسول الله ﷺ يَقْدَمُ عَلَيْكُمُ اللَّيْلَةَ رَجُلٌ حَكِيمٌ مُهَاجِرٌ فَقَدِمَ عَمْرُو بْنُ الْعَاصِ فَأَسْلَمَ تاريخ ابن أبي خيثمة خط في موضح أوهام الجمع والتفريق كر

Abū Mūsā al-Ashʿarī ؓ

Ibn Saʿd and al-Bayhaqī narrated from Anas ؓ that the Prophet ﷺ said: 198 "Tomorrow shall come to you a people more sensitive in their hearts than you." Then the Ashʿarīs came, Abū Mūsā with them. [The continuation states: On their approach to Madīna they sang poetry, saying: "Tomorrow we meet our beloved ones, Muhammad and his group!" Anas said: "When they arrived they began to shake hands with the people, and they were the first to introduce hand-shaking."][274]

عَنْ أَنَسٍ قَالَ قَالَ رَسُولُ اللهِ ﷺ يَقْدَمُ عَلَيْكُمْ أَقْوَامٌ هُمْ أَرَقُّ مِنْكُمْ قُلُوبًا قَالَ فَقَدِمَ الْأَشْعَرِيُّونَ فِيهِمْ أَبُو مُوسَى الْأَشْعَرِيُّ
حم ن في الكبرى ز ابن سعد حب

ʿAbd al-Razzāq said that Maʿmar told them: "I was told that the Prophet ﷺ was sitting with his Companions one day when he said: 199 "Save those on board the ship!" Then some time passed and he said: "She sailed on." When they neared al-Madīna, he said: [a] "They have come with a holy man leading them." He [the narrator] said: "Those on board were the Ashʿarīs and their leader

Ibn ʿAsākir (70:129).

[274]Narrated from Anas with a sound chain by Ahmad and Ibn ʿAbd al-Barr in al-Tamhīd (21:15) as well as – without mention of the handshake – Ibn Saʿd (4:106), Ahmad, al-Nasāʾī in al-Kubrā (5:92 §8352) and Fadāʾil al-Sahāba (p. 73 §247), Abū Yaʿlā (6:454 §3845), Ibn Hibbān (16:164-165 §7192-7193 both isnād sahīh), and al-Bayhaqī in the Dalāʾil (5:351). The Ashʿarīs are from Yemen. Abū Mūsā was returning from Yemen after having entered Islam in Mecca and having emigrated to Abyssinia.

was ʿAmr b. al-Ḥamiq al-Khuzāʿī." <The Messenger of Allah ﷺ said: "From where did you come?" They said, "From Zabīd." He said: [b] "Allah bless Zabīd!" They said, "And Rimaʿ?" He said: "Allah bless Zabīd!" They said, "And Rimaʿ?" The third time he added: "And Rimaʿ."> Al-Bayhaqī narrated it.[275]

عَبْدُ الرَّزَّاقِ قَالَ أَخْبَرَنَا مَعْمَرٌ قَالَ بَلَغَنِي أَنَّ النَّبِيَّ ﷺ كَانَ جَالِساً فِي أَصْحَابِهِ يَوماً فَقَالَ اللهُمَّ أَنْجِ أَصْحَابَ السَّفِينَةِ ثُمَّ مَكَثَ سَاعَةً فَقَالَ قَدِ اسْتَمَرَّتْ فَلَمَّا دَنَوا مِنَ الْمَدِينَةِ قَالَ قَدْ جَاؤُوا وَيَقُودُهُمْ رَجُلٌ صَالِحٌ قَالَ وَالَّذِينَ جَاؤُوا فِي السَّفِينَةِ الأَشْعَرِيُّونَ وَالَّذِي قَادَهُم عَمْرُو بْنُ الْحَمِقِ الْخُزَاعِيُّ قَالَ قَالَ النَّبِيُّ ﷺ مِنْ أَيْنَ جِئْتُمْ قَالُوا مِنْ زَبِيدٍ قَالَ النَّبِيُّ ﷺ بَارَكَ اللهُ فِي زَبِيدٍ قَالُوا وَفِي زَمْعٍ قَالَ بَارَكَ اللهُ فِي زَبِيدٍ قَالُوا وَفِي زَمْعٍ يَا رَسُولَ اللهِ فَقَالَ فِي الثَّالِثَةِ وَفِي زَمْعٍ جامع معمر بن راشد هق في الدلائل كر حم في فضائل الصحابة مختصرا

Ibn Saʿd narrated that ʻIyāḍ al-Ashʻarī [ﷺ] said that, concerning the saying of Allah ﷻ ﴾**[O you who believe! Whoever among you turns back from his Religion, know that in his stead] Allah shall bring a people whom He loves and who love Him, [humble towards believers, stern toward disbelievers, striving in the way of Allah, and fearing not the blame of any blamer. Such is the grace of Allah which He gives to whom He will. Allah is All-**

[275]Narrated through ʿAbd al-Razzāq, from Maʻmar b. Rāshid in the latter's *Jāmiʿ* (appended to ʿAbd al-Razzāq's *Musannaf* 11:54), al-Bayhaqī in the *Dalāʾil* (6:298), Ibn ʿAsākir (45:496), and – without the bracketed segment – through ʿAbd al-Razzāq, from Maʻmar, from Qatāda by Aḥmad in *Faḍāʾil al-Saḥāba* (2:863 §1612). The latter is a sound *mursal* chain missing the Companion-link. Rimaʻ (misspelt Zimaʻ in al-Nabhānī) lies between Zabīd and Ghassān cf. Yāqūt (3:68).

Embracing, All-Knowing]﴾ (5:54), the Prophet ﷺ said: 200 "They are that man's people." Meaning, Abū Mūsā al-Ash'arī.[276]

عَنْ عِيَاضٍ الأَشْعَرِيِّ رَضِيَ اللهُ عَنْهُ قَالَ قَالَ رَسُولُ اللهِ ﷺ لأَبِي مُوسَى رَضِيَ اللهُ عَنْهُ هُمْ قَوْمُ هَذَا يَعْنِي قَوْلَهُ ﴿ يَٰٓأَيُّهَا ٱلَّذِينَ ءَامَنُوا۟ مَن يَرْتَدَّ مِنكُمْ عَن دِينِهِۦ فَسَوْفَ يَأْتِى ٱللَّهُ بِقَوْمٍ يُحِبُّهُمْ وَيُحِبُّونَهُۥٓ أَذِلَّةٍ عَلَى ٱلْمُؤْمِنِينَ أَعِزَّةٍ عَلَى ٱلْكَٰفِرِينَ يُجَٰهِدُونَ فِى سَبِيلِ ٱللَّهِ وَلَا يَخَافُونَ لَوْمَةَ لَآئِمٍ ۚ ذَٰلِكَ فَضْلُ ٱللَّهِ يُؤْتِيهِ مَن يَشَآءُ ۚ وَٱللَّهُ وَٰسِعٌ عَلِيمٌ ﴿٥٤﴾ ﴾

المائدة ش ابن أبي عاصم في الآحاد ابن سعد طب ورجاله ورجال الصحيح مج ك قال صحيح على شرط مسلم تفسير الطبري خط هق في الدلائل

Abū Hurayra, Samura b. Jundub رضي الله عنهما, and a Third Man

'Abd al-Razzāq said that Ma'mar narrated to them that he heard Ibn Ṭāwūs and others say that the Prophet ﷺ said **[495]** to Abū Hurayra, Samura b. Jundub and another man: 201 "The last of you to die shall be in the fire." The man died before the two of them, then Abū Hurayra and Samura remained.[277]

[276]Narrated from the Companion 'Iyāḍ b. 'Amr by Ibn Sa'd (4:107), al-Ṭabarī in his *Tafsīr* (6:284), Ibn Abī Shayba (6:387 §32261), Ibn Abī 'Āṣim in *al-Āḥād wal-Mathānī* (4:460-462 §2515), Abū Nu'aym in *Tārīkh Aṣbahān* (1:59), al-Khaṭīb (2:39) cf. Aḥdab, *Zawā'id Tārīkh Baghdād* (1:466-470 §127 *ḥadīth ṣaḥīḥ*), al-Ḥākim (with the wording: "They are your people, Abū Mūsā!" 2:313=1990 ed. 2:342 *ṣaḥīḥ* by Muslim's criterion), al-Bayhaqī in the *Dalā'il* (5:351), and al-Ṭabarānī in *al-Kabīr* (17:371) with a chain of *Ṣaḥīḥ* narrators according to al-Haythamī (7:16). Another narration states the verse refers to "Abū Bakr al-Ṣiddīq and those with him" according to 'Alī, al-Ḥasan al-Baṣrī, Qatāda, al-Ḍaḥḥāk, and Ibn Jurayj cf. al-Rāzī, *al-Tafsīr al-Kabīr* (3:427); al-Qurṭubī, *al-Jāmi' li Aḥkām al-Qur'ān*, and others.

[277]Narrated from the Companion Abū Maḥdhūra [Aws b. Mi'yar] by al-Ṭabarānī in *al-Awsaṭ* (6:208) and *al-Kabīr* (7:177), Ṭaḥāwī and others with weak chains cf. al-Haythamī (8:290) but it is corroborated by other chains cf. al-Bukhārī, *al-Tārīkh al-Ṣaghīr* (1:106-107 §446-447), al-Ṭaḥāwī, *Sharḥ Mushkil al-Āthār* (14:485-488 §5776-5780), Abū

الحَسَنُ عَنْ أَنَسِ بْنِ حَكِيمٍ الضَبِّيِّ قَالَ كُنْتُ أَمُرُّ بِالْمَدِينَةِ
فَأَلْقَى أَبَا هُرَيْرَةَ فَلا يَبْدَأُ بِشَيْءٍ يَسْأَلُنِي حَتَّى يَسْأَلَنِي عَنْ سَمُرَةَ
فَإِذَا أَخْبَرْتُهُ بِحَيَاتِهِ وَصِحَّتِهِ فَرِحَ فَقَالَ إِنَّا كُنَّا عَشْرَةً فِي بَيْتٍ
وَإِنَّ رَسُولَ اللهِ ﷺ قَامَ فِينَا فَنَظَرَ فِي وُجُوهِنَا وَأَخَذَ بِعِضَادَتَيِ
الْبَابِ ثُمَّ قَالَ آخِرُكُمْ مَوْتاً فِي النَّارِ فَقَدْ مَاتَ مِنَّا ثَمَانِيَةٌ وَلَمْ يَبْقَ
غَيْرِي وَغَيْرُهُ فَلَيْسَ شَيْءٌ أَحَبَّ إِلَيَّ مِنْ أَنْ أَكُونَ ذُقْتُ الْمَوْتَ
هق في الدلائل وجاء من طريق علي بن زيد عن أبي أويس أوس بن خالد بلفظ كُنَّا
سَبْعَةً فِي بَيْتٍ طب وعن أوس أيضاً كُنْتُ إِذَا نَزَلْتُ عَلَى سَمُرَةَ بْنِ
جُنْدُبٍ سَأَلَنِي عَنْ أَبِي مَحْذُورَةَ وَإِذَا قَدِمْتُ عَلَى أَبِي مَحْذُورَةَ
سَأَلَنِي عَنْ سَمُرَةَ بْنِ جُنْدُبٍ فَقُلْتُ لِأَبِي مَحْذُورَةَ مَا شَأْنُكَ إِذَا
قَدِمْتُ عَلَيْكَ سَأَلْتَنِي عَنْ سَمُرَةَ وَإِذَا قَدِمْتُ عَلَى سَمُرَةَ سَأَلَنِي
عَنْكَ فَقَالَ أَبُو مَحْذُورَةَ كُنْتُ أَنَا وَأَبُو هُرَيْرَةَ وَسَمُرَةَ فِي بَيتٍ
فَجَاءَ النَّبِيُّ ﷺ فَأَخَذَ بِعِضَادَتَيِ الْبَابِ فَقَالَ آخِرُكُمْ مَوتاً فِي
النَّارِ قَالَ فَمَاتَ أَبُو هُرَيرَةَ ثُمَّ مَاتَ أَبُو مَحْذُورَةَ ثُمَّ مَاتَ سَمُرَةُ
قَالَ أَبُو بَكْرٍ زَعَمُوا أَنَّهُ وَقَعَ فِي كَانُونَ ش طب أبو نعيم في الدلائل وجاء
أيضاً بلفظ عَنْ أَبِي هُرَيْرَةَ قَالَ انْطَلَقْتُ أَنَا وَعَبْدُ اللهِ بْنُ عَمْرٍو

Nuʿaym, *Dalā'il* (p. 556), al-'Irāqī, *Takhrīj Aḥādīth al-Iḥyā'* (2:385), *Iṣāba* (3:178), *Bidāya* (6:231-232), and *Siyar* (Risāla ed. 3:184) where Dhahabī said: *"gharīb jiddan"*.

وَسَمُرَةُ بْنُ جُنْدُبٍ نَطْلُبُ النَّبِيَّ ﷺ فَقِيلَ لَنَا تَوَجَّهَ نَحْوَ مَسْجِدِ التَّقْوَى قَالَ فَانْطَلَقْنَا فَإِذَا هُوَ قَدْ أَقْبَلَ فَلَمَّا رَأَيْنَاهُ جَلَسْنَا فَلَمَّا دَنَا قُمْنَا فَسَلَّمْنَا عَلَيْهِ فَإِذَا يَدُهُ الْيُمْنَى عَلَى كَاهِلِ أَبِي بَكْرٍ وَيَدِهِ الْيُسْرَى عَلَى كَاهِلِ عُمَرَ قَالَ فَقَالَ مَنْ هَؤُلاءِ يَا أَبَا بَكْرٍ فَقَالَ هَؤُلاءِ يَا رَسُولَ اللهِ أَبُو هُرَيْرَةَ وَعَبْدُ اللهِ بْنُ عَمْرٍو وَسَمُرَةُ بْنُ جُنْدُبٍ فَقَالَ أَمَا إِنَّ آخِرَهُمْ مَوْتًا فِي النَّارِ الطحاوي في شرح المشكل مسند الحارث قال الهيثمي في في بغية الباحث سَقَطَ سَمُرَةُ فِي قِدْرٍ مُسَخَّنٍ بِالنَّارِ فَمَاتَ فِيهَا

Whenever someone wanted to upset Abū Hurayra he would tell him that Samura died, hearing which, he would faint and remain in shock. Then Abū Hurayra died before Samura.[278]

مَعْمَرٌ قَالَ سَمِعْتُ ابْنَ طَاوُوسٍ وَغَيْرَهُ يَقُولُونَ قَالَ النَّبِيُّ ﷺ لأَبِي هُرَيْرَةَ وَلِسَمُرَةَ بْنِ جُنْدُبٍ وَلِرَجُلٍ آخَرَ آخِرُكُمْ موتاً فِي النَّارِ فَمَاتَ الرَّجُلُ قَبْلَهُمْ وَبَقِيَ أَبُو هُرَيْرَةَ بِالْمَدِينَةِ فَكَانَ إِذَا أَرَادَ الرَّجُلُ أَنْ يَغِيظَ أَبَا هُرَيْرَةَ يَقُولُ مَاتَ سَمُرَةُ بْنُ جُنْدُبٍ يَعْنِي فَإِذَا سَمِعَهُ غُشِيَ عَلَيْهِ وَصَعِقَ وَمَاتَ أَبُو هُرَيْرَةَ قَبْلَ سَمُرَةَ هق في الدلائل

Ibn Wahb narrated that Abū Yazīd al-Madanī said that when Samura fell fatally ill, he was afflicted with severe chills. A fire

[278]Narrated by al-Bayhaqī in the *Dalā'il* (6:459).

was lit for him and they placed a coal stove in front of him, another one behind him, another one to his right, and another one to his left. Yet he was not relieved. He remained in this state until he died. Ibn ʿAsākir narrated from Muḥammad b. Sīrīn that Samura had been afflicted with chronic tetanus *(kuzāz)* and nothing seemed to warm him up. He ordered for a huge tub to be filled with water and a fire lit under it, and he sat above it. Its steam rose to him and warmed him up. As he was there, he fell and was burnt.[279]

عَنْ أَبِي يَزِيدٍ الْمَدِينِي قَالَ لَمَّا مَرِضَ سَمُرَةُ مَرَضَهُ الَّذِي مَاتَ فِيهِ أَصَابَهُ بَرْدٌ شَدِيدٌ فَأُوْقِدَتْ لَهُ نَارٌ فَجَعَلَ كَانُونَ بَيْنَ يَدَيْهِ وَكَانُونَ خَلْفَهُ وَكَانُونَ عَنْ يَمِينِهِ وَكَانُونَ عَنْ شِمَالِهِ فَجَعَلَ لاَ يَنْتَفِعُ بِذَلِكَ فَلَمْ يَزَلْ كَذَلِكَ حَتَّى مَاتَ قال في الخصائص الكبرى أخرجه ابن وهب وَعَنْ مُحَمَّدِ بْنِ سِيرِينَ أَنَّ سَمُرَةَ أَصَابَهُ كُزَازٌ شَدِيدٌ فَكَانَ لا يَكَادُ يَدْفَأُ فَأَمَرَ بِقِدْرٍ عَظِيمَةٍ فَمُلِئَتْ مَاءً وَأَوْقَدَ تَحْتَهَا وَاتَّخَذَ فَوْقَهَا مَجْلِساً وَكَانَ يَصْعَدُ إِلَيْهِ بُخَارُهَا فَيُدْفِئُهُ فَبَيْنَا هُوَ كَذَلِكَ خُسِفَ بِهِ فَحَصَلَ فِي النَّارِ فَنَظُنُّ أَنَّ ذَلِكَ الَّذِي قَالَ لَهُ كر الطحاوي في مشكل الآثار قال وهذا الحديث فمستفيض في أيدي الناس في سمرة فعقلنا بذلك أن النار التي كان رسول الله ﷺ عناها في الآثار المروية عنه فيها كانت من نيران الدنيا لا من نيران الآخرة فعاد ما في هذه الآثار مما عاد إلى سمرة فضيلة يستحقها في الآخرة

[279] Narrated from Ibn Sīrīn by al-Ṭaḥāwī in *Sharḥ Mushkil al-Āthār* (14:489) and Ibn ʿAsākir (7:50-51), both through Dāwūd b. al-Muḥabbar al-Bakrāwī who is discarded although al-Ṭaḥāwī said the narration is widespread *(mustafīd)* among the scholars. Cited without chain in *al-Istīʿāb* (2:654), *Tahdhīb al-Kamāl* (12:133), and Ibn al-Athīr, *Nihāya*, and al-Khaṭṭābī's *Gharīb al-Ḥadīth*, art. *nār*.

Similarly worded is the report narrated by al-Wāqidī, Ṭabarānī, Abū Nu'aym and Ibn 'Asākir from Rāfi' b. Khadīj ﵁: "Al-Rajjāl [or Raḥḥāl] b. 'Unfuwa [or 'Athmūyah, or Ghathmūyah, or Ghanmūyah] was superlatively devout and assiduous in reading the Qur'ān. One day, the Prophet ﷺ came out to us while al-Rajjāl was sitting with us and said: 202 'One person in this group shall end up in the Fire.' I looked at the group. There was Abū Hurayra, Abū Arwā al-Dawsī, al-Ṭufayl b. 'Amr, and Rajjāl b. 'Unfuwa [of the Banū Ḥanīfa]. I looked and wondered, saying to myself, 'Who is this wretch?' When the Messenger of Allah ﷺ passed on and the Banū Ḥanīfa apostatized, I enquired to see what al-Rajjāl b. 'Unfuwa had done. I was told, 'He was seduced and is the one that bore witness for Musaylima that the Messenger of Allah ﷺ had [supposedly] made him a partner in his status after him.' I said, 'What the Messenger of Allah ﷺ said came true!'"[280] Ibn 'Asākir said that he is also called al-Raḥḥāl but this is a nickname and his actual name is Nahār.

عَنْ رَافِعٍ قَالَ كَانَ بِالرَّحَّالِ بْنِ عَثْمُويَهْ أو غَثْمُويَهْ مِنَ الْخُشُوعِ وَاللُّزُومِ لِقِرَاءَةِ الْقُرْآنِ وَالْخَيرِ فِيمَا يُرِي رَسُولَ اللهِ ﷺ شَيْءٌ عَجِيبٌ فَخَرَجَ عَلَينَا رَسُولُ اللهِ ﷺ يوماً وَالرَّحَّالُ مَعَنَا جَالِسٌ مَعَ نَفَرٍ فَقَالَ: أَحَدُ هَؤُلَاءِ النَّفَرِ فِي النَّارِ قَالَ رَافِعٌ فَنَظَرْتُ فِي الْقَومِ فَإِذَا أَبُو هُرَيرَةَ الدَّوْسِيُّ وَأَبُو أَرْوَى الدَّوْسِيُّ وَالطُّفَيْلُ بْنُ عَمْرٍو الدَّوْسِيُّ وَرَجَّالُ بْنُ عَثْمُويَهْ [الحَنَفِيُّ] فَجَعَلْتُ أَنْظُرُ وَأَتَعَجَّبُ وَأَقُولُ مَنْ هَذَا الشَّقِيُّ فَلَمَّا تُوُفِّيَ رَسُولُ اللهِ ﷺ

[280]Narrated from Rāfi' b. Khadīj by al-Tabarānī in *al-Kabīr* (4:283 §4434), al-Dāraquṭnī in *al-Mu'talif wal-Mukhtalif* (2:1063), Ibn 'Asākir (53:157), and al-Ṭabarī in his *Tārīkh* (3:287), all through al-Wāqidī, from 'Abd Allāh b. Nūḥ who is discarded. Sayf b. 'Umar narrated it in his *Futūḥ* with a different chain, from Makhlad b. Qays al-Bajalī cf. *Iṣāba* (2:539). See also *Bidāya*, year 11, chapter on Musaylima.

رَجَعَتْ بَنُو حَنِيفَةَ فَسَأَلْتُ مَا فَعَلَ الرَّحَّالُ بْنُ عَثْمُويَهْ فَقَالُوا
افْتَتَنَ هُوَ الَّذِي شَهِدَ لِمُسَيْلِمَةَ عَلَى رَسُولِ اللهِ ﷺ أَنَّهُ أَشْرَكَهُ
فِي الأَمْرِ بَعْدَهُ فَقُلْتُ مَا قَالَ رَسُولُ اللهِ ﷺ فَهُوَ حَقٌّ وَسَمِعَ
الرَّحَّالُ وَهُوَ يَقُولُ كَبْشَانِ انْتَطَحَا فَأَحَبُّهُمَا إِلَيْنَا كَبْشُنَا كر قال
كذا في الأصل في المواضع كلها والصواب ابن عنفرة والرجال بالجيم ويقال بالحاء وهو
لقب واسمه نهار اه وفي المؤتلف والمختلف للدارقطني وتاريخ الطبري والإصابة ومجمع الزوائد
رَجَّال بن عُنْفُوَة وفي المعجم الكبير الرَّجَّال بن غَنْمُويَه لكن قال الهيثمي
رواه الطبراني وقال فيه الرحال بالحاء المهملة المشددة وهكذا قاله الواقدي والمدائني وتبعهما
عبد الغني بن سعيد ووهم في ذلك والاكثرون قالوا إنه بالجيم الدار قطني وابن ماكولا مج

Sayf b. ʿUmar narrated something similar in *al-Futūḥ*[281] from Makhlad b. Qays al-Bajalī, "Furāt b. Ḥayyān, al-Rajjāl b. ʿUnfuwa, and Abū Hurayra had just come out after seeing the Messenger of Allah ﷺ when the latter said: 203 'Truly, the molar tooth of one of them in the Fire shall be greater than Mount Uḥud and he shall have, near him, a well-spring that eludes him.' News of this reached them. When Abū Hurayra and Furāt b. Ḥayyān finally heard the news of Rajjāl, they fell prostrate."[282]

281 As stated by Ibn Ḥajar, *Iṣāba* and al-Suyūṭī in the *Khaṣāʾiṣ*; however, Ibn Ḥudayda (d. 783) in *al-Miṣbāḥ al-Muḍiyy* (1:246 §35) refers it to Sayf b. ʿUmar's *Kitāb al-Ridda.*

282 I.e. in thanksgiving after they heard Zayd b. al-Khaṭṭāb had killed Rajjāl at Yamāma. Cited from Sayf b. ʿUmar in *al-Istīʿāb* (3:1258) and *al-Isāba* (2:539, 5:357). Narrated also through Sayf by al-Ṭabarī in his *Tārīkh* (2:278); al-Ḥumaydī in his *Musnad* (2:297298 §1211) with a passable chain if the unnamed link is Ḥakīm b. Saʿd al-Ḥanafī; and al-Ṭabarī in his *Tārīkh* (2:279) with another chain also containing an unnamed link. Cited without chain by Ibn ʿAbd al-Barr in *al-Istīʿāb* (2:551-552). The "molar" version is also that cited by al-Dāraquṭni (cf. previous note). Sayf b. ʿUmar, like al-Wāqidī, is reliable in history and unreliable in ḥadīth (cf. p. xvii).

عَنْ أَحْمَدَ بْنِ فُرَاتِ بْنِ حَيَّانَ قَالَ خَرَجَ فُرَاتٌ وَالرَّحَّالُ وَأَبُو هُرَيْرَةَ مِنْ عِنْدِ رَسُولِ اللهِ ﷺ فَقَالَ لَضِرْسُ أَحَدِكُمْ فِي النَّارِ أَعْظَمُ مِنْ أُحُدٍ وَإِنَّهُ مَعَهُ لَقَفَا غَادِرٍ فَبَلَغَنَا ذَلِكَ فَمَا أَمِنَّا حَتَّى صَنَعَ الرَّجَّالُ مَا صَنَعَ ثُمَّ قُتِلَ فَخَرَّ أَبُو هُرَيْرَةَ وَفُرَاتُ بْنُ حَيَّانَ سَاجِدَيْنِ لِلَّهِ عَزَّ وَجَلَّ سيف بن عمر كما في تاريخ الطبري والإستيعاب والإصابة والخصائص ورواه الحميدي في مسنده مختصراً

'Attāb b. Asīd, Jubayr b. Muṭ'im, Ḥakīm b. Ḥizām, Suhayl b. ʿAmr رضي الله عنهم

Ibn ʿAsākir narrated from 'Aṭā' – saying, "I believe he raised it to Ibn ʿAbbās رضي الله عنهما" – that the Messenger of Allah ﷺ said: 204
"There are four in Mecca I deem above any suspicion (*arba'uhum*) of *shirk* and I wish they embraced Islam." He was asked, "Who are they, Messenger of Allah?" He said: "'Attāb b. Asīd, Jubayr b. Muṭ'im, Ḥakīm b. Ḥizām, and Suhayl b. ʿAmr." He ﷺ said this the night of his approach to Mecca in the raid that led to its conquest.[283] They all entered Islam – Allah be well-pleased with them!

عَنِ ابْنِ عَبَّاسٍ رَضِيَ اللهُ عَنْهُمَا عَنِ النَّبِيِّ ﷺ قَالَ إِنَّ بِمَكَّةَ لَأَرْبَعَةَ نَفَرٍ مِنْ قُرَيْشٍ أَرْبَأُ بِهِمْ عَنِ الشِّرْكِ وَأَرْغَبُ لَهُمْ فِي الْإِسْلَامِ عَتَّابُ بْنُ أَسِيدٍ وَجُبَيْرُ بْنُ مُطْعِمٍ وَحَكِيمُ بْنُ حِزَامٍ وَسُهَيْلُ بْنُ عَمْرٍو الزبير بن بكار في جمهرة نسب قريش ك سكت عنه كر

[283]Narrated by al-Zubayr b. Bakkār in *Jamharat Nasab Quraysh wa-Akhbārihā* (p. 362-363 §640) and through him al-Ḥākim (3:595) and Ibn ʿAsākir (15:106) cf. *al-Khaṣā'is al-Kubrā* (1:438) and *Kanz* (§33692).

Suhayl b. ʿAmr ؓ

Yūnus b. Bukayr ؓ narrated in the *Maghāzī* together with Ibn Saʿd, through Ibn Isḥāq, from Muḥammad b. ʿAmr b. 'Aṭā' who said that when Suhayl b. ʿAmr was captured ʿUmar said: "Messenger of Allah, pull out his front teeth and his tongue shall show, so that he will never speak in public again!" Suhayl was harelipped. The Messenger of Allah ﷺ said: [205] "I shall not mutilate lest Allah mutilate me, even if I am a Prophet. But [a] perhaps he shall, one day, take a stand of which you will not disapprove." When news of the death of the Messenger of Allah ﷺ reached Suhayl in Mecca, he stood and said exactly what Abū Bakr had said **[496]** as if he had heard the words of the latter. When ʿUmar heard of Suhayl's speech, he said, "I bear witness that Muḥammad is the Messenger of Allah! He had said, 'Perhaps he shall, one day, take a stand of which you will not disapprove.'"[284] Another version has it that when ʿUmar heard of this, he said, "I bear witness that Muhammad is the Messenger of Allah and that what he brought is the truth! This is the station that the Messenger of Allah ﷺ meant when he said, 'perhaps he shall rise to a station of which you will not disapprove.'" Abū Bakr's speech, which he delivered in Madīna at the time of the death of the Prophet ﷺ, is the one in which he said, [206] "Whoever worshipped Muḥammad, then truly, Muḥammad has died; and whoever worshipped Allah, truly, Allah is living and never dies."[285]

عَنْ يَحْيَى بْنِ أَبِي كَثِيرٍ وَمُحَمَّدِ بْنِ عَمْرِو بْنِ عَطَاءٍ وَالْحَسَنِ بْنِ مُحَمَّدٍ قَالُوا لَمَّا أُسِرَ سُهَيْلُ بْنُ عَمْرٍو قَالَ عُمَرُ رَضِيَ اللهُ عَنْهُ يَا رَسُولَ اللهِ انْزِعْ ثَنِيَّتَيْهِ يَدْلُعْ لِسَانُهُ فَلاَ يَقُومُ عَلَيْكَ خَطِيبًا أَبَدًا

[284] Narrated *mursal* by al-Wāqidī (1:107), Ibn Saʿd (6:122), al-Ṭabarī in his *Tārīkh* (2:41), al-Ḥākim (3:282), al-Bayhaqī in the *Dalā'il* (6:367), and Abū Nuʿaym in the chapter on Suhayl in *Maʿrifat al-Ṣaḥāba*, cf. *Isāba* (6:206) and *Kanz* (§37137). Suhayl b. 'Amr was the Quraysh deputy who made difficulties at the time of signing the Ḥudaybiya truce.

[285] Narrated from ʿĀ'isha by al-Bukhārī, Ibn Mājah, and Aḥmad.

فَقَالَ رَسُولُ اللهِ ﷺ لاَ أُمَثِّلُ بِهِ فَيُمَثِّلَ اللهُ بِي وَإِنْ كُنْتُ نَبِيًّا وَلَعَلَّهُ يَقُومُ مَقَامًا لاَ تَكْرَهُهُ فَقَامَ سُهَيْلُ بْنُ عَمْرٍو حِينَ جَاءَهُ وَفَاةُ النَّبِيِّ ﷺ بِخُطْبَةِ أَبِي بَكْرٍ رَضِيَ اللهُ عَنْهُ بِمَكَّةَ كَأَنَّهُ كَانَ يَسْمَعُهَا قَالَ عُمَرُ حِينَ بَلَغَهُ كَلاَمُ سُهَيْلٍ أَشْهَدُ أَنَّكَ لَرَسُولُ اللهِ يُرِيدُ حَيْثُ قَالَ النَّبِيُّ ﷺ لَعَلَّهُ يَقُومُ مَقَامًا لاَ تَكْرَهُهُ الواقدي ابن سعد الطبري في التاريخ ك هق في الدلائل أبو نعيم في المعرفة وفي رواية عَنْ أَبِي عَمْرِو بْنِ عَدِيِّ بْنِ الْحَمْرَاءِ الْخُزَاعِيِّ قَالَ لَمَّا بَلَغَ عُمَرَ كَلاَمُ سُهَيلٍ بِمَكَّةَ قَالَ أَشْهَدُ أَنَّ مُحَمَّداً رَسُولُ اللهِ وَأَنَّ مَا جَاءَ بِهِ حَقٌّ هَذِهِ هُوَ الْمَقَامُ الَّذِي عَنَى رَسُولُ اللهِ ﷺ حِينَ قَالَ لَعَلَّهُ يَقُومُ مَقَامًا لاَ تَكْرَهُهُ ابن سعد كر وعندهم جميعا فَلَمَّا مَاتَ النَّبِيُّ ﷺ نَفَرَ أَهْلُ مَكَّةَ فَقَامَ سُهَيْلُ بْنُ عَمْرٍو عِنْدَ الْكَعْبَةِ فَقَالَ مَنْ كَانَ مُحَمَّدٌ ﷺ إِلاَهَهُ فَإِنَّ مُحَمَّداً قَدْ مَاتَ وَاللهُ حَيٌّ لاَ يَمُوتُ

Suhayl b. ʿAmr spoke similarly in Mecca when news of the death of the Prophet ﷺ came. The author of *al-Sīra al-Nabawiyya* said, after mentioning some of what preceded, that he رضي الله عنه entered Islam the year of the conquest of Mecca, excelled in his Islam, and took his place among the elite of the Companions. When the Messenger of Allah ﷺ died, most of the people of Mecca intended to recant Islam so Suhayl b. ʿAmr stood and addressed them publicly. He thanked Allah and praised Him then mentioned the death of the Messenger of Allah ﷺ and delievered a speech by which Allah kept the people firm in their faith, similar to the speech of Abū Bakr رضي الله عنه in Madīna the day the Prophet ﷺ died. Suhayl said in his address:

"People! 207 Whoever worshipped Muḥammad, truly, Muḥammad has died; and whoever worshipped Allah, truly, Allah is living and never dies. Do you not know that Allah said, ﴾**Lo! you will die, and lo! they will die**﴿ (39:30) and he said, ﴾**Muḥammad is but a messenger, messengers (the like of whom) have passed away before him. Will it be that, when he dies or is slain, you will turn back on your heels? He who turns back does no hurt to Allah, and Allah will reward the thankful**﴿ (3:144)." Then he said: "I know with absolute certitude that this Religion shall spread far and wide like the sun wherever it rises and sets. Therefore, trust in your Lord! The Religion of Allah is on the march. The Word of Allah is complete. Allah shall aid whoever aids Him. He shall strengthen His Religion. Allah has made you agree upon the best [choice] – meaning Abū Bakr ؓ – and this [loss] shall only increase Islam in strength. Therefore, whoever we see recant, we shall cut off his head!" Hearing this, the people ceased and desisted from what they had intended to do.[286] His stance at the time evidently constitutes a stunning miracle for the Prophet ﷺ since he predicted it many years before it took place, namely, on the day of Badr, when he said to ʿUmar, "perhaps he will, one day, take a stand of which you will not disapprove."

قَالَ ابْنُ هِشَامٍ حَدَّثَنِي أَبُو عُبَيدَةَ وَغَيْرُهُ مِنْ أَهْلِ الْعِلْمِ أَنَّ أَكْثَرَ أَهْلِ مَكَّةَ لَمَّا تُوُفِّيَ رَسُولُ اللهِ ﷺ هَمُّوا بِالرُّجُوعِ عَنِ الإِسْلاَمِ وَأَرَادُوا ذَلِكَ حَتَّى خَافَهُم عَتَّابُ بْنُ أَسِيدٍ فَتَوَارَى فَقَامَ سُهَيْلُ بْنُ عَمْرٍو فَحَمِدَ اللهَ وَأَثْنَى عَلَيْهِ ثُمَّ ذَكَرَ وَفَاةَ رَسُولِ اللهِ ﷺ وَقَالَ إِنَّ ذَلِكَ لَمْ يَزِدِ الإِسْلاَمَ إِلاَّ قُوَّةً فَمَنْ رَابَنَا ضَرَبْنَا عُنُقَهُ فَتَرَاجَعَ النَّاسُ وَكَفُّوا عَمَّا هَمُّوا بِهِ وَظَهَرَ عَتَّابُ بْنُ أَسِيدٍ فَهَذَا

[286]Cf. Ibn Hishām, *Sīra* (6:88-89), *Iktifā'* (2:445 and 3:7), al-Ḥalabī, *Muqtafā* (p. 199) and *Sīra Ḥalabiyya* (2:455), and Ibn Ḥajar, *Iṣāba* (3:213) in addition to the sources mentioned in the next to previous note.

الْمَقَامُ الَّذِي أَرَادَ رَسُولُ اللهِ ﷺ فِي قَوْلِهِ لِعُمَرَ بْنِ الْخَطَّابِ إِنَّهُ عَسَى أَنْ يَقُومَ مَقَاماً لاَ تَذُمُّهُ سيرة ابن هشام

Abū Sufyān b. Ḥarb رضي الله عنه

Al-Ṭabarānī narrated from Maymūna رضي الله عنها–Ibn Hishām narrated it in the *Sīra* from Ibn Isḥāq–that when the Quraysh violated their treaty with the Messenger of Allah ﷺ by assisting the Banū Bakr against the Khuzāʿa, the Messenger of Allah ﷺ said to his Companions: 208 "You are about to see Abū Sufyān coming and saying, 'Renew the treaty and give it a longer term,' after which he will leave in anger." Then Abū Sufyān came to al-Madīna, exactly as the Prophet ﷺ had foretold, and asked to renew the treaty and increase its term. The Prophet ﷺ did not respond to his request and he left disappointed.[287]

عَنْ حِزَامِ بْنِ هِشَامٍ عَنْ أَبِيهِ قَالَ رَسُولُ اللهِ ﷺ لَكَأَنَّكُمْ بِأَبِي سُفْيَانَ قَدْ جَاءَ يَقُولُ جَدِّدِ الْعَهْدَ وَزِدْ فِي الْهُدْنَةِ وَهُوَ رَاجِعٌ بِسَخَطِهِ وَأَقْبَلَ أَبُو سُفْيَانَ حَتَّى قَدِمَ الْمَدِينَةَ فَدَخَلَ عَلَى النَّبِيِّ ﷺ فَقَالَ يَا مُحَمَّدُ إِنِّي كُنْتُ غَائِبًا فِي صُلْحِ الْحُدَيْبِيَةِ فَاشْدُدِ الْعَهْدَ وَزِدْنَا فِي الْمُدَّةِ فَقَالَ رَسُولُ اللهِ ﷺ هَلْ كَانَ قَبْلَكُمْ حَدَثٌ قَالَ مَعَاذَ اللهِ فَقَالَ رَسُولُ اللهِ ﷺ فَنَحْنُ عَلَى مُدَّتِنَا وَصُلْحِنَا يَوْمَ الْحُدَيْبِيَةِ، لا نُغِيرُ وَلا نُبَدِّلُ الواقدي وفي السيرة الحلبية فَأَعَادَ أَبُو سُفْيَانَ الْقَوْلَ عَلَى رَسُولِ اللهِ ﷺ فَلَمْ يَرُدَّ عَلَيْهِ شَيْئاً

[287]Narrated by al-Wāqidī (2:791) cf. *Fath al-Bārī* (8:6) and Dahlān's *Sīra* (2:78).

Al-Ṭabarānī narrated that Abū Laylā said, "We were with the Messenger of Allah ﷺ in the Ẓahrān pass – meaning, the day of the conquest of Mecca – when he said: 209 'Abū Sufyān is in al-Arāk. Catch him.' We took him **[497]** and brought him to the Prophet ﷺ."[288]

عَنْ أَبِي لَيْلَى ﷺ قَالَ كُنَّا مَعَ النَّبِيِّ ﷺ يَوْمَ الْفَتْحِ فَقَالَ إِنَّ أَبَا سُفْيَانَ فِي الْأَرَاكِ فَدَخَلْنَا فَأَخَذْنَاهُ فَجَعَلَ الْمُسْلِمُونَ يَجِيئُونَهُ يُخْفُونَ سُيُوفَهُمْ حَتَّى جَاؤُوا بِهِ إِلَى رَسُولِ اللهِ ﷺ طب

Ibn Saʿd, al-Bayhaqī and Ibn ʿAsākir narrated from Abū Isḥāq al-Sabīʿī that Abū Sufyān b. Ḥarb was sitting, after the conquest of Mecca, thinking to himself, "What if I gathered a huge army against Muḥammad?" Suddenly, the Messenger of Allah ﷺ slapped him between the shoulder-blades and said: 210 "Then Allah shall disgrace you!" He raised his head and there was the Messenger of Allah ﷺ, standing next to him. Abū Sufyān said: "I was never certain, until this moment, that you were truly a Prophet. Indeed, I was saying this to myself just now!"[289]

عَنْ أَبِي إِسْحَاقَ السَّبِيعِيِّ أَنَّ أَبَا سُفْيَانَ بْنَ حَرْبٍ ﷺ بَعْدَ فَتْحِ مَكَّةَ كَانَ جَالِساً فَقَالَ فِي نَفْسِهِ لَوْ جَمَعْتُ لِمُحَمَّدٍ جَمْعاً إِنَّهُ لَيُحَدِّثُ نَفْسَهُ بِذَلِكَ إِذْ ضَرَبَ النَّبِيُّ ﷺ بَيْنَ كَتِفَيْهِ وَقَالَ إِذاً يُخْزِيكَ اللهُ قَالَ فَرَفَعَ رَأْسَهُ فَإِذَا النَّبِيُّ ﷺ قَائِمٌ عَلَى رَأْسِهِ

---

[288]Narrated by al-Ṭabarānī in *al-Kabīr* (7:76 §6419) cf. Dahlān's *Sīra* (2:83). Ibn ʿAsākir (23:454) narrates something similar *mursal* from the *Tābiʿī* Abū al-Walīd Saʿīd b. Mīnā. Abū Sufyān entered Islam at Marr al-Zahrān, a valley 22 km north of Mecca ending at the seashore south of Jedda and al-Arāk is a place near ʿArafa on the side of Syria cf. Shurrāb, *al-Maʿālim* (p. 184, 25).

[289]Narrated by Ibn Saʿd (10:10), al-Bayhaqī in the *Dalāʾil* (4:102), and Ibn ʿAsākir (23:458) cf. *Iṣāba* (3:414), *Bidāya* (4:304), and *Khaṣāʾis* (1:441).

فقال مَا أَيْقَنْتُ أَنَّكَ نَبِيٌّ حَتَّى السَّاعَةِ إِنْ كُنْتُ لأُحَدِّثُ
نَفْسِي بِذَلِكَ هق في الدلائل ابن سعد كر وعندهما إِذاً أَخْزَاكَ اللهُ

Al-Bayhaqī and Ibn ʿAsākir [also Ibn Saʿd] narrated from Ibn ʿAbbās رضي الله عنهما that when Abū Sufyān saw the Messenger of Allah ﷺ walking with the people close on his heels he <became jealous of him and> said to himself, "What if I resumed fighting this man?" Whereupon the Messenger of Allah ﷺ walked over to him and slapped him in the chest, saying: [211] "Then Allah shall disgrace you!" He said: "I repent to Allah and seek forgiveness of Allah of what I said! <I did not say it but was only thinking it.>"[290]

عَنِ ابْنِ عَبَّاسٍ رَضِيَ اللهُ عَنْهُمَا قَالَ رَأَى أَبُو سُفْيَانَ رَسُولَ اللهِ
ﷺ يَمْشِي وَالنَّاسُ يَطَئُونَ عَقِبَهُ فَقَالَ بَيْنَهُ وَبَيْنَ نَفْسِهِ لَوْ
عَاوَدْتُ هَذَا الرَّجُلَ الْقِتَالَ فَجَاءَ رَسُولُ اللهِ ﷺ حَتَّى ضَرَبَ
بِيَدِهِ فِي صَدْرِي فَقَالَ إِذاً يُخْزِيَكَ اللهُ قَالَ أَتُوبُ إِلَى اللهِ
وَأَسْتَغْفِرُ اللهَ مِمَّا تَفَوَّهْتُ بِهِ هق كر وجاء بلفظ عَنْ أَبِي السَّفَرِ هُوَ
سَعِيدُ بْنُ يُحْمِدَ تَابِعِيٌّ قَالَ لَمَّا رَأَى أَبُو سُفْيَانَ النَّاسَ يَطَئُونَ
عَقِبَيْ رَسُولِ اللهِ ﷺ حَسَدَهُ فَقَالَ بَيْنَهُ وَبَيْنَ نَفْسِهِ لَوْ عَاوَدْتُ
هَذَا الرَّجُلَ فَجَاءَ رَسُولُ اللهِ ﷺ حَتَّى ضَرَبَ بِيَدِهِ فِي صَدْرِهِ ثُمَّ
قَالَ إِذاً يُخْزِيَكَ اللهُ إِذاً يُخْزِيَكَ اللهُ فَقَالَ أَتُوبُ إِلَى اللهِ وَأَسْتَغْفِرُهُ
وَاللهِ مَا تَفَوَّهْتُ بِهِ مَا هُوَ إِلاَّ شَيْءٌ حَدَّثْتُ بِهِ نَفْسِي ابن سعد

[290] Narrated from Ibn ʿAbbās by Ibn Saʿd (10:10), al-Bayhaqī in the *Dalāʾil* (4:102), Ibn ʿAsākir (23:457-458) and others cf. *Iṣāba* (3:413), *Bidāya* (4:304), *Khaṣāʾiṣ* (1:441), and Daḥlān's *Sīra* (2:84). The bracketed clauses are only in Ibn Saʿd.

[Ṭāwūs said in *al-Shifā*: "The Prophet ﷺ never struck anyone in the chest suffering from satanic influence (*mass*) except he was cured on the spot." The slapping in the chest or back is a Prophetic gesture associated with driving away evil influence and conferring blessing as shown by the following reports in addition to the above:

(i) ʿĀmir b. Rabʿa and Sahl b. Ḥunayf went out to bathe. ʿĀmir took off his woolen robe. He [Sahl] narrates: "I looked at him and I cast the evil eye on him. He went down into the water then I heard a noise coming from him. I called out to him three times. There was no answer. I went to call the Messenger of Allah ﷺ who came on foot and waded his way into the water. Then he slapped his chest with his hand, saying: [212] "O Allah! drive away from him its heat and its coolness and its harm." Then he ﷺ rose up and said: "If one of you sees something that pleases him in his brother – whether in his person or property – let him invoke blessing for him, for the evil eye is a reality."[291]

(ii) A report from Abū Ṭalḥa states: A man recited [the Qur'an] before ʿUmar b. al-Khaṭṭāb ؓ who corrected him, so the man said: "I recited before the Messenger of Allah ﷺ and he did not correct me. They went for arbitration before the Messenger of Allah ﷺ where the man said: "Messenger of Allah, did you not made me recite such-and-such a verse?" He said yes. Something stirred in ʿUmar's breast. Realizing this from ʿUmar's face, [213] the Prophet ﷺ slapped his chest and said three times: [a] "Away, devil!" *(abʿid shayṭānan)*. Then he said: [b] "ʿUmar, the Qur'an is all correct as long as you do not turn mercy into punishment or punishment into mercy."[292]

(iii) In similar circumstances, Ubay b. Kaʿb said: "There occurred in my mind a sort of denial which never occurred to me before, even during the Days of Ignorance. When the Messenger of Allah ﷺ saw how I was affected, [214] he slapped my chest, whereupon I broke into a sweat and felt as if I were looking at Allah in fear."[293]

(iv) A woman brought to the Prophet ﷺ a black slave-girl, saying, "Messenger of Allah, I am obliged to free a Muslim slave. Does this girl fulfill this obligation of mine?" The Messenger of Allah ﷺ asked her: [215] "Who is your Lord?" She said, "Allah." He asked, [a] "And what is your religion?" She said, "Islam." He asked, [b] "And who am I?" She replied, "You are the Messenger of Allah." He asked: [c] "Do you pray the five [prayers] and do you accept what I have brought from Allah?" She said yes. Then [d] he ﷺ slapped her on the chest and said: [e] "Free her!"[294]

(v) Jarīr b. ʿAbd Allāh al-Bajalī was sent by the Prophet ﷺ on a mission to destroy Dhūl-Khalaṣa, the idol-house of Khathʿam, nicknamed the Yemenite Kaʿba. Jarīr

[291] Ibn Kathir, *Tafsīr* (1981 Dār al-Fikr ed. 4:412) through ʿAbd Allāh b. ʿĀmir.

[292] Al-Tabarī, *Tafsīr*, Introduction, dialects in which the Qur'an was revealed cf. Ibn Ḥajar, *Fatḥ al-Bārī* (9:26). Aḥmad narrates it without mention of the slap, both with the same good chain.

[293] Narrated by Muslim.

[294] Narrated – with a chain authenticated by al-Dāraquṭnī in his *ʿIlal* (5:194) – through Abū ʿĀṣim al-Nabīl, from Abū Maʿdān, from ʿAwn b. ʿAbd Allāh b. ʿUtba from his father, from his grandfather, by al-Ṭabarānī in *al-Kabīr* (17:136), al-Bayhaqī (7:388), and al-Ḥākim (1990 ed. 3:289).

narrates: "I went along with a hundred and fifty horsemen but I could not sit steadily on my horse. I mentioned it to the Messenger of Allah ﷺ who then struck his hand on my chest so hard that I could see the trace of his fingers on it, saying: 216 'O Allah! Grant him steadfastness and make him a guide of righteousness and a rightly guided one!'"[295]

(vi) When the Prophet ﷺ dispatched ʿAlī to the Yemen as a judge the latter said, "You send me, a young man, to judge among them when I do not know how to judge?" "Whereupon he slapped his hand on my chest then said, 217 'O Allah! Guide his heart and make firm his tongue.' After this I never experienced a doubt over my judgment between two disputants."[296]

(vii) One time the Prophet ﷺ went to al-Baqīʿ at night and ʿĀ'isha followed him surreptitiously. After his visit, he turned to walk back home. ʿĀ'isha narrates: "He hastened his steps and I hastened mine. He ran and I ran. He arrived as I arrived except that I preceded him and entered first. As I lay down in the bed, he entered and said: 218 'Why is it, ʿĀ'ish, that you are out of breath?' I said: 'No reason!' He said: 'Tell me, or the Subtle and Aware will inform me!' I said: 'Messenger of Allah, my father and mother be your ransom!' Then I told him. He said: 'So it was your form I saw in front of me?' I said yes. a He gave me a push or slap on the chest which made me sore and said: b 'Did you think that Allah and His Messenger would deal unjustly with you?'"[297]

(viii) Jaʿfar b. Muḥammad reported on the authority of his father: "We went to see Jābir b. ʿAbd Allāh who began attending to his visitors until it was my turn. I said: 'I am Muḥammad b. ʿAlī b. al-Ḥusayn.' a He placed his hand upon my head and opened my upper button and then the lower one and placed his palm on my chest. I was, in those days, a young boy. He said: 'You are welcome, my nephew.'"[298]

(ix) A report states that a as Yūsuf ﷷ neared the King's wife, his father Yaʿqūb ﷷ appeared and slapped him in the chest, whereupon Yūsuf's lust exited through his fingertips.[299]

[295]Narrated by al-Bukhārī and Muslim.

[296]Narrated by Ibn Mājah, al-Nasā'ī in the *Kubrā* (5:116), Ibn Abī Shayba (6:13 §29098, 6:356 §32068), Abū Yaʿlā (1:323 §401), ʿAbd b. Ḥumayd in his *Musnad* (p. 61 §94), Ibn Saʿd (2:337), and Aḥmad in *Faḍā'il al-Ṣaḥāba* (2:580), all with a chain missing a link from ʿAlī while that link is cited but unidentified by al-Bayhaqī in the *Kubrā* (10:86) cf. al-Būṣīrī, *Miṣbāḥ* (3:42), al-Zaylaʿī, *Naṣb* (4:61), and Ibn Ḥajar, *Talkhīṣ al-Ḥabīr* (4:182)

[297]Narrated by Muslim. The Prophet ﷺ called her "ʿĀ'ish" according to a still current Arabian practice called *tarkhīm* and consisting of suppressing the last vowel or consonant of a name or both: Māli for Mālik, Fāṭim for Fāṭima, Marw for Marwān, Ḥār for Ḥārith cf. al-Qurṭubī, *Tafsīr* (16:116) and below, report on al-Ḥārith b. Suwayd (p. 253).

[298]Narrated by Muslim as part of a longer ḥadīth.

[299]Narrated from Ibn ʿAbbās, Mujāhid, al-Ḥasan, Saʿīd b. Jubayr and ʿIkrima in the *Tafsīr*s of Sufyān al-Thawrī, ʿAbd al-Razzāq, al-Ṭabarī, (12:187), Ibn Abī Ḥātim, al-Wāḥidī, al-Baghawī, Ibn al-Mundhir, Abū al-Shaykh, al-Thaʿlabī and al-Qurṭubī (9:170), cf. Ibn Kathīr (2:475), al-Jalālayn, Abū al-Suʿūd and al-Shawkānī while latter-day scholars reject this and similar reports as inauthentic (cf. Abū Ḥayyān, al-Ālūsī, al-Shinqīṭī) or as out-

(x) The report of Abū Sufyān cited above: "The a Messenger of Allah ﷺ walked over to him and slapped him in the chest."

(xi)Shayba b. ʿUthmān b. Ṭalḥa's report of his attempted assassination below: "The a Prophet ﷺ placed his hand on my chest."

(xii) Wābiṣa's report below: a He joined three fingers together and poked my chest."

(xiii) Faḍāla b. ʿUmayr al-Laythī's story of his attempted assassination of the Prophet during circumambulation. after which the Prophet put his hand on his chest and prayed for him.[300]]

Al-Bayhaqī, Abū Nuʿaym and Ibn ʿAsākir narrated that Saʿīd b. al-Musayyib said that the night the people entered Mecca when it was conquered, they did not stop making *takbīr* and *tahlīl* and circumambulating the House until morning. Abū Sufyān said to [his wife] Hind, "Do you consider that this is from Allah?" The next morning he went to see the Messenger of Allah ﷺ and the latter said: 219 "You asked Hind, 'Do you consider that this is from Allah?' Yes, it is from Allah!" Abū Sufyān said, "I bear witness that you are the servant of Allah and His Messenger! By Allah, none heard these words of mine except Allah and Hind."[301]

عَنْ سَعِيدِ بْنِ المسَيَّبِ قَالَ لَمَّا كَانَ لَيْلَةَ دَخَلَ النَّاسُ مَكَّةَ لَيْلَةَ
الْفَتْحِ لَمْ يَزَالُوا فِي تَكْبِيرٍ وَتَهْلِيلٍ وَطَوَافٍ بِالْبَيْتِ حَتَّى أَصْبَحُوا
فَقَالَ أَبُو سُفْيَانَ لِهِنْدٍ أَتَرَيْنَ هَذَا مِنَ اللهِ ثُمَّ أَصْبَحَ فَغَدَا أَبُو

right forgeries (al-Zamakhsharī, al-Rāzī), with contemporary scholars vying in stridency (Abū Shahba, *al-Isrāʾīliyyāt wal-Mawḍūʿāt* p. 220-225, Ramzī Naʿnāʿa, *al-Isrāʾīliyyāt wa-Atharuhā* p. 272-274, Ṭāhir Maḥmūd Yaʿqūb, *Asbāb al-Khaṭaʾ fil-Tafsīr* p. 610-616 and ʿAbd Allāh al-Ghumārī, *Bidaʿ al-Tafāsīr* p. 70-71). However, the *burhān Rabbih* (12:24) which Yūsuf saw is authentically narrated by al-Ṭabarī as being his father Yaʿqūb, upon our Prophet and them blessings and peace cf. Ḥikmat Bashīr Yasīn, *al-Tafsīr al-Ṣaḥīḥ* (3:84).

300 Ibn Hishām, *Sīra* (*kayfa aslama Faḍāla*).

301 Narrated from Ibn al-Musayyib by al-Bayhaqī in the *Dalāʾil* (4:103), Ibn ʿAsākir (23:457) and others cf. *Iṣāba* (3:413), *Bidāya* (4:304), *Khaṣāʾiṣ* (1:441), and Dahlān's *Sīra* (2:84).

سُفْيَانَ إِلَى رَسُولِ اللهِ ﷺ فَقَالَ لَهُ رَسُولُ اللهِ ﷺ قُلْتَ لِهِنْدٍ
أَتَرَيْنَ هَذَا مِنَ اللهِ نَعَمْ هُوَ مِنَ اللهِ فَقَالَ أَبُو سُفْيَانَ أَشْهَدُ
أَنَّكَ عَبْدُ اللهِ وَرَسُولُهُ وَالَّذِي يَحْلِفُ بِهِ أَبُو سُفْيَانَ مَا سَمِعَ قَوْلِي
هَذَا أَحَدٌ مِنَ النَّاسِ إِلاَّ اللهُ عَزَّ وَجَلَّ وَهِنْدٌ هق في الدلائل كر

Al-ʿUqaylī and Ibn ʿAsākir narrated that Ibn ʿAbbās رضي الله عنهما said that the Messenger of Allah ﷺ met Abū Sufyān b. Ḥarb in *ṭawāf* and said to him: 220 "Abū Sufyān, did you say such-and-such to Hind?" Abū Sufyān replied, "Hind betrayed my confidence! I shall make her pay dearly for this!" When the Messenger of Allah ﷺ finished his *ṭawāf* he caught up with Abū Sufyān and said: "Abū Sufyān, do not talk to Hind. She did not betray your confidence in the least." Abū Sufyān said, "I bear witness that you are the Messenger of Allah!"[302]

عَنِ ابْنِ عَبَّاسٍ رَضِيَ اللهُ عَنْهُمَا قَالَ لَقِيَ رَسُولُ اللهِ ﷺ أَبَا
سُفْيَانَ بْنَ حَرْبٍ فِي الطَّوَافِ فَقَالَ يَا أَبَا سُفْيَانَ كَانَ بَيْنَكَ
وَبَيْنَ هِنْدٍ كَذَا وَكَذَا فَقَالَ أَبُو سُفْيَانَ أَفْشَتْ عَلَيَّ
سِرِّي لَأَفْعَلَنَّ بِهَا وَلَأَفْعَلَنَّ فَلَمَّا فَرِغَ رَسُولُ اللهِ ﷺ مِنْ طَوَافِهِ
لَحِقَ أَبَا سُفْيَانَ فَقَالَ يَا أَبَا سُفْيَانَ لاَ تُكَلِّمْ هِنْداً لأَنَّهَا لَمْ تُفْشِ
مِنْ سِرِّكَ فَقَالَ أَبُو سُفْيَانَ أَشْهَدُ أَنَّكَ رَسُولُ اللهِ العقيلي كر

Ibn Saʿd, al-Ḥārith b. Abī Usāma and Ibn ʿAsākir narrated that ʿAbd Allāh b. Abī Bakr b. Ḥazm said the Messenger of Allah ﷺ came out as Abū Sufyān was sitting in the Mosque, saying [to

[302]Narrated from Ibn ʿAbbās by ʿUqaylī (3:810) and, through him, Ibn ʿAsākir (23:459).

himself], "I have no idea how Muḥammad is beating us." The Prophet ﷺ came over to him and slapped his chest, saying: [221] "With Allah he is beating you!" Abū Sufyān said, "I bear witness that you are the Messenger of Allah!"[303]

عَنْ عَبْدِ اللهِ بْنِ أَبِي بَكْرِ بْنِ حَزْمٍ قَالَ خَرَجَ النَّبِيُّ ﷺ مُلْتَحِفاً بِثَوْبٍ مِنْ بَعْضِ بُيُوتِ نِسَائِهِ وَأَبُو سُفْيَانَ جَالِسٌ فِي الْمَسْجِدِ فَقَالَ أَبُو سُفْيَانَ مَا أَدْرِي بِمَ يَغْلِبُنَا مُحَمَّدٌ فَأَتَى النَّبِيُّ ﷺ حَتَّى ضَرَبَ فِي ظَهْرِهِ وَقَالَ بِاللهِ يَغْلِبُكَ قَالَ أَبُو سُفْيَانَ أَشْهَدُ أَنَّكَ رَسُولُ اللهِ ابن سعد كر

The erudite Scholar, Sayyid Aḥmad Daḥlān – Allah have mercy on him! – said:

> The gist of these reports is that Abū Sufyān, at first, was being coerced; but the Messenger of Allah ﷺ did not stop treating him gently and winning him over until Islam gained a firm foothold in his heart. His eye was plucked out in the raid on Ṭā'if and he came to the Prophet ﷺ carrying it in his hand. The Prophet ﷺ said to him: [222] "If you wish, Allah shall return it to you in a better state than it used to be; or, if you wish, [He shall give you] better than that in Paradise." He threw it away and said, "Better than that in Paradise!"[304] His other eye was plucked out in the battle of Yarmūk during the caliphate of ʿUmar ؓ at which time he urged on the people and pushed them to fight, saying, "This is one of the days of Allah, help the Religion of Allah and He shall help you!"[305]

[303]Narrated from ʿAbd Allāh b. Abī Bakr b. Ḥazm by Ibn Saʿd (10:10) and Ibn ʿAsākir (23:458-459) cf. *Iṣāba* (3:414) and Daḥlān's *Sīra* (2:84).

[304]Cited by Ibn Ḥajar, *Iṣāba* (3:414).

[305]Narrated by Ya'qūb b. Sufyān and Ibn Saʿd with a sound chain cf. al-Balādhūrī, *Ansāb al-Ashrāf* (5:14=p.1858), Ibn Ḥajar, *Iṣāba* (3:414), Daḥlān, *Sīra* (2:84).

الزُّبَيْرُ بْنُ بَكَّارٍ مِنْ طَرِيقِ سَعِيدِ بْنِ عُبَيدٍ الثَّقَفِيِّ قَالَ رَمَيْتُ أَبَا سُفْيَانَ يَوْمَ الطَّائِفِ فَأَصَبْتُ عَينَهُ فَأَتَى النَّبِيَّ ﷺ فَقَالَ هَذِهِ عَيْنِي أُصِيبَتْ فِي سَبِيلِ اللهِ قَالَ إِنْ شِئْتَ دَعَوْتُ فَرُدَّتْ عَلَيْكَ وَإِنْ شِئْتَ فَالْجَنَّةُ قَالَ الْجَنَّةُ وَرَوَى يَعْقُوبُ بْنُ سُفْيَانَ وَابْنُ سَعْدٍ بِإِسْنَادٍ صَحِيحٍ عَنْ سَعِيدِ بْنِ الْمسَيِّبِ عَنْ أَبِيهِ قَالَ فُقِدَتِ الأَصْوَاتُ يَوْمَ الْيَرْمُوكِ إِلاَّ صَوْتُ رَجُلٍ يَقُولُ يَا نَصْرُ اللهِ اقْتَرِبْ قَالَ فَنَظَرْتُ فَإِذَا هُوَ أَبُو سُفْيَانَ تَحْتَ رَايَةِ ابْنِهِ يَزِيدَ وَيُقَالُ فُقِئَتْ عَيْنُهُ يَوْمَئِذٍ إصابة

[When the Prophet ﷺ escaped to Madīna and Abū Jahl was searching for him, the latter questioned Fāṭima and slapped her. When Abū Sufyān heard of this, he took her by the hand, led her to Abū Jahl, and said to her "Slap him back" which she did. Hearing of this, the Prophet ﷺ said: 223 "O Allah! Count it as a good deed for Abū Sufyān and guide him with it."][306]

Muʿāwiya ؓ

Ibn Abī Shayba narrated in his *Musnad* through ʿAbd al-Malik b. ʿUmayr from Muʿāwiya ؓ **[498]**, "I never stopped longing for the caliphate after the Messenger of Allah ﷺ said to me: 224 'Muʿāwiya, when you rule, rule well' *(idhā malakta fa'aḥsin)*."[307]

306Narrated from al-Madā'inī by al-Balādhūrī in *Ansāb al-Ashrāf* (5:14=p.1858). Dahlān mentions it in his *Sīra*.

307Narrated *mursal* by Ibn Abī Shayba (6:207 §30715), al-Ṭabarānī in *al-Kabīr* (19:361), Ibn ʿAsākir (59:110), and al-Bayhaqī in the *Dalā'il* (6:446) all with a weak chain because of Ismā'īl b. Ibrāhīm b. Muhājir, and ʿAbd al-Malik b. 'Umayr did not meet Muʿāwiya cf. *Siyar* (Fikr ed. 4:294=Risāla ed. 3:131), but Bayhaqī said the hadith has witness-reports.

عَنْ عَبْدِ المِلِكِ بْنِ عُمَيرٍ قَالَ قَالَ مُعَاوِيَةُ رَضِيَ اللهُ عَنْهُ مَا زِلْتُ أَطْمَعُ فِي الخِلاَفَةِ مُنْذُ قَالَ رَسُولُ اللهِ ﷺ مَا قَالَ يَا مُعَاوِيَةُ إِنْ مَلَكْتَ فَأَحْسِنْ ش طب طس كر الشريعة للآجري هق دلائل وفيه إسماعيل بن إبراهيم بن مهاجر ضعيف والخبر مرسل قال هق إلا أن للحديث شواهد

Al-Bayhaqī narrated from Saʿīd b. al-ʿĀṣ that Muʿāwiya carried the ablution water for the Prophet ﷺ one time when Abū Hurayra was unwell, at which time the Prophet ﷺ looked at him once or twice and said: 225 "Muʿāwiya, when you receive authority over a certain affair, fear Allah and be just!" Muʿāwiya said: "After this, I never stopped expecting to be tried with some act because of what the Prophet ﷺ said."[308]

عَنْ أَبِي أُمَيَّةَ عَمْرِو بْنِ يَحْيَى بْنِ سَعِيدٍ قَالَ سَمِعْتُ جَدِّي يُحَدِّثُ أَنَّ مُعَاوِيَةَ أَخَذَ الإِدَاوَةَ بَعْدَ أَبِي هُرَيْرَةَ رَضِيَ اللهُ عَنْهُ يَتْبَعُ رَسُولَ اللهِ ﷺ بِهَا وَاشْتَكَى أَبُو هُرَيْرَةَ فَبَيْنَا هُوَ يُوَضِّئُ رَسُولَ اللهِ ﷺ رَفَعَ رَأْسَهُ إِلَيْهِ مَرَّةً أَوْ مَرَّتَيْنِ فَقَالَ يَا مُعَاوِيَةُ إِنْ وُلِّيتَ أَمْرًا فَاتَّقِ اللهَ عَزَّ وَجَلَّ وَاعْدِلْ قَالَ فَمَا زِلْتُ أَظُنُّ أَنِّي مُبْتَلًى بِعَمَلٍ لِقَوْلِ النَّبِيِّ ﷺ حَتَّى ابْتُلِيتُ حم ع ابن سعد هق في الدلائل كر قال الهيثمي رواه أحمد وهو مرسل ورجاله رجال الصحيح ورواه أبو يعلى عن سعيد عن معاوية فوصله ورجاله رجال الصحيح

[308]Narrated by Aḥmad and Abū Yaʿlā (13:370 §7380) with a strong chain cf. Haythamī (5:186), among others.

Al-Ṭabarānī narrated from ʿĀ'isha رضي الله عنها that the Prophet ﷺ said to Muʿāwiya: 226 "What will happen to you when Allah vests you with a certain shirt?" meaning the caliphate. Umm Ḥabība said, "Messenger of Allah, will Allah really vest my brother with a certain shirt?" He said: "Yes, but there shall be in it flaws here and there" meaning aberration. Then the Prophet supplicated for him.[309]

عَنْ عَائِشَةَ رَضِيَ اللهُ عَنْهَا قَالَتْ لَمَّا كَانَ يَوْمُ أُمِّ حَبِيبَةَ مِنَ النَّبِيِّ ﷺ دَقَّ الْبَابَ دَاقٌّ فَقَالَ النَّبِيُّ ﷺ انْظُرُوا مَنْ هَذَا قَالُوا مُعَاوِيَةُ فَقَالَ ائْذَنُوا لَهُ وَدَخَلَ وَعَلَى أُذُنِهِ قَلَمٌ لَهُ يَخُطُّ بِهِ فَقَالَ مَا هَذَا الْقَلَمُ عَلَى أُذُنِكَ يَا مُعَاوِيَةُ قَالَ أَعْدَدْتُهُ لِلَّهِ وَلِرَسُولِهِ قَالَ جَزَاكَ اللهُ عَنْ نَبِيِّكَ خَيْراً وَاللهِ مَا اسْتَكْتَبْتُكَ إِلاَّ بِوَحْيٍ مِنَ اللهِ عَزَّ وَجَلَّ وَمَا أَفْعَلُ مِنْ صَغِيرَةٍ وَلاَ كَبِيرَةٍ إِلاَّ بِوَحْيٍ مِنَ اللهِ عَزَّ وَجَلَّ كَيْفَ بِكَ لَوْ قَدْ قَمَّصَكَ اللهُ قَمِيصاً يَعْنِي الْخِلاَفَةَ فَقَامَتْ أُمُّ حَبِيبَةَ فَجَلَسَتْ بَيْنَ يَدَيْهِ فَقَالَتْ يَا رَسُولَ اللهِ وَإِنَّ اللهَ مُقَمِّصٌ أَخِي قَمِيصاً قَالَ نَعَمْ وَلَكِنْ فِيهِ هَنَاتٌ وَهَنَاتٌ وَهَنَاتٌ فَقَالَتْ يَا رَسُولَ اللهِ فَادْعُ لَهُ فَقَالَ اللهُمَّ اهْدِهِ بِالْهُدَى وَجَنِّبْهُ الرَّدَى وَاغْفِرْ لَهُ فِي الآخِرَةِ وَالأُولَى طب طس من طريق السري بن عاصم ضعيف مج

[309]Narrated from ʿĀ'isha by al-Ṭabarānī in *al-Awsat* (2:233 §1838) and Ibn ʿAsākir (59:69) through al-Sarī b. ʿĀṣim who is weak and by al-Khallāl in *al-Sunna* (2:458) with a chain of unknowns.

Ibn ʿAsākir narrated it from ʿĀ'isha رضي الله عنها with the wording: 227 "Muʿāwiya, truly Allah has given you some responsibility over this Community, so watch what you will do." Umm Ḥabība said, "Will Allah really give my brother this?" He said: "Yes, but there will be in him defects here and there."[310]

وعنها جاء بلفظ يَا مُعَاوِيَةُ إِنَّ اللهَ وَلاَّكَ مِنْ أَمْرِ هَذِهِ الأُمَّةِ فَانْظُرْ مَا أَنْتَ صَانِعٌ كر

Ibn ʿAsākir also narrated through al-Ḥasan from Muʿāwiya رضي الله عنه, "The Messenger of Allah ﷺ said to me: 228 'As for you, you will take charge of my Community after me. When this happens, accept those of them who do good and overlook those of them who do wrong.' Since then, I never ceased expecting it until I reached my position."[311]

عَنِ الْحَسَنِ رَضِيَ اللهُ عَنْهُ قَالَ سَمِعْتُ مُعَاوِيَةَ يَقُولُ صَبَبْتُ يَوْماً عَلَى رَسُولِ اللهِ ﷺ وَضُوءَهُ فَرَفَعَ رَأْسَهُ إِلَيَّ فَقَالَ أَمَا إِنَّكَ سَتَلِي أَمْرَ أُمَّتِي بَعْدِي فَإِذَا كَانَ ذَلِكَ فَاقْبَلْ مِنْ مُحْسِنِهِمْ وَتَجَاوَزْ عَنْ مُسِيئِهِمْ فَمَا زِلْتُ أَرْجُوهَا حَتَّى قُمْتُ مَقَامِي هَذَا طس كر

Al-Daylamī narrated that al-Ḥasan b. ʿAlī رضي الله عنهما said that he heard ʿAlī say, "I heard the Messenger of Allah ﷺ say: 229 'The days and nights will not be long until Muʿāwiya rules.'"[312]

[310]Narrated from ʿĀ'isha by Ibn ʿAsākir (59:69-70)

[311]Narrated from Muʿāwiya by al-Ṭabarānī in *al-Awsat* (2:351-352 §2204) and Ibn ʿAsākir (59:109), both through Yaḥyā b. Ghālib, from his father, a forged report according to Ibn ʿAdī in *al-Kāmil* (2:742 §7030) and al-Dhahabī in the *Mīzān* (7:211).

[312]Narrated from ʿAlī by Ibn ʿAsākir (59:151) cf. Daylamī, *Firdaws* (5:77 §7507) through al-Sarī b. Ismāʿīl who is a discarded narrator cf. Dhahabī, *Siyar* (Risāla ed. 3:147).

عَنِ الْحَسَنِ بْنِ عَلِيٍّ رَضِيَ اللّٰهُ عَنْهُمَا قَالَ سَمِعْتُ أَبِي يَقُولُ لاَ تَذْهَبُ الأَيَّامُ وَاللَّيَالِي حَتَّى يَمْلِكُ مُعَاوِيَةُ كر وفي سير النبلاء فيه السري بن إسماعيل تالف ورفعه صاحب البداية والنهاية

Ibn Sa'd and Ibn 'Asākir narrated that Maslama b. Mukhallad ﷺ said that he heard the Prophet ﷺ say before Mu'āwiya: 230 "O Allah, teach him the Book [or writing], make firm his power over the world, and spare him from punishment."[313]

عَنْ مَسْلَمَةَ بْنِ مَخْلَدٍ أَنَّهُ قَالَ لِعَمْرِو بْنِ الْعَاصِ سَمِعْتُ النَّبِيَّ ﷺ يَقُولُ اللهُمَّ عَلِّمْ مُعَاوِيَةَ الْكِتَابَ وَمَكِّنْ لَهُ فِي الْبِلاَدِ وَقِهِ الْعَذَابَ تاريخ ابن أبي خيثمة حم في فضائل الصحابة طب ابن سعد الآجري في الشريعة ابن قتيبة في غريب الحديث كر قال في الميزان الخبر منكر بمرة اهـ قلت له طرق وشواهد وجاء بلفظ عَلِّمْهُ الْكِتَابَ وَالْحِسَابَ كر

Ibn 'Asākir narrated that [the *Tābi'ī*] 'Urwa b. Ruwaym ﷺ said that a Bedouin came to the Prophet ﷺ and said, "Wrestle with me." Mu'āwiya got up and said, "I shall wrestle with you!" The Prophet ﷺ said: 231 "Mu'āwiya will never lose!" Then he wrestled down the

[313]A "completely disclaimed report" *(munkar bi-marra)* according to al-Dhahabī in the *Mīzān* (2:112) cf. Ibn Ḥajar, *Lisān* (2:96), narrated from Maslama b. Mukhallad by al-Ṭabarānī in *al-Kabīr* (19:439 §1065) with a passable *mursal* chain cf. al-Haythamī (9:356-357) strengthened by other chains cf. *Siyar* (Risāla ed. 3:124-125), *Iṣāba* (2:193, 4:342) such as from 'Alī and 'Amr b. al-'Āṣ by Ibn 'Asākir (59:74, 59:78) and Aḥmad in *Faḍā'il al-Saḥāba* (2:915). Also narrated with the wording: "O Allah, teach him the Book and arithmetic (*al-ḥisāb*) , and spare him from punishment" from Ibn 'Abbās, al-'Irbāḍ, and Abū Hurayra cf. Ibn al-Jawzī, *al-'Ilal al-Mutanāhiya* (1:272-274 §436-438 and §440) and Ibn 'Asākir (59:77, 59:106), from Shurayḥ b. 'Ubayd by Aḥmad in *Faḍā'il al-Saḥāba* (2:914) with a sound *mursal* chain, from Maslama by al-Ṭabarānī in *Musnad al-Shāmiyyīn* (1:190 §333), also from the Companion 'Abd al-Raḥmān b. Abī 'Umayra al-Muzanī and – *mursal* – from al-Zuhrī, 'Urwa b. Ruwaym, Ḥarīz b. Ùthmān al-Raḥabī, and Yūnus b. Maysara b. Ḥalbas in Ibn 'Asākir (35:230, 59:79, 59:85, 59:106).

Bedouin. At Ṣiffīn, ʿAlī ؓ said, "Had I remembered that saying I would have never fought Muʿāwiya!"[314]

عَنْ عُرْوَةَ بْنِ رُوَيْمٍ قَالَ جَاءَ أَعْرَابِيٌّ إِلَى النَّبِيِّ ﷺ فَقَالَ يَا رَسُولَ
اللهِ صَارِعْنِي فَقَامَ إِلَيْهِ مُعَاوِيَةُ فَقَالَ يَا أَعْرَابِيُّ أَنَا أُصَارِعُكَ
فَقَالَ النَّبِيُّ ﷺ لَنْ يُغْلَبَ مُعَاوِيَةُ أَبَداً فَصَرَعَ الأَعْرَابِيَّ قَالَ فَلَمَّا
كَانَ يَوْمُ صِفِّينَ قَالَ عَلِيٌّ لَوْ ذَكَرْتُ هَذَا الْحَدِيثَ مَا قَاتَلْتُ
مُعَاوِيَةَ كر وجاء بلفظ عَنِ ابْنِ عَبَّاسٍ قَالَ جَاءَ أَعْرَابِيٌّ إِلَى النَّبِيِّ
ﷺ لِيُصَارِعَهُ فَقَالَ قُمْ يَا مُعَاوِيَةُ فَصَارِعْهُ فَقَامَ مُعَاوِيَةُ فَصَارَعَهُ
فَصَرَعَهُ فَقَالَ رَسُولُ اللهِ ﷺ أَمَا عَلِمْتُمْ أَنَّ مُعَاوِيَةَ لاَ يُصَارِعُ
أَحَداً إِلاَّ صَرَعَهُ مُعَاوِيَةُ أبو نعيم في رياضة الأبدان

Al-Bayhaqī narrated that al-Shaʿbī said that when ʿAlī returned from the battle of Ṣiffīn he said, "People! Do not loathe Muʿāwiya's leadership. If you were to lose him, you would see heads parting with their necks <like colocynths *(kal-ḥanẓal)*>!"[315]

عَنْ عَلِيٍّ قَالَ لاَ تَكْرَهُوا إِمْرَةَ مُعَاوِيَةَ فَوَاللهِ لَئِنْ فَقَدْتُمُوهُ لَتَرَوُنَّ
الرُّؤُوسَ تَنْدِرُ عَنْ كَوَاهِلِهَا ش كر وفي رواية زيادة كَالْحَنْظَلِ كر أبو

[314]Narrated *mursal* from ʿUrwa b. Ruwaym by Ibn ʿAsākir (59:87). Abū Nuʿaym narrates something similar with a strong chain in his *Riyāḍat al-Abdān* (§2) and al-Daylamī chainless in the *Firdaws* (1:232 §891): "Muʿāwiya never wrestles anyone but wins!" as adduced by al-Suyūṭī at the very end of his *al-Musāraʿa ilā al-Muṣāraʿa* (p. 89).

[315]Narrated through al-Shaʿbī from al-Ḥārith al-Aʿwar by Ibn Abī Shayba (7:548 §37854) and Ibn ʿAsākir (59:152). Another version in the latter (59:151) includes the bracketed phrase.

نعيم في المعرفة وفي رواية تَنْزُو مِنْ كَوَاهِلِهَا كَالْحَنْظَلِ كر هق في الدلائل أي
تَثِبُ

ʿIkrima b. Abī Jahl ﷜

Ibn ʿAsakir narrated that Anas ﷜ said that ʿIkrima b. Abī Jahl killed – before his Islam – Ṣakhr al-Anṣārī. When news of this reached the Prophet ﷺ, he smiled. The Anṣār said, "Messenger of Allah, are you smiling because a man of your people killed a man of ours?" He said: 232 "I am not smiling because of this but because he killed him and yet shares his high rank"[316] – meaning, in Paradise. Later, ʿIkrima entered Islam, may Allah be well-pleased with him.

عَنْ أنس رَضِيَ اللهُ عَنْهُ قَالَ قَتَلَ عِكْرِمَةُ بْنُ أَبِي جَهْلٍ صَخْراً الأَنْصَارِيَّ فَبَلَغَ ذَلِكَ النَّبِيَّ ﷺ فَضَحِكَ فَقَالَ الأَنْصَارُ يَا رَسُولَ اللهِ تَضْحَكُ أَنْ قَتَلَ رَجُلٌ مِنْ قَومِكَ رَجُلاً مِنْ قَومِنَا قَالَ مَا ذَاكَ أَضْحَكَنِي وَلَكِنَّهُ قَتَلَهُ وَهُوَ مَعَهُ فِي دَرَجَتِهِ كر قال المصنف رحمه الله ثم أسلم عكرمة رضي الله عنه

ʿUthmān b. Ṭalḥa ﷜

Ibn Saʿd narrated that al-Wāqidī told them Ibrāhīm b. Muḥammad al-ʿAbdarī narrated to them from his father that ʿUthmān b. Ṭalḥa said, "The Messenger of Allah ﷺ met me in Mecca before the *Hijra* and called me to Islam. I said, 'Muḥammad, how strange you are! How can you expect me to follow you when you have gone against the religion of your people and brought a new religion?' We used to open the Kaʿba, in *Jāhiliyya*, every first and fifth day of the week *(al-ithnayn wal-khamīs)*. He ﷺ came one

[316]Narrated from Anas by Ibn ʿAsākir (41:59) cf. Ibn Ḥajar, *Isāba* (3:419).

day, intending to enter the Ka‘ba with the people. I treated him rudely and abused him but he reciprocated with kindness and dignity. Then he said: [233] ‘‘Uthman, you may see this key **[499]** in my hand one day; then I shall dispose of it in any way I wish.’ I said, ‘The Quraysh must have perished and fallen low then!’ He replied: ‘On the contrary, they will have become stronger and mightier.’ Then he entered the Ka‘ba. His words had such an effect on me that I became convinced that what he said would eventually take place. I began to desire Islam. My relatives scolded me harshly. The day Makka was conquered, he ﷺ said to me: ‘‘Uthmān, bring me the key!’ I brought him the key and gave it to him. He took it then gave it back to me, saying: <[a] ‘Take it, [a right] revered and time-honored>, and none shall usurp it from you except wrong-doers.’ When I walked away, he called me back and said: ‘Did not what I had told you take place?’ Then I remembered what he had said in Mecca before the *Hijra* – ‘You may see this key in my hand one day, then I shall dispose of it in any way I wish’ – and I said, ‘Yes, it did, and I bear witness that you are the Messenger of Allah!’’’[317]

عَنْ مُحَمَّدٍ العَبْدَرِيِّ قَالَ قَالَ عُثْمَانُ بْنُ طَلْحَةَ لَقِيَنِي رَسُولُ اللهِ
ﷺ بِمَكَّةَ قَبْلَ الهِجْرَةِ فَدَعَانِي إِلَى الإِسْلَامِ فَقُلْتُ يَا مُحَمَّدُ
العَجَبُ لَكَ حَيْثُ تَطْمَعُ أَنْ أَتَّبِعَكَ وَقَدْ خَالَفْتَ دِينَ قَوْمِكَ
وَجِئْتَ بِدِينٍ مُحْدَثٍ وَكُنَّا نَفْتَحُ الْكَعْبَةَ فِي الْجَاهِلِيَّةِ يَوْمَ الاِثْنَيْنِ
وَالْخَمِيسِ فَأَقْبَلَ رَسُولُ اللهِ ﷺ يَوْمًا يُرِيدُ أَنْ يَدْخُلَ الْكَعْبَةَ مَعَ
النَّاسِ فَأَغْلَظْتُ لَهُ وَنِلْتُ مِنْهُ فَحَلُمَ عَنِّي ثُمَّ قَالَ يَا عُثْمَانُ
لَعَلَّكَ سَتَرَى هَذَا الْمِفْتَاحَ يَوْمًا بِيَدِي أَضَعُهُ حَيْثُ شِئْتُ

317 Narrated from ʿUthmān b. Ṭalḥa through Ibn Saʿd and al-Wāqidī by Ibn ʿAsākir (38:382-383, 387, cf. 23:259), cf. *Fatḥ* (8:18). Ibn Saʿd (2:137) narrates the bracketed phrase as spoken to the Banū Abī Ṭalḥa collectively.

فَقُلْتُ لَقَدْ هَلَكَتْ قُرَيْشٌ يَوْمَئِذٍ وَذَلَّتْ فَقَالَ بَلْ عَمَرَتْ
وَعَزَّتْ يَوْمَئِذٍ وَدَخَلَ الْكَعْبَةَ فَوَقَعَتْ كَلِمَتُهُ مِنِّي مَوْقِعًا ظَنَنْتُ
يَوْمَئِذٍ أَنَّ الأَمْرَ سَيَصِيرُ إِلَى مَا قَالَ فَلَمَّا كَانَ يَوْمُ الْفَتْحِ قَالَ يَا
عُثْمَانُ ائْتِنِي بِالْمِفْتَاحِ فَأَتَيْتُهُ بِهِ فَأَخَذَهُ مِنِّي ثُمَّ دَفَعَهُ إِلَيَّ وَقَالَ
خُذُوهَا خَالِدَةً تَالِدَةً لاَ يَنْزِعُهَا مِنْكُمْ إِلّا ظَالِمٌ يَا عُثْمَانُ إِنَّ اللهَ
اسْتَأْمَنَكُمْ عَلَى بَيْتِهِ فَكُلُوا مِمَّا يَصِلُ إِلَيْكُمْ مِنْ هَذَا الْبَيْتِ
بِالْمَعْرُوفِ قَالَ فَلَمَّا وَلَّيْت نَادَانِي فَرَجَعْتُ إِلَيْهِ فَقَالَ أَلَمْ يَكُنْ
الَّذِي قُلْتُ لَكَ قَالَ فَذَكَرْت قَوْلَهُ لِي بِمَكَّةَ قَبْلَ الْهِجْرَةِ لَعَلَّك
سَتَرَى هَذَا الْمِفْتَاحَ بِيَدِي أَضَعُهُ حَيْثُ شِئْت فَقُلْتُ بَلَى
أَشْهَدُ أَنَّكَ رَسُولُ اللهِ كر وأخبار مكة للأزرقي والخبر مذكور في الاكتفاء
والمنتظم والزاد والخصائص وعزواه لابن سعد ولم أجده في الطبقات الكبرى سوى قوله ﷺ
خُذُوهَا يَا بَنِي أَبِي طَلْحَةَ تَالِدَةً خَالِدَةً لاَ يَنْزَعُهَا مِنْكُمْ أَحَدٌ
إِلاَّ ظَالِمٌ

Shayba b. ʿUthmān b. Ṭalḥa ﵁

Ibn Saʿd and Ibn ʿAsākir narrated that ʿAbd al-Malik b. ʿUbayd and others said that Shayba b. ʿUthmān told of his Islam and said, "The year of the Conquest the Messenger of Allah ﷺ entered Mecca by force. I said to myself, let me join up with the Quraysh and the Hawāzin in Ḥunayn. Perhaps, in the fray of battle, I shall be able to fall upon Muḥammad unguarded and I shall be the one who obtains revenge for the Quraysh. I also used to say, even if no one [non-Muslim] is left among the Arabs and *ʿAjam*, I shall still not follow Muḥammad! I shall never follow him! I was, therefore, very determined against him when I rode out and my determination only increased in intensity. When the people entered the fray, the fighting caused the Messenger of Allah ﷺ to dismount his mule. I drew my sword and approached to carry out my intent against him. I raised my sword and was almost standing over him when he put up, in front of me, a blaze of fire like a lightning bolt, which almost charred me! I put up my hand before my eyes, fearing to lose my sight, then I turned towards the Messenger of Allah ﷺ. At this time he called me: [234] 'Shayba, come here!' I went near him and he wiped my breast then said: [a] 'O Allah, protect him from the devil.' I swear it by Allah! – at that very moment, he became more beloved to me than my hearing, my sight and my own life! Allah took away everything that was in me. Then he said: [b] 'Advance and fight.' I went ahead of him and struck sword-blows. Allah knew best that I loved to protect him with my own life from any harm, even if I had met my own father at that time, had he been alive – I would have used the sword against him. <I stayed near him along with others until the Muslims retreated then moved forward like one man. The mule of the Messenger of Allah ﷺ was brought and he mounted it and pursued them until they dispersed in every direction.> Later he ﷺ went back to his camp and entered his tent. I went in to see him <and no one else entered but myself, out of love for him, longing to see his face, in joy and elation.> He said: [c] 'Shayba, what Allah desired for you is better than what you desired for yourself.' Then he revealed to me all that I had harbored in my heart – things I had never mentioned to anyone. I said, 'I bear witness that there is no God but Allah and that you are the Messenger of Allah.' Then I said, 'Ask forgiveness for me, Messenger of Allah!' He replied, [d] 'Allah forgive you.'"[318]

[318]Narrated by al-Wāqidī (2:909-910) and through him by Ibn Sa'd in the *Juz' al-Mutammam* (Salūmī ed. 1:256-258 §110) as well as through a different chain by al-Ṭabarānī in the *Kabīr* (7:358-359 §7192), Ibn 'Asākir (23:255-256), al-Ṭabarī in the *Tārīkh* and others. Al-Nabhānī omitted the bracketed segments.

عَنْ شَيْبَةَ بْنِ عُثْمَانَ الْحَجَبِيِّ قَالَ لَمَّا كَانَ عَامُ الْفَتْحِ دَخَلَ رَسُولُ اللهِ ﷺ مَكَّةَ عَنْوَةً قُلْت أَسِيرُ مَعَ قُرَيْشٍ إِلَى هَوَازِنَ بِحُنَيْنٍ فَعَسَى إِنْ اخْتَلَطُوا أَنْ أُصِيبَ مِنْ مُحَمَّدٍ غِرَّةً فَأَثْأَرَ مِنْهُ فَأَكُونَ أَنَا الَّذِي قُمْتُ بِثَأْرِ قُرَيْشٍ كُلِّهَا وَأَقُولُ لَوْ لَمْ يَبْقَ مِنْ الْعَرَبِ وَالْعَجَمِ أَحَدٌ إِلَّا اتَّبَعَ مُحَمَّدًا مَا تَبِعْتُهُ أَبَدًا وَكُنْت مُرْصِدًا لِمَا خَرَجْتُ لَهُ لاَ يَزْدَادُ الأَمْرُ فِي نَفْسِي إِلا قُوَّةً فَلَمَّا اخْتَلَطَ النَّاسُ اقْتَحَمَ رَسُولُ اللهِ ﷺ عَنْ بَغْلَتِهِ فَأَصْلَتُّ السَّيْفَ فَدَنَوْتُ أُرِيدُ مَا أُرِيدُ مِنْهُ وَرَفَعْتُ سَيْفِي حَتَّى كِدْتُ أُشْعِرَهُ إِيَّاهُ فَرُفِعَ لِي شُوَاظٌ مِنْ نَارٍ كَالْبَرْقِ كَادَ يَمْحَشُنِي فَوَضَعْتُ يَدَيَّ عَلَى بَصَرِي خَوْفًا عَلَيْهِ فَالْتَفَتَ إِلَيَّ رَسُولُ اللهِ ﷺ فَنَادَانِي يَا شَيْبُ اُدْنُ مِنِّي فَدَنَوْتُ مِنْهُ فَمَسَحَ صَدْرِي ثُمَّ قَالَ اللهُمَّ أَعِذْهُ مِنْ الشَّيْطَانِ قَالَ فَوَاللهِ لَهُوَ كَانَ سَاعَتَئِذٍ أَحَبَّ إِلَيَّ مِنْ سَمْعِي وَبَصَرِي وَنَفْسِي وَأَذْهَبَ اللهُ مَا كَانَ فِي نَفْسِي ثُمَّ قَالَ اُدْنُ فَقَاتِلِ بِنَفْسِي كُلَّ شَيْءٍ وَلَوْ لَقِيتُ تِلْكَ السَّاعَةَ أَبِي لَوْ كَانَ حَيًّا لأَوْقَعْتُ بِهِ السَّيْفَ فَجَعَلْتُ أَلْزَمُهُ فِيمَنْ لَزِمَهُ حَتَّى تَرَاجَعَ الْمُسْلِمُونَ فَكَرُّوا كَرَّةَ رَجُلٍ وَاحِدٍ وَقُرِّبَتْ بَغْلَةُ رَسُولِ اللهِ ﷺ فَاسْتَوَى عَلَيْهَا وَخَرَجَ فِي أَثَرِهِمْ حَتَّى تَفَرَّقُوا فِي كُلِّ وَجْهٍ وَرَجَعَ إِلَى مُعَسْكَرِهِ فَدَخَلَ خِبَاءَهُ فَدَخَلْتُ عَلَيْهِ مَا دَخَلَ عَلَيْهِ أَحَدٌ

غَيْرِي حُبًّا لِرُؤْيَةِ وَجْهِهِ وَسُرُورًا بِهِ فَقَالَ يَا شَيْبُ الَّذِي أَرَادَ اللهُ
بِكَ خَيْرٌ مِمَّا أَرَدْتَ لِنَفْسِكَ ثُمَّ حَدَّثَنِي بِكُلِّ مَا أَضْمَرْتُ فِي
نَفْسِي مَا لَمْ أَكُنْ أَذْكُرُهُ لِأَحَدٍ قَطُّ قَالَ فَقُلْتُ فَإِنِّي أَشْهَدُ أَنْ
لاَ إِلَهَ إِلَّا اللهُ وَأَنَّكَ رَسُولُ اللهِ ﷺ ثُمَّ قُلْتُ اِسْتَغْفِرْ لِي فَقَالَ
غَفَرَ اللهُ لَكَ الواقدي ابن سعد وذكره الماوردي في أعلام النبوة

Abū al-Qāsim al-Baghawī, al-Bayhaqī, Abū Nuʿaym, and Ibn ʿAsākir narrated through Ibn al-Mubārak from Abū Bakr al-Hudhalī from ʿIkrima who said that Shayba b. ʿUthmān said, "When the Prophet ﷺ raided Ḥunayn, I remembered my father and uncle and how they were killed by ʿAlī and Ḥamza – that is, in Uḥud – so I said to myself, 'Today I have a chance to get my revenge from Muḥammad.' I came to him until I saw al-ʿAbbās to his right. I said to myself, 'His uncle is not going to desert him.' I came towards him from his left but there was Abū Sufyān b. al-Ḥārith. I said to myself, 'His paternal cousin is not going to desert him.' Then I came towards him from his back until all I had to do was close in on him with my sword. At that time a flame of fire rose in front of me like lightning, and I feared lest it scorched me. I went backwards without turning around, face down. The Prophet ﷺ turned towards me and said: [235] 'Come, Shayba!' Then [a] the Messenger of Allah ﷺ placed his hand on my chest and Allah removed the devil from my heart. I raised my eyes to look at him and he had become more beloved to me than my hearing and sight and everything else. He said to me: [b] 'Shayba, fight the disbelievers.' Then he said: [c] 'ʿAbbās! **[500]** Rally the Emigrants who pledged their oath under the Tree and the Helpers who gave shelter and aid.' Truly, nothing resembled the fierce attention of a mother camel for her kids more than the concern of the *Anṣār* for the Messenger of Allah ﷺ. Then the Messenger of Allah ﷺ was left in an area resembling a thicket. I viewed the spears of the *Anṣār* as more dangerous [there] for the Messenger of Allah ﷺ than those of the disbelievers. Then he said: [d] 'ʿAbbās! Hand me some pebbles.'

Allah made the mule understand his words because she stooped with him on her back until her belly almost touched the ground. <The Messenger of Allah ﷺ collected some pebbles then threw them in their faces, saying: ｅ 'May they be disfigured!'> **{Hā Mīm}**. They shall not be victorious!' Then they were routed and the Muslims vanquished them as is well-known."[319] This is what the ḥadīth Master al-Suyūṭī mentioned in *al-Khaṣā'iṣ*.

عَنْ عِكْرِمَةَ قَالَ قَالَ شَيْبَةُ بْنُ عُثْمَانَ لَمَّا غَزَا النَّبِيُّ ﷺ حُنَيْنٍ تَذَكَّرْتُ أَبِي وَعَمِّي قَتَلَهُمَا عَلِيٌّ وَحَمْزَةُ فَقُلْتُ الْيَوْمَ أُدْرِكُ ثَأْرِي فِي مُحَمَّدٍ فَجِئْتُهُ فَإِذَا الْعَبَّاسُ مِنْ يَمِينِهِ عَلَيْهِ دِرْعٌ بَيْضَاءُ كَأَنَّهَا الْفِضَّةُ فَكَشَفَ عَنْهَا الْعَجَاجَ فَقُلْتُ عَمُّهُ لَنْ يَخْذُلَهُ فَجِئْتُ عَنْ يَسَارِهِ فَإِذَا أَنَا بِأَبِي سُفْيَانَ بْنِ الْحَارِثِ فَقُلْتُ ابْنُ عَمِّهِ وَلَنْ يَخْذُلَهُ فَجِئْتُهُ مِنْ خَلْفِهِ فَدَنَوْتُ وَدَنَوْتُ حَتَّى إِذَا لَمْ يَبْقَ إِلَّا أَنْ أَسَوِّرَهُ سَوْرَةً بِالسَّيْفِ رُفِعَ إِلَيَّ شُوَاظٌ مِنْ نَارٍ كَأَنَّهُ الْبَرْقُ فَخِفْتُ أَنْ يَمْحَشَنِي فَنَكَصْتُ الْقَهْقَرَى فَالْتَفَتَ إِلَيَّ النَّبِيُّ ﷺ قَالَ تَعَالَ يَا شَيْبُ فَوَضَعَ رَسُولُ اللهِ ﷺ يَدَهُ عَلَى صَدْرِي فَاسْتَخْرَجَ اللهُ الشَّيْطَانَ مِنْ قَلْبِي فَرَفَعْتُ إِلَيْهِ بَصَرِي وَهُوَ أَحَبُّ إِلَيَّ مِنْ سَمْعِي وَمِنْ بَصَرِي وَمِنْ كَذَا فَقَالَ لِي يَا شَيْبُ

---

[319] Narrated with very weak chains by Ṭabarānī, *Kabīr* (7:298), al-Fākihī in *Akhbār Makka* (5:92), Baghawī, *Muʿjam al-Ṣaḥāba* (3:291 §1229), Abū Nuʿaym in his and Ibn ʿAsākir (23:256-257) all through Abū Bakr al-Hudhalī who is discarded *(matrūk)* although Ibn al-Mubārak and Wakīʿ b. al-Jarrāḥ took ḥadīth from him cf. Haythamī (6:184) and Suyūṭī, *Khaṣā'iṣ* (1:449). Ibn Kathīr adduces it in his *Tafsīr* (2:346) as it is strenghtened by the previous report and another weak-chained report in Taymī's *Dalā'il* (p. 228) and Ibn ʿAsākir (23:254) in which Shayba sees the piebald horse of an angel. The bracketed segment is narrated from Salama b. al-Akwaʿ by Muslim, Aḥmad, Dārimī cf. *Sīra Ḥalabiyya* (3:66).

قَاتِلِ الْكُفَّارَ ثُمَّ قَالَ يَا عَبَّاسُ اصْرُخْ بِالْمُهَاجِرِينَ الَّذِينَ بَايَعُوا تَحْتَ الشَّجَرَةِ وَبِالأَنْصَارِ الَّذِينَ آوَوْا وَنَصَرُوا فَمَا شَبَّهْتُ عَطْفَةَ الأَنْصَارِ عَلَى رَسُولِ اللهِ ﷺ إِلا الْبَقَرَ عَلَى أَوْلادِهَا حَتَّى نَزَلَ عَلَى رَسُولِ اللهِ ﷺ كَأَنَّهُ حَرَجَةٌ قَالَ فَلَرِمَاحُ الأَنْصَارِ كَانَتْ عِنْدِيَ أَخْوَفَ عَلَى رَسُولِ اللهِ ﷺ مِنْ رِمَاحِ الْكُفَّارِ ثُمَّ قَالَ يَا عَيَّاشُ نَاوِلْنِي مِنَ الْبَطْحَاءِ قَالَ فَأَفْقَهَ اللهُ الْبَغْلَةَ كَلامَهُ فَأَخْفَضَتْ بِهِ حَتَّى كَادَ بَطْنُهَا يَمَسُّ الأَرْضَ فَتَنَاوَلَ رَسُولُ اللهِ ﷺ مِنَ الْحَصْبَاءِ فَنَفَخَ فِي وُجُوهِهِمْ وَقَالَ شَاهَتِ الْوُجُوهُ حم لا يُنْصَرُونَ طب البغوي في معجم الصحابة أبو نعيم في المعرفة هق في الدلائل كر الفاكهي في أخبار مكة

Ibn al-Athīr said in *Usd al-Ghāba*, in the biographical notice on Shayba:

> Al-Zubayr said that Shayba went out with the Messenger of Allah ﷺ on the day of Ḥunayn intending to assassinate the Messenger of Allah ﷺ. When he saw the latter unguarded he came forward to carry out his intent. The Messenger of Allah ﷺ saw him and said: 236 "Shayba, come on!" by which Allah jolted his heart with fear. He approached the Messenger of Allah ﷺ and the latter placed his hand on his chest and said: a "Quit chattering in him, devil!" whereupon Allah cast faith into his heart. He accepted Islam and fought alongside the Messenger of Allah ﷺ. He was with those who remained steadfast that day.[320] Other ver-

[320]Cited from al-Zubayr by Ibn ʿAbd al-Barr in *al-Istīʿāb* (2:712-713), al-Khuzāʿī in *Takhrīj al-Dilālāt* (1995 ed. p. 149=1985 ed. p. 161), and Ibn al-Athīr in *Usd al-Ghāba*

sions are related concerning why he refrained from trying to kill the Prophet ﷺ. Abū Ja'far ʿAbd Allāh b. Aḥmad narrated to us with his chain to Yūnus b. Bukayr from Ibn Isḥāq, about the day of Ḥunayn: When the Muslims were being routed, Shayba b. ʿUthmān b. Abī Ṭalḥa said, "Today I shall obtain my revenge"—his father ʿUthmān b. Abī Ṭalḥa had been killed among the disbelievers in the battle of Uḥud—"and I shall kill Muḥammad today." [Shayba said,] "I approached the Messenger of Allah ﷺ to kill him but something came at me and overwhelmed me until I could not bear it. I realized he was thoroughly guarded."[321] [Later] Shayba was among the elite of the Muslims and the Messenger of Allah ﷺ gave him and his paternal cousin ʿUthmān b. Ṭalḥa b. Abī Ṭalḥa the key to the Ka'ba, saying: 237 "Take it, Banū Ṭalḥa, [a right] revered, immortal, and time-honored until the Day of Judgment, and none shall usurp it from you except wrong-doers!" He is the ancestor of the Banū Shayba that are in charge of the gatekeeping of the House and have had custody of the key to the Ka'ba until our time.[322]

قَالَ الزُّبَيْرُ خَرَجَ شَيْبَةُ مَعَ رَسُولِ اللهِ ﷺ يَوْمَ حُنَيْنٍ يُرِيدُ أَنْ
يَغْتَالَ رَسُولَ اللهِ ﷺ فَرَأَى مِنْ رَسُولِ اللهِ ﷺ غِرَّةً فَأَقْبَلَ يُرِيدُهُ
فَرَآهُ رَسُولُ اللهِ ﷺ فَقَالَ يَا شَيْبَةَ هَلُمَّ فَقَذَفَ اللهُ فِي قَلْبِهِ
الرُّعْبَ وَدَنَا مِنْ رَسُولِ اللهِ ﷺ فَوَضَعَ يَدَهُ عَلَى صَدْرِهِ ثُمَّ قَالَ

(2:645). Eighty to one hundred of the *Muhājirūn* and *Anṣār* remained steadfast in the battle of Ḥunayn including Abū Bakr, ʿUmar, ʿAlī, al-ʿAbbās, his son al-Faḍl, Sufyān b. al-Ḥārith, Rabīʿa b. al-Ḥārith, Ayman b. ʿUbayd, Usāma b. Zayd b. Ḥāritha, and a man of Ḥawzān mounted on a red camel and carrying a black flag cf. al-Ṭabarī, *Tārīkh* (2:167-168), Aḥmad from Jābir with a sound chain, Ibn Hisham (4:124), al-Ṭabarī in his *Tafsīr* (3:74), Ibn Saʿd (2:150), al-Haythamī (6:262-264 §10264-10265), al-Dhahabī's *Tārīkh al-Islām* (*Maghāzī* p. 574), Ibn Kathīr, *Bidāya* (4:332), and *Sīra Ḥalabiyya* (3:255).

[321]Cited to here through Ibn Abī Khaythama in al-Ṭabarī's *Tārīkh* (2:168), *al-Iktifā'* (2:243), al-Māwardī, *Aʿlām al-Nubuwwa* (p. 133), *al-Bidāya* (4:433-434), and al-Suhaylī's *Rawd* (4:214).

[322]Cf. *Istīʿāb* (2:713).

إِخْسَأْ عَنْهُ يَا شَيْطَانُ فَقَذَفَ اللهُ فِي قَلْبِهِ الإِيمَانَ فَأَسْلَمَ وَقَاتَلَ
مَعَ رَسُولِ اللهِ ﷺ وَكَانَ مِمَّنْ صَبَرَ يَوْمَئِذٍ وَقِيلَ فِي امْتِنَاعِهِ مِنْ
قَتْلِ النَّبِيِّ ﷺ غَيْرُ ذَلِكَ أسد الغابة

Those same Banū Shayba have had custody of the key to the Ka'ba until our own time, in this seventeenth year of the fourteenth century [1317=1899]. In the statement of the Prophet ﷺ, "Take it, Banū Ṭalḥa, revered, immortal, and time-honored until the Day of Judgment," there is another astounding miracle for him ﷺ. Namely, his acquaintance of the remainder of their lineage and effective inheritance, as well as glad tidings for them in informing them that their line shall remain until the Day of Judgment, inheriting that right except if Allah should empower a wrongdoer that shall usurp it from them. This has not taken place so far.

Tamīm al-Dārī رضي الله عنه

It was mentioned in the Prophetic *Sīra* and elsewhere that the Dārī delegation came to him ﷺ – Tamīm [b. Aws] al-Dārī, his brother Nuʿaym, and four others. They were Christians, entered Islam, and excelled thereafter – Allah be well-pleased with them! Their delegation visited him ﷺ twice, once in Mecca before the Emigration, and once **[501]** after it. The first time <they asked the Messenger of Allah ﷺ to give them a plot of land in al-Shām. He said to them: [238] "Ask [for land] wherever you wish." Abū Hind – one of Tamīm's companions – said, "We retired to discuss among ourselves where we wished to have land." Tamīm said, "Let us ask him for Bayt al-Maqdis [Jerusalem] and its vicinity." Abū Hind said to him, "This is the place of the King of the *'Ajam*,> after which it shall become the place of the King of the Arabs, so I fear we cannot own it." Tamīm said, "Let us ask him for Bayt Ḥibrūn [Hebron] and its vicinity." [Abū Hind said,] "We returned to the Messenger of Allah ﷺ and mentioned this to him. He said: [239] "Tamīm, if you wish, you tell me what you discussed or, if you wish, I shall tell you!" He replied: "Messenger of Allah, you tell us so that our faith will increase." Whereupon the Prophet ﷺ told him what had transpired. Then he called for a piece of leather and wrote for us a document stating:

> In the Name of Allah All-Beneficent, Most Merciful. [a] This is a writ in which is stated what Muḥammad the Messenger of Allah granted to the Dāriyyīn. Allah has given him the earth and he has granted them, from it, Bayt 'Aynūn, Ḥibrūn, al-Marṭūm, and Bayt Ibrāhīm – forever. Witnessed by ʿAbbās b. ʿAbd al-Muṭṭalib, [Abū] Khuzayma b. Qays, and Shuraḥbīl b. Ḥasana. It has been written.

Then he gave us the writ and said: [b] 'Go, until you hear that I have migrated.'" Abū Hind said, "We left. Then, when the Prophet ﷺ migrated to al-Madīna, we came to him and asked him to renew the writ for us with another one. He wrote for us a writ stating:

> In the Name of Allah All-Beneficent, Most Merciful. [c] This is what Muḥammad the Messenger of Allah has appropriated for Tamīm al-Dārī and his companions. I have appropriated for you Bayt 'Aynūn, Ḥibrūn, al-Marṭūm, and Bayt Ibrāhīm, in their entirety and as far as their boundaries reach. I have settled, concluded, and delivered this [property] to them and to their descendents forever and ever. If anyone should harm them over it, may Allah harm him! Witnessed by Abū Bakr b. Abī Quḥāfa, ʿUmar b. al-Khaṭṭāb, ʿUthmān b. 'Affān, ʿAlī b. Abī Ṭālib, and Muʿāwiya b. Abī Sufyān. It has been written."[323]

عَنْ زِيَادِ بْنِ أَبِي هِنْدٍ رَضِيَ اللهُ عَنْهُ قَالَ قَدِمْنَا عَلَى رَسُولِ اللهِ ﷺ وَنَحْنُ سِتَّةُ نَفَرٍ تَمِيمُ بْنُ أَوْسِ بن خارجة وَأَخُوهُ نُعَيمُ بْنُ أَوْسٍ وَيَزِيدُ بْنُ قَيْسٍ وَأَبُو هِنْدِ بْنِ عَبْدِ اللهِ الَّذِي حَدَّث

[323]Narrated from Abū Hind al-Dārī and *mursal* from Rāshid b. Saʿd by Ibn Abī ʿĀṣim in *al-Āḥād wal-Mathānī* (5:12-13 §2549) and Ibn ʿAsākir (11:64-68) cf. *Tarātīb* (Arqam ed. 1:163-164=ʿArabī ed. 1:144-145) and *Sīra Halabiyya* (3:236-237) while Ibn Saʿd (1:344) narrates something similar and mentions a delegation of ten cf. also *Iṣāba* (2:611) and *Khaṣā'is* (2:45). bracketed segment narrated by al-Ṭabarānī in *al-Kabīr*. Abū Khuzayma is Jahm b. Qays who was part of the first emigration to Abyssinia.

الحَدِيثَ وَأَخُوهُ الطَّيِّبُ بْنُ عَبْدِ اللهِ فَسَمَّاهُ رَسُولُ اللهِ ﷺ عَبْدَ الرَّحْمَنِ وَفَاكِهُ بْنُ النُّعْمَانِ فَسَأَلْنَاهُ أَنْ يُقْطِعَنَا أَرْضاً مِنْ أَرْضِ الشَّامِ وَهُوَ يَوْمَئِذٍ بِمَكَّةَ فَقَالَ رَسُولُ اللهِ ﷺ حَيْثُ أَحْبَبْتُمْ فَنَهَضْنَا مِنْ عِنْدِهِ نَتَشَاوَرُ فِي مَوْضِعٍ نَسْأَلُهُ فِيهِ فَقَالَ تَمِيمٌ الدَّارِيُّ رَضِيَ اللهُ عَنْهُ أَسْأَلُهُ بِبَيْتِ المَقْدِسِ وَكُورِهَا فَقَالَ أَبُو هِنْدٍ أَرَأَيْتَ مَلِكَ الْعَجَمِ الَّذِي هُوَ فِي بَيْتِ المَقْدِسِ فَقَالَ تَمِيمٌ رَضِيَ اللهُ عَنْهُ نَعَمْ قَالَ فَكَذَلِكَ يَكُونُ بَيْتُ مَلِكِ الْعَرَبِ فِيهَا وَأَخَافُ أَنْ لاَ يَتِمَّ لَنَا هَذَا فَقَالَ تَمِيمٌ فَنَسْأَلُ بَيْتَ جَبْرِينَ وَكُورَهَا فَقَالَ أَبُو هِنْدٍ هَذَا أَعْظَمُ وَأَكْبَرُ فَقَالَ تَمِيمٌ فَأَيْنَ تَرَى أَنْتَ فَقَالَ الْقُرَى الَّتِي تَضَعُ حَضَرُهَا فِيهَا مَعَهَا فِيهَا مِنْ أَثَرِ إِبْرَاهِيمَ عَلَيْهِ السَّلاَمُ قَالَ تَمِيمٌ رَضِيَ اللهُ عَنْهُ أَصَبْتَ فَنَهَضْنَا إِلَى رَسُولِ اللهِ ﷺ فَقَالَ يَا تَمِيمُ إِنْ شِئْتَ أَخْبِرْنِي وَإِنْ شِئْتَ أَخْبَرْتُكَ بِمَا كُنْتُمْ فِيهِ فَقَالَ تَمِيمٌ رَضِيَ اللهُ عَنْهُ بَلْ أَخْبِرْنَا يَا رَسُولَ اللهِ لِنَزْدَادَ إِيمَاناً فَقَالَ أَرَدْتَ أَمْراً وَأَرَادَ هَذَا غَيْرَهُ وَنِعْمَ الَّذِي رَأَى وَكَتَبَ لَهُ كِتَاباً فِي قِطْعَةِ جِلْدٍ مِنْ قِطْعَةِ آدَمٍ ثُمَّ دَخَلَ بِهِ إِلَى بَيْتِهِ فَعَالَجَ فِي زَاوِيَةِ الرُّقْعَةِ مِنْ أَسْفَلَ خَاتَمًا وَغَشَّاهُ بِشَيْءٍ لاَ يُعْرَفُ وَعَقَدَ بِسَيْرٍ مِنْ خَارِجِ الرُّقْعَةِ عِقْدَيْنِ وَفِي الْكِتَابِ بِسْمِ اللهِ الرَّحْمَنِ الرَّحِيمِ هَذَا مَا وَهَبَ مُحَمَّدٌ رَسُولُ اللهِ

ﷺ لِلدَّارِيِّينَ إِذَا أَعْطَاهُ اللهُ عَزَّ وَجَلَّ الأَرْضَ وَهَبَ لَهُمْ بَيْتَ عَيْنٍ وَجَبْرُونَ وَبَيْتَ إِبْرَاهِيمَ نُمُرٌّ فِيهِنَّ أَبَداً شَهِدَ الْعَبَّاسُ بْنُ عَبْدِ المطَّلِبِ وَجَهْمُ بْنُ قَيْسٍ وَشُرَحْبِيلُ بْنُ حَسَنَةَ وَكَتَبَ قَالَ ثُمَّ قَدِمْنَا عَلَيْهِ المدِينَةَ فَجَدَّدَ لَنَا كِتَاباً آخَرَ هَذَا مَا أَعْطَى مُحَمَّدٌ رَسُولُ اللهِ ﷺ تَمِيمَ الدَّارِيَّ أَعْطَيْتُهُمْ بَيْتَ عَيْنٍ وَبَيْتَ جَبْرُونَ وَالمرْطُونَ بَيْتَ إِبْرَاهِيمَ عَطِيَّةً تَبْقَى لَهُمْ وَلاَ تَبْقَى بِهِمْ وَنُفِّذَتْ وَسُلِّمَتْ ذَلِكَ بِهِمْ أَبَدَ الأَبَدِ فَمَنْ أَذَاهُمْ فِيهِمْ فَآذَاهُ اللهُ عَزَّ وَجَلَّ شَهِدَ أَبُو بَكْرٍ ابْنُ أَبِي قُحَافَةَ وَعُمَرُ بْنُ الخَطَّابِ وَعُثْمَانُ بْنُ عَفَّانَ وَعَلِيُّ بْنُ أَبِي طَالِبٍ وَمُعَاوِيَةُ رَضِيَ اللهُ عَنْهُمْ وَكَتَبَ

ابن أبي عاصم في الآحاد والمثاني كر وروى نحوه ابن سعد وكذلك طب مختصرا

[Tamīm narrated from the Prophet ﷺ the foundational ḥadīth: "Religion is absolute good faith" *(al-dīn al-nasīḥa)*.[324] He and al-Miqdād b. al-Aswad also narrated that the Prophet ﷺ said: "This great cause will reach wherever the night and the day reach. Allah will not leave a single mud-house nor one camel-hair tent except He will cause this Religion to enter it, raising and honoring some while humbling and lowering others. He will raise and honor Islam while humbling and lowering disbelief." Tamīm would say: "I have seen this among my own relatives. Whoever among them entered Islam got wealth, nobility, and honor; and whoever remained in his disbelief got humiliation, lowliness, and the non-Muslim poll-tax *(al-jizya)*."[325] The Prophet ﷺ

[324]Narrated from Abū Hurayra by Tirmidhī *(ḥasan ṣaḥīḥ)* and Aḥmad, and from Tamīm al-Dārī by Abū Dāwūd. Also narrated – without repetition – from Tamīm by Muslim and Nasā'ī, from Abū Hurayra by Nasā'ī and Aḥmad, from Ibn ʿUmar by al-Bazzār, and from Thawbān by al-Bukhārī in *al-Tārīkh al-Kabīr*. This ḥadīth is §7 of al-Nawawī's "Forty".

[325]Narrated from Tamīm al-Dārī by Aḥmad with a chain of *Ṣaḥīḥ* narrators cf. al-Haythamī (6:14, 8:262); al-Bukhārī in *al-Tārīkh al-Kabīr* (2:150 §2016); al-Ṭaḥāwī, *Sharḥ Mushkil al-Āthār*; al-Ṭabarānī, *al-Kabīr* (2:58 §1280) and *Musnad al-Shāmiyyīn* (2:79 §951); Ibn Mandah, *al-Īmān* (2:982 §1085); al-Hakim (4:330=1990 ed. 4:477 "*ṣaḥīḥ* per the criterion of al-Bukhārī and Muslim"); and al-Bayhaqī, *al-Sunan al-Kubrā* (9:181) cf. *Iṣāba* (5:265). Also narrated from al-Miqdād b. al-Aswad by Aḥmad with a strong chain.

said of him, "There is no one like him left on the face of the earth."[326] During the Caliphate of ʿUmar, a fire appeared in al-Ḥarra [near Madīna]. ʿUmar summoned Tamīm al-Dārī, saying to him, "You control it!" Tamīm replied, "And who am I and what am I, O Commander of the Believers?" But ʿUmar did not stop insisting until they both went near the area of the fire. There, Tamīm began to goad *(yaḥūsh)* the fire with his hands until the fire went into [a hole in] a mountain gorge. ʿUmar said, "the one who sees is not like the one who does not see!" He said this three times.[327] Ibrāhīm b. Rustum al-Marwazī said: "Four are the Imams that recited the entire Qur'ān in a single *rakʿa*: ʿUthmān b. 'Affān, Tamīm al-Dārī, Saʿīd b. Jubayr, and Abū Ḥanīfa."[328] He was also known to recite a single verse all night long. Masrūq narrated that he saw Tamīm recite at night and until morning the single verse ﴾**Or do those who commit ill deeds suppose that We shall make them as those who believe and do good works, the same life and death? Bad is their judgment!**﴿ (45:21). Abū Nuʿaym said that Tamīm was the first to install lighting in mosques.[329] ʿUmar gathered the people in Ramaḍān to pray behind Ubay b. Ka'b [the men] and behind Tamīm al-Dārī [the women] for twenty-one *rakʿas*, reciting some 200 verses [per *rakʿa*] then leaving before the rising of the dawn.[330] ʿUmar also gave him exclusive permission to stand and address public gatherings. Al-Sā'ib b. Yazīd said this was unprecedented in the time of the Prophet ﷺ and Abū Bakr, and calls Tamīm the first story-teller *(qāss)* in Islam.[331] 'Uthman also employed Tamīm as imam for *tarāwīḥ*.[332] He moved to al-Qudus after the murder of ʿUthmān ؓ and died in al-Khalīl in the year 40. Eighteen Prophetic ḥadīths are narrated from him.]

ʿAbd Allāh b. Busr ؓ

Al-Ḥākim, al-Bayhaqī, and Abū Nuʿaym narrated from ʿAbd Allāh b. Busr ؓ that the Prophet ﷺ placed his hand on his head and said: 240 "This boy shall live for a century *(qarnan)*." He lived for one hundred years. There was a wart in his face and he

[326]Narrated by al-Bukhārī in *al-Tārīkh al-Kabīr* (2:150 §2016).

[327]Narrated from Muʿāwiya b. Ḥarmal by al-Bayhaqī and Abū Nuʿaym cf. Ibn Kathīr, *al-Bidāya* (6:153) and al-Dhahabī, *Siyar* (Risāla ed. 2:447) and *Tārīkh al-Islām* (*Khulafā'* p. 615). The latter commented that "This Muʿāwiya is not known" but Ibn Ḥajar in the *Iṣāba* (3:497) identifies him as Musaylima al-Kadhdhāb's brother-in-law. He saw the Prophet ﷺ, fought on the side of Musaylima, and entered Islam in the time of ʿUmar.

[328]Cited by al-Khaṭīb (13:356), al-Dhahabī in *Manāqib Abī Ḥanīfa* (p. 22), and al-Suyūṭī in *Tabyīd al-Saḥīfa* (p. 94-95).

[329]Narrated by al-Sam'ānī in *al-Ansāb* cf. al-Nawawī, *al-Tibyān* (p. 84), al-Haytamī, *Fath al-Mubīn* (p. 108), al-Khazrajī in his *Khulāsa* (p. 55), and al-Lacknawī in *Iqāmat al-Ḥujja* (p. 62-63).

[330]Narrated by ʿAbd al-Razzāq (4:260 §7730) with a good chain. The *matn* is confirmed independently.

[331]Narrated by Aḥmad.

[332]Narrated by Ibn Saʿd (5:26) and Ibn Ḥazm, *al-Muḥallā* (3:139).

said: [a] "He will not die until the wart disappears." It disappeared before he died.[333]

عَنْ عَبْدِ اللهِ بْنِ بُسْرٍ أَنَّ النَّبِيَّ ﷺ وَضَعَ يَدَهُ عَلَى رَأْسِهِ وَقَالَ يَعِيشُ هَذَا الْغُلامُ قَرْنًا قَالَ فَعَاشَ مِائَةَ سَنَةٍ وَكَانَ فِي وَجْهِهِ ثُؤْلُولٌ فَقَالَ لاَ يَمُوتُ هَذَا حَتَّى يَذْهَبَ هَذَا الثُّؤْلُولُ مِنْ وَجْهِهِ فَلَمْ يَمُتْ حَتَّى ذَهَبَ الثُّؤْلُولُ مِنْ وَجْهِهِ طب في مسند الشاميين ك هق في الدلائل الحارث في مسنده أبو نعيم في معرفة الصحابة كر وجاء بلفظ عَنْ أَبِي عَبْدِ اللهِ الحَسَنِ بْنِ أَيُّوبَ الحَضْرَمِيّ قَالَ أَرَانِي عَبْدُ اللهِ بْنُ بُسْرٍ شَامَةً فِي قَرْنِهِ فَوَضَعْتُ أُصْبُعِي عَلَيْهَا فَقَالَ وَضَعَ رَسُولُ اللهِ ﷺ أُصْبُعَهُ عَلَيْهَا ثُمَّ قَالَ لَيَبْلُغَنَّ قَرْناً قَالَ أَبُو عَبْدِ اللهِ وَكَانَ ذَا جُمَّةٍ حم ابن أبي عاصم في الآحاد والمثاني الدولابي في الكنى والأسماء جميعهم برجال ثقات مج إتحاف الخيرة

ʿUrwa b. Masʿud al-Thaqafī ﷺ

Al-Ḥākim, al-Bayhaqī, and Abū Nuʿaym narrated through ʿUrwa b. al-Zubayr who said that ʿUrwa b. Masʿūd al-Thaqafī came to see the Messenger of Allah ﷺ then asked permission to return to his people. The Messenger of Allah ﷺ said to him: [241] "They are going to kill you." He replied, "They would not even wake me up

[333]Narrated from ʿAbd Allāh b. Busr by al-Ṭabarānī in *Musnad al-Shāmiyyīn* (2:17 §836), Abū Nuʿaym in *Maʿrifat al-Ṣaḥāba*, al-Ḥārith in his *Musnad* (*Bughyat al-Bāḥith* 2:937 §1032), al-Ḥākim (4:500=1990 ed. 4:545), Bayhaqī in the *Dalāʾil* and al-Maqdisī in *al-Mukhtāra* (9:90), as well as al-Bazzār, all through trustworthy narrators according to al-Būṣīrī, *Itḥāf* and al-Haythamī (9:404) and al-Bukhārī in *al-Tārīkh al-Kabīr* (1:323). This narration is proof that *qarn* in the Sunna refers to a hundred-year span.

if they saw me sleeping." He went back to them and called them to Islam. They rejected him and abused him. One morning, as the dawn was rising, he stood outside a high room of his and raised the call to prayer, reciting the testimony of faith. A man of Thaqīf shot an arrow at him and killed him. <As he lay dying he was asked: "What do you think about your death now?" He replied: "It is a gift granted me out of the generosity of Allah."> When news of this reached the Messenger of Allah ﷺ he said: a "The example ʿUrwa set is that of the man in Sūrat Yā Sīn. He called his people to Allah, so they killed him." [A reference to the verses ﴾**And there came from the uttermost part of the city a man running. He cried: O my people! Follow those who have been sent!**﴿ to His statement ﴾**It was said (unto him): Enter Paradise. He said: Would that my people knew With what (munificence) my Lord has pardoned me and made me of the honored ones**﴿ (36:20-27).] Later, the delegation of Thaqīf came, – between ten and twenty men – among them Kināna b. ʿAbd Yālīl and ʿUthmān b. Abī al-ʿĀṣ, and they entered Islam.[334]

عَنْ عُرْوَةَ بْنِ الزُّبَيْرِ قَالَ قَدِمَ عُرْوَةُ بْنُ مَسْعُودٍ الثَّقَفِيُّ عَلَى
رَسُولِ اللهِ ﷺ فَأَسْلَمَ ثُمَّ اسْتَأْذَنَ لِيَرْجِعَ إِلَى قَوْمِهِ فَقَالَ لَهُ
رَسُولُ اللهِ ﷺ إِنَّهُمْ قَاتِلُوكَ قَالَ لَوْ وَجَدُونِي نَائِماً مَا أَيْقَظُونِي
فَرَجَعَ إِلَيْهِمْ فَدَعَاهُمْ إِلَى الإِسْلاَمِ فَعَصَوْهُ وَأَسْمَعُوهُ مِنَ الأَذَى
فَلَمَّا أَسْحَرَ وَطَلَعَ الْفَجْرُ قَامَ عَلَى غُرْفَةٍ لَهُ فَأَذَّنَ بِالصَّلاَةِ

[334]Narrated by Mūsā b. ʿUqba in his *Maghāzī* (p. 308), Ibn Shabba in *Tārīkh al-Madīna* (2:470), al-Ṭabarānī in *al-Kabīr* (17:147), al-Ḥākim (3:616=1990 ed. 3:713), and in the *Dalāʾil* of al-Bayhaqī (5:299) and Abū Nuʿaym (p. 533-534), some with a fair *mursal* chain from ʿUrwa cf. al-Haythamī (9:386), corroborated by another chain as in the next narration cf. *Iṣāba* (4:492-493), and *Istīʿāb* (8:1066-1067). The bracketed segment was omitted by al-Nabhānī. The Prophet ﷺ also said that ʿUrwa was the closest Companion in physical resemblance to ʿĪsā b. Maryam عليه السلام as narrated from Abū Hurayra by Muslim. Ibn Ḥajar also mentions that it is from this ʿUrwa that Abū Nuʿaym narrated – with a weak chain – that the Prophet ﷺ took the women's pledge of allegiance at Ḥudaybiya by touching the water of a pail in which they dipped their hands.

وَتَشَهَّدَ فَرَمَاهُ رَجُلٌ مِنْ ثَقِيفٍ بِسَهْمٍ فَقَتَلَهُ فَقَالَ رَسُولُ اللهِ ﷺ حِينَ بَلَغَهُ قَتْلُهُ مَثَلُ عُرْوَةَ مَثَلُ صَاحِبِ يس دَعَا قَوْمَهُ إِلَى اللهِ عَزّ وَجَلّ فَقَتَلُوه ثُمَّ أَقْبَلَ بَعْدَ قَتْلِهِ مِنْ وَفْدِ ثَقِيفٍ بِضْعَةَ عَشَرَ رَجُلاً فِيهِمْ كِنَانَةُ بْنُ عَبْدِ يَالِيلَ وَعُثْمَانُ بْنُ أَبِي الْعَاصِ فَأَسْلَمُوا المغازي لموسى بن عقبة ابن شبة في تاريخ المدينة طب ك هق في الدلائل أبونعيم فيها أيضا

Ibn Sa'd narrated something similar through al-Wāqidī from 'Abd Allāh b. Yaḥyā, from more than one authority. The latter version mentions that when he was shot, he said, "I bear witness that Muḥammad is the Messenger of Allah! He told me that this would happen and that you would kill me."[335]

عَنْ الواقدي في المغازي وابن سعد نحوه وفيه فَرَمَاهُ رَجُلٌ مِنْ رَهْطِهِ مِنْ الأَحْلافِ يُقَالُ لَهُ وَهْبُ بْنُ جَابِرٍ وَيُقَالُ رَمَاهُ أَوْسُ بْنُ عَوْفٍ مِنْ بَنِي مَالِكٍ وَهَذَا أَثْبَتُ عِنْدَنَا وَكَانَ عُرْوَةُ رَجُلاً مِنْ الأَحْلافِ فَأَصَابَ أَكْحَلَهُ فَلَمْ يَرْقَأْ دَمُهُ وَحُشِدَ قَوْمُهُ فِي السّلاحِ وَجُمِعَ الآخَرُونَ وَتَجَايَشُوا فَلَمّا رَأَى عُرْوَةُ مَا يَصْنَعُونَ قَالَ لا تَقْتَتِلُوا فِيّ فَإِنّي قَدْ تَصَدّقْت بِدَمِي عَلَى صَاحِبِهِ لِيُصْلِحَ بِذَلِكَ بَيْنَكُمْ فَهِيَ كَرَامَةُ اللهِ أَكْرَمَنِي اللهُ بِهَا الشّهَادَةُ سَاقَهَا اللهُ إِلَيّ أَشْهَدُ أَنّ مُحَمّدًا رَسُولُ اللهِ أَخَبَرَنِي عَنْكُمْ هَذَا أَنّكُمْ

[335]Narrated through al-Wāqidī (3:960) by Ibn Sa'd (5:503).

تَقْتُلُونَنِي ثُمَّ قَالَ لِرَهْطِهِ ادْفِنُونِي مَعَ الشُّهَدَاءِ الَّذِينَ قُتِلُوا مَعَ
رَسُولِ اللهِ ﷺ قَبْلَ أَنْ يَرْتَحِلَ عَنْكُمْ قَالَ فَدَفَنُوهُ مَعَهُمْ وَبَلَغَ
رَسُولَ اللهِ ﷺ قَتْلُهُ فَقَالَ مَثَلُ عُرْوَةَ مَثَلُ صَاحِبِ يس دَعَا
قَوْمَهُ إِلَى اللهِ عَزّ وَجَلّ فَقَتَلُوه

Abū Nuʿaym narrated through al-Wāqidī who said that when the Prophet ﷺ returned from al-Ṭā'if, ʿUrwa b. Masʿūd said to Ghaylān b. Maslama, "Do you not see how much Allah has helped the cause of that man, and people have all followed him [until none is left] except those who aspire and those are afraid? We are the shrewdest of the Arabs and our likes are not **[502]** unaware of what Muḥammad is calling to nor of the fact that he is a Prophet! I shall tell you of something I have not told anyone before. I went to Najrān for some trading before Muḥammad appeared in Mecca. The bishop there was a friend of mine. He said to me, 'Abū Yaʿfūr, 242 over you looms the shadow of a Prophet that shall come out in your sanctuary and who is the last Prophet. He will slaughter his people like 'Ād was slaughtered. When he appears and calls [people] unto Allah, follow him!' I never mentioned one word of this to anyone in Thaqīf nor to anyone else until now. In truth, I will follow him!" Then ʿUrwa came to the Prophet ﷺ and entered Islam.[336]

وزاد أبو نعيم في سياقه القصة بسنده عن الواقدي أَلْقَى اللهُ عَزَّ وَجَلَّ فِي قَلْبِ
عُرْوَةَ الإِسْلاَمَ فَلَقِيَ غَيلاَنَ بْنَ سَلَمَةَ فَقَالَ أَلاَ تَرَى إِلَى مَا قَدْ
قَرَّبَ اللهُ مِنْ أَمْرِ هَذَا الرَّجُلِ وَإِنَّ النَّاسَ قَدْ دَخَلُوا مَكَّةَ كُلُّهُمْ
فَرَاغِبٌ فِيهِ وَخَائِفٌ أَنْ يُوقَعَ بِهِ وَنُحْنُ عِنْدَ النَّاسِ أَدْهَى الْعَرَبِ

[336]Narrated *mursal* from al-Wāqidī by Abū Nuʿaym in the *Dalā'il* (p. 531-534 §461) cf. *Khasā'is* (2:23). Ghaylān is identified as "b. Salama" in al-Wāqidī.

وَمِثْلُنَا لاَ يَجْهَلُ مَا يَدْعُو إِلَيْهِ مُحَمَّدٌ ﷺ وَأَنَّهُ نَبِيٌّ قَالَ غَيْلاَنُ لاَ تَقُلْ هَذَا يَا أَبَا يَعْقُوبَ وَلاَ يُسْمَعْ مِنْكَ إِنِّي لاَ آمَنُ عَلَيْكَ ثَقِيفاً وَإِنْ كَانَ لَكَ فِيهِمْ مِنَ الشَّرَفِ مَا لَكَ فِيهَا قَالَ عُرْوَةُ فَأَنَا مُتَّبِعُهُ وَسَائِرٌ إِلَيْهِ قَالَ غَيْلاَنُ لاَ تَعْجَلْ حَتَّى تَنْظُرَ وَتَدَبَّرَ قَالَ عُرْوَةُ أَيُّ أَمْرٍ هُوَ أَبْيَنُ مِنْ أَمْرِ مُحَمَّدٍ ﷺ إِنِّي ذَاكِرٌ لَكَ أَمْراً لَمْ أَذْكُرْهُ لأَحَدٍ قَطُّ وَأَنَا ذَاكِرُهُ لَكَ السَّاعَةَ قَالَ غَيْلاَنُ وَمَا هُوَ قَالَ عُرْوَةُ قَدِمْتُ نَجْرَانَ فِي تِجَارَةٍ وَذَلِكَ قَبْلَ أَنْ يَظْهَرَ مُحَمَّدٌ بِمَكَّةَ وَكَانَ أُسْقُفُهَا لِي صَدِيقاً فَقَالَ يَا أَبَا يَعْقُوبَ أَظَلَّكُمْ نَبِيٌّ يَخْرُجُ فِي حَرَمِكُمْ قُلْتُ مَا تَقُولُ قَالَ إِي وَالمَسِيحِ وَهُوَ آخِرُ الأَنْبِيَاءِ وَلَيَقْتُلَنَّ قَوْمَهُ قَتْلَ عَادٍ فَإِذَا ظَهَرَ وَدَعَا إِلَى اللهِ فَاتَّبِعْهُ وَكُنْ أَوَّلَ مَنْ يَسْبُقُ إِلَيْهِ لَمْ أَذْكُرْ مِنْ ذَلِكَ حَرْفاً وَاحِداً لأَحَدٍ مِنْ ثَقِيفٍ وَلاَ غَيْرِهِمْ لِمَا كُنْتُ أَرَى مِنْ شِدَّتِهِمْ عَلَيهِ وَكُنْتُ أَنَا مِنْ أَشَدِّهِمْ عَلَيهِ بَعْدَ مَا سَمِعْتُ مِنَ الأُسْقُفِ مَا سَمِعْتُ ثُمَّ غَيَّرَ اللهُ قَلْبِي مِنْ سَاعَتِي هَذِهِ وَأَنَا مُتَّبِعُهُ فَخَرَجَ عُرْوَةُ وَأَسْلَمَ

Jarīr b. ʿAbd Allāh al-Bajalī ؓ

Al-Bayhaqī narrated that Jarīr al-Bajalī ؓ said, "I came to see the Prophet ﷺ. I wore my tunic and entered as he was delivering a speech. The people stared at me, gaping. I asked the man next to whom I sat, 'Did the Messenger of Allah ﷺ say anything about me?' He said, 'Yes, he mentioned you in the best possible way. As he was speaking, something came over him and he said: 243 About to come into your presence through this door or opening is a man from among the best of those who were granted good fortune, on his face the streak of an angel.'"[337]

قَالَ جَرِيرٌ رَضِيَ اللهُ عَنْهُ لَمَّا دَنَوْتُ مِنَ الْمَدِينَةِ أَنَخْتُ رَاحِلَتِي ثُمَّ حَلَلْتُ عَيْبَتِي ثُمَّ لَبِسْتُ حُلَّتِي ثُمَّ دَخَلْتُ الْمَسْجِدَ فَإِذَا النَّبِيُّ ﷺ يَخْطُبُ فَرَمَانِي النَّاسُ بِالْحَدَقِ قَالَ فَقُلْتُ لِجَلِيسِي يَا عَبْدَ اللهِ هَلْ ذَكَرَ رَسُولُ اللهِ ﷺ مِنْ أَمْرِي شَيْئًا قَالَ نَعَمْ ذَكَرَكَ بِأَحْسَنِ الذِّكْرِ بَيْنَمَا هُوَ يَخْطُبُ إِذْ عَرَضَ لَهُ فِي خُطْبَتِهِ فَقَالَ إِنَّهُ سَيَدْخُلُ عَلَيْكُمْ مِنْ هَذَا الْفَجِّ مِنْ خَيْرِ ذِي يَمَنٍ أَلاَ وَإِنَّ عَلَى وَجْهِهِ مَسْحَةُ مَلَكٍ قَالَ جَرِيرٌ فَحَمِدْتُ اللهَ عَزَّ وَجَلَّ حم

ن في الكبرى وفضائل الصحابة ش خز حب طب طس ك هق في السنن والدلائل الحميدي خد ابن سعد ابن أبي عاصم في الآحاد

[244 After Jarīr entered Islam whenever the Prophet ﷺ saw him he ﷺ laughed or smiled and ʿUmar used to call Jarīr "the Yūsuf of this *Umma.*"[338]]

[337]Narrated from Jarīr by Aḥmad (31:516-518 §19180) with three chains, al-Nasā'ī in *al-Sunan al-Kubrā* (5:82 §8304) and *Faḍā'il al-Saḥāba* (p. 60 §199), Ibn Abī Shayba (6:397 §32341, 7:342 §36607), Ibn Khuzayma (3:150), Ibn Ḥibbān (16:174 §7199), al-Ṭabarānī in *al-Kabīr* (2:352 §2483), al-Ḥākim (1:285=1990 ed. 1:422), and al-Bayhaqī in his *Sunan* (3:222) and *Dalā'il* (5:346-347), all with a fair chain because of Yūnus b. Abī Isḥāq but the ḥadīth is also narrated from Jarīr with a sound chain by al-Ḥumaydī in his *Musnad* (2:350 §800), al-Bukhārī in *al-Adab al-Mufrad* (p. 97 §250), Ibn Abī ʿĀṣim in *al-Āḥād* (§2523), al-Nasā'ī in *al-Kubrā* (5:82 §8302) and *Faḍā'il al-Saḥāba* (p. 59 §197), and al-Ṭabarānī in *al-Kabīr* (2:301 §2258), also with a third and fourth chain by al-Ṭabarānī in *al-Awsat* (6:74-75 §5834, 6:179 §6124) and *al-Kabīr* (2:356 §2498) from Jarīr and al-Barā', also with a fifth, very weak chain from ʿAbd al-Hamīd b. ʿAbd Allāh b. al-Ḥakam through al-Wāqidī by Ibn Saʿd (1:347).

[338]Cf. *Istīʿāb* (1:237), *Siyar* (Risāla ed. 2:531), and *Sifat al-Safwa* (1:740).

Zayd al-Khayr ﵁

Al-Bayhaqī narrated that Ibn Isḥāq said that the delegation of Ṭayyi' came, among them Zayd al-Khayl ("Zayd of the horses"). They entered Islam and the Messenger of Allah ﷺ renamed him Zayd al-Khayr ("Zayd of goodness"). Then he rode out, returning to his people, whereupon the Messenger of Allah ﷺ said: 245 "Zayd will not survive the fever of the town." When he reached a certain oasis at the border of Najd, fever seized him and he died.[339]

قَالَ ابْنُ إِسْحَاقَ : وَقَدِمَ عَلَى رَسُولِ اللهِ ﷺ وَفْدُ طَيِّئٍ فِيهِمْ زَيْدُ الْخَيْلِ وَهُوَ سَيِّدُهُمْ فَلَمَّا انْتَهَوْا إِلَيْهِ كَلَّمُوهُ وَعَرَضَ عَلَيْهِمْ رَسُولُ اللهِ ﷺ الإِسْلاَمَ فَأَسْلَمُوا فَحَسُنَ إِسْلاَمُهُمْ وَقَالَ رَسُولُ اللهِ ﷺ كَمَا حَدَّثَنِي مَنْ لاَ أَتَّهِمُ مِنْ رِجَالِ طَيِّئٍ مَا ذُكِرَ لِي رَجُلٌ مِنْ الْعَرَبِ بِفَضْلٍ ثُمَّ جَاءَنِي إِلَّا رَأَيْته دُونَ مَا يُقَالُ فِيهِ إِلَّا زَيْدَ الْخَيْلِ فَإِنَّهُ لَمْ يَبْلُغْ كُلَّ مَا كَانَ فِيهِ ثُمَّ سَمَّاهُ رَسُولُ اللهِ ﷺ زَيْدَ الْخَيْرِ وَقَطَعَ لَهُ فَيْدًا وَأَرَضِينَ مَعَهُ وَكَتَبَ لَهُ بِذَلِكَ فَخَرَجَ مِنْ عِنْدِ رَسُولِ اللهِ ﷺ رَاجِعًا إِلَى قَوْمِهِ فَقَالَ رَسُولُ اللهِ ﷺ إِنْ يَنْجُ زَيْدٌ مِنْ حُمَّى الْمَدِينَةِ فَإِنَّهُ غَالِبٌ قَالَ قَدْ سَمَّاهَا رَسُولُ اللهِ ﷺ بِاسْمٍ غَيْرِ الْحُمَّى وَغَيْرِ أُمِّ مَلْدَمٍ فَلَمْ يُثْبِتْهُ فَلَمَّا انْتَهَى مِنْ بَلَدِ نَجْدٍ إِلَى مَاءٍ مِنْ مِيَاهِهِ يُقَالُ لَهُ فَرَدَةُ أَصَابَتْهُ

[339]Narrated by al-Ṭabarī in his *Tārīkh* (2:203), Ibn Hishām (5:274), and al-Bayhaqī in the *Dalā'il* cf. *Sīra Ḥalabiyya* (3:257), *Iktifā'* (2:352), *Iṣāba* (2:623), *Rawḍ* (4:358-360), *Bidāya* (5:63), and *Zād* (Risāla ed. 3:539=3:616) while al-Suyūṭī, *Khaṣā'iṣ* (2:34) cites the wording "Zayd will not survive *(lan yanjua)*...".

الْحُمَّى بِهَا فَمَاتَ رَضِيَ اللهُ عَنْهُ ابن هشام تاريخ الطبري هق في الدلائل
حلبية اكتفاء إصابة روض بداية زاد خصائص

Wā'il b. Ḥujr ﵁

Al-Bukhārī in his *Tārīkh* and al-Bayhaqī narrated that Wā'il b. Ḥujr said, "We heard news of the appearance of the Messenger of Allah ﷺ so I travelled to meet him. His Companions later told me [246] he had announced my coming to them three days before my arrival."[340]

عَنْ وَائِلِ بْنِ حُجْرٍ رَضِيَ اللهُ عَنْهُ قَالَ بَلَغَنِي ظُهُورُ النَّبِيِّ ﷺ فَتَرَكْتُ مُلْكاً عَظِيماً وَطَاعَةً عَظِيمَةً فَهَبَطْتُ إِلَى النَّبِيِّ ﷺ فَأَخْبَرَنِي أَصْحَابُهُ فَقَالُوا بَشَّرَنَا النَّبِيُّ ﷺ بِمَقْدَمِكَ قَبْلَ أَنْ تَقْدَمَ بِثَلَاثَةِ أَيَّامٍ تخ طب عق حب في الثقات مجمع

Ṣurad b. ʿAbd Allāh al-Azdī ﵁

Al-Bayhaqī and Abū Nuʿaym narrated from Ibn Isḥāq that Ṣurad b. ʿAbd Allāh al-Azdī came and entered Islam in a delegation sent by the Azd. The Messenger of Allah ﷺ then put him in command of the Muslims among his people and ordered him to struggle against the polytheists that were in their immediate vicinity. He rode out until he alighted at al-Jurash and lay siege to it for nearly a month. Then he raised the siege and went away. When he reached the mountain which they call Kushar, the people of Jurash, believing that he had raised the siege in defeat, rode out in his pursuit. When they reached him, he turned upon them and

[340]Narrated from Wā'il b. Ḥujr by al-Bukhārī in *al-Tārīkh al-Kabīr* (8:175), al-Ṭabarānī in *al-Kabīr* (2:284, 22:46), al-ʿUqaylī in *al-Duʿafā'* (4:59) and Ibn Ḥibbān in *al-Thiqāt* (3:425) cf. al-Haythamī (9:374).

fought them fiercely. The people of Jurash had sent two of their countrymen to the Messenger of Allah ﷺ in al-Madīna to explore and observe. As they were with the Messenger of Allah ﷺ one evening after the meal, he ﷺ said: [247] "Where among the lands of Allah is Shukar?" The two Jurashīs said, "In our lands there is a mountain called Kushar." He said: "It is not Kushar but Shukar." They said, "What about it?" He replied: [a] "The sacrifices to Allah are being slaughtered there as we speak." Later, the two men sat with Abū Bakr and ʿUthmān who said to them, "Woe to the two of you! The Messenger of Allah ﷺ is announcing to you the funeral of your people. Go and ask him to supplicate Allah so that He ward off disaster from your people." They got up and asked him. He said: [b] "O Allah, ward it off from them." Later, they left the Messenger of Allah ﷺ and rode out to return to their people. They found that they had been routed by Ṣurad b. ʿAbd Allāh the very day the Messenger of Allah ﷺ had first said what he had said, at the moment he had said it. Then they went back and accepted Islam.[341]

قَالَ ابْنُ إِسْحَاقَ وَقَدِمَ عَلَى رَسُولِ اللَّهِ ﷺ صُرَدُ بْنُ عَبْدِ اللَّهِ الْأَزْدِيُّ فَأَسْلَمَ وَحَسُنَ إِسْلَامُهُ فِي وَفْدٍ مِنَ الْأَزْدِ فَأَمَرَهُ رَسُولُ اللَّهِ ﷺ عَلَى مَنْ أَسْلَمَ مِنْ قَوْمِهِ وَأَمَرَهُ أَنْ يُجَاهِدَ بِمَنْ أَسْلَمَ مَنْ كَانَ يَلِيهِ مِنْ أَهْلِ الشِّرْكِ مِنْ قِبَلِ الْيَمَنِ فَخَرَجَ صُرَدُ بْنُ عَبْدِ اللَّهِ يَسِيرُ بِأَمْرِ رَسُولِ اللَّهِ ﷺ حَتَّى نَزَلَ بِجُرَشَ وَهِيَ يَوْمَئِذٍ مَدِينَةٌ مُعَلَّقَةٌ وَبِهَا قَبَائِلُ مِنْ قَبَائِلِ الْيَمَنِ وَقَدْ ضَوَتْ إِلَيْهِمْ خَثْعَمُ فَدَخَلُوهَا مَعَهُمْ حِينَ سَمِعُوا بِسَيْرِ الْمُسْلِمِينَ إِلَيْهِمْ فَحَاصَرُوهُمْ فِيهَا قَرِيبًا مِنْ شَهْرٍ وَامْتَنَعُوا فِيهَا مِنْهُ ثُمَّ إِنَّهُ رَجَعَ

---

[341] Narrated from Ibn Isḥāq from ʿAbd Allāh b. Abī Bakr b. Ḥazm by Ṭabarī in his *Tārīkh* (2:196) and Ibn Hishām in his *Sīra* (5:285). Al-Jurash is a city in Hadramawt, Yemen.

عَنْهُمْ قَافِلًا حَتّى إِذَا كَانَ إِلَى جَبَلٍ لَهُمْ يُقَالُ لَهُ شَكْرٌ ظَنّ أَهْلُ جُرَشَ أَنّهُ إِنّمَا وَلّى عَنْهُمْ مُنْهَزِمًا فَخَرَجُوا فِي طَلَبِهِ حَتّى إِذَا أَدْرَكُوهُ عَطَفَ عَلَيْهِمْ فَقَتَلَهُمْ قَتْلًا شَدِيدًا وَقَدْ كَانَ أَهْلُ جُرَشَ بَعَثُوا رَجُلَيْنِ مِنْهُمْ إِلَى رَسُولِ اللهِ ﷺ بِالْمَدِينَةِ يَرْتَادَانِ وَيَنْظُرَانِ فَبَيْنَمَا هُمَا عِنْدَ رَسُولِ اللهِ ﷺ عَشِيّةً بَعْدَ صَلاةِ الْعَصْرِ إِذْ قَالَ رَسُولُ اللهِ ﷺ بِأَيِّ بِلادِ اللهِ شَكْرٌ فَقَامَ إِلَيْهِ الْجُرُشِيّانِ فَقَالاَ يَا رَسُولَ اللهِ بِبِلاَدِنَا جَبَلٌ يُقَال لَهُ شَكْرٌ وَكَذَلِكَ يُسَمّيهِ أَهْلُ جُرَشَ فَقَالَ إِنّهُ لَيْسَ بِكَشْرٍ وَلَكِنّهُ شَكْرٌ قَالاَ فَمَا شَأْنُهُ يَا رَسُولَ اللهِ قَالَ إِنّ بُدْنَ اللهِ لَتُنْحَرُ عِنْدَهُ الْآنَ قَالَ فَجَلَسَ الرّجُلاَنِ إِلَى أَبِي بَكْرٍ أَوْ إِلَى عُثْمَانَ فَقَالَ لَهُمَا وَيْحَكُمَا إِنّ رَسُولَ اللهِ ﷺ لَيَنْعَى لَكُمَا قَوْمَكُمَا فَقُومَا إِلَى رَسُولِ اللهِ ﷺ فَاسْأَلاَهُ أَنْ يَدْعُوَ اللهَ أَنْ يَرْفَعَ عَنْ قَوْمِكُمَا فَقَامَا إِلَيْهِ فَسَأَلاَهُ ذَلِكَ فَقَالَ اللهُمّ ارْفَعْ عَنْهُمْ فَخَرَجَا مِنْ عِنْدِ رَسُولِ اللهِ ﷺ رَاجِعِينَ إِلَى قَوْمِهِمَا فَوَجَدَا قَوْمَهُمَا قَدْ أُصِيبُوا يَوْمَ أَصَابَهُمْ صُرَدُ بْنُ عَبْدِ اللهِ فِي الْيَوْمِ الّذِي قَالَ فِيهِ رَسُولُ اللهِ ﷺ مَا قَالَ وَفِي السّاعَةِ الّتِي ذَكَرَ فِيهَا مَا ذَكَرَ ابن هشام تاريخ الطبري

Al-Ḥārith the father of *Umm al-Mu'minīn* Juwayriya رضي الله عنها

Ibn ʿAsākir narrated through Ibn 'Ā'idh **[503]** that Muḥammad b. Shuʿayb narrated to him from ʿAbd Allāh b. Zyād that Allah ﷻ bestowed as booty to the Messenger of Allah ﷺ – the year of al-Muraysī' in the campaign of the Banū Muṣṭaliq – Juwayriya bint al-Ḥārith so her father came to ransom her. When he arrived at al-'Aqīq he looked at his camels, which he had brought as ransom for his daughter, and longed to keep two prize animals among them. He hid them in one of the woodlands of al-'Aqīq then came to the Messenger of Allah ﷺ with the rest of the camels. He said: "Muḥammad, you have captured my daughter and this is her ransom." The Messenger of Allah ﷺ said: 248 "Where are the two camels you hid in al-'Aqīq, in such-and-such a woodland?" Al-Ḥārith said, "I bear witness that you are the Messenger of Allah! I did hide those two camels and no one saw me do it except Allah." Thus he entered Islam.[342]

عَنْ عَبْدِ اللهِ بْنِ زِيَادٍ مُرْسَلاً قَالَ وَأَفَاءَ اللهُ عَلَى رَسُولِهِ ﷺ عَامَ المُرَيْسِيعِ فِي غَزْوَةِ بَنِي المصْطَلِقِ جُوَيْرِيَةَ ابْنَةَ الحَارِثِ بْنِ أَبِي ضِرَارٍ فَقَدِمَ رَسُولُ اللهِ ﷺ المدِينَةَ وَأَقْبَلَ أَبُوهَا الحَارِثُ بْنُ أَبِي ضِرَارٍ وَكَانَ مِنْ أَشْرَافِ قَوْمِهِ يَفْدِي ابْنَتَهُ فَلَمَّا قَدِمَ فَكَانَ بِالعَقِيقِ نَظَرَ إِلَى إِبِلِهِ الَّتِي تَفْدِي بِهَا بِنْتُهُ فَرَغِبَ فِي بَعِيرَيْنِ مِنْهَا كَانَا مِنْ أَفْضَلِهَا فَغَيَّبَهُمَا فِي شِعْبٍ مِنْ أَشْعابِ العَقِيقِ ثُمَّ أَقْبَلَ إِلَى رَسُولِ اللهِ ﷺ بِسَايِرِ الإِبِلِ فَقَالَ يَا مُحَمَّدُ أَصَبْتُمْ

[342] Narrated *mursal* from the *Tābiʿī* ʿAbd Allāh b. Zyād by Ibn ʿAsākir (3:217-218) and without chain by Ibn Hishām (4:259, 6:59-60) cf. *Iṣāba* (1:579), *Khaṣā'iṣ* (1:392), *Sīra Ḥalabiyya* (2:589) etc. Al-'Aqīq is a blessed valley and river near al-Madīna. Al-Bukhārī and *Ma'ālim*.

إِبْنَتِي فَهَذَا فِدَاؤُهَا فَقَالَ رَسُولُ اللهِ ﷺ فَأَيْنَ الْبَعِيرَانِ اللَّذَانِ
غَيَّبْتَ بِالْعَقِيقِ بِشِعْبِ كَذَا وَكَذَا فَقَالَ الْحَارِثُ أَشْهَدُ أَنْ لاَ إِلَهَ
إِلاَّ اللهُ وَأَشْهَدُ أَنَّكَ رَسُولُ اللهِ وَلَقَدْ كَانَ ذَلِكَ مِنِّي فِي الْبَعِيرَيْنِ
وَمَا اطَّلَعَ عَلَى ذَلِكَ إِلاَّ اللهُ تَعَالَى فَأَسْلَمَ ابن هشام كر إستيعاب أسد
الغابة إصابة خصائص حلبية

ʿAdī b. Ḥātim ﷺ

Al-Bukhārī narrated that ʿAdī b. Ḥātim said, "As I was visiting the Prophet ﷺ a man came to him complaining of destitution and another one complaining of highway robbery. He said: 249 ʻʿAdī b. Ḥātim, if you live long, you shall certainly see the lone woman traveller journey from al-Ḥīra [all the way to Mecca] until she circumambulates the Kaʿba, not fearing anyone but Allah.' I said to myself, 'I wonder what will happen to the robbers of Ṭayyi' whose mischief has spread far and wide!' 'And if you live long, [you will see that] a the treasures of Chosroes shall certainly be conquered.' I said to myself, 'Chosroes the son of Hurmuz?' 'And if you live long, b you shall behold a man bring out his two hands' fill of gold or silver, looking for someone to accept it from him, to no avail.'" ʿAdī said: "I have witnessed the lone woman traveller journey from al-Ḥīra until she circumambulated the Kaʿba, not fearing anyone but Allah, and I was among those who conquered the treasures of Chosroes. And if you all live long enough, you shall see the third item."[343]

[343]Narrated by al-Būkhārī and Ahmad. Al-Hīra is in Iraq between al-Najaf and Kūfa cf. *Maʿālim*. Kisrā's full name is Kisrā b. Barwīz b. Hurmuz b. Anūsharwān, Kisrā al-Kabīr cf. *Fath* (8:127).

عَنْ عَدِيِّ بْنِ حَاتِمٍ رَضِيَ اللهُ عَنْهُ قَالَ بَيْنَا أَنَا عِنْدَ النَّبِيِّ ﷺ إِذْ أَتَاهُ رَجُلٌ فَشَكَا إِلَيْهِ الْفَاقَةَ ثُمَّ أَتَاهُ آخَرُ فَشَكَا إِلَيْهِ قَطْعَ السَّبِيلِ فَقَالَ يَا عَدِيُّ هَلْ رَأَيْتَ الْحِيرَةَ قُلْتُ لَمْ أَرَهَا وَقَدْ أُنْبِئْتُ عَنْهَا قَالَ فَإِنْ طَالَتْ بِكَ حَيَاةٌ لَتَرَيَنَّ الظَّعِينَةَ تَرْتَحِلُ مِنْ الْحِيرَةِ حَتَّى تَطُوفَ بِالْكَعْبَةِ لاَ تَخَافُ أَحَدًا إِلاَّ اللهَ قُلْتُ فِيمَا بَيْنِي وَبَيْنَ نَفْسِي فَأَيْنَ دُعَّارُ طَيِّئٍ الَّذِينَ قَدْ سَعَّرُوا الْبِلاَدَ وَلَئِنْ طَالَتْ بِكَ حَيَاةٌ لَتُفْتَحَنَّ كُنُوزُ كِسْرَى قُلْتُ كِسْرَى بْنِ هُرْمُزَ قَالَ كِسْرَى بْنِ هُرْمُزَ وَلَئِنْ طَالَتْ بِكَ حَيَاةٌ لَتَرَيَنَّ الرَّجُلَ يُخْرِجُ مِلْءَ كَفِّهِ مِنْ ذَهَبٍ أَوْ فِضَّةٍ يَطْلُبُ مَنْ يَقْبَلُهُ مِنْهُ فَلاَ يَجِدُ أَحَدًا يَقْبَلُهُ مِنْهُ وَلَيَلْقَيَنَّ اللهَ أَحَدُكُمْ يَوْمَ يَلْقَاهُ وَلَيْسَ بَيْنَهُ وَبَيْنَهُ تَرْجُمَانٌ يُتَرْجِمُ لَهُ فَلَيَقُولَنَّ لَهُ أَلَمْ أَبْعَثْ إِلَيْكَ رَسُولاً فَيُبَلِّغَكَ فَيَقُولُ بَلَى فَيَقُولُ أَلَمْ أُعْطِكَ مَالاً وَأُفْضِلْ عَلَيْكَ فَيَقُولُ بَلَى فَيَنْظُرُ عَنْ يَمِينِهِ فَلاَ يَرَى إِلاَّ جَهَنَّمَ وَيَنْظُرُ عَنْ يَسَارِهِ فَلاَ يَرَى إِلاَّ جَهَنَّمَ قَالَ عَدِيٌّ سَمِعْتُ النَّبِيَّ ﷺ يَقُولُ اتَّقُوا النَّارَ وَلَوْ بِشِقَّةِ تَمْرَةٍ فَمَنْ لَمْ يَجِدْ شِقَّةَ تَمْرَةٍ فَبِكَلِمَةٍ طَيِّبَةٍ قَالَ عَدِيٌّ فَرَأَيْتُ الظَّعِينَةَ تَرْتَحِلُ مِنْ الْحِيرَةِ حَتَّى تَطُوفَ بِالْكَعْبَةِ لاَ تَخَافُ إِلاَّ اللهَ وَكُنْتُ فِيمَنْ افْتَتَحَ كُنُوزَ كِسْرَى بْنِ هُرْمُزَ وَلَئِنْ طَالَتْ بِكُمْ حَيَاةٌ لَتَرَوُنَّ مَا قَالَ النَّبِيُّ أَبُو الْقَاسِمِ ﷺ يُخْرِجُ مِلْءَ كَفِّهِ خ حم

Al-Bayhaqī said, "The third item took place in the rule of ʿUmar b. ʿAbd al-ʿAzīz." Then he narrated from ʿUmar b. Usayd that ʿAbd al-Raḥmān b. Zayd b. al-Khaṭṭāb said, "ʿUmar b. ʿAbd al-ʿAzīz ruled only for two and a half years; by Allah! – he did not die before a man would come with huge wealth, saying, 'Spend this as you see fit for the good of the poor,' but then he would return still carrying his wealth. We would consult each other as to whom he might spend it upon and not find anyone, so he would have to return together with his wealth. c ʿUmar b. ʿAbd al-ʿAzīz made everyone rich."[344]

عَنْ عُمَرَ بْنِ أَسِيدِ بْنِ عَبْدِ الرَّحْمَنِ بْنِ أَسِيدِ بْنِ عَبْدِ الرَّحْمَنِ بْنِ زَيْدِ بْنِ الخَطَّابِ قَالَ إِنَّمَا وَلِيَ عُمَرُ بْنُ عَبْدِ العَزِيزِ سَنَتَيْنِ وَنِصْفاً ثَلاَثِينَ شَهْراً وَاللهِ مَا مَاتَ عُمَرُ بْنُ عَبْدِ العَزِيزِ حَتَّىٰ جَعَلَ الرَّجُلُ يَأْتِينَا بِالمَالِ العَظِيمِ فَيَقُولُ اجْعَلُوا هَذَا حَيْثُ تَرَوْنَ فِي الفُقَرَاءِ فَمَا نَبْرَحُ حَتَّىٰ يَرْجِعَ بِمَالِهِ يَتَذَكَّرُ مَنْ يَضَعُهُ فِيهِمْ فَلاَ يَجِدُهُمْ فَيَرْجِعُ بِمَالِهِ قَدْ أَغْنَىٰ عُمَرُ بْنُ عَبْدِ العَزِيزِ النَّاسَ تاريخ يعقوب بن سفيان تهذيب فتح خصائص

[Additional combined reports give a detailed account of how ʿAdī accepted Islam:

[1] "I came to the Messenger of Allah ﷺ as he was sitting in the Mosque. The people said, 'This is ʿAdī b. Ḥātim.' I had come without advance guarantee nor writ of safety. When I was forwarded to him, 250 he took me by the hand – he had said before: a 'I dearly hope that Allah shall place his (ʿAdī's) hand in my hand!' – then set forth. A woman met him on the way – a boy was accompanying her – saying, 'We need something from you.' He attended to them until he took care of their need. Then he took me by the hand and brought me to his home. A slave-girl placed a cushion for him and he sat on it. I sat in front of him. He glorified Allah and praised Him then said: b 'Why are you terrified of saying *Lā ilāha illa-l-Lāh*? Do you know of a god

[344]Narrated from ʿAbd al-Raḥmān b. Zayd by Yaʿqūb b. Sufyān in his *Tārīkh* and al-Mizzī in *Tahdhīb al-Kamāl* (21:444) with a good chain cf. Ibn Hajar, *Fatḥ* (13:83) and al-Bayhaqī cf. *Khaṣāʾis* (2:35).

other than the One God?' I said no. Then he spoke for a while, after which he said: [c] 'Are you terrified to say *Allāhu akbar* because you know something greater than Allah?' I said no. He said: [d] 'In truth, the Jews ﴿**earned Divine anger**﴾ (1:7) and the Christians are misguided *(ḍullāl).*' I said: 'In truth, I came to be a Muslim.' I saw elation on his face."[345]

[2] "The cavalry – or the envoys – of the Messenger of Allah ﷺ came when I was in 'Aqrab and took my aunt and other people [prisoners]. [She related that] when they brought them to the Messenger of Allah ﷺ and they lined up she said, 'Messenger of Allah, our representative is far away, I was separated from my son(s), and I am a hoary old woman who is helpless, so be kind to me – may Allah be kind to you!' He said: [251] 'Who is your representative?' She said, ʿAdī b. Ḥātim. He said: [a] 'The one who fled from Allah and His Messenger!' She related, 'Then he showed me kindness.' She said that when he came back [later], a man was accompanying him – apparently ʿAlī – who told her, 'Ask him for mounts.' She did, and he ordered that she be given mounts. Then she travelled to me and said: 'You have done a deed that your father never did! Go to him whether you like it or not! So-and-so went to him and he obtained such-and-such from him, while So-and-so went to him and he obtained such-and such from him!' I came to him as he was conferring with a woman accompanied by boys or by one boy, without any formalities. I knew then and there that it was nothing like the throne of Chosroes or Caesar. He said: [b] 'ʿAdī b. Ḥātim! What terrifies you about saying *Lā ilāha illa-l-Lāh*? Is there a god other than the One God? What terrifies you about saying *Allāhu akbar*? Is there something greater than Allah?' Then I became Muslim. I saw elation in his face."[346]

[3] "No man among the Arabs hated the Messenger of Allah ﷺ upon hearing of him more than myself. I was a man of noble ancestry and a Christian. I received from my people a fourth-part annual levy *(mirbāʿ)*. I thought of myself as one who possessed religion and I was a king among my people because of the way they treated me. When I first heard of the Messenger of Allah ﷺ, I hated him. I told a boyservant who belonged to me, a Bedouin who grazed my camels, 'Scamp! Get some of my best, fattest camels ready and wait near me for my signal. As soon as you hear that the army of Muḥammad has entered these parts, let me know.' When he did, ... I took my wife and children and told myself 'I shall join my coreligionists among the Christians in Shām'... – leaving behind two of Ḥātim's daughters – and I took up residence there. Then the cavalry of the Messenger of Allah ﷺ raided us. Ḥātim's daughter was taken prisoner and brought to the Messenger of Allah ﷺ among other prisoners from Ṭayyi'. News of my flight to Shām had reached the Messenger of Allah ﷺ. Ḥātim's daughter was placed in an enclosure by the gate of the Mosque where captives were kept. The Messenger of Allah ﷺ passed by her. She rose to meet him – she was a prudent woman – and said: 'Messenger of Allah! My son died and my representative is absent, so be kind to me – may Allah be kind to you!' He said: 'Who is your representative?' She said, ʿAdī b. Ḥātim. He said: 'The one who fled from Allah and His Messenger!'" She continued: "Then the Messenger of Allah ﷺ left me until the

[345]Narrated from ʿAdī b. Ḥātim by al-Tirmidhī *(ḥasan gharīb)* as part of a longer ḥadīth.

[346]Narrated from ʿAdī b. Ḥātim by Ibn Abī ʿĀṣim in *al-Awāʾil* (p. 104) and Aḥmad as part of a longer ḥadīth with trustworthy narrators per al-Haythamī (6:208) but Àbbād b. Ḥubaysh is unknown. 'Aqrab is one of the districts of Damascus frequented by the Ghassanī kings cf. Yāqūt (4:135).

next day, when he passed by me again. I repeated my words and he repeated his. The day after that, I had despaired of him when a man that stood behind him motioned to me to get up and ask him again. I got up and said: 'Messenger of Allah! My son died and my representative is absent, so be kind to me – may Allah be kind to you!' He said: 'I have done. Do not hasten to leave until you find a trustworthy escort from your people with whom you can reach your country, and let me know.' Then I asked about the man who had motioned to me and was told it was ʿAlī b. Abī Ṭālib ﷺ. I tarried until a mounted group arrived from Bulay or Quḍāʿa. All I wanted was to reach my brother in Shām. I came to the Messenger of Allah ﷺ and said, 'Messenger of Allah, a group came from my country and I trust them.' He gave me clothes, provision and money. I went out with them until I reached Shām." ʿAdī said: "By Allah, I was sitting with my household when I saw a woman's traveling party reaching our parts. I said it must be the daughter of Ḥātim and, lo and behold, it was she! When she faced me she said, without pausing, 'You unnatural felon! You took your wife and children and left the last of your father's family behind, for shame!' I said to her, 'Sister, say only good, for I admit – by Allah! – that I have no excuse. Yes, I did all that you said.' Then she alighted and stayed with me. I asked her – she was a shrewd woman: 'What do you want [me to do] concerning that man?' She said: 'In my opinion, by Allah, you should join up with him as soon as possible. If he is a Prophet, then the early ally gets more credit. And if he is a king, then you will not be put to shame in the glory of Yemen with the name you carry!' I said, 'By Allah! You have spoken right.' I set out until I reached the Messenger of Allah ﷺ in al-Madīna. I went in to see him as he was sitting in his Mosque. I greeted him. He asked: 252 'Who is the man?' I replied, "ʿAdī b. Ḥātim.' He rose and took me to his home. He turned his whole attention to me – by Allah! – but a decrepit, old woman met him on the way and stopped him. He stood there with her a long time as she went on and on explaining her need to him. I said to myself, 'By Allah! This is not a king.' Then the Messenger of Allah ﷺ went on his way with me until we entered his home. He took a cushion of hide stuffed with leaves and handed it to me, saying: a 'Sit on this.' I said, 'No, you sit on it,' but he insisted, so I took it and b he sat on the floor. I said to myself, 'By Allah! This is definitely not a king.' Then he said: c "ʿAdī b. Ḥātim, were you not a *Rakūsī*?' I said yes. d 'Did you not take a fourth-part annual levy from your people?' I said yes. He said: 'If only such were permissible to you in your religion!' I said, 'Yes, by Allah!' I knew, at that time, that he was a Prophet-Messenger and knew what is not usually known. He continued: 'Perhaps, ʿAdī, what is preventing you from entering this Religion is that you see them in need? But, by Allah! e The time has almost come when wealth shall flow among them to the point no one can be found to take it [from you]! And perhaps what is preventing you from entering it is that you see how many enemies they have? But, by Allah! f The time has almost come when you will hear that a woman can travel out of al-Qādisiyya on her camel all the way to visit this House and fear none. And perhaps what is preventing you from entering it is that you see kingdom and power in the hands of others? I swear it by Allah! g The time has almost come when you will hear that the white palaces of Babylon have been conquered by them.' I entered Islam and have seen two of the three signs.[347]

[347]Narrated by Ibn Hishām (5:275-278) without chain cf. Ibn Kathīr, *Bidāya* (5:63-65) who said it is partly confirmed by the other reports on ʿAdī. *Rakūsī* is glossed by Ibn Sīrīn as "adherent to a religion between Sabeanism and Christianity" (cf. Ibn Sallām, *Gharīb*

[4] "When I heard that the Messenger of Allah ﷺ had come out, I hated nothing worse. I went away until I reached the regions of the Romans. (One narrator has: "Until I reached Caesar.") But I hated my situation there even worse! I said to myself, 'Why not go to that man? If he lies, I have nothing to lose, and he tells the truth, I will know it.' So I came to him. When I arrived, the people were saying, "'Adī b. Ḥātim! 'Adī b. Ḥātim!' I went in to see the Messenger of Allah ﷺ. He told me: 253 "'Adī b. Ḥātim, surrender and you will be safe *(aslim taslam)*,' three times. I said, 'I already have Religion.' He said: a 'I know better than you about your religion.' I said, 'You know better than I about my religion?' He said: 'Yes. b Are you not a *Rakūsī*? Do you not get a fourth-part annual levy from your people?' I said yes. He said: 'And this is impermissible to you in your religion!' As soon as he said this, I was humbled to my soul. He continued: c 'I also know what is keeping you away from Islam. You are thinking: Only the weaklings follow him, and the Arabs are fighting them! Do you know al-Ḥīra?' I said, 'I have not seen it but I heard of it.' He continued: 'By the One in Whose Hand is my life! d Allah shall most certainly bring this endeavor to perfection to the point that a woman traveller shall come all the way from al-Ḥīra to circumambulate this House, without escort, and He shall most certainly lay open the treasures of Chosroes, the son of Hurmuz.' I said, 'Chosroes, the son of Hurmuz?' He said: 'Yes, Chosroes, the son of Hurmuz! And e money shall flow to the point that no one will accept it from you!'" 'Adī b. Ḥātim said: "Now, you can see the woman traveller come out of al-Ḥīra until she circumambulates the House without escort and I was among those who conquered the treasures of Chosroes, the son of Hurmuz. By the One in Whose Hand is my life! You will most certainly see the third thing, because the Messenger of Allah ﷺ said so."[348]

[5] Al-Sha'bī said: "When 'Adī b. Ḥātim came to al-Kūfa we visited him as part of a group of the *Fuqahā'* of Kūfa. We said to him: 'Tell us what you heard from the Messenger of Allah ﷺ.' He said: 'I came to see the Messenger of Allah ﷺ and he said: 254 "'Adī b. Ḥātim! Surrender and you will be safe." I said, "And what is Islam?" He said: a "Your bearing witness that there is no God but Allah and that I am the Messenger of Allah; and your believing in the foreordained events – all of them whether good or bad, sweet or bitter."'"'[349]]

'Amr b. al-Ghafwā' al-Khuzā'ī ﷺ

Abū Nu'aym in the *Ma'rifat* [*al-Aṣḥāb*] and Ibn Sa'd narrated that 'Amr b. al-Ghafwā' al-Khuzā'ī said, "The Messenger of Allah ﷺ summoned me to send me to Abū Sufyān with money that was to be divided among the Quraysh after the conquest, in Mecca.

al-Ḥadīth) and might be connected to Marcionism or Mandeanism or else a corruption of *rakūzī* < *rikz* pl. *rikāz* and *rakā'iz*, buried treasures. In Islam, their five-part allotment is identical to that of war spoils. The *rakūzī* may have garnered a fourth-part share in comparable fashion. Al-Qādisiyya in Iraq is fifteen parasangs from Kūfa and was conquered under 'Umar ﷺ, a decisive victory which led to the seizure of all of Iraq.

[348] Narrated by Aḥmad with three chains ('Ālamiyya ed. §17548, §18569, and §18578).

[349] Narrated by Ibn Mājah with a very weak chain through 'Abd al-A'lā b. Abī al-Musāwir.

He told me: [255] 'Look for a travel companion.' 'Amr b. Umayya al-Ḍamrī came to me, saying, 'I heard you intended to travel, so I will be your travel companion.' I told the Prophet ﷺ and he said: [a] 'When you arrive at the land of his people, beware of him. It is said, [b] do not trust even your own firstborn brother!' We went out and rode until we reached al-Abwā' whereupon he said, 'I need something from my people, so wait for me here.' I told him to take care. When he left, I remembered the warning of the Messenger of Allah ﷺ so I prodded my camel and searched for him at top speed. When I reached al-'Aṣāfir I caught sight of him as he was going towards a group of riders. I galloped and overtook him. When his people saw my strength they moved away. He came towards me and said, 'I needed something from my people!' I said, 'Indeed!' We travelled on until we reached Mecca.[350]

عَنْ عَبْدِ اللهِ بْنِ عَمْرِو بْنِ الْفَغْوَاءِ الْخُزَاعِيِّ عَنْ أَبِيهِ قَالَ دَعَانِي رَسُولُ اللهِ ﷺ وَقَدْ أَرَادَ أَنْ يَبْعَثَنِي بِمَالٍ إِلَى أَبِي سُفْيَانَ يَقْسِمُهُ فِي قُرَيْشٍ بِمَكَّةَ بَعْدَ الْفَتْحِ فَقَالَ الْتَمِسْ صَاحِبًا قَالَ فَجَاءَنِي عَمْرُو بْنُ أُمَيَّةَ الضَّمْرِيُّ فَقَالَ بَلَغَنِي أَنَّكَ تُرِيدُ الْخُرُوجَ وَتَلْتَمِسُ صَاحِبًا قَالَ قُلْتُ أَجَلْ قَالَ فَأَنَا لَكَ صَاحِبٌ قَالَ فَجِئْتُ رَسُولَ اللهِ ﷺ قُلْتُ قَدْ وَجَدْتُ صَاحِبًا قَالَ فَقَالَ مَنْ قُلْتُ عَمْرُو بْنُ أُمَيَّةَ الضَّمْرِيُّ قَالَ إِذَا هَبَطْتَ بِلَادَ قَوْمِهِ فَاحْذَرْهُ فَإِنَّهُ

---

[350]Narrated with a passable chain by Abū Dāwūd, Ahmad, Ibn Saʿd (4:296), Ibn Qāniʿ in *Muʿjam al-Ṣaḥāba* (2:214 §717), al-Ṭabarānī in *al-Kabīr* (17:36 §73), al-Bayhaqī in *al-Sunan al-Kubrā* (10:129), Abū Nuʿaym in *Maʿrifat al-Ṣaḥāba*, and Ibn ʿAsākir (45:424) cf. *Isāba* (4:558) while the bracketed segment alone is narrated from ʿAmr by al-Bukhārī in *al-Tārīkh al-Kabīr* (7:39) with a strong chain; from ʿUmar by al-Bazzār (1:414-415 §291) with a very weak chain cf. *Mīzān* (Indian ed. 2:508 "Zayd b. ʿAbd al-Raḥmān b. Zayd"); and from Abū Hurayra by al-Ṭabarānī cf. al-Haythamī (3:215). Al-Abwā' is a water-rich valley in Ḥijāz in which is said to be the grave of Āmina bint Wahb the mother of the Prophet ﷺ and in which is found present-day al-Khurayba cf. *Maʿālim*. Al-Aṣāfir is a woodland near Badr cf. *Lisān al-ʿArab*.

قَدْ قَالَ الْقَائِلُ أَخُوكَ الْبِكْرِيُّ وَلاَ تَأْمَنْهُ فَخَرَجْنَا حَتَّى إِذَا كُنْتُ بِالأَبْوَاءِ قَالَ إِنِّي أُرِيدُ حَاجَةً إِلَى قَوْمِي بِوَدَّانَ فَتَلَبَّثْ لِي قُلْتُ رَاشِدًا فَلَمَّا وَلَّى ذَكَرْتُ قَوْلَ النَّبِيِّ ﷺ فَشَدَدْتُ عَلَى بَعِيرِي حَتَّى خَرَجْتُ أُوضِعُهُ حَتَّى إِذَا كُنْتُ بِالأَصَافِرِ إِذَا هُوَ يُعَارِضُنِي فِي رَهْطٍ قَالَ وَأَوْضَعْتُ فَسَبَقْتُهُ فَلَمَّا رَآنِي قَدْ فُتُّهُ انْصَرَفُوا وَجَاءَنِي فَقَالَ كَانَتْ لِي إِلَى قَوْمِي حَاجَةٌ قَالَ قُلْتُ أَجَلْ وَمَضَيْنَا حَتَّى قَدِمْنَا مَكَّةَ فَدَفَعْتُ الْمَالَ إِلَى أَبِي سُفْيَانَ د حم ابن سعد ابن قانع طب هق كر خد مختصرا وعن عمر ز وعن أبي هريرة طب مجمع وفي بعض الروايات خالد بن الوليد بدل عمرو بن الفغواء

Al-Ḥārith b. Sawā' ﷺ

Ibn Shāhīn and Ibn Mandah narrated that al-Muṭṭalib b. ʿAbd Allāh said: "I said to the sons of al-Ḥārith b. Sawā', 'Your father is the one who belied his sale to the Messenger of Allah ﷺ!' They said: 'Do not say such a thing! **[504]** For the Messenger of Allah gave him a young she-camel and said: 256 "Allah shall bless you with it." Since then, we never transported cargoes near or far except with her!'"[351]

عَنِ الْمُطَّلِبِ بْنِ عَبْدِ اللهِ بْنِ حَنْطَبٍ قَالَ قُلْتُ لِبَنِي سَوَاءِ بْنِ الحَارِثِ أَبُوكُم الَّذِي جَحَدَ بَيْعَةَ رَسُولِ اللهِ ﷺ فَقَالَ لاَ تَقُلْ

[351]Narrated by Abū Nuʿaym in *Maʿrifat al-Ṣaḥāba* (3:1410 §3564). Thus cited in *Usd al-Ghāba* (2:587 §2328), *al-Isaba* (3:215) and *al-Khasā'is* (2:98) while al-Khaṭīb and Ibn Saʿd identify the (grand?)father as Sawā' b. Qays al-Muhāribī.

إِلاَّ خَيْراً قَدْ أَعْطَاهُ بَكْرَةً وَقَالَ إِنَّ اللهَ سَيُبَارِكُ لَكَ فِيهَا فَمَا أَصْبَحْنَا نَسُوقُ مِنَ الْغَنَمِ سَارِحاً وَلاَ بَارِحاً وَلاَ مَمْلُوكاً إِلاَّ مِنْهَا

أبو نعيم في المعرفة

[A reference to the Bedouin Sawā' b. al-Hārith al-Muhāribī who accepted Islam together with his son then agreed with the Prophet ﷺ to the sale of a horse, after which he received better offers from unwitting buyers and denied this sale, demanding a witness, whereupon Khuzayma b. Thābit bore witness in favor of the Prophet ﷺ. The latter asked him on what basis he could bear witness, since he was not present at the time of the sale. Khuzayma replied: "On the basis of your truthfulness." 257 The Prophet ﷺ then gave Khuzayma's testimony the weight of two testimonies[352] and said: 258 "Whoever Khuzayma witnesses for or against, it is enough for him."[353] Subsequently, the Rightly-Guided Caliphs counted Khuzayma's word as that of two men.]

Mas'ūd b. al-Ḍaḥḥāk al-Lakhmī

Abū Nu'aym narrated from Mas'ūd b. al-Ḍaḥḥāk al-Lakhmī ؓ that the Prophet ﷺ named him Muṭā' ["Obeyed"] and said to him: 259 "You shall be obeyed among your people." Then he told him: a "Go to your friends. Whoever joins under this banner of yours is safe." He went and they obeyed him and came back with him to the Prophet ﷺ.[354]

عَنْ مَسْعُودٍ أَبِي مُحَمَّدٍ الأَنْصَارِيِّ ثُمَّ الْخَزْرَجِيِّ الْبَدْرِيِّ أَنَّ النَّبِيَّ ﷺ سَمَّاهُ مُطَاعًا وَقَالَ لَهُ يَا مُطَاعُ أَنْتَ مُطَاعٌ فِي قَوْمِكَ وَقَالَ لَهُ امْضِ إِلَى أَصْحَابِكَ وَحَمَلَهُ عَلَى فَرَسٍ أَبْلَقَ وَأَعْطَاهُ الرَّايَةَ

---

[352] Narrated from 'Umāra b. Khuzayma's uncle by Abū Dāwūd, al-Nasā'ī, and Aḥmad with sound chains.

[353] Narrated by al-Ṭabarānī in *al-Kabīr* (4:87) through trustworthy narrators cf. al-Haythamī (9:320), al-Bukhārī in *al-Tārīkh al-Kabīr* (1:86), and al-Khaṭīb in *Muwaḍḍiḥ al-Jam' wal-Tafrīq* (2:96-97).

[354] Narrated by al-Ṭabarānī in *al-Kabīr* (20:331) and *al-Awsaṭ* (5:97-98), Abū Nu'aym in the *Ma'rifa* (5:2532-2533 §6130) and Ibn 'Asākir (35:393), all with a patrilinear chain of unknowns cf. al-Haythamī (8:54-55 and 9:407), *Iṣāba* (6:100), and *Khaṣā'iṣ* (2:179).

وَقَالَ مَنْ دَخَلَ تَحْتَ رايَتِي هَذِهِ فَقَدْ أَمِنَ مِنَ الْعَذَابِ طب طس

وفي إسناده من لم أعرفهم مج أبو نعيم في المعرفة كر قال الطيالسى لا يروى إلا بهذا الاسناد

Ḥabīb b. Maslama al-Fihrī رضي الله عنهما

Abū Nuʿaym and Ibn ʿAsākir narrated from Abū Mulayka that Ḥabīb b. Maslama al-Fihrī رضي الله عنهما came to the Prophet ﷺ in al-Madīna to join in raids. When his father saw him in al-Madīna he said, "Prophet of Allah, I have no other son except him to care for my property, my house, and my dependants, whereupon the Prophet ﷺ turned him back together with Maslama himself and said: 260 "Perhaps the way will open for you this year, so go back, Ḥabīb, with your father!" He returned, then Maslama died that year and after that Ḥabīb joined up.[355]

عَنْ عَبْدِ اللهِ بْنِ أَبِي مُلَيْكَةَ أَنَّ حَبِيبَ بْنَ مَسْلَمَةَ قَدِمَ عَلَى النَّبِيِّ ﷺ بِالمدِينَةِ غَازِياً وَأَنَّ أَبَاهُ أَدْرَكَهُ بِالمدِينَةِ فَقَالَ مَسْلَمَةُ لِلنَّبِيِّ ﷺ يَا نَبِيَّ اللهِ إِنِّي لَيْسَ لِي وَلَدٌ غَيْرُهُ يَقُومُ فِي مَالِي وَضَيْعَتِي وعَلَى أَهْلِ بَيْتِي وَأَنَّ رَسُولَ اللهِ ﷺ رَدَّهُ مَعَهُ وَقَالَ لَعَلَّكَ أَنْ يَخْلُوَ لَكَ وَجْهُكَ فِي عَامِكَ فَارْجِعْ يَا حَبِيبُ مَعَ أَبِيكَ فَرَجَعَ فَمَاتَ مَسْلَمَةُ فِي ذَلِكَ الْعَامِ وَغَزَا حَبِيبٌ فِيهِ أبو نعيم في المعرفة كر

[355]Narrated by Abū Nuʿaym in the *Maʿrifa* (2:825-826 §2167) and Ibn ʿAsākir (12:66) cf. *Isāba* (2:203 and 6:115) and *Khasāʾis* (2:243).

Ibn Sa'd, al-Baghawī, Abū Nu'aym, and Bayhaqī narrated from Ḥabīb himself that he came to Madīna to see him and that when his father saw him there he said: "Messenger of Allah! My son is my arm and my leg!" The Prophet ﷺ said to Ḥabīb: [261] "Return with him for he is going to die soon." He died the same year.[356]

عَنْ حَبِيبِ بْنِ مَسْلَمَةَ الفِهْرِيِّ أَنَّهُ أَتَى النَّبِيَّ ﷺ فَأَدْرَكَهُ أَبُوهُ
فَقَالَ يَا نَبِيَّ اللهِ اِبْنِي يَدِي وَرِجْلِي فَقَالَ اِرْجِعْ مَعَهُ فَإِنَّهُ يُوشِكُ
أَنْ يَهْلِكَ فَهَلَكَ تِلْكَ السَّنَةَ ابن سعد ابن قانع البغوي في الصحابة كر

Surāqa b. Mālik ؓ

Al-Bayhaqī narrated that the Prophet ﷺ said to Surāqa b. Mālik – who had tried to intercept him as he was emigrating to al-Madīna, then entered Islam the year of the Conquest of Mecca: [262] "I can almost see you wearing the armlets of Chosroes."[357] When Allah took away his empire from Chosroes in 'Umar's Caliphate, they brought his two armlets to 'Umar who gave them to Surāqa to wear as his own, just as the Prophet ﷺ had foretold. 'Umar said: [a] "Glory to Allah Who took them away from Kisrā and adorned Surāqa with them, a Bedouin Arab from the Banū Mudlij!" They were made of gold.

[356]Narrated from Ḥabīb b. Maslama by Ibn Sa'd (7:409), Ibn Qāni', *Mu'jam al-Ṣaḥāba* (1:191), al-Baghawī in his (2:120 §492) and Ibn 'Asākir (12:65-66) cf. Ibn Ḥajar and al-Suyūṭī. The Madanīs denied that Ḥabīb was a Companion. He was one of the famed *mujāhidīn* of Shām against the Byzantines and was thus nicknamed Ḥabīb al-Rūm.

[357]Narrated from al-Shāfi'ī chainless by Bayhaqī, *Sunan* (6:357), *Ma'rifa* (9:290 §13197), and *Dalā'il* (6:325), which also narrate the report from 'Umar with full chains; also in al-Shāfi'ī, *al-Umm* (4:157), *al-Istī'āb* (2:581) and elsewhere; also narrated in this wording from Sufyān b. 'Uyayna in *al-Iktifā'* (4:277) cf. al-Māwardī, *A'lām al-Nubuwwa* (p. 155), al-Nawawī, *Tahdhīb al-Asmā'* (1:205), *Bidāya* (6:194, 7:67), *Iṣāba* (3:41), *Khaṣā'is* (2:193), *Halabiyya* (2:221), *Iktifā'* (1:348), *Rawḍ* (2:323), *Shifā* cf. hadīth at note 502.

عَنِ الشَّافِعِيِّ أَنَّ النَّبِيَّ ﷺ قَالَ لِسُرَاقَةَ وَنَظَرَ إِلَى ذِرَاعَيْهِ كَأَنِّي بِكَ قَدْ لَبِسْتَ سِوَارَيْ كِسْرَى هق وفي الدلائل والمعرفة من بلاغاته عَنِ الحَسَنِ أَنَّ عُمَرَ بْنَ الْخَطَّابِ رَضِيَ اللهُ عَنْهُ أُتِيَ بِفَرْوَةِ كِسْرَى فَوُضِعَتْ بَيْنَ يَدَيهِ وَفِي القَوْمِ سُرَاقَةُ بْنُ جُعْشُمٍ قَالَ فَأَلْقَى إِلَيْهِ سَوَارِيَ كِسْرَى بْنِ هُرْمُزَ فَجَعَلَهُمَا فِي يَدَيْهِ فَبَلَغَا مَنْكِبَيهِ فَلَمَّا رَآهُمَا فِي يَدَي سُرَاقَةَ قَالَ الحَمْدُ للهِ سَوَارِي كِسْرَى بْنِ هُرْمُزَ فِي يَدِ سُرَاقَةَ بْنِ مَالِكِ بْنِ جُعْشُمٍ أَعْرَابِيٍّ مِنْ بَنِي مُدْلِجٍ هق وفي الدلائل والمعرفة

Qudad or Qudar b. ʿAmmār ؓ

Ibn Saʿd narrated that Hishām b. Muḥammad informed them that a man from the Banū Sulaym told him: "One of us – his name was Qudad b. ʿAmmār – went in a delegation to see the Prophet ﷺ in Madīna. He accepted Islam and promised the Prophet ﷺ to bring him one thousand mounted troops of his people. He died but sent nine hundred riders under the command of three men he deputized while one hundred remained behind in their region. The Messenger of Allah ﷺ asked: 263 "Where is the remainder of the thousand?" They said: "One hundred stayed behind in our region in precaution against a war that has been raging between the Banū Kināna and us." The Prophet ﷺ said: a "Send for that force. No harm will come your way this year." They sent for them and they came. When people heard the clatter of horses they said "Messenger of Allah! We are under attack!" He said: b "On the contrary, these are allies not foes. Sulaym b. Manṣūr's tribe have come."[358]

[358]Narrated by Ibn Saʿd (1:308) cf. *Khaṣāʾis* (2:32).

عَنْ رَجُلٍ مِنْ بَنِي سُلَيْمٍ مِنْ بَنِي الشَّرِيدِ قَالَ وَفَدَ رَجُلٌ مِنَّا يُقَالُ لَهُ قُدَدُ أَوْ قُدَرُ بْنُ عَمَّارٍ عَلَى النَّبِيِّ ﷺ بِالمَدِينَةِ فَأَسْلَمَ وَعَاهَدَهُ عَلَى أَنْ يَأْتِيَهُ بِأَلْفٍ مِنْ قَوْمِهِ عَلَى الخَيْلِ ثُمَّ أَتَى إِلَى قَوْمِهِ فَأَخْبَرَهُم الخَبَرَ فَخَرَجَ تِسْعُمِائَةٍ وَخَلَّفَ فِي الحَيِّ مِائَةً فَقَالَ رَسُولُ اللهِ ﷺ أَيْنَ تَكْمِلَةُ الأَلْفِ الَّذِينَ عَاهَدَنِي عَلَيْهِمْ قَالُوا قَدْ خَلَّفَ مِئَةً بِالحَيِّ مَخَافَةَ حَرْبٍ كَانَ بَيْنَنَا وَبَيْنَ بَنِي كِنَانَةَ قَالَ ابْعَثُوا إِلَيْهَا فَإِنَّهُ لاَ يَأْتِيكُمْ فِي عَامِكُمْ هَذَا شَيْءٌ تَكْرَهُونَهُ فَبَعَثُوا إِلَيْهَا فَأَتَتْهُ بِالهَدَّةِ وَهِيَ مِائَةٌ عَلَيْهَا المُنَقَّعُ بْنُ مَالِكِ بْنِ أُمَيَّةَ بْنِ عَبْدِ العُزَّى فَلَمَّا سَمِعُوا وَئِيدَ الخَيْلِ قَالُوا يَا رَسُولَ اللهِ أُتِينَا قَالَ لاَ بَلْ لَكُمْ لاَ عَلَيْكُمْ هَذِهِ سُلَيْمُ بْنُ مَنْصُورٍ قَدْ جَاءَتْ ابن سعد

Dhūl-Jawshan ﷺ

Ibn Saʿd narrated that Abū Isḥāq al-Sabīʿī said: "Dhūl-Jawshan ["Busty"] al-Kilābī [Abū Shimr al-Ḍibābī] came to see the Prophet ﷺ. The latter told him: [264] 'What is stopping you from accepting Islam?' He replied: 'The fact that your people called you a liar, expelled you and fought you. I am keeping watch; if you overcome them, I shall believe in you and follow you; but if they overcome you, I shall not follow you.' The Messenger of Allah ﷺ said to him: [a] 'Dhūl-Jawshan! You might live to see me overcome them after a little while.' Dhūl-Jawshan later said: 'I swear I was in Ḍariyya when a rider from Mecca came to us. We asked him for news and he said: Muḥammad has overcome the people of

Mecca!'" Thenceforth, Dhūl-Jawshan bitterly grieved his declining Islam at the time the Messenger of Allah ﷺ invited him.[359] **[505]**

عَنْ أَبِي إِسْحَاقَ الْهَمْدَانِيِّ قَالَ قَدِمَ عَلَى النَّبِيِّ ﷺ ذُو الْجَوْشَنِ وَأَهْدَى لَهُ فَرَسًا وَهُوَ يَوْمَئِذٍ مُشْرِكٌ فَأَبَى رَسُولُ اللهِ ﷺ أَنْ يَقْبَلَهُ ثُمَّ قَالَ إِنْ شِئْتَ بِعْتَنِيهِ أَوْ هَلْ لَكَ أَنْ تَبِيعَنِيهِ بِالْمُتَخَيَّرَةِ مِنْ دُرُوعِ بَدْرٍ ثُمَّ قَالَ لَهُ ﷺ هَلْ لَكَ أَنْ تَكُونَ أَوَّلَ مَنْ يَدْخُلُ فِي هَذَا الأَمْرِ فَقَالَ لاَ فَقَالَ لَهُ النَّبِيُّ ﷺ مَا يَمْنَعُكَ مِنْ ذَلِكَ قَالَ رَأَيْتُ قَوْمَكَ قَدْ كَذَّبُوكَ وَأَخْرَجُوكَ وَقَاتَلُوكَ فَانْظُرْ مَا تَصْنَعُ فَإِنْ ظَهَرْتَ عَلَيْهِمْ آمَنْتُ بِكَ وَاتَّبَعْتُكَ وَإِنْ ظَهَرُوا عَلَيْكَ لَمْ أَتَّبِعْكَ فَقَالَ لَهُ رَسُولُ اللهِ ﷺ يَا ذَا الْجَوْشَنِ لَعَلَّكَ إِنْ بَقِيتَ قَرِيباً أَنْ تَرَى ظُهُورِي عَلَيْهِمْ قَالَ فَوَاللهِ إِنِّي لَبِضَرِيَّةَ إِذْ قَدِمَ عَلَيْنَا رَاكِبٌ مِنْ قِبَلِ مَكَّةَ فَقُلْنَا مَا الْخَبَرُ قَالَ ظَهَرَ مُحَمَّدٌ عَلَى أَهْلِ مَكَّةَ قَالَ فَكَانَ ذُو الْجَوْشَنِ يَتَوَجَّعُ عَلَى تَرْكِهِ الإِسْلاَمَ حِينَ دَعَاهُ رَسُولُ اللهِ ﷺ حم ابن سعد الآحاد لابن أبي عاصم كر

[359]Narrated from Abū Isḥāq al-Hamdānī al-Sabī'ī – most likely from Shimr the son of Dhūl-Jawshan – by Aḥmad with several strong chains, Ibn Sa'd (6:46-47), Ibn Abī 'Āṣim in *al-Āḥād wal-Mathānī* (3:175-176), and Ibn 'Asākir (23:187-188) cf. *Istī'āb* (2:467-468), *Iṣāba* (2:410), and *Khaṣā'iṣ* (1:437). Dhūl-Jawshan's name was Aws b. al-A'war b. 'Amr. He was nicknamed "Busty" because of his bulging chest. Ḍariyya was a protected oasis in Najd but Aḥmad's version only has: "I was in a valley with my wife."

Abū Ṣufra ؓ

Ibn Mandah and Ibn ʿAsākir narrated that Muḥammad b. Ghālib b. ʿAbd al-Raḥmān b. Yazīd b. al-Muhallab b. Abī Ṣufra said: "My father mentioned, on the authority of his forefathers, that Abū Ṣufra ['Bright Yellow'] came to pledge his loyalty to the Prophet ﷺ wearing a yellow tunic that trailed behind him. He was tall, handsome, articulate, a striking sight. The Prophet ﷺ asked him who he was. He replied, 'I am Qāṭiʿ (Scoundrel), son of Sāriq (Thief), son of Ẓālim (Felon), son of ʿAmr, son of Shihāb, son of Murra (Bitter), son of al-Halqām (Jowly), son of al-Julandī, son of al-Mustakbir (Arrogant), son of al-Julandī, the sea-pirate. I am a king son of a king!' The Prophet ﷺ said: 265 'You are Abū Ṣufra. Rid yourself of "Thief" and "Felon."' He said: 'I bear witness that there is no god but Allah and that you are His servant and Messenger. In truth! I have eighteen boys and was only lately blessed with a daughter, whom I named Ṣufra!'"[360]

عَنْ مُحَمَّدِ بْنِ غَالِبِ بْنِ عَبْدِ الرَّحْمَنِ بْنِ يَزِيدَ بْنِ الْمُهَلَّبِ بْنِ أَبِي صُفْرَةَ قَالَ ذَكَرَ أَبِي عَنْ آبَائِهِ أَنَّ أَبَا صُفْرَةَ قَدِمَ عَلَى النَّبِيِّ ﷺ عَلَى أَنْ يُبَايِعَهُ وَعَلَيْهِ حِلَّةٌ صَفْرَاءُ يَسْحَبُهَا خَلْفَهُ ذِرَاعَيْنِ وَلَهُ طُولٌ وَمَنْظَرٌ وَجَمَالٌ وَفَصَاحَةُ اللِّسَانِ فَلَمَّا نَظَرَ إِلَيْهِ النَّبِيُّ ﷺ أَعْجَبَهُ جَمَالُهُ وَخَلْقُهُ فَقَالَ لَهُ النَّبِيُّ ﷺ مَنْ أَنْتَ قَالَ أَنَا قَاطِعُ بْنُ سَارِقِ بْنِ ظَالِمِ بْنِ عَمْرِو بْنِ شِهَابِ بْنِ مُرَّةَ بْنِ الهَلْقَامِ بْنِ الجُلَنْدِيِّ بْنِ المسْتَكْبِرِ بْنِ الجُلَنْدِيِّ الَّذِي كَانَ يَأْخُذُ كُلَّ سَفِينَةٍ غَصْباً أَنَا مَلِكٌ اِبْنُ مَلِكٍ فَقَالَ لَهُ النَّبِيُّ ﷺ أَنْتَ

[360] Narrated by Abū Nuʿaym in the *Maʿrifa* (4:2363-2364 §5803) and Ibn al-Sakan in *al-Saḥāba* per Ibn Ḥajar, *Isāba* (7:219-220) cf. Ibn ʿAsākir (61:287) and *Khasā'is* (2:56).

أَبُو صُفْرَةَ وَدَعْ عَنْكَ سَارِقاً وَظَالِماً فَقَالَ أَشْهَدُ أَنْ لاَ إِلَهَ إِلاَّ
اللهُ وَأَنَّكَ عَبْدُهُ وَرَسُولُهُ حَقّاً حَقّاً وَإِنَّ لِي لَثَمَانِيَةَ عَشَرَ ذَكَراً
وَقَدْ رُزِقْتُ بِأَخَرَةٍ بِنْتاً فَسَمَّيْتُهَا صُفْرَةَ أبو نعيم في معرفة الصحابة

Al-Ḥārith b. ʿAbd Kulāl al-Ḥimyarī ﵁

Al-Hamdānī said in *al-Ansāb* ("The Genealogies") that al-Ḥārith b. ʿAbd Kulāl al-Ḥimyarī – one of the chieftains *(aqyāl)* of Yemen – came in a delegation to the Prophet ﷺ who said before his arrival: 266 "From this opening a man is going to enter into your presence who is of noble male and female ancestry *(karīm al-jaddayn)*." Then al-Ḥārith entered. The Prophet ﷺ embraced him and spread his cloak for him [to sit on].[361]

قال الهَمْداني في الأنساب وَفَدَ الحَارِثُ بْنُ عَبْدِ كُلاَلٍ الحِمْيَرِيُّ
أَحَدُ أَقْيَالِ اليَمَنِ إِلَى النَّبِيِّ ﷺ فَقَالَ قَبْلَ أَنْ يَدْخُلَ عَلَيْهِ
يَدْخُلُ عَلَيْكُمْ مِنْ هَذَا الفَجِّ رَجُلٌ كَرِيمُ الجَدَّينِ صَبِيحُ الخَدَّيْنِ
فَدَخَلَ الحَارِثُ فَأَسْلَمَ فَاعْتَنَقَهُ وَأَفْرَشَهُ رِدَاءَهُ إصابة خصائص سبل الهدى وزاد قال الحافظ رحمه الله تعالى والذي تضافرت به الروايات أنه أرسل بإسلامه وأقام باليمن

[361]Narrated by the ḥadīth Master Abū Bakr Muḥammad b. Mūsā b. ʿUthmān al-Ḥāzimī al-Hamadhānī (548-584) in *ʿUjālat al-Mubtadī wa-Fuḍālat al-Muntahī fīl-Nasab*, cf. Ibn Ḥajar in *al-Iṣāba* (1:296-297 §1437) who said multiple reports state he declared his *islām* in writing but stayed in Yemen; Suyūṭī, *Khaṣāʾiṣ* (2:46); Ṣāliḥī, *Subul*. Note: the title "of noble male and female ancestry" *(karīm al-ṭarafayn)* is also a Prophetic attribute. The Prophet had written them summoning them to Islam as mentioned in Qalqashandī's *Nihāyat al-Arab fī Maʿrifat Ansāb al-ʿArab*, al-Ṣaḥārī al-ʿAwtabī in his *Tārīkh Ansāb al-ʿArab* and others.

Umm Waraqa رضي الله عنها

Abu Dāwūd and Abū Nu'aym narrated from Umm Waraqa bint Nawfal رضي الله عنها that when the Prophet ﷺ was leaving for his Badr campaign she asked him, "Messenger of Allah, give me permission to battle with you and perhaps Allah will grant me martyrdom!" He said: [267] "Sit quietly in your house *(qarrī fī baytiki)* for Allah shall certainly grant you martyrdom." After that she was nicknamed the Martyr *(al-Shahīda)*. She had recited the [whole] Qur'an [and may have assisted 'Umar in collating the text]. She announced that her slave and slavegirl would be free after her death. One night they went to her and suffocated her to death with a sheet of cloth. This took place in the caliphate of 'Umar. He put out a search for them and had them crucified. This was the first crucifixion in Madīna. 'Umar said: "Truly the Messenger of Allah ﷺ spoke truth! He would say: 'Let us go and visit the *shahīda*.'"[362]

عَنْ عَنْ أُمِّ وَرَقَةَ رَضِيَ اللهُ عَنْهَا بنتِ نَوْفَلٍ قَالَتْ لَمَّا غَزَا النَّبِيُّ
ﷺ بَدْرًا قُلْتُ يَا رَسُولَ اللهِ ائْذَنْ لِي أَنْ أَغْزُوَ مَعَكَ أُدَاوِي
جَرْحَاكُمْ وَأُمَرِّضَ مَرْضَاكُمْ لَعَلَّ اللهُ يَرْزُقَنِي شَهَادَةً فَقَالَ قَرِّي
فِي بَيْتِكِ فَإِنَّ اللهَ يَرْزُقُكِ الشَّهَادَةَ وَكَانَتْ تُسَمَّى الشَّهِيدَةَ
وَكَانَتْ قَدْ قَرَأَتِ الْقُرْآنَ وَكَانَتْ دَبَّرَتْ غُلَاماً لَهَا وَجَارِيَةً فَقَامَا
إِلَيْهَا بِاللَّيْلِ فَغَمَّاهَا بِقَطِيفَةٍ لَهَا حَتَّى مَاتَتْ وَدَفَنَاهَا فَأَصْبَحَ
عُمَرُ رَضِيَ اللهُ عَنْهُ فَقَامَ فِي النَّاسِ فَقَالَ مَنْ عِنْدَهُ مِنْ هَذَيْنِ
مِنْ عِلْمٍ أَوْ مَنْ رَآهُمَا فَلْيَجِئْ بِهِمَا فَجِيءَ بِهِمَا فَأَمَرَ بِهِمَا فَصُلِبَا

[362]Narrated by Abū Dāwūd with three chains, Aḥmad, Ibn Abī 'Āṣim in *al-Āḥād wal-Mathānī* (6:139), Ibn Abī Shayba (6:538), al-Ṭabarānī, Abū Nu'aym, al-Bayhaqī and others cf. *Bidāya* (6:202), *Iṣāba* (8:321), and *Khaṣā'is* (2:228).

فَكَانَ أَوَّلَ مَصْلُوبٍ بِالْمَدِينَةِ فَقَالَ عُمَرُ صَدَقَ رَسُولُ اللهِ ﷺ
كَانَ يَقُولُ انْطَلِقُوا بِنَا نَزُورُ الشَّهِيدَةَ حم د ع ابن أبي عاصم في الآحاد
ش طب ابن سعد ابن الجارود في المنتقى حل وفي المعرفة هق وفي الدلائل

Wābiṣat al-Asadī ؓ

Al-Imām Aḥmad and others narrated that Wābiṣat al-Asadī said: "I came to ask the Prophet ﷺ about virtue and vice. He said, before I asked him about it: 268 'Wābiṣa! Shall I tell you what you came to ask me about?' I said, 'Tell me, Messenger of Allah!' He said: a 'You came to ask me about virtue and vice.' I said, 'Yes, by Him Who sent you with the truth!' He ﷺ said: b 'Virtue is what sets your mind at rest [lit. "dilates your breast"] *(mā-nsharaḥa lahu ṣadruk)* and vice is what pricks your conscience [lit. "becomes fixed in yourself"] *(mā ḥāka fī nafsik)*, no matter what people recommend about it.'"363

> [In another version the Prophet ﷺ replies: 269 "Consult yourself, consult your heart *(istafti nafsak istafti qalbak)*, Wābiṣa!" three times while poking Wābiṣa's chest with his [first] three fingers, adding: a "Virtue is what sets the soul and heart at rest *(mā-tma'annat ilayhi al-nafsu wamā-tma'anna ilayhi al-qalb)* while vice is what pricks the conscience [lit. "goes back and forth in"] the breast *(mā ḥāka fil-nafsi wa taraddada fil-ṣadr)*, no matter what people keep recommending to you."364
>
> In another version Wābiṣa said: "I came to the Messenger of Allah ﷺ, not wanting to leave out anything about virtue and vice except I should ask him about it. There was a crowd around him so I began to step over [the shoulders of] the people. They said: 'Away, away with you, Wābiṣa, from the Messenger of Allah!' But I said: 'So I am Wābiṣa! Leave me so I can get near him! I love no one more that I want to get near to!' He said to me: 270 'Come near, Wābiṣa, come near, Wābiṣa!' I approached until my knees touched his. He said: 'Wābiṣa! Shall I tell you what you came to ask me about or do you want to ask me first?' I said, 'Messenger of Allah, tell me!' He said: 'You came to ask me about virtue and vice.' I said, 'Yes, by the One Who sent you with the truth!' a He joined three fingers together and poked my chest, saying: b 'Wābiṣa! Consult yourself! Virtue is whatever sets the heart and soul at rest, while vice is what pricks the conscience [lit. "becomes fixed in the heart"] and nags the breast, no matter what people keep recommending to you."365

363Narrated by Aḥmad with a chain of trustworthy narrators.
364Narrated by al-Dārimī with a weak chain.
365Narrated by Aḥmad, Abū Ya'lā (3:160-162), and Abū Nu'aym (1985 ed. 2:24 and

In another version from al-Khushanī, the Prophet ﷺ said: 271 "Virtue is what sets the soul at rest and brings peace of mind *(mā sakanat ilayhi al-nafsu wa-ṭma'anna ilayhi al-qalb)* while vice is what does not set the soul at rest and does not bring peace of mind, no matter what people recommend."[366]

In another version from al-Nawwās, the Prophet ﷺ said: 272 "Virtue consists in good character and vice is that which disquiets you and which you would hate for people to see."[367]

Wābiṣa also narrated the Prophetic ḥadīth: 273 "Leave what seems dubious to you for what does not seem dubious to you."[368]

In another narration from Abū Hurayra, Anas, and Wāthila b. al-Asqa', the Prophet ﷺ said, pointing to the heart: 274 "Fear of Allah is right here" *(al-taqwā hāhunā)*.[369]

Another Prophetic narration states: 275 "Verily, Allah looks not at your bodies nor at your faces but He looks at your hearts."[370]

Ibn 'Umar said: a "One does not attain true God-wariness until one leaves alone all that troubles the conscience."[371]

Imam al-Nawawī stated that these narrations were used as proof that the seat of the mind is the heart and Ibn Ḥajar similarly adduced all the above texts as evidence of the same together with the verses ﴾**Have they not travelled in the land, and have they hearts wherewith to understand?**﴿ (22:46) and ﴾**Therein verily is a reminder for him who has a heart or gives ear with full intelligence**﴿ (50:37).[372]

'Alī b. Abī Ṭālib ﷺ said at the battle of Ṣiffīn: b "The seat of reason is the heart *(al-'aqlu fī al-qalb)*, that of mercy the liver, that of sympathy the spleen, and that of breath the lung."[373] Imam Aḥmad also said the seat of reason is the heart.[374]

6:255), all with the same weak chain as al-Dārimī.

[366]Narrated from Abū Tha'laba al-Khushanī by Aḥmad with a sound chain as stated by al-Haythamī (1:175) and Aḥmad Shākir in the *Musnad* (13:479 §17671).

[367]Narrated from al-Nawwās b. Sim'ān by Muslim, Tirmidhī *(ḥasan ṣaḥīḥ)* and Aḥmad.

[368]Narrated from al-Ḥasan b. 'Alī by al-Tirmidhī *(ḥasan ṣaḥīḥ)*, al-Nasā'ī, Aḥmad, al-Dārimī, 'Abd al-Razzāq (3:117-118 §4984), al-Ṭabarānī in *al-Kabīr* (3:75-77 §2708-2711), al-Ṭayālisī (p. 163 §1178), Abū Nu'aym in *Akhbār Aṣbahān* (1:45) and the *Ḥilya* (8:264), al-Bayhaqī in *al-Sunan al-Kubrā* (5:335), Ibn Ḥibbān in his *Ṣaḥīḥ* (2:498 §722, *ṣaḥīḥ* per al-Arna'ūṭ), al-Baghawī in *Sharḥ al-Sunna* (7:16-17 §2032), al-Ḥākim (2:13, 4:99, *ṣaḥīḥ* per al-Dhahabī); from Anas by Aḥmad; Wābiṣa b. Ma'bad by al-Ṭabarānī in *al-Kabīr*; and Ibn 'Umar by al-Ṭabarānī in *al-Saghīr* (1:102), Abū al-Shaykh in *al-Amthāl* (§40), Abū Nu'aym in *Akhbār Aṣbahān* (2:243) and the *Ḥilya* (6:352), al-Khaṭīb (2:220, 2:387, 6:386) and al-Quḍā'ī in *Musnad al-Shihāb* (§645).

[369]Narrated from Abū Hurayra by Muslim, Ibn Mājah, and Aḥmad.

[370]Narrated from Abū Hurayra by Muslim and Aḥmad; and from Anas, Wāthila b. al-Asqa' and an unnamed elderly Companion from the Banū Salīt by Aḥmad.

[371]Narrated by al-Bukhārī.

[372]Respectively in *Sharḥ Ṣaḥīḥ Muslim* (16:122) and *Fatḥ al-Bārī* (1959 ed. 1:129).

[373]Narrated from 'Iyāḍ b. Khalifa by al-Bukhārī in *al-Adab al-Mufrad* (p. 192) with a fair chain through Muḥammad b. Muslim al-Ṭā'ifī, and Bayhaqī, *Shu'ab al-Īmān* (3-4:161).

Imam Ibn Fūrak said: "Every instance in which you see scholarly endeavor but upon which there is no light, know that it is a surreptitious innovation *(bid'a khafiyya)*." Ibn al-Subkī said: "This is truly well-said and shows the great refinement of the Teacher. Its foundation is the Prophet's ﷺ ḥadīth: 'Virtue is what sets the soul at rest.'"[375]]

عَنْ وَابِصَةَ بْنِ مَعْبَدٍ قَالَ أَتَيْتُ رَسُولَ اللهِ ﷺ وَأَنَا أُرِيدُ أَنْ لاَ أَدَعَ شَيْئًا مِنَ الْبِرِّ وَالإِثْمِ إِلاَّ سَأَلْتُهُ عَنْهُ وَإِذَا عِنْدَهُ جَمْعٌ فَذَهَبْتُ أَتَخَطَّى النَّاسَ فَقَالُوا إِلَيْكَ يَا وَابِصَةُ عَنْ رَسُولِ اللهِ ﷺ إِلَيْكَ يَا وَابِصَةُ فَقُلْتُ أَنَا وَابِصَةُ دَعُونِي أَدْنُو مِنْهُ فَإِنَّهُ مِنْ أَحَبِّ النَّاسِ إِلَيَّ أَنْ أَدْنُوَ مِنْهُ فَقَالَ لِي ادْنُ يَا وَابِصَةُ ادْنُ يَا وَابِصَةُ فَدَنَوْتُ مِنْهُ حَتَّى مَسَّتْ رُكْبَتِي رُكْبَتَهُ فَقَالَ يَا وَابِصَةُ أُخْبِرُكَ مَا جِئْتَ تَسْأَلُنِي عَنْهُ أَوْ تَسْأَلُنِي فَقُلْتُ يَا رَسُولَ اللهِ فَأَخْبِرْنِي قَالَ جِئْتَ تَسْأَلُنِي عَنِ الْبِرِّ وَالإِثْمِ قُلْتُ نَعَمْ فَجَمَعَ أَصَابِعَهُ الثَّلاَثَ فَجَعَلَ يَنْكُتُ بِهَا فِي صَدْرِي وَيَقُولُ يَا وَابِصَةُ اسْتَفْتِ نَفْسَكَ الْبِرُّ مَا اطْمَأَنَّ إِلَيْهِ الْقَلْبُ وَاطْمَأَنَّتْ إِلَيْهِ النَّفْسُ وَالإِثْمُ مَا حَاكَ فِي الْقَلْبِ وَتَرَدَّدَ فِي الصَّدْرِ وَإِنْ أَفْتَاكَ النَّاسُ وَأَفْتَوْكَ حم وأصله في م والسنن وفي بعض ألفاظه الْبِرُّ حُسْنُ الْخُلُقِ والإثْمُ مَا حَاكَ فِي صَدْرِكَ وَكَرِهتَ أَن يَطَّلِعَ عليه النَّاسُ م ت حم خد

[374]Ahmad b. Ḥanbal in *Ṭabaqāt al-Ḥanābila* (2:281).

[375]Ibn al-Subkī, *Ṭabaqāt al-Shāfi'iyya al-Kubrā* (4:134).

Qays b. Kharasha ﷺ

Al-Ṭabarānī and al-Bayhaqī narrated that Muḥammad b. Yazīd b. Abī Zyād al-Thaqafī ﷺ said that Qays b. Kharasha came to the Prophet ﷺ and said: "I pledge to you [submission] to all that came from Allah and promise I shall always speak the truth!" The Prophet ﷺ said: 276 "Qays! Perhaps, if you live long enough, you might serve, after me, under rulers to whom you will be unable to speak the truth." Qays said: "By Allah! I do not pledge anything to you except I shall fulfill it!" The Prophet ﷺ said: "In that case, no man shall ever harm you." Qays [later] became known for criticizing Zyād and his son ʿUbayd Allāh b. Zyād. News of this reached ʿUbayd Allāh who sent for him [and said]: "Are you the one who makes up lies against Allah and His Prophet?" Qays replied: "No, but if you wish, I shall tell you who makes up lies against Allah and His Prophet: whoever stops applying the Book of Allah **[506]** and the Sunna of His Prophet." "And who is that?" "You, your father, and the one who put you both in charge!" Then Qays said: "And what lie have I made up against Allah and His Prophet?" ʿUbayd Allāh said: "You claim that no man shall ever harm you?" He said yes. ʿUbayd Allāh continued: "You will learn today that you are lying. Call the torturer!" At that moment Qays leaned forward and died.[376]

عَنْ مُحَمَّدِ بْنِ أَبِي زِيَادٍ الثَّقَفِيِّ قَالَ قَدِمَ قَيْسُ بْنُ خَرَشَةَ عَلَى النَّبِيِّ ﷺ فَقَالَ أُبَايِعُكَ عَلَى مَا جَاءَكَ مِنَ اللهِ وَعَلَى أَنْ أَقُولَ بِالْحَقِّ فَقَالَ النَّبِيُّ ﷺ يَا قَيْسُ إِنْ مَدَّ بِكَ الدَّهْرُ أَنْ يَلِيَكَ بَعْدِي وُلاةٌ لا تَسْتَطِيعُ أَنْ تَقُولَ الْحَقَّ مَعَهُمْ فَقَالَ قَيْسٌ وَاللهِ

[376]Narrated by al-Ṭabarānī in *al-Kabīr* (16:349 §15271), Abū Nuʿaym in *Maʿrifat al-Ṣaḥāba* (4:2322-2323 §2438), Ibn Abī ʿĀṣim in *al-Āḥād* (5:179 §2712) and al-Ḥasan b. Sufyān in his *Musnad* cf. *Iṣāba* (5:464), *Istīʿāb* (3:1288), *Usd* (4:419), *Bidāya* (6:235), *Sīra Ḥalabiyya* (3:354), and *Khasāʾis* (2:254).

لا أُبَايِعُكَ عَلَى شَيْءٍ إِلا وَفَّيْتُ لَكَ بِهِ فَقَالَ رَسُولُ اللهِ ﷺ
إِذًا لا يَضُرُّكَ شَيْءٌ قَالَ فَكَانَ قَيْسٌ يَعِيبُ زِيَادًا وَابْنَهُ عُبَيْدَ اللهِ
بن زِيَادٍ فَأَرْسَلَ إِلَيْهِ فَقَالَ أَنْتَ الَّذِي تَفْتَرِي عَلَى اللهِ وَعَلَى
رَسُولِهِ فَقَالَ لا لَكِنْ إِنْ شِئْتَ أَخْبَرْتُكَ مَنْ يَفْتَرِي عَلَى اللهِ
وَعَلَى رَسُولِهِ مَنْ تَرَكَ الْعَمَلَ بِكِتَابِ اللهِ عَزَّ وَجَلَّ وَسُنَّةِ رَسُولِهِ
ﷺ قَالَ وَمَنْ ذَاكَ قَالَ أَنْتَ وَأَبُوكَ وَالَّذِي أَمَّرَكُمَا قَالَ قَيْسٌ
وَمَا الَّذِي افْتَرَيْتُ عَلَى رَسُولِ اللهِ ﷺ قَالَ تَزْعُمُ أَنَّهُ لَنْ يَضُرَّكَ
بَشَرٌ قَالَ نَعَمْ قَالَ لَتَعْلَمَنَّ الْيَوْمَ أَنَّكَ قَدْ كَذَبْتَ ائْتُونِي
بِصَاحِبِ الْعَذَابِ وَبِالْعَذَابِ قَالَ فَمَالَ قَيْسٌ عِنْدَ ذَلِكَ فَمَاتَ

طب أبو نعيم في المعرفة هق في الدلائل ابن أبي عاصم في الآحاد وفيه عَنْ قَيْسِ بْنِ
خَرَشَةَ رَضِيَ اللهُ عَنْهُ قَالَ جِئْتُ رَسُولَ اللهِ ﷺ فَقُلْتُ يَا رَسُولَ
اللهِ أُبَايِعُكَ عَلَى أَنْ لاَ أَخَافَ فِي الحَقِّ أَحَداً قَالَ فَتَبَسَّمَ
رَسُولُ اللهِ ﷺ الحديث

Abū Rayḥāna ﷺ

Muḥammad b. al-Rabīʿ al-Jīzī narrated from Abū Rayḥāna that the Messenger of Allah ﷺ said to him: 277 "How will you fare, Abū Rayḥāna, when you pass by certain people who use a live animal as their shooting target, then you tell them that the Messenger of Allah ﷺ forbade such an act, and they will reply: 'Recite to us the verse that was revealed concerning this'?" Abū

Rayḥāna said: "Allah and His Messenger of Allah ﷺ told the truth."[377]

عَنْ عُبَيْدِ اللهِ بْنِ أَبِي جَعْفَرٍ أَنَّهُ بَلَغَهُ عَنْ أَبِي رَيْحَانَةَ صَاحِبِ رَسُولِ اللهِ ﷺ قَالَ قَالَ رَسُولُ اللهِ ﷺ كَيْفَ بِكَ يَا أَبَا رَيْحَانَةَ لَوْ قَدْ مَرَرْتَ عَلَى قَوْمٍ قَدْ نَصَبُوا دَابَّةً يَرْمُونَهَا بِنُبْلٍ فَقُلْتُ لَهُمْ إِنَّ رَسُولَ اللهِ ﷺ قَدْ نَهَى عَنْ هَذَا فَيَقُولُونَ لَكَ اقْرَأْ عَلَيْنَا الآيَةَ الَّتِي فِيهَا هَذَا فَمَرَّ أَبُو رَيْحَانَةَ يَوْماً عَلَى قَوْمٍ قَدْ نَصَبُوا دَجَاجَةً يَرْمُونَهَا فَقَالَ إِنَّ رَسُولَ اللهِ ﷺ قَدْ نَهَى عَنْ هَذَا فَقَالُوا اقْرَأْ عَلَيْنَا الآيَةَ الَّتِي فِيهَا هَذَا فَقَالَ أَبُو رَيْحَانَةَ صَدَقَ اللهُ وَرَسُولُهُ تَأْكُلُونَهَا حَرَاماً قِمَاراً حَرَاماً وَمَيْتَةً لاَ تُذْبَحُ ابن المبارك في الزهد ابن الربيع الجيزي في مسند الصحابة الذين نزلوا مصر كما في الخصائص وقال السيوطي في درّ السحابة فيمن دخل مصر من الصحابة رضي الله عنهم أبو ريحانة الأزدي أسمه شمغون بالغين المعجمة وقيل بالمهملة ابن زيد حليف الأنصار له صحبة ورواية شهد فتح مصر ولهم عنه حديثان أو ثلاثة

ʿAmr b. al-Ḥamiq ؓ

Ibn ʿAsākir narrated that Rifāʿa b. Shaddād al-Bajalī went with ʿAmr b. al-Ḥamiq when the latter was summoned by Muʿāwiya. ʿAmr told Rifāʿa: "Rifāʿa, they are going to kill me. 278 The Messenger of Allah ﷺ told me that both jinn and human beings shall share responsibility in [shedding] my blood." Rifāʿa said:

---

[377] Narrated by Ibn al-Mubārak in *al-Zuhd* (p. 308 §883) and Ibn al-Rabīʿ al-Jīzī in *Musnad al-Saḥābat al-Ladhīna Nazalū Miṣr* as cited in al-Suyūṭī's *al-Khaṣāʾis al-Kubrā* (2:252-253).

"No sooner did he speak that I saw the reins of horses closing in so I left him. After I left a snake lunged at him and bit him. Then the riders reached him and decapitated him. His was the first head gifted in Islam."[378]

عَنْ رِفَاعَةَ بْنِ شَدَّادٍ البَجَلِيِّ وَكَانَ مُؤَاخِياً لِعَمْرِو بْنِ الحَمِقِ أَنَّهُ خَرَجَ مَعَهُ حِينَ طُلِبَ فَقَالَ لِي يَا رِفَاعَةَ إِنَّ القَوْمَ قَاتِلِي إِنَّ رَسُولَ اللهِ ﷺ أَخْبَرَنِي أَنَّ الجِنَّ وَالإِنْسَ تَشْتَرِكُ فِي دَمِي وَقَالَ لِي يَا عَمْرُو إِنْ أَمَّنَكَ رَجُلٌ عَلَى دَمِهِ فَلاَ تَقْتُلْهُ فَتَلْقَى اللهَ بِوَجْهِ غَادِرٍ قَالَ رِفَاعَةُ فَمَا أَتَمَّ حَدِيثَهُ حَتَّى رَأَيْتُ أَعِنَّةَ الخَيْلِ فَوَدَّعْتُهُ وَوَاثَبَتْهُ حَيَّةٌ فَلَسَعَتْهُ وَأَدْرَكُوهُ فَاحْتَزُّوا رَأْسَهُ فَكَانَ أَوَّلَ رَأْسٍ أُهْدِيَ فِي الإِسْلاَمِ كر

Al Aqraʿ b. Shufay al-ʿAkkī ﷺ

Ibn al-Sakan, Ibn Mandah and Ibn ʿAsākir narrated with various chains that al-Aqraʿ b. Shufay al-ʿAkkī said: "The Prophet ﷺ visited me in my sickness. I said: 'I reckon I shall die of my sickness.' The Prophet ﷺ said: [279] 'Not at all! You will definitely live on, you will definitely emigrate to the land of Shām, and you will die and be buried in al-Ramla in Palestine.'" He died in the caliphate of ʿUmar and was buried in al-Ramla.[379]

[378]Narrated by Ibn ʿAsākir (45:498). See also Ibn Ḥibbān, *Thiqāt* (3:275), *Istīʿāb* (3:1174), *Iṣāba* (4:623-624), *Khaṣāʾiṣ* (2:241), and Ibn al-Jawzī, *Talqīḥ* (p. 330 and p. 339). ʿAmr was one of ʿUthmān's killers: Ibn Saʿd (3:74), al-Ṭabarī, *Tārīkh* (2:677), *Bidāya* (7:185) but the Prophet ﷺ called him a saintly man (cf. above, section on Abū Mūsā al-Ashʿarī, second hadith) and supplicated for long life for him: al-Taymī, *Dalāʾil al-Nubuwwa* (p. 173) cf. *Iṣāba*. He was 80 when he died.

[379]Narrated from al-Aqraʿ b. Shufay al-ʿAkkī (spelt ʿUkkī or ʿUkī in al-Nabhānī but corrected after al-Suyūṭī's *Lubb al-Lubāb fīl-Ansāb*, where he says the initial *hamza* takes a *fatḥa* as the name originates from the Arab progenitor ʿAkk or the palestinian city

عَنِ الْأَقْرَعِ بْنِ شُفَيٍّ الْعَكِّيِّ قَالَ دَخَلَ عَلَيَّ النَّبِيُّ ﷺ فِي مَرَضٍ فَقُلْتُ لَا أَحْسَبُ إِلَّا أَنِّي مَيِّتٌ مِنْ مَرَضِي قَالَ النَّبِيُّ ﷺ كَلَّا لَتَبْقَيَنَّ وَلَتُهَاجِرَنَّ إِلَى أَرْضِ الشَّامِ وَتَمُوتُ وَتُدْفَنُ بِالرَّبْوَةِ مِنْ أَرْضِ فِلَسْطِينَ ابن قانع في المعجم أبو نعيم في المعرفة كر زاد السيوطي في الجامع الكبير والدر المنثور والخصائص فَمَاتَ فِي خِلَافَةِ عُمَرَ وَدُفِنَ بِالرَّمْلَةِ كذا أيضا في سبل الهدى والرشاد وزاد وروى ابن أبي حاتم وابن جرير والطبراني عَنْ مُرَّةَ الْبَهْزِيِّ سَمِعْتُ النَّبِيَّ ﷺ يَقُولُ لِرَجُلٍ إِنَّكَ تَمُوتُ بِالرَّبْوَةِ فَمَاتَ بِالرَّمْلَةِ

Al-Nuḍayr b. al-Ḥārith

Al-Wāqidī said that Ibrāhīm b. Muḥammad b. Shuraḥbīl narrated to him that his father said al-Nuḍayr b. al-Ḥārith said: "I rode out with the Quraysh to Ḥunayn. Our intention was to help against Muḥammad in case he was being routed, to no avail. When he reached al-Jiʿrāna, by Allah! I had not changed my mind in the least, when none other than the Messenger of Allah ﷺ met me face to face, exclaiming: 280 "Al- Nuḍayr!" I replied: "At your service!" He said: a "Is this better, or what you wanted to do at Ḥunayn and which Allah prevented you from doing?" I hastened to him and he said: "It is time for you to understand where you are camping in ambush!" I said: "I do see that if there were another with Allah it

---

of ʿAkkā) by Ibn Qāniʿ in *Muʿjam al-Saḥāba* (1:68 §66), Abū Nuʿaym in the *Maʿrifa* (1:339 §1058) and Ibn ʿAsākir (1:211 through Ibn Mandah) with a *musnad* chain the latter termed *gharīb gharīb* and with another, broken *(munqatiʿ)* chain cf. *Isāba* (1:103, mentioning three chains), *Khaṣāʾis* (2:218), *Istīʿāb* (1:103 -104) including also al-Ṭabarānī, Ibn Mandah and Ibn al-Sakan per al-Suyūṭī in *al-Durr al-Manthūr* (6:102) and elsewhere as well as Ibn Kathīr in *Jāmiʿ al-Asānīd* (1:377 §386).

would have helped us. I truly bear witness that there is no god but Allah and that Muḥammad is the Messenger of Allah!" He ﷺ said: b "O Allah! Make him more steadfast." Al-Nuḍayr said: "By the One Who sent him with the truth! My heart became as firm as a rock in the Religion and in recognition of the truth." Ibn Sa'd and al-Bayhaqī narrated it.[380]

عَنْ النَّضِيرِ بْنِ الحَارِثِ خَرَجَ رَسُولُ اللهِ ﷺ إِلَى حُنَيْنٍ فَخَرَجْتُ مَعَ قَوْمِي مِنْ قُرَيشٍ وَهُمْ عَلَى دِينِهِمْ بَعْدُ وَنَحْنُ نُرِيدُ إِنْ كَانَتْ دَبْرَةٌ عَلَى مُحَمَّدٍ أَنْ نُعِينَ عَلَيْهِ فَلَمْ يُمْكِنَّا ذَلِكَ فَلَمَّا صَارَ بِالجِعْرَانَةِ فَوَاللهِ إِنِّي لَعَلَى مَا أَنَا عَلَيْهِ إِنْ شَعَرْتُ إِلاَّ بِرَسُولِ اللهِ ﷺ تَلَقَّانِي كَفَّةً كَفَّةً فَقَالَ النَّضِيرُ قُلْتُ لَبَّيْكَ قَالَ هَذَا خَيْرٌ مِمَّا أَرَدْتَ يَوْمَ حُنَيْنٍ مِمَّا حَالَ اللهُ بَيْنَكَ وَبَيْنَهُ قَالَ فَأَقْبَلْتُ إِلَيْهِ مُسْرِعاً فَقَالَ قَدْ آنَ لَكَ أَنْ تُبْصِرَ مَا أَنْتَ فِيهِ مُوضِعٌ قُلْتُ قَدْ أَرَى أَنَّهُ لَوْ كَانَ مَعَ اللهِ غَيْرُهُ لَقَدْ أَغْنَى شَيْئاً وَإِنِّي أَشْهَدُ أَنْ لاَ إِلَهَ إِلاَّ اللهُ وَحْدَهُ لاَ شَرِيكَ لَهُ فَقَالَ رَسُولُ اللهِ ﷺ اللهُمَّ زِدْهُ ثَبَاتاً قَالَ النَّضِيرُ فَوَالَّذِي بَعَثَهُ بِالحَقِّ لَكَانَ قَلْبِي حَجَراً ثَبَاتاً فِي الدِّينِ وَبَصِيرَةً فِي الحَقِّ فَقَالَ رَسُولُ اللهِ ﷺ الحَمْدُ للهِ الَّذِي هَدَاكَ ابن سعد هق في الدلائل

[380]Narrated by through Wāqidī by Ibn Sa'd (Sallūmī ed. 1:261); Bayhaqī, *Dalā'il* (5:205-206) cf. *Isāba* (6:436) and *Bidāya* (4:364). Neither Ibrāhīm b. Muhammad b. Shuraḥbīl nor his father are known and there may be a link missing between the latter and al-Nuḍayr. Nabhānī has al-Naḍr but that is the name of his brother who was killed as an unbeliever cf. Suyūṭī, *Khasā'is* (1:447), killed by 'Alī at al-Ṣafrā' on the day of Badr. Ji'rāna (also al-Ji'irrāna but Ibn Ḥajar prefers *takhfīf*) is an oasis between Mecca and Ṭā'if cf. Yāqūt.

Qabāth b. Ashyam al-Laythī ؓ

Al-Ṭabarānī narrated from [Zabbān] b. Salmān that his father said the reason Qabāth b. Ashyam entered Islam was that some Bedouin Arabs visited him, saying: "Muḥammad has taken up arms and is calling people to a different religion from ours." Qabāth went to see the Messenger of Allah ﷺ. When he entered his presence the Prophet ﷺ said to him: [281] "Sit, Qabāth." Qabāth became speechless. The Messenger of Allah ﷺ said to him: [a] "Are you the one who said that if the women of Quraysh came out with their claws *(akimmatihā)* they could repel Muḥammad and his friends?" Qabāth said: "By the One Who sent you with the truth! My tongue did not form such words nor did my lips mumble them, nor did anyone hear me say them, but it was only something that stirred in myself! I bear witness that there is no God but Allah alone, without partner; that Muḥammad is the Messenger of Allah; and that what you brought is the truth!"[381]

عَنْ أَصْبَغُ بن عَبْدِ الْعَزِيزِ حَدَّثَنِي أَبِي عَنْ جَدِّهِ أَبَانَ عَنْ أَبِيهِ سُلَيْمَانَ قَالَ كَانَ إِسْلامُ قَبَاثِ بن أَشْيَمَ اللَّيْثِيُّ أَنَّ رَجُلا مِنْ قَوْمِهِ وَغَيْرِهِمْ مِنَ الْعَرَبِ أَتَوْهُ فَقَالُوا إِنَّ مُحَمَّدَ بن عَبْدِ الْمُطَّلِبِ قَدْ خَرَجَ يَدْعُو إِلَى دَيْنٍ غَيْرِ دِينِنَا فَقَامَ قَبَاثٌ حَتَّى أَتَى رَسُولَ اللهِ ﷺ فَلَمَّا دَخَلَ عَلَيْهِ قَالَ لَهُ اِجْلِسْ يَا قَبَاثُ فَأَوْجَمَ قَبَاثٌ (أي بُهِتَ) فَقَالَ لَهُ رَسُولُ اللهِ ﷺ أَنْتَ الْقَائِلُ لَوْ خَرَجَتْ نِسَاءُ قُرَيْشٍ بِأَكِمَّتِهَا رَدَّتْ مُحَمَّدًا وَأَصْحَابَهُ فَقَالَ قَبَاثٌ

[381] Narrated by al-Ṭabarānī in *al-Kabīr* (19:35) and *al-Awsat* (5:146), Abū Nuʿaym in the *Maʿrifa*, Ibn ʿAsākir (49:232-233) and al-Ḥākim (1990 ed. 3:724) cf. *Bidāya* (3:301) and *Khasā'is* (1:343-344), all through unknown narrators cf. al-Haythamī (8:287). Al-Nabhānī spells Ibn Salmān's name Abān after al-Ḥākim but see "Zabbān" in al-Mizzī's *Tahdhīb* and Ibn Ḥajar's *Taqrīb*. Some of the Scholars prefer the spelling Qubāth.

وَالَّذِي بَعَثَكَ بِالْحَقِّ مَا تَحَرَّكَ بِهِ لِسَانِي وَلَا تَزَمْزَمَتْ بِهِ شَفَتَايَ وَلَا سَمِعَهُ مِنِّي أَحَدٌ وَمَا هُوَ إِلَّا شَيْءٌ هَجَسَ فِي نَفْسِي أَشْهَدُ أَنْ لَا إِلَهَ إِلَّا اللَّهُ وَحْدَهُ لَا شَرِيكَ لَهُ وَأَشْهَدُ أَنَّ مُحَمَّدًا رَسُولُ اللَّهِ وَأَنَّ مَا جِئْتَ بِهِ لَحَقٌّ ك طب طس أبو نعيم في المعرفة كر

Al-Bayhaqī narrated that al-Wāqidī said the authorities said that Qabāth b. Ashyam al-Kinānī said: "I fought at Badr with the polytheists. [507] Verily I saw the small number of Muḥammad's friends and how many we were with our horses and our men, yet I was routed together with the rest of them! I found myself staring at the pagans from every possible side and saying to myself: 'I never saw anything like this. They all fled from him except the women!' After the battle of the Trench I became convinced of the truth of Islam so I went to see the Messenger of Allah ﷺ. I greeted him and he said: 282 'Qabāth! Are you the one who said, the day of the battle of Badr: I never saw anything like this, they all fled from him except the women?' Hearing this, I said, 'I bear witness that you are the Messenger of Allah! I never told anyone what you just said nor did I even mumble it, but it was something I thought to myself! If you were not a Prophet, Allah would not have shown it to you.' Then he invited me to Islam and I accepted."[382]

عَنِ الْوَاقِدِيِّ قَالُوا وَكَانَ قُبَاثُ بْنُ أَشْيَمَ الْكِنَانِيُّ يَقُولُ شَهِدْتُ مَعَ الْمُشْرِكِينَ بَدْرًا وَإِنِّي لَأَنْظُرُ إِلَى قِلَّةِ أَصْحَابِ مُحَمَّدٍ ﷺ فِي عَيْنِي وَكَثْرَةِ مَا مَعَنَا مِنَ الْخَيْلِ وَالرِّجَالِ فَانْهَزَمْتُ فِيمَنِ انْهَزَمَ فَلَقَدْ رَأَيْتُنِي وَإِنِّي لَأَنْظُرُ إِلَى الْمُشْرِكِينَ فِي كُلِّ وَجْهٍ وَإِنِّي لَأَقُولُ

---

[382] Narrated by al-Wāqidī (1:97-98), al-Bayhaqī in the *Dalā'il* (3:150) and Ibn ʿAsākir (49:232-234) cf. *Khaṣā'is* (1:343), *Bidāya* (3:301).

فِي نَفْسِي مَا رَأَيْتُ مِثْلَ هَذَا الأَمْرِ فَرَّ مِنْهُ إِلاَّ النِّسَاءُ فَلَمَّا كَانَ بَعْدَ الْخَنْدَقِ قُلْتُ لَوْ قَدِمْتُ الْمَدِينَةَ فَنَظَرْتُ مَا يَقُولُ مُحَمَّدٌ ﷺ وَقَدْ وَقَعَ فِي قَلْبِي الإِسْلاَمُ فَقَدِمْت الْمَدِينَةَ فَسَأَلْتُ عَنْ رَسُولِ اللهِ ﷺ فَقَالُوا هُوَ ذَاكَ فِي ظِلِّ الْمَسْجِدِ مَعَ مَلأٍ مِنْ أَصْحَابِهِ فَأَتَيْتُهُ وَأَنَا لاَ أَعْرِفُهُ مِنْ بَيْنِهِمْ فَسَلَّمْتُ فَقَالَ يَا قُبَاث بْنَ أَشْيَمَ أَنْتَ الْقَائِلُ يَوْمَ بَدْرٍ مَا رَأَيْتُ مِثْلَ هَذَا الأَمْرِ فَرَّ مِنْهُ إِلاَّ النِّسَاءُ قُلْتُ أَشْهَدُ أَنَّكَ رَسُولُ اللهِ وَأَنَّ هَذَا الأَمْرَ مَا خَرَجَ مِنِّي إِلَى أَحَدٍ قَطُّ وَمَا تَرَمْرَمْتُ بِهِ إِلاَّ شَيْئًا حَدَّثْتُ بِهِ نَفْسِي فَلَوْلاَ أَنَّك نَبِيٌّ مَا أَطْلَعَكَ اللهُ عَلَيْهِ فَعَرَضَ عَلَيَّ الإِسْلاَمَ فَأَسْلَمْتُ الواقدي وعنه هق في الدلائل كلاهما معلق وأسنده كر من طريق ابن منده

Muʿāwiya al-Laythī ؓ

Ibn Saʿd and al-Bayhaqī narrated that al-ʿAlā' b. Muḥammad al-Thaqafī said <that Anas said>: "We were with the Messenger of Allah ﷺ in Tabūk when the sun rose all white, with its full heat and light, as I never saw it happen before. Jibrīl came to the Prophet ﷺ who said: [283] 'Jibrīl, why did the sun rise today all white, with its full heat and light, as I never saw it happen before?' He replied: 'This is because Muʿāwiya b. Muʿāwiya al-Laythī died in Madīna today, so Allah sent down 70,000 angels to pray over him.' The Prophet ﷺ asked why and Jibrīl said: 'Because he used to recite in abundance ﴾***Qul huwa Allāhu aḥad***﴿ [Sūra 112] by night and by day, walking, standing and sitting. Shall I fold up the earth so you can pray over him?' He said yes, and he prayed over him."[383]

عَنْ أَنَسَ بْنَ مَالِكٍ رَضِيَ اللهُ عَنْهُ قَالَ كُنَّا مَعَ رَسُولِ اللهِ ﷺ بِتَبُوكَ فَطَلَعَتِ الشَّمْسُ بَيْضَاءَ وَنُورٌ وَشُعَاعٌ لَمْ نَرَهَا طَلَعَتْ فِيمَا مَضَى فَأَتَى جِبْرِيلُ النَّبِيَّ ﷺ فَقَالَ لَهُ يَا جِبْرِيلُ مَا لِي أَرَى الشَّمْسَ الْيَوْمَ طَلَعَتْ بَيْضَاءَ وَنُورٌ وَشُعَاعٌ لَمْ أَرَهَا طَلَعَتْ بِهِ فِيمَا مَضَى قَالَ ذَاكَ أَنَّ مُعَاوِيَةَ بْنَ مُعَاوِيَةَ اللَّيْثِيَّ مَاتَ الْيَوْمَ فَبَعَثَ اللهُ إِلَيْهِ سَبْعِينَ أَلْفَ مَلَكٍ يُصَلُّونَ عَلَيْهِ قَالَ وَفِيمَ ذَاكَ قَالَ كَانَ يُكْثِرُ قِرَاءَةَ ﴿**قُلْ هُوَ اللهُ أَحَدٌ**﴾ بِاللَّيْلِ وَالنَّهَارِ فِي مَمْشَاهُ وَقِيَامِهِ وَقُعُودِهِ فَهَلْ لَكَ يَا رَسُولَ اللهِ أَنْ أَقْبِضَ لَكَ الأَرْضَ فَتُصَلِّيَ عَلَيْهِ قَالَ نَعَمْ فَصَلَّى عَلَيْهِ ثُمَّ رَجَعَ أحمد بن منيع في المسند ع أبو نعيم في المعرفة هق وفي الدلائل كر وفي معجم الشيوخ جميعهم من طريق العلاء بن محمد الثقفي متروك مج

[383]Narrated from Anas by Abū Ya'lā (7:256-257 §4267), Ibn 'Asākir (45:69-70) and al-Bayhaqī in the *Sunan al-Kubrā* (4:50 §6823) and *Dalā'il al-Nubuwwa* (5:245-246), all through al-'Alā' b. Zayd Abū Muḥammad al-Thaqafī who is discarded as a narrator and accused of forgery cf. Ibn Ḥibbān, *Majrūḥīn* (2:181 *munkar*), Ibn al-Jawzī, *'Ilal* (1:298), al-Haythamī (9:378), *Zād* (1:520), *Mīzān* (5:123), Ibn Kathīr, *Tafsīr* (4:570). The latter and Ibn Ḥajar (*Iṣāba* 6:160) mention that the report comes through other chains, among them that of 'Aṭā' b. Abī Maymūna as in al-Nabhānī's next entry cf. Abū Ya'lā (7:258 §4268), al-Ṭabarānī in the *Kabīr* (19:429-429 §1040), Abū Nu'aym in the *Ma'rifa*, and al-Bayhaqī in the *Sunan* (4:51) and *Dalā'il* (5:246), all through Maḥbūb b. Hilāl who is unknown cf. al-Haythamī (3:37-38) and al-Dhahabī. Cited in al-Nawawī's *al-Majmū'* (5:253 *ḍa'īf*), *al-Khaṣā'is* (1:461), *al-Bidāya* (5:14-15 *munkar*), *Fatḥ* (3:188), *Sifat al-Safwa* (1:677), *Nayl* (4:89), and al-Zurqānī's *Sharḥ al-Muwaṭṭa'* (2:81).

Ibn Saʿd and al-Bayhaqī also narrated through another chain from ʿAṭāʾ b. Abī Maymūna, and Abū Yaʿlā from Anas, with the wording: Jibrīl came and said: "Muḥammad! Muʿāwiya b. Muʿāwiya al-Muzanī died. Do you wish to pray over him?" He said yes, whereupon Jibrīl struck down his two wings and neither tree nor elevation remained except they shrank and his bier was raised up before him so that he could gaze upon it. He prayed on him with two rows of angels [praying] behind him, each row numbering seventy thousand angels. He [the narrator] said that the Prophet ﷺ said, "I asked: [284] 'Jibrīl! How was he granted such a rank by Allah?' He said, 'Through his love for ﴿***Qul huwa Allāhu aḥad***﴾ which he recited standing and sitting, coming and going, and on every occasion.'"[384]

عَنْ أَنَسِ بْنِ مَالِكٍ قَالَ نَزَلَ جِبْرِيلُ عَلَى النَّبِيِّ ﷺ قَالَ يَا مُحَمَّدُ مَاتَ مُعَاوِيَةُ بْنُ مَعَاوِيَةَ اللَّيْثِيُّ أَفَتُحِبُّ أَنْ تُصَلِّيَ عَلَيْهِ قَالَ نَعَمْ فَضَرَبَ بِجَنَاحِهِ الأَرْضَ فَلَمْ تَبْقَ شَجَرَةٌ وَلاَ أَكْمَةٌ إِلاَّ تَضَعْضَعَتْ فَرَفَعَ سَرِيرَهُ فَنَظَرَ إِلَيْهِ وَصَلَّى عَلَيْهِ وَخَلْفَهُ صَفَّانِ مِنَ الْمَلاَئِكَةِ فِي كُلِّ صَفٍّ سَبْعُونَ أَلْفَ مَلَكٍ فَقَالَ النَّبِيُّ ﷺ يَا جِبْرِيلُ لِمَ نَالَ هَذِهِ الْمَنْزِلَةَ مِنَ اللهِ قَالَ بِحُبِّهِ ﴿**قُلْ هُوَ اللهُ أَحَدٌ**﴾ وَقِرَاءَتِهِ إِيَّاهَا ذَهَابًا وَإِيَابًا وَقَائِمًا وَقَاعِدًا عَلَى كُلِّ حَالٍ

ع طب هق وفي الدلائل جميعهم من طريق محبوب بن هلال قال الذهبي مجهول لا يتابع على هذا

[384] See previous note.

'Awf b. Mālik al-Ashja'ī

Ibn Ishāq and al-Bayhaqī narrated that 'Awf b. Mālik al-Ashja'ī said: "I was in the raid of al-Salāsil together with Abū Bakr and 'Umar when I passed by people that had slaughtered a camel but were unable to cut it up and divide its meat. I was a knowledgeable butcher, so I told them: 'If you give me a tenth of the meat, I will cut it and divide it among you.' They agreed. I divided it, took one tenth and carried it to my companions. We ate our fill then Abū Bakr and 'Umar asked, 'From where did you get this meat, 'Awf?' I told them. They said, 'You were wrong to feed us from this!' Then they got up and began to vomit. When everyone returned home, I was the first one to come to the Messenger of Allah ﷺ. He said, ''Awf <b. Mālik>?' I said yes. He continued: 'The camel-meat man?' He did not add anything."[385]

عَنْ عَوْفِ بْنِ مَالِكٍ الأَشْجَعِيّ قَالَ كُنْتُ فِي الْغَزَاةِ الَّتِي بَعَثَ فِيهَا رَسُولُ اللهِ ﷺ عَمْرَو بْنَ الْعَاصِ إِلَى ذَاتِ السَّلاَسِلِ قَالَ فَصَحِبْتُ أَبَا بَكْرٍ وَعُمَرَ فَمَرَرْتُ بِقَوْمٍ عَلَى جَزُورٍ لَهُمْ قَدْ نَحَرُوهَا وَهُمْ لاَ يَقْدِرُونَ عَلَى أَنْ يُبَعْضُوهَا قَالَ وَكُنْتُ امْرَأً لَبِقًا جَازِرًا قَالَ فَقُلْتُ أَتُعْطُونَنِي مِنْهَا عَشِيرًا عَلَى أَنْ أَقْسِمَهَا بَيْنَكُمْ قَالُوا نَعَمْ قَالَ فَأَخَذْتُ الشَّفْرَتَيْنِ فَجَزَّأْتُهَا مَكَانِي وَأَخَذْتُ مِنْهَا جُزْءًا فَحَمَلْتُهُ إِلَى أَصْحَابِي فَاطَّبَخْنَاهُ فَأَكَلْنَاهُ فَقَالَ لِي أَبُو بَكْرٍ وَعُمَرُ رَضِيَ اللهُ عَنْهُمَا أَنَّى لَكَ هَذَا اللَّحْمُ

---

[385]Narrated by Ahmad with a strong chain, al-Tabarānī in *al-Kabīr* (18:71), al-Bayhaqī in *al-Sunan al-Kubrā* (6:120 §11433), all three with 'Umar and Abū 'Ubayda b. al-Jarrāh instead of Abū Bakr and they did not eat then vomit but both refused to touch the meat in the first place. Al-Nabhānī is citing the broken-chained version of Ibn Hishām (6:38) cf. *Bidāya* (4:275), *Iktifā'* (2:305), and *Khasā'is* (1:434).

يَا عَوْفُ قَالَ فَأَخْبَرْتهمَا خَبَرَهُ فَقَالاَ وَاللهِ مَا أَحْسَنْت حِينَ قَالَ فَلَمّا قَفَلَ النّاسُ مِنْ ذَلِكَ السّفَرِ كُنْت أَوّلَ قَادِمٍ عَلَى رَسُولِ اللهِ ﷺ قَالَ فَجِئْته وَهُوَ يُصَلّي فِي بَيْتِهِ قَالَ فَقُلْت السّلاَمُ عَلَيْك يَا رَسُولَ اللهِ وَرَحْمَةُ اللهِ وَبَرَكَاتُهُ قَالَ أَعَوْفُ بْنُ مَالِكٍ قَالَ قُلْت نَعَمْ بِأَبِي أَنْتَ وَأُمّي قَالَ أَصَاحِبُ الْجَزُورِ وَلَمْ يَزِدْنِي رَسُولُ اللهِ ﷺ عَلَى ذَلِكَ شَيْئًا ابن هشام هق في الدلائل بإسناد منقطع لكن وصله غيرهما واختلفت ألفاظه فعند حم وهق غَزَوْنَا وَعَلَيْنَا عَمْرُو بْنُ الْعَاصِ فَأَصَابَتْنَا مَخْمَصَةٌ فَمَرُّوا عَلَى قَوْمٍ قَدْ نَحَرُوا جَزُورًا فَقُلْتُ أُعَالِجُهَا لَكُمْ عَلَى أَنْ تُطْعِمُونِي مِنْهَا شَيْئًا وَقَالَ إِبْرَاهِيمُ فَتُطْعِمُونِي مِنْهَا فَعَالَجْتُهَا ثُمَّ أَخَذْتُ الَّذِي أَعْطَوْنِي فَأَتَيْتُ بِهِ عُمَرَ بْنَ الْخَطَّابِ فَأَبَى أَنْ يَأْكُلَهُ ثُمَّ أَتَيْتُ بِهِ أَبَا عُبَيْدَةَ بْنَ الْجَرَّاحِ فَقَالَ مِثْلَ مَا قَالَ عُمَرُ بْنُ الْخَطَّابِ وَأَبَى أَنْ يَأْكُلَ ثُمَّ إِنِّي بُعِثْتُ إِلَى رَسُولِ اللهِ ﷺ بَعْدَ ذَاكَ فِي فَتْحِ مَكَّةَ فَقَالَ أَنْتَ صَاحِبُ الْجَزُورِ فَقُلْتُ نَعَمْ يَا رَسُولَ اللهِ لَمْ يَزِدْنِي عَلَى ذَلِكَ وفي طب فَذَكَرْتُ ذَلِكَ لِعُمَرَ بن الْخَطَّابِ فَقَالَ قَدْ تَعَجَّلْتَ أَجْرَهُ وَمَا أَنَا بِآكِلِهِ وَقَالَ أَبُو عُبَيْدَةَ مِثْلَ ذَلِكَ فَتَقَدَّمَ عَلَى النَّبِيِّ ﷺ فَلَمَّا رَآنِي قَالَ يَا صَاحِبَ الْجَزُورِ وفي الواقدي ثُمّ قَامَا يَتَقَيّآنِ فَلَمّا فَعَلَ ذَلِكَ أَبُو بَكْرٍ وَعُمَرُ فَعَلَ ذَلِكَ الْجَيْشُ وَقَالَ أَبُو

بَكْرٍ وَعُمَرُ رَضِيَ اللهُ عَنْهُمَا لِعَوْفٍ تَعَجَّلْتَ أَجْرَكَ ثُمَّ أَتَى أَبَا عُبَيْدَةَ فَقَالَ لَهُ مِثْلَ ذَلِكَ

The Delegation of ʿAbd al-Qays ﷺ

Abū Yaʿlā and al-Bayhaqī narrated that Mazīda [b. Mālik b. Hammām b. Muʿāwiya b. Shabāba b. ʿĀmir b. Ḥuṭma b. 'Āmr b. Muḥārib b. ʿAbd al-Qays al-'Abdī] al-'Aṣarī said: "As the Prophet ﷺ was talking to his Companions, suddenly, he said to them: 286 'A group of riders are about to come into your sight from this direction who are the best of the people of the East *(khayr ahl al-mashriq)*!' ʿUmar rose and went in that direction. He met thirteen riders. He asked, 'Who are you?' They said: 'From the Banū ʿAbd al-Qays.'"[386] **[508]**

عَنْ مَزِيدَةَ جَدِّ هُودٍ الْعَصَرِيِّ قَالَ بَيْنَمَا رَسُولُ اللهِ ﷺ يُحَدِّثُ أَصْحَابَهُ إِذْ قَالَ لَهُمْ سَيَطْلُعُ عَلَيْكُمْ مِنْ هَذَا الْوَجْهِ رَكْبٌ هُمْ خَيْرُ أَهْلِ الْمَشْرِقِ فَقَامَ عُمَرُ بن الْخَطَّابِ يَتَوَجَّهُ فِي ذَلِكَ الْوَجْهِ فَلَقِيَ ثَلاثَةَ عَشَرَ رَاكِبًا فَرَحَّبَ وَقَرَّبَ وَقَالَ مَنِ الْقَوْمُ

[386]Narrated from Mazīda as part of a long ḥadīth by Abū Yaʿlā (12:245-247 §6850), al-Ṭabarānī in *al-Kabīr* (20:345) through trustworthy narrators cf. al-Haythamī (9:388), Ibn Saʿd, al-Bukhārī in *al-Adab al-Mufrad* (p. 308-309 §1198), Ibn Abī ʿĀṣim in *al-Āḥād wal-Mathānī* (3:314 §1690), al-Bayhaqī, and Ibn al-Muqrī in *Taqbīl al-Yad* (p. 66 §6), the latter with the addition "some of them walked, some of them made haste, and some of them ran to the Prophet ﷺ. They took his hand and kissed it." Cited in al-Hakīm al-Tirmidhī's *Nawādir* (4:47), *Fath* (1:131 and 8:58), and *Bidāya* (5:47) all with the same chain as Imam al-Tirmidhī's lone-narrator ḥadīth in the *Sunan*: "The Prophet ﷺ entered [Mecca] the day of the Conquest carrying a sword adorned with gold and silver," which he graded *ḥasan gharīb* while al-Dhahabī in the *Mīzān* (3:456) endorses Ibn al-Qaṭṭān's weakening of al-Tirmidhī's chain, but Ibn Ḥajar strengthens the hadith in the *Fatḥ*. Mazīda's *nasab* is spelled al-Ghaḍarī in al-Nabhānī and al-Qaṣarī elsewhere but al-'Aṣarī in Ibn Ḥajar who adds that Ibn Mandah identifies Mazīda's father as Jābir while Ibn al-Kalbī and Ibn Saʿd have Mālik.

قَالُوا نَفَرٌ مِنْ عَبْدِ الْقَيْسِ طب ع ابن سعد ابن أبي عاصم في الآحاد ورواه خد مطولا

Ibn Shāhīn narrated that Ḥusayn b. Muhammad said: My father narrated to us: Ja'far b. al-Ḥākim al-'Abdī narrated to us from Ṣuḥār b. al-ʿAbbās and Mazīda b. Mālik among others from ʿAbd al-Qays that al-Ashajj – Ashajj ʿAbd al-Qays [al-'Abdī] – had a friendship with a monk in Dārayn. One year that monk told him that a Prophet was about to appear in Mecca who accepted gifts but not alms, bore a certain mark between his shoulders, and would gain supremacy over all the religions. Then the monk died. Al-Ashajj sent out his nephew who arrived in Mecca the year of the Emigration. He met the Prophet ﷺ and ascertained the truth of the portent then entered Islam. 287 The Prophet ﷺ taught him ﴿**al-Ḥamd**﴾ [Sūrat al-Fātiḥa] and ﴿**Iqra' bismi Rabbik**﴾ [Sūra 96] then told him: a "Invite your maternal uncle to Islam." He returned and recounted everything to al-Ashajj. The latter entered Islam but kept it secret for a while, then rode out in a group of sixteen men and came to Madīna. The Prophet ﷺ came out the night before the morning they arrived and said: "Lo! A group of riders from the East are about to come who were not forced to enter Islam. Their leader bears a mark." Then al-Ashajj ["Headwounded"][387] of ʿAbd al-Qays came with a group of his people. This took place in the year of the Conquest [of Mecca].[388]

عَنْ صَحَّارِ بْنِ العَبَّاسِ وَمَزِيدَةَ بْنِ مَالِكٍ عَنْ نَفَرٍ مِنْ عَبْدِ الْقَيْسِ قَالُوا كَانَ الأَشَجُّ أَشَجُّ عَبْدِ الْقَيْسِ وَاسْمُهُ المُنْذِرُ بْنُ

[387]His face was scarred from the kick of a mule in his childhood.

[388]Cited from Ibn Shāhīn in the *Iṣāba* (3:410) and *Khasā'is* (1:224). Ibn Saʿd (5:564) narrates it without chain. Al-Nabhānī has the spelling Ṣukhār. Ibn Shāhīn and Ibn Ḥajar identify al-Ashajj's full name as al-Mundhir b. ʿĀ'idh b. al-Ḥārith al-ʿAṣarī and his nephew as ʿAmr b. ʿAbd Qays while Ibn Saʿd and al-Baghawī identify al Ashajj as ʿAbd Allāh b. ʿAwf. Ibn Ḥajar said there could be two men thus nicknamed. Dārīn was a coastal marketplace in Baḥrayn for musk traders coming from India cf. Yāqūt.

عَائِذِ بْنِ الْحَارِثِ بْنِ الْمُنْذِرِ بْنِ النُّعْمَانِ الْعَصَرِيُّ صَدِيقاً لِرَاهِبٍ يَنْزِلُ بِدَارَيْنِ فَكَانَ يَلْقَاهُ فِي كُلِّ عَامٍ فَلَقِيَهُ عَاماً بِالزَّارَةِ فَأَخْبَرَ الْأَشَجَّ أَنَّ نَبِيّاً يَخْرُجُ بِمَكَّةَ يَأْكُلُ الْهَدِيَّةَ وَلَا يَأْكُلُ الصَّدَقَةَ بَيْنَ كَتِفَيْهِ عَلَامَةٌ يَظْهَرُ عَلَى الْأَدْيَانِ ثُمَّ مَاتَ الرَّاهِبُ فَبَعَثَ الْأَشَجُّ ابْنَ أُخْتٍ لَهُ مِنْ بَنِي عَامِرِ بْنِ عَصَرٍ يُقَالُ لَهُ عَمْرُو بْنُ عَبْدِ الْقَيْسِ وَهُوَ عَلَى بِنْتِهِ أُمَامَةَ بِنْتِ الْأَشَجِّ فَأَتَى مَكَّةَ عَامَ الْهِجْرَةِ فَذَكَرَ الْقِصَّةَ فِي لُقِيِّهِ النَّبِيَّ ﷺ وَصِحَّةِ الْعَلَامَاتِ وَإِسْلَامِهِ وَأَنَّهُ عَلَّمَهُ ﴿اَلْحَمْدُ﴾ وَ﴿اِقْرَأْ بِاسْمِ رَبِّكَ﴾ وَقَالَ لَهُ ادْعُ خَالَكَ إِلَى الْإِسْلَامِ فَرَجَعَ وَجَاءَ الْأَشَجُّ فَأَخْبَرَهُ الْخَبَرَ فَأَسْلَمَ الْأَشَجُّ وَكَتَمَ الْإِسْلَامَ حِيناً ثُمَّ خَرَجَ فِي سِتَّةَ عَشَرَ رَجُلاً مِنْ أَهْلِ هَجَرَ فَقَدِمُوا الْمَدِينَةَ فَخَرَجَ النَّبِيُّ ﷺ فِي اللَّيْلَةِ الَّتِي قَدِمُوا فِي صُبْحِهَا فَقَالَ لَيَأْتِيَنَّ رَكْبٌ مِنْ قِبَلِ الْمَشْرِقِ وَلَمْ يُكْرَهُوا عَلَى الْإِسْلَامِ لِصَاحِبِهِمْ عَلَامَةٌ فَقَدِمُوا فَقَالَ اللهُمَّ اغْفِرْ لِعَبْدِ الْقَيْسِ وَكَانَ قُدُومُهُمْ عَامَ الْفَتْحِ ابن شاهين كما ذكره ابن حجر بإسناده في الإصابة ونحوه ابن سعد

Ibn Saʿd narrated from ʿUrwa that the Prophet ﷺ looked at the horizon in the early morning preceding the night in which the delegation of ʿAbd al-Qays arrived: "Lo! [288] A group of riders from the East are about to come who were not forced to enter Islam. They have exhausted their mounts and supplies. Their leader bears a distinguishing mark. [a] O Allah! Forgive ʿAbd al-

Qays. They came without asking me for wealth. They are the best of the people of the East." They arrived in a group of twenty men led by ʿAbd Allāh b. ʿAwf al-Ashajj as the Messenger of Allah ﷺ was in the Mosque. They greeted him and he greeted them. The Messenger of Allah ﷺ then asked them: [b] "Which of you is ʿAbd Allāh b. ʿAwf al-Ashajj?" He said: "I, Messenger of Allah!" He was a diminutive man *(damīm)*. The Messenger of Allah ﷺ looked at him. Al-Ashajj said: "The hides of men are not used to make water-pails *(lā yusta[s]qā fī musūk al-rijāl)*.[389] All that is needed from a man is the two smallest parts of him: his tongue and his heart." <The Messenger of Allah ﷺ said: [c] "In you are two well-defined traits Allah loves: forbearance *(ḥilm)* and equanimity *(anāt)*.">[390] He said: "Is it something that happened over time or was I created thus?" The Prophet ﷺ said: "No, [d] you were created thus."[391]

[In Abū Dāwūd and Aḥmad: He said: "Messenger of Allah, did I acquire those two traits or did Allah create me possessing them?" The Prophet ﷺ said: "Nay, [289] Allah created you possessing them." He replied: "Praise and thanks to Allah Who created me with two traits Allah and His Prophet love."]

[389]Singular *mask*, animal leather hide. I.e. my smallness is not

[390]The bracketed segment is narrated from Abū Saʿīd al-Khudrī by Muslim, Ibn Mājah, and Aḥmad; Ibn ʿAbbās by Muslim, al-Tirmidhī *(hasan saḥīḥ gharīb)* and Ibn Mājah; Zāriʿ b. ʿĀmir al-ʿAbdī by Abū Dāwūd, al-Bukhārī in *al-Adab al-Mufrad* (§975), and Ibn Abī ʿĀṣim in *al-Āḥād wal-Mathānī* (3:304-306 §1684); Ashajj himself by al-Bukhārī in *al-Adab al-Mufrad* (p. 205 §584) and Aḥmad both with a broken chain cf. al-Haythamī (9:387-388) contrary to the grading of *saḥīḥ* forwarded by Shuʿayb and ʿAbd al-Qādir al-Arna'ūṭ in their edition of Ibn al-Qayyim's *Zād al-Maʿād* (3:532n.); Ibn ʿUmar by al-Ṭabarānī with two good chains cf. al-Haythamī (9:388); Mazīda (cf. note 386); and an unnamed Companion by Aḥmad in *Faḍā'il al-Ṣaḥāba* (2:830 §1515). Some versions have *ḥayā'* instead of *anāt*.

[391]Narrated *mursal* from ʿUrwa b. al-Zubayr through al-Wāqidī and from ʿAbd al-Ḥamīd b. Jaʿfar b. ʿAbd Allāh b. al-Ḥakam from his father by Ibn Saʿd (1:314) cf. *Khaṣā'is* (2:26) and *Sīra Ḥalabiyya* (3:251). The delegation were forty in al-Ṭabarānī and al-Dūlābī cf. *Iṣāba* (7:111). The Prophet's ﷺ calling the Banū ʿAbd al-Qays the best of the people of the East is narrated from Ibn ʿAbbās by Aḥmad, Ṭabarānī in *al-Kabīr* (12:230, 20:345), Abū Yaʿlā (12:246), Ibn Ḥibbān (16:283) and Ibn Abī ʿĀṣim, *al-Āḥād* (3:257); Abū Hurayra by al-Ṭabarānī in *al-Awsat* (2:171) and Abū Yaʿlā (10:449); Murthid b. ʿAdī al-Ṭā'ī by Ibn Qāniʿ b. *Muʿjam al-Saḥāba* (3:69); and Mazīda (cf. note 386).

عَنْ عُرْوَةَ بْنِ الزُّبَيْرِ وَجَعْفَر بْنِ عَبْدِ اللهِ الأَنْصَارِيِّ قَالاَ نَظَرَ رَسُولُ اللهِ ﷺ إِلَى الأُفُقِ صَبِيحَةَ لَيْلَةِ قُدُومِ وَفْدِ عَبْدِ الْقَيْسِ وَقَالَ لَيَأْتِيَنَّ رَكْبٌ مِنَ المشْرِكِينَ لَمْ يُكْرَهُوا عَلَى الإِسْلاَمِ قَدْ أَنْضَوا الرِّكَابَ وَأَفْنَوا الزَّادَ بِصَاحِبِهِمْ عَلاَمَةٌ اللهُمَّ اغْفِرْ لِعَبْدِ الْقَيْسِ أَتَونِي لاَ يَسْأَلُونِي مَالاً هُمْ خَيْرُ أَهْلِ المشْرِقِ قَالَ فَجَاؤُوا فِي ثِيَابِهِمْ وَرَسُولُ اللهِ ﷺ فِي المسْجِدِ فَسَلَّمُوا عَلَيهِ وَسَأَلَهُمْ رَسُولُ اللهِ ﷺ أَيُّكُمْ عَبْدُ اللهِ الأَشَجُّ قَالَ أَنَا يَا رَسُولَ اللهِ وَكَانَ رَجُلاً دَمِيماً فَنَظَرَ إِلَيْهِ رَسُولُ اللهِ ﷺ فَقَالَ إِنَّهُ لاَ يُسْتَسْقَى فِي مُسُوكِ الرِّجَالِ إِنَّمَا يُحْتَاجُ مِنَ الرَّجُلِ إِلَى أَصْغَرَيْهِ لِسَانِهِ وَقَلْبِهِ فَقَالَ رَسُولُ اللهِ ﷺ فِيكَ خِصْلَتَانِ يُحِبُّهُمَا اللهُ فَقَالَ عَبْدُ اللهِ وَمَا هُمَا قَالَ الحِلْمُ وَالأَنَاةُ قَالَ أَشَيْءٌ حَدَثٌ أَمْ جُبِلْتُ عَلَيْهِ قَالَ بَلْ جُبِلْتَ عَلَيْهِ ابن سعد

Al-Ḥākim narrated from Anas that a delegation from ʿAbd al-Qays from the people of Hajar came to see the Messenger of Allah ﷺ. He came to to them and said: 290 "You have a date that you call such-and-such," and he went on to list all the various types of dates they grew. One of them said: "My father and mother be your ransom, Messenger of Allah! I swear that if I had been born in the heart of Hajar I would not know more than you. Here and now I bear witness that you are the Messenger of Allah!" The Prophet ﷺ said: a "Your land was displayed for me to see from the moment you sat with me, so I could see it from its nearest point to its farthest. <b The best of your dates is the *barnī*. It removes disease and contains nothing harmful.>"[392]

عَنْ أَنَسِ بْنِ مَالِكٍ رَضِيَ اللّٰهُ عَنْهُ أَنَّ وَفْدَ عَبْدِ الْقَيسِ مِنْ أَهْلِ الهَجَرِ قَدِمُوا عَلَى رَسُولِ اللّٰهِ ﷺ فَبَيْنَمَا هُمْ قُعُودٌ عِنْدَهُ إِذْ أَقْبَلَ عَلَيْهِمْ فَقَالَ لَهُمْ تَمْرَةٌ تَدْعُونَهَا كَذَا وَتَمْرَةٌ تَدْعُونَهَا كَذَا حَتَّى عَدَّ أَلْوَانَ تَمَرَاتِهِمْ أَجْمَعَ فَقَالَ لَهُ رَجُلٌ مِنَ الْقَوْمِ بِأَبِي أَنْتَ وَأُمِّي يَا رَسُولَ اللّٰهِ لَوْ كُنْتَ وُلِدْتَ فِي جَوْفِ هَجَرَ مَا كُنْتَ بِأَعْلَمَ مِنْكَ السَّاعَةَ أَشْهَدُ أَنَّكَ رَسُولُ اللّٰهِ فَقَالَ إِنَّ أَرْضَكُمْ رُفِعَتْ لِي مُنْذُ قَعَدْتُمْ إِلَيَّ فَنَظَرْتُ مِنْ أَدْنَاهَا إِلَى أَقْصَاهَا فَخَيْرُ تَمَرَاتِكُمْ الْبَرْنِيُّ يُذْهِبُ الدَّاءَ وَلاَ دَاءَ فِيهِ ك وقال صحيح الإسناد ولم يخرجاه وله شاهد من حديث أبي سعيد الخدري وقال الذهبي قي التلخيص الحديث منكر اه نعم من حيث الإسناد والتحقيق أنه حسن لغيره والله أعلم

Aḥmad narrated from Shihāb b. 'Abbād [from an unnamed Companion] that al-Ashajj said: "Messenger of Allah! Our land is sluggish and insalubrious. Unless we use those potent bev-

[392]*Khasā'is* (2:26-27). Narrated by al-Ḥākim (4:203-204=1990 ed. 4:226) and al-Ṭabarānī in *al-Awsat* (6:166), both through 'Ubayd b. Wāfid al-Qaysī who is weak cf. Haythamī (5:40) and 'Uthmān b. 'Abd Allāh [misspelt "b. 'Abd al-Raḥmān" in many editions] al-'Abdī who is unknown cf. al-'Uqaylī (3:206). Hence it was declared forged by Ibn al-Jawzī in his *Mawḍū'āt* and disclaimed by al-Dhahabī in *Talkhīṣ al-Mustadrak*. Nevertheless the bracketed segment is also narrated independently from Burayda and Abū Sa'īd al-Khudrī as is the entire incident in the following narration in Aḥmad's *Musnad*, thus the hadith itself is "fair overall" (*ḥasan li-ghayrih*) cf. in his marginalia on Ibn al-Mulaqqin's *Mukhtaṣar Istidrāk al-Dhahabī 'alā al-Mustadrak* (6:2763). The word *hajar* or "town" served to denote outlying localities as in "Hajar Baḥrayn" (meant here), "Hajar Najrān," "Hajar Jāzān," "Hajar al-Madīna," etc. but it is also the eponym of an ancient Baḥraynī queen, Hajar bint al-Mukaffaf cf. Yāqūt. The *barniyya* is a prized round, yellow date cf. *Lisān al-'Arab*.

erages we lose our colors and our bellies swell up. Give us permission to drink this much"– and he gestured with his two hands. The Messenger of Allah ﷺ said: [291] "Ashajj! If I give you permission to drink this much"–he gestured with his hands–"then you are going to drink this much" – he opened wide between his two hands to mean much more. "In the end, one of you will get drunk and then get up and maim his very cousin with his sword." There was, among them, a man named al-Ḥarith whose leg had been struck **[509]** in a drinking bout because of poetry verses he had declaimed about a certain woman. Al-Ḥārith said: "When I heard this from the Messenger of Allah ﷺ I slowly let down my garment to cover up the wound which Allah had revealed to His Prophet ﷺ."[393]

عَنْ شِهَابُ بْنُ عَبَّادٍ أَنَّهُ سَمِعَ بَعْضَ وَفْدِ عَبْدِ الْقَيْسِ وَهُمْ
يَقُولُونَ قَالَ الأَشَجُّ يَا رَسُولَ اللهِ إِنَّ أَرْضَنَا أَرْضٌ ثَقِيلَةٌ وَخِمَةٌ
وَإِنَّا إِذَا لَمْ نَشْرَبْ هَذِهِ الأَشْرِبَةَ هِيجَتْ أَلْوَانُنَا وَعَظُمَتْ بُطُونُنَا
فَقَالَ رَسُولُ اللهِ ﷺ لاَ تَشْرَبُوا فِي الدُّبَّاءِ وَالْحَنْتَمِ وَالنَّقِيرِ
وَلْيَشْرَبْ أَحَدُكُمْ فِي سِقَاءٍ يُلاَثُ عَلَى فِيهِ فَقَالَ لَهُ الأَشَجُّ بِأَبِي
وَأُمِّي يَا رَسُولَ اللهِ رَخِّصْ لَنَا فِي مِثْلِ هَذِهِ وَأَوْمَأَ بِكَفَّيْهِ فَقَالَ
يَا أَشَجُّ إِنِّي إِنْ رَخَّصْتُ لَكَ فِي مِثْلِ هَذِهِ وَقَالَ بِكَفَّيْهِ هَكَذَا
شَرِبْتَهُ فِي مِثْلِ هَذِهِ وَفَرَّجَ يَدَيْهِ وَبَسَطَهَا يَعْنِي أَعْظَمَ مِنْهَا حَتَّى
إِذَا ثَمِلَ أَحَدُكُمْ مِنْ شَرَابِهِ قَامَ إِلَى ابْنِ عَمِّهِ فَهَزَرَ سَاقَهُ
بِالسَّيْفِ وَكَانَ فِي الْوَفْدِ رَجُلٌ مِنْ بَنِي عَضَلٍ يُقَالُ لَهُ الْحَارِثُ

[393]Narrated by Aḥmad with a chain containing Yaḥyā b. ʿAbd al-Raḥmān al-ʿAṣarī who is unknown but Ibn Ḥibbān included him in his *Thiqāt*, hence al-Haythamī's (5:59, 8:178) verdict that "its men are trustworthy."

قَدْ هُزِرَ سَاقُهُ فِي شَرَابٍ لَهُمْ فِي بَيْتٍ تَمَثَّلَهُ مِنَ الشِّعْرِ فِي امْرَأَةٍ
مِنْهُمْ فَقَامَ بَعْضُ أَهْلِ ذَلِكَ الْبَيْتِ فَهَزَرَ سَاقَهُ بِالسَّيْفِ فَقَالَ
الْحَارِثُ لَمَّا سَمِعْتُهَا مِنْ رَسُولِ اللهِ ﷺ جَعَلْتُ أَسْدُلُ ثَوْبِي
فَأُغَطِّي الضَّرْبَةَ بِسَاقِي وَقَدْ أَبْدَاهَا اللهُ تَبَارَكَ وَتَعَالَى لنبيه ﷺ

حم رجاله ثقات مج أي على شرط ابن حبان

A Desert Arab Companion

Ibn Khuzayma, al-Bayhaqī, and al-Ṭabarānī narrated from Kudayr al-Ḍibbī that a desert Arab came to the Prophet ﷺ asking him, "Tell me of a deed that shall bring me close to Paradise and far from the Fire." The Prophet ﷺ replied: [292] "Speak justice and give away your surplus *(taqūlu al-'adl wa tu'ṭī al-faḍl)*." He said, "By Allah! I cannot speak justice every moment nor give away my surplus." The Prophet ﷺ said: [a] "Then feed people and greet them with the greeting of peace." The man said: "That, too, is very difficult." The Prophet ﷺ said: "Do you own any camels?" The man said yes. The Prophet ﷺ continued: [b] "Choose one of your camels and take your waterskin then go to people that hardly have any access to drinking water. Give them to drink. Then your camel will not die nor your waterskin wear out until Paradise becomes guaranteed for you." The man departed and his waterskin never wore out nor did his camel die until he was killed as a martyr. Al-Mundhirī said its narrators are those of the *Ṣaḥīḥ* collections except that Kudayr is a Successor *(Tābi'ī)*, so the ḥadīth is *mursal*. The ḥadīth master al-Suyūṭī said that another report with as connected chain corroborates it.[394]

[394]Narrated with several chains from Kudayr by al-Tayālisī in his *Musnad* (p. 194 §1361), Hannād b. al-Sarī in *al-Zuhd* (1:349 and 2:516), Ma'mar b. Rāshid in his *Jāmi'* (in ʿAbd al-Razzāq 10:456), Ibn Abī ʿĀṣim in *al-Āḥād wal-Mathānī* (5:199-200 §2728-2730), al-Tabarānī in *al-Kabīr* (19:187) with trustworthy narrators cf. al-Haythamī (3:132), Ibn Khuzayma (4:125-126), Abū Nuʿaym (4:346), al-Khatīb (13:456), and al-Bayhaqī in *al-Sunan al-Kubrā* (4:186) and *Shuʿab al-Īmān* (3:219), also – as stated in *al-*

عَنْ كُدَيْرٍ الضَّبِّيِّ أَنَّ رَجُلا أَعْرَابِيًّا أَتَى رَسُولَ اللهِ ﷺ فَقَالَ أَخْبِرْنِي بِعَمَلٍ يُقَرِّبُنِي مِنْ طَاعَتِهِ وَيُبَاعِدُنِي مِنَ النَّارِ قَالَ أَوَهُمَا أَعْمَلَتَاكَ قَالَ نَعَمْ قَالَ تَقُولُ الْعَدْلَ وَتُعْطِي الْفَضْلَ قَالَ وَاللهِ مَا أَسْتَطِعُ أَنْ أَقُومَ الْعَدْلَ كُلَّ سَاعَةٍ وَمَا أَسْتَطِيعُ أَنْ أُعْطِيَ فَضْلَ مَالِي قَالَ فَتُطْعِمُ الطَّعَامَ وَتُفْشِي السَّلامَ قَالَ هَذِهِ أَيْضًا شَدِيدَةٌ قَالَ فَقَالَ فَهَلْ لَكَ إِبِلٌ قَالَ نَعَمْ قَالَ فَانْظُرْ بَعِيرًا مِنْ إِبِلِكَ وَسِقَاءً ثُمَّ اعْمِدْ إِلَى أَهْلِ أَبْيَاتٍ لاَ يَشْرَبُونَ الْمَاءَ إِلاَّ غِبًّا فَاسْقِهِمْ فَلَعَلَّكَ أَنْ لاَ يَهْلِكَ بَعِيرُكَ وَلا يَنْخَرِقَ سِقَاؤُكَ حَتَّى تَجِبَ لَكَ الْجَنَّةُ قَالَ فَانْطَلَقَ الأَعْرَابِيُّ يُكَبِّرُ قَالَ فَمَا انْخَرَقَ سِقَاؤُهُ وَلا هَلَكَ بَعِيرُهُ حَتَّى قُتِلَ شَهِيدًا عق ط خز طب أبو نعيم في المعرفة خط هق هب كر وغيرهم وهو مرسل لكن قواه الحافظ السيوطي باعتبار ما روي

عَنِ ابْنِ عَبَّاسٍ قَالَ أَتَى النَّبِيَّ ﷺ رَجُلٌ فَقَالَ مَا عَمَلٌ إِنْ عَمِلْتُ بِهِ دَخَلْتُ الْجَنَّةَ قَالَ أَنْتَ بِبَلَدٍ يُجْلَبُ بِهِ الْمَاءُ قَالَ نَعَمْ

Iṣāba (5:575-576) – Aḥmad b. Manīʿ in his *Musnad*, al-Baghawī in *Muʿjam al-Ṣaḥāba*, Ibn Qāniʿ in his (2:384) and Ibn Shāhīn. Ibn Ḥajar quotes Imam Aḥmad's opinion that Kudayr never saw the Prophet ﷺ while others identify him as a weak Shīʿī *Tābiʿī* narrator cf. al-Bukhārī in *al-Tārīkh al-Kabīr* (7:242 §1034) and *al-Duʿafā' al-Saghīr* (p. 97 §308), Ibn Abī Ḥātim in *al-Marāsīl* (p. 178 §648), al-Nasā'ī in his *al-Duʿafā' wal-Matrūkīn* (p. 89 §502), Ibn al-Jawzī in his (3:24 §2795), Ibn Ḥibbān in *al-Majrūḥīn* (2:221 §892), al-ʿUqaylī in *al-Duʿafā'* (4:13 §1568), al-Mundhirī in *al-Targhīb* (1997 ed. 2:39-40), Ibn ʿAdī in the *Kāmil* (6:79) and al-Dhahabī in the *Mīzān* (5:497) but the report is independently confirmed as stated by al-Suyūṭī, *Khasā'is* (2:224) while Abū Ḥātim (Ibn Abī Ḥātim, *al-Jarḥ wal-Taʿdīl* 7:174) considered Kudayr strong and al-Bukhārī's verdict on him erroneous.

قَالَ فَاشْتَرِ بِهَا سِقَاءً جَدِيدًا ثُمَّ اسْتَقِ فِيهَا حَتَّى تَخْرِقَهَا فَإِنَّكَ
لَنْ تَخْرِقَهَا حَتَّى تَبْلُغَ بِهَا عَمَلَ الْجَنَّةِ طب قال المنذري رواة إسناده ثقات
إلا يحيى الحماني

[A man came to the Prophet ﷺ asking, "What can I do that shall let me enter into Paradise?" The Prophet ﷺ said: [293] "Do you live in a place where there is water?" The man said yes. The Prophet ﷺ said: [a] "Buy a new waterskin and use it to bring water to people until it wears out. Truly, you will not wear it out before you reach the works of Paradise with it."[395]]

A Hypocrite Who Then Accepted Islam

Al-Bayhaqī and Abū Nuʿaym narrated from Mūsā b. ʿUqba and ʿUrwa [b. al-Zubayr] that <the Prophet ﷺ, upon his return from the raid on Banū al-Muṣṭaliq, was nearing al-Madīna when the wind began to blow so strongly that riders were almost buried [in the sand]. The Messenger of Allah ﷺ said: [294] "This wind was sent because of the death of a hypocrite." When we arrived, lo and behold, one of the great leaders of the *munāfiqūn* had indeed died> – Rifāʿa b. Zayd b. al-Tābūt. The wind died down towards day's end. The people collected their pack beasts but the mount of the Messenger of Allah was nowhere to be found among the other camels. The men began searching everywhere. One of the hypocrites said in a gathering of the *Anṣār*: "Muḥammad is telling us about far greater things than a trivial camel! Does Allah not tell him where his own mount is?" Then he got up and left. He went straight to the Messenger of Allah ﷺ to look for news. He found that Allah had already revealed to the Prophet ﷺ what he had just said! The Messenger of Allah ﷺ said: [a] "Some hypocrite has gloated that the she-camel of the Messenger of Allah had gotten lost and he said, 'Why does Allah not tell him where his she-camel is?' Indeed, Allah has informed me of her place and none knows the unseen except Allah. She is in the wood that is facing you and her

[395] Narrated from Ibn ʿAbbās by al-Ṭabarānī in *al-Kabīr* (12:104 §12605) through trustworthy narrators but for Yaḥyā al-Ḥammānī, yet some declared him trustworthy: *Khasā'is* (2:224), al-Haythamī (3:132).

reins have got entangled in a tree branch." They went, found her, and brought her. The hypocrite rushed back to the group to whom he had spoken his words and said, "I ask you on oath to tell me truly, did any of you go to Muḥammad and tell him what I had just said to you?" They said, "By Allah, no! We did not even get up from our seats." He said: "I swear I just found him aware of every word I said! I was truly undecided about him, but now, I bear witness that he is the Messenger of Allah!"[396]

عَنْ جَابِرٍ أَنَّ رَسُولَ اللهِ ﷺ قَدِمَ مِنْ سَفَرٍ فَلَمَّا كَانَ قُرْبَ الْمَدِينَةِ هَاجَتْ رِيحٌ شَدِيدَةٌ تَكَادُ أَنْ تَدْفِنَ الرَّاكِبَ فَزَعَمَ أَنَّ رَسُولَ اللهِ ﷺ قَالَ بُعِثَتْ هَذِهِ الرِّيحُ لِمَوْتِ مُنَافِقٍ فَلَمَّا قَدِمَ الْمَدِينَةَ فَإِذَا مُنَافِقٌ عَظِيمٌ مِنَ الْمُنَافِقِينَ قَدْ مَاتَ م حم ع عبد بن حميد ش البغوي في الأنوار حب حل هق في الدلائل وجاء عَن ابْنِ إِسْحَاقَ عَنْ شُيُوخِهِ الَّذِينَ رَوَى عَنْهُمْ قِصَّةَ بَنِي الْمُصْطَلِقِ قَالُوا فَوَجَدُوا رُفَاعَةَ بْنَ زَيْدِ بْنِ التَّابُوتِ قَدْ مَاتَ يَوْمَئِذٍ وَكَانَ مِنْ بَنِي قَيْنُقَاعٍ وَكَانَ قَدْ أَظْهَرَ الإِسْلاَمَ وَكَانَ كَهْفاً لِلْمُنَافِقِينَ عبد بن حميد الواقدي هق في الدلائل الذهبي في التاريخ ثم زاد بعضهم وَسَكَنَت الرِّيحُ آخِرَ النَّهَارِ فَجَمَعَ النَّاسُ ظَهْرَهُم أو ظُهُورَهُمْ وقال الواقدي فَحَدَّثَنِي عَبْدُ الْحَمِيدِ بْنُ جَعْفَرٍ عَنْ ابْنِ رُومَانَ وَمُحَمَّدُ بْنُ صَالِحٍ عَنْ عَاصِمِ

[396]Narrated *mursal* by Wāqidī (1:423-424), Mūsā b. ʻUqbā, *Maghāzī* (p. 232-233), Ibn Shabba, *Tārīkh* (1:353-354), Abū Nuʿaym, *Dalā'il al-Nubuwwa* (p. 515-516 §443) and Bayhaqī in his (3:59-60) as cited in the *Khaṣā'iṣ* (1:391-392). The narration adds: "They said that he [the hypocrite] did not cease to tergiversate (*yafsul*) until he died." Wāqidī adds: "and he did it again at Tabūk." Ibn Isḥāq, Wāqidī and Ibn Shabba identify him as Zayd b. al-Luṣayt al-Qaynuqāʻī. The bracketed segment is cited by Ibn Hishām (3:60-61) and narrated without mention of the Banū al-Muṣṭaliq from Jābir by Muslim and Aḥmad.

بْنِ عُمَرَ بْنِ قَتَادَةَ قَالاَ وَفُقِدَتْ نَاقَةُ رَسُولِ اللهِ ﷺ الْقَصْوَاءُ مِنْ بَيْنِ الإِبِلِ فَجَعَلَ الْمُسْلِمُونَ يَطْلُبُونَهَا فِي كُلِّ وَجْهٍ فَقَالَ زَيْدُ بْنُ اللُّصَيْتِ وَكَانَ مُنَافِقًا وَهُوَ فِي رِفْقَةِ قَوْمٍ مِنْ الأَنْصَارِ مِنْهُمْ عَبّادُ بْنُ بِشْرِ بْنِ وَقَشٍ وَسَلَمَةُ بْنُ سَلاَمَةَ بْنِ وَقَشٍ وَأُسَيْدُ بْنُ حُضَيْرٍ فَقَالَ أَيْنَ يَذْهَبُ هَؤُلاَءِ فِي كُلّ وَجْهٍ قَالُوا يَطْلُبُونَ نَاقَةَ رَسُولِ اللهِ ﷺ قَدْ ضَلّتْ قَالَ أَفَلاَ يُخْبِرُهُ اللهُ بِمَكَانِ نَاقَتِهِ فَأَنْكَرَ الْقَوْمُ ذَلِكَ عَلَيْهِ فَقَالُوا قَاتَلَكَ اللهُ يَا عَدُوَّ اللهِ نَافَقْتَ ثُمَّ أَقْبَلَ عَلَيْهِ أُسَيْدُ بْنُ حُضَيْرٍ فَقَالَ وَاللهِ لَوْلاَ أَنِّي لاَ أَدْرِي مَا يُوَافِقُ رَسُولُ اللهِ ﷺ مِنْ ذَلِكَ لأَنْفَذْتُ خُصْيَتَكَ بِالرُّمْحِ يَا عَدُوَّ اللهِ فَلِمَ خَرَجْتَ مَعَنَا وَهَذَا فِي نَفْسِكَ قَالَ خَرَجْتُ لِأَطْلُبَ مِنْ عَرَضِ الدُّنْيَا وَلَعَمْرِي إِنَّ مُحَمّدًا لَيُخْبِرُنَا بِأَعْظَمَ مِنْ شَأْنِ النَّاقَةِ يُخْبِرُنَا عَنْ أَمْرِ السّمَاءِ فَوَقَعُوا بِهِ جَمِيعًا وَقَالُوا وَاللهِ لاَ يَكُونُ مِنْكَ سَبِيلٌ أَبَدًا وَلاَ يُظِلُّنَا وَإِيّاكَ ظِلٌّ أَبَدًا وَلَوْ عَلِمْنَا مَا فِي نَفْسِكَ مَا صَحِبْتَنَا سَاعَةً مِنْ نَهَارٍ ثُمّ وَثَبَ هَارِبًا مُنْهَزِمًا مِنْهُمْ أَنْ يَقَعُوا بِهِ وَنَبَذُوا مَتَاعَهُ فَعَمَدَ لِرَسُولِ اللهِ ﷺ فَجَلَسَ مَعَهُ فِرَارًا مِنْ أَصْحَابِهِ مُتَعَوّذًا بِهِ وَقَدْ جَاءَ رَسُولَ اللهِ ﷺ خَبَرُ مَا قَالَ مِنْ السّمَاءِ فَقَالَ رَسُولُ اللهِ ﷺ وَالْمُنَافِقُ يَسْمَعُ إِنَّ رَجُلًا مِنْ الْمُنَافِقِينَ شَمِتَ أَنْ ضَلّتْ نَاقَةُ رَسُولِ اللهِ وَقَالَ أَلاَ يُخْبِرُهُ

اللهُ بِمَكَانِهَا فَلَعَمْرِي إِنّ مُحَمّدًا لَيُخْبِرُنَا بِأَعْظَمَ مِنْ شَأْنِ النّاقَةِ وَلاَ يَعْلَمُ الْغَيْبَ إِلّا اللهُ وَإِنّ اللهَ تَعَالَى قَدْ أَخْبَرَنِي بِمَكَانِهَا وَإِنّهَا فِي هَذَا الشّعْبِ مُقَابِلَكُمْ قَدْ تَعَلّقَ زِمَامُهَا بِشَجَرَةٍ فَاعْمِدُوا عَمْدَهَا فَذَهَبُوا فَأَتَوْا بِهَا مِنْ حَيْثُ قَالَ رَسُولُ اللهِ ﷺ فَلَمّا نَظَرَ الْمُنَافِقُ إِلَيْهَا قَامَ سَرِيعًا إِلَى رُفَقَائِهِ الّذِينَ كَانُوا مَعَهُ فَإِذَا رَحْلُهُ مَنْبُوذٌ وَإِذَا هُمْ جُلُوسٌ لَمْ يَقُمْ رَجُلٌ مِنْ مَجْلِسِهِ فَقَالُوا لَهُ حِينَ دَنَا لاَ تَدْنُ مِنّا قَالَ أُكَلّمُكُمْ فَدَنَا فَقَالَ أُذَكّرُكُمْ بِاللهِ هَلْ أَتَى أَحَدٌ مِنْكُمْ مُحَمّدًا فَأَخْبَرَهُ بِالّذِي قُلْتُ قَالُوا لاَ وَاللهِ وَلاَ قُمْنَا مِنْ مَجْلِسِنَا هَذَا قَالَ فَإِنّي قَدْ وَجَدْتُ عِنْدَ الْقَوْمِ مَا تَكَلّمْتُ بِهِ وَإِنّي قَدْ كُنْتُ فِي شَكٍّ مِنْ شَأْنِ مُحَمّدٍ فَأَشْهَدُ أَنّهُ رَسُولُ اللهِ وَاللهِ لَكَأَنّي لَمْ أُسْلِمْ إِلاّ الْيَوْمَ قَالُوا لَهُ فَاذْهَبْ إِلَى رَسُولِ اللهِ يَسْتَغْفِرْ لَك فَذَهَبَ إِلَى رَسُولِ اللهِ ﷺ فَاسْتَغْفَرَ لَهُ وَاعْتَرَفَ بِذَنْبِهِ وَيُقَالُ إِنّهُ لَمْ يَزَلْ فَسْلًا حَتّى مَاتَ وَصَنَعَ مِثْلَ هَذَا فِي غَزْوَةِ تَبُوكَ الواقدي موسى بن عقبة ابن شبّة في التاريخ هق في الدلائل

Something similar took place in the expedition of Tabūk. Al-Bayhaqī and Abū Nuʿaym narrated through Ibn Isḥāq that [the *Tābiʿī*] ʿĀṣim b. ʿUmar b. Qatāda said: "Some among my people – meaning the *Anṣār* – told me that the she-camel of the Messenger of Allah ﷺ got lost during the raid on Tabūk, whereupon one of the well-known hypocrites [Zayd b. al-Lasīt al-Qaynuqāʿī] said: 'Does not Muḥammad claim that he is a Prophet and that he is bringing you news from the heaven? Now he does not know where his own camel is!' The Messenger of Allah ﷺ said – as 'Umāra b. Ḥazm was with him: 295 'Someone said, "Here is Muhammad **[510]** telling you he is a Prophet and bringing you news from heaven, and he does not know where his own she-camel is!" Truly, I know only what Allah has taught me, and Allah has shown me where she is! She is in such-and-such a vale with its reins entangled in a tree.' The people went off and brought her. 'Umāra returned to his convoy and reported to them what the Messenger of Allah ﷺ had said about the words the man spoke. One of those present said: 'I swear by Allah that that hypocrite just spoke those words, just before you came.'"'[397]

قَالَ ابْنُ إِسْحَاقَ سَارَ رَسُولُ اللهِ ﷺ إِلَى تَبُوكَ حَتَّى إِذَا كَانَ بِبَعْضِ الطَّرِيقِ ضَلَّتْ نَاقَتُهُ فَخَرَجَ أَصْحَابُهُ فِي طَلَبِهَا وَعِنْدَ رَسُولِ اللهِ ﷺ يُقَالُ لَهُ عُمَارَةُ بْنُ حَزْمٍ وَكَانَ عَقَبِيًّا بَدْرِيًّا وَهُوَ عَمّ بَنِي عَمْرِو بْنِ حَزْمٍ وَكَانَ فِي رَحْلِهِ زَيْدُ بْنُ اللُّصَيْتِ الْقَيْنُقَاعِيّ وَكَانَ مُنَافِقًا قَالَ ابْنُ هِشَامٍ وَيُقَالُ ابْنُ لُصَيْبٍ بِالْبَاءِ قَالَ ابْنُ إِسْحَاقَ فَحَدَّثَنِي عَاصِمُ بْنُ عُمَرَ بْنِ قَتَادَةَ عَنْ مَحْمُودِ بْنِ لَبِيدٍ عَنْ رِجَالٍ مِنْ بَنِي عَبْدِ الأَشْهَلِ قَالُوا فَقَالَ زَيْدُ بْنُ اللُّصَيْتِ وَهُوَ فِي رَحْلِ عُمَارَةَ وَعُمَارَةُ عِنْدَ رَسُولِ اللهِ ﷺ

[397]Narrated from the Companions Maḥmūd b. Labīd and 'Umāra b. Ḥazm al-Anṣārīyyayn by Ibn Isḥāq in *al-Maghāzī* as stated by Ibn Hishām (3:60 and 5:203) and al-Ṭabarī, *Tārīkh* (2:184); Ibn Ḥazm in *al-Muhallā* (11:222) and Ibn Ḥajar in *Fath al-Bārī* (1959 ed. 13:364) and *al-Iṣāba* (2:619), and *mursal* from 'Urwa by Ibn 'Abd al-Barr in *al-Istī'āb* (1:288) who identifies the man who found the she-camel and brought it as al-Ḥārith b. Khazama while Ibn Ḥibbān cites it without chain in *al-Thiqāt* (2:93-94) cf. *Sīra Ḥalabiyya* (3:107), *Iktifā'* (1:368 and 2:275-276), al-Māwardī, *A'lām al-Nubuwwa* (p. 159), *Zād* (3:467 *rijāluhu thiqāt*), and *Bidāya* (3:240 and 5:9). Also narrated by al-Taymī in *Dalā'il al-Nubuwwa* (p. 137) citing Ibn Qutayba's report. 'Umāra's name is misspelt as Ibn Ḥazn in al-Nabhānī. The camel of the Prophet ﷺ was similarly reported lost and found in the expedition of Ḥudaybiya, cf. n. 204.

أَلَيْسَ مُحَمَّدٌ يَزْعُمُ أَنَّهُ نَبِيٌّ وَيُخْبِرُكُمْ عَنْ خَبَرِ السَّمَاءِ وَهُوَ لَا يَدْرِي أَيْنَ نَاقَتُهُ فَقَالَ رَسُولُ اللهِ ﷺ وَعُمَارَةُ عِنْدَهُ إِنَّ رَجُلًا قَالَ هَذَا مُحَمَّدٌ يُخْبِرُكُمْ أَنَّهُ نَبِيٌّ وَيَزْعُمُ أَنَّهُ يُخْبِرُكُمْ بِأَمْرِ السَّمَاءِ وَهُوَ لَا يَدْرِي أَيْنَ نَاقَتُهُ وَإِنِّي وَاللهِ مَا أَعْلَمُ إِلَّا مَا عَلَّمَنِي اللهُ وَقَدْ دَلَّنِي اللهُ عَلَيْهَا وَهِيَ فِي هَذَا الْوَادِي فِي شِعْبِ كَذَا وَكَذَا قَدْ حَبَسَتْهَا شَجَرَةٌ بِزِمَامِهَا فَانْطَلِقُوا حَتَّى تَأْتُونِي بِهَا فَذَهَبُوا فَجَاءُوا بِهَا فَرَجَعَ عُمَارَةُ بْنُ حَزْمٍ إِلَى رَحْلِهِ فَقَالَ وَاللهِ لَعَجَبٌ مِنْ شَيْءٍ حَدَّثَنَاهُ رَسُولُ اللهِ ﷺ آنِفًا عَنْ مَقَالَةِ قَائِلٍ أَخْبَرَهُ اللهُ عَنْهُ بِكَذَا وَكَذَا لِلَّذِي قَالَ زَيْدُ بْنُ لُصَيْتٍ فَقَالَ رَجُلٌ مِمَّنْ كَانَ فِي رَحْلِ عُمَارَةَ وَلَمْ يَحْضُرْ رَسُولَ اللهِ ﷺ زَيْدٌ وَاللهِ قَالَ هَذِهِ الْمَقَالَةَ قَبْلَ أَنْ تَأْتِيَ ابن هشام تاريخ الطبري هق في الدلائل

Al-Ḥārith b. Suwayd

Ibn Saʿd narrated from al-Wāqidī, from his authorities, that Suwayd b. al-Ṣāmit had killed Zyād the father of Mujadhdhar in battle, after which Mujadhdhar found Suwayd and killed him. This all took place before Islam. When the Messenger of Allah ﷺ came to Madīna, both al-Ḥārith the son of Suwayd and Mujadhdhar the son of Zyād accepted Islam and fought at Badr. Al-Ḥārith kept looking for Mujadhdhar to kill him but was unsuccessful. When the day of the battle of Uḥud came and the Muslims spread over great distances, al-Ḥārith came from behind Mujadhdhar and struck him dead. When the Messenger of Allah ﷺ returned from Ḥamrāʾ al-Asad, Jibrīl came to him and informed him that al-Ḥārith b. Suwayd had ambushed and murdered Mujadhdhar b. Zyād and ordered him to have him killed. The Messenger of Allah ﷺ rode to Qubā' that day – it was a very hot day – and entered the mosque there where he prayed two *rak'a*s. The *Anṣār* heard that he was there and came to greet him. They were puzzled that he had come at such a time on such a day. Then came al-Ḥārith b. Suwayd, wearing a saffron-dyed cloak. When the Messenger of Allah ﷺ saw him, he summoned 'Uwaym b. Sā'ida and said: 296 "Take al-Ḥārith b. Suwayd outside the door of the mosque and strike his neck for ambushing and murdering Mujadhdhar b. Zyād!" Al-Ḥārith said, "I did, by Allah, kill him! However, my killing him was in no way a recanting of Islam nor doubt in it but rather fanaticism inspired by the devil and a matter in which I followed my lust. I repent with all my heart to Allah and His Prophet of what I did to him! I shall pay his blood money, fast two months in a row, and free a slave!" When he finished speaking, the Prophet ﷺ said: "Take him, 'Uwaym, and strike his neck." He took him and executed him. Ḥassān declaimed:

O Ḥār fatigued from your first father's sleep,
Were you – woe to you! – oblivious to Jibrīl?
Or to Ziyād's son when you killed him
Ambushed in some desert void, unknown?

You said we'll go unnoticed but Allah saw you;
And among you is the Definer of Verses and Sayings,
Muḥammad, whom Allah the Almighty informs
Of all your secrets and intrigues.[398]

[398]Narrated through Wāqidī (1:304-305) by 'Askarī in *Tashīfāt al-Muhaddithīn* (2:699-701) and Bayhaqī in *al-Sunan al-Kubrā* (8:57). Cited by al-Suyūṭī in the *Khasā'is* (1:362-363) after Ibn Sa'd. Al-Nabhānī has the spelling Mujaddar. Ḥamrā' al-Asad is a red mountain twenty km south of al-Madīna out to which the Prophet ﷺ rode in search of enemy fighters during the battle of Uḥud cf. Yāqūt and *Ma'ālim*. Ibn 'Abd al-Barr in *al-Istī'āb* (3:912) identifies Mujadhdhar as 'Abd Allāh b. Zyād b. 'Amr al-Balawī. On the shortening of Ḥārith's name to "Ḥār" see note 297. Ibn Ḥajar in *al-Iṣāba* (1:577) cites the opinion of some of the authorities who averred that it was al-Ḥārith's brother, Julās b. Suwayd, who murdered Mujadhdhar and was then executed. Al-Julās b. Suwayd is the one who reportedly said concerning the campaign of Tabūk: "If what Muḥammad says is true, we are worse than donkeys." 'Umayr b. Sa'd heard it and said: "By Allah, I fear that if I do not report it to the Prophet ﷺ, [something of] the Qur'ān will be revealed [about it] and I shall be involved in a sin when the Prophet ﷺ is like a father to me. So he reported

رَوَى الوَاقِدِيُّ عَنْ شُيُوخِهِ قَالَ كَانَ سُوَيْدُ بْنُ الصَّامِتِ قَدْ قَتَلَ زِيَاداً أَبَا مُجَذَّرٍ فِي وَقْعَةٍ اِلْتَقَوْا فِيهَا فَظَفَرَ المُجَذَّرُ بِسُوَيْدٍ فَقَتَلَهُ وَذَلِكَ قَبْلَ الإِسْلاَمِ فَلَمّا قَدِمَ رَسُولُ اللهِ ﷺ الْمَدِينَةَ أَسْلَمَ الْحَارِثُ بْنُ سُوَيْدِ بْنِ الصَّامِتِ وَمُجَذَّرُ بْنُ زِيَادٍ فَشَهِدَا بَدْرًا فَجَعَلَ الْحَارِثُ يَطْلُبُ مُجَذَّرًا لِيَقْتُلَهُ بِأَبِيهِ فَلاَ يَقْدِرُ عَلَيْهِ يَوْمَئِذٍ فَلَمَّا كَانَ يَوْمُ أُحُدٍ وَجَالَ الْمُسْلِمُونَ تِلْكَ الْجَوْلَةَ أَتَاهُ الْحَارِثُ مِنْ خَلْفِهِ فَضَرَبَ عُنُقَهُ فَرَجَعَ رَسُولُ اللهِ ﷺ إِلَى الْمَدِينَةِ ثُمَّ خَرَجَ إِلَى حَمْرَاءِ الأَسَدِ فَلَمّا رَجَعَ مِنْ حَمْرَاءِ الأَسَد أَتَاهُ جِبْرِيلُ عَلَيْهِ السّلاَمُ فَأَخْبَرَهُ أَنّ الْحَارِثَ بْنَ سُوَيْدٍ قَتَلَ مُجَذّرًا غِيلَةً وَأَمَرَهُ بِقَتْلِهِ فَرَكِبَ رَسُولُ اللهِ ﷺ إِلَى قُبَاءٍ فِي الْيَوْمِ الّذِي أَخْبَرَهُ جِبْرِيلُ فِي يَوْمٍ حَارٍّ وَكَانَ ذَلِكَ يَوْمًا لاَ يَرْكَبُ فِيهِ رَسُولُ اللهِ ﷺ إِلَى قُبَاءٍ إِنّمَا كَانَتْ الأَيّامُ الّتِي يَأْتِي فِيهَا رَسُولُ اللهِ ﷺ قُبَاءَ يَوْمَ السَّبْتِ وَيَوْمَ الاِثْنَيْنِ فَلَمّا دَخَلَ رَسُولُ اللهِ ﷺ مَسْجِدَ

it to the Prophet ﷺ who summoned al-Julās. When the latter was asked about it, he swore he did not say it. At that time was revealed: ﴾**They swear by Allah that they did not say it, but indeed they uttered words of disbelief, and they did it after professing their submission; and they plotted what they were unable to carry out; this revenge of theirs was their only return for the favor of Allah with which Allāh and His Messenger had enriched them. If they repent, it will be best for them.**﴿ Julās said: Ask repentance from my Lord for me, for I repent to Allah, and I bear witness He has spoken the truth." Narrated through ʿAbd al-Razzāq by Ibn ʿAbd al-Barr, *Istīʿāb* (3:1215-1216). Suyūṭī, *Asbāb al-Nuzūl* cites Ibn Abī Ḥātim as relating the same from Ibn ʿAbbās and Kaʿb b. Mālik, and Ibn Saʿd, *Tabaqāt* as relating something similar through ʿUrwa.

قُبَاءٍ صَلَّى فِيهِ مَا شَاءَ اللهُ أَنْ يُصَلِّيَ وَسَمِعَتْ الأَنْصَارُ فَجَاءَتْ تُسَلِّمُ عَلَيْهِ وَأَنْكَرُوا إِتْيَانَهُ فِي تِلْكَ السَّاعَةِ وَفِي ذَلِكَ الْيَوْمِ فَجَلَسَ رَسُولُ اللهِ ﷺ يَتَحَدَّثُ وَيَتَصَفَّحُ النَّاسَ حَتَّى طَلَعَ الْحَارِثُ بْنُ سُوَيْدٍ فِي مِلْحَفَةٍ مُوَرَّسَةٍ فَلَمَّا رَآهُ رَسُولُ اللهِ ﷺ دَعَا عُوَيْمَ بْنَ سَاعِدَةَ فَقَالَ لَهُ قَدِمَ الْحَارِثُ بْنُ سُوَيْدٍ إِلَى بَابِ الْمَسْجِدِ فَاضْرِبْ عُنُقَهُ بِمُجَذَّرِ بْنِ زِيَادٍ فَإِنَّهُ قَتَلَهُ يَوْمَ أُحُدٍ فَأَخَذَهُ عُوَيْمٌ فَقَالَ الْحَارِثُ دَعْنِي أُكَلِّمْ رَسُولَ اللهِ فَأَبَى عُوَيْمٌ عَلَيْهِ فَجَابَذَهُ يُرِيدُ كَلاَمَ رَسُولِ اللهِ ﷺ وَنَهَضَ رَسُولُ اللهِ ﷺ يُرِيدُ أَنْ يَرْكَبَ وَدَعَا بِحِمَارِهِ عَلَى بَابِ الْمَسْجِدِ فَجَعَلَ الْحَارِثُ يَقُولُ قَدْ وَاللهِ قَتَلْتُهُ يَا رَسُولَ اللهِ وَاللهِ مَا كَانَ قَتْلِي إِيَّاهُ رُجُوعًا عَنِ الإِسْلاَمِ وَلاَ ارْتِيَابًا فِيهِ وَلَكِنَّهُ حَمِيَّةَ الشَّيْطَانِ وَأَمْرٌ وُكِلْتُ فِيهِ إِلَى نَفْسِي وَإِنِّي أَتُوبُ إِلَى اللهِ وَإِلَى رَسُولِهِ مِمَّا عَمِلْتُ وَأُخْرِجُ دِيَتَهُ وَأَصُومُ شَهْرَيْنِ مُتَتَابِعَيْنِ وَأُعْتِقُ رَقَبَةً وَأُطْعِمُ سِتِّينَ مِسْكِينًا إِنِّي أَتُوبُ إِلَى اللهِ وَرَسُولِهِ وَجَعَلَ يُمْسِكُ بِرِكَابِ رَسُولِ اللهِ لإِ وَبَنُو الْمُجَذَّرِ حُضُورٌ لاَ يَقُولُ لَهُمْ رَسُولُ اللهِ ﷺ شَيْئًا حَتَّى إِذَا اسْتَوْعَبَ كَلاَمَهُ قَالَ قَدِّمْهُ يَا عُوَيْمُ فَاضْرِبْ عُنُقَهُ وَرَكِبَ رَسُولُ اللهِ ﷺ وَقَدِمَهُ عُوَيْمُ عَلَى بَابِ الْمَسْجِدِ فَضَرَبَ عُنُقَهُ وَقَالَ حَسَّانُ بْنُ ثَابِتٍ:

يَا حَارِ فِي سِنَةٍ مِنْ نَوْمِ أَوَّلِكُمْ أَمْ كُنْتَ وَيْلَكَ مُغْتَرّاً[٣] بِجِبْرِيـــلِ

أَمْ كُنْتَ بِابْنِ زِيَادٍ حِينَ تَقْتُلُـهُ بِغِرَّةٍ فِي فَضَاءِ الأَرْضِ مجْهُولِ

وَقُلْتُمُ لَنْ نُرَى وَاللهُ مُبْصِرُكُـــمْ وَفِيكُمْ مُحْكِمُ الآيَاتِ وَالْقِيـــلِ

مُحَمَّدٌ وَالْعَزِيزُ اللـــــّـــهُ يُخْبِرُهُ بِمَا تَكِنُّ سَرِيرَاتُ الأَقَاوِيـــلِ

الواقدي هق

An Anṣārī and a Thaqafī

Al-Bayhaqī and Abū Nuʿaym narrated that Anas ؓ said: "I was sitting with the Messenger of Allah ﷺ in the mosque of al-Khayf when two men came, one from the *Anṣār* and one from Thaqīf. They said: 'We came to you, Messenger of Allah, to ask you something.' He said: [297] 'If you wish, I can tell you what you came to ask me, and if you wish, I can remain silent until you ask me.' They said, 'Tell us, Messenger of Allah, so that our faith will increase.' He said to the Thaqafī: [a] 'You came to ask about your late-night prayer, your bowing, your prostrating, your fasting, and your washing off the state of major impurity.' Then he said to the Anṣārī: [b] 'You came to ask about your leaving your home to head for the Ancient Mosque and what you should do there, your standing in ʿArafāt, the shaving of your head, your circumambulation of the House, and your stoning of the pelting-posts.' They said: 'By the One Who sent you with the truth, this is precisely what we came to ask you about!'" Something similar came to us as narrated by Ibn ʿUmar رضي الله عنهما.[399] **[511]** [The Prophet ﷺ relatedly said: [298] "In the Mosque of al-Khayf is the grave of seventy Prophets."][400]

[399] *Khaṣāʾiṣ* (2:65, 2:171). Narrated from [1] Anas broken-chained by Musaddad in his *Musnad* cf. Ibn Ḥajar, *Maṭālib* (6:262-264 §1131), al-Bazzar cf. al-Haythamī (3:601-603) and his *Kashf al-Astār* (2:9-10 §1083), al-Ṭabarānī in *al-Aḥādīth al-Ṭiwāl* (p. 152 §61), Qawwām al-Sunna al-Taymī in *al-Targhīb* (2:5-7 §1036), al-Azraqī in *Akhbār Makka* (1:495-496 §552) and al-Fākihī in *Akhbār Makka* (1:425 §919); [2] Ibn ʿUmar by ʿAbd

عَنْ عَبْدِ اللهِ بْنِ عُمَرَ رَضِيَ اللهُ عَنْهُمَا قَالَ كُنْتُ جَالِساً عِنْدَ نَبِيِّ اللهِ ﷺ فَجَاءَهُ رَجُلاَنِ أَحَدُهُمَا أَنْصَارِيٌّ وَالآخَرُ ثَقَفِيٌّ فَقَالَ رَسُولُ اللهِ ﷺ قَالَ إِنْ شِئْتُمَا أُخْبِرْكُمَا بِمَا تَسْأَلاَنِي عَنْهُ وَإِنْ شِئْتُمَا أَنْ أَسْكُتَ وَتَسْأَلاَنِي قَالاَ أَخْبِرْنَا يَا رَسُولَ اللهِ نَزْدَدْ إِيمَاناً فَقَالَ لِلثَّقَفِيِّ فَإِنَّكَ جِئْتَ تَسْأَلُ عَنْ صَلاَتِكَ بِاللَّيْلِ وَعَنْ رُكُوعِكَ وَعَنْ سُجُودِكَ وَعَنْ صِيَامِكَ وَعَنْ غُسْلِكَ مِنَ الجَنَابَةِ وَقَالَ لِلأَنْصَارِيِّ جِئْتَ تَسْأَلُ عَنْ خُرُوجِكَ مِنْ بَيْتِكَ تَؤُمُّ البَيْتَ الْعَتِيقَ وَتَقُولُ مَاذَا لِي فِيهِ وَعَنْ وُقُوفِكَ بِعَرَفَاتٍ وَتَقُولُ مَاذَا لِي فِيهِ وَعَنْ حَلْقِكَ رَأْسَكَ وَتَقُولُ مَاذَا لِي فِيهِ وَعَنْ طَوَافِكَ بِالْبَيْتِ وَتَقُولُ مَاذَا لِي فِيهِ وَعَنْ رَمْيِكَ الجِمَارَ وَتَقُولُ مَاذَا لِي فِيهِ قَالاَ وَالَّذِي بَعَثَكَ بِالحَقِّ إِنَّ ذَلِكَ لَلَّذِي جِئْنَا نَسْأَلُكَ عَنْهُ عق ز وحسّنه طب هق في الدلائل الفاكهي في أخبار مكة وفي الباب عن عبادة بن الصامت طب وأنس بن مالك مسند مسدد ز طب في الأحاديث الطوال التيمي في الترغيب الفاكهي والأزرقي كلاهما في أخبار مكة

al-Razzāq (5:15-16 §8830), al-Bazzār (12:317-318 §6177 cf. *Kashf al-Astār* 2:8-9 §1082), al-Ṭabarānī in *al-Kabīr* (12:425 §13566), al-Fākihī in *Akhbār Makka* (1:423-424 §918) and al-Bayhaqī in the *Dalā'il* (6:293), the latter three through ʿAbd al-Wahhāb b. Mujāhid who is discarded while the first two have simply "Mujāhid," hence al-Haythamī's (3:599-601) favorable verdict on al-Bazzār's chain and the latter's statement that his is the best chain; [3] 'Ubāda b. al-Ṣāmit by al-Ṭabarānī in *al-Awsaṭ* (3:16 §2320) with a passable chain cf. al-Haythamī (3:603-604).

[400]Narrated from Ibn ʿUmar by al-Fākihī in *Akhbār Makka* (4:266 §2594), al-Tabarānī in *al-Kabīr* (12:414 §13525), and al-Bazzār with a chain of trustworthy narrators according to al-Haythamī (3:297) but al-Suyūṭi grades it weak in *al-Jāmiʿ al-Saghīr* (§5965).

ʿUyayna b. Ḥiṣn al-Fazārī ﵁

Al-Bayhaqī and Abū Nuʿaym narrated from ʿUrwa that ʿUyayna b. Ḥiṣn asked the Messenger of Allah ﷺ permission to go to the people of al-Ṭā'if and talk to them so that, perhaps, Allah will guide them. He gave permission. ʿUyayna went and told them: "Hold fast to your position. By Allah! We are lowlier than slaves. I solemnly swear by Allah that if something happens to him [the Prophet ﷺ], the Arabs will be in a decisive position of superiority! Therefore, hold your fort, never let it go from your hands, and do not yield even if they hack down all of those trees!" Then he returned. The Messenger of Allah ﷺ asked him what he had told them. He said, "I spoke to them and ordered them to embrace Islam. I invited them to it and warned them of the Fire and induced them to seek Paradise." The Prophet ﷺ said: 299 "You are lying! You said to them such-and-such." He replied, "You are right, Messenger of Allah! I repent to Allah and to you."[401]

عَنْ عُرْوَةَ أَقْبَلَ عُيَيْنَةُ بْنُ حِصْنٍ حَتَّى جَاءَ إِلَى رَسُولِ اللهِ ﷺ
فقال إِئْذَنْ لِي أَنْ أُكَلِّمَهُمْ لَعَلَّ اللهَ أَنْ يَهْدِيَهُمْ فَأَذِنَ لَهُ
فَانْطَلَقَ حَتَّى دَخَلَ الحِصْنَ فَقَالَ بِأَبِي أَنْتُمْ تَمَسَّكُوا بِمَكَانِكُمْ
وَاللهِ لَنَحْنُ أَذَلُّ مِنَ الْعَبِيدِ وَأَقْسَمَ بِاللهِ لَئِنْ حَدَثَ بِهِ حَدَثٌ
لَيَمْلَكَنَّ الْعَرَبُ عِزّاً وَمَنْعَةً فَتَمَسَّكُوا بِحِصْنِكُمْ وَإِيَّاكُمْ أَنْ تُعْطُوا
بِأَيْدِيكُمْ وَلاَ يَتَكَابَرْنَ عَلَيْكُمْ قَطْعُ هَذِهِ الشَّجَرِ ثُمَّ خَرَجَ فَقَالَ

[401] Narrated *mursal* from ʿUrwa by Abū Nuʿaym in his *Dalā'il* (p. 531 §460) and al-Bayhaqī in his (4:163) cf. *Bidāya* (4:348-349), *Sīra Ḥalabiyya* (3:81), and *Khaṣā'is* (1:451). In Ibn ʿAbd al-Barr, *Durar* (1:255): "ʿUyayna was a coarse, rude, mad and 'foolish desert Arab obeyed among his people' *(al-aḥmaq al-mutāʿ)* [hadīth]." Ibn Ḥajar in *al-Iṣāba* (4:769) cites al-Shāfiʿī's statement in *al-Umm*, book of *zakāt*, that ʿUmar had ʿUyayna b. Ḥiṣn killed as an apostate but said it is likely that ʿUmar issued the order, then ʿUyayna reiterated his Islam and lived on until ʿUthmān's time cf. *Istīʿāb* (3:1249).

لَهُ النَّبِيُّ ﷺ مَاذَا قُلْتَ قَالَ دَعَوْتُهُمْ إِلَى الإِسْلَامِ وَحَذَّرْتُهُمُ النَّارَ وَفَعَلْتُ فَقَالَ كَذَبْتَ بَلْ قُلْتَ كَذَا وَكَذَا قَالَ صَدَقْتَ يَا رَسُولَ اللهِ أَتُوبُ إِلَى اللهِ وَإِلَيْكَ أبو نعيم وهق كلاهما في الدلائل

His ﷺ Foretelling the Death of a Group of Quraysh Idolaters

Ibn Isḥāq, al-Bayhaqī, and Abū Nuʿaym narrated that ʿUrwa said to ʿAbd Allāh b. ʿAmr b. al-ʿĀṣ: "What is the greatest extent of enmity you have seen from the Quraysh against the Messenger of Allah ﷺ?" He said: "I saw them when their foremost leaders assembled in the Chamber [of Ismāʿīl ﷺ] one day to discuss the Messenger of Allah ﷺ. They said: 'We have never seen the like of our patience with him before. He has ridiculed us, insulted our forefathers, defamed our religion, destroyed our unity and cursed our gods! We have suffered too much from him.' As they were saying this, the Messenger of Allah ﷺ came up and kept walking until he touched the [Black Stone] Corner. Then he passed them by while circumambulating the House, so they taunted him with certain words. I realized this from the look on the face of the Messenger of Allah ﷺ. He moved on. When he passed them by the second time they taunted him again with certain words. I realized this from the look on his face. When he passed them by the third time they taunted him again, so he stopped and said: 300 'Hear, O Quraysh! By the One in Whose Hand is my soul, I bring you slaughter!' His word sank into them to the point that each and every one of them froze as if birds had nested on top of their heads. Even the most violently opposed to him moments before began to entreat him in the gentlest terms and, in the end, said to him: 'Godspeed, Abū al-Qāsim! You are no fool.'"[402]

[402]Narrated as part of a longer ḥadīth with a sound chain from ʿUrwa, from ʿAbd Allāh b. ʿAmr b. al-ʿĀṣ by Ibn Isḥāq (§308) and, through him, al-Bazzār (6:457-459 §2497), Aḥmad (11:609-611 §7036 *isnād ḥasan*), Ibn Hishām (2:127), al-Ṭabarī in his *Tārīkh* (1:548), Ibn Ḥibbān (14:525-527 §6567 *isnād qawī*), al-Bayhaqī in the *Dalā'il* (2:275) and others cf. *Iktifā'* (1:224-225), *Bidāya* (3:46), *Fatḥ* (7:168-169), *Khaṣā'iṣ* (1:240), al-Haythamī (6:15-16), and Ibn Ḥajar in *Taghlīq al-Ta'līq* (4:86-87).

عَنْ عَبْدِ اللهِ بْنِ عَمْرِو بْنِ الْعَاصِ قَالَ قُلْتُ لَهُ مَا أَكْثَرَ مَا رَأَيْتَ قُرَيْشًا أَصَابَتْ مِنْ رَسُولِ اللهِ ﷺ فِيمَا كَانَتْ تُظْهِرُ مِنْ عَدَاوَتِهِ قَالَ حَضَرْتُهُمْ وَقَدْ اجْتَمَعَ أَشْرَافُهُمْ يَوْمًا فِي الْحِجْرِ فَذَكَرُوا رَسُولَ اللهِ ﷺ فَقَالُوا مَا رَأَيْنَا مِثْلَ مَا صَبَرْنَا عَلَيْهِ مِنْ هَذَا الرَّجُلِ قَطُّ سَفَّهَ أَحْلَامَنَا وَشَتَمَ آبَاءَنَا وَعَابَ دِينَنَا وَفَرَّقَ جَمَاعَتَنَا وَسَبَّ آلِهَتَنَا لَقَدْ صَبَرْنَا مِنْهُ عَلَى أَمْرٍ عَظِيمٍ أَوْ كَمَا قَالُوا قَالَ فَبَيْنَمَا هُمْ كَذَلِكَ إِذْ طَلَعَ عَلَيْهِمْ رَسُولُ اللهِ ﷺ فَأَقْبَلَ يَمْشِي حَتَّى اسْتَلَمَ الرُّكْنَ ثُمَّ مَرَّ بِهِمْ طَائِفًا بِالْبَيْتِ فَلَمَّا أَنْ مَرَّ بِهِمْ غَمَزُوهُ بِبَعْضِ مَا يَقُولُ قَالَ فَعَرَفْتُ ذَلِكَ فِي وَجْهِهِ ثُمَّ مَضَى فَلَمَّا مَرَّ بِهِمْ الثَّانِيَةَ غَمَزُوهُ بِمِثْلِهَا فَعَرَفْتُ ذَلِكَ فِي وَجْهِهِ ثُمَّ مَضَى ثُمَّ مَرَّ بِهِمْ الثَّالِثَةَ فَغَمَزُوهُ بِمِثْلِهَا فَقَالَ تَسْمَعُونَ يَا مَعْشَرَ قُرَيْشٍ أَمَا وَالَّذِي نَفْسُ مُحَمَّدٍ بِيَدِهِ لَقَدْ جِئْتُكُمْ بِالذَّبْحِ فَأَخَذَتِ الْقَوْمَ كَلِمَتُهُ حَتَّى مَا مِنْهُمْ رَجُلٌ إِلَّا كَأَنَّمَا عَلَى رَأْسِهِ طَائِرٌ وَاقِعٌ حَتَّى إِنَّ أَشَدَّهُمْ فِيهِ وَصَاةً قَبْلَ ذَلِكَ لَيَرْفَؤُهُ بِأَحْسَنِ مَا يَجِدُ مِنْ الْقَوْلِ حَتَّى إِنَّهُ لَيَقُولُ انْصَرِفْ يَا أَبَا الْقَاسِمِ انْصَرِفْ رَاشِدًا فَوَاللهِ مَا كُنْتَ جَهُولًا قَالَ فَانْصَرَفَ

حم ابن هشام الطبري في التاريخ ابن أبي حاتم في التفسير ز حب هق في الدلائل

Abū Nuʿaym also narrated it with another chain from ʿAbd Allāh b. ʿUmar and also with a fair chain from ʿAmr b. al-ʿĀṣ.

The latter version states that after the Prophet ﷺ said, [301] "I was not sent to you except to bring you slaughter," Abū Jahl said, "O Muḥammad! You are no fool." The Prophet ﷺ said: "You are one of them."[403]

عَنْ عَمْرِو بْنِ الْعَاصِ قَالَ مَا رَأَيْتُ قُرَيْشًا أَرَادُوا قَتْلَ رَسُولِ اللهِ ﷺ إِلاَّ يَوْمَ ائْتَمَرُوا بِهِ وَهُمْ جُلُوسٌ فِي ظِلِّ الْكَعْبَةِ وَرَسُولُ اللهِ ﷺ يُصَلِّي عِنْدَ الْمَقَامِ فَقَامَ إِلَيْهِ عُقْبَةُ بْنُ أَبِي مُعَيْطٍ فَجَعَلَ رِدَاءَهُ فِي عُنُقِهِ ثُمَّ جَذَبَهُ حَتَّى وَجَبَ لِرُكْبَتَيْهِ وَتَصَايَحَ النَّاسُ وَظَنُّوا أَنَّهُ مَقْتُولٌ قَالَ وَأَقْبَلَ أَبُو بَكْرٍ يَشْتَدُّ حَتَّى أَخَذَ بِضَبْعِ رَسُولِ اللهِ ﷺ مِنْ وَرَائِهِ وَهُوَ يَقُولُ أَيَقْتُلُونَ رَجُلًا أَنْ يَقُولَ رَبِّيَ اللهُ ثُمَّ انْصَرَفُوا عَنِ النَّبِيِّ ﷺ فَقَامَ رَسُولُ اللهِ ﷺ فَلَمَّا قَضَى صَلاتَهُ مَرَّ بِهِمْ وَهُمْ جُلُوسٌ فِي ظِلِّ الْكَعْبَةِ فَقَالَ يَا مَعْشَرَ قُرَيْشٍ أَمَا وَالَّذِي نَفْسِي بِيَدِهِ مَا أُرْسِلْتُ إِلَيْكُمْ إِلا بِالذَّبْحِ وَأَشَارَ بِيَدِهِ إِلَى حَلْقِهِ قَالَ لَهُ أَبُو جَهْلٍ يَا مُحَمَّدُ مَا كُنْتَ جَهُولاً فَقَالَ رَسُولُ اللهِ ﷺ أَنْتَ مِنْهُمْ ع ش حب أبو نعيم في الدلائل

Al-Bazzār narrated that Ṭalḥa b. ʿUbayd Allāh said: "A group of the Quraysh were around the Ka'ba, among them Abū Jahl, when the Messenger of Allah ﷺ came and stood in front of them. He said: [302] 'Perish these faces!' *(qabuḥat al-wujūh)*. They all fell

[403]Narrated from ʿAmr b. al-ʿĀṣ by Ibn Abī Shayba (7:331 §36561) and, through him, Abū Yaʿlā (13:325-326 §7339), Ibn Ḥibbān (14:529 §6569 *isnād ḥasan*), Abū Nuʿaym in the *Dalā'il* (p. 208-209 §159), and Ibn Ḥajar in *Taghlīq al-Taʿlīq* (4:88); also, with another chain, by al-Bukhārī in *Khalq Afʿāl al-ʿIbād* (p. 75) cf. *Fatḥ* (7:169).

mute without exception and I actually saw Abū Jahl apologizing to the Messenger of Allah ﷺ and saying, 'Spare us.' But the Messenger of Allah ﷺ kept saying: [a] 'I shall not spare you until I kill you!' Abū Jahl said: 'Are you able to do that?' The Prophet ﷺ said: [b] 'Allah shall kill you!'"[404]

عَنْ طَلْحَةَ بْنِ عُبَيْدِ اللهِ قَالَ كَانَ نَفَرٌ مِنَ الْمُشْرِكِينَ حَوْلَ الْكَعْبَةِ فِيهِمْ أَبُو جَهْلٍ لَعَنَهُ اللهُ فَأَقْبَلَ رَسُولُ اللهِ ﷺ فَوَقَفَ عَلَيْهِمْ فَقَالَ قَبُحَتِ الْوُجُوهُ فَخَرِسُوا فَمَا أَحَدٌ مِنْهُمْ تَكَلَّمَ بِكَلِمَةٍ وَلَقَدْ نَظَرْتُ إِلَى أَبِي جَهْلٍ وَهُوَ يَعْتَذِرُ إِلَى رَسُولِ اللهِ ﷺ فَقَالَ أَمْسِكْ عَنَّا وَيَقُولُ رَسُولُ اللهِ ﷺ لاَ أَمْسِكُ عَنْكُمْ أَوْ أَقْتُلُكُمْ فَقَالَ أَبُو جَهْلٍ أَنْتَ تَقْدِرُ عَلَى ذَلِكَ فَقَالَ رَسُولُ اللهِ ﷺ اللهُ يَقْتُلُكُمْ ز عن شيخه علي بن شبيب لا يعرف وبقية رجاله ثقات مج

Abū Nu'aym also narrated through 'Urwa: 'Amr b. 'Uthmān narrated to me that 'Uthmān b. 'Affān said: "The worst provocation the Quraysh committed against the Messenger of Allah ﷺ was when I saw him one day circumambulating the House while three of them were sitting in the Chamber – 'Uqba b. Abī Mu'ayṭ,[405] Abū Jahl, and Umayya b. Khalaf. When he came up to their level they taunted him. This was evident from the expression on the face of the Messenger of Allah ﷺ. They did this again and again in the second and third circumambulation. Then he stopped and said: 'Lo! [303] By Allah, **[512]** you will never stop until His

[404]Narrated from Talha b. 'Ubayd Allāh by al-Bazzār (3:165-166 §952) through trustworthy narrators except that his direct source, 'Alī b. Shabīb, is not known cf. al-Haythamī (8:228-229).

[405]He was executed after his capture at Badr.

punishment comes to pass, and that very soon!'" ʿUthmān said: "By Allah! Not a single one of them remained except he was seized with trembling. Then he went home and we followed him. He said: [a] 'Be glad! For Allah will grant the upper hand to His Religion, complete His Word, and grant victory to His Religion! [b] Those men you see are among those Allah shall slaughter at your very hands, and that very soon.' By Allah! I saw them as Allah slaughtered them at our hands [in the battle of Badr]."[406]

عَنْ عُثْمَانَ بْنِ عَفَّانَ رَضِيَ اللهُ تَعَالَى عَنْهُ كَانَ رَسُولُ اللهِ ﷺ يَطُوفُ بِالْبَيْتِ وَيَدُهُ فِي يَدِ أَبِي بَكْرٍ وَفِي الحِجْرِ ثَلاَثَةُ نَفَرٍ جُلُوسٌ عُقْبَةُ بْنُ أَبِي مُعَيْطٍ وَأَبُو جَهْلِ بْنُ هِشَامٍ وَأُمَيَّةُ بْنُ خَلَفٍ فَمَرَّ رَسُولُ اللهِ ﷺ فَلَمَّا حَاذَاهُمْ أَسْمَعُوهُ بَعْضَ مَا يَكْرَهُ فَعَرَفْتُ ذَلِكَ فِي وَجْهِ النَّبِيِّ ﷺ فَدَنَوْتُ مِنْهُ حَتَّى كَانَ بَيْنِي وَبَيْنَ أَبِي بَكْرٍ فَأَدْخَلَ أَصَابِعَهُ فِي أَصَابِعِي حَتَّى طُفْنَا جَمِيعاً فَلَمَّا حَاذَاهُمْ قَالَ أَبُو جَهْلٍ وَاللهِ لاَ نُصَالِحُكَ مَا بَلَّ بَحْرٌ صُوفَةً وَأَنْتَ تَنْهَانَا أَنْ نَعْبُدَ مَا يَعْبُدُ آبَاؤُنَا فَقَالَ رَسُولُ اللهِ ﷺ أَنَا ذَلِكَ ثُمَّ مَضَى عَنْهُمْ فَصَنَعُوا بِهِ فِي الشَّوْطِ الثَّالِثِ مِثْلَ ذَلِكَ حَتَّى إِذَا كَانَ الشَّوْطُ الرَّابِعُ نَاهَضُوهُ فَوَثَبَ أَبُو جَهْلٍ يُرِيدُ أَنْ يَأْخُذَ بِمَجْمَعِ ثَوْبِهِ فَدَفَعْتُ فِي صَدْرِهِ فَوَقَعَ عَلَى أُسْتِهِ وَدَفَعَ

[406]Narrated through al-Zubayr b. Bakkār by al-Dāraquṭnī in *al-Afrād* (Ibn Ṭāhir al-Maqdisī, *Aṭrāf* 1:74 §211) and through him by al-Khaṭīb in *Talkhīṣ al-Mutashābih* (1:14-15 §11). The *Khaṣā'is* (1:240-241) references it to Abū Nuʿaym cf. Ḍyā' al-Dīn al-Maqdisī in *al-Mukhtāra* (1:514-515 §382), *Fatḥ* (7:168) and *Sīra Ḥalabiyya* (1:472). Al-Nabhānī has 'Utba instead of ʿUqba.

أَبُو بَكْرٍ أُمَيَّةَ بْنَ خَلَفٍ وَدَفَعَ رَسُولُ اللهِ ﷺ عُقْبَةَ بْنَ أَبِي مُعَيْطٍ ثُمَّ انْفَرَجُوا عَنْ رَسُولِ اللهِ ﷺ وَهُوَ وَاقِفٌ ثُمَّ قَالَ لَهُمْ أَمَا وَاللهِ لاَ تَنْتَهُونَ حَتَّى يَحِلَّ عِقَابُهُ عَاجِلاً قَالَ عُثْمَانُ فَوَاللهِ مَا مِنْهُمْ رَجُلٌ إِلاَّ وَقَدْ أَخَذَهُ الْخَوْفُ وَجَعَلَ يَرْتَعِدُ فَجَعَلَ رَسُولُ اللهِ ﷺ يَقُولُ بِئْسَ الْقَوْمُ أَنْتُم لِنَبِيِّكُمْ ثُمَّ انْصَرَفَ إِلَى بَيْتِهِ وَتَبِعْنَاهُ حَتَّى انْتَهَى إِلَى بَابِ بَيْتِهِ فَوَقَفَ عَلَى السُّدَّةِ ثُمَّ أَقْبَلَ عَلَيْنَا بِوَجْهِهِ ثُمَّ قَالَ أَبْشِرُوا فَإِنَّ اللهَ عَزَّ وَجَلَّ مُظْهِرٌ دِينَهُ وَمُتِمٌّ كَلِمَتَهُ وَنَاصِرٌ نَبِيَّهُ إِنَّ هَؤُلاَءِ الَّذِينَ تَرَوْنَ مِمَّا يَذْبَحُ اللهُ بِأَيْدِيكُمْ عَاجِلاً ثُمَّ انْصَرَفْنَا إِلَى بُيُوتِنَا فَوَاللهِ لَقَدْ رَأَيْتُهُمْ قَدْ ذَبَحَهُمُ اللهُ عَزَّ وَجَلَّ بِأَيْدِينَا قط في الأفراد ومن طريقه خط في التلخيص وأورده الضياء في المختارة

In Muslim's *Ṣaḥīḥ* and elsewhere: the Messenger of Allah ﷺ stated before battling the idolaters on the day of Badr: 304 "Here is where So-and-so will find his demise" *(hādhā maṣra'u fulān)*, and he put his hand on the ground. Then [at another spot] he said: "Here is where So-and-so will find his demise," and he put his hand on it. Then he mentioned the rest of them one by one, pointing out the place where each would be killed. They were all killed precisely where he had said. Not one of them was killed in a different place than that pointed out by the Messenger of Allah ﷺ.[407]

[407]Narrated from Anas and 'Umar by Muslim, al-Nasā'ī, Abū Dāwūd, Aḥmad and others.

عَنْ أَنَسٍ رَضِيَ اللهُ عَنْهُ نَدَبَ رَسُولُ اللهِ ﷺ النَّاسَ فَانْطَلَقُوا حَتَّى نَزَلُوا بَدْرًا فَقَالَ رَسُولُ اللهِ ﷺ هَذَا مَصْرَعُ فُلَانٍ قَالَ وَيَضَعُ يَدَهُ عَلَى الْأَرْضِ هَا هُنَا وَهَا هُنَا قَالَ فَمَا مَاطَ أَحَدُهُمْ عَنْ مَوْضِعِ يَدِ رَسُولِ اللهِ ﷺ م ن د حم ط ز مسند أبي عوانة ش طس طس تهذيب الآثار للطبري حب هق وفي الدلائل

Abū Nuʿaym narrated from Jābir ؓ that Abū Jahl said, "Muḥammad is claiming that if you do not obey him, he is going to slaughter all of you!" The Messenger of Allah ﷺ said: 305 "This is what I say – and you are among the slaughtered." When he saw him lying dead the day of Badr, he said: a "O Allah! You have completed for me what You had promised."[408]

عَنْ جَابِرٍ رَضِيَ اللهُ عَنْهُ قَالَ قَالَ أَبُو جَهْلِ بْنِ هِشَامٍ إِنَّ مُحَمَّدًا يَزْعُمُ أَنَّكُمْ إِنْ لَمْ تُطِيعُوهُ كَانَ فِيكُمْ ذَبْحٌ فَقَالَ رَسُولُ اللهِ ﷺ وَأَنَا أَقُولُ ذَلِكَ وَأَنْتَ مِنْ ذَلِكَ الذَّبْحِ فَلَمَّا نَظَرَ إِلَيْهِ يَوْمَ بَدْرٍ مَقْتُولًا قَالَ اللَّهُمَّ قَدْ أَنْجَزْتَ لِي مَا وَعَدْتَنِي طس وفيه عبد العزيز بن عمران وهو ضعيف مج وروى الشطر الأخير الواقدي وجاء من وجه آخر عَنْ مُحَمَّدِ بْنِ كَعْبٍ الْقُرَظِيِّ قَالَ اجْتَمَعُوا لَهُ ﷺ وَفِيهِمْ أَبُو جَهْلٍ

---

[408] Narrated as part of a longer ḥadīth from Jābir by al-Ṭabarānī in *al-Awsaṭ* (9:60) through the genealogist ʿAbd al-ʿAzīz b. ʿImrān al-Madanī who is discarded as he narrated only from memory after the burning of his library cf. al-Haythamī (6:78) and *Khaṣāʾis* (1:241). The last clause is in al-Wāqidī (1:90) while Abū Jahl's statement is part of a longer hadith narrated by Ibn Hishām, al-Ṭabarī in his *Tārīkh*, and Abū Nuʿaym in the *Dalāʾil* (p. 203-204 §154).

فَقَالَ وَهُمْ عَلَى بَابِهِ إِنَّ مُحَمَّداً زَعَمَ أَنَّكُمْ إِنْ تَابَعْتُمُوهُ عَلَى أَمْرِهِ كُنْتُمْ مُلُوكَ الْعَرَبِ وَالْعَجَمِ ثُمَّ يَبْعَثُكُمْ مِنْ بَعْدِ مَوْتِكُمْ لَكُمْ جِنَانُ الأُرْدُنِ وَإِنْ لَمْ تَفْعَلُوا كَانَ لَكُمْ مِنْهُ ذَبْحٌ ثُمَّ بُعِثْتُمْ مِنْ بَعْدِ مَوْتِكُمْ فَجُعِلَتْ لَكُمْ نَارٌ تُحْرَقُونَ فِيهَا فَخَرَجَ رَسُولُ اللهِ ﷺ وَأَخَذَ حَفْنَةً مِنْ تُرَابٍ فِي يَدِهِ ثُمَّ قَالَ نَعَمْ أَنَا أَقُولُ ذَلِكَ وَأَنْتَ أَحَدُهُمْ وَأَخَذَ اللهُ عَلَى أَبْصَارِهِمْ فَلاَ يَرَوْنَهُ فَجَعَلَ يَنْثُرُ ذَلِكَ التُّرَابَ عَلَى رُؤُوسِهِمْ وَهُوَ يَتْلُو هَذِهِ الآيَاتِ ﴿ يسٓ ﴿١﴾ وَٱلْقُرْءَانِ ٱلْحَكِيمِ ﴿٢﴾ إِنَّكَ لَمِنَ ٱلْمُرْسَلِينَ ﴿٣﴾ ﴾ إِلَى قَوْلِهِ تَعَالَى ﴿ وَجَعَلْنَا مِنۢ بَيْنِ أَيْدِيهِمْ سَدًّا وَمِنْ خَلْفِهِمْ سَدًّا فَأَغْشَيْنَٰهُمْ فَهُمْ لَا يُبْصِرُونَ ﴿٩﴾ ﴾ حَتَّى فَرَغَ ابن هشام الطبري في التاريخ أبو نعيم في الدلائل

Aḥmad, al-Ḥākim, al-Bayhaqī, and Abū Nu'aym narrate through Ibn 'Abbās that Fāṭima رضي الله عنها said the idolaters of Quraysh gathered in the Chamber and plotted that when Muḥammad passed them by, each of them should strike him one blow. She heard them and went to her mother and told her. She mentioned this to him but he said: 306 "Little daughter, be still." Then he went out and and entered the Mosque in full sight of them. When they saw him, they said, "Here he is!" But they cast down their eyes, buried their chins into their chests, and remained seated one and all. They did not even raise their eyes to look at him nor did even one of them address him. He approached until he was standing over them, a took a handful of dust and threw it in their direction, saying: b "Perish the faces!" *(shāhat al-wujūh)*. None of the men that were hit by a pebble that day survived but all were killed with the disbelievers at Badr.[409]

عَنْ ابْنِ عَبَّاسٍ رَضِيَ اللهُ عَنْهُمَا أَنَّ الْمَلَأَ مِنْ قُرَيْشٍ اجْتَمَعُوا
فِي الْحِجْرِ فَتَعَاهَدُوا بِاللَّاتِ وَالْعُزَّى ﴿ وَمَنَوٰةَ ٱلثَّالِثَةَ ٱلْأُخْرَىٰ ﴿٢٠﴾ ﴾
النجم لَوْ قَدْ رَأَيْنَا مُحَمَّدًا قُمْنَا إِلَيْهِ قِيَامَ رَجُلٍ وَاحِدٍ فَلَمْ نُفَارِقْهُ
حَتَّى نَقْتُلَهُ قَالَ فَأَقْبَلَتْ فَاطِمَةُ تَبْكِي حَتَّى دَخَلَتْ عَلَى أَبِيهَا
فَقَالَتْ هَؤُلَاءِ الْمَلَأُ مِنْ قَوْمِكَ فِي الْحِجْرِ قَدْ تَعَاهَدُوا أَنْ لَوْ
قَدْ رَأَوْكَ قَامُوا إِلَيْكَ فَقَتَلُوكَ فَلَيْسَ مِنْهُمْ رَجُلٌ إِلَّا قَدْ عَرَفَ
نَصِيبَهُ مِنْ دَمِكَ قَالَ يَا بُنَيَّةُ أَدْنِي وَضُوءًا فَتَوَضَّأَ ثُمَّ دَخَلَ
عَلَيْهِمْ الْمَسْجِدَ فَلَمَّا رَأَوْهُ قَالُوا هُوَ هَذَا فَخَفَضُوا أَبْصَارَهُمْ
وَعُقِرُوا فِي مَجَالِسِهِمْ فَلَمْ يَرْفَعُوا إِلَيْهِ أَبْصَارَهُمْ وَلَمْ يَقُمْ مِنْهُمْ
رَجُلٌ فَأَقْبَلَ رَسُولُ اللهِ ﷺ حَتَّى قَامَ عَلَى رُءُوسِهِمْ فَأَخَذَ قَبْضَةً
مِنْ تُرَابٍ فَحَصَبَهُمْ بِهَا وَقَالَ شَاهَتْ الْوُجُوهُ قَالَ فَمَا أَصَابَتْ
رَجُلًا مِنْهُمْ حَصَاةٌ إِلَّا قَدْ قُتِلَ يَوْمَ بَدْرٍ كَافِرًا حم بإسنادين ورجال

[409]Narrated from Ibn ʿAbbās by Aḥmad with two sound chains cf. al-Haythamī (8:228), Saʿīd b. Manṣūr in his *Sunan* (2:378 §2913), Ibn Abī Ḥātim in his *ʿIlal* (2:397-398 §2702), in the *Dalā'il* of Abū Nuʿaym (p. 192-193 §139), al-Taymī (p. 65-66 §48), and al-Bayhaqī (6:240), Ibn Ḥibbān (14:430 §6502 *ṣaḥīḥ*), and al-Ḥākim (3:157 *isnād ṣaḥīḥ* cf. 1:163=1990 ed. 3:170 cf. 1:268), cf. al-Maqdisī in *al-Aḥādīth al-Mukhtāra* (10:218-220 §230-231), *Fatḥ al-Bārī* (7:169) and *Sīra Ḥalabiyya* (1:474) The curse of the Prophet ﷺ *(shāhat al-wujūh)* is narrated from several Companions in Muslim and elsewhere as also pronounced both before Badr and before Ḥunayn.

أحدهما رجال الصحيح مج ز سعيد بن منصور حب ك التيمي أبو نعيم هق ثلاثتهم في الدلائل

Al-Bayhaqī narrated through Isrā'īl from Abū Isḥāq that the Prophet ﷺ passed by Abū Jahl and Abū Sufyān as they were sitting. Abū Jahl said: "This is your Prophet, O Banū ʿAbd Shams!" Abū Sufyān said: "And why are you so surprised that there should be a Prophet from among us?" Abū Jahl said: "I am surprised a boy should emerge from the elders!" The Messenger of Allah ﷺ heard all this. He came to them and said: 307 "As for you, Abū Sufyān, it is neither for Allah nor for His Prophet that you became angry but you only jumped to defend your origins *(ḥamīta lil-aṣli)*. And as for you, Abū al-Ḥakam, by Allah! You shall laugh little and weep much." He replied, "Evil is what you promise me, nephew, with your Prophethood!"[410]

عَنْ أَبِي إِسْحَاقَ قَالَ مَرَّ النَّبِيُّ ﷺ عَلَى أَبِي جَهْلٍ وَأَبِي سُفْيَانَ وَهُمَا جَالِسَانِ فَقَالَ أَبُو جَهْلٍ هَذَا نَبِيُّكُمْ يَا بَنِي عَبْدِ شَمْسٍ فَقَالَ أَبُو سُفْيَانَ وَتَعْجَبُ أَنْ يَكُونَ مِنَّا نَبِيٌّ وَالنَّبِيُّ يَكُونُ فِيمَنْ هُوَ أَقَلُّ مِنَّا وَأَذَلُّ فَقَالَ أَبُو جَهْلٍ عَجِبْتُ أَنْ يَخْرُجَ غُلَامٌ مِنْ بَيْنِ شُيُوخٍ نَبِيّاً وَرَسُولُ اللهِ ﷺ يَسْمَعُ فَأَتَاهُمْ فَقَالَ أَمَّا أَنْتَ يَا أَبَا سُفْيَانَ فَمَا لِلَّهِ وَرَسُولِهِ غَضِبْتَ وَلَكِنَّكَ حَمِيتَ لِلأَصْلِ وَأَمَّا أَنْتَ يَا أَبَا الحَكَمِ فَوَاللهِ لَتَضْحَكَنَّ قَلِيلاً وَلَتَبْكِيَنَّ كَثِيراً قَالَ بِئْسَمَا تَعِدُنِي ابْنَ أَخِي مِنْ نُبُوَّتِكَ هق في الدلائل

[410]Narrated *mursal* from the Successor Abū Isḥāq al-Sabīʿī by al-Bayhaqī in his *Dalā'il* (2:284) and as cited in *al-Bidāya* (3:65). Al-Nabhānī misidentifies him as Ibn Isḥāq and has "O Banū ʿAbd Manāf."

Muslim, Abū Dāwūd, and al-Bayhaqī narrated from Anas: "The Prophet ﷺ said the night before Badr: [308] 'Here is where So-and-so will find his demise tomorrow, if Allah wills,' and he put his hand on the ground. 'And this [at another spot] is where So-and-so will find his demise tomorrow, if Allah wills,' and he put his hand on the ground. 'And this [at another spot] is where So-and-so will find his demise tomorrow, if Allah wills,' and he put his hand on the ground. By the One Who sent him with the truth! They did not trespass those limits one whit. They died precisely within them. Then they were thrown into the well. <The Prophet ﷺ came and said: [a] 'O So-and-so son of So-and-so! And O So-and-so son of So-and-so! Did you find true what your Lord had promised? For my part, I found true what my Lord had promised!' They said, 'Messenger of Allah, are you addressing bodies devoid of souls?' He replied: [b] 'You do not hear better than they do but they are unable to reply to me.'>"[411]

عَنْ أَنَسٍ رَضِيَ اللهُ عَنْهُ قَالَ رَسُولُ اللهِ ﷺ هَذَا مَصْرَعُ فُلَانٍ
غَداً وَوَضَعَ يَدَهُ عَلَى الأَرْضِ وَهَذَا مَصْرَعُ فُلَانٍ غَداً وَوَضَعَ
يَدَهُ عَلَى الأَرْضِ وَهَذَا مَصْرَعُ فُلَانٍ غَداً وَوَضَعَ يَدَهُ عَلَى
الأَرْضِ فقَالَ وَالَّذِي نَفْسِي بِيَدِهِ ما جَاوَزَ أَحَدٌ مِنْهُمْ عَنْ
مَوْضِعِ يَدِ رَسُولِ اللهِ ﷺ فَأَمَرَ بِهِمْ رَسُولُ اللهِ ﷺ فَأُخِذَ
بِأَرْجُلِهِمْ فَسُحِبُوا فَأُلْقُوا فِي قَلِيبِ بَدْرٍ د وَعَنْ أَنَسٍ قَالَ كُنَّا
مَعَ عُمَرَ بَيْنَ مَكَّةَ وَالْمَدِينَةِ فَأَنْشَأَ يُحَدِّثُنَا عَنْ أَهْلِ بَدْرٍ فَقَالَ

[411] Narrated from Anas by al-Nasā'ī, Abū Dāwūd, and Aḥmad and from ʿUmar by al-Ṭayālisī, Abū ʿAwāna in his *Mustakhraj*, al-Ṭabarī in *Tahdhīb al-Āthār*, Ibn Abī Shayba, al-Bayhaqī in the *Dalā'il*, and ohers. This narration was mentioned earlier in this section with a slightly different wording. The bracketed segment is also narrated independently from Ibn ʿUmar by al-Bukhārī and – with the specific names of the disbelievers – from Anas by Aḥmad.

إِنَّ رَسُولَ اللهِ ﷺ كَانَ يُرِينَا مَصَارِعَ أَهْلِ بَدْرٍ بِالأَمْسِ يَقُولُ
هَذَا مَصْرَعُ فُلاَنٍ غداً إِنْ شَاءَ اللهُ قَالَ فَقَالَ عُمَرُ فَوَالَّذِي بَعَثَهُ
بِالْحَقِّ مَا أَخْطَأُوا الْحُدُودَ الَّتِي حَدَّ رَسُولُ اللهِ ﷺ قَالَ فَجُعِلُوا
فِي بِئْرٍ بَعْضُهُمْ عَلَى بَعْضٍ فَانْطَلَقَ رَسُولُ اللهِ ﷺ حَتَّى انْتَهَى
إِلَيْهِمْ فَقَالَ يَا فُلاَنَ بْنَ فُلاَنٍ وَيَا فُلاَنَ بْنَ فُلاَنٍ هَلْ وَجَدْتُمْ مَا
وَعَدَكُمُ اللهُ وَرَسُولُهُ حَقّاً فَإِنِّي قَدْ وَجَدْتُ مَا وَعَدَنِي اللهُ حَقّاً
قَالَ عُمَرُ يَا رَسُولَ اللهِ كَيْفَ تُكَلِّمُ أَجْسَاداً لاَ أَرْوَاحَ فِيهَا قَالَ
مَا أَنْتُمْ بِأَسْمَعَ لِمَا أَقُولُ مِنْهُمْ غَيْرَ أَنَّهُمْ لاَ يَسْتَطِيعُونَ أَنْ يَرُدُّوا
عَلَيَّ شَيْئاً م ن وفي الكبرى حم د ط أبو عوانة ش طس طص ش الطبري في الآثار
هق وفي الدلائل

[The dead pagans of Badr were thrown into a dry well and the Prophet ﷺ addressed them in the same manner as the Prophets Ṣāliḥ ﷺ and Shuʿayb ﷺ had harangued the Thamūd and Madyan after their destruction as mentioned in Sūrat al-Aʿrāf (7:78-79, 91-93):

> The Prophet ﷺ ordered that the bodies of the idolaters slain on the Day of Badr be thrown into a well whose interior was lined with stones. After three days he approached the well and began addressing the unbelievers by their names and their fathers' names, saying: "O So-and-so son of So-and-so, and So-and-so son of So-and-so, it would have been easier if you had obeyed Allah and His Messenger. We have found our Lord's promise to be true; have you found your Lord's promise to be true?" To which ʿUmar said: "Messenger of Allah, why do you speak to lifeless bodies?" (in Muslim: "How can they hear, and how can they answer when they have turned into carcasses?") He replied: "By Him in whose hand is the soul of Muḥammad, you do not hear my words better than they do." In Muslim: "By Him in whose hand is the soul of Muḥammad, you do not hear my words better than they do, only they are unable to answer."[412]]

[412]Bukhārī (*Maghāzī, Qatl Abī Jahl*); Muslim (*al-Janna wa-Ṣifat Naʿīmihā, ʿArḍ maqʿad al-mayyit min al-janna aw al-nār ʿalayh*); Aḥmad (21:451-452 §14064). Al-Ṭabarī relies heavily upon the above narrations in his long validation of the proofs for the hearing of the dead in *Tahdhīb al-Āthar* (2:491-519).

Al-Bayhaqī narrated through Mūsā b. ʿUqba from Ibn Shihāb and through ʿUrwa b. al-Zubayr that when the Prophet ﷺ consulted his Companions about going to battle at **[513]** Badr he said: 309 "Say the Name of Allah and go *(sīrū 'alā-smi-l-Lāh)*! Truly, I have seen the spots where they are going to be killed."[413]

عَنْ مُوسَى بْنِ عُقْبَةَ قَالَ قَالَ ابْنُ شِهَابٍ قَالَ رَسُولُ اللهِ ﷺ سِيرُوا عَلَى اسْمِ اللهِ عَزَّ وَجَلَّ فَإِنِّي قَدْ أُرِيتُ مَصَارِعَ الْقَوْمِ فَعَمَدَ لِبَدْرٍ مغازي موسى بن عقبة هق في الدلائل وجاء بلفظ سِيرُوا عَلَى بَرَكَةِ اللهِ فَإِنَّ اللهَ قَدْ وَعَدَنِي إِحْدَى الطَّائِفَتَيْنِ فَوَاللهِ لَكَأَنِّي أَنْظُرُ إِلَى مَصَارِعَ الْقَوْمِ ابن هشام ابن سعد تاريخ الطبري الواقدي سيرة ابن حبان هق في الدلائل وأصله في صحيح مسلم عن عمر رضي الله عنه

Abū Nuʿaym narrated from Ibn Masʿūd ؓ that when the Messenger of Allah ﷺ looked at the idolaters the day of Badr, he said: 310 "Enemies of Allah! You look already slain in that red ridge of mountain."[414]

الحديثُ أنّه ﷺ لماَّ نَظَرَ إِلَى المُشْرِكِينَ يَوْمَ بَدْرٍ قَالَ كَأَنَّكُمْ يَا أَعْدَاءَ اللهِ بِهَذِهِ الضِّلَعِ الحَمْراءِ مُقَتَّلِينَ لا أصل له وكذا كَأَنِّي بِكُمْ

[413]Narrated *mursal* by Mūsā b. ʿUqba in his *Maghāzī* (p. 128) and Bayhaqī in the *Dalā'il* (3:107). Something similar is narrated with a broken chain from Ibn Mas'ūd by Nasā'ī in *'Amal al-Yawm wal-Layla* (p. 394 §606), Ṭabarānī in *al-Kabīr* (10:147), and Bayhaqī in *al-Sunan al-Kubrā* (5:187, 6:155) and the *Dalā'il* cf. al-Haythamī (6:82) with the wording *sīrū 'alā barakati-l-Lāh*, also cf. Ibn Hishām (3:162); Ibn Saʿd (2:14); Ibn Ḥibbān in *al-Thiqāt* (1:161). Its basis is in *Ṣaḥīḥ Muslim* from ʿUmar (*Janna, ʿarḍ maqʿad al-mayyit*).

[414]Thus cited and referenced in the *Khaṣā'is* (1:329) but it has no known chain and is not found other than in the lexical dictionaries such as al-Zamakhsharī's *Fā'iq*, al-Azharī's *Tahdhīb al-Lugha*, the *Nihāya*, the *Qāmūs*, and *Tāj al-'Arūsi*, all under *ḍ-l-ʿ*. What is authentically related is from ʿAlī b. Abī Ṭālib ؓ that the Prophet ﷺ said at Badr: "The host of Quraysh are under that red ridge of mountain." Narrated by Aḥmad, al-Bayhaqī in the *Dalā'il* (3:63), and Ibn ʿAsākir (38:249).

يَا أَعْدَاءَ اللهِ مُقَتَّلِينَ بِهَذِهِ الضِّلَعِ الْحَمْرَاءِ إنما ذكره أصحاب معاجم اللغة دون سند كالفائق وتهذيب اللغة والنهاية والقاموس وتاج العروس عزاه للعُباب للصغاني وليس في المطبوع والله تعالى أعلم وقال في الخصائص رواه أبو نعيم عن ابن مسعود وهو وهم والذي ورد عَنْ عَلِيٍّ رَضِيَ اللهُ عَنْهُ قَالَ سَارَ رَسُولُ اللهِ ﷺ إِلَى بَدْرٍ فَلَمَّا أَنْ طَلَعَ الْفَجْرُ نَادَى الصَّلَاةَ عِبَادَ اللهِ فَجَاءَ النَّاسُ مِنْ تَحْتِ الشَّجَرِ وَالْحَجَفِ فَصَلَّى بِنَا رَسُولُ اللهِ ﷺ وَحَرَّضَ عَلَى الْقِتَالِ ثُمَّ قَالَ إِنَّ جَمْعَ قُرَيْشٍ تَحْتَ هَذِهِ الضِّلَعِ الْحَمْرَاءِ مِنَ الْجَبَلِ حم هق في الدلائل كر

Al-Bukhārī and al-Bayhaqī narrated from Ibn Mas'ūd ؓ that Sa'd b. Mu'adh went to *'Umra* and stayed with Umayya b. Khalaf b. Ṣafwān. (When Umayya travelled to Shām and passed by al-Madīna, he would reside with Sa'd.) Umayya said to Sa'd: "Wait for noonday. When people are napping, go and circumambulate." As Sa'd was circumambulating, Abū Jahl came and asked, "Who is this circumambulating the Ka'ba?" Sa'd b. Mu'ādh said: "I am Sa'd." Abū Jahl said: "Are you circumambulating the Ka'ba in all safety when you have all given shelter to Muḥammad and his friends?" They began to quarrel. Umayya said to Sa'd: "Do not raise your voice over that of Abū al-Ḥakam – he is the leader of the people of this Valley!" Sa'd replied: "By Allah! If you prevent me from circumambulating the House, I shall cut off your trading in Shām." Umayya kept saying to Sa'd: "Do not raise your voice," trying to calm him down. Sa'd became angry and said: "Off with you! [311] I have heard Muḥammad ﷺ say that he will kill you." He said: "Is this true?" Sa'd said yes. Umayya said: "By Allah! Muḥammad never lies <when he says something>." He returned to his wife and said to her: "Did you hear what my brother from Yathrib said?" She said, "What did he say?" He said: "He claimed that he heard Muḥammad say he was going to kill me!" She said: "By Allah! Muḥammad does not lie." When they were about to go to Badr and they mobilized, his wife said to him: "Do you not remember what your Yathribī brother said to you?" He decided not to go. Abū Jahl said to him: "You are one of the eminent leaders of the people of this Valley. March with us for one or two days." He marched with them and got killed.[415]

عَنْ عَبْدِ اللهِ بْنِ مَسْعُودٍ رَضِيَ اللهُ عَنْهُ قَالَ انْطَلَقَ سَعْدُ بْنُ مُعَاذٍ مُعْتَمِرًا قَالَ فَنَزَلَ عَلَى أُمَيَّةَ بْنِ خَلَفٍ أَبِي صَفْوَانَ وَكَانَ أُمَيَّةُ إِذَا انْطَلَقَ إِلَى الشَّأْمِ فَمَرَّ بِالْمَدِينَةِ نَزَلَ عَلَى سَعْدٍ فَقَالَ أُمَيَّةُ لِسَعْدٍ انْتَظِرْ حَتَّى إِذَا انْتَصَفَ النَّهَارُ وَغَفَلَ النَّاسُ انْطَلَقْتُ فَطُفْتُ فَبَيْنَا سَعْدٌ يَطُوفُ إِذَا أَبُو جَهْلٍ فَقَالَ مَنْ هَذَا الَّذِي يَطُوفُ بِالْكَعْبَةِ فَقَالَ سَعْدٌ أَنَا سَعْدٌ فَقَالَ أَبُو جَهْلٍ تَطُوفُ بِالْكَعْبَةِ آمِنًا وَقَدْ آوَيْتُمْ مُحَمَّدًا وَأَصْحَابَهُ فَقَالَ نَعَمْ فَتَلَاحَيَا بَيْنَهُمَا فَقَالَ أُمَيَّةُ لِسَعْدٍ لَا تَرْفَعْ صَوْتَكَ عَلَى أَبِي الْحَكَمِ فَإِنَّهُ سَيِّدُ أَهْلِ الْوَادِي ثُمَّ قَالَ سَعْدٌ وَاللهِ لَئِنْ مَنَعْتَنِي أَنْ أَطُوفَ بِالْبَيْتِ لَأَقْطَعَنَّ مَتْجَرَكَ بِالشَّامِ قَالَ فَجَعَلَ أُمَيَّةُ يَقُولُ لِسَعْدٍ لَا تَرْفَعْ صَوْتَكَ وَجَعَلَ يُمْسِكُهُ فَغَضِبَ سَعْدٌ فَقَالَ دَعْنَا عَنْكَ فَإِنِّي سَمِعْتُ مُحَمَّدًا ﷺ يَزْعُمُ أَنَّهُ قَاتِلُكَ قَالَ إِيَّايَ قَالَ نَعَمْ قَالَ وَاللهِ مَا يَكْذِبُ مُحَمَّدٌ إِذَا حَدَّثَ فَرَجَعَ إِلَى امْرَأَتِهِ

[415]Narrated from Ibn Mas'ūd by Bukhārī, Aḥmad, Ṭabarānī in *al-Kabīr*, Bayhaqī in the *Dalā'il* and others. Yathrib is the pre-Islamic name of al-Madīna. The bracketed segment is corrupted to *fakāda yuḥdith* in al-Nabhānī instead of the correct *idhā ḥaddatha*.

فَقَالَ أَمَا تَعْلَمِينَ مَا قَالَ لِي أَخِي الْيَثْرِبِيُّ قَالَتْ وَمَا قَالَ قَالَ
زَعَمَ أَنَّه سَمِعَ مُحَمَّدًا يَزْعُمُ أَنَّهُ قَاتِلِي قَالَتْ فَوَاللهِ مَا يَكْذِبُ
مُحَمَّدٌ قَالَ فَلَمَّا خَرَجُوا إِلَى بَدْرٍ وَجَاءَ الصَّرِيخُ قَالَتْ لَهُ امْرَأَتُهُ
أَمَا ذَكَرْتَ مَا قَالَ لَكَ أَخُوكَ الْيَثْرِبِيُّ قَالَ فَأَرَادَ أَنْ لَا يَخْرُجَ
فَقَالَ لَهُ أَبُو جَهْلٍ إِنَّكَ مِنْ أَشْرَافِ الْوَادِي فَسِرْ يَوْمًا أَوْ
يَوْمَيْنِ فَسَارَ مَعَهُمْ فَقَتَلَهُ اللهُ خ حم طب هق في الدلائل

Abū Nuʿaym narrated with a sound chain from Ibn ʿAbbās رضي الله عنهما that [ʿUqba] Ibn Abī Muʿayṭ invited the Prophet ﷺ to a meal, whereupon the Prophet ﷺ said: 312 "I shall not eat until you bear witness that there is no God but Allah and that I am the Messenger of Allah!" He bore witness. Later, one of his friends met him and blamed him for what he had done. He said: "What can I do to regain the trust of the Quraysh?" His friend said: "You must approach him while he is sitting and spit in his face." When he did, the Prophet ﷺ only wiped his face and said: a "When I find you outside the mountains of Mecca, I will execute you." On the day of Badr, when all his friends went out, ʿUqba refused to leave, saying, "The man has said he shall execute me when he finds me outside the mountains of Mecca!" They told him, "We will give you a red camel that can never be caught. If we are routed, you will fly!" He went out with them. When the idolaters were routed, his camel got mired in and he was captured. Then the Prophet ﷺ had him executed.[416]

[416]This wording is from Ibn Mardūyah's *Tafsīr* or from the lost/unpublished part of Abū Nuʿaym's *Dalā'il* and Allah knows best. Narrated through several *mursal* chains from Mujāhid, Miqsam and al-Sha'bī by al-Ṭabarī in his *Tafsīr* (19:8 under 25:27) and, in the terms of the Arabic wording, from Ibn ʿAbbās by Abū Nuʿaym in the *Dalā'il* (p. 470-471 §401) cf. *Khasā'is* (1:341), *Sīra Ḥalabiyya* (1:508). See also Aḥmad, *ʿIlal* (1:130) on those said to have been executed at Badr.

عَنِ ابْنِ عَبَّاسٍ رَضِيَ اللهُ عَنْهُمَا أَنَّ عُقْبَةَ بْنَ أَبِي مُعَيْطٍ دَعَا رَسُولَ اللهِ ﷺ إِلَى طَعَامٍ فَقَالَ لَهُ رَسُولُ اللهِ ﷺ مَا أَنَا بِالَّذِي آكُلُ مِنْ طَعَامِكَ حَتَّى تَشْهَدَ أَنْ لاَ إِلَهَ إِلاَّ اللهُ وَأَنِّي رَسُولُ اللهِ فَقَالَ لَهُ يَابْنَ أَخِي دَعْنِي وَاطْعَمْ قَالَ مَا أَنَا بِالَّذِي أَفْعَلُ حَتَّى تَقُولَ قَالَ فَشَهِدَ عُقْبَةُ بِذَلِكَ وَطَعِمَ رَسُولُ اللهِ ﷺ مِنْ طَعَامِهِ فَبَلَغَ ذَلِكَ أُبَيَّ بْنَ خَلَفٍ فَأَتَاهُ فَقَالَ لَهُ أَصَبَوْتَ يَا عُقْبَةَ قَالَ لاَ وَلَكِنْ دَخَلَ عَلَيَّ فَأَبَى أَنْ يَطْعَمَ مِنْ طَعَامِي إِلاَّ أَنْ أَشْهَدَ لَهُ فَاسْتَحْيَيْتُ أَنْ يَخْرُجَ مِنْ بَيْتِي قَبْلَ أَنْ يَطْعَمَ فَشَهِدْتُ لَهُ فَطَعِمَ فَقَالَ مَا أَنَا بِالَّذِي أَرْضَى عَنْكَ حَتَّى تَأْتِيَهُ فَتَبْزُقَ فِي وَجْهِهِ وَتَطَأَ عَلَى عُنُقِهِ قَالَ فَفَعَلَ عُقْبَةُ ذَلِكَ فَقَالَ لَهُ رَسُولُ اللهِ ﷺ وَاللهِ لاَ أَلْقَاكَ خَارِجاً مِنْ مَكَّةَ إِلاَّ عَلَوْتُ رَأْسَكَ بِالسَّيْفِ فَأُسِرَ عُقْبَةُ يَوْمَ بَدْرٍ فَقُتِلَ صَبْراً أبو نعيم في الدلائل وروى أطرافه الطبري في التفسير من وجوه مختلفة مرسلة صحيحة

[ʿUqba also tried to strangle the Prophet ﷺ with his cloak as the latter was praying at the Kaʿba but Abū Bakr pushed him back and said: 313 "Will you kill a man because he says, 'My Sovereign Lord is Allah'?" ʿAbd Allāh b. ʿAmr b. al-ʿĀṣ said it was the worst act of provocation ever committed by the idolaters against the Prophet ﷺ.][417]

Al-Bayhaqī narrated through Mūsā b. ʿUqba, from Ibn Shihāb, from Saʿīd b. al-Musayyib, that Ubay b. Khalaf swore when he paid his ransom [after being captured at Badr]: "By Allah! I have a steed which I am feeding every day a portion of corn, and I

[417]Narrated from ʿAbd Allāh b. ʿAmr b. al-ʿĀṣ by al-Bukhārī and Aḥmad.

shall kill Muḥammad riding it!" News of this reached the Messenger of Allah ﷺ who said: 314 "Nay, I shall kill him if Allah wills." [At Uḥud] Ubay came in his armor, riding that horse of his, shouting "May I not survive if Muḥammad survives!" He charged the Messenger of Allah ﷺ, intent on killing him. Mūsā b. ʿUqba said that Saʿīd b. al-Musayyib said that several men among the Believers intercepted him[418] then the Messenger of Allah ﷺ ordered them to clear the way. a The Messenger of Allah ﷺ sighted the clavicle *(tarquwa)* of Ubay b. **[514]** Khalaf showing through a gap between the helmet and the breastplate. b He speared him there. Ubay fell off his horse but no blood came out of his wound. Saʿīd said he broke a rib. Thereupon was revealed the verse **﴾You threw not when you did throw, but Allah threw﴿** (8:17). His friends came and found him drooping like a tired bull. They said: "What is ailing you? It is only a scratch!" But he reminded them of the saying of the Messenger of Allah ﷺ – "I shall kill Ubay" – then he said, "By the One in Whose Hand is my soul! If the wound I just received were in the people of Dhūl-Majāz they would all die!" He died on his way to Mecca.[419] Al-Bayhaqī said ʿAbd al-Raḥmān b. Khālid b. Musāfir also related it from Ibn Shihāb from Saʿīd b. al-Musayyib. Al-Suyūṭī said: "Ibn Saʿd and Abū Nuʿaym narrated it with the latter chain while al-Bayhaqī and Abū Nuʿaym also narrated something identical from ʿUrwa b. al-Zubayr but without mention of the breaking of the rib nor the revelation of the verse."[420]

[418]Among them Muṣʿab b. ʿUmayr who got killed, Umm ʿUmāra Nasība bint Kaʿb al-Anṣāriyya al-Khazrajiyya al-Najjāriyya al-Māziniyya, her husband Ghaziyya b. ʿAmr, and her two sons Khubayb b. Zayd b. ʿĀṣim whom Musaylima cut to pieces and ʿAbd Allāh b. Zayd al-Māzinī who killed Musaylima at al-Yamāma and got killed at al-Ḥarra. She got gashed in her shoulder (among twelve wounds in total) and nursed that wound for a full year. The Prophet ﷺ praised her during battle and later. She also saw Ḥunayn and her hand got cut off at al-Yamāma. She referred to Ubay b. Khalaf as Ibn Qami'a ("Son of Trash"). Her brother ʿAbd Allāh b. Kaʿb al-Māzinī fought at Badr. Al-Dhahabī, *Siyar* (3:520-523 §146). *Al-Ḥarra* is the name of a place near Madīna and refers to the sacking of Madīna by the armies of Shām under Yazīd b. Muʿāwiya in the last days of Dhūl-Hijja in the year 63, at which time al-Zuhrī stated that ten thousand of the people of Madīna were killed, among them 300 to 700 of the *Muhājirūn* and *Anṣār*.

[419]Narrated by al-Bayhaqī in the *Dalā'il* (3:211-212) after Mūsā b. ʿUqbā, *Maghāzī* (p. 188) cf. Ibn Hishām also.

[420]Something similar was narrated from the Companion al-Musayyib b. Hazn by al-Ḥākim (2:327=1990 ed. 2:357) with a sound chain per al-Bukhārī's criterion; *mursal* from his son Saʿīd b. al-Musayyib by Ibn Saʿd (2:46); and – in part – by al-Wāqidī (1:250); also,

كَانَ أُبَيُّ بْنُ خَلَفٍ قَالَ حِينَ افْتُدِيَ وَاللهِ إِنَّ عِنْدِي لَفَرَساً أَعْلِفُهَا كُلَّ يَوْمٍ فِرْقَ ذُرَةٍ وَلَأَقْتُلَنَّ عَلَيْهَا مُحَمَّداً فَبَلَغَتْ رَسُولَ اللهِ ﷺ حَلْفَتُهُ فَقَالَ بَلْ أَنَا أَقْتُلُهُ إِنْ شَاءَ اللهُ فَأَقْبَلَ أُبَيٌّ مُقَنَّعاً فِي الحَدِيدِ عَلَى فَرَسِهِ تِلْكَ يَقُولُ لاَ نَجَوْتُ إِنْ نَجَا مُحَمَّدٌ فَحَمَلَ عَلَى رَسُولِ اللهِ ﷺ يُرِيدُ قَتْلَهُ قَالَ مُوسَى بْنُ عُقْبَةَ قَالَ سَعِيدُ بْنُ المسَيِّبِ فَاعْتَرَضَ لَهُ رِجَالٌ مِنَ المؤْمِنِينَ فَأَمَرَهُمْ رَسُولُ اللهِ ﷺ فَخَلَّوا طَرِيقَهُ وَاسْتَقْبَلَهُ مُصْعَبُ بْنُ عُمَيْرٍ أَخُو بَنِي عَبْدِ الدَّارِ يَقِي رَسُولَ اللهِ ﷺ فَقُتِلَ مُصْعَبُ بْنُ عُمَيْرٍ وَأَبْصَرَ رَسُولُ اللهِ ﷺ تَرْقُوَةَ أُبَيِّ بْنِ خَلَفٍ مِنْ فُرْجَةٍ بَيْنَ سَابِغَةِ الْبَيْضَةِ وَالدِّرْعِ فَطَعَنَهُ بِحَرْبَتِهِ فَوَقَعَ أُبَيٌّ عَنْ فَرَسِهِ وَلَمْ يَخْرُجْ مِنْ طَعْنَتِهِ دَمٌ قَالَ سَعِيدٌ فَكَسَرَ ضِلْعاً مِنْ أَضْلاَعِهِ فَفِي ذَلِكَ نَزَلَ ﴿وَمَا رَمَيْتَ إِذْ رَمَيْتَ وَلَٰكِنَّ ٱللَّهَ رَمَىٰ﴾ الأنفال فَأَتَاهُ أَصْحَابُهُ وَهُوَ يَخُورُ خُوَارَ الثَّوْرِ فَقَالُوا مَا جَزَعَكَ إِنَّمَا هُوَ خَدْشٌ فَذَكَرَ لَهُمْ قَوْلَ رَسُولِ اللهِ ﷺ بَلْ أَنَا أَقْتُلُ أُبَيّاً ثُمَّ قَالَ وَالَّذِي نَفْسِي بِيَدِهِ

without mention of the broken rib and the verse, *mursal* from ʿUrwa b. al-Zubayr by Abū Nuʿaym in the *Dalā'il* (p. 483 §415). Cf. *Khasā'is* (1:352-353), al-Qurṭubī's (7:385) and Ibn Kathīr's *Tafsīr* (1:416), *Bidāya* (4:32), *Zād* (3:178, 188), and *Sīra Ḥalabiyya* (2:511). Dhūl-Majāz is an oasis of Hudhayl behind 'Arafa where a market was held in pre-Islamic times cf. Yāqūt (5:55 and 5:58). After this encounter the Prophet ﷺ bugled to head for Ḥamrā' al-Asad. *Siyar* (3:521).

لَوْ كَانَ هَذَا الَّذِي بِي بِأَهْلِ ذِي المَجَازِ لَمَاتُوا أَجْمَعُونَ فَمَاتَ
أُبَيٌّ قَبْلَ أَنْ يَقْدَمَ مَكَّةَ هق في الدلائل من طريق موسى بن عقبة في المغازي
ونحوه عند الواقدي

Al-Bayhaqī narrated through Ibn Isḥāq that al-Zuhrī mentioned: "Ubay b. Khalaf faced the Prophet ﷺ saying, 'Muḥammad! May I not survive if you survive!' They said: 'Messenger of Allah! Shall one of us turn to face him?' He said: [315] 'Leave him!' When he approached, the Prophet ﷺ took the spear from al-Ḥārith b. al-Ṣimma [al-Badrī]. One of the witnesses said – as was related to me – that [a] the Prophet ﷺ jumped up with a motion that sent us scampering away from him like gadflies off the back of a camel. Then he faced him and stabbed him in the neck with a thrust that sent him tumbling off his horse in a great fall.[421]

عَنِ الزُّهْرِيِّ فَلَمَّا أُسْنِدَ رَسُولُ اللهِ ﷺ فِي الشِّعْبِ أَدْرَكَهُ أُبَيُّ بْنُ خَلَفٍ وَهُوَ يَقُولُ إِيْ مُحَمَّدُ لاَ نَجَوْتُ إِنْ نَجَوْتَ فَقَالَ الْقَوْمُ يَا رَسُولَ اللهِ أَيَعْطِفُ عَلَيْهِ رَجُلٌ مِنَّا فَقَالَ رَسُولُ اللهِ ﷺ دَعُوهُ فَلَمَّا دَنَا تَنَاوَلَ رَسُولُ اللهِ ﷺ الْحَرْبَةَ مِنَ الْحَارِثِ بْنِ الصِّمَّةِ يَقُولُ بَعْضُ الْقَوْمِ فِيمَا ذُكِرَ لِي فَلَمَّا أَخَذَهَا رَسُولُ اللهِ ﷺ مِنْهُ انْتَفَضَ بِهَا انْتِفَاضَةً تَطَايَرْنَا عَنْهُ تَطَايُرَ الشَّعْرَاءِ عَنْ ظَهْرِ الْبَعِيرِ إِذَا انْتَفَضَ بِهَا قَالَ ابْنُ هِشَامٍ الشَّعْرَاءُ ذُبَابٌ لَهُ لَدْغٌ ثُمَّ

[421]Narrated from Ka'b b. Mālik by al-Wāqidī (1:251-252) and Ibn Isḥāq (§511), and through the latter Ibn Hishām (4:33), Ibn Abī ʿĀṣim, *Jihād* (2:601-602 §253), al-Ṭabarī, *Tārīkh* (2:67), and Abū Nuʿaym, *Dalā'il* (p. 482 §414) cf. Ibn Ḥibbān, *Thiqāt* (1:229), *Iktifā'* (2:77), Ibn Kathīr, *Tafsīr* (1:416-417), *Bidāya* (4:32).

اسْتَقْبَلَهُ فَطَعَنَهُ فِي عُنُقِهِ طَعْنَةً تَدَأْدَأَ مِنْهَا عَنْ فَرَسِهِ مِرَارًا قَالَ ابْنُ هِشَامٍ تَدَأْدَأَ يَقُولُ تَقَلَّبَ عَنْ فَرَسِهِ فَجَعَلَ يَتَدَحْرَجُ ابن هشام تاريخ الطبري هق في الدلائل وجاء مسنداً عَنْ كَعْبِ بْنِ مَالِكٍ كَانَ رَسُولُ اللهِ ﷺ فِي الْقِتَالِ لاَ يَلْتَفِتُ وَرَاءَهُ فَكَانَ يَقُولُ لِأَصْحَابِهِ إِنِّي أَخْشَى أَنْ يَأْتِيَ أُبَيُّ بْنُ خَلَفٍ مِنْ خَلْفِي فَإِذَا رَأَيْتُمُوهُ فَآذِنُونِي بِهِ فَإِذَا بِأُبَيٍّ يَرْكُضُ عَلَى فَرَسِهِ وَقَدْ رَأَى رَسُولَ اللهِ ﷺ فَعَرَفَهُ فَجَعَلَ يَصِيحُ بِأَعْلَى صَوْتِهِ يَا مُحَمَّدُ لاَ نَجَوْتُ إِنْ نَجَوْتَ فَقَالَ الْقَوْمُ يَا رَسُولَ اللهِ مَا كُنْتَ صَانِعًا حِينَ يَغْشَاكَ فَقَدْ جَاءَكَ وَإِنْ شِئْتَ عَطَفَ عَلَيْهِ بَعْضُنَا فَأَبَى رَسُولُ اللهِ ﷺ وَدَنَا أُبَيٌّ فَتَنَاوَلَ رَسُولُ اللهِ ﷺ الْحَرْبَةَ مِنَ الْحَارِثِ بْنِ الصِّمَّةِ ثُمَّ انْتَفَضَ بِأَصْحَابِهِ كَمَا يَنْتَفِضُ الْبَعِيرُ فَتَطَايَرْنَا عَنْهُ تَطَايُرَ الشَّعَارِيرِ وَلَمْ يَكُنْ أَحَدٌ يُشْبِهُ رَسُولَ اللهِ ﷺ إِذَا جَدَّ الْجِدُّ

الواقدي ابن أبي عاصم في الجهاد

Abū Nuʿaym also narrated it through other chains, such as from Maʿmar [from] Miqsam, in which Ubay says, "By Allah! If he hit me only with his spittle he would kill me! Did he not say 'I shall kill him'?"[422]

[422]Narrated *mursal* from Miqsam b. Bujra the freedman of Ibn ʿAbbās by ʿAbd al-Razzāq (5:355-357 §9731) through his Shaykh Maʿmar b. Rāshid cf. *Khasāʾis* (1:353) and by Ibn Hishām (4:33) through Ibn Isḥāq. Al-Nabhānī's text has the lapsus "from Maʿmar b. Miqsam."

عَنْ مِقْسَمٍ بِهِ وَفِيهِ فَقَالَ وَاللهِ لَوْ لَمْ يُصِبْنِي إِلاَّ بِرِيقِهِ لَقَتَلَنِي
أَلَيْسَ قَدْ قَالَ أَنَا أَقْتُلُهُ عق

Al-Wāqidī said that Ibn ʿUmar would say: "Ubay b. Khalaf died in the clan of Rābigh. I was travelling in the clan of Rābigh for a while after nightfall when I saw a fire blazing before me. I felt dread. Lo and behold! A man came out of it, dragging a chain and crying thirst. Another man said, 'Do not give him water! This man was killed by the Messenger of Allah ﷺ. This is Ubay b. Khalaf.'"[423]

قَالَ الوَاقِدِيُّ كَانَ ابْنُ عُمَرَ يَقُولُ مَاتَ أُبَيُّ بْنُ خَلَفٍ بِبَطْنِ
رَابِغٍ فَإِنِّي لأَسِيرُ بِبَطْنِ رَابِغٍ بَعْدَ هَوِيٍّ مِنَ اللَّيْلِ إِذَا نَارٌ تَأَجَّجُ
فَهِبْتُهَا وَإِذَا رَجُلٌ يَخْرُجُ مِنْهَا فِي سِلْسِلَةٍ يَجْتَذِبُهَا يَصِيحُ الْعَطَشَ
وَإِذَا رَجُلٌ يَقُولُ لا تَسْقِهِ فَإِنَّ هَذَا قَتِيلُ رَسُولِ اللهِ ﷺ هَذَا أُبَيُّ
بْنُ خَلَفٍ فَقُلْتُ أَلاَ سُحْقًا الواقدي هق في الدلائل

His ﷺ Revealing that Woodworms Had Devoured the Charter of the Quraysh, which Proved True

Al-Bayhaqī and Abū Nuʿaym narrated through Mūsā b. ʿUqba that al-Zuhrī said the idolaters bore down on the Muslims as hard as they could to the point that the Muslims felt unendurable hardship. This hardship increased after the Muslims emigrated to the Negus and news of the latter's hospitality toward them reached the idolaters. Quraysh unanimously decided to kill the Messenger of Allah ﷺ and made no secret of it. When Abū Ṭālib saw them do

[423]Narrated by al-Wāqidī (1:252) as cited by Bayhaqī in the *Dalāʾil* (3:259) cf. *Khasāʾis* (1:353), *Zād* (3:188), *Bidāya* (4:32), Ibn Kathīr (1:417), *Sīra Ḥalabiyya* (2:512), etc.

this, he convened the Banū al-Muṭṭalib and ordered them to conceal the Messenger of Allah ﷺ inside their mountain trails and defend him against anyone that might try to kill him. They all agreed to this, both their believers and their unbelievers. When Quraysh found out that they were defending the Messenger of Allah ﷺ, they convened and unanimously decided to cease sitting with them, trading with them, and entering their houses until they handed over the Messenger of Allah ﷺ. They transcribed the plot they had hatched in a charter *(ṣaḥīfa)* of pacts and covenants stipulating that they would not accept any truce with the Banū Hāshim until they handed him over to be killed. The Banū Hāshim stood firm for three years. During that time, hardships increased against them and they cut off all supplies from them. They left no provisions reach Mecca nor any kind of goods except they preceded them in buying it. At the end of the third year, men from the Banū ʿAbd Manāf, from **[515]** the Banū Quṣay, and others from the Quraysh whose mothers and foremothers were of the Banū Hāshim began to blame one another for cutting off blood ties and making light of justice. One night, they all decided to rescind the pact of treachery they had covenanted together and to wash their hands of it. Allah had sent the woodworms against their charter and they had devoured all the pacts and covenants that it contained. It had been hanged from the roof of the House. The woodworms did not leave a single Name of Allah in it except it devoured it, leaving the rest of its content of idolatry, wrongdoing, and the desertion of kindred. Allah disclosed to His Prophet what had happened to their charter and the Messenger of Allah ﷺ informed Abū Ṭālib of it. Abū Ṭālib said: "By the falling stars *(lā wal-thawāqib)*! You never once lied to me." He went out in a throng of the Banū ʿAbd al-Muṭṭalib until he reached the Mosque which was filled with the Quraysh. When the Quraysh saw them coming out in full resolve they found it unusual and thought they had come out due to hardship and in order to surrender the Messenger of Allah ﷺ. Abū Ṭālib said: "Certain things took place among you which we shall not mention to you. Bring your charter to which you agreed with one another. Perhaps there will be a truce between us and you after all!" He only said this lest they look at the charter before bringing it out in full view. They brought their charter with pomp and pride, not doubting for a moment that the Messenger of Allah ﷺ was going to be surrendered to them. They placed the charter between them. Abū Ṭālib said: "I came to you only to give you something in all fairness to you *(lakum fīhi naṣaf)*. [316] My nephew has informed me – and he never once lied to me! – that Allah wants nothing to do with this charter you are holding in your hands and that He has erased every Name of His that was in it, leaving only your treachery, your severing ties with us, and your oppression of us! If what my nephew said is as he said, then be on guard! For, by Allah! He will never be given over, not until the last one of us dies! And if what he said is false, then we shall give him over to you to kill or spare." They said, "We accept your terms." Then they opened the charter and found that the Truthful and Confirmed Prophet ﷺ had indeed described it accurately. When the Qurasyh realized that it was just as he had told, they said, "By Allah! This is nothing but sorcery from your friend!" The Banū ʿAbd al-Muṭṭalib said: "It is not we but others who are more deserving of the charge of falsehood and sorcery! We know well that what you all did together – severing your ties with us – is nearer to Satan and sorcery. Had you not acted together in sorcery, your charter would not have decayed in your very hands! Allah caused every Name of His that was in it to vanish and He left only its perfidy in it. Are we the sorcerers or you?" At this the Banū ʿAbd Manāf and Banū Quṣay said: "We no longer have anything to do with this charter." Thereafter, the Prophet ﷺ and his band came out into the open and lived freely among the people.[424]

عَنِ ابْنِ شِهَابٍ الزُّهْرِيِّ قَالَ ثُمَّ إِنَّ الْمُشْرِكِينَ اشْتَدُّوا عَلَى الْمُسْلِمِينَ كَأَشَدِّ مَا كَانُوا حَتَّى بَلَغَ الْمُسْلِمِينَ الْجَهْدُ وَاشْتَدَّ عَلَيْهِمُ الْبَلَاءُ وَاجْتَمَعَتْ قُرَيْشٌ فِي مَكْرِهَا أَنْ يَقْتُلُوا رَسُولَ اللهِ

[424]Narrated *mursal* through ʿUrwa b. al-Zubayr by Abū Nuʿaym, *Dalā'il* (p. 272-275 §205), and through Mūsa b. ʿUqba in his *Maghāzī* (p. 82-85) from al-Zuhrī in the *Dalā'il* of al-Taymī (p. 200-202) and al-Bayhaqī (2:311-314), also in Ibn ʿAbd al-Barr's *Durar* (1:53-56) cf. *Khaṣā'is* (1:249-251). Also narrated *mursal* by Ibn Isḥāq (§209). Al-Bayhaqī cites part of it in *al-Sunan al-Kubrā* (6:365).

ﷺ عَلاَنِيَةً فَلَمَّا رَأَى أَبُو طَالِبٍ عَمَلَ الْقَوْمِ جَمَعَ بَنِي عَبْدِ
المطَّلِبِ وَأَمَرَهُمْ أَنْ يُدْخِلُوا رَسُولَ اللهِ ﷺ شِعْبَهُمْ وَيَمْنَعُوهُ مِمَّنْ
أَرَادَ قَتْلَهُ فَاجْتَمَعُوا عَلَى ذَلِكَ مُسْلِمُهُمْ وَكَافِرُهُمْ فَمِنْهُمْ مَنْ
فَعَلَهُ حَمِيَّةً وَمِنْهُمْ مَنْ فَعَلَهُ إِيْمَاناً وَيَقِيناً فَلَمَّا عَرفَتْ قُرَيْشٌ أَنَّ
الْقَومَ قَدْ مَنَعُوا رَسُولَ اللهِ ﷺ وَاجْتَمَعُوا عَلَى ذَلِكَ اجْتَمَعَ
المشْرِكُونَ مِنْ قُرَيْشٍ فَأَجْمَعُوا أَمْرَهُمْ أَنْ لاَ يُجَالِسُوهُمْ وَلاَ
يُبَايِعُوهُمْ وَلاَ يَدْخُلُوا بُيُوتَهُمْ حَتَّى يُسَلِّمُوا رَسُولَ اللهِ ﷺ لِلْقَتْلِ
وَكَتَبُوا فِي مَكْرِهِمْ صَحِيفَةً وعهودا وَمَوَاثِيقَ لاَ يَقْبَلُوا مِنْ بَنِي
هَاشِمٍ أَبَداً صُلْحاً وَلاَ تَأْخُذَهُمْ بِهِ رَأْفَةٌ حَتَّى يُسَلِّمُوهُ لِلْقَتْلِ
فَلَبِثَ بَنُو هَاشِمٍ فِي شِعْبِهِمْ يَعْنِي ثَلاَثَ سِنِينَ وَاشْتَدَّ عَلَيْهِمُ
الْبَلاَءُ وَالْجَهْدُ وَقَطَعُوا عَنْهُمُ الأَسْوَاقَ فَلاَ يَتْرُكُوا طَعَاماً يَقْدَمُ
مَكَّةَ وَلاَ بَيْعاً إِلاَّ بَادَرُوهُمْ إِلَيْهِ فَاشْتَرَوْهُ يُرِيدُونَ بِذَلِكَ أَنْ يُدْرِكُوا
سَفْكَ دَمَ رَسُولِ اللهِ ﷺ وَكَانَ أَبُو طَالِبٍ إِذَا أَخَذَ النَّاسَ
مَضَاجِعَهُمْ أَمَرَ رَسُولَ اللهِ ﷺ فَاضْطَجَعَ عَلَى فِرَاشِهِ حَتَّى يَرَى
ذَلِكَ مَنْ أَرَادَ مَكْراً بِهِ وَاغْتِيَالَهُ فَإِذَا نَامَ النَّاسُ أَمَرَ أَحَدَ بَنِيهِ أَوْ
إِخْوَتِهِ أَوْ بَنِي عَمِّهِ فَاضْطَجَعَ عَلَى فِرَاشِ رَسُولِ اللهِ ﷺ وَأَمَرَ
رَسُولَ اللهِ ﷺ أَنْ يَأْتِيَ بَعْضَ فُرُشِهِمْ فَيَنَامَ عَلَيْهِ فَلَمَّا كَانَ رَأْسَ
ثَلاَثَ سِنِينَ تَلاَوَمَ رِجَالٌ مِنْ بَنِي عَبْدِ مَنَافٍ وَمِنْ بَنِي قُصَيٍّ

وَرِجَالٌ سِوَاهُمْ مِنْ قُرَيْشٍ قَدْ وَلَدَتْهُمْ نِسَاءٌ مِنْ بَنِي هَاشِمٍ وَرَأَوْا أَنَّهُمْ قَدْ قَطَعُوا الرَّحِمَ وَاسْتَخَفُّوا بِالْحَقِّ وَاجْتَمَعَ أَمْرُهُمْ مِنْ لَيْلَتِهِمْ عَلَى نَقْضِ مَا تَعَاهَدُوا عَلَيْهِ مِنَ الْغَدْرِ وَالْبَرَاءَةِ مِنْهُ وَبَعَثَ اللهُ عَزَّ وَجَلَّ عَلَى صَحِيفَتِهِمُ الَّتِي الْمَكْرُ فِيهَا بِرَسُولِ اللهِ ﷺ الْأَرَضَةَ فَلَحِسَتْ كُلَّ مَا كَانَ فِيهَا مِنْ عَهْدٍ وَمِيثَاقٍ وَيُقَالُ كَانَتْ مُعَلَّقَةً فِي سَقْفِ الْبَيْتِ وَلَمْ تَتْرُكْ اسْماً لِلَّهِ عَزَّ وَجَلَّ فِيهَا إِلَّا لَحِسَتْهُ وَبَقِيَ مَا كَانَ فِيهَا مِنْ شِرْكٍ أَوْ ظُلْمَةٍ أَوْ قَطِيعَةِ رَحِمٍ وَأَطْلَعَ اللهُ عَزَّ وَجَلَّ رَسُولَهُ ﷺ عَلَى الَّذِي صُنِعَ بِصَحِيفَتِهِمْ فَذَكَرَ ذَلِكَ رَسُولُ اللهِ ﷺ لِأَبِي طَالِبٍ فَقَالَ أَبُو طَالِبٍ لَا وَالثَّوَاقِبِ مَا كَذَبَنِي فَانْطَلَقَ يَمْشِي بِعِصَابَةٍ مِنْ بَنِي عَبْدِ الْمُطَّلِبِ حَتَّى أَتَى الْمَسْجِدَ وَهُوَ حَافِلٌ مِنْ قُرَيْشٍ فَلَمَّا رَأَوْهُمْ عَامِدِينَ لِجَمَاعَتِهِمْ أَنْكَرُوا ذَلِكَ وَظَنُّوا أَنَّهُمْ خَرَجُوا مِنْ شِدَّةِ الْبَلَاءِ فَأَتَوْا لِيُعْطُوهُمْ رَسُولَ اللهِ ﷺ فَتَكَلَّمَ أَبُو طَالِبٍ فَقَالَ قَدْ حَدَثَتْ أُمُورٌ بَيْنَكُمْ لَمْ نَذْكُرْهَا لَكُمْ فَأْتُوا بِصَحِيفَتِكُمُ الَّتِي تَعَاهَدْتُمْ عَلَيْهَا فَلَعَلَّهُ أَنْ يَكُونَ بَيْنَنَا وَبَيْنَكُمْ صُلْحٌ وَإِنَّمَا قَالَ ذَلِكَ خَشْيَةَ أَنْ يَنْظُرُوا فِي الصَّحِيفَةِ قَبْلَ أَنْ يَأْتُوا بِهَا فَأَتَوْا بِصَحِيفَتِهِمْ مُعْجَبِينَ بِهَا لَا يَشُكُّونَ أَنَّ رَسُولَ اللهِ ﷺ مَدْفُوعٌ إِلَيْهِمْ فَوَضَعُوهَا بَيْنَهُمْ وَقَالُوا قَدْ آنَ لَكُمْ أَنْ تَقْبَلُوا وَتَرْجِعُوا إِلَى

أَمْرٍ يَجْمَعُ قَوْمَكُمْ فَإِنَّمَا قَطَعَ بَيْنَنَا وَبَيْنَكُمْ رَجُلٌ وَاحِدٌ جعَلْتُمُوهُ خَطَراً لِهَلَكَةِ قَوْمِكُمْ وَعَشِيرَتِكُمْ وَفَسَادِهِمْ فَقَالَ أَبُو طَالِبٍ إِنَّمَا أَتَيْتُكُمْ لِأُعْطِيَكُمْ أَمْراً لَكُمْ فِيهِ نَصَفٌ إِنَّ ابْنَ أَخِي قَدْ أَخْبَرَنِي وَلَمْ يَكْذُبْنِي أَنَّ اللهَ عَزَّ وَجَلَّ بَرِيءٌ مِنْ هَذِهِ الصَّحِيفَةِ الَّتِي فِي أَيْدِيكُمْ وَمَحَا كُلَّ اسْمٍ هُوَ لَهُ فِيهَا وَتَرَكَ فِيهَا غَدْرَكُمْ وَقَطِيعَتَكُمْ إِيَّانَا وَتَظَاهُرَكُمْ عَلَيْنَا بِالظُّلْمِ فَإِنْ كَانَ الحَدِيثُ الَّذِي قَالَ ابْنُ أَخِي كَمَا قَالَ فَأَفِيقُوا فَوَاللهِ لاَ نُسَلِّمُهُ أَبَداً حَتَّى نَمُوتَ مِنْ عِنْدِ آخِرِنَا وَإِنْ كَانَ الَّذِي قَالَ بَاطِلاً دَفَعْنَاهُ إِلَيْكُمْ فَقَتَلْتُمْ أَوِ اسْتَحْيَيْتُمْ قَالُوا قَدْ رَضِينَا بِالَّذِي يَقُولُ فَفَتَحُوا الصَّحِيفَةَ فَوَجَدُوا الصَّادِقَ المصْدُوقَ ﷺ قَدْ أَخْبَرَ خَبَرَهَا فَلَمَّا رَأَتْهَا قُرَيْشٌ كَالَّذِي قَالَ أَبُو طَالِبس قَالُوا وَاللهِ إِنْ كَانَ هَذَا قَطُّ إِلاَّ سِحْراً مِنْ صَاحِبِكُمْ فَارْتَكَسُوا وَعَادُوا بِشَرِّ مَا كَانُوا عَلَيْهِ مِنْ كُفْرِهِمْ وَالشِّدَّةِ عَلَى رَسُولِ اللهِ ﷺ وَعَلَى المسْلِمِينَ رَهْطِهِ وَالْقِيَامِ بِمَا تَعَاهَدُوا عَلَيْهِ فَقَالَ أُولَئِكَ النَّفَرُ مِنْ بَنِي عَبْدِ المطَّلِبِ إِنَّ أَوْلَى بِالْكَذِبِ وَالسِّحْرِ غَيْرُنَا فَكَيْفَ تَرَوْنَ فَإِنَّا نَعْلَمُ أَنَّ الَّذِي اجْتَمَعْتُمْ عَلَيْهِ مِنْ قَطِيعَتِنَا أَقْرَبُ إِلَى الْجِبْتِ وَالسِّحْرِ مِنْ أَمْرِنَا وَلَوْلاَ أَنَّكُم اجْتَمَعْتُمْ عَلَى السِّحْرِ لَمْ تَفْسُدْ صَحِيفَتُكُمْ وَهِيَ فِي أَيْدِيكُمْ طَمَسَ اللهُ مَا كَانَ فِيهَا مِنْ إِسْمٍ

وَمَا كَانَ مِنْ بَغْيٍ تَرَكَهُ أَفَنَحْنُ السَّحَرَةُ أَمْ أَنْتُمْ فَقَالَ عِنْدَ ذَلِكَ النَّفَرُ مِنْ بَنِي عَبْدِ مَنَافٍ وَبَنِي قُصَيٍّ وَرِجَالٌ مِنْ قُرَيْشٍ وَلَدَتْهُمْ نِسَاءٌ مِنْ بَنِي هَاشِمٍ نَحْنُ بُرَآءُ مِمَّا فِي هَذِهِ الصَّحِيفَةِ قَالَ مُوسَى بْنُ عُقْبَةَ فَلَمَّا أَفْسَدَ اللهُ عَزَّ وَجَلَّ صَحِيفَةَ مَكْرِهِمْ خَرَجَ النَّبِيُّ وَرَهْطُهُ فَعَاشُوا وَخَالَطُوا النَّاسَ هق وأبو نعيم كلاهما في الدلائل ومغازي موسى بن عقبة

Ibn Saʿd said: Muḥammad b. ʿUmar [al-Wāqidī] told us: al-Ḥakam b. al-Qāsim narrated to me, from Zakariyyā b. ʿAmr, from an old man of the Quraysh, that after Quraysh wrote its charter and three years had passed, Allah disclosed to His Prophet ﷺ what had happened to their charter and the fact that the woodworms had eaten away its content of defiance and injustice so that there only remained in it whatever mentions of Allah it contained before. The Messenger of Allah ﷺ mentioned this to Abū Ṭālib who said: "By Allah! [317] My nephew never once told me a lie." Then he went out to confront the Quraysh and informed them of the disclosure. The charter was brought and was found in the state the Messenger of Allah ﷺ had described. They were crestfallen. Abū Ṭālib said, "O Quraysh! Why should we be ostracized and confined when it is plain for all to see that you are the ones guilty of the desertion of kindred and wrongdoing?"[425]

[425]The version in which the woodworms devour everything except the Name of Allah ﷻ is narrated from Ibn Isḥāq (§210) – through him Ibn Hishām (2:219-221), al-Ṭabarī in his *Tārīkh* (1:552-553), and Abū Nuʿaym, *Dalā'il* (p. 275-278) – and al-Wāqidī – through him Ibn Saʿd (1:188-189 and 1:209-210) and al-Taymī in the *Dalā'il* (p. 198-200 §267) – cf. *Bidāya* (3:95-97). Al-Ḥalabī said the discrepancy between the two versions is resolved by the possibility that there were several documents that were variously moth-eaten so that the Divine Names were nowhere to be found side by side with the offenses cf. *Sīra Ḥalabiyya* (2:34-38), *Bidāya* (6:297), *Khaṣā'is* (1:250-251)

عَنْ زَكَرِيَّا بْنِ عَمْرٍو عَنْ شَيْخٍ مِنْ قُرَيْشٍ فَلَمَّا مَضَتْ ثَلَاثَ سِنِينَ أَطْلَعَ اللهُ نَبِيَّهُ عَلَى أَمْرِ صَحِيفَتِهِمْ وَأَنَّ الأَرَضَةَ قَدْ أَكَلَتْ مَا كَانَ فِيهَا مِنْ جَوْرٍ أَوْ ظُلْمٍ وَبَقِيَ مَا كَانَ فِيهَا مِنْ ذِكْرِ اللهِ فَذَكَرَ ذَلِكَ رَسُولُ اللهِ ﷺ لِأَبِي طَالِبٍ فَقَالَ أَبُو طَالِبٍ أَحَقٌّ مَا تُخْبِرُنِي يَا ابْنَ أَخِي قَالَ نَعَمْ وَاللهِ قَالَ فَذَكَرَ ذَلِكَ أَبُو طَالِبٍ لِإِخْوَتِهِ فَقَالُوا لَهُ مَا ظَنُّكَ بِهِ قَالَ فَقَالَ أَبُو طَالِبٍ وَاللهِ مَا كَذَبَنِي قَطُّ فَخَرَجُوا حَتَّى دَخَلُوا المَسْجِدَ فَأَرْسَلُوا إِلَى الصَّحِيفَةِ فَلَمَّا فَتَحُوهَا إِذَا هِيَ كَمَا قَالَ رَسُولُ اللهِ ﷺ قَدْ أُكِلَتْ كُلُّهَا إِلاَّ مَا كَانَ مِنْ ذِكْرِ اللهِ فِيهَا قَالَ فَسُقِطَ فِي أَيْدِي الْقَوْمِ ثُمَّ نَكَسُوا عَلَى رُؤُوسِهِمْ فَقَالَ أَبُو طَالِبٍ هَلْ تَبَيَّنَ لَكُمْ أَنَّكُمْ أَوْلَى بِالظُّلْمِ وَالْقَطِيعَةِ وَالإِسَاءَةِ ابن سعد أبو نعيم في الدلائل

Ibn Saʿd narrated from Ibn ʿAbbās [رضي الله عنهما], **[516]** ʿĀṣim b. ʿĀmir b. Qatāda, Abū Bakr b. ʿAbd al-Raḥmān b. Hishām, and ʿUthmān b. Abī Sulaymān b. Jubayr b. Muṭʿim – their narrations overlap – that when news of the Negus' hospitality and munificence toward Jaʿfar and his companions reached the Quraysh, they were greatly irritated and drew up a writ against the Banū Hāshim stipulating that none should intermarry with them, nor trade, nor mix in any way whatsoever. The one who wrote that charter was Manṣūr b. 'Ikrima al-'Abdarī whose hand was subsequently paralyzed. They tied up the charter inside the Kaʿba and confined the Banū Hāshim to the mountain trails of Abū Ṭālib starting on the new moon of Muḥarram on the seventh year after the beginning of Prophethood. They prevented even pedestrians from reaching them. They would come out only in the market season, until their hardship became too much to bear. Those that disagreed with this state of affairs among the Quraysh would say "See what happened to Manṣūr b. 'Ikrima!" So they stayed in the mountain trails for three years, after which Allah disclosed to His Prophet what had happened to their charter and told him that the wood-worms had eaten away its content of defiance and injustice so that there only remained in it the mention of Allah.[426]

الوَاقِدِيُّ عَنِ ابْنِ عَبَّاسٍ وَعَاصِمِ بْنِ عُمَرَ بْنِ قَتَادَةَ وَأَبِي بَكْرِ بْنِ عَبْدِ الرَّحْمَنِ بْنِ الحَارِثِ بْنِ هِشَامٍ وَجُبَيْرِ بْنِ مُطْعِمٍ دَخَلَ حَدِيثُ بَعْضِهِمْ فِي حَدِيثِ بَعْضٍ قَالُوا لَمَّا بَلَغَ قُرَيْشاً فِعْلُ النَّجَاشِيِّ لِجَعْفَرٍ وَأَصْحَابِهِ وَإِكْرَامِهِ إِيَّاهُمْ كَبُرَ ذَلِكَ عَلَيْهِمْ وَكَتَبُوا كِتَاباً عَلَى بَنِي هَاشِمٍ أَلاَّ يُنَاكِحُوهُمْ وَلاَ يُبَايِعُوهُمْ وَلاَ يُخَالِطُوهُمْ وَكَانَ الَّذِي كَتَبَ الصَّحِيفَةَ مَنْصُورَ بْنَ عِكْرِمَةَ الْعَبْدَرِيَّ فَشُلَّتْ يَدُهُ وَعَلَّقُوا الصَّحِيفَةَ فِي جَوْفِ الْكَعْبَةِ وَحَصَرُوا بَنِي هَاشِمٍ فِي شِعْبِ أَبِي طَالِبٍ لَيْلَةَ هِلاَلِ المُحَرَّمِ سَنَةَ سَبْعٍ مِنْ حِينِ تَنَبَّأَ رَسُولُ اللهِ ﷺ وَقَطَعُوا عَنْهُمُ المِيرَةَ وَالمَادَّةَ فَكَانُوا لاَ يَخْرُجُونَ إِلاَّ مِنْ مَوْسِمٍ إِلَى مَوْسِمٍ حَتَّى بَلَغَهُمُ الجُهْدُ وَسُمِعَ أَصْوَاتُ صِبْيَانِهِمْ مِنْ وَرَاءِ الشِّعْبِ فَمِنْ قُرَيْشٍ مَنْ سَرَّهُ ذَلِكَ وَمِنْهُمْ مَنْ سَاءَهُ وَقَالَ انْظُرُوا مَا أَصَابَ مَنْصُورَ بْنَ عِكْرِمَةَ فَأَقَامُوا فِي الشِّعْبِ ثَلاَثَ سِنِينَ ثُمَّ أَطْلَعَ اللهُ رَسُولَهُ عَلَى

[426]Narrated from Ibn ʿAbbās and others by Ibn Saʿd (1:208-209).

أَمْرِ صَحِيفَتِهِمْ وَأَنَّ الأَرَضَةَ قَدْ أَكَلَتْ مَا كَانَ فِيهَا مِنْ جَوْرٍ وَظُلْمٍ وَبَقِيَ مَا كَانَ فِيهَا مِنْ ذِكْرِ اللهِ عَزَّ وَجَلَّ ابن سعد

Ibn Saʿd also narrated from ʿIkrima and Muḥammad b. ʿAlī [b. al-Ḥusayn b. ʿAlī b. Abī Ṭālib] that Allah sent insects that ate up everything in the charter except the name of Allah – in one version, "In Your Name, O Allah" *(bismik Allāhumma)*.[427]

عَنْ عِكْرِمَةَ قَالَ كَتَبَتْ قُرَيْشٌ بَيْنَهُمْ وَبَيْنَ رَسُولِ اللهِ ﷺ كِتَاباً وَخَتَمُوا عَلَيْهِ ثَلاَثَةَ خَوَاتِيمَ فَأَرْسَلَ اللهُ عَزَّ وَجَلَّ عَلَى الصَّحِيفَةِ دَابَّةً فَأَكَلَتْ كُلَّ شَيْءٍ إِلاَّ اسْمَ اللهِ عَزَّ وَجَلَّ وَعَنْ مُحَمَّدِ بْنِ عَلِيٍّ وَعِكْرِمَةَ قَالاَ أُكِلَ كُلُّ شَيْءٍ كَانَ فِي الصَّحِيفَةِ إِلاَّ بِاسْمِكَ اللَّهُمَّ ابن سعد

Ibn ʿAsākir narrated from al-Zubayr b. Bakkār that Abū Ṭālib said at the time of the incident of the charter:

Did the news not reach you that the charter was torn to pieces
And that everything Allah dislikes is destined to ruin?
(Alam ya'tikum anna al-ṣaḥīfata muzziqat
wa'in kāna mā lam yarḍahu-l-Lāhu yafsudu?)[428]

عَنِ الزُّبَيْرِ بْنِ بَكَّارٍ قَالَ: هِشَامُ بْنُ عَمْرٍو يَعْنِي الْعَامِرِيَّ هُوَ الَّذِي قَامَ فِي نَقْضِ الصَّحِيفَةِ الَّتِي كَتَبَ مُشْرِكُو قُرَيْشٍ عَلَى

[427]Narrated *mursal* through two chains as cited by Ibn Saʿd (1:209).

[428]Narrated *mursal* from al-Zubayr b. Bakkār (d. 256) by al-Muṣʿab al-Zubayrī in *Nasab Quraysh* (p. 431), Ibn ʿAsākir (66:320), and without chain by Ibn Isḥāq (§209) and, through him, Ibn Hishām (2:222) cf. *Istīʿāb* (2:660), *Bidāya* (3:97), *Khaṣā'is* (1:251), *Iktifā'* (1:271). This is one of six verses spoken by Abū Ṭālib at the time.

بَنِي هَاشِمٍ فِي نَفَرٍ قَامُوا مَعَهُ وَفِي ذَلِكَ يَقُولُ أَبُو طَالِبِ بْنُ
عَبْدِ الْمُطَّلِبِ

أَلَمْ يَأْتِكُمْ أَنَّ الصَّحِيفَةَ مُزِّقَتْ وَإِنْ كَانَ مَا لَمْ يَرْضَهُ اللهُ يَفْسُدُ

الزبيري في نسب قريش كر ونحوه في سيرة ابه هشام

Abū Nu'aym narrated that 'Uthmān b. Abī Sulaymān b. Jubayr b. Muṭ'im said, "Manṣūr b. 'Ikrima al-'Abdarī wrote the charter, after which his hand became paralyzed and dried up so that he could no longer use it for anything anymore. The Quraysh would say in private, 'What we did to the Banū Hāshim is wrong – see what happened to Manṣūr b. 'Ikrima."[429]

His ﷺ Foretelling the Killing of Certain People and Conquest of Cities

Al-Bukhārī narrated from Abū Hurayra ؓ that the Messenger of Allah ﷺ said: [318] "The Hour will not rise until you fight Khūz and Karmān, two non-Arab nations, red-faced, flat-nosed, beady-eyed, their faces resembling well-hammered bucklers. The Hour will not rise until you fight a nation that wears shoes of hair [*i.e.* untanned leather]."[430] Al-Bayhaqī said: "This took place when a party of the Khawārij came out near al-Ray wearing shoes of hair. They were defeated."

عَنْ أَبِي هُرَيْرَةَ رَضِيَ اللهُ عَنْهُ أَنَّ النَّبِيَّ ﷺ قَالَ لاَ تَقُومُ السَّاعَةُ
حَتَّى تُقَاتِلُوا خُوزًا وَكَرْمَانَ مِنْ الأَعَاجِمِ حُمْرَ الْوُجُوهِ فُطْسَ

[429]Thus cited and referenced in the *Khasā'is* (1:252) but this is the same report as in Ibn Sa'd (1:208-209) already mentioned.

[430]Narrated from Abū Hurayra by Muslim and al-Bukhārī. These are identified in another narration in al-Bukhārī and the *Sunan* as "the Turks" (*al-atrāk*), meaning Tartars.

الْأُنُوفِ صِغَارَ الأَعْيُنِ وُجُوهُهُمْ الْمَجَانُّ الْمُطْرَقَةُ نِعَالُهُمْ الشَّعَرُ

خ هق في الدلائل وزاد هم قوم من الخوارج خرجوا في ناحية الري فأكثروا الفساد والقتل في المسلمين حتى قوتلوا وأهلكهم الله عز وجل

Al-Bayhaqī narrated that Abū Hurayra said: 319 "The Messenger of Allah ﷺ foretold us our raiding India."[431] [The Prophet ﷺ said: 320 "There are two groups in my Community whom Allah has protected from the Fire; one is a group that shall raid India and another is a group that shall be with 'Īsā b. Maryam."[432]]

عَنْ أَبِي هُرَيْرَةَ رَضِيَ اللهُ عَنْهُ قَالَ وَعَدَنَا رَسُولُ اللهِ ﷺ غَزْوَةَ الهِنْدِ حم ن وفي الكبرى ز هق وفي الدلائل ك خط

Ibn Sa'd and al-Ḥākim narrated—the latter declaring it *ṣaḥīḥ*—Dhū Mikhmar [al-Ḥabashī] said "I heard the Messenger of Allah ﷺ say: 321 'The Romans will enter into a secure truce with you.'"[433]

عَنْ ذِي مِخْمَرٍ رَجُلٍ مِنْ أَصْحَابِ النَّبِيِّ ﷺ قَالَ سَمِعْتُ رَسُولَ اللهِ ﷺ يَقُولُ سَتُصَالِحُكُمْ الرُّومُ صُلْحًا آمِنًا ثُمَّ تَغْزُونَ وَهُمْ

[431]Narrated from Abū Hurayra by al-Nasā'ī with three chains in the *Sunan* and *al-Sunan al-Kubrā* (3:28 §4382-4383), Aḥmad (al-Arna'ūṭ ed. 12:28-29 §7128 *isnād ḍa'īf*), al-Bukhārī in *al-Tārīkh al-Kabīr* (2:243 §2333), Sa'īd b. Manṣur in his *Sunan* (2:178 §2374), Nu'aym b. Ḥammād in *al-Fitan* (1:409 §1237), Abū Nu'aym (8:316-317), al-Ḥākim (3:514=1990 ed. 3:588), and al-Bayhaqī in the *Sunan* (9:176) and *Dalā'il* (6:336), all only through Jabr b. 'Abīda who is unknown cf. al-Mizzī, *Tahdhīb al-Kamāl* (4:494 §893) and Ibn Ḥajar, *Tahdhīb al-Tahdhīb* (2:52 §90); but the narration is strengthened by [1] a similar weak-chained report from al-Ḥasan al-Baṣrī from Abū Hurayra in the *Musnad* (14:419 §8823); [2] another similar report with another chain in Ibn Abī 'Āṣim's *al-Jihād* (2:668 §291); and [3] Thawbān's sound report of the same prediction (see next note). Cf. *Khaṣā'iṣ* (2:190) and *Bidāya* (6:233).

[432]A sound narration from Thawbān by al-Nasā'ī in his *Sunan* and *al-Sunan al-Kubrā* (3:28 §4384), Aḥmad (37:81 §22396 *ḥasan*), al-Bukhārī in *al-Tārīkh al-Kabīr* (6:72 §1747), Ibn Abī 'Āṣim in *al-Jihād* (2:665 §288), al-Ṭabarānī in *al-Awsaṭ* (7:23-24 §6737 cf. al-Haythamī 5:282) and *Musnad al-Shāmiyyīn* (§1851), al-Bayhaqī in *al-Sunan al-Kubrā* (9:176), and Ibn 'Asākir (15:197).

[433]Part of a longer ḥadīth from Dhū Mikhmar by Ibn Mājah, Abū Dāwūd, Aḥmad and others with several chains. His name is misspelt Dhū Mikhbar in al-Nabhānī.

عَدُوًّا فَتُنْصَرُونَ وَتَسْلَمُونَ وَتَغْنَمُونَ ثُمَّ تَنْصُرُونَ الرُّومَ حَتَّى
تَنْزِلُوا بِمَرْجٍ ذِي تُلُولٍ فَيَرْفَعُ رَجُلٌ مِنَ النَّصْرَانِيَّةِ صَلِيبًا فَيَقُولُ
غَلَبَ الصَّلِيبُ فَيَغْضَبُ رَجُلٌ مِنَ الْمُسْلِمِينَ فَيَقُومُ إِلَيْهِ فَيَدُقُّهُ
فَعِنْدَ ذَلِكَ يَغْدِرُ الرُّومُ وَيَجْمَعُونَ لِلْمَلْحَمَةِ حم جه ش ك ورواه ابن
سعد مختصرا

Al-Bayhaqī and al-Ḥākim narrated – the latter declaring it sound – from ʿAbd Allāh b. Ḥawāla al-Azdī ؓ that the Prophet ﷺ said: [322] "You will all be joining [opposite] armies: one army in al-Shām, one in Yemen, and one in Iraq." ʿAbd Allāh b. Ḥawāla said: "Choose for me, Messenger of Allah <, in case I live to see that day>!" The Prophet ﷺ said: [a] "You must go to Shām[434] <for it is the chosen land of Allah in all His earth *(khīratullāhi min arḍih)*! The chosen ones among His servants will recur to its protection>. Whoever does not wish to go there, let him go to his Yemen and drink from its streams *(ghudur)*. For [b] **Allah has given me a guarantee concerning Shām and its people**" *(fa-inna-l-Lāha tawakkala lī bish-Shāmi wa-ahlih)*.[435]

[434]Repeated three times in one of Aḥmad's several reports of this ḥadīth.

[435]Narrated from ʿAbd Allāh b. Ḥawāla by Abū Dāwūd and Aḥmad with sound chains, Ibn Ḥibbān (16:295), al-Ḥākim (4:510=1990 ed. 4:555) who said it is *ṣaḥīḥ* cf. al-Dhahabī in *Tārīkh al-Islām* (1:378), al-Ṭaḥāwī in *Sharḥ Mushkil al-Āthār* (2:35), al-Bayhaqī in *al-Sunan al-Kubrā* (9:179), al-Fasawī in *al-Maʿrifa wal-Tārīkh* (2:302), al-Samʿānī in *Faḍā'il al-Shām* (p. 31-32 §1), and Ibn ʿAbd al-Salām in *Targhīb Ahl al-Islām* (p. 15) among others. Al-Nabhānī omits the bracketed segments. ʿAbd Allāh b. Ḥawāla would add after narrating the above: "And whoever has Allāh as his guarantor shall suffer no loss." Also narrated from Abū al-Dardā' by al-Bazzār and al-Ṭabarānī with a sound chain as indicated by al-Haythamī (10:58) after al-Mundhirī in *al-Targhīb* (4:104 §4504=1997 ed. 4:30). Something similar is narrated from ʿAbd Allāh b. Yazīd by al-Ṭabarānī with a very weak chain as indicated by al-Haythamī (10:58) and from Wāthila b. al-Asqaʿ by al-Ṭabarānī in *al-Kabīr* (22:55-58) – specifying that those who were asking the Prophet ﷺ were Muʿādh and Ḥudhayfa – with two chains, one of them fair as per al-Mundhirī in *al-Targhīb* (4:105 §4507=1997 ed. 4:30) but al-Haythamī (10:59) stated that all al-Ṭabarānī's chains of the latter narration were weak. Something similar is also narrated from al-ʿIrbāḍ b. Sāriya by al-Ṭabarānī in *al-Kabīr* (18:251) with a sound chain according to al-Mundhirī in *al-Targhīb* (4:104-105 §4506=1997 ed. 4:30) and al-Haythamī

عَنْ ابْنِ حَوَالَةَ رَضِيَ اللهُ عَنْهُ قَالَ قَالَ رَسُولُ اللهِ ﷺ سَيَصِيرُ الأَمْرُ إِلَى أَنْ تَكُونُوا جُنُودًا مُجَنَّدَةً جُنْدٌ بِالشَّامِ وَجُنْدٌ بِالْيَمَنِ وَجُنْدٌ بِالْعِرَاقِ قَالَ ابْنُ حَوَالَةَ خِرْ لِي يَا رَسُولَ اللهِ إِنْ أَدْرَكْتُ ذَلِكَ فَقَالَ عَلَيْكَ بِالشَّامِ فَإِنَّهَا خِيرَةُ اللهِ مِنْ أَرْضِهِ يَجْتَبِي إِلَيْهَا خِيرَتَهُ مِنْ عِبَادِهِ فَأَمَّا إِنْ أَبَيْتُمْ فَعَلَيْكُمْ بِيَمَنِكُمْ وَاسْقُوا مِنْ غُدُرِكُمْ فَإِنَّ اللهَ تَوَكَّلَ لِي بِالشَّامِ وَأَهْلِهِ د حم وفي الباب عن أبي الدرداء وعبدالله بن يزيد وواثلة بن الأسقع وابن عمر ومعاذ وحذيفة بن أسيد والعرباض بن سارية وفي رواية فَإِنَّ اللهَ قَدْ تَكَفَّلَ لِي بِالشَّامِ وَأَهْلِهِ عق ع طب طس وفي جزء أبي مسهر قال كان أبو إدريس الخولانى إذا حدث بهذا الحديث التفت إلى ابن عامر فقال مَنْ تَكَفَّلَ اللهُ بِهِ فَلاَ ضَيْعَةَ عَلَيْهِ قال شيخ الإسلام النووي في الإرشاد هذا من فضائل الشام مناسب لائق بالحال

[Another version states that some Companions said: "We are herdsmen, we cannot adapt to Shām," whereby the Prophet ﷺ said: 323 "Whoever cannot adapt to Shām, let him go to Yemen. Truly, Allah has given me a guarantee concerning Shām."[436]

In another version Ibn Ḥawāla states: "When he noticed my dislike for Shām he said: 324 'Do you know what Allah says about Shām? Truly, Allah said: Shām, you are the quintessence of My lands *(ṣafwatī min bilādī)* and I shall inhabit you with the chosen ones among My servants *(khīratī min 'ibādī)*."[437]

Another time, 325 the Prophet ﷺ compared the world to a little rain water on a mountain plateau of which the *safw* had already been drunk and from which only the *kadar* or dregs remained.[438]]

(10:58), chapter entitled *Faḍā'il al-Shām*, and from Ibn 'Umar by al-Ṭabarānī and al-Bazzār with a weak chain per al-Suyūṭī in *al-Durr al-Manthūr*. The latter said Ibn 'Asākir also narrates it from Thābit b. Ma'bad.

436 Narrated from Abū al-Dardā' by al-Bazzār and al-Ṭabarānī with a sound chain as indicated by al-Haythamī (10:58).

437 Narrated by al-Ṭabarānī with two chains of which one is good according to al-Mundhirī in *al-Targhīb* (4:104 §4505=1997 ed. 4:30) and al-Haythamī (10:59).

438 Narrated from Ibn Mas'ūd by al-Ḥākim (4:320 *isnād saḥīh*) as well as *mawqūf* by al-

Ibn Saʿd narrated from Saʿd b. Ibrāhīm that ʿAbd al-Raḥmān b. ʿAwf said, "The Messenger of Allah ﷺ endowed me with a land in al-Shām known as "the Valley" (al-Salīl). He passed on without giving me a document to that effect. He only said to me: [326] 'When Allah opens for us Syro-Palestine, that land is yours.'"[439]

عَنْ سَعْدِ بْنِ إِبْرَاهِيمَ وَغَيْرِهِ مِنْ وَلَدِ إِبْرَاهِيمَ بْنِ عَبْدِ الرَّحْمَنِ بْنِ
عَوْفٍ قَالُوا قَالَ عَبْدُ الرَّحْمَنِ بْنُ عَوْفٍ قَطَعَ لِي رَسُولُ اللهِ ﷺ
أَرْضاً بِالشَّامِ يُقَالُ لَهَا السَّلِيلُ فَتُوُفِّيَ النَّبِيُّ ﷺ وَلَمْ يَكْتُبْ لِي بِهَا
كِتَاباً وَإِنَّمَا قَالَ لِي إِذَا فَتَحَ اللهُ عَلَيْنَا بِالشَّامِ فَهِيَ لَكَ ابن سعد

Ibn Saʿd narrated **[517]** that Dhūl-Aṣābiʿ ؓ said: "I said, 'Messenger of Allah! If we are tried with surviving you, where do you command me to live?' He said: [327] 'Go and live in Bayt al-Maqdis. Perhaps, Allah will give you offspring that will frequent <that> Mosque *(dhālik al-masjid)* and visit it in the early mornings and late nights.'"[440]

عَنْ ذِي الْأَصَابِعِ رَضِيَ اللهُ عَنْهُ قُلْتُ يَا رَسُولَ اللهِ إِنِ ابْتُلِينَا
بَعْدَكَ بِالْبَقَاءِ أَيْنَ تَأْمُرُنَا قَالَ عَلَيْكَ بِبَيْتِ الْمَقْدِسِ فَلَعَلَّهُ أو
عَسَى أَنْ يَنْشَأَ أو يَنْشُوَ لَكَ ذُرِّيَّةٌ يَغْدُونَ إِلَى ذَلِكَ الْمَسْجِدِ
وَيَرُوحُونَ حم طب كر وجاء بلفظ وَلَعَلَّ اللهَ يَرْزُقُكَ ذُرِّيَّةً يُعَمِّرُونَ

Bukhārī. Al-Suyūṭī declared it sound in *al-Jāmiʿ al-Saghīr* (§1710). Al-Huwjirī and al-Qushayrī mention it in their chapters on *tasawwuf* respectively in *Kashf al-Mahjūb* and *al-Risāla al-Qushayriyya*. Ibn al-Athīr defines *safw* and *safwa* in his dictionary *al-Nihāya* as "the best of any matter, its quintessence, and purest part."

[439]Narrated from ʿAbd al-Raḥmān b. ʿAwf by Ibn Saʿd (3:126) cf. *Khasāʾis* (2:187). The land is misspelled "al-Sabīl" in al-Nabhānī.

[440]*Khasāʾis* (2:188). Narrated from Dhūl-Aṣābiʿ by Aḥmad, Ibn Saʿd (7:424), al-Ṭabarānī in *al-Kabīr* (4:238 §4237-4238), al-Baghawī in *Sharḥ al-Sunna* (14:211-212 §4010), Ibn ʿAsākir (22:339), and Abū Nuʿaym in the *Maʿrifa*, chapter on Dhūl-Aṣābiʿ.

ذَلِكَ المَسْجِدَ يَغْدُونَ إِلَيْهِ وَيَرُوحُونَ   ابن سعد طب شرح السنة للبغوي
أبو نعيم في المعرفة وفي سند جميعهم عثمان بن عطاء وثقه دحيم وضعفه الناس مج

Muslim narrated from Abū Dharr ؓ that the Messenger of Allah ﷺ said: 328 "You will conquer a land where the *qīrāṭ* is mentioned. Treat its people well. They have inviolable rights and kinship with us.[441] But when you see two men fight with one another over the placement of a brick, leave it!" He said that, eventually, he passed by Rabīʿa and [his brother] ʿAbd al-Raḥmān b. Shuraḥbīl b. Ḥasana fighting over the placement of an unburnt brick, so he went out of that land, meaning Egypt *(Miṣr)*.[442]

عَنْ أَبِي ذَرٍّ رَضِيَ اللهُ عَنْهُ قَالَ رَسُولُ اللهِ ﷺ إِنَّكُمْ سَتَفْتَحُونَ أَرْضاً يُذْكَرُ فِيهَا القِيرَاطُ فَاسْتَوْصُوا بِأَهْلِهَا خَيْراً فَإِنَّ لَهُمْ ذِمَّةً وَرَحِماً فَإِذَا رَأَيْتُمْ رَجُلَيْنِ يَقْتَتِلَانِ فِي مَوْضِعِ لَبِنَةٍ فَاخْرُجْ مِنْهَا قَالَ فَرَأَيْتُ عَبْدَ الرَّحْمَنِ بْنَ شُرَحْبِيلَ بْنِ حَسَنَةَ وَأَخَاهُ رَبِيعَةَ يَخْتَصِمَانِ فِي مَوْضِعِ لَبِنَةٍ فَخَرَجْتُ مِنْهَا   م مشكل الآثار هق وفي الدلائل

Al-Ṭabarānī and al-Ḥākim narrated from Kaʿb b. Mālik ؓ that the Messenger of Allah ﷺ said: "When Egypt is conquered, treat the Copts *(al-qibṭ)* well! For they have inviolable rights and kinship with us." He meant that Hājar, the mother of Ismāʿīl ؑ,

---

[441] See al-Nabhānī's explanation of the next hadith.
[442] Narrated from Abū Dharr by Muslim and Aḥmad. Cf. Abū al-Dardāʾ (note 228). The *qīrāṭ* is [1] a currency or measure per Nawawī; [2] a Coptic name for feasts per Sakhāwī; or [3] a euphemism – referring to the use of expletives – current in the language of the Egyptians at the time and consisting in saying, "I gave X his *qarārīṭ* = I told him off" cf. al-Ṭaḥāwī, *Sharḥ Mushkil al-Āthār* (3:296) and Ibn al-Athīr, *Nihāya* (s.v. qirāṭ).

was one of them.[443] Māriya the mother of Ibrāhīm – the son of the Prophet ﷺ – was also Coptic.

عَنْ عَبْدِ اللهِ بْنِ كَعْبِ بْنِ مَالِكٍ عَنْ أَبِيهِ قَالَ سَمِعْتُ رَسُولَ اللهِ ﷺ يَقُولُ إِذَا فُتِحَتْ مِصْرُ فَاسْتَوْصُوا بِالْقِبْطِ خَيْرًا فَإِنَّ لَهُمْ ذِمَّةً وَرَحِمًا يَعْنِي أَنَّ أُمَّ إِسْمَاعِيلَ كَانَتْ مِنْهُمْ طب ك أبو نعيم في الدلائل هق كذلك وشرح الرحم قول الزهري راوي الحديث عن عبد الله

A bū Nuʿaym narrated that Umm Salama رضي الله عنها said, "The Messenger of Allah ﷺ recommended [the Copts] to our care at the time of his death and said: '[I remind you by] 329 Allah! [I remind you by] Allah concerning the Copts of Egypt! Truly you are going to hold sway over them, then they will provide you material and helpers in the way of Allah.'"[444] [There is also the narration: 330 "Egypt shall be conquered after my time so seek out its benefits but a do not take up residence there, for the shortest-lived of people are driven there."[445]]

---

[443]Narrated from Kaʿb b. Mālik by Ibn Saʿd (8:214), ʿAbd al-Razzāq (6:58 §9996), al-Bukhārī in *al-Tārīkh al-Kabīr* (5:309), al-Ṭabarānī in *al-Kabīr* (19:61) with several chains, one of which al-Haythamī (10:63) said through trustworthy narrators, and al-Ḥākim (1990 ed. 2:603). A *ṣaḥīḥ* narration according to al-Suyūṭī in *al-Jāmiʿ al-Ṣaghīr* (§772). Cf. al-Taymī, *Dalāʾil al-Nubuwwa* (p. 226 §322), al-Māwardī, *Aʿlām al-Nubuwwa* (p. 154), *Istīʿāb* (1:59), *Bidāya* (6:193), *Khaṣāʾis* (2:189), *Kanz* (§14304). Al-Ṭabarī in his *Tārīkh* (1:150) narrates it with the phrase "treat its people well" without mention of the Copts, through Ibn Isḥāq from Kaʿb's son with a "fine" *(malīḥ) mursal* chain according to al-Dhahabī in *Tārīkh al-Islām* (1:376). Al-Ghumārī in *al-Mudāwī* (1:428) said that Ibn ʿAbd al-Ḥakam collected all the chains and wordings of this narration in the introduction to his *Futūḥ Miṣr*. ʿAbd al-Razzāq reported Maʿmar's query concerning the kinship: "Because of [Māriya the Copt] the mother of Ibrāhīm the son of the Prophet ﷺ?" Al-Zuhrī replied: "Rather, the mother of Ismāʿīl [Hājar]!" See also al-Ṭaḥāwī's evidence in *Sharḥ Mushkil al-Āthār* (3:296).

[444]Narrated from Umm Salama by al-Ṭabarānī in *al-Kabīr* (23:265) with a chain of *Ṣaḥīḥ* narrators cf. al-Haythamī (10:63-64) and al-Suyūṭī's grading in his *Khaṣāʾis* (2:189) and *Ḥusn al-Muḥāḍara*. Ibn Ḥibbān (15:69) narrates a similar but *mursal* report.

[445]Narrated by Abū Nuʿaym, al-Ṭabarānī in the *Kabīr*, Ibn Shāhīn, Ibn al-Sakan in *Maʿrifat al-Ṣaḥāba*, Ibn Yūnus, and others, all of them through the governor of Egypt Mūsā b. ʿUlay b. Rabāḥ, from his father, from his grandfather Rabāḥ, from the Prophet ﷺ. Al-Qārī in *al-Asrār al-Marfūʿa* said: "Ibn Yūnus said it is 'extremely disclaimed' *(munkar jiddan)*, adding, 'Allah forbid that Mūsā should narrate such as this for he is more scrupulous than that!' Ibn al-Jawzī followed him and adduced it in the *Mawḍūʿāt*

عَنْ أُمِّ سَلَمَةَ رَضِيَ اللهُ عَنْهَا أَنَّ رَسُولَ اللهِ ﷺ أَوْصَى عِنْدَ
وَفَاتِهِ فَقَالَ اللهَ اللهَ فِي قِبْطِ مِصْرَ فَإِنَّكُمْ سَتَظْهَرُونَ عَلَيْهِمْ
وَيَكُونُ لَكُمْ عِدَّةً وَأَعْوَانًا فِي سَبِيلِ اللهِ طب

Ibn Isḥāq said: "A source I consider reliable narrated to me that Abū Hurayra رضي الله عنه used to say, when these regions were conquered in the time of ʿUmar and ʿUthmān رضي الله عنهما: "Conquer what you will – by the One in Whose Hand lies Abū Hurayra's soul! [331] You do not, nor shall you ever conquer any city until the Day of Resurrection except Muhammad ﷺ had long been given its keys before that!""[446]

ابنُ إِسْحَقَ عَمَّنْ لاَ يَتَّهِمُ عَنْ أَبِي هُرَيرَةَ رَضِيَ اللهُ عَنْهُ أَنَّهُ كَانَ
يَقُولُ حِينَ فُتِحَتْ هَذِهِ الأَمْصَارُ فِي زَمَنِ عُمَرَ وَعُثْمَانَ وَمَا
بَعْدَهُ اِفْتَتِحُوا مَا بَدَا لَكُمْ فَوَالَّذِي نَفْسُ أَبِي هُرَيْرَةَ بِيَدِهِ مَا
افْتَتَحْتُمْ مِنْ مَدِينَةٍ وَلاَ تَفْتَتِحُونَهَا إِلَى يَوْمِ الْقِيَامَةِ إِلاَّ وَقَدْ
أُعْطِيَ مُحَمَّدٌ مَفَاتِيحَهَا قَبْلَ ذَلِكَ تاريخ الطبري ابن هشام هق في الدلائل

Abū Nuʿaym narrated from Anas رضي الله عنه that the Prophet ﷺ struck [a rock] with a pick on the Day of the Trench when a great spark flashed and light came out in the direction of Yemen. Then he struck another time and light came out in the direction of Persia. Then he struck another time and light came out in the direction of the Eastern Romans. Salmān was astounded at this event. The Messenger of Allah ﷺ said: [332] "Did you see it?" He said yes. The

while al-Bukhārī said it is inauthentic."

[446]Narrated by Ibn Hishām (4:176), al-Ṭabarī in the *Tārīkh* (2:570) and al-Bayhaqī in the *Dalāʾil* (3:418), cf. al-Suhaylī, Ibn Sayyid al-Nās, al-Kilāʿī, al-Dhahabī, and Ibn Kathīr in their *Sīra*s.

Prophet ﷺ continued: [a] "This [light] illumined the cities for me. Truly, Allah has given me the glad tidings, at this spot where I am standing, that Yemen, the Romans, and Persia would be conquered."[447]

وَأَخْرَجَ أَبُو نُعَيْمٍ عَنْ أَنَسٍ رَضِيَ اللهُ عَنْه قَالَ ضَرَبَ النَّبِيُّ ﷺ
يَوْمَ الخَنْدَقِ بِمِعْوَلِهِ ضَرْبَةً فَبَرِقَتْ بَرْقَةً فَخَرَجَ نُورٌ مِنْ قِبَلِ الْيَمَنِ
ثُمَّ ضَرَبَ أُخْرَى فَخَرَجَ نُورٌ مِنْ قِبَلِ فَارِسٍ ثُمَّ ضَرَبَ أُخْرَى
فَخَرَجَ نُورٌ مِنْ قِبَلِ الرُّومِ فَعَجِبَ سَلْمَانُ مِنْ ذَلِكَ فَقَالَ رَسُولُ
اللهِ ﷺ أَرَأَيْتَ قُلْتُ نَعَمْ قَالَ لَقَدْ أَضَاءَتْ لِيَ المَدَائِنُ وَإِنَّ اللهَ
بَشَّرَنِي فِي مَقَامِي هَذَا بِفَتْحِ الْيَمَنِ وَالرُّومِ وَفَارِسٍ كذا في الخصائص
ولم نجده

Abū Nuʾaym narrated from ʿAbd Allāh b. ʿAmr b. al-ʿĀṣ رضي الله عنهما that **[518]** the Prophet ﷺ struck once with the ax on the Day of the Trench, saying: [333] "With this strike Allah shall lay open for us the treasures of the Romans." Then he struck again and said: [a] "With this strike Allah shall lay open for us the treasures of Persia." Then he struck again and said: [b] "With this strike Allah shall bring me the people of Yemen as helpers and supporters."[448]

عَنْ عَبْدِ اللهِ بْنِ عَمْرِو بْنِ الْعَاصِ رَضِيَ اللهُ عَنْهُمَا أَنَّ رَسُولَ
اللهِ ﷺ خَرَجَ يَوْمَ الخَنْدَقِ وَهُمْ مُحْدِقُونَ حَوْلَ المدِينَةِ فَتَنَاوَلَ
رَسُولُ اللهِ ﷺ الْفَأْسَ فَضَرَبَ بِهَا ضَرْبَةً فَقَالَ هَذِهِ الضَّرْبَةُ يَفْتَحُ

[447] Thus cited and referenced in the *Khaṣāʾis* (1:379).

[448] Narrated from ʿAbd Allāh b. ʿAmr b. al-ʿĀṣ by Abū Nuʿaym in *Dalāʾil al-Nubuwwa* (p. 498-499 §429) cf. *Khaṣāʾis* (1:377).

اللهُ تَعَالَى بِهَا كُنُوزَ الرُّومِ ثُمَّ ضَرَبَ الثَّانِيَةَ فَقَالَ هَذِهِ الضَّرْبَةُ يَفْتَحُ اللهُ تَعَالَى بِهَا كُنُوزَ فَارِسٍ ثُمَّ ضَرَبَ الثَّالِثَةَ فَقَالَ هَذِهِ الضَّرْبَةُ يَأْتِينِي اللهُ عَزَّ وَجَلَّ بِأَهْلِ الْيَمَنِ أَنْصَاراً وَأَعْوَاناً أبو نعيم في الدلائل ابن عبد الحكم في فتوح مصر

Al-Bayhaqī narrated through Ibn Isḥāq that it was narrated to him that Salmān said: "I was digging in one corner of the trench at which time one rock gave me difficulty. The Messenger of Allah ﷺ came near and saw my predicament. He came down and took the pick from my hands. Then he struck and a great spark flashed under the pick. He struck again and another spark flashed. He struck a third time and a third spark flashed. I said to him: 'My father and mother be ransomed for you, Messenger of Allah! What is that I saw flashing under the pick as you were striking?' He said: 334 'Did you see it, Salmān?' I said: 'Yes!' He said: a 'The first time, Allah opened Yemen for me; the second time, He opened al-Shām and al-Maghrib for me; and the third time, he opened the East.'"449 Abū Nuʿaym also narrated it through Ibn Isḥāq from al-Kalbī, from Abū Ṣāliḥ, from Salmān ؓ.

قَالَ ابْنُ إِسْحَاقَ حُدِّثْتُ عَنْ سَلْمَانَ قَالَ ضَرَبْتُ فِي نَاحِيَةٍ مِنَ الْخَنْدَقِ فَغَلُظَتْ عَلَيَّ صَخْرَةٌ فَعَطَفَ عَلَيَّ رَسُولُ اللهِ ﷺ وَهُوَ قَرِيبٌ مِنِّي فَلَمَّا رَآنِي أَضْرِبُ وَرَأَى شِدَّةَ الْمَكَانِ عَلَيَّ نَزَلَ فَأَخَذَ الْمِعْوَلَ مِنْ يَدِي فَضَرَبَ بِهِ ضَرْبَةً فَلَمَعَتْ تَحْتَ الْمِعْوَلِ بَرْقَةٌ ثُمَّ ضَرَبَ ضَرْبَةً أُخْرَى فَلَمَعَتْ تَحْتَهُ بَرْقَةٌ أُخْرَى ثُمَّ ضَرَبَ

---

[449]Narrated through Ibn Isḥāq by Ibn Hishām (4:175-176) and al-Bayhaqī in the *Dalāʾil* (3:417-418), both without chain cf. *Khaṣāʾiṣ* (1:378), *Bidāya* (4:99-101), and *Sīra Halabiyya* (2:634).

الثَّالِثَةَ فَلَمَعَتْ تَحْتَهُ بَرْقَةٌ أُخْرَى فَقُلْتُ يَا رَسُولَ اللهِ بِأَبِي أَنْتَ
وَأُمِّي مَا هَذَا الَّذِي رَأَيْتُ يَلْمَعُ تَحْتَ المِعْوَلِ وَأَنْتَ تَضْرِبُ بِهِ
فَقَالَ أَوَقَدْ رَأَيْتَ ذَلِكَ يَا سَلْمَانُ فَقُلْتُ نَعَمْ فَقَالَ أَمَّا الأُولَى
فَإِنَّ اللهَ عَزَّ وَجَلَّ فَتَحَ عَلَيَّ بِهَا الْيَمَنَ وَأَمَّا الثَّانِيَةُ فَإِنَّ اللهَ عَزَّ
وَجَلَّ فَتَحَ عَلَيَّ بِهَا الشَّامَ وَالمَغْرِبَ وَأَمَّا الثَّالِثَةُ فَإِنَّ اللهَ فَتَحَ
عَلَيَّ بِهَا المَشْرِقَ ابن هشام هق في الدلائل

Al-Bayhaqī and Abū Nu'aym narrated that al-Barā' b. 'Āzib said: "We faced, in a certain part of the Trench, a huge rock that caused us great difficulties. The picks were useless against it. We complained of this to the Prophet ﷺ. When he saw it, he took the pick, saying: [335] *'Bismillāh!'* He struck it once and broke one third of it. He exclaimed: *'Allāhu akbar!* [a] I have been given the keys to *Shām*. I swear it by Allah, I can see her red palaces!' Then he struck a second time and broke another third. He exclaimed: *'Allāhu akbar!* [b] I have been given the keys to Persia! <I swear it by Allah! I can see the white palace of al-Madā'in.' Then he struck a third time, saying: *'Bismillāh!'* and he broke off the remainder of the rock. He exclaimed: *'Allāhu akbar!* [c] I have been given the keys to Yemen.> I swear it by Allah! I can see the gates of Ṣan'ā' right now, from where I stand!'[450]

[450]Narrated from al-Barā' b. 'Āzib by Aḥmad (30:625-626 §18694), Ibn Abī Shayba (7:378 §36820= 'Awwāma ed. 20:385-386 §37975), al-Nasā'ī in *al-Sunan al-Kubrā* ('Ilmiyya ed. 5:269 §8858), Abū Ya'la (3:244 §1685), al-Rūyānī (through Ibn Isḥāq) in his *Musnad* (1:276-277 §410), Abū Nu'aym in *Dalā'il al-Nubuwwa* (p. 499 §430), and through him al-Khaṭīb (1:131-132), al-Bayhaqī in his *Dalā'il*, and Ibn 'Asākir, all with a chain of *Ṣaḥīḥ* narrators except for Maymūn Abū 'Abd Allāh who is weak cf. al-Haythamī (6:130-131) although the chain was declared fair *(ḥasan)* by Ibn Ḥajar in the *Fath* (7:397) and "good" *(jayyid)* by al-Ṣāliḥī in *Subul al-Hudā* (4:518). The ḥadīth itself is "fair due to its corroborations" *(ḥasan li-ghayrih)* cf. al-Aḥdab in *Zawā'id Tārīkh Baghdād* (1:173-177 §30) and is "nearly mass-narrated" *(mashhūr)* from no less than six Companions. Cf. *Sīra Ḥalabiyya* (2:635), *Khaṣā'iṣ* (1:378), *Iktifā'* (4:260-261), al-Māwardī, *A'lām al-Nubuwwa* (p. 154), and *Bidāya* (4:101 *ḥadīth gharīb*). The bracketed

عَنْ الْبَرَاءِ بْنِ عَازِبٍ رَضِيَ اللهُ عَنْهُ قَالَ لَمَّا كَانَ حَيْثُ أَمَرَنَا رَسُولُ اللهِ ﷺ أَنْ نَحْفُرَ الْخَنْدَقَ عَرَضَ لَنَا فِي بَعْضِ الْجَبَلِ صَخْرَةٌ عَظِيمَةٌ شَدِيدَةٌ لَا تَدْخُلُ فِيهَا الْمَعَاوِلُ فَاشْتَكَيْنَا ذَلِكَ إِلَى رَسُولِ اللهِ ﷺ فَجَاءَ رَسُولُ اللهِ ﷺ فَلَمَّا رَآهَا أَلْقَى ثَوْبَهُ وَأَخَذَ الْمِعْوَلَ فَقَالَ بِسْمِ اللهِ ثُمَّ ضَرَبَ ضَرْبَةً فَكَسَرَ ثُلُثَهَا وَقَالَ اللهُ أَكْبَرُ أُعْطِيتُ مَفَاتِيحَ الشَّامِ وَاللهِ إِنِّي لَأُبْصِرُ قُصُورَهَا الْحُمْرَ السَّاعَةَ ثُمَّ ضَرَبَ الثَّانِيَ فَقَطَعَ ثُلُثًا آخَرَ فَقَالَ اللهُ أَكْبَرُ أُعْطِيتُ مَفَاتِيحَ فَارِسَ وَاللهِ إِنِّي لَأُبْصِرُ قَصْرَ الْمَدَائِنِ الْأَبْيَضِ ثُمَّ ضَرَبَ الثَّالِثَةَ وَقَالَ بِسْمِ اللهِ فَقَطَعَ بَقِيَّةَ الْحَجَرِ وَقَالَ اللهُ أَكْبَرُ أُعْطِيتُ مَفَاتِيحَ الْيَمَنِ وَاللهِ إِنِّي لَأُبْصِرُ أَبْوَابَ صَنْعَاءَ ن الكبرى حم ش ع

وهذا لفظه مسند الروياني أبو نعيم هق كلاهما في الدلائل خط كر

Ibn Sa'd, Ibn Jarīr, Ibn Abī Ḥātim and Abū Nu'aym narrated through Kathīr b. 'Abd Allāh b. 'Amr b. 'Awf al-Muzanī from his father, from his grandfather who ﷺ said: "A white, round rock emerged before us from the trench that broke our blades and gave us great difficulty. We complained to the Prophet ﷺ. He took the pick from Salmān and struck the rock, cracking it, whereupon a great light glimmered, illuminating al-Madīna from one boundary-stone to another until it seemed like a light in the midst of a dark night. The Messenger of Allah ﷺ exclaimed *Allāhu Akbar!* Then he struck it a second time cracking it whereupon a great light glimmered, illuminating al-Madīna from one boundary-stone to another.

segment was dropped out in al-Nabhānī. On al-Ḥīra see above, first hadith in the section on 'Adī b. Ḥātim.

He exclaimed [336] *Allāhu Akbar!* Then he struck it a third time shattering it, whereupon a great light glimmered, illuminating al-Madīna from one boundary-stone to another. He exclaimed *Allāhu Akbar!* We said: 'Messenger of Allah, we saw you strike and lightning would come out like waves, and we saw you exclaim *Allāhu Akbar!*' He said '[a] The first time the palaces of al-Ḥīra and Kisrā's Madā'in were illuminated for me as bright as the canine teeth of a dog, and Jibrīl informed me that my Community would prevail over them. The second time the red palaces of Shām in Byzantine lands were illuminated for me as bright as the canine teeth of a dog, and Jibrīl informed me that my Community would prevail over them. The third time the palaces of Ṣan'ā' were illuminated for me as bright as the canine teeth of a dog, and Jibrīl informed me that my Community would prevail over them. Receive the glad news of victory!' Hearing this, the hypocrites said: 'Muḥammad is telling you that he is seeing the palaces of al-Ḥīra and al-Madā'in from Yathrib and that you will conquer them and here you are entrenching yourselves, unable to have the upper hand!' At that time was revealed ﴿**And When the hypocrites, and those in whose hearts is a disease, were saying: Allah and His Messenger promised us naught but delusion**﴾ (33:12)."[451]

عَنْ عَمْرِو بْنِ عَوْفٍ المُزَنِيِّ قَالَ خَرَجَتْ لَنَا مِنَ الخَنْدَقِ صَخْرَةٌ
بَيْضَاءُ مُدَوَّرَةٌ فَكَسَرَتْ حَدِيدَنَا وَشَقَّتْ عَلَيْنَا فَشَكَوْنَا إِلَى
رَسُولِ اللهِ ﷺ فَأَخَذَ المِعْوَلَ مِنْ سَلْمَانَ فَضَرَبَ الصَّخْرَةَ ضَرْبَةً
صَدَعَهَا وَبَرِقَتْ مِنْهَا بَرْقَةٌ أَضَاءَ مَا بَيْنَ لَابَتَيِ المَدِينَةِ حَتَّى
لَكَأَنَّ مِصْبَاحاً فِي جَوْفِ لَيْلٍ مُظْلِمٍ فَكَبَّرَ رَسُولُ اللهِ ﷺ ثُمَّ
ضَرَبَهَا الثَّانِيَةَ فَصَدَّهَا وَبَرِقَ مِنْهَا بَرْقَةٌ أَضَاءَ مَا بَيْنَ لَابَتَيْهَا

[451]Narrated from ʿAmr b. ʿAwf by Ibn Saʿd (4:83), in the *Tafsīr*s of al-Ṭabarī, Ibn Abī Ḥātim, al-Wāḥidī, and al-Thaʿlabī, al-Ṭabarī in his *Tārīkh* (2:568-570), al-Bayhaqī in his *Dalā'il* (3:418-419), and *mursal* from Qatāda by al-Ṭabarī in his *Tafsīr* (21:133) cf. Ibn Hishām (3:55-56), *Bidāya* (4:101), and *Sīra Ḥalabiyya* (2:640).

فَكَبَّرَ ثُمَّ ضَرَبَهَا الثَّالِثَةَ فَكَسَرَهَا وَبَرِقَ مِنْهَا بَرْقَةٌ أَضَاءَ مَا بَيْنَ
لاَبَتَيْهَا فَكَبَّرَ فَقُلْنَا يَا رَسُولَ اللهِ قَدْ رَأَيْنَاكَ تَضْرِبُ فَيَخْرُجُ بَرْقٌ
كَالمَوْجِ وَرَأَيْنَاكَ تُكَبِّرُ فَقَالَ أَضَاءَ لِي فِي الأُوْلَى قُصُورُ الحِيرَةِ
وَمَدَائِنُ كِسْرَى كَأَنَّهَا أَنْيَابُ الكِلاَبِ فَأَخْبَرَنِي جِبْرَئِيلُ أَنَّ أُمَّتِي
ظَاهِرَةٌ عَلَيْهَا وَأَضَاءَ لِي فِي الثَّانِيَةِ قُصُورُ الحُمُرِ مِنْ أَرْضِ الرُّومِ
كَأَنَّهَا أَنْيَابُ الكِلاَبِ فَأَخْبَرَنِي جِبْرَئِيلُ أَنَّ أُمَّتِي ظَاهِرَةٌ عَلَيْهَا
وَأَضَاءَ لِي فِي الثَّالِثَةِ قُصُورُ صَنْعَاءَ كَأَنَّهَا أَنْيَابُ الكِلاَبِ
فَأَخْبَرَنِي جَبْرَئِيلُ أَنَّ أُمَّتِي ظَاهِرَةٌ عَلَيْهَا فَأَبْشِرُوا بِالنَّصْرِ فَقَالَ
المنَافِقُونَ يُخْبِرُكُمْ مُحَمَّدٌ أَنَّهُ يُبْصِرُ مِنْ يَثْرِبَ قُصُورَ الحِيرَةِ وَمَدَائِنَ
كِسْرَى وَأَنَّهَا تُفْتَحُ لَكُمْ وَأَنْتُمْ تَحْفُرُونَ الخَنْدَقَ وَلاَ تَسْتَطِيعُونَ
أَنْ تَبْرُزُوا فَنَزَلَ ﴿ **وَإِذْ يَقُولُ ٱلْمُنَٰفِقُونَ وَٱلَّذِينَ فِى قُلُوبِهِم مَّرَضٌ مَّا**
وَعَدَنَا ٱللَّهُ وَرَسُولُهُۥٓ إِلَّا غُرُورًا ﴿١٢﴾ ﴾ الأحزاب ابن سعد في ترجمة سلمان
الواحدي في أسباب النزول الطبري ابن أبي حاتم الثعلبي البغوي جميعهم في التفسير
والطبري أيضا في التاريخ هق في الدلائل وكثير بن عبد الله المزني ضعفه الجمهور وحسن
الترمذي حديثه وبقية رجاله ثقات مج

[Jābir ﷺ said: "The Prophet ﷺ and his friends dug the Trench for three days during which they ate no food. The people said, 'Messenger of Allah! There is a boulder *(kudya)* here that is part of the mountain.' The Messenger of Allah ﷺ said: 337 'Spray it with water.' They sprayed it then the Prophet ﷺ came, seized the pick, said *'Bismillāh!'* and struck it three times. The boulder turned into a brittle dune. At one point I turned around and noticed that the Messenger of Allah ﷺ had tied up his belly with a stone [to control the pangs of hunger]."⁴⁵²

Another version states: "They said, 'Messenger of Allah! We came upon a rock *(safāh)* which we are unable to dig up.' The Prophet ﷺ went and we went with him. He was given a pick and struck [the rock] with it, saying, *'Allāhu akbar!'* I heard a tremor I never heard the like of. He said: 338 'The good things of Persia!' He struck again, saying, *'Allāhu akbar!'* I heard a tremor I never heard the like of. He said: a 'The good things of Byzantium!' He struck again, saying, *'Allāhu akbar!'* I heard a tremor I never heard the like of. He said: *'Allāhu akbar!* b Allah has brought us Himyar as supporters and helpers!'"⁴⁵³]

Imām [519] Aḥmad and Muslim narrated from ʿUqba b. ʿĀmir ؓ that the Messenger of Allah ﷺ said: 339 "Many lands shall be laid open for you. Allah will suffice you [for defense]. But let it not make anyone quit practicing [archery] with his arrows!"⁴⁵⁴

عَنْ عُقْبَةَ بْنِ عَامِرٍ قَالَ سَمِعْتُ رَسُولَ اللهِ ﷺ يَقُولُ سَتُفْتَحُ عَلَيْكُمْ أَرَضُونَ وَيَكْفِيكُمُ اللهُ فَلاَ يَعْجِزْ أَحَدُكُمْ أَنْ يَلْهُوَ بِأَسْهُمِهِ

م حم ت سعيد بن منصور طب هق وفي الصغرى

Al-Ṭabarānī narrated from Abū Juḥayfa [Wahb b. ʿAbd Allāh ؓ] with a sound chain that the Messenger of Allah ﷺ said: 340 "The world shall be laid open for you to the point that you will be furnishing your houses the way the Kaʿba is furnished. Today you are better than you will be then."⁴⁵⁵

---

⁴⁵²Narrated from Jābir by Aḥmad, Bukhārī, and Dārimī. Tirmidhī *(gharīb)* independently narrates from Abū Ṭalḥa that the Prophet ﷺ at one point tied two stones to his belly because of hunger.

⁴⁵³Narrated from ʿAbd Allāh b. ʿAmr b. al-ʿĀṣ by al-Ḥārith in his *Musnad* (*Zawā'id* 2:704 §692) and al-Ṭabarānī with two chains according to Haythamī (6:131). Ibn Ḥajar in the *Fatḥ* (7:396-397) and al-Ṣāliḥī in *Subul al-Hudā* (4:518-519) cite all these narrations.

⁴⁵⁴Narrated from ʿUqba b. ʿĀmir by Muslim, Aḥmad, al-Tirmidhī and others.

⁴⁵⁵Narrated from [1] Abū Juḥayfa by Aḥmad in *al-Zuhd* (p. 139 §278), al-Bazzār (10:157 §4227), and al-Ṭabarānī in *al-Kabīr* (22:108) through trustworthy narrators per al-Haythamī (8:291 cf. 10:323) cf. *Khaṣā'is* (2:185-186); [2] Ṭalḥa b. ʿAmr al-Baṣrī by Ibn Abī ʿĀṣim in *al-Āḥād wal-Mathānī* (3:112 §1434) and *al-Zuhd* (p. 25-26), al-Ḥākim (1990 ed. 3:16 and 4:591), al-Bayhaqī in *al-Sunan al-Kubrā* (2:445) and the *Shuʿab* (2:76-77 §1200 and 7:284 §10325), and (only the phrase "you will be furnishing your

عَنْ أَبِي جُحَيْفَةَ قَالَ رَسُولُ اللهِ ﷺ سَتُفْتَحُ عَلَيْكُمُ الدُّنْيَا حَتَّى تُنَجِّدُوا بُيُوتَكُمْ كَمَا تُنَجَّدُ الْكَعْبَةُ قُلْنَا وَنَحْنُ عَلَى دِينِنَا قَالَ نَعَمْ فَأَنْتُمُ الْيَوْمَ خَيْرٌ مِنْ يَوْمَئِذٍ قُلْنَا يَوْمَئِذٍ قَالَ بَلْ أَنْتُمُ الْيَوْمَ خَيْرٌ طب ز حم في الزهد وفي الباب عن طلحة بن عمرو البصري ابن أبي عاصم في الآحاد ك هق هب حم مختصرا والزبير بن العوام ك وعلي ت ع هناد في الزهد وعبد الله بن يزيد بن زيد ابن أبي عاصم في الزهد ابن قانع هق وغيرهم مرسلاً

Abū Nuʿaym narrated in the *Ḥilya* from al-Ḥasan al-Baṣrī that the Messenger of Allah ﷺ said: 341 "The world east and west shall be laid open for my Community. Truly, a its agents shall enter the Fire except those that fear Allah and remit their trust."[456]

عَنِ الْحَسَنِ الْبَصْرِيِّ مُرْسَلاً قَالَ رَسُولُ اللهِ ﷺ سَتُفْتَحُ مَشَارِقُ الْأَرْضِ وَمَغَارِبُهَا عَلَى أُمَّتِي أَلاَ وَعُمَّالُهَا فِي النَّارِ إِلاَّ مَنِ اتَّقَى اللهَ وَأَدَّى الْأَمَانَةَ عبد الله بن أحمد في زوائد الزهد حل

houses the way the Kaʿba is furnished") Aḥmad cf. *Bidāya* (6:255); [3] al-Zubayr b. al-ʿAwwām as related by al-Nabhānī below (see note 489); [4] Muḥammad b. Kaʿb al-Quraẓī, from someone, from ʿAlī by Ibn Isḥāq (§246) and, through him, al-Tirmidhī *(ḥasan* and in some versions *ḥasan gharīb)*, Hannād in *al-Zuhd* (2:389 §758), and Abū Yaʿlā (1:387 §502). The unnamed narrator could be another Companion or one of the *Tābiʿī*s ʿAbd Allāh b. Shaddād b. al-Hād *(thiqa)* or Shabath b. Ribʿī *("sadūq yukhtiʾ")* – one of the killers of ʿUthmān and al-Ḥusayn رضي الله عنهما – but it is also narrated in full from [5] Muhammad b. Kaʿb, from the Companion ʿAbd Allāh b. Yazīd b. Zayd by Ibn Abī ʿĀṣim: see note 512, section entitled "His ﷺ Foretelling that Allah Would Grant Empire to the Community"; and [6] *mursal* from *Tābiʿīn* such as al-Hasan, Qatāda, Ibn Kaʿb, and Saʿd b. Masʿūd al-Sadafī.

[456]Narrated from an unnamed Companion by Aḥmad with a weak chain because of two unknown *Tābiʿī* narrators and from al-Ḥasan with a fair to weak *mursal* chain by Aḥmad in *al-Zuhd* (p. 277) and Abū Nuʿaym (1985 ed. 6:199) cf. *al-Jāmiʿ al-Saghīr* (§4668). Al-Munāwī in *Fayd al-Qadīr* (4:98) said al-Suyūṭī erred in documenting it only as *mursal* since it is found *mawsūl* in Aḥmad, but the beginnings of the respective narrations differ and the chains have nothing in common.

[The Prophet ﷺ also said, when he saw hunger in the faces of his Companions: 342 "Receive the glad tidings! A day shall come when one of you will have meat and bread for breakfast, and meat and bread for dinner!" They said, "Messenger of Allah, will we be in a better state at that time?" He replied: "Nay, you are in a better state today than you will be then!"][457]

His ﷺ Foretelling the Deaths of Chosroes and Caesar and the Conquest of the Persians and Eastern Romans

Al-Bazzār, Abū Nuʿaym, and al-Bayhaqī narrated from Diḥya رضي الله عنه that when the Prophet ﷺ wrote to Chosroes, the latter wrote to his friend in Ṣanʿāʾ threatening him and saying, "Will you not rid me of a man that came out in your parts and is summoning me to his religion? Either you will rid me of him or I shall do this and that to you!" The ruler of Ṣanʿāʾ then sent word of this to the Prophet ﷺ. When the Prophet ﷺ read about the letter, he let them [the emissaries] wait for fifteen days. Then he said: <"Go to your friend and say to him, 343 'My Lord killed your Lord [Chosroes] last night' *(inna rabbī qatala rabbaka al-layla)*!"> They left and reported it. Diḥya said: "Then the news came that Chosroes was killed that night."[458]

عَنْ دِحْيَةَ رَضِيَ اللهُ عَنْهُ أَنَّ كِسْرَى لَمَّا كَتَبَ إِلَيْهِ رَسُولُ اللهِ
ﷺ كَتَبَ كِسْرَى إِلَى صَاحِبِهِ بِصَنْعَاءَ يَتَوَعَّدُهُ وَيَقُولُ أَلاَ
تَكْفِينِي رَجُلاً بِأَرْضِكَ يَدْعُونِي إِلَى دِينِهِ لَتَكْفِيَنَّهُ أَوْ لأَفْعَلَنَّ بِكَ
فَبَعَثَ صَاحِبُ صَنْعَاءَ إِلَى النَّبِيِّ ﷺ فَلَمَّا قَرَأَ رَسُولُ اللهِ ﷺ

[457]Narrated from Ibn Masʿūd by al-Bazzār (5:323 §1941) with a good chain per al-Haythamī (10:323), from Wāthila b. al-Asqaʿ by Khaythama b. Sulayman cf. *Min Ḥadīthi Khaythama* (p. 190), Abū Nuʿaym (1985 ed. 2:23), and al-Bayhaqī in *Shuʿab al-Īmān* (7:283 §10322), from Jābir and al-Zubayr in the same work (7:286-287 §10334, §10329) and al-Ḥākim (1990 ed. 3:728) cf. note 489.

[458]Narrated with a very weak chain through two discarded narrators from Diḥya by Abū Nuʿaym in the *Dalāʾil* (p. 347-348 §240) as part of a longer report confirmed through six chains by Ibn Saʿd (see below) and elsewhere but in most reports the emissaries wait overnight instead of a fortnight while al-Taymī mentions a full month in his *Dalāʾil* (p. 234).

كِتَابَ صَاحِبِهِمْ تَرَكَهُمْ خَمْسَ عَشْرَةَ لَيْلَةً لاَ يُكَلِّمُهُمْ وَلاَ يَنْظُرُ إِلَيْهِمْ إِلاَّ إِعْرَاضاً فَلَمَّا مَضَتْ خَمْسَ عَشْرَةَ لَيْلَةً تَقَدَّمُوا إِلَيْهِ فَلَمَّا رَآهُمْ دَعَاهُمْ وَقَالَ اِذْهَبُوا إِلَى صَاحِبِكُمْ فَقُولُوا إِنَّ رَبِّي قَتَلَ رَبَّكَ اللَّيْلَةَ فَانْطَلَقُوا فَأَخْبَرُوهُ قَالَ دِحْيَةُ ثُمَّ جَاءَ الخَبَرُ بِأَنَّ كِسْرَى قُتِلَ تِلْكَ اللَّيْلَةَ أبو نعيم في الدلائل

Ibn Isḥāq, al-Bayhaqī, Abū Nuʿaym, and [Abū Bakr Muḥammad b. Ja'far] al-Kharā'iṭī (d. 327) narrated that [the *Tābiʿī*] Abū Salama [ʿAbd Allāh] b. ʿAbd al-Raḥmān b. ʿAwf heard that as Chosroes was sitting in his imperial palace one day, a certain incident took place in which the truth appeared clearly to him. Suddenly, he saw a man walking with a staff in his hand and saying to him: [344] "Kisrā! Are you going to accept Islam before I break *(aksira)* this staff?" Chosroes replied, "Yes, do not break it, do not break it." After the man left, Chosroes sent for his gatekeepers and asked, "Who authorized this man to enter and see me?" They replied, "No-one entered to see you." He said, "Liars!" and became angry at them, threatening them with dire consequences. After one year passed, the same man came, carrying his staff and saying: "Kisrā! Are you going to accept Islam before I break this staff?" Chosroes said, "Yes, do not break it, do not break it." After the man left, Chosroes again sent for his gatekeepers, asking who had authorized the man to enter. They denied that anyone had entered. He said the same thing he had said to them the first time. Another year passed and the same man came again, staff in hand, saying: "Kisrā! Are you going to accept Islam before I break this staff?" Chosroes said, "Yes, do not break it, do not break it." But the man broke the staff. Then Allah brought to pass the destruction of Chosroes.[459] • The ḥadīth Master al-Suyūṭī said

[459]Narrated *mursal* from al-Zuhrī, from Abū Salama in the *Dalā'il* of al-Bayhaqī (4:392) and al-Taymī (p. 179-180 §229) cf. *Khaṣā'iṣ* (2:15), *Bidāya* (4:271), *Iktifā'* (2:388), and al-Māwardī, *A'lām al-Nubuwwa* (p. 239).

this narration was *mursal ṣaḥīḥ* and that it was narrated from Abū Salama by al-Zuhrī and ʿUmar b. ʿAbd al-Qawī; and, from al-Zuhrī, 'Uqayl [b. Khālid al-Īlī], ʿAbd Allāh b. Abī Bakr, Ṣāliḥ b. Kaysān, and others; and that al-Wāqidī and Abū Nuʿaym had narrated it with an unbroken chain *(mawṣūlan)* from Abū Salama, from Abū Hurayra.

عَنْ أَبِي سَلَمَةَ أَنَّهُ بَلَغَهُ أَنَّ كِسْرَى بَيْنَمَا هُوَ فِي دَسْكَرَةِ مُلْكِهِ بُعِثَ لَهُ أَوْ قُيِّضَ لَهُ عَارِضٌ فَعُرِضَ عَلَيْهِ الحَقُّ فَلَمْ يَفْجَأْ كِسْرَى إِلاَّ الرَّجُلُ يَمْشِي وَفِي يَدِهِ عَصَا فَقَالَ يَا كِسْرَى هَلْ لَكَ فِي الإِسْلاَمِ قَبْلَ أَنْ أَكْسِرَ هَذِهِ الْعَصَا قَالَ كِسْرَى نَعَمْ فَلاَ تَكْسِرْهَا فَوَلَّى الرَّجُلُ فَلَمَّا ذَهَبَ أَرْسَلَ كِسْرَى إِلَى حُجَّابِهِ فَقَالَ مَنْ أَذِنَ لِهَذَا الرَّجُلِ عَلَيَّ فَقَالُوا مَا دَخَلَ عَلَيْكَ أَحَدٌ قَالَ كَذَبْتُمْ قَالَ فَغَضِبَ عَلَيْهِمْ وَتَلْتَلَهُمْ ثُمَّ تَرَكَهُمْ فَلَمَّا كَانَ رَأْسُ الحَوْلِ أَتَاهُ ذَلِكَ الرَّجُلُ المَعْهُودُ مَعَهُ الْعَصَا فَقَالَ يَا كِسْرَى هَلْ لَكَ فِي الإِسْلاَمِ قَبْلَ أَنْ أَكسِرَ هَذِهِ الْعَصَا قَالَ نَعَمْ لاَ تَكْسِرْهَا لاَ تَكْسِرْهَا فَلَمَّا انْصَرَفَ عَنْهُ دَعَا كِسْرَى حُجَّابَهُ فَسَأَلَهُمْ مَنْ أَذِنَ لَهُ فَأَنْكَرُوا أَنْ يَكُونَ دَخَلَ عَلَيْهِ أَحَدٌ فَلَقُوا مِنْ كِسْرَى مِثْلَ مَا لَقُوا فِي المَرَّةِ الأُولَى حَتَّى إِذَا كَانَ الحَوْلُ المُسْتَقْبَلُ أَتَاهُ ذَلِكَ الرَّجُلِ مَعَهُ الْعَصَا فَقَالَ لَهُ هَلْ لَكَ يَا كِسْرَى فِي الإِسْلاَمِ قَبْلَ أَنْ أَكسِرَ الْعَصَا قَالَ لاَ تَكْسِرْهَا فَكَسَرَهَا فَأَهْلَكَ اللهُ كِسْرَى عِنْدَ ذَلِكَ التيمي هق في دلائلهما

Abū Nuʿaym narrated something similar from ʿIkrima, adding: "This is why Chosroes' son wrote Bādhān, his representative in Yemen, forbidding him from interfering with the Prophet ﷺ in fear of what he had seen before."[460]

Abū Nuʿaym narrated from Abū Umāma al-Bāhilī that a man appeared before Chosroes dressed in two green garments and carrying a green stick, his back bent, saying **[520]** 345 "Kisrā! Surrender *(aslim)*, or else I shall break *(aksiru)* your kingdom as I break this stick!" Chosroes said, "Do not!" The man left him.[461]

عَنْ أَبِي أُمَامَةَ البَاهِلِيِّ قَالَ مَثَلَ بَيْنَ يَدَي كِسْرَى رَجُلٌ فِي بُرْدَيْنِ أَخْضَرَينِ مَعَهُ قَضِيبٌ أَخْضَرُ قَدْ حَنَى ظَهْرَهُ وَهُوَ يَقُولُ يَا كِسْرَى أَسْلِمْ وَإِلاَّ كَسَرْتُ مُلْكَكَ كَمَا أَكْسِرُ هَذِهِ الْعَصَا فَقَالَ كِسْرَى لاَ تَفْعَلْ ثُمَّ تَوَلَّى عَنْهُ كذا في الخصائص وعزاه لأبي نعيم ولم يوجد في المطبوع من الدلائل ولا الحلية

Abū Nuʿaym also narrated from Saʿīd b. Jubayr that Chosroes wrote to Bādhān, the king of Yemen: "Send word to that man that he must return to the faith of his people and, if not, let him promise to meet you on a certain day in which the two of you shall meet and fight." Bādhān then sent two men to the Messenger of Allah ﷺ who told them to stay for a while. They stayed for a few days when, one morning, he summoned them and told them: 346 "Go to Bādhān and tell him that my Lord killed Kisrā last night." They set out and conveyed the message to him, after which the same news reached him.

[460]*Khasā'is* (2:15) cf. Abū Nuʿaym, *Dalā'il* (p. 351). I.e. Chosroes's patricidal successor Shīrawayh as in the reports adduced further down. On Bādhān b. Sāsān who accepted Islam after which it spread in Yemen, see *Zād* (1:125) and Ibn Khaldūn's *Muqaddima.* Al-Nabhānī states here: "Something similar was mentioned towards the end of the first part of this book *[Ḥujjatullāh]* narrated by Ibn al-Jawzī through Ibn Isḥāq.

[461]This and the next report are thus cited and referenced in the *Khasā'is* (2:16-17).

أَخْرَجَ أَبُو نُعَيْمٍ عَنْ سَعِيدِ بْنِ جُبَيْرٍ قَالَ كَتَبَ كِسْرَى إِلَى بَاذَانَ
عَامِلِ اليَمَنِ أَنِ ابْعَثْ إِلَى هَذَا الرَّجُلِ فَمُرْهُ فَلْيَرْجِعْ إِلَى دِينِ
قَوْمِهِ وَإِلاَّ فَلْيُوَاعِدْكَ يَوْماً تَلْتَقُونَ فِيهِ فَبَعَثَ بَاذَانُ إِلَى رَسُولِ
اللهِ ﷺ رَجُلَيْنِ فَأَمَرَهُمَا رَسُولُ اللهِ ﷺ بِالمَقَامِ فَأَقَامَا أَيَّاماً ثُمَّ
أَرْسَلَ إِلَيْهِمَا ذَاتَ غَدَاةٍ فَقَالَ إِنْطَلِقَا إِلَى بَاذَانَ فَأَعْلِمَاهُ إِنَّ
رَبِّي قَدْ قَتَلَ كِسْرَى فِي هَذِهِ اللَّيْلَةِ فَانْطَلَقَا فَأَخْبَرَاهُ فَأَتَاهُ الخَبَرُ
كَذَلِكَ كذا في الخصائص الكبرى ولم نجده

Ibn Saʿd narrated through al-Wāqidī from Ibn ʿAbbās and [the *Tābiʿī*] al-Miswar b. Rifāʿa and [the Companion] al-ʿAlāʾ b. al-Ḥaḍramī [and others] – their reports partly overlap – that when the Prophet ﷺ wrote to Chosroes, the latter wrote to Bādhān, his representative in Yemen: "Send two of your strong men to that man in the Ḥijāz and let them bring me news of him." Bādhān then sent his right hand man (*qahramān*) and another man bearing a letter from him. They came to al-Madīna and handed the letter to the Prophet ﷺ after a formal announcement. He smiled and invited them to Islam as they were trembling from head to toe. He said: [347] "Leave me be today and come back tomorrow, then I will inform you of my decision." They came back the next day. The Prophet ﷺ said: [a] "Tell your friend that my Lord has killed his lord Chosroes last night, seven hours ago <– to wit, the night of the third day of the week on the tenth of Jumāda al-Ūlā of the year seven –> and that Allah has empowered over him his son Shīrawayh, who killed him." They returned to Bādhān <with the news>. He entered Islam together with all the Persian subjects in Yemen.[462]

[462]*Khaṣāʾis* (2:17). Narrated from Ibn ʿAbbās, the *Tābiʿīs* al-Miswar b. Rifāʿa and Jaʿfar b. ʿAbd Allāh b. al-Hakam, and the Companions al-Shifāʾ bint ʿAbd Allāh b. ʿAbd Shams, al-ʿAlāʾ b. al-Ḥaḍramī, and ʿAmr b. Umayya by Ibn Saʿd (1:260) and Ibn ʿAsākir (27:357). The bracketed passage was omitted by al-Nabhānī.

عَنْ ابْنِ عَبَّاسٍ وَآخَرِينَ كَتَبَ كِسْرَى إِلَى بَاذَانَ عَامِلِهِ عَلَى
اليَمَنِ أَنِ ابْعَثْ مِنْ عِنْدِكَ رَجُلَين جَلْدَيْنِ إِلَى هَذَا الرَّجُلِ
الَّذِي بِالحِجَازِ فَلْيَأْتِيَانِي بِخَبَرِهِ فَبَعَثَ بَاذَانَ قَهْرَمَانَهُ وَرَجُلاً آخَرَ
وَكَتَبَ مَعَهُمَا كِتَاباً فَقَدِمَا المَدِينَةَ فَدَفَعَا كِتَابَ بَاذَانَ إِلَى النَّبِيِّ
ﷺ فَتَبَسَّمَ رَسُولُ اللهِ ﷺ وَدَعَاهُمَا إِلَى الإِسْلَامِ وَفَرَائِصُهُمَا
تَرْعُدُ وَقَالَ إِرْجِعَا عَنِّي يَوْمَكُمَا هَذَا حَتَّى تَأْتِيَانِي الْغَدَ فَأُخْبِرُكُمَا
بِمَا أُرِيدُ فَجَاءَاهُ مِنَ الْغَدِ فَقَالَ لَهُمَا أَبْلِغَا صَاحِبَكُمَا أَنَّ رَبِّي قَدْ
قَتَلَ رَبَّهُ كِسْرَى فِي هَذِهِ اللَّيْلَةِ لِسَبْعِ سَاعَاتٍ مَضَتْ مِنْهَا
وَهِيَ لَيْلَةُ الثَّلَاثَاءِ لِعَشْرِ لَيَالٍ مَضِينَ مِنْ جُمَادَى الأُولَى سَنَةَ
سَبْعٍ وَأَنَّ اللهَ تَبَارَكَ وَتَعَالَى سَلَّطَ عَلَيْهِ ابْنَهُ شِيرَوَيْهِ فَقَتَلَهُ فَرَجَعَا
إِلَى بَاذَانَ بِذَلِكَ فَأَسْلَمَ هُوَ وَالأَبْنَاءُ الَّذِينَ بِالْيَمَنِ ابن سعد كر

Abū Nuʿaym and Ibn Saʿd in *Sharaf al-Muṣṭafā* [*sic*][463] narrated through Ibn Isḥāq, from al-Zuhrī, that Abū Salama b. ʿAbd al-Raḥmān [b. ʿAwf] said that when the letter of the Messenger of Allah ﷺ reached Chosroes, the latter wrote to Bādhān, his representative in Yemen, "Send two of your strong men to that man in the Ḥijāz and let them bring him to me." Bādhān then sent his right hand man and another man, sending word with them to the Messenger of Allah ﷺ to go with them to Chosroes. He said to his

[463]Thus in the *Khaṣā'is* (2:17-18). "The mention of *Sharaf al-Muṣṭafā* here appears to be a lapse since the report is in Ibn Saʿd's *Ṭabaqāt* (1:260) and Abū Nuʿaym's *Dalā'il* (§241) through various paths in the wording mentioned by al-Suyūṭī and not in *Sharaf al-Muṣṭafā*, and Allah knows best": al-Ghamrī, notes on Abū Saʿd al-Kharkūshī's *Sharaf al-Muṣṭafā* (4:18).

right hand man: "Observe the man, speak to him, then come back and tell me about him." They came to the Prophet ﷺ and conveyed the message to him. He said: 348 "Come back tomorrow." The next morning, the Messenger of Allah ﷺ informed them that Allah ﷻ had empowered over Chosroes his son Shīrawayh who killed him in such-and-such a month in such-and-such a night, at a certain period of time that very night. They said: "Do you realize what you just said? Are we to report this to the King?" He said: "Yes, tell him what I just said. Tell him that, truly, a my Faith and authority *(inna dīnī wa-sulṭānī)* shall reach the full extent of Chosroes' empire up to wherever shoes and hooves can tread. Tell him also: b If you submit, I shall give you whatever is presently under your authority." They came back to Bādhān with the news. He said, "By Allah! This is not the speech of a king. We shall wait and see about what he said." Soon after this, a letter from Shīrawayh came to Bādhān, saying, "To proceed: I have killed Chosroes and did this deed only in anger for Persia, because of his excesses in killing her noblemen. Declare your obedience to my emissary facing you. Do not in the least provoke the man about whom Chosroes wrote you." When Bādhān read this he said, "Indeed, the man is a Divine Messenger!" He entered Islam together with all the Persian subjects that were in Yemen. He asked his right hand man, "How does he look?" He said, "I spoke to no man that awed me more than him." He asked, "Were there guards with him?" He said no.[464]

Aḥmad, al-Bazzār, al-Ṭabarānī, and Abū Nuʿaym narrated that Abū Bakrah ﷺ said that when **[521]** the Messenger of Allah ﷺ wrote to Chosroes, the latter wrote to his representative in Yemen, Bādhān: "News have reached me that a certain man has come out in your region who claims that he is a Prophet. Tell him to cease and desist or else I shall send him a force that will destroy him and his nation." Bādhān conveyed the message to the Prophet ﷺ who replied: 349 "If this were something I was claiming on my own, I would cease and desist; but it is Allah that sent me." The emissary

[464]Al-Nabhānī misspells the word for "guards" (*shuraṭ*) as *sharaf*, "honor," and then glosses: "By *sharaf* he meant the pageantry and pomp of kings." This is the same report he mentions a few hadiths down.

stayed with him. The Prophet ﷺ told him later: a "My Lord has destroyed Chosroes and there will be no Chosroes after today, just as Caesar was killed and there will be no more Caesar!" The emissary recorded his statement and the exact time, day and month he had said it, then returned to Bādhān. Lo and behold! Chosroes had died and Caesar had died.[465]

عَنْ أَبِي بَكْرَةَ رَضِيَ اللهُ عَنْهُ قَالَ لَمَّا بُعِثَ رَسُولُ اللهِ ﷺ بَعَثَ كِسْرَى إِلَى عَامِلِهِ عَلَى أَرْضِ اليَمَنِ وَمَنْ يَلِيهِ مِنَ الْعَرَبِ وَكَانَ يُقَالُ لَهُ بَاذَامُ أَنَّهُ بَلَغَنِي أَنَّهُ خَرَجَ رَجُلٌ قِبَلَكَ يَزْعُمُ أَنَّه نَبِيٌّ فَقُلْ لَهُ فَلْيَكُفَّ عَنْ ذَلِكَ أَوْ لَأَبْعَثَنَّ إِلَيْهِ مَنْ يَقْتُلُهُ أَوْ يَقْتُلُ قَوْمَهُ قَالَ فَجَاءَ رَسُولُ بَاذَامَ إِلَى النَّبِيِّ ﷺ فَقَالَ لَهُ هَذَا فَقَالَ رَسُولُ اللهِ ﷺ لَوْ كَانَ شَيْءٌ فَعَلْتُهُ مِنْ قِبَلِي كَفَفْتُ وَلَكِنِ اللهَ عَزَّ وَجَلَّ بَعَثَنِي فَأَقَامَ الرَّسُولُ عِنْدَهُ فَقَالَ لَهُ رَسُولُ اللهِ ﷺ إِنَّ رَبِّي قَتَلَ كِسْرَى وَلاَ كِسْرَى بَعْدَ الْيَوْمِ وَقَتَلَ قَيْصَرَ وَلاَ قَيْصَرَ بَعْدَ اليَوْمِ قَالَ فَكَتَبَ قَوْلَهُ فِي السَّاعَةِ الَّتِي حَدَّثَهُ وَالْيَوْمِ الَّذِي حَدَّثَهُ والشَّهْرِ الَّذِي حَدَّثَهُ فِيهِ ثُمَّ رَجَعَ إِلَى بَاذَامَ فَإِذَا كِسْرَى قَدْ مَاتَ وَإِذَا قَيْصَرُ قَدْ قُتِلَ طب ورجاله رجال الصحيح غير كثير بن زياد وهو ثقة مج

[The Prophet ﷺ <said to the Persian emissary: "My Lord has killed your Lord" – meaning Chosroes. Then he> was told that his daughter had been made to succeed him, so he said: 350 "No people shall prosper who are ruled by a woman."[466]]

[465]Narrated from Abū Bakrah by al-Ṭabarānī through trustworthy narrators per al-Haythamī (8:287-288), and by Aḥmad and al-Bazzār in shorter form with the addition mentioned below (next note).

[466]Narrated from Abū Bakrah by Aḥmad and al-Bazzār (9:106 §3647), and – without the bracketed segment but with the wording "who have a woman rule them" – by al-Bukhārī,

Al-Daylamī narrated from ʿUmar b. al-Khaṭṭāb ؓ that the Messenger of Allah ﷺ said to the two emissaries of Chosroes, the ruler of Persia, when he sent them to him: 351 "Truly, my Lord killed your Lord last night. His son killed him. Allah empowered him over him. Therefore, say to your master: If you submit, I shall give you whatever is presently under your authority and, if not, Allah shall cause your demise."[467]

عَنْ عُمَرَ بْنِ الخَطَّابِ قَالَ رَسُولُ اللهِ ﷺ لِرَسُولَي كِسْرَى لَمَّا
بَعَثَهُمَا إِلَى رَسُولِ اللهِ ﷺ إِنَّ رَبِّي قَدْ قَتَلَ رَبَّكُمَا اللَّيلَةَ فِي
خَمْسِ سَاعَاتٍ مَضَيْنَ مِنْهَا قَتَلَهُ ابْنُهُ شِيرَوَيْهْ سَلَّطَهُ اللهُ عَلَيْهِ
فَقُولاَ لِصَاحِبِكُمَا إِنْ تُسْلِمْ أُعْطِكَ مَا تَحْتَ يَدَيْكَ فِي بِلاَدِكَ
وَإِنْ لاَ تَفْعَلْ يُغْنِ اللهُ عَنْكَ إِرْجِعَا إِلَيْهِ فَأَخْبِرَاهُ الديلمى في الفردوس

Al-Bayhaqī narrated through Ibn Shihāb who said, ʿAbd al-Raḥmān b. 'Abdin al-Qārī said that the Messenger of Allah ﷺ sent his missive to Chosroes. When it reached him he tore it up. The Messenger of Allah ﷺ said: 352 "Chosroes has just torn up his kingdom" *(mazzaqa Kisrā mulkah)*.[468]

al-Tirmidhī *(ḥasan saḥīḥ)*, al-Nasā'ī, and Aḥmad, and from Jābir b. Samura by al-Ṭabarānī in *al-Awsat* (5:123 §4855) cf. Haythamī (5:209) but al-Bazzār (9:106) said this narration is not known except through Abū Bakrah. Ibn Ḥazm said this Prophetic stipulation pertains strictly to the office of caliphate: *Muḥallā* (9:429-430).

[467]Narrated from ʿUmar by al-Daylamī in *al-Firdaws* (1:242 §933) cf. *Khaṣā'is* (2:18).

[468]Narrated *mursal* from the *Tābiʿī* ʿAbd al-Raḥmān b. 'Abdin al-Qārī by Abū Muḥammad ʿAbd Allāh b. Wahb b. Muslim al-Qurashī al-Mālikī (d. 197) [perhaps in his *Muwatta' al-Saghīr*] cf. *Bidāya* (4:268-269) and *Sīra Ḥalabiyya* (3:291) and by al-Bayhaqī in his *Dalā'il* (4:388) cf. *Khaṣā'is* (2:14) as well as from Ibn Isḥāq without chain by Abū Nuʿaym in his *Dalā'il* (p. 349). Misspelt *muzziqa Kisrā wa-mulkuh* in al-Nabhānī. Something similar is narrated from the *Tābiʿī* Abū Salama by al-Ṭabarī in his *Tārīkh* (2:133) through Ibn Isḥāq cf. *Bidāya* (4:269); from the Companion ʿAbd Allāh b. Ḥudhāfa by al-Wāqidī cf. *Iktifā'* (2:386); from Abū Saʿīd al-Khudrī by Abū al-Shaykh in *Tabaqāt al-Muḥaddithīn bi-Aṣbahān* (3:350-351 §404); and, *mursal*, from Abū Ma'shar Najīḥ b. ʿAbd al-Raḥmān al-Madanī – who is very weak – by al-Khaṭīb (1:131-132). Also narrated by al-Shāfi'ī without chain in *al-Umm* (4:171) cf. al-Bayhaqī, *Sunan* (9:181) and

عَنْ عَبْدِ الرَّحْمَنِ بْنِ عَبْدٍ الْقَارِيِّ أَنَّ رَسُولَ اللهِ ﷺ بَعَثَ إِلَى كِسْرَى بِكِتَابِهِ فَمَزَّقَهُ كِسْرَى فَقَالَ رَسُولُ اللهِ ﷺ مَزَّقَ كِسْرَى مُلْكَهُ أبو نعيم هق كلاهما في الدلائل ويروى مُزِّقَ مُلْكُهُ تاريخ الطبري هق كر

وفي رواية اللهُمَّ مَزِّقْ مُلْكَهُ ابن سعد

Al-Bayhaqī narrated through Ibn ʿAwf that ʿUmayr b. Isḥāq said the Messenger of Allah ﷺ wrote to Chosroes and Caesar. The latter put down the message but Chosroes tore it up. News of both reached the Messenger of Allah ﷺ who said: 353 "These shall be torn asunder but those shall have some remnants."[469]

عَنْ عُمَيْرِ بْنِ إِسْحَاقَ قَالَ كَتَبَ رَسُولُ اللهِ ﷺ إِلَى كِسْرَى وَقَيْصَرَ فَأَمَّا قَيْصَرُ فَوَضَعَهُ وَأَمَّا كِسْرَى فَمَزَّقَهُ فَبَلَغَ ذَلِكَ رَسُولَ اللهِ ﷺ فَقَالَ أَمَّا هَؤُلَاءِ فَيُمَزَّقُونَ وَأَمَّا هَؤُلَاءِ فَسَتَكُونُ لَهُمْ بَقِيَّةٌ

هق وفي الدلائل القاسم بن سلام ابن زنجويه كلاهما في الأموال

The author of a *Sīra Nabawiyya* quoted al-Bayhaqī as narrating that 354 the Prophet ﷺ informed Chosroes' envoy of the death of Chosroes the same day he died. When the Messenger of Allah ﷺ wrote Chosroes, inviting him to Islam, the latter wrote to his governor in Yemen, named Bādhān, telling him, "A man from Quraysh has come out in Mecca claiming that he is a Prophet. Seize him and summon him to repent. If he does, [leave him] and,

Bidāya (4:271). Al-Nabhānī has "Kisrā and his kingdom are torn up" *(muzziqa Kisrā wa mulkuh)* but this wording is not found anywhere.

469Narrated with passable *mursal* chains from the *Tābiʿī* ʿUmayr b. Isḥāq in *al-Amwāl* by Abū ʿUbayd (1:64-65 §59) and Ibn Zanjūyah (1:121 §101) cf. *Fatḥ* (1:44) and al-Bayhaqī in *al-Sunan al-Kubrā* (9:179) and the *Dalāʾil* (4:394) cf. *Khaṣāʾis* (2:16) and *Tarātīb* (1:157).

if not, send me his head."[470] Another version states that he said to his representative: "Will you not rid me of a man that came out in your parts and is summoning me to his religion? Either you will rid me of him or I shall do this and that to you!"[471] [Ibn Isḥāq said that] Chosroes wrote to Badhān, his governor in Yemen: "Send two of your strong men to that man in the Ḥijāz and let them bring him to me." Bādhān then sent Chosroes' reply to the Prophet ﷺ with his right hand man <named, Abābūh, a scribe and secretary, with the Persian king's letter,> and another Persian <by the name of Khurkhusrū,> sending word with them to the Messenger of Allah ﷺ to go with them at once to Chosroes. <He said to Abābūh: "Observe the man, speak to him, then come back and tell me about him."> They went out and reached al-Ṭā'if where they enquired about him. They met a Qurayshite who told them he was in al-Madīna. <The people rejoiced greatly at the two of them, gloating, "Good news! Chosroes the King of kings is now his enemy, and you are about to be rid of that man!"> When they reached him in Madīna they said <–Abābūh spoke to him>: "Shāhān Shāh, the King of kings, Chosroes, wrote to King Bādhān ordering him to send out emissaries to bring you to him! He has sent me so that you should come with me! <If you do, he will write to the King of kings a letter that will benefit you and placate him so he will not harm you!> If you refuse, <you know who and what he is!> He will destroy you and your nation and ruin your countries!" At the time they went in to see the Messenger of Allah ﷺ they had shaven their beards and let their moustaches grow freely in the Persian fashion so that he disliked looking at them. He said: [355] "Woe to you! Who told you to do such a thing?" They replied, "Our Lord!" meaning Chosroes. The Messenger of Allah ﷺ said: [a] "My Lord has told me to let grow my beard freely and cut my moustache."> He then said: "Come back tomorrow." News then came from the heaven to the Messenger of Allah ﷺ that Allah ﷻ had empowered over Chosroes his son Shīrawayh who killed him in such-and-such a month in **[522]** such-and-such a night, at a certain period of time

[470] Narrated by Ibn Hishām (1:191) cf. *Iktifā'* (1:114), *Bidāya* (2:180), and *Sīra Ḥalabiyya* (3:291).

[471] This is Diḥya's narration cf. note 458.

that very night.[472] He informed them of this the next morning. <They said: "Do you realize what you just said? We have already taken you to task for less than that by far! Are we to report this to the King and tell him what you just said?" He said: "Yes, tell him what I just said. Tell him that truly [b] my faith and power *(dīnī wa sulṭānī)* shall reach the full extent of Chosroes' empire up to wherever shoes and hooves tread. Tell him also: [c] If you submit, I shall give you whatever is presently under your authority and give you kingship over your nation of the citizens [of Persia]." Then he gave Khurkhusrū a girdle *(minṭaqa)* adorned with gold and silver which he had received from some king. They left him and came back to Bādhān with the news. He said, "By Allah! This is not the speech of a king. I can see that this man is a Prophet just as he says he is. We will certainly verify what he said."> In one version, the Messenger of Allah ﷺ wrote to Bādhān: "Allah has promised me that He would kill Chosroes on such-and-such a day of such-and-such a month. When the letter reached Bādhān, he suspended his judgment, saying, "If he is a Prophet, it will happen." Then Allah killed Kisrā at the hand of his son Shīrawayh.[473] In another version, the Prophet ﷺ said to Bādhān's envoy: [d] "Go to your friend and say to him, 'My Lord killed your Lord last night.'" The news came that Chosroes was killed that night exactly as the Prophet ﷺ had said.[474] [In Ibn Isḥāq Badhān said:] <"If what he said turns out to be true, there remains no dispute that the is a Prophet sent from above. If not, then we shall see."> Soon after this, a letter from Shīrawayh came to Bādhān, saying, "To proceed: I have killed Chosroes and did not do this deed except in anger for Persia because of his excesses in killing her noblemen <and keeping her armies in forced exile>. When my letter reaches you, declare your obedience to my emissary facing you. Wait in the matter of the man about whom Chosroes wrote you. Do not provoke him in the least[475] until my orders reach you!" <When the letter of Shīrawayh

[472]In Ibn Saʿd's report from Ibn ʿAbbās already cited: "To wit, the night of the third day of the week on the tenth of Jumāda al-Ūlā of the Year Seven."

[473]This version only in Ibn Hishām (1:191) cf. *Iktifā'* (1:114), *Bidāya* (2:180), and *Sīra Ḥalabiyya* (3:292).

[474]Cf. the report from Diḥya already cited.

[475]*Fa-lā tuhayyij-hu* in the sources. Nabhānī has the more genteel *fa-lā tuzʿij-hu*.

to Bādhān finished, the latter said, "Indeed, this man is a Divine Messenger!"> He entered Islam together with all the Persian subjects that were in Yemen. <Ḥimyar used to call Kurkhusrū Dhūl-Miʻjaza – "He of the girdle" – in reference to the girdle the Messenger of Allah ﷺ had given him, *miʻjaza* being the term for girdle in the tongue of Ḥimyar. His descendants today are known by that name: Kurkhusrū Dhūl-Miʻjaza. Abābūh said to Bādhān, |e| "I never spoke to any man that awed me more than him." Bādhān asked him, "Does he have guards?" He said no.>[476] Bādhān sent news to the Prophet ﷺ of his Islam and that of all those that were with him. After that, Allah bestowed Chosroes' empire, his people, his treasures and all his possessions on the Muslims during the caliphate of ʻUmar ؓ and tore them asunder in every way just as the Prophet ﷺ had prayed.

رَوَى ابنُ إِسْحَاقَ مِنْ طُرُقٍ كَتَبَ كِسْرَى إِلَى بَاذَانَ وَهُوَ عَلَى الْيَمَنِ إِنْعَثْ إِلَى هَذَا الرَّجُلِ الَّذِي بِالحِجَازِ مِنْ عِنْدِكَ رَجُلَيْنِ جَلْدَيْنِ فَلْيَأْتِيَانِي بِهِ، فَبَعَثَ بَاذَانُ قَهْرَمَانَهُ وَهُوَ أَبَابُوهُ وَكَانَ كَاتِباً حَاسِباً بِكِتَابِ مَلِكِ فَارِسٍ وَبَعَثَ مَعَهُ بِرَجُلٍ مِنَ الفُرْسِ خُرْخُسْرُو وَكَتَبَ مَعَهُمَا إِلَى رَسُولِ اللهِ ﷺ يَأْمُرُهُ أَنْ يَنْصَرِفَ مَعَهُ إِلَى كِسْرَى وَقَالَ لِأَبَابُوهُ وَيْلَكَ أُنْظُرْ مَا الرَّجُلُ وَكَلِّمْهُ

---

[476]Narrated to here through Ibn Isḥāq by al-Ṭabarī in his *Tārīkh* (2:133-134=2:655-656) and Abū Nuʻaym in the *Dalāʼil* (p. 349-351 §241) cf. *Iṣāba* (1:532), *Iktifāʼ* (1:114), *Sīra Ḥalabiyya* (3:292) and *Bidāya*. Also narrated from Ibn Isḥāq without chain by Ibn Abī al-Dunyā in his *Dalāʼil al-Nubuwwa* cf. *Iṣāba* (1:337) with the names Bābawayh or Baʼbawayh instead of Abābūh and Khusra instead of Khurkhusrū. Al-Nabhānī replaces "Abābūh" with "Qahramānah" and omits all bracketed passages. Ibn Hishām (1:191) cites the report in short form from al-Zuhrī without chain cf. *Bidāya* (2:180) and *Fatḥ* (8:127). Shārūyah only ruled for six months cf. *Bidāya* (2:180), which explains the attribution of Chosroes' successorship to his daughter in Abū Bakrah's reports (see below). Her name was Būrān cf. *Fatḥ* (13:56) from Ibn Qutayba's *Maghāzī*. Her sister Arzamīdukht also ruled cf. *Fatḥ* (8:128) citing al-Ṭabarī, but Ibn al-Athīr in *al-Kāmil* (1:387) identifies the latter as the daughter of Abrawīz succeeding Khashnashbandah.

وَائْتِنِي بِخَبَرِهِ فَخَرَجَا حَتَّى قَدِمَا الطَّائِفَ فَوَجَدُوا رِجَالاً بِنَدْبٍ مِنْ قُرَيْشٍ مِنْ أَرْضِ الطَّائِفِ فَسَأَلُوهُمْ عَنْهُ فَقَالُوا هُوَ بِالمَدِينَةِ وَاسْتَبْشَرُوا بِهِمَا وَفَرِحُوا وَقَالَ بَعْضُهُمْ لِبَعْضٍ أَبْشِرُوا فَقَدْ نَصَبَ لَهُ كِسْرَى مَلِكُ المُلُوكِ وَكُفِيتُمُ الرَّجُلَ فَخَرَجَا حَتَّى قَدِمَا إِلَى المَدِينَةِ عَلَى رَسُولِ اللهِ ﷺ فَكَلَّمَهُ أَبَابُوه وَقَالَ إِنَّ شَاهَانْ شَاهْ مَلِكَ المُلُوكِ كِسْرَى كَتَبَ إِلَى المَلِكِ بَاذَانَ يَأْمُرُهُ أَنْ يَبْعَثَ إِلَيْكَ مَنْ يَأْتِيهِ بِكَ وَقَدْ بَعَثَنِي إِلَيْكَ لِتَنْطَلِقَ مَعِي فَإِنْ فَعَلْتَ كَتَبَ فِيكَ إِلَى مَلِكِ المُلُوكِ بِكِتَابٍ يَنْفَعُكَ وَيَكُفُّ بِهِ عَنْكَ وَإِنْ أَبَيْتَ فَهُوَ مَنْ قَدْ عَلِمْتَ وَهُوَ مُهْلِكُكَ وَمُهْلِكُ قَوْمَكَ وَمُخَرِّبُ بِلاَدَكَ وَقَدْ دَخَلاَ عَلَى رَسُولِ اللهِ ﷺ وَقَدْ حَلَقَا لِحَاهُمَا وَأَعْفَيَا شَوَارِبَهُمَا فَكَرِهَ النَّظَرَ إِلَيْهِمَا وَقَالَ وَيْلُكُمَا مَنْ أَمَرَكُمَا بِهَذَا قَالاَ أَمَرَنَا بِهَذَا رَبُّنَا يَعْنِيَانِ كِسْرَى فَقَالَ رَسُولُ اللهِ ﷺ لَكِنْ رَبِّي قَدْ أَمَرَنِي بِإِعْفَاءِ لِحْيَتِي وَقَصِّ شَارِبِي ثُمَّ قَالَ لَهُمَا إِرْجِعَا حَتَّى تَأْتِيَانِي غَداً وَأَتَى رَسُولَ اللهِ ﷺ الخَبَرُ أَنَّ اللهَ عَزَّ وَجَلَّ قَدْ سَلَّطَ عَلَى كِسْرَى ابْنَهُ شِيرَوَيْهْ فَقَتَلَهُ فِي شَهْرِ كَذَا وَكَذَا فِي لَيْلَةِ كَذَا وَكَذَا لِعِدَّةِ مَا مَضَى مِنَ اللَّيْلِ فَلَمَّا أَعْلَمَهُمَا رَسُولَ اللهِ ﷺ بِذَلِكَ قَالاَ هَلْ تَدْرِي مَا تَقُولُ قَدْ نَقَمْنَا مِنْكَ مَا هُوَ يَسِيرٌ أَيْسَرُ مِنْ هَذَا فَنَكْتُبُ بِهَذَا عَنْكَ وَنُخْبِرُ المَلِكَ قَالَ

نَعَمْ أَخْبِرَاهُ ذَلِكَ عَنِّي وَقُولَا لَهُ إِنَّ دِينِي وَسُلْطَانِي سَيَبْلُغُ مَا بَلَغَ مُلْكُ كِسْرَى وَيَنْتَهِي إِلَى مُنْتَهَى الْخُفِّ وَالْحَافِرِ وَقُولَا لَهُ إِنَّكَ إِنْ أَسْلَمْتَ أَعْطَيْتُكَ مَا تَحْتَ يَدَيْكَ وَمَلَّكْتُكَ عَلَى قَوْمِكَ مِنَ الْأَبْنَاءِ ثُمَّ أَعْطَى خُرْخُسْرُو مِنْطَقَةً فِيهَا ذَهَبٌ وَفِضَّةٌ كَانَ أَهْدَاهَا لَهُ بَعْضُ الْمُلُوكِ فَخَرَجَا مِنْ عِنْدِهِ حَتَّى قَدِمَا عَلَى بَاذَانَ وَأَخْبَرَاهُ الْخَبَرَ فَقَالَ وَاللهِ مَا هَذَا بِكَلَامِ مَلِكٍ وَإِنِّي لَأَرَى هَذَا الرَّجُلَ نَبِيًّا كَمَا يَقُولُ وَلَنَنْظُرَنَّ مَا قَدْ قَالَ فَلَئِنْ كَانَ مَا قَالَ حَقًّا مَا فِيهِ كَلَامٌ أَنَّهُ لَنَبِيٌّ مُرْسَلٌ وَإِنْ لَمْ يَكُنْ فَسَنَرَى فِيهِ رَأْيَنَا فَلَمْ يَنْشَبْ بَاذَانُ إِذْ قَدِمَ عَلَيْهِ كِتَابُ شِيرَوَيْهْ أَمَّا بَعْدُ فَإِنِّي قَدْ قَتَلْتُ كِسْرَى وَلَمْ أَقْتُلْهُ إِلَّا غَضَبًا لِفَارِسٍ لِمَا كَانَ قَدِ اسْتَحَلَّ مِنْ قَتْلِ أَشْرَافِهِمْ وَتَجْمِيرِ بُعُوثِهِمْ فَإِذَا جَاءَكَ كِتَابِي هَذَا فَخُذْ لِي الطَّاعَةَ مِمَّنْ قِبَلَكَ وَانْظُرِ الرَّجُلَ الَّذِي كَتَبَ إِلَيْكَ كِسْرَى فِيهِ فَلَا تُهَيِّجْهُ حَتَّى يَأْتِيَكَ أَمْرِي فَلَمَّا انْتَهَى كِتَابُ شِيرَوَيْهْ إِلَى بَاذَانَ قَالَ إِنَّ هَذَا الرَّجُلَ لَرَسُولٌ فَأَسْلَمَ وَأَسْلَمَتِ الْأَبْنَاءُ مِنْ فَارِسٍ مَنْ كَانَ مِنْهُمْ بِالْيَمَنِ فَكَانَتْ حِمْيَرُ تَقُولُ لِخُرْخُسْرُو ذُو الْمِعْجَزَةِ الْمِنْطَقَةِ الَّتِي أَعْطَاهُ رَسُولُ اللهِ ﷺ وَالْمِنْطَقَةُ بِلِسَانِ حِمْيَرَ الْمِعْجَزَةُ فَبَنُوهُ الْيَوْمَ يُنْسَبُونَ إِلَيْهَا خُرْخُسْرُو ذُو الْمِعْجَزَةِ وَقَدْ كَانَ قَالَ أَبَابُوهُ لِبَاذَانَ مَا كَلَّمْتُ رَجُلًا أَهْيَبَ عِنْدِي مِنْهُ فَقَالَ

لَهُ بَاذَانُ هَلْ مَعَهُ شُرَطٌ قَالَ لاَ الطبري في التاريخ أبو نعيم في الدلائل وروى أطرافه ابن هشام

The Destruction of al-Ḥārith b. Abī Shimr al-Ghassānī

Ibn Saʿd narrated through al-Wāqidī that the latter's authorities said, the Messenger of Allah ﷺ sent Shujāʿ b. Wahb al-Asadī to al-Ḥārith b. Abī Shimr al-Ghassānī with a letter from him. Shujāʿ said, "I reached him in the Ghūṭa outskirt of Damascus. I went to his gatekeeper and said, 'I am the messenger of the Messenger of Allah ﷺ.' He said, 'You cannot see him until he comes out on such-and-such a day.' His gatekeeper, an Eastern Roman named Murayy, began to ask me about the Messenger of Allah ﷺ and I described him and his mission until he was overcome by tears and said, 'I read the Evangel and find him described there to the letter. I believe in him and confirm the truth of his call. I fear that al-Ḥārith will kill me.' Later, al-Ḥārith came out and had the crown placed on his head. The letter was handed to him. He read it then threw it down and said, 'Who dares take my kingdom from me? I shall march against him! Even if he is in Yemen, I shall come to him!' He did not stop this until he got up and asked for his horse. He put on his riding-boots and said, 'Inform your master of what you just saw.' Then he wrote to Caesar and told him of his intention. Caesar replied, 'Do not march against him but ignore him.' When Caesar's reply reached him he called me and asked me when I was leaving. I said, 'Tomorrow.' He ordered for one hundred gold *mithqāl*s [over 1 kg.] to be given to me and <his gatekeeper gave me money and clothes and> said, 'Give the Messenger of Allah my greeting <and tell him that I am following his religion.>' I returned to the Messenger of Allah ﷺ and recounted everything to him. He said: 356 'His kingdom has ended.' Al-Ḥārith died the year of the conquest of Mecca."[477]

[477]This is part of the report already narrated above through al-Wāqidī from Ibn ʿAbbās by Ibn Saʿd (1:261, 3:94), Ibn ʿAsākir (57:366-368), and al-Tabarī in his *Tārīkh* (2:131=2:652), cf. *Naṣb* (4:424), *Isāba* (6:287), *Khaṣā'is* (2:18-19), *Iktifā'* (2:406), *Bidāya* (24:268), *Zād* (3:509-510), *Sīra Ḥalabiyya* (3:304-305), al-Dhahabī, *Tārīkh*

عَنْ رَسُولَ اللهِ صَلَّى اللهُ عَلَيْهِ وَسَلَّمَ بَعَثَ شُجَاعَ بْنَ وَهْبٍ
الأَسَدِيَّ إِلَى الْحَارِثِ بْنِ أَبِي شِمْرٍ وَهُوَ بِغُوطَةِ دِمَشْقَ قَالَ فَلَمَّا
قَدِمْتُ عَلَيْهِ انْتَهَيْتُ إِلَى حَاجِبِهِ فَقُلْتُ لَهُ إِنِّي رَسُولُ رَسُولِ
اللهِ ﷺ إِلَيْهِ فَقَالَ لِي إِنَّكَ لَا تَصِلُ إِلَيْهِ إِلَى يَوْمِ كَذَا فَأَقَمْتُ
عَلَى بَابِهِ يَوْمَيْنِ أَوثلاثة وَجَعَلَ حَاجِبُهُ وَكَانَ رُومِيًّا اسْمُهُ مُرَيٌّ
يَسْأَلُنِي عَنْ رَسُولِ اللهِ ﷺ وَمَا يَدْعُو إِلَيْهِ فَكُنْتُ أُحَدِّثُهُ فَيَرِقُّ
قَلْبُهُ حَتَّى يَغْلِبَهُ الْبُكَاءُ وَقَالَ إِنِّي قَرَأْتُ فِي الْإِنْجِيلِ صِفَةَ هَذَا
النَّبِيِّ وَكُنْتُ أَرَى أَنَّهُ يَخْرُجُ بِالشَّامِ وَأَنَا أُؤْمِنُ بِهِ وَأُصَدِّقُهُ وَكَانَ
يُكْرِمُنِي وَيُحْسِنُ ضِيَافَتِي وَيُخْبِرُنِي عَنْ الْحَارِثِ بِالْيَأْسِ مِنْهُ وَيَقُولُ
هُوَ يَخَافُ قَيْصَرَ قَالَ فَلَمَّا خَرَجَ الْحَارِثُ يَوْمَ جُلُوسِهِ أَذِنَ لِي
عَلَيْهِ فَدَفَعْتُ إِلَيْهِ الْكِتَابَ فَقَرَأَهُ ثُمَّ رَمَى بِهِ وَقَالَ مَنْ يَنْتَزِعُ مِنِّي
مُلْكِي أَنَا سَائِرٌ إِلَيْهِ وَلَوْ كَانَ بِالْيَمَنِ جِئْتُهُ عَلَيَّ بِالنَّاسِ فَلَمْ
يَزَلْ يَسْتَعْرِضُ حَتَّى اللَّيْلِ وَأَمَرَ بِالْخَيْلِ أَنْ تُنْعَلَ ثُمَّ قَالَ أَخْبِرْ
صَاحِبَكَ بِمَا تَرَى وَكَتَبَ إِلَى قَيْصَرَ يُخْبِرُهُ خَبَرِي فَصَادَفَ قَيْصَرَ
بِإِيلِيَاءَ وَعِنْدَهُ دِحْيَةُ الْكَلْبِيُّ وَقَدْ بَعَثَهُ إِلَيْهِ رَسُولُ اللهِ ﷺ فَلَمَّا

(*Maghāzī* p. 622), and Ibn al-Qayyim, *Hidāyat al-Ḥayārā* (p. 38). The gatekeeper's name is misspelled Turayy in Nabhānī who omits the bracketed segment as does the *Khasā'is*. The king is elsewhere identified as al-Mundhir b. al-Ḥārith b. Abī Shimr al-Ghassānī: narrated from al-Miswar b. Makhrama by al-Ṭabarānī in *al-Kabīr* through Muḥammad b. Ismā'īl b. 'Ayyāsh who is weak cf. al-Haythamī (5:306).

قَرَأَ قَيْصَرُ كِتَابَ الْحَارِثِ كَتَبَ أَنْ لَا تَسِرْ إِلَيْهِ وَالْهُ عَنْهُ وَوَافِنِي
بِإِيلِيَاءَ قَالَ وَرَجَعَ الْكِتَابُ وَأَنَا مُقِيمٌ فَدَعَانِي وَقَالَ مَتَى تُرِيدُ أَنْ
تَخْرُجَ إِلَى صَاحِبِكَ قُلْتُ غَدًا فَأَمَرَ لِي بِمِائَةِ مِثْقَالِ ذَهَبٍ
وَوَصَّلَنِي الْحَاجِبُ بِنَفَقَةٍ وَكِسْوَةٍ وَقَالَ لِي اقْرَأْ عَلَى رَسُولِ اللهِ
ﷺ مِنِّي السَّلَامَ وَأَخْبِرْهُ أَنِّي مُتَّبِعٌ دِينَهُ قَالَ شُجَاعٌ فَقَدِمْتُ
عَلَى النَّبِيِّ ﷺ فَأَخْبَرْتُهُ فَقَالَ بَادَ مُلْكُهُ وَمَاتَ الْحَارِثُ بْنُ أَبِي
شِمْرٍ عَامَ الْفَتْحِ ابن سعد كر

Destruction of One of the Pagan Leaders

Al-Bayhaqī narrated from Anas ؓ that the Messenger of Allah ﷺ sent one of his Companions to one of the pagan leaders, calling him unto Allah. The *mushrik* said: "That God unto Whom you call, is He made of gold? Silver? Copper?" The envoy returned [after three trips back and forth], after which Allah ﷻ sent down a thunderstorm that burnt him to cinders. The envoy of the Messenger of Allah ﷺ was still travelling and was unaware of this. The Prophet ﷺ said to him **[523]**: 357 "Allah has destroyed your friend!" The verse was then revealed: ﴾**He launches the thunderbolts and smites with them whom He will while they dispute (in doubt) concerning Allah, and He is mighty in wrath**﴿ (13:13).[478]

[478]Narrated from Anas by al-Nasā'ī in *al-Sunan al-Kubrā* (6:370 §11259), Ibn Abī ʿĀṣim in *al-Sunna* (p. 304 §692), Abū Yaʿlā (6:183 §3468), al-Ṭabarānī in *al-Awsat* (3:96 §2602), and al-Bazzār, the latter through trustworthy narrators cf. al-Haythamī (7:42), al-Maqdisī, *Mukhtāra* (5:89-90 §1711), Ibn Kathīr, *Tafsīr* (2:506 and 3:207) and *Khasā'is* (2:22); from Ibn ʿAbbās by al-Rabīʿ in his *Musnad* (p. 308 §821); *mursal* from Abū Ka'b al-Makkī by Ibn Abī Ḥātim cf. Ibn Kathīr, *Tafsīr* (3:207); and *mursal* from ʿAbd al-Raḥmān b. Ṣuḥār al-'Abdī by al-Ṭabarī in his *Tafsīr* (13:125).

عَنْ أَنَسٍ قَالَ أَرْسَلَ رَسُولُ اللهِ ﷺ رَجُلا مِنْ أَصْحَابِهِ إِلَى رَأْسِ الْمُشْرِكِينَ يَدْعُوهُ إِلَى اللهِ تَعَالَى فَقَالَ الْمُشْرِكُ هَذَا الَّذِي تَدْعُونِي إِلَيْهِ مِنْ ذَهَبٍ أَوْ فِضَّةٍ أَوْ نُحَاسٍ فَتَعَاظَمَ مَقَالَتُهُ فِي صَدْرِ رَسُولِ رَسُولِ اللهِ فَرَجَعَ إِلَى رَسُولِ اللهِ ﷺ فَأَخْبَرَهُ فَقَالَ ارْجِعْ إِلَيْهِ فَرَجَعَ إِلَيْهِ بِمِثْلِ ذَلِكَ وَأَرْسَلَ اللهُ تَبَارَكَ وَتَعَالَى عَلَيْهِ صَاعِقَةً مِنَ السَّمَاءِ فَأَهْلَكَتْهُ وَرَسُولُ رَسُولِ اللهِ ﷺ فِي الطَّرِيقِ لا يَدْرِي فَقَالَ لَهُ النَّبِيُّ ﷺ إِنَّ اللهَ قَدْ أَهْلَكَ صَاحِبَكَ بَعْدَكَ وَنَزَلَتْ عَلَى رَسُولِ اللهِ ﷺ ﴿وَيُسَبِّحُ ٱلرَّعْدُ بِحَمْدِهِۦ وَٱلْمَلَٰٓئِكَةُ مِنْ خِيفَتِهِۦ وَيُرْسِلُ ٱلصَّوَٰعِقَ فَيُصِيبُ بِهَا مَن يَشَآءُ وَهُمْ يُجَٰدِلُونَ فِى ٱللَّهِ وَهُوَ شَدِيدُ ٱلْمِحَالِ ﴿١٣﴾﴾ الرعد ن في الكبرى ابن أبي عاصم في السنة ز ع طس الطبري هق في الدلائل ض

[Jaz' b. Suhayl al-Sulamī ؓ]

Al-Bayhaqī, Abū Nuʿaym, and Thābit in his *Dalā'il* narrated that ʿAbd Allāh b. Ḥawāla ؓ said, "We were with the Messenger of Allah ﷺ when we complained to him of our destitution and poverty and how little we had. He replied: [358] 'Be glad! By Allah! [a] I surely fear more for you your having much than your having little. By Allah! [b] This power shall continue to remain with you until Allah opens up the lands of Persia, the Eastern Romans, and Ḥimyar. [c] You will divide into three armies: one in Syro-Palestine, one in Iraq, one in Yemen. At that time [d] a man might be given a hundred [dinars] but he will scorn it.' I said, 'Messenger of Allah! Who can enter Syro-Palestine with the many-headed Romans in it?' He said: 'I swear by Allah that Allah is going to open it up for you and give it to you. e You will see a legion of their fleshy-rumped white men under the command of a little bald black man from among you – whatever he orders them to do, they will do it!'" Al-Suyūṭī said that this ḥadīth contains the description of Jaz' b. Suhayl al-Sulamī who was given command over the non-Arabs in that time. When they [=the Companions] went to the mosque they would look at him with the *'Ajam* standing around him and they marvelled at the accuracy of the Prophet's ﷺ description of him and them.[479]

عَنْ عَبْدِ اللهِ بْنِ حَوَالَةَ ؓ كُنَّا عِنْدَ رَسُولِ اللهِ ﷺ فَشَكَوْنَا إِلَيْهِ الْعُرْيَ وَالْفَقْرَ وَقِلَّةَ الشَّيْءِ فَقَالَ رَسُولُ اللهِ ﷺ أَبْشِرُوا فَوَاللهِ لَأَنَا بِكَثْرَةِ الشَّيْءِ أَخْوَفُنِي عَلَيْكُمْ مِنْ قِلَّتِهِ وَاللهِ لَا يَزَالُ هَذَا الْأَمْرُ فِيكُمْ حَتَّى يَفْتَحَ اللهُ أَرْضَ فَارِسَ وَأَرْضَ الرُّومِ وَأَرْضَ حِمْيَرَ وَحَتَّى تَكُونُوا أَجْنَادًا ثَلَاثَةً جُنْدًا بِالشَّامِ وَجُنْدًا بِالْعِرَاقِ وَجُنْدًا بِالْيَمَنِ وَحَتَّى يُعْطَى الرَّجُلُ الْمِائَةَ فَيَسْخَطُهَا قَالَ ابْنُ حَوَالَةَ قُلْتُ يَا رَسُولَ اللهِ وَمَنْ يَسْتَطِيعُ الشَّامَ وَبِهِ الرُّومُ ذَوَاتُ الْقُرُونِ قَالَ وَاللهِ لَيَفْتَحَنَّهَا اللهُ عَلَيْكُمْ وَلَيَسْتَخْلِفَنَّكُمْ فِيهَا حَتَّى

[479]Narrated from ʿAbd Allāh b. Ḥawāla by Ibn Abī ʿĀṣim in *al-Āḥād* (4:274 §2295); al-Fasawī in *al-Maʿrifa wal-Tārīkh* (2:288-289); Thābit b. Ḥazm in *al-Dalā'il* as cited in the *Isāba* (1:478) and *Khasā'is* (2:191); al-Ṭabarānī with two chains, one through trustworthy narrators cf. al-Haythamī (6:211-212); Abū Nuʿaym, *Dalā'il* (p. 546-547 §478) and *Ḥilya* (1985 ed. 2:3-4); Ibn ʿAsākir (1:73-74); and al-Bayhaqī in *al-Sunan al-Kubrā* (9:179) and the *Dalā'il* (6:327-328) cf. also al-Maqdisī, *Mukhtāra* (9:278-279 §241), *Bidāya* (6:195), and Yāqūt (3:314). The comment al-Nabhānī attributes to al-Suyūṭī is actually that of ʿAbd al-Raḥmān b. Jubayr b. Nufayr as narrated by the sources. Thābit is the Andalusian Imam, qādi, philologist and ḥadīth Master Abū al-Qāsim Ibn Ḥazm b. Abd al-Raḥmān al-Saraqasṭī al-Sharīṭī (d. 313/314) the author – with his son Qāsim – of a glossary of difficulties – *al-Dalā'il fī Gharīb al-Ḥadīth* that rivals those of al-Qāsim b. Sallām and Ibn Qutayba's cf. al-Dhahabī, *Siyar* (Risāla ed. 14:562-563).

تَظَلَّ الْعِصَابَةُ الْبِيضُ مِنْهُمْ قُمُصُهُمْ الْمُلْحِمَةُ أَقْفَاؤُهُمْ قِيَامًا
عَلَى الرُّوَيْجِلِ الأَسْوَدِ مِنْكُمُ الْمَحْلُوقِ مَا أَمَرَهُمْ مِنْ شَيْءٍ فَعَلُوهُ
قَالَ أَبُو عَلْقَمَةَ فَسَمِعَتُ عَبْدَ الرَّحْمَنِ بْنَ جُبَيْرٍ يَقُولُ فَعَرَفَ
أَصْحَابُ رَسُولِ اللهِ ﷺ نَعْتَ هَذَا الْحَدِيثِ فِى جَزْءِ بْنِ سُهَيْلٍ
السُّلَمِيِّ وَكَانَ عَلَى الأَعَاجِمِ فِى ذَلِكَ الزَّمَانِ فَكَانَ إِذَا رَاحُوا
إِلَى مَسْجِدٍ نَظَرُوا إِلَيْهِ وَإِلَيْهِمْ قِيَامًا حَوْلَهُ فَعَجِبُوا لِنَعْتِ رَسُولِ
اللهِ ﷺ فِيهِ وَفِيهِمْ الفسوي في المعرفة آحاد ابن أبي عاصم حل هق وفي دلائلهما كر

[Conquest of the Persians and Eastern Romans Continued]

The Two Masters [al-Bukhārī and Muslim] narrated that Khabbāb b. al-Arathth ﷺ said, "I came to see the Messenger of Allah ﷺ as he was lying down with his head resting on his cloak in the shade of the Ka'ba. We had experienced great hardships on the part of the idolaters. I said, 'Messenger of Allah! Will you not supplicate on our behalf?'[480] He sat up, face reddened, and said: 'Truly, 359 Before your time, a man might be raked with iron rakes and skinned alive without budging one whit from his faith! A see-saw might be placed on top of his head and he might be sawed in half without budging one whit from his religion! Allah shall certainly accomplish this great matter until a rider can travel from Ṣan'ā' to Ḥaḍramawt without fearing any but Allah <or a wolf for his flock. But you are impatient>!'"[481]

[480]Narrated to here by al-Nasā'ī.

[481]Narrated by Bukhārī, Abū Dāwūd and Aḥmad. Nabhānī omits the bracketed segment.

عَنْ خَبَّابِ بْنِ الْأَرَتِّ رَضِيَ اللهُ عَنْهُ قَالَ شَكَوْنَا إِلَى رَسُولِ اللهِ ﷺ وَهُوَ مُتَوَسِّدٌ بُرْدَةً لَهُ فِي ظِلِّ الْكَعْبَةِ قُلْنَا لَهُ أَلَا تَسْتَنْصِرُ لَنَا أَلَا تَدْعُو اللهَ لَنَا قَالَ كَانَ الرَّجُلُ فِيمَنْ قَبْلَكُمْ يُحْفَرُ لَهُ فِي الْأَرْضِ فَيُجْعَلُ فِيهِ فَيُجَاءُ بِالْمِنْشَارِ فَيُوضَعُ عَلَى رَأْسِهِ فَيُشَقُّ بِاثْنَتَيْنِ وَمَا يَصُدُّهُ ذَلِكَ عَنْ دِينِهِ وَيُمْشَطُ بِأَمْشَاطِ الْحَدِيدِ مَا دُونَ لَحْمِهِ مِنْ عَظْمٍ أَوْ عَصَبٍ وَمَا يَصُدُّهُ ذَلِكَ عَنْ دِينِهِ وَاللهِ لَيُتِمَّنَّ هَذَا الْأَمْرَ حَتَّى يَسِيرَ الرَّاكِبُ مِنْ صَنْعَاءَ إِلَى حَضْرَمَوْتَ لَا يَخَافُ إِلَّا اللهَ أَوْ الذِّئْبَ عَلَى غَنَمِهِ وَلَكِنَّكُمْ تَسْتَعْجِلُونَ خ

د حم ورواه ن مختصراً

[Mafrūq b. ʿAmr and Hāni' b. Qubayṣa]

Al-Bayhaqī and Abū Nuʿaym narrated from Ibn ʿAbbās that ʿAlī b. Abī Ṭālib [ﷺ] told him: "When the Messenger of Allah ﷺ was ordered to address himself to the Arabian tribes he went out [among them]. I and Abū Bakr were with him. We ended up at a tribal gathering in which were sitting Mafrūq b. ʿAmr and Hāni' b. Qubayṣa, two of the elders of the Banū Shaybān. Mafrūq asked, 'To what do you call us?' The Messenger of Allah ﷺ said: 360 'I call you to the witnessing that there is no God but Allah alone without partner, that Muḥammad is His servant and Messenger, and to giving me haven and help, for Quraysh are opposing the command of Allah and have belied His Messengers. They content themselves with falsehood to do without truth, but Allah is the All-Glorious, True Sovereign!' Mafrūq said, 'By Allah! I never heard better speech than this.' Then the Messenger of Allah ﷺ recited, ﴾**Say: Come, I will recite unto you that which your Lord has made a sacred duty for you: that you ascribe no thing as partner unto Him and that you do good to parents, and that**

you slay not your children because of penury – We provide for you and for them – and that you draw not nigh to lewd things whether open or concealed. And that you slay not the life which Allah has made sacred, save in the course of justice. This He has commanded you, in order that you may discern﴿ (6:151), whereupon Mafrūq said, 'This is not human speech.' Then the Messenger of Allah ﷺ recited ﴾**Lo! Allah enjoins justice and kindness, and giving to kinsfolk, and forbids lewdness and abomination and wickedness. He exhorts you in order that you may take heed**﴿ (16:90), whereupon Mafrūq said, 'I swear by Allah that you are calling unto high morals and excellent deeds! And that those who belied and opposed you are liars!' **[524]** The Messenger of Allah ﷺ then said: a 'Wait and see! It will not be long until Allah causes you to inherit the land of Chosroes and their houses and properties, and give all of you their women while you glorify Allah and exalt Him!'''[482]

عَنِ ابْنِ عَبَّاسٍ قَالَ حَدَّثَنِي عَلِيُّ بْنُ أَبِي طَالِبٍ رَضِيَ اللهُ عَنْهُمْ
مِنْ فِيهِ قَالَ لَمَّا أَمَرَ اللهُ رَسُولَ اللهِ ﷺ أَنْ يَعْرِضَ نَفْسَهُ عَلَى
قَبَائِلِ الْعَرَبِ خَرَجَ وَأَنَا مَعَهُ وَأَبُو بَكْرٍ فَدَفَعْنَا إِلَى مَجْلِسٍ مِنْ
مَجَالِسِ الْعَرَبِ فِيهِمْ مَفْرُوقُ بْنُ عَمْرٍو وَهَانِئُ بْنُ قَبِيصَةَ وَالْمُثَنَّى
بْنُ حَارِثَةَ وَالنُّعْمَانُ بْنُ شَرِيكٍ وَكَانَ مَفْرُوقُ قَدْ غَلَبَهُمْ جَمَالاً
وَلِسَاناً فقال فَإِلَى مَا تَدْعُو يَا أَخَا قُرَيْشٍ فَقَالَ رَسُولُ اللهِ ﷺ
أَدْعُوكُمْ إِلَى شَهَادَةِ أَنْ لاَ إِلَهَ إِلاَّ اللهُ وَحْدَهُ لاَ شَرِيكَ لَهُ وَأَنَّ

[482]Narrated as part of a longer hadīth from ʿAlī by Ibn Hibbān, *Thiqāt* (1:80-88), in the *Dalā'il* of Abū Nuʿaym (p. 282-288 §214) and al-Bayhaqī (2:422-426), al-Samʿanī through the latter in his *Ansāb* (1:64-67), and Ibn ʿAsākir (17:295) cf. *Bidāya* (3:143-145 *gharīb*), *Khasā'is* (1:301), *Iktifā'* (1:307-308), *Sīra Halabiyya* (2:156-157), *Kanz* (§35684), *Rawd* (2:239-240), and al-Muhibb al-Tabarī, *Riyād* (2:54-56).

مُحَمَّداً عَبْدُهُ وَرَسُولُهُ وَإِلَى أَنْ تَؤْوُونِي وَتَنْصُرُونِي فَإِنَّ قُرَيْشاً قَدْ
ظَاهَرَتْ عَلَى أَمْرِ اللهِ وَكَذَّبَتْ رُسُلَهُ وَاسْتَغْنَتْ بِالْبَاطِلِ عَنِ
الحَقِّ وَاللهُ هُوَ الغَنِيُّ الحَمِيدُ فَقَالَ مَفْرُوقُ بْنُ عَمْرٍو وَإِلامَ
تَدْعُونَا يَا أَخَا قُرَيْشٍ فَوَاللهِ مَا سَمِعْتُ كَلاماً أَحْسَنَ مِنْ هَذَا
فَتَلاَ رَسُولُ اللهِ ﷺ ﴿ قُلْ تَعَالَوْا۟ أَتْلُ مَا حَرَّمَ رَبُّكُمْ
عَلَيْكُمْ ۖ أَلَّا تُشْرِكُوا۟ بِهِۦ شَيْـًٔا ۖ وَبِٱلْوَٰلِدَيْنِ إِحْسَـٰنًا ۖ وَلَا تَقْتُلُوٓا۟
أَوْلَـٰدَكُم مِّنْ إِمْلَـٰقٍ ۖ نَّحْنُ نَرْزُقُكُمْ وَإِيَّاهُمْ ۖ وَلَا تَقْرَبُوا۟
ٱلْفَوَٰحِشَ مَا ظَهَرَ مِنْهَا وَمَا بَطَنَ ۖ وَلَا تَقْتُلُوا۟ ٱلنَّفْسَ ٱلَّتِى حَرَّمَ
ٱللَّهُ إِلَّا بِٱلْحَقِّ ۚ ذَٰلِكُمْ وَصَّىٰكُم بِهِۦ لَعَلَّكُمْ تَعْقِلُونَ ﴿١٥١﴾ وَلَا تَقْرَبُوا۟ مَالَ
ٱلْيَتِيمِ إِلَّا بِٱلَّتِى هِىَ أَحْسَنُ حَتَّىٰ يَبْلُغَ أَشُدَّهُۥ ۖ وَأَوْفُوا۟ ٱلْكَيْلَ وَٱلْمِيزَانَ
بِٱلْقِسْطِ ۖ لَا نُكَلِّفُ نَفْسًا إِلَّا وُسْعَهَا ۖ وَإِذَا قُلْتُمْ فَٱعْدِلُوا۟ وَلَوْ كَانَ
ذَا قُرْبَىٰ ۖ وَبِعَهْدِ ٱللَّهِ أَوْفُوا۟ ۚ ذَٰلِكُمْ وَصَّىٰكُم بِهِۦ لَعَلَّكُمْ تَذَكَّرُونَ
﴿١٥٢﴾ وَأَنَّ هَـٰذَا صِرَٰطِى مُسْتَقِيمًا فَٱتَّبِعُوهُ ۖ وَلَا تَتَّبِعُوا۟ ٱلسُّبُلَ فَتَفَرَّقَ
بِكُمْ عَن سَبِيلِهِۦ ۚ ذَٰلِكُمْ وَصَّىٰكُم بِهِۦ لَعَلَّكُمْ تَتَّقُونَ ﴿١٥٣﴾ ﴾ الأنعام
فَقَالَ مَفْرُوقٌ وَإِلامَ تَدْعُونَا يَا أَخَا قُرَيْشٍ فَوَاللهِ مَا هَذَا مِنْ
كَلامِ أَهْلِ الأَرْضِ فَتَلاَ رَسُولُ اللهِ ﷺ ﴿ إِنَّ ٱللَّهَ يَأْمُرُ بِٱلْعَدْلِ

وَٱلۡإِحۡسَٰنِ وَإِيتَآيِٕ ذِي ٱلۡقُرۡبَىٰ وَيَنۡهَىٰ عَنِ ٱلۡفَحۡشَآءِ
وَٱلۡمُنكَرِ وَٱلۡبَغۡيِۚ يَعِظُكُمۡ لَعَلَّكُمۡ تَذَكَّرُونَ ﴿٩٠﴾ النحل
فَقَالَ مَفْرُوقُ بْنُ عَمْرٍو دَعَوْتَ وَاللهِ يَا أَخَا قُرَيْشٍ إِلَى مَكَارِمِ
الأَخْلاَقِ وَمَحَاسِنِ الأَعْمَالِ وَلَقَدْ أَفِكَ قَوْمٌ كَذَّبُوكَ وَظَاهَرُوا
عَلَيْكَ فَقَالَ رَسُولُ اللهِ ﷺ أَرَأَيْتُمْ إِنْ لَمْ تَلْبَثُوا إِلاَّ قَلِيلاً حَتَّى
يُورِثَكُمُ اللهُ أَرْضَهُمْ وَدِيَارَهُمْ وَأَمْوَالَهُمْ وَيُفْرِشَكُمْ نِسَاءَهُمْ
أَتُسَبِّحُونَ اللهَ وَتُقَدِّسُونَهُ حب في الثقات أبو نعيم في المعرفة والدلائل هق في
الدلائل السمعاني في الأنساب كر

[Khuraym b. Uways b. Ḥāritha b. Lām ؓ]

Al-Bukhārī in his *Tārīkh*, al-Ṭabarānī, al-Bayhaqī and Abū Nuʿaym narrated that Khuraym b. Uways b. Ḥāritha b. Lām ؓ said, <"We were with the Messenger of Allah ﷺ when al-ʿAbbās b. ʿAbd al-Muṭṭalib said to him: 'Messenger of Allah, I wish to praise you.' He replied: 'Let us hear it, and may Allah preserve your mouth!' Al-ʿAbbās declaimed:

Before time you were blessed in the shades
and the repository where leaves were used for garments.
Then you alighted upon earth, neither a human being yet
nor a piece of flesh nor clot,
But as a drop that boarded the Ark when
the flood destroyed Nasr and the rest of the idols:
Transported from the loins to the wombs
in the succession of worlds and centuries.
Until your noble House, proclaiming [your merit],
took hold of the highest summit of the line of Khindif.
And then, when you were born, the sun rose
over the earth and the horizon was illuminated with your light.

So we – in that radiance and that light
and paths of guidance – can pierce through.>

"I heard the Messenger of Allah ﷺ say [361] 'This glittering Ḥīra [in Iraq] was brought up before my eyes. I can see al-Shaymā' the daughter of Nufayla al-Azdiyya sitting on a white mule, veiled from head to toe in a black *khimār*!' I said, 'Messenger of Allah! If we, here present, enter al-Ḥīra, and if I find her as you have just described her, is she for me?' He said: [a] 'She is for you.' Later, in the time of Abū Bakr, after we finished with Musaylima, we came to al-Ḥīra and the first person we saw when we entered was al-Shaymā' bint Nufayla, just as the Messenger of Allah ﷺ had described her, on a white mule, covered from head to toe in a black *khimār*. I stood fast by her and said, 'This woman was bestowed upon me by the Messenger of Allah ﷺ!' Khalid b. al-Walīd summoned me to produce a proof. I gave him one, in the form of the testimony to that effect of the two *Anṣār*s Muḥammad b. Maslama [b. Salama] and Muḥammad b. Bashīr. Then he gave her to me. Her brother ʿAbd al-Masīḥ came to visit us and said, 'Sell her to me.' I said, 'I will not accept less than ten hundred something for her.' He gave me a thousand dirhams [and took her]. I was told, 'Had you said ten thousand he would have paid it to you.' I said, 'I did not reckon there was a number greater than ten hundred!'"[483]

483 Narrated from Khuraym – misspelt Khuzaym in al-Nabhānī –by al-Ṭabarānī in *al-Kabīr* (4:213-214 §4168), Abū Bakr al-Shāfiʿī in *al-Ghaylāniyyāt* (Ḥilmī-Salmān ed. 1:282-284 §285), Abū Nuʿaym in his *Dalā'il* (p. 540 §469) and *Maʿrifa* (under Khuraym b. Aws), and al-Bayhaqī in the *Dalā'il* (5:267-268); and without mention of al-ʿAbbās's poetry by al-Bukhārī, *al-Tārīkh al-Kabīr* (1:18), Abū Nuʿaym (1:364), Ibn Zanjūyah in *al-Amwāl* (2:437-438 §711), al-Taymī in his *Dalā'il* (p. 150 §161), and Ibn Bashkuwāl, *Ghawāmiḍ* (1:438-439 §407) cf. *Khaṣā'iṣ* (2:186-187) (also omitted in al-Nabhānī), *Iṣāba* (2:274 and 6:6), *Bidāya* (5:28), *Nasb* (3:433), and al-Dāraquṭnī, *al-Mu'talif wal-Mukhtalif* (2:850-851). Shaymā' is misspelt Shahbā' in al-Nabhānī cf. al-Suyūṭī and Buqayla instead of Nufayla in some narrations. This is the same chain and report in which al-ʿAbbās declaims to the Prophet ﷺ his famous *mawlid* poem which al-Ḥākim (3:327=1990 ed. 3:369) narrates by itself, without the Shaymā' story. Al-Haythamī (8:217-218=8:288-289 and 6:223) said it contains unknown narrators. These are Khuraym's grandson Ḥumayd b. Manhab and the latter's grandson Zahr b. Ḥiṣn. Al-Ḥākim said that these Bedouin narrators are not the type that forge ḥadīths while al-Suyūṭī in *al-La'āli' al-Maṣnūʿa* (1:265=1996 ed. 1:244) said: "There is no question that these verses are by al-ʿAbbās." Also cited by al-Qāḍī 'Iyāḍ in *al-Shifā'* (p. 216 §393), Ibn al-Athīr in *Usd al-Ghaba* (2:129 §1348), Ibn ʿAbd al-Barr in *al-Istīʿāb* (8:447), also from Khuraym's brother Jarīr

عَنْ خُرَيْمِ بْنِ أَوْسِ بْنِ حَارِثَةَ بْنِ لَامٍ كُنَّا عِنْدَ النَّبِيِّ ﷺ فَقَالَ لَهُ الْعَبَّاسُ يَا رَسُولَ اللهِ إِنِّي أُرِيدُ أَنْ أَمْتَدِحَكَ فَقَالَ لَهُ النَّبِيُّ ﷺ هَاتْ لَا يَفْضُضِ اللهُ فَاكَ قَالَ فَأَنْشَأَ الْعَبَّاسُ يَقُولُ:

مِنْ قَبْلِهَا طِبْتَ فِي الظِّلَالِ وَفِي مُسْتَوْدَعٍ حَيْثُ يُخْصَفُ الْوَرَقُ

ثُمَّ هَبَطْتَ الْبِلَادَ لَا بَشَرٌ أَنْتَ وَلَا مُضْغَةٌ وَلَا عَلَقُ

بَلْ نُطْفَةٌ تَرْكَبُ السَّفِينَ وَقَدْ أَلْجَمَ نَسْرًا وَأَهْلَهُ الْغَرَقُ

تُنْقَلُ مِنْ صَالِبٍ إِلَى رَحِمٍ إِذَا مَضَى عَالَمٌ بَدَا طَبَقُ

حَتَّى احْتَوَى بَيْتُكَ الْمُهَيْمِنُ مِنْ خِنْدِفَ عَلْيَا تَحْتَهَا النُّطُقُ

وَأَنْتَ لَمَّا وُلِدْتَ أَشْرَقَتِ الْأَرْضُ وَضَاءَتْ بِنُورِكَ الْأُفُقُ

فَنَحْنُ فِي ذَلِكَ الضِّيَاءِ وَفِي النُّورِ وَسُبُلِ الرَّشَادِ نَخْتَرِقُ

قَالَ وَسَمِعْتُ رَسُولَ اللهِ ﷺ يَقُولُ هَذِهِ الْحِيرَةُ الْبَيْضَاءُ قَدْ رُفِعَتْ لِي وَهَذِهِ الشَّيْمَاءُ بِنتُ بُقَيْلَةَ الْأَزْدِيَّةُ عَلَى بَغْلَةٍ شَهْبَاءَ مُعْتَجِرَةٌ بِخِمَارٍ أَسْوَدَ فَقُلْتُ يَا رَسُولَ اللهِ فَإِنْ نَحْنُ دَخَلْنَا الْحِيرَةَ

b. Aws, Ibn Hajar in *al-Isāba* – in the entry "Khuraym" –, al-Dhahabī in the *Siyar* (1-2:36-37 and 3:415=al-Arna'ūṭ ed. 2:102-103), Ibn Sayyid al-Nās in *Minaḥ al-Madḥ* (p. 192-193), Ibn Kathīr in *al-Sīra al-Nabawiyya* (ed. Muṣṭafā ʿAbd al-Wāḥid 4:51) and Ibn al-Qayyim in *Zād al-Ma'ād* (3:482-483). The poem is cited in *Amālī Ibn al-Shajarī* (2:337), *al-Fā'iq* (3:123), etc..

وَوَجَدْتُهَا عَلَى هَذِهِ الصِّفَةِ فَهِيَ لِي قَالَ هِيَ لَكَ فَلَمَّا فَرَغْنَا مِنْ مُسَيْلِمَةَ وَأَصْحَابِهِ أَقْبَلْنَا إِلَى نَاحِيَةِ الْبَصْرَةِ ثُمَّ سِرْنَا عَلَى طَرِيقِ الطَّفِّ حَتَّى دَخَلْنَا الْحِيرَةَ فَكَانَ أَوَّلَ مِنْ تَلَقَّانَا فِيهَا شَيْمَاءُ بنتُ بُقَيْلَةَ الأَزْدِيَّةُ عَلَى بَغْلَةٍ لَهَا شَهْبَاءَ بِخِمَارٍ أَسْوَدَ كَمَا قَالَ رَسُولُ اللهِ ﷺ فَتَعَلَّقْتُ بِهَا وَقُلْتُ هَذِهِ وَهَبَهَا لِي رَسُولُ اللهِ ﷺ فَدَعَانِي خَالِدٌ عَلَيْهَا الْبَيِّنَةَ فَأَتَيْتُهُ بِهَا فَسَلَّمَهَا إِلَيَّ وَنَزَلَ إِلَيْنَا أَخُوهَا عَبْدُ الْمَسِيحِ فَقَالَ لِي بِعْنِيهَا فَقُلْتُ لا أَنْقُصُهَا وَاللهِ مِنْ عَشْرِ مِائَةٍ شَيْئًا فَدَفَعَ إِلَيَّ أَلْفَ دِرْهَمٍ فَقِيلَ لِي لَوْ قُلْتَ مِائَةَ أَلْفٍ لَدَفَعَهَا إِلَيْكَ فَقُلْتُ مَا أَحْسِبُ أَنَّ مَالا أَكْثَرَ مِنْ عَشْرِ مِائَةٍ قَالَ الطَّبَرَانِيُّ وَبَلَغَنِي فِي غَيْرِ هَذَا الْحَدِيثِ أَنَّ الشَّاهِدَيْنِ كَانَا مُحَمَّدَ بْنَ مَسْلَمَةَ وَعَبْدَ اللهِ بْنَ عُمَرَ وَقَالَ ابْنُ زَنْجُويَهْ بَشِيرُ بْنُ سَعْدٍ وَمُحَمَّدُ بْنُ مَسْلَمَةَ الأَنْصَارِيَّانِ طب غيلانيات أبو نعيم في المعرفة والدلائل هق في الدلائل ورواه دون سرد الشعر خت حل ابن زنجويه في الأموال ابن بشكوال في الغوامض قط في المؤتلف وعنده وعند ابن أبي خيثمة هَاجَرْتُ إِلَى رَسُولِ اللهِ ﷺ فَقَدِمْتُ عَلَيْهِ مُنْصَرَفَهُ مِنْ تَبُوكٍ فَأَسْلَمْتُ وقال الذهبي في التاريخ الظلال: ظلال الجنة قال الله تعالى {إن المتقين في ظلال وعيون} . والمستودع: هو الموضع الذي كان فيه آدم وحواء يخصفان عليهما من الورق أي يضمان بعضه إلى بعض يتستران به ثم هبطت إلى الدنيا في صلب آدم وأنت لا بشر ولا مضغة. وقوله: (تركب السفين) يعني في صلب نوح. وصالب لغة غريبة في الصُّلْب ويجوز في الصلب الفتحتان كسُقْم وسَقَم. والطبق: القرن كلما مضى عالم وقرن جاء قرن ولأن القرن يطبق الأرض بسكناه بها

ومنه قوله عليه السلام في الاستسقاء: اللهم اسقنا غيثا مغيثا طبقا غدقا أي يطبق الأرض. وأما قوله تعالى {لتركبن طبقا عن طبق} أي حالا بعد حال. والنطق: جمع نطاق وهو ما يشد به الوسط ومنه المنطقة. أي أنت أوسط قومك نسبا. وجعله في علياء وجعلهم تحته نطاقا وقال ابن الأثير أراد شَرفه، فجعلَه في أعْلَى خِنْدِف بَيْتاً. والمهيْمن: الشَّاهد بِفَضْلك

Al-Bayhaqī and Abū Nuʿaym narrated from ʿAdī b. Ḥātim ؓ that the Prophet ﷺ said: [362] "Al-Ḥīra was displayed before me, [shining] like canine teeth! You shall conquer it." A man stood and said, "Messenger of Allah! Can I have the daughter of Nufayla?" He said: [a] "She is yours." They gave her to him. Her father came and said, "Will you sell her to me?" He said yes. "How much do you ask?" "A thousand dirhams." He [paid and took her then] said, "Had you asked for thirty thousand I would have still taken her!" He said: "As if there were a number greater than a thousand!"[484]

عَنْ عَدِيِّ بْنِ حَاتِمٍ رَضِيَ اللهُ عَنْهُ قَالَ النَّبِيُّ ﷺ مُثِّلَتْ لِي الْحِيرَةُ كَأَنْيَابِ الْكِلَابِ وَإِنَّكُمْ سَتَفْتَحُونَهَا فَقَامَ رَجُلٌ فَقَالَ يَا رَسُولَ اللهِ هَبْ لِي ابْنَةَ بُقَيْلَةَ قَالَ هِيَ لَكَ فَأَعْطَوْهُ إِيَّاهَا فَجَاءَ أَبُوهَا فَقَالَ أَتَبِيعُهَا قَالَ نَعَمْ قَالَ بِكَمْ أُحْكُمْ مَا شِئْتَ قَالَ أَلْفُ دِرْهَمٍ قَالَ قَدْ أَخَذْتُهَا قَالُوا لَهُ لَوْ قُلْتَ ثَلَاثِينَ أَلْفًا لَأَخَذَهَا قَالَ وَهَلْ عَدَدٌ أَكْثَرُ مِنْ أَلْفٍ ابن أبي عاصم في الآحاد حب الإسماعيلي مي معجم الشيوخ هق وفي الدلائل وإسناده صحيح لكن قال أبو حاتم الرازي

484 *Khaṣā'is* (2:187). Narrated from ʿAdī b. Ḥātim by Ibn Abī ʿĀṣim in his *Āḥād* (4:437 §2490), Ibn Ḥibbān (15:65 §6674), al-Bayhaqī in the *Sunan* (9:136) and *Dalā'il* (6:326) while al-Ṭabarānī in *al-Kabīr* (17:81 §183) narrates it with her brother as the ransomer rather than her father, with a chain of *Ṣaḥīḥ* narrators cf. al-Haythamī (6:212), Abū Bakr al-Ismāʿīlī, *Muʿjam al-Shuyūkh* (3:789-790 §397), Ibn Bashkuwāl, *Ghawāmid* (1:437-438 §406), al-Wādyāshī, *Tuḥfat al-Muḥtāj* (2:515 §1660).

في العلل هذا حديث باطل وقال الهيثمي في موارد الظمآن هكذا وقع في هذه الرواية أن الذي اشتراها أبوها و المشهور أن الذي اشتراها عبد المسيح أخوها وروي بلفظ **فَجَاءَ أَخُوهَا** طب ورجاله رجال الصحيح مج

[Continuation: Conquest of the Persians and Eastern Romans]

Al-Bayhaqī and Abū Nuʿaym narrated from ʿUthmān b. Abī al-ʿĀṣ ☸, "I heard the Messenger of Allah ﷺ say: 363 'The Muslims shall have three chief regions *(amṣār)*: a chief region at the meeting of the two seas (al-Baḥrayn), a chief region in al-Jīza [in Egypt], and a chief region in Syro-Palestine (al-Shām). <The people will suffer three terrors *(fazaʿāt)*. Al-Dajjāl will come out in their midst. He will wreak havoc towards the East *(al-mashriq)*. The first region he goes to is the region at the meeting of the Two Seas. The people there will split into three groups. One group will say, 'We will test him and see what he is.' Another group will join the desert Arabs. A third group will join the chief region next to them. With al-Dajjāl there will be seventy thousand in full armor. Most of his followers will be Jews and women. He will proceed to the next chief region. Again, its people will split into three groups, one saying we will test him and see what he is, another joining the desert Arabs, and a third joining the next chief region, in the West, in Syro-Palestine *(bi-gharbī al-Shām)*. The Muslims will fold back to ʿAqabat Afīq and send out their infantry but ehy will be defeated. This will bring great pressure upon them. They will suffer great famine and hardship. Some will cook the strings of their bows and eat them. While they are in this state, someone will call out before the dawn, 'People! Help is here!' three times. They will say to each other, 'This is the voice of hope!' ʿĪsā عليه السلام will descend at the dawn prayer. Their leader will say to him, 'Spirit of Allah! Go forward and pray [as imām].' But he will reply: 'This Community has its own leaders presiding over one another.' Their leader will come forward and lead them in prayer. Once he finishes praying, ʿĪsā عليه السلام will take up his spear and go toward al-Dajjāl. When al-Dajjāl sees ʿĪsā, he will melt like lead. ʿĪsā will spear him between the breasts and kill him. His supporters will be

routed. That day, nothing will serve to hide them anymore. Even the trees will say, 'O Believer! Here is an unbeliever [hiding behind me]!' And the rocks will say, 'O Believer! Here is an unbeliever [hiding behind me]!>'''[485]

عَنْ عُثْمَانَ بْنِ أَبِي الْعَاصِ رَضِيَ اللهُ عَنْهُ قَالَ سَمِعْتُ رَسُولَ اللهِ ﷺ يَقُولُ يَكُونُ لِلْمُسْلِمِينَ ثَلاَثَةُ أَمْصَارٍ مِصْرٌ بِمُلْتَقَى الْبَحْرَيْنِ وَمِصْرٌ بِالْحِيرَةِ وَمِصْرٌ بِالشَّامِ فَيَفْزَعُ النَّاسُ ثَلاَثَ فَزَعَاتٍ فَيَخْرُجُ الدَّجَّالُ فِي أَعْرَاضِ النَّاسِ فَيَهْزِمُ مَنْ قِبَلَ الْمَشْرِقِ فَأَوَّلُ مِصْرٍ يَرِدُهُ الْمِصْرُ الَّذِي بِمُلْتَقَى الْبَحْرَيْنِ فَيَصِيرُ أَهْلُهُ ثَلاَثَ فِرَقٍ فِرْقَةٌ تَقُولُ نُشَامُّهُ نَنْظُرُ مَا هُوَ وَفِرْقَةٌ تَلْحَقُ بالأَعْرَابِ وَفِرْقَةٌ تَلْحَقُ بِالْمِصْرِ الَّذِي يَلِيهِمْ وَمَعَ الدَّجَّالِ سَبْعُونَ أَلْفًا عَلَيْهِمْ السِّيجَانُ وَأَكْثَرُ تَبَعِهِ الْيَهُودُ وَالنِّسَاءُ ثُمَّ يَأْتِي الْمِصْرَ الَّذِي يَلِيهِ فَيَصِيرُ أَهْلُهُ ثَلاَثَ فِرَقٍ فِرْقَةٌ تَقُولُ نُشَامُّهُ وَنَنْظُرُ مَا هُوَ وَفِرْقَةٌ تَلْحَقُ بالأَعْرَابِ وَفِرْقَةٌ تَلْحَقُ بِالْمِصْرِ الَّذِي يَلِيهِمْ

[485]*Khasā'is* (2:257) and al-Nabhānī omitted the bracketed passage. Narrated from ʿUthmān b. Abī al-ʿĀṣ by Aḥmad (Arna'ūṭ ed. 29:430-432 §17900 *isnād ḍaʿīf*) cf. Ibn Kathīr's *Tafsīr* (1:580), Ibn Abī Shayba (7:491 §37478), al-Ṭabarānī in *al-Kabīr* (9:60 §8392) cf. al-Haythamī (7:342), Ibn ʿAsākir (2:467), and al-Ḥākim (4:478-479= 1990 ed. 4:525 through the very weak Saʿīd b. Hubayra), all but the latter with a fair-to-weak chain because of ʿAlī b. Zayd b. Judʿān cf. al-Būṣirī in *Miṣbāḥ al-Zujāja* (2:95) although al-Tirmidhī considers him "truthful" *(sadūq)*, he is retained by Ibn Khuzayma in his *Sahīh*, Muslim in his as an auxiliary narrator *(maqrūn)*, Ibn Ḥajar grades his chain fair in the *Fatḥ* (7:39), al-Haythamī (7:183, 4:310, 9:71-72) grades him "trustworthy with a poor memory" *(thiqa sayyi' al-hafz)* and his narrations "fair," al-Dhahabī in his marginalia on al-Ḥākim (3:190=1990 ed. 3:210) grades his chain passable *(sālih)*, and Ibn Kathīr in *al-Bidāya* (6:137-138) grades him as meeting the authenticity criteria of the *Sunan*. "ʿAqabat Afīq is a town between Ḥawrān and al-Ghawr" (al-Sindī).

بِغَرْبِيِّ الشَّامِ وَيَنْحَازُ الْمُسْلِمُونَ إِلَى عَقَبَةِ أَفِيقٍ فَيَبْعَثُونَ سَرْحًا لَهُمْ فَيُصَابُ سَرْحُهُمْ فَيَشْتَدُّ ذَلِكَ عَلَيْهِمْ وَتُصِيبُهُمْ مَجَاعَةٌ شَدِيدَةٌ وَجَهْدٌ شَدِيدٌ حَتَّى إِنَّ أَحَدَهُمْ لَيُحْرِقُ وَتَرَ قَوْسِهِ فَيَأْكُلُهُ فَبَيْنَمَا هُمْ كَذَلِكَ إِذْ نَادَى مُنَادٍ مِنَ السَّحَرِ يَا أَيُّهَا النَّاسُ أَتَاكُمُ الْغَوْثُ ثَلَاثًا فَيَقُولُ بَعْضُهُمْ لِبَعْضٍ إِنَّ هَذَا لَصَوْتُ رَجُلٍ شَبْعَانَ وَيَنْزِلُ عِيسَى ابْنُ مَرْيَمَ عَلَيْهِ السَّلَامُ عِنْدَ صَلَاةِ الْفَجْرِ فَيَقُولُ لَهُ أَمِيرُهُمْ رُوحَ اللهِ تَقَدَّمْ صَلِّ فَيَقُولُ هَذِهِ الْأُمَّةُ أُمَرَاءُ بَعْضُهُمْ عَلَى بَعْضٍ فَيَتَقَدَّمُ أَمِيرُهُمْ فَيُصَلِّي فَإِذَا قَضَى صَلَاتَهُ أَخَذَ عِيسَى حَرْبَتَهُ فَيَذْهَبُ نَحْوَ الدَّجَّالِ فَإِذَا رَآهُ الدَّجَّالُ ذَابَ كَمَا يَذُوبُ الرَّصَاصُ فَيَضَعُ حَرْبَتَهُ بَيْنَ ثَنْدُوَتِهِ فَيَقْتُلُهُ وَيَنْهَزِمُ أَصْحَابُهُ فَلَيْسَ يَوْمَئِذٍ شَيْءٌ يُوَارِي مِنْهُمْ أَحَدًا حَتَّى إِنَّ الشَّجَرَةَ لَتَقُولُ يَا مُؤْمِنُ هَذَا كَافِرٌ وَيَقُولُ الْحَجَرُ يَا مُؤْمِنُ هَذَا كَافِرٌ حم طب ش ك كر

Al-Bayhaqī and Abū Nuʿaym narrated from ʿAbd Allāh b. Busr ؓ that <he gave the Prophet ﷺ a sheep as a gift. In those days food was scarce. He said to his wives: "Cook this sheep and look for that cracked wheat, bake bread out of it and mix it with the meat." The Messenger of Allah ﷺ had a tray they called *al-ghabrā'* or *al-ʿazzā'* which it took four men to carry. After he/they rose in the morning and prayed the Ḍuḥā prayer he brought that tray and they all surrounded it. When many people came the Messenger of Allah ﷺ sat on his knees. A bedouin said: "What

kind of sitting is this?" The Prophet ﷺ replied: "Truly Allah has made me a noble servant and he did not make me a stubborn tyrant." Then he said: "Eat from its sides and leave its top alone so that blessing will descend on it." Then he said: "Eat!> By the One in Whose Hand is the soul of Muḥammad! [364] Persia and Byzantium shall be laid open for you until food becomes plentiful and the name of Allah ﷻ is no longer pronounced over it."[486]

عَنْ عَبْدِ اللهِ بْنُ بُسْرٍ رَضِيَ اللهُ عَنْهُ قَالَ أَهْدَيْتُ النَّبِيَّ ﷺ شَاةً وَالطَّعَامُ يَوْمَئِذٍ قَلِيلٌ فَقَالَ لأَهْلِهِ اطْبُخُوا هَذِهِ الشَّاةَ وَانْظُرُوا إِلَى هَذَا الدَّقِيقِ فَاخْبِزُوهُ وَأَثْرِدُوا عَلَيْهِ وَكَانَتْ لِلنَّبِيِّ ﷺ قَصْعَةٌ يُقَالُ لَهَا الْغَبْرَاءُ أَوِ الْعَزَّاءُ يَحْمِلُهَا أَرْبَعَةُ رِجَالٍ فَلَمَّا أَصْبَحَ وَسَجَدَ الضُّحَى أَتَى بِتِلْكَ الْقَصْعَةِ وَالْتَفُّوا عَلَيْهَا فَلَمَّا كَثُرَ النَّاسُ جَثَى رَسُولُ اللهِ ﷺ فَقَالَ أَعْرَابِيٌّ مَا هَذِهِ الْجِلْسَةُ فَقَالَ النَّبِيُّ ﷺ إِنَّ اللهَ جَعَلَنِي عَبْدًا كَرِيمًا وَلَمْ يَجْعَلْنِي جَبَّارًا عَنِيدًا ثُمَّ قَالَ رَسُولُ اللهِ ﷺ كُلُوا مِنْ جَوَانِبِهَا وَذَرُوا ذُرْوَتَهَا يُبَارَكْ فِيهَا ثُمَّ قَالَ كُلُوا فَوَالَّذِي نَفْسِي بِيَدِهِ لَتُفْتَحَنَّ عَلَيْكُمْ أَرْضُ فَارِسَ وَالرُّومِ حَتَّى يَكْثُرَ الطَّعَامُ فَلا يُذْكَرُ اسْمُ اللهِ عَلَيْهِ المعرفة والتاريخ غيلانيات هق هب وفي الآداب والدلائل كر

[486]*Khaṣā'iṣ* (2:191) and al-Nabhānī omitted the bracketed passage, which is narrated by Abū Dāwūd and Ibn Mājah without the remaining text. Narrated in full from ʿAbd Allāh b. Busr by al-Fasawī in *al-Maʿrifa wal-Tārīkh* (2:351-352), Abū Bakr al-Shāfiʿī in *al-Ghaylāniyyāt* (Ḥilmī-Salmān ed. 2:694 §942), al-Bayhaqī in *al-Sunan al-Kubrā* (7:283 §14430), the *Shuʿab* (5:79 §5847), *al-Ādāb* (p. 181 §538), and *Dalā'il al-Nubuwwa* (6:334), and Ibn ʿAsākir (27:140-141), all with Abū Dāwūd's chain which al-Nawawī graded fair in *Riyāḍ al-Ṣāliḥīn* cf. *Mukhtāra* (9:91-92 §73), *Bidāya* (6:197).

Al-Bayhaqī and Abū Nu'aym narrated from Ibn 'Umar رضي الله عنهما that the Messenger of Allah ﷺ said: 365 "When my Community struts in pomp *(mashat ummatī al-muṭayṭā')* and the children of Persia and Byzantium serve them, at that time the worst of them will preside over the best of them."[487] [Another version has: "at that time they will exert power over one another."][488]

عَنِ ابْنِ عُمَرَ رَضِيَ اللهُ عَنْهُمَا قَالَ رَسُولُ اللهِ ﷺ إِذَا مَشَتْ أُمَّتِي المطَيْطَاءَ وَخَدَمَهَا أَبْنَاءُ الملُوكِ أَبْنَاءُ فَارِسَ وَالرُّومِ سُلِّطَ شِرَارُها عَلَى خِيَارِهَا ت ابن المبارك في الزهد بحشل في تاريخ واسط أبو نعيم في أخبار أصبهان والدلائل هق في الدلائل التيمي في الترغيب شرح السنّة وفي الباب عن أبي هريرة طس وإسناده حسن مج وخولة بنت قيس الأنصارية حب وأبي موسى يُحَنَّس ابن أبي الدنيا في التواضع والخمول هق في الدلائل وقال الزيلعي في تخريج الكشاف قَالَ إِبْرَاهِيم الْحَرْبِيّ فِي كِتَابه غَرِيب الحَدِيث الْمُطَيْطَاء بِالْمدِّ أَن يفتح يَدَيْهِ عَن جَنْبَيْهِ وَيَمْشي وَهُوَ التَّبَخْتُر نَقله عَن أبي عُبَيْدَة وَالْفراء وَابْن الْأَعرَابِي وقال قوّام السنّة فيها لغة أخرى المطَيْطِيَاء

Al-Ḥākim narrated from al-Zubayr رضي الله عنه that the Messenger of Allah ﷺ <was sitting in Qubā' with a group when Muṣ'ab b. 'Umayr got up [to go], wearing a cloak that barely covered his nakedness. Everyone looked down. He came and gave his greeting and they answered back. The Prophet ﷺ said good things about him and praised him then> said: "<I have seen this man with his parents in Mecca indulging him and pampering him like no other

[487]Narrated from Ibn 'Umar by al-Tirmidhī *(gharīb)* with three chains, one of them *mursal* through Mālik, from the *Tābi'ī* Yaḥyā b. Sa'īd al-Anṣārī; Ibn al-Mubārak with a fourth chain in *al-Zuhd* (p. 51-52 §187); Baḥshal in *Tārīkh Wāsiṭ* (p. 223); graded unsound by al-Dhahabī in his *Mīzān* (6:136 Muhammad b. Khulayd b. 'Amr).

[488]Narrated from Ibn 'Umar by al-Tirmidhī (*gharīb*), Abū Nu'aym in the *Dalā'il* (p. 539 §466) and *Akhbār Aṣbahān* (1:308), al-Bayhaqī in the *Dalā'il* (6:525), al-Baghawī in *Sharḥ al-Sunna* (14:395 §4200) and al-Taymī in *al-Targhīb* (1:370 §636); from Umm Muḥammad Khawla bint Qays al-Anṣāriyya by Ibn Ḥibbān (15:112 §6716); from Abū Hurayra by al-Ṭabarānī in *al-Awsat* (1:47-48 §132) with a fair chain per al-Haythamī (10:237); and *mursal* from the *Tābi'ī* Yuḥannas the *mawlā* of al-Zubayr by Ibn Abī al-Dunyā in *al-Tawāḍu' wal-Khumūl* (p. 220 §249), and al-Bayhaqī in the *Dalā'il* (6:525).

young man of the young men of Quraysh! Then he left all that behind, seeking the good pleasure of Allah and to help His Messenger. Behold!> [366] Little time shall pass before Persia and the Eastern Romans are laid open for you. At that time, one of you will wear a tunic in the morning and a different tunic in the evening, and you will have a dish for ten *(qaṣʿatun)* to eat in the morning and another in the evening."[489]

عَنْ عُرْوَةَ بْنِ الزُّبَيْرِ عَنْ أَبِيهِ رَضِيَ اللهُ تَعَالَى عَنْهُ قَالَ كَانَ
رَسُولُ اللهِ ﷺ جَالِساً بِقُبَاءَ وَمَعَهُ نَفَرٌ فَقَامَ مُصْعَبُ بْنُ عُمَيْرٍ
عَلَيْهِ بُرْدَةٌ مَا تَكَادُ تُوَارِيهِ وَنَكَسَ الْقَوْمُ فَجَاءَ فَسَلَّمَ فَرَدُّوا عَلَيْهِ
فَقَالَ فِيهِ النَّبِيُّ ﷺ خَيْراً وَأَثْنَى عَلَيْهِ ثُمَّ قَالَ لَقَدْ رَأَيْتُ هَذَا عِنْدَ
أَبَوَيْهِ بِمَكَّةَ يُكْرِمَانِهِ يُنَعِّمَانِهِ وَمَا فَتىً مِنْ فِتْيَانِ قُرَيْشٍ مِثْلُهُ ثُمَّ
خَرَجَ مِنْ ذَلِكَ ابْتِغَاءَ مَرْضَاةِ اللهِ وَنُصْرَةِ رَسُولِهِ أَمَا أَنَّهُ لاَ يَأْتِي
عَلَيْكُمْ إِلاَّ كَذَا وَكَذاَ حَتَّى يُفْتَحُ عَلَيْكُمْ فَارِسٌ وَالرُّومُ فَيَغْدُو
أَحَدُكُمْ فِي حِلَّةٍ وَيَرُوحُ فِي حِلَّةٍ وَيُغْدَى عَلَيْكُمْ بِقَصْعَةٍ وَيُرَاحُ
عَلَيْكُمْ بِقَصْعَةٍ ابن أبي الدنيا في الزهد وذم الدنيا ك هب الأخير مرسلا

Abū Nuʿaym narrated from ʿAwf b. Mālik ؓ that the Messenger of Allah ﷺ stood among his Companions and said: [367] "Is it poverty you fear when Allah is about to open up to you the lands of Persia and the Eastern Romans, and pour upon you the world

[489]*Khasā'is* (2:191) and al-Nabhānī omit the bracketed passage. Narrated from al-Zubayr b. al-ʿAwwām by by Ibn Abī al-Dunyā in *al-Zuhd* (p. 218 §575) and *Dhamm al-Dunyā* (p. 174-175 §428), al-Ḥākim (3:628=1990 ed. 3:728) and—*mursal* from his son ʿUrwa b. al-Zubayr—al-Bayhaqī in the *Shuʿab* (7:286 §10329); also narrated from others cf. above, section entitled "His ﷺ Foretelling the Killing of Certain People and Conquest of Cities" note 455.

without stint, so that nothing should lead you astray – if you were to go astray – except that?"[490]

عَنْ عَوْفِ بْنِ مَالِكٍ أَنَّهُ قَالَ إِنَّ رَسُولَ اللهِ ﷺ قَامَ فِي أَصْحَابِهِ فَقَالَ آلْفَقْرَ تَخَافُونَ أَوْ الْعَوَزَ أَوَتُهِمُّكُمْ الدُّنْيَا فَإِنَّ اللهَ فَاتِحٌ لَكُمْ أَرْضَ فَارِسَ وَالرُّومِ وَتُصَبُّ عَلَيْكُمْ الدُّنْيَا صَبًّا حَتَّى لَا يُزِيغُكُمْ بَعْدِي إِنْ أَزَاغَكُمْ إِلَّا هِيَ حم طب أبو نعيم في الدلائل كر وفي الباب عن أبي الدّرداء آلْفَقْرَ تَخَافُونَ؟ والَّذِي نَفْسِي بِيَدِهِ لَتُصَبَّنَّ عَلَيْكُمُ الدُّنْيَا صَبّاً حَتَّى لا يُزِيغَ قَلْبَ أَحَدِكُمْ إِنْ أَزَاغَهُ إِلاَّ هِيَ وَآيْمُ اللهِ لَقَدْ تَرَكْتُكُمْ عَلَى مِثْلِ البَيْضَاءِ لَيْلُهَا وَنَهَارُهَا سَوَاءٌ جه ز قال إسناده حسن

Al-Ḥākim and Abū Nuʿaym narrated from Nāfiʿ[491] b. ʿUtba [b. Abī Waqqāṣ] ؓ, "I was with the Prophet ﷺ during a certain raid. <People from the West came to him wearing woolen garments and they met him on top of a stony hill. There they were, standing, and the Messenger of Allah ﷺ was sitting. I told myself: 'Go over there and stand between him and them lest they assassinate him.' Then I thought, 'Maybe he wants to talk to them in private.' I went over and stood between him and them. I memorized from him four words which I counted on the fingers of my hand.> He said: [368] 'You will raid the Arabian peninsula **[525]** and Allah shall lay it open; then you will raid Persia and Allah shall lay

[490]Narrated from ʿAwf b. Mālik al-Ashjaʿī by Aḥmad in the *Musnad* and *al-Zuhd* (p. 106-107 §210), al-Ṭabarānī in *al-Kabīr* (18:52 §93), and Abū Nuʿaym in the *Dalāʾil* (p. 539 §467) and, in slightly shorter form, al-Bazzār (7:189-190 §2758) and al-Ṭabarānī in *Musnad al-Shāmiyyīn* (2:181 §1150) through trustworthy narrators cf. Haythamī (10:245) and *Khaṣāʾiṣ* (2:192). Ibn ʿAsākir (1:395) narrates both versions. Something similar is also narrated from Abū al-Dardāʾ by Ibn Mājah and al-Bazzār (10:76-77 §4141).

[491]Misidentified as his brother Hāshim b. ʿUtba b. Abī Waqqāṣ in al-Nabhānī.

it open; then you will raid Byzantium and Allah shall lay it open; then you will raid the Anti-Christ (al-Dajjāl) and Allah shall lay him open."[492]

عَنْ نَافِعِ بْنِ عُتْبَةَ قَالَ كُنَّا مَعَ رَسُولِ اللهِ ﷺ فِي غَزْوَةٍ قَالَ فَأَتَى النَّبِيَّ ﷺ قَوْمٌ مِنْ قِبَلِ الْمَغْرِبِ عَلَيْهِمْ ثِيَابُ الصُّوفِ فَوَافَقُوهُ عِنْدَ أَكَمَةٍ فَإِنَّهُمْ لَقِيَامٌ وَرَسُولُ اللهِ ﷺ قَاعِدٌ قَالَ فَقَالَتْ لِي نَفْسِي ائْتِهِمْ فَقُمْ بَيْنَهُمْ وَبَيْنَهُ لَا يَغْتَالُونَهُ قَالَ ثُمَّ قُلْتُ لَعَلَّهُ نَجِيٌّ مَعَهُمْ فَأَتَيْتُهُمْ فَقُمْتُ بَيْنَهُمْ وَبَيْنَهُ قَالَ فَحَفِظْتُ مِنْهُ أَرْبَعَ كَلِمَاتٍ أَعُدُّهُنَّ فِي يَدِي قَالَ تَغْزُونَ جَزِيرَةَ الْعَرَبِ فَيَفْتَحُهَا اللهُ ثُمَّ فَارِسَ فَيَفْتَحُهَا اللهُ ثُمَّ تَغْزُونَ الرُّومَ فَيَفْتَحُهَا اللهُ ثُمَّ تَغْزُونَ الدَّجَّالَ فَيَفْتَحُهُ اللهُ م حم خت ابن أبي عاصم في الآحاد ش طس ابن قانع في المعجم حب وفي الثقات أبو نعيم في المعرفة التيمي في الدلائل وجاء نحوه عن أخيه هاشم بن عتبة مرفوعا ك وهو وهم قط في العلل

Al-Bayhaqī narrated from ʿUmar b. Shuraḥbīl ؓ that the Messenger of Allah ﷺ said: [369] "I saw, last night, as if black sheep were following me. Then white sheep succeeded them until no more black was seen among them." Abū Bakr said: "Messenger of Allah! These are the Arabs following you, succeeded by the

[492]*Khasā'is* (2:192) and al-Nabhānī omitted the bracketed passage. Narrated from Nāfiʿ b. ʿUtba b. Abī Waqqās by Muslim, Aḥmad with four chains, Ibn Abī Shayba (7:494 §37504), al-Bukhārī in *al-Tārīkh al-Kabīr* (8:81 §2254), Ibn Qāniʿ in *Muʿjam al-Saḥāba* (3:139 §1111), Ṭabarānī in *al-Awsaṭ* (4:93 §3691), Ibn Ḥibbān (15:62 §6672 and 15:220 §6809), Ḥākim (1990 ed. 3:487 and 4:472), Abū Nuʿaym in the *Maʿrifa* (under Nāfiʿ b. ʿUtba), Taymī in *Dalā'il al-Nubuwwa* (p. 226 §323), and al-Mizzī in *Tahdhīb al-Kamāl* (29:285) and from his brother Hāshim by al-Ḥākim (1990 ed. 3:446) cf. *Istīʿāb* (4:1547) and *Iṣāba* (6:515). Al-Dāraquṭnī in the *ʿIlal* termed the latter version an inadvertance and Ibn Hajar cites the ḥadīth Masters' precedence for the attribution to Nāfiʿ.

non-Arabs [in huge numbers] until the Arabs can no longer be seen among them." The Prophet ﷺ said: "Yes, [a] just so did the angel interpret it [to me] before the dawn."[493] This narration is *mursal*.

عَنْ عَمْرِو بْنِ شُرَحْبِيلَ قَالَ قَالَ رَسُولُ اللهِ ﷺ إِنِّي رَأَيْتُ اللَّيْلَةَ
كَأَنَّمَا تَتْبَعُنِي غَنَمٌ سُودٌ ثُمَّ أَرْدَفَتْهَا غَنَمٌ بِيضٌ حَتَّى لَمْ تُرَ السُّودُ
فِيهَا فَقَصَّهَا عَلَى أَبِي بَكْرٍ رَضِيَ اللهُ عَنْهُ فَقَالَ يَا رَسُولَ اللهِ
هِيَ الْعَرَبُ تَبِعَتْكَ ثُمَّ أَرْدَفَتْهَا الْعَجَمُ حَتَّى لَمْ يُرَوْا فِيهَا قَالَ
أَجَلْ كَذَلِكَ عَبَّرَهَا الْمَلَكُ سَحَراً هذا مرسل هق في الدلائل وفي الباب
عن أبي هريرة وحذيفة والنعمان بن بشير وجبير بن مطعم وأبي بكر الصديق وعبد الرحمن
بن أبي ليلى ورجل من الصحابة أخرجها جميعا أبو نعيم في أخبار أصبهان ونحوه عن ابن
عمر ك قال صحيح على شرط البخاري

[Another, *musnad* narration states that the Prophet ﷺ said: [370] "I saw in dream black sheep succeeded by dirt-white sheep. Abū Bakr! Interpret it." The latter said, "Messenger of Allah, these are the Arabs following you, then the non-Arabs succeed them until they completely engulf them in their number." The Prophet ﷺ said: "Just so did the angel interpret it [to me] before the dawn."[494]

In another *musnad* narration the Prophet ﷺ said: [371] "I saw a great flock of black sheep with which a great flock of white sheep intermingled. I interpreted it as the non-Arabs joining with you in both your Religion and your lineages." They said: "The non-Arabs, Messenger of Allah?" He replied: [a] "Were faith hanging upon the Pleiades, men among the non-Arabs would certainly fetch it from there and bring felicity to people."[495]

[493]*Khasā'is* (2:192). Narrated *mursal* from the *Tābi'ī* Abū Maysara 'Amr [not 'Umar] b. Shurahbīl al-Hamdānī by al-Bayhaqī in the *Dalā'il* (6:337) cf. al-Muhibb al-Ṭabarī in *al-Ryād al-Nadira* (2:64 §478) and something similar from several Companions by Abū Nu'aym in *Akhbār Asbahān* (1:8-10), from Ibn 'Umar in al-Ḥākim (4:395), and *mursal* from Qatāda by Ma'mar b. Rāshid in his *Majma'* ('Abd al-Razzāq 11:66).

[494]Narrated from 'Abd al-Rahmān b. Abī Laylā, [1] from Abū Ayyūb al-Anṣārī by al-Ḥākim (4:395= 1990 ed. 4:437) and [2] from Abū Bakr himself but al-Dāraqutnī in his *'Ilal* (1:289) avers that this narration is more probably *mursal* from Ibn Abī Laylā. Yet the *mursal* has a different wording cf. n. 497.

[495]Narrated from Ibn 'Umar by al-Ḥākim (4:395=1990 ed. 4:437 *sahīh 'alā shart al-Bukhārī*). The Prophet's ﷺ reply is also narrated from Abū Hurayra by al-Bukhārī and

In a similar narration the Prophet ﷺ said: 372 "Last night as [I dreamt] I was hoisting up [water from a well] I saw a flock of black sheep and dirt-white sheep. Abū Bakr came and hoisted a bucket or two. I saw some weakness in his hoisting and Allah forgives him. Then ʿUmar came and the bucket changed into a pail. The drinking-basin became full and quenched the thirst of all that came to it. a I never saw any strong master of his people hoisting water better than ʿUmar. b I interpreted the black [sheep] to refer to the Arabs and the dirt-white to refer to the non-Arabs."[496]

In another narration the interpretation of the hoisting dream is given by Abū Bakr.[497]

Al-Shāfiʿī glossed the word "weakness" as referring to the short duration of Abū Bakr's caliphate and the fact that his turning to the *Ridda* wars delayed him from the conquests and expansions achieved by ʿUmar during the latter's longer tenure.[498]]

M uslim and al-Bayhaqī narrated from Jābir b. Samura رضي الله عنهما : "The Messenger of Allah ﷺ said: 373 'A band *(ʿiṣāba)* of Muslims shall conquer the treasures of Chosroes that are in the white palace.' <I and my father were part of that group. We got one thousand dirhams.">[499]

عَنْ جَابِرِ بْنِ سَمُرَةَ رَضِيَ اللهُ عَنْهُمَا قَالَ سَمِعْتُ رَسُولَ اللهِ ﷺ يَقُولُ لَتُفْتَحَنَّ عِصَابَةٌ مِنَ الْمُسْلِمِينَ أَوْ مِنَ الْمُؤْمِنِينَ كَنْزَ آلِ كِسْرَى الَّذِي فِي الْأَبْيَضِ م حم قَالَ جَابِرٌ فَكُنْتُ فِيهِمْ

Muslim as "a man from the non-Arabs" in the singular.

[496]Narrated from Abū al-Ṭufayl ʿĀmir b. Wāthila through ʿAlī b. Zayd b. Judʿān (cf. n. 485) by Aḥmad, al-Bazzār (7:211 §2785), Abū Yaʿlā (2:198 §904), Ibn Abī ʿĀṣim in *al-Āḥād wal-Mathānī* (2:200-201 §951), and al-Ṭabarānī "with a fair chain" per Ibn Ḥajar in the *Fatḥ* (7:39 and 12:414) and al-Haythamī (5:180, 7:183, 9:71-72) cf. also al-Muḥibb al-Ṭabarī, *al-Ryāḍ al-Naḍira* (1:350), also with a strong *mursal* chain from al-Ḥasan al-Baṣrī by Aḥmad in *Faḍāʾil al-Ṣaḥāba* (1:163 §150). Something very similar is also narrated from Abū Qatāda by Muslim, Aḥmad, Abū ʿAwāna in his *Musnad* (2:259), Bayhaqī in *al-Iʿtiqād* (p. 340) and *al-Madkhal* (p. 122), al-Firyābī and Abū Nuʿaym each in their *Dalāʾil al-Nubuwwa*, and the Jahmī ḥadīth Master ʿAlī b. al-Jaʿd (d. 230) in his *Musnad* (p. 450)

[497]Narrated *mursal* from the *Tābiʿī* ʿAbd al-Raḥmān b. Abī Laylā by Ibn Abī Shayba (6:176 §30479).

[498]In *Fatḥ al-Bārī* (7:32).

[499]Narrated from Jābir b. Samura by Muslim, Aḥmad, and al-Bayhaqī in the *Dalāʾil* (4:389) but the bracketed segment is only in the latter two, Aḥmad mentioning the speaker alone while al-Bayhaqī's version includes his father Samura b. Jundub, who was also a Companion.

فَأَصَابَنِي أَلْفُ دِرْهَمٍ حم وفي رواية فَكُنْتُ أَنَا وَأَبِي فِيهِمْ فَأَصَبْنَا مِنْ ذَلِكَ أَلْفُ دِرْهَمٍ هق في الدلائل

Aḥmad, Abū Yaʿlā, and al-Ṭabarānī narrated that 'Afīf al-Kindī ﷺ said: "I came to Mecca and went to al-ʿAbbās to buy goods from him. I was with him in Minā when 374 a man came out of a tent nearby and looked at the sky. When he saw that it [the sun] passed its zenith, he stood and prayed. Then a woman came out and stood praying behind him. Then a boy came out and stood praying with him. I asked al-ʿAbbās what this was and he said: 375 'This is Muḥammad, my nephew, together with his wife Khadīja and his paternal cousin ʿAlī; he claims that he is a Prophet but no one followed him except his wife and cousin. He claims that the treasures of Chosroes and Caesar will be laid open for him.'"[500]

عَنْ إِسْمَاعِيلَ بْنِ إِيَاسِ بْنِ عَفِيفٍ الْكِنْدِيِّ عَنْ أَبِيهِ عَنْ جَدِّهِ قَالَ كُنْتُ امْرَأً تَاجِرًا فَقَدِمْتُ الْحَجَّ فَأَتَيْتُ الْعَبَّاسَ بْنَ عَبْدِ الْمُطَّلِبِ لِأَبْتَاعَ مِنْهُ بَعْضَ التِّجَارَةِ وَكَانَ امْرَأً تَاجِرًا فَوَاللهِ إِنِّي لَعِنْدَهُ بِمِنًى إِذْ خَرَجَ رَجُلٌ مِنْ خِبَاءٍ قَرِيبٍ مِنْهُ فَنَظَرَ إِلَى الشَّمْسِ فَلَمَّا رَآهَا مَالَتْ يَعْنِي قَامَ يُصَلِّي قَالَ ثُمَّ خَرَجَتْ امْرَأَةٌ مِنْ ذَلِكَ الْخِبَاءِ الَّذِي خَرَجَ مِنْهُ ذَلِكَ الرَّجُلُ فَقَامَتْ خَلْفَهُ تُصَلِّي ثُمَّ خَرَجَ غُلَامٌ حِينَ رَاهَقَ الْحُلُمَ مِنْ ذَلِكَ الْخِبَاءِ فَقَامَ

[500]Narrated from 'Afīf by Aḥmad, al-Ṭabarānī in *al-Kabīr* (18:100), and al-Ḥākim (3:183= 1990 ed. 3:201 *saḥīh*) all with a weak chain – contrary to al-Dhahabī and al-Haythamī (9:103) cf. al-Maqdisī in *al-Mukhtārā* (8:388) and *Nasb* (3:459) – through three unknowns: Yaḥyā b. Abī al-Ash'ath, Ismā'īl b. Iyās b. 'Afīf al-Kindī, and his father Iyās, both of whom al-Bukhārī doubted cf. al-Bukhārī, *al-Tārīkh al-Kabīr* (7:74), *al-Istīʿāb* (3:1242), Ibn Ḥibbān, *al-Thiqāt* (4:35 and 6:35), Ibn al-Jawzī, *al-Duʿafāʾ* (1:110 §360), *Mīzān* (1:380), *Lisān* (1:395), *Kāmil* (1:310), and al-ʿUqaylī (1:79).

مَعَهُ يُصَلِّي قَالَ فَقُلْتُ لِلْعَبَّاسِ مَنْ هَذَا يَا عَبَّاسُ قَالَ هَذَا مُحَمَّدُ بْنُ عَبْدِ اللهِ بْنِ عَبْدِ الْمُطَّلِبِ ابْنُ أَخِي قَالَ فَقُلْتُ مَنْ هَذِهِ الْمَرْأَةُ قَالَ هَذِهِ امْرَأَتُهُ خَدِيجَةُ ابْنَةُ خُوَيْلِدٍ قَالَ قُلْتُ مَنْ هَذَا الْفَتَى قَالَ هَذَا عَلِيُّ بْنُ أَبِي طَالِبٍ ابْنُ عَمِّهِ قَالَ فَقُلْتُ فَمَا هَذَا الَّذِي يَصْنَعُ قَالَ يُصَلِّي وَهُوَ يَزْعُمُ أَنَّهُ نَبِيٌّ وَلَمْ يَتْبَعْهُ عَلَى أَمْرِهِ إِلاَّ امْرَأَتُهُ وَابْنُ عَمِّهِ هَذَا الْفَتَى وَهُوَ يَزْعُمُ أَنَّهُ سَيُفْتَحُ عَلَيْهِ كُنُوزُ كِسْرَى وَقَيْصَرَ قَالَ فَكَانَ عَفِيفٌ وَهُوَ ابْنُ عَمِّ الأَشْعَثِ بْنِ قَيْسٍ يَقُولُ وَأَسْلَمَ بَعْدَ ذَلِكَ فَحَسُنَ إِسْلاَمُهُ لَوْ كَانَ اللهُ رَزَقَنِي الإِسْلاَمَ يَوْمَئِذٍ فَأَكُونُ ثَالِثًا مَعَ عَلِيِّ بْنِ أَبِي طَالِبٍ رَضِيَ اللهُ عَنْهُ حم طب ك ض نصب فيه يحيى بن أبي الأشعث مجهول

Al-Bayhaqī narrated from al-Ḥasan [al-Baṣrī] that ʿUmar ﷺ was brought the armlets of Chosroes and gave them to Surāqa b. Mālik. They reached to his shoulders. ʿUmar said: [376] "Glory to Allah! The armlets of Kisrā b. Hurmuz on the arms of Surāqa b. Mālik, a Bedouin Arab from the Mudlij tribe!" Al-Suyūṭī said that al-Shāfiʿī specified ʿUmar only gave them to Surāqa to wear because the Prophet ﷺ said to Surāqa, as he looked at his arms: [377] "I can already see you wearing the armlets of Chosroes, his girdle *(minṭaqa)*, and his crown!" Al-Bayhaqī also narrated through Ibn [ʿUyayna][501] from Isrā'il Abī Mūsā, from al-Ḥasan, that the Messenger of Allah ﷺ said to Surāqa b. Mālik: [378] "What will you do when you wear the armlets of Chosroes?" When ʿUmar was brought the armlets he summoned Surāqa and made him wear

[501]Corrupted to Ibn ʿUtba in the printed edition.

them then said: [a] "Glory to Allah Who took them away from Kisrā b. Hurmuz and made Surāqa the Bedouin Arab wear them!"[502]

Al-Ḥārith b. Abī Usāma narrated from [the *Tābiʿī*] Abū Muḥayrīz ﵁ that the Messenger of Allah ﷺ said: [379] "Persia will give one or two head-butts then there will be no more Persia ever after, while the Romans regenerate: every time one generation perishes, another replaces it. <They are a people of rocks and sea, and so on to the end of time. They will be with you as long as there is something to be gained from living.>"[503]

عَنِ ابْنِ مُحَيرِيزٍ قَالَ قَالَ رَسُولُ اللهِ ﷺ ثُمَّ فَارِسُ نَطْحَةٌ أَوْ
نَطْحَتَانِ ثُمَّ لا فَارِسَ بَعْدَهَا أَبَدًا وَالرُّومُ ذَاتُ الْقُرُونِ كُلَّمَا
هَلَكَ قَرْنٌ خَلَّفَ مَكَانَهُ قَرْنَ أَهْلُ صَخْرٍ وَأَهْلُ بَحْرٍ
هَيْهَاتَ لآخِرِ الدَّهْرِ هُمْ أَصْحَابُكُمْ مَا كَانَ فِي الْعَيْشِ خَيْرٌ

الحارث بن أبي أسامة ش ابن قتيبة في الغريب تفسيرا الوسيط للواحدي والثعلبي

The Two Masters [al-Bukhārī and Muslim] narrated from Jābir b. Samura رضي الله عنهما that the Messenger of Allah ﷺ said: [380] "When Chosroes perishes there will be no more Chosroes after him and when Caesar perishes there will be no more Caesar after him. By the One in Whose Hand is my soul! You will certainly spend their treasures in the way of Allah."[504] • Al-Bukhārī also narrated it from Abū Hurayra ﵁.

[502]All three reports were already cited above, in section on Surāqa b. Mālik, note 357.

[503]*Khasāʾis* (2:193) and al-Nabhanī omit the bracketed passage. Narrated *mursal* from Abū Mujaylīz by al-Ḥārith in his *Musnad* (2:713), Ibn Abī Shayba (4:206), Ibn Qutayba in *Gharīb al-Ḥadīth*, al-Wāḥidī in *al-Wasīt*, al-Thaʿlabī in his *Tafsīr*, and Nuʿaym b. Ḥammād in the *Fitan* (2:479).

[504]Narrated from Jābir b. Samura and Abū Hurayra by al-Bukhārī, Muslim, al-Tirmidhī, and Aḥmad.

عَنْ جَابِرِ بْنِ سَمُرَةَ رَضِيَ اللهُ عَنْهُمَا قَالَ رَسُولُ اللهِ ﷺ إِذَا هَلَكَ كِسْرَى فَلَا كِسْرَى بَعْدَهُ وَإِذَا هَلَكَ قَيْصَرُ فَلَا قَيْصَرَ بَعْدَهُ وَالَّذِي نَفْسِي بِيَدِهِ لَتُنْفَقَنَّ كُنُوزُهُمَا فِي سَبِيلِ اللهِ ق ت حم

Al-Nawawī said that al-Shāfi'ī and all the Ulema said that it means there will no longer be a Chosroes in Iraq nor a Caesar in Syro-Palestine as there had been in the Prophet's ﷺ own time. So he informed us that their rule would come to an end in those two regions and this proved true exactly as he had said.[505] As for Chosroes, his rule came to an end and was completely dismantled and eradicated from the face of the earth through the supplication of the Prophet ﷺ after Chosroes tore up the Prophet's letter to him.[506] As for Caesar, he was routed in Syro-Palestine and retreated to the far end of his territories, after which the Muslims conquered his territories and settled them. **[526]** This took place – to Allah belongs the glory – in the caliphate of our Master 'Umar b. al-Khaṭṭāb ﷺ. The meaning of this ḥadīth and of other narrations with the same meaning is confirmed by the statement of Allah ﷻ, **﴾Allah has promised such of you as believe and do good works that He will surely make them to succeed (the present rulers) in the earth even as He caused those who were before them (to succeed others); and that He will surely establish for them their faith which He has approved for them, and will give them in exchange safety after their fear﴿** (24:55). The author of the *Mawāhib* said:

> This is a promise on the part of Allah ﷻ to His Messenger ﷺ that He will cause his Community to be successors over the earth, leaders and governors for the people, by whom all regions will achieve peace and prosperity and to whose rule all God's servants will submit. Allah fulfilled His promise – to Him belongs all glory and bounty! – for the Prophet ﷺ did not

[505] Cf. *Fatḥ* (6:626).

[506] See above, section entitled "His ﷺ Foretelling the Deaths of Chosroes and Caesar."

die before Allah first conquered, at his hands, Mecca, Khaybar, al-Baḥrayn, and the rest of the Arabian peninsula as well as the territories of Yemen in their entirety. He also took the non-Muslim poll tax *(jizya)* from the Zoroastrians of Hajar and from some of the territories bordering Syro-Palestine while Heraclius the king of the Eastern Romans, al-Muqawqis the ruler of Alexandria, the king of ʿAmmān, al-Najāshī the Abyssinian king who succeeded Aṣḥama – Allah have mercy on him! – all entered into a truce with him. Then the Messenger of Allah ﷺ died and Allah chose to lavish upon him all the blessings of His presence, his successor Abū Bakr al-Ṣiddīq ؓ took command. When weakness became widespread in the wake of the death of the Prophet ﷺ he cleared the way again in the Arabian peninsula and sent out the Muslim armies to the territories of Persia with Khālid b. al-Walīd. They conquered some of its border regions. He sent another army with Abū ʿUbayda to the land of Syro-Palestine and a third army with ʿAmr b. al-ʿĀṣ to the lands of Egypt. Allah opened up for the army of Syro-Palestine, in the time of Abū Bakr, Buṣrā,[507] Damascus, and their vicinities in and around the territory of Ḥawrān. Then Allah ﷻ took him back to Him and chose for him His own presence. Yet He lavished His bounty on Islam and its people by inspiring Abū Bakr to appoint ʿUmar al-Fārūq as his successor. The latter took up the task with utmost diligence, to an extent the sky never saw the like of after the Prophets with regard to strength of character and perfection of justice. The conquest of the territories of Syro-Palestine was completed in his time as well as those of Egypt and most of Persia. He routed Chosroes and humiliated him until the latter retreated to the far end of his kingdom. He cut down Caesar to size *(qaṣṣara Qayṣara)* and left him no influence at all in Syro-Palestine until the latter retreated to Constantinople. He spent their spoils in the way of Allah just as the Messenger of Allah ﷺ had predicted and promised. In the time of the Caliphate of ʿUthmān ؓ, the possessions of Islam extended to the far Eastern ends of the earth and the far West [Spain] as well. The Maghreb territo-

[507]Said to be the site of Bahīra's sighting of the Prophet ﷺ as a young boy.

ries were conquered to their farthest tip: Andalus, Qayrawān, Sabta and the lands bordering the ocean. On the Eastern side, lands were conquered to the farthest end of China. Chosroes was killed, his empire collapsed entirely, and the cities of Iraq, Kurāsān and Ahwāz were conquered. The Muslims killed a vast number of non-Arabs. Land tax was brought from East and West to the Commander of the Believers, ʿUthmān b. ʿAffān.

His Foretelling that Allah Would Grant Empire to the Community and that All Worldly Things Would Become Available to Them

Muslim narrated from Abū Saʿīd al-Khudrī ؓ **[527]** that the Prophet ﷺ said: [381] "The world is sweet and verdant. Allah will surely make you inherit it. He will observe to see what you do with it. Beware of the world and beware of women! The first trial of the Israelites was because of women."[508]

عَنْ أَبِي سَعِيدٍ الْخُدْرِيِّ رَضِيَ اللهُ عَنْهُ عَنِ النَّبِيِّ ﷺ قَالَ إِنَّ الدُّنْيَا حُلْوَةٌ خَضِرَةٌ وَإِنَّ اللهَ مُسْتَخْلِفُكُمْ فِيهَا فَيَنْظُرُ كَيْفَ تَعْمَلُونَ فَاتَّقُوا الدُّنْيَا وَاتَّقُوا النِّسَاءَ فَإِنَّ أَوَّلَ فِتْنَةِ بَنِي إِسْرَائِيلَ كَانَتْ فِي النِّسَاءِ م هب وفي الدلائل شرح السنّة ورواه غيرهم مختصراً ومطولاً قال الطحاوي رحمه الله في شرح المشكل فكان في هذا الحديث ذكره فتنة النساء التي ذكرها في حديث أبي عثمان النهدي وذكر فتنة الدنيا وفيها الفتنة بالمال المذكورة في حديث كعب بن عياض والفتن بما سوى ذلك والله الموفق

Abū Nuʿaym narrated from Ibn Masʿūd ؓ that a man <stood while the Prophet ﷺ was speaking and> said, "Messenger of Allah, the hyenas have devoured us!" He meant a year of drought. <People shoved him until he fell. Then he stood up again and

[508]Narrated from Abū Saʿīd al-Khudrī by Muslim and others and, without the last sentence, al-Tirmidhī and Aḥmad.

called out. Finally> the Prophet ﷺ replied: [382] "For my part I fear other than the hyenas for you. I fear the world pouring down on you like rain. <So would that my Umma did not wear gold.>"[509]

عَنْ أَبِي ذَرٍّ رَضِيَ اللهُ عَنْهُ قَالَ قَامَ رَجُلٌ وَرَسُولُ اللهِ ﷺ يَخْطُبُ
فَقَالَ يَا رَسُولَ اللهِ أَكَلَتْنَا الضُّبُعُ أَيِ السَّنَةُ قَالَ فَدَفَعَهُ النَّاسُ
حَتَّى وَقَعَ ثُمَّ قَامَ أَيْضًا فَنَادَى بِصَوْتِهِ ثُمَّ الْتَفَتَ إِلَيْهِ رَسُولُ اللهِ
ﷺ عِنْدَ ذَلِكَ فَقَالَ أَخْوَفُ عَلَيْكُمْ عِنْدِي مِنْ ذَلِكَ أَنْ تُصَبَّ
عَلَيْكُمُ الدُّنْيَا صَبًّا فَلَيْتَ أُمَّتِي لاَ يَلْبَسُونَ الذَّهَبَ ش ط حم طس
ز أبو نعيم في الدلائل الحارث هب ض

Abū Dāwūd narrated from Ibn Mas'ūd ؓ that the Prophet ﷺ said: [383] "Victory is yours, much booty and many conquests. Whoever among you sees that day, let him fear Allah! Let him command good and forbid evil!"[510]

عَنْ عَبْدِ اللهِ بنِ مَسْعُودٍ يحدّثُ عن أَبِيهِ قَالَ سَمِعْتُ رَسُولَ اللهِ
ﷺ يَقُولُ إِنَّكُمْ مَنْصُورُونَ وَمُصِيبُونَ وَمَفْتُوحٌ لَكُمْ فَمَنْ أَدرَكَ
ذَلِكَ مِنْكُمْ فَلْيَتَّقِ اللهَ وَلْيَأْمُرْ بِالْمَعْرُوفِ وَلْيَنْهَ عَنِ المنْكَرِ وَمَنْ

[509]The *Khaṣā'iṣ* and al-Nabhānī omit the bracketed passages. Narrated from Abū Dharr by Ibn Abī Shayba (7:85 §34385) with a sound chain and by Aḥmad, al-Ṭabarānī in *al-Awsaṭ* (9:166 §9437), al-Bazzār (9:396 §3984), al-Ḥārith in his *Musnad* (2:616 §586), al-Ṭayālisī in his (p. 60 §447), and al-Bayhaqī in *Shu'ab al-Īmān* (7:282 §10315), all six with the same chain through Yazīd b. Abī Zyād – al-Tirmidhī considered his narrations fair. Al-Ṭabarānī narrates something similar from Hudhayfa in *al-Awsat* (9:166 §9437) and from Abū al-Dardā' with weak chains cf. al-Haythamī. The expression "The hyenas have devoured us" means "We have suffered a year of drought that left us so weak the hyenas now prey on us" cf. *Majma' al-Amthāl* (§2805) and *al-Nihāya* (*s.v. ḍ-b-'*).

[510]Narrated from Ibn Mas'ūd by al-Tirmidhī *(ḥasan ṣaḥīḥ)* and Aḥmad, both with the ending: "And whoever lies about me, let him take his seat in the Fire" while one version in Aḥmad adds: "And let each respect his family ties" as does Abū Ya'lā (9:205 §5304).

يَكْذِبْ عَلَيَّ مُتَعَمِّداً فَلْيَتَبَوَّأْ مَقْعَدَهُ مِنَ النَّارِ   ت حم ك ويروى
بزيادة وَلْيَصِلْ رَحِمَهُ حم ع

Muslim and others narrated from Thawbān that the Messenger of Allah ﷺ said: [384] "Allah has folded up the earth for me so that I saw it from east to west. Truly, my Community's dominion shall reach all that I saw. [a] I was granted the two treasures, the red and the white [gold and silver]. [b] I begged my Lord that my Umma not be destroyed by famine, nor be dominated by a foreign enemy – other than themselves – who will violate their hearth *(fa-yastabīḥ bayḍatahum)*. My Lord ﷻ said: 'Muḥammad, when I decree something none repels it! I have granted you for your Umma that I shall not destroy it by famine nor impose over them a foreign enemy – other than themselves – who will violate their most sacred home, even if all the regions of the world joined together against them, until they themselves destroy one another <and take each other prisoners>.'"[511]

عَنْ ثَوْبَانَ رَضِيَ اللهُ عَنْهُ قَالَ قَالَ رَسُولُ اللهِ ﷺ إِنَّ اللهَ زَوَى
لِي الأَرْضَ فَرَأَيْتُ مَشَارِقَهَا وَمَغَارِبَهَا وَإِنَّ مُلْكَ أُمَّتِي سَيَبْلُغُ مَا
زُوِيَ لِي مِنْهَا وَأُعْطِيتُ الْكَنْزَيْنِ الأَحْمَرَ وَالأَبْيَضَ وَإِنِّي سَأَلْتُ
رَبِّي لأُمَّتِي أَنْ لاَ يُهْلِكَهَا بِسَنَةٍ عَامَّةٍ وَأَنْ لاَ يُسَلِّطَ عَلَيْهِمْ عَدُوّاً
مِنْ سِوَى أَنْفُسِهِمْ فَيَسْتَبِيحَ بَيْضَتَهُمْ وَإِنَّ رَبِّي قَالَ يَا مُحَمَّدُ إِنِّي
إِذَا قَضَيْتُ قَضَاءً فَإِنَّهُ لاَ يُرَدُّ وَإِنِّي أَعْطَيْتُكَ لأُمَّتِكَ أَنْ لاَ
أُهْلِكَهُمْ بِسَنَةٍ عَامَّةٍ وَأَنْ لاَ أُسَلِّطَ عَلَيْهِمْ عَدُوّاً مِنْ سِوَى

[511]Narrated from Thawbān by Muslim, Tirmidhī *(ḥasan ṣaḥīḥ)*, Abū Dāwūd, Ibn Mājah, and Aḥmad. "Their hearth" is their society, the seat of their collective power, their lives, and the center of their Religion cf. *Sharḥ Ṣaḥīḥ Muslim* and *al-Nihāya fī Gharīb al-Athar*.

أَنْفُسِهِمْ يَسْتَبِيحُ بَيْضَتَهُمْ وَلَوِ اجْتَمَعَ عَلَيْهِمْ مَنْ بِأَقْطَارِهَا أَوْ قَالَ مَنْ بَيْنَ أَقْطَارِهَا حَتَّى يَكُونَ بَعْضُهُمْ يُهْلِكُ بَعْضاً وَيَسْبِي بَعْضُهُمْ بَعْضاً م ت د جه حم

Abū Nuʿaym narrated that ʿAbd Allāh b. Yazīd [b. Zayd al-Khaṭmī al-Anṣārī] was once invited to a meal; when he arrived, he saw that the house was furnished *(munajjadan)*. He sat outside and wept. Asked why, he replied, "Truly, the Messenger of Allah said: 385 'The world will certainly glut you *(taṭalaʿat ilaykum al-dunyā)* three times. Then he said: [a] 'You are better off today than you will be when a dish for ten *(qaṣʿatun)* is served to you in the morning and another is served to you in the evening; when one of you wears a tunic in the morning and a different tunic in the evening; and when you decorate your houses the way you decorate the Kaʿba.' Should I not weep when I can see you decorating your houses the way you decorate the Kaʿba?"[512]

عَنْ مُحَمَّدِ بْنِ كَعْبٍ قَالَ دُعِيَ عَبْدُ اللهِ بْنُ يَزِيدَ إِلَى طَعَامٍ فَلَمَّا جَاءَ رَأَى الْبَيْتَ مُنَجَّدًا فَقَعَدَ خَارِجًا وَبَكَى قَالَ فَقِيلَ لَهُ مَا يُبْكِيكَ قَالَ كَانَ رَسُولُ اللهِ ﷺ إِذَا شَيَّعَ جَيْشًا فَبَلَغَ عَقَبَةَ الْوَدَاعِ قَالَ أَسْتَوْدِعُ اللهَ دِينَكُمْ وَأَمَانَاتِكُمْ وَخَوَاتِيمَ أَعْمَالِكُمْ قَالَ فَرَأَى رَجُلاً ذَاتَ يَوْمٍ قَدْ رَقَّعَ بُرْدَةً لَهُ بِقِطْعَةٍ قَالَ فَاسْتَقْبَلَ مَطْلِعَ الشَّمْسِ وَقَالَ هَكَذَا وَمَدَّ يَدَيْهِ وَقَالَ تَطَالَعَتْ عَلَيْكُمْ

---

[512] Narrated from Muhammad b. Kaʿb al-Quraẓī by Aḥmad in *al-Zuhd* (p. 197), Ibn Qāniʿ in *Muʿjam al-Ṣaḥāba* (2:113-114 §570), and al-Bayhaqī in the *Sunan* (7:272) and *al-Ādāb* (p. 217 §657) cf. *Siyar* (Risāla ed. 21:436), *al-Mughnī* (Fikr ed. 7:217), note 455 §5, and hadiths at notes 457 and 489.

الدُّنْيَا ثَلاَثَ مَرَّاتٍ أَىْ أَقْبَلَتْ حَتَّى ظَنَنَّا أَنْ يَقَعَ عَلَيْنَا ثُمَّ قَالَ
أَنْتُمُ الْيَوْمَ خَيْرٌ أَمْ إِذَا غَدَتْ عَلَيْكُمْ قَصْعَةٌ وَرَاحَتْ أُخْرَى
وَيَغْدُو أَحَدُكُمْ فِى حُلَّةٍ وَيَرُوحُ فِى أُخْرَى وَتَسْتُرُونَ بُيُوتَكُمْ كَمَا
تُسْتَرُ الْكَعْبَةُ فَقَالَ عَبْدُ اللهِ بْنُ يَزِيدَ أَفَلاَ أَبْكِى وَقَدْ بَقِيتُ حَتَّى
تَسْتُرُونَ بُيُوتَكُمْ كَمَا تُسْتَرُ الْكَعْبَةُ أحمد في الزهد ابن قانع هق وفي الآداب

[Some versions add: "Truly, b I fear for my Community misguiding leaders. c When the sword is thrust at my Community it will not be lifted from them until the Day of Judgment. d The Hour will not rise until entire tribes of my Community join the pagans and until entire tribes of my Community worship the idols. Truly, e there will be in my Community thirty arch-liars, all claiming that he or she is a Prophet; but f I am the Seal of Prophets: there is no Prophet after me! And g there will not cease to be a group in my Community that follows truth – one narrator added: and will be victorious. Those who oppose them cannot harm them in the least, and so until the command of Allah comes."[513]]

Imām Aḥmad, al-Ḥākim – he declared it *ṣaḥīḥ* – and al-Bayhaqī narrated from Ṭalḥa al-Naḍrī that the Prophet ﷺ said: 386 "You might reach a time in which a dish for ten will be served to each of you in the morning and another in the evening; and you will wear garments [as luxurious] as the ones hanging on the Ka'ba." <They asked, "Messenger of Allah, are we better off now or will be better off then?" He said: "Nay! a Today, you love one another, but that day, you will hate one another and strike one another's necks!">[514]

[513]In Abū Dāwūd, Ibn Mājah, and Aḥmad.

[514]Narrated from Ṭalḥa b. 'Amr al-Naḍrī or al-Baṣrī (which Shaykh Aḥmad Shākir said is the correct spelling in *Tahdhīb al-Āthār*) or al-Naṣrī – he was from the *Ahl al-Suffa* – (without the bracketed segment) by Aḥmad, al-Bazzār with a sound chain (*Zawā'id* §3673), al-Ṭabarānī in *al-Kabīr* (8:371 §8160), Hannād in *al-Zuhd* (2:395), Ibn al-Aʿrābī in his *Muʿjam* (1:348-349 §668), Abū Nuʿaym (1:374-375) and in the *Maʿrifa*, Ḥammād b. Isḥāq, *Tarikat al-Nabī* ﷺ, ed. Akram Ḍiyā' al-ʿUmarī (p. 57-58), al-Fākihī, *Akhbār Makka* (3:94-95), Ibn Ḥibbān (15:77-78 §6684), al-Taymī, *Dalā'il al-Nubuwwa* (p. 116), al-Khaṭīb, *Muwaḍḍiḥ Awhām al-Jamʿ wal-Tafrīq* (1:498-499); (with the bracketed segment) Ibn Abī ʿĀṣim in *al-Āḥād* (3:112 §1434), Aḥmad in *al-Zuhd*, al-Ḥākim (1990 ed. 3:16, 4:591 *isnād ṣaḥīḥ*) and in *Maʿrifat ʿUlūm al-Ḥadīth* (p. 225), Ibn Bishrān in his *Amālī* 1:185 §426), and al-Bayhaqī, *Sunan* (2:445), *Shuʿab* (7:284 §10325), and *Dalā'il*

عَنْ طَلْحَةَ رَضِيَ اللهُ عَنْهُ قَالَ قَالَ رَسُولُ اللهِ ﷺ أَمَا إِنَّكُمْ تُوشِكُونَ أَنْ تُدْرِكُوا وَمَنْ أَدْرَكَ ذَلِكَ مِنْكُمْ أَنْ يُرَاحَ عَلَيْكُمْ بِالْجِفَانِ وَتَلْبَسُونَ مِثْلَ أَسْتَارِ الْكَعْبَةِ حم ز طب هناد في الزهد مسند الروياني الطبري في تهذيب الآثار ويروى بلفظ يُغْدَى وَيُرَاحُ عَلَيْكُمْ بِالْجِفَانِ الطبري حب ك معجم ابن الأعرابي حل وفي المعرفة التيمي في الدلائل وجاء بزيادة قَالُوا يَا رَسُولَ اللهِ أَنَحْنُ يَوْمَئِذٍ خَيْرٌ أَوِ الْيَوْمَ قَالَ لَا بَلْ أَنْتُمُ الْيَوْمَ خَيْرٌ مِنْكُمْ يَوْمَئِذٍ أَنْتُمُ الْيَوْمَ إِخْوَانٌ وَأَنْتُمْ يَوْمَئِذٍ يَضْرِبُ بَعْضُكُمْ رِقَابَ بَعْضٍ ابن أبي عاصم في الآحاد حم في الزهد والورع الطبري في الآثار المعرفة والتاريخ ك هق هب وفي الدلائل وعندهما أيضا أَنْتُمْ مُتَحَابُّونَ وَأَنْتُمْ يَوْمَئِذٍ مُتَبَاغِضُونَ ك هب والجفان جمع جَفْنَة وهي القصعة قال في الحماسة

تَرَى الْجِفَانَ مِنَ الشِّيزَى مُكَلَّلَةً * قُدَّامَهُ زَانَهَا التَّشْرِيفُ وَالْكَرَمُ

الشيزى خشب يصنع منه الجفان وتكليل الجفان جعلها مغطاة بقطع كبار من اللحم وقوله زانها الخ يريد ما يستعمله من اللطف

The Two Masters [al-Bukhārī and Muslim] narrated that Jābir said: "The Messenger of Allah said: 387 'Do you have fringed rugs *(anmāṭ)*?' I said, 'Messenger of Allah, how can I own fringed rugs?' He replied: a 'You will own fringed rugs.' Now, I tell my wife, 'Remove your rugs from my way,' but she replies,

---

(6:524). Al-Ṭabarī narrates both versions in *Tahdhīb al-Āthār* (*Musnad 'Umar* 2:707-710 §1029-1030) cf. *Iṣāba* (3:534), *Istī'āb* (3:965), *Mukhtāra* (8:146-147), and al-Muhibb al-Ṭabarī, *al-Ryāḍ al-Naḍira* (1:459-460 §381-382) through trustworthy narrators cf. *Fatḥ al-Bārī* (7:237) and al-Haythamī (10:322).

'Did not the Messenger of Allah ﷺ say, You will have rugs after my time?'"[515]

عَنْ جَابِرٍ رَضِيَ اللهُ عَنْهُ قَالَ قَالَ النَّبِيُّ ﷺ هَلْ لَكُمْ مِنْ أَنْمَاطٍ قُلْتُ وَأَنَّى يَكُونُ لَنَا الْأَنْمَاطُ قَالَ أَمَا إِنَّهُ سَيَكُونُ لَكُمْ الْأَنْمَاطُ فَأَنَا أَقُولُ لَهَا يَعْنِي امْرَأَتَهُ أَخِّرِي عَنِّي أَنْمَاطَكِ فَتَقُولُ أَلَمْ يَقُلْ النَّبِيُّ ﷺ إِنَّهَا سَتَكُونُ لَكُمْ الْأَنْمَاطُ فَأَدَعُهَا ق ت د ن والأنماط ضرب من البسط له خمل رقيق واحدها نمطٌ

The Two Masters also narrated from ʿAmr b. ʿAwf رضي الله عنه that the Prophet ﷺ said: "By Allah! 388 I do not fear poverty for you but I fear for you that the world be spread open for you **[528]** as it was spread open for those before you, so that you will compete as they competed and it will distract you as it distracted them *(wa-tulhiakum kamā alhat-hum)*."[516] [Some versions have: "and it will destroy you as it destroyed them *(wa-tuhlikakum kamā ahlakat-hum)*."][517]

عَنْ عَمْرِو بْنِ عَوْفٍ رَضِيَ اللهُ عَنْهُ تَبَسَّمَ رَسُولُ اللهِ ﷺ حِينَ رَآهُمْ أي الْأَنْصَارَ وَقَالَ وَاللهِ مَا الْفَقْرَ أَخْشَى عَلَيْكُمْ وَلَكِنْ أَخْشَى عَلَيْكُمْ أَنْ تُبْسَطَ عَلَيْكُمْ الدُّنْيَا كَمَا بُسِطَتْ عَلَى مَنْ كَانَ قَبْلَكُمْ فَتَنَافَسُوهَا كَمَا تَنَافَسُوهَا وَتُلْهِيَكُمْ كَمَا أَلْهَتْهُمْ ق حم طب الأخير بلفظ وَيُلْهِيَكُمْ وعنه وَتُهْلِكَكُمْ كَمَا أَهْلَكَتْهُمْ ق حم

[515]Narrated from Jābir by al-Bukhārī, Muslim, al-Tirmidhī, al-Nasā'ī, and Abū Dāwūd.

[516]Narrated from ʿAmr b. ʿAwf al-Anṣārī by al-Bukhārī, Muslim, and Aḥmad.

[517]In al-Bukhārī, Muslim, and others.

في الزهد طب ومسند الشاميين الآحاد والمثاني ابن أبي الدنيا في الزهد وذم الدنيا مشكل الآثار ن في الكبرى هق في الآداب

His ﷺ Foretelling the Caliphs After Him Then the Kings

Muslim narrated from Abū Hurayra ﵁ that the Prophet ﷺ said: [389] "The Israelites were ruled by Prophets. Every time one of them died, another succeeded him. Truly, [a] there is no Prophet after me! There will be successors *(khulafā')*, and many of them!" They asked, "What do you order us to do?" He replied: [b] "Be true *(fū)* to the pledge made to the first then the first one after him. Give them their due right. Then Allah shall ask them about the rule which he entrusted to them."[518]

عَنْ أَبِي حَازِمٍ قَالَ قَاعَدْتُ أَبَا هُرَيْرَةَ ﵁ خَمْسَ سِنِينَ فَسَمِعْتُهُ يُحَدِّثُ عَنِ النَّبِيِّ ﷺ قَالَ كَانَتْ بَنُو إِسْرَائِيلَ تَسُوسُهُمُ الأَنْبِيَاءُ كُلَّمَا هَلَكَ نَبِيٌّ خَلَفَهُ نَبِيٌّ وَإِنَّهُ لاَ نَبِيَّ بَعْدِي وَسَتَكُونُ خُلَفَاءُ فَتَكْثُرُ قَالُوا فَمَا تَأْمُرُنَا قَالَ فُوْا بِبَيْعَةِ الأَوَّلِ فَالأَوَّلِ وَأَعْطُوهُمْ حَقَّهُمْ فَإِنَّ اللهَ سَائِلُهُمْ عَمَّا اسْتَرْعَاهُمْ ق حم هق وفي الصغرى والدلائل شرح السنة كر في معجم الشيوخ وجاء بلفظ أَوْفُوْا جه ش ع حب

Muslim narrated that Jābir b. Samura ﵄ said, "I heard the Messenger of Allah ﷺ say <on the day of Jumu'a, on the eve of the lapidation of al-Aslamī>: [390] 'The Religion will not cease to be strong until <the rising of the Hour of Judgment or until> twelve caliphs first rule over you, all of them from the Quraysh.' <And I heard him say: [a] 'A small band *('uṣaybatun)* of Muslims will conquer the White House – the house of Chosroes or of his family.'

[518]Narrated from Abū Hurayra by al-Bukhārī, Muslim, Ibn Mājah, Aḥmad, and others.

And I heard him say:> b 'There will be arch-liars just before the Hour <so beware of them!' And I heard him say: c 'When Allah gives one of you material goods, let him begin with himself and his dependants.' And I heard him say: d 'I am the scout at the Basin.'"519

عَنْ جَابِرِ بْنِ سَمُرَةَ سَمِعْتُ رَسُولَ اللهِ ﷺ يَوْمَ جُمُعَةٍ عَشِيَّةَ رُجِمَ الأَسْلَمِيُّ يَقُولُ لَا يَزَالُ الدِّينُ قَائِماً حَتَّى تَقُومَ السَّاعَةُ أَوْ يَكُونَ عَلَيْكُمُ اثْنَا عَشَرَ خَلِيفَةً كُلُّهُمْ مِنْ قُرَيْشٍ وَسَمِعْتُهُ يَقُولُ عُصَيْبَةٌ مِنَ الْمُسْلِمِينَ يَفْتَتِحُونَ الْبَيْتَ الأَبْيَضَ بَيْتَ كِسْرَى أَوْ آلِ كِسْرَى وَسَمِعْتُهُ يَقُولُ إِنَّ بَيْنَ يَدَيِ السَّاعَةِ كَذَّابِينَ فَاحْذَرُوهُمْ وَسَمِعْتُهُ يَقُولُ إِذَا أَعْطَى اللهُ أَحَدَكُمْ خَيْراً فَلْيَبْدَأْ بِنَفْسِهِ وَأَهْلِ بَيْتِهِ وَسَمِعْتُهُ يَقُولُ أَنَا الْفَرَطُ عَلَى الْحَوْضِ م ومثله عند حم وهق في الدلائل بلفظ عِصَابَةٌ مِنَ الْمُسْلِمِينَ وبلفظ فَرَطُكُمْ عَلَى الْحَوْضِ

The Two Masters [al-Bukhārī and Muslim] narrated from Ibn Mas'ūd ؓ that the Messenger of Allah ﷺ said: 391 "There will be [after me] favoritism and things you will find reprehensible." They asked, "What should we do if we live to see this?" He replied: a "Pay the right you owe and ask Allah for the right owed to you."520

519Narrated from Jābir b. Samura by Muslim and Aḥmad. Al-Nabhānī omits the bracketed segments.

520Narrated from Ibn Mas'ūd by al-Bukhārī, Muslim, al-Tirmidhī (ḥasan ṣaḥīḥ), Ahmad and others. On favoritism cf. above, section on the Anṣār (hadiths at notes 235-236).

عَنِ ابْنِ مَسْعُودٍ رَضِيَ اللهُ عَنْهُ عَنِ النَّبِيِّ ﷺ قَالَ سَتَكُونُ أَثَرَةٌ وَأُمُورٌ تُنْكِرُونَهَا قَالُوا يَا رَسُولَ اللهِ فَمَا تَأْمُرُنَا قَالَ تُؤَدُّونَ الْحَقَّ الَّذِي عَلَيْكُمْ وَتَسْأَلُونَ اللهَ الَّذِي لَكُمْ ق ت حم ط ش ع ز طب طص حب هق هب وفي الدلائل وغيرهم

Ibn Mājah, al-Ḥākim, and al-Bayhaqī narrated from al-ʿIrbāḍ b. Sāriya ﷺ: "The Messenger of Allah ﷺ admonished us so intensely that hearts trembled and the eyes wept. They said: 'Messenger of Allah! This seems to be the admonishment of one who bids farewell, therefore, what solemn promise do you require of us?" He replied: 392 "I exhort you to beware of Allah ﷻ! a I exhort you to hear and obey, even if your leader should be a black Abyssinian. Lo! b Whoever of you lives shall see great divisions. c Therefore you must follow my Sunna and the Sunna of the rightly-guided, upright successors after me. Bite upon it with your very jaws! d Beware of newfangled matters: they are misguidance."[521]

[521]Narrated from al-ʿIrbāḍ b. Sāriya by al-Tirmidhī *(ḥasan saḥīḥ)* with four chains [this is his wording], Abū Dāwūd, Ibn Mājah with two chains, Aḥmad – he declared it *saḥīḥ* according to Ibn Rajab – with four chains in his *Musnad* (Arnaʾūṭ ed. 28:367-377 §17142-17147 *saḥīḥ*=Zayn ed. 13:278-280 §17077-17080 *ṣaḥīḥ*), al-Dārimī, Ibn Ḥibbān (1:178-179 §5 *ṣaḥīḥ*), al-Ḥākim with five chains (1:95-97=1990 ed. 1:174-177) – declaring it *saḥīḥ* – and in *al-Madkhal ilā al-Saḥīḥ* (p. 80-81), al-Ājurrī with four chains in *al-Sharīʿa* (p. 54-55 §79-82=p. 46 *ṣaḥīḥ*), Ibn Abī ʿĀṣim in *al-Sunna* (p. 29 §54 *saḥīḥ*), al-Taḥāwī in *Mushkil al-Āthār* (2:69=3:221-224 §1185-1187 *saḥīḥ*), Muḥammad b. Naṣr al-Marwazī with four chains in *al-Sunna* (p. 26-27 §69-72 *saḥīḥ*), al-Ḥārith b. Abī Usāma in his *Musnad* (1:197-198), al-Rūyānī in his *Musnad* (1:439), Abū Nuʿaym who cited it "among the *saḥīḥ* narrations of the people of Shām" in *Ḥilyat al-Awliyāʾ* (1985 ed. 5:220-221, 10:115), al-Ṭabarānī with several chains in *Musnad al-Shāmiyyīn* (1:254, 1:402, 1:446, 2:197, 2:298) and *al-Kabīr* (18:245-257), al-Bayhaqī in *al-Sunan al-Kubrā* (10:114), *al-Madkhal* (p. 115-116), *al-Iʿtiqād* (p. 229), and *Shuʿab al-Īmān* (6:67), al-Baghawī who declared it *ḥasan* in *Sharḥ al-Sunna* (1:205 §102 *isnād saḥīḥ*), Ibn al-Athīr in *Jāmiʿ al-Uṣūl* (1:187, 1:279), Ibn ʿAsākir in *al-Arbaʿīn al-Buldāniyya* (p. 121), Ibn ʿAbd al-Barr in *al-Tamhīd* (21:278-279) and *Jāmiʿ Bayān al-ʿIlm* (2:924 §1758) where he declared it *saḥīḥ*, and others.

عَنِ الْعِرْبَاضِ بْنِ سَارِيَةَ رَضِيَ اللهُ عَنْهُ صَلَّى بِنَا رَسُولُ اللهِ ﷺ الصُّبْحَ ذَاتَ يَوْمٍ ثُمَّ أَقْبَلَ عَلَيْنَا فَوَعَظَنَا مَوْعِظَةً بَلِيغَةً ذَرَفَتْ مِنْهَا الْعُيُونُ وَوَجِلَتْ مِنْهَا الْقُلُوبُ فَقَالَ قَائِلٌ يَا رَسُولَ اللهِ كَأَنَّ هَذِهِ مَوْعِظَةُ مُوَدِّعٍ فَمَاذَا تَعْهَدُ إِلَيْنَا فَقَالَ أُوصِيكُمْ بِتَقْوَى اللهِ وَالسَّمْعِ وَالطَّاعَةِ وَإِنْ كَانَ عَبْدًا حَبَشِيًّا فَإِنَّهُ مَنْ يَعِشْ مِنْكُمْ بَعْدِي فَسَيَرَى اخْتِلَافًا كَثِيرًا فَعَلَيْكُمْ بِسُنَّتِي وَسُنَّةِ الْخُلَفَاءِ الرَّاشِدِينَ الْمَهْدِيِّينَ فَتَمَسَّكُوا بِهَا وَعَضُّوا عَلَيْهَا بِالنَّوَاجِذِ وَإِيَّاكُمْ وَمُحْدَثَاتِ الْأُمُورِ فَإِنَّ كُلَّ مُحْدَثَةٍ بِدْعَةٌ وَكُلَّ بِدْعَةٍ ضَلَالَةٌ ت د جه حم مي ابن أبي عاصم في السنة مشكل الآثار طب وفي مسند الشاميين ك حب مسند الحارث وغيرهم

Ibn ʿAsākir narrated from ʿAbd al-Raḥmān b. Sahl al-Anṣārī al-Ḥārithī [ؓ], a veteran of Uḥud, that the Messenger of Allah ﷺ said: 393 "Never was there Prophethood *(nubuwwa)* but Caliphate *(khilāfa)* followed it; nor was there ever Caliphate but Kingship *(mulk)* followed it; nor was there ever alms *(ṣadaqa)* but it became a tithe *(maks)*."[522]

عَنْ عَبْدِ الرَّحْمَنِ بْنِ سَهْلٍ رَضِيَ اللهُ عَنْهُ قَالَ رَسُولُ اللهِ ﷺ مَا كَانَتْ نُبُوَّةٌ قَطُّ إِلاَّ تَبِعَتْهَا خِلَافَةٌ وَلاَ كَانَتْ خِلَافَةٌ قَطُّ إِلاَّ

[522]Narrated by Ibn Ṭuhmān in his *Mashyakha* (p. 94 §42) and through him Ibn ʿAsākir (34:420-421) as well as Ibn Mandah and Ibn Shāhīn cf. *Iṣāba* (4:313), *Kanz* (§31447, §32246) and *al-Jāmiʿ al-Saghīr* (§7969 *daʿīf*).

تَبِعَهَا مُلْكٌ وَلاَ كَانَتْ صَدَقَةٌ إِلاَّ صَارَتْ مَكْساً ابن طُهْمَان في مشيخته ومن طريقه كر وقال الحافظ في الإصابة أخرجه ابن شاهين وابن منده

[Ibn ʿAsākir narrates that in the time of ʿUthmān, during a military expedition, ʿAbd al-Raḥmān came by a convoy carrying wine-caskets which he proceeded to puncture one by one with his spear. His accusers went to Muʿāwiya – the governor of Syro-Palestine at the time – who said: "Leave him, he is an old man who lost his mind." ʿAbd al-Raḥmān said: "You are lying! By Allah, I have not lost my mind at all but 394 the Messenger of Allah ﷺ forbade us from putting this substance into our bellies and our cups, and I swear a solemn oath by Allah that if I live to see inside Muʿāwiya what I heard from the Messenger of Allah ﷺ I will certainly puncture his belly twice!"][523]

Al-Tirmidhī– he declared it fair–and others narrated from Safīna ؓ that the Messenger of Allah ﷺ said: 395 "Caliphate *(al-khilāfa)* after me shall last for thirty years. Then there will be kingship."[524] This was precisely the duration of the caliphate of the Four with al-Ḥasan:

Abū Bakr al-Ṣiddīq ؓ,	two years, three months, nine days;
ʿUmar ؓ,	ten years, six months, five days;
ʿUthmān ؓ,	eleven years, eleven months, nine days;
ʿAlī ؓ,	four years, nine months, seven days;
Al-Ḥasan ؓ,	six months, totalling thirty years.

عَنْ سَفِينَةَ رَضِيَ اللهُ عَنْهُ قَالَ قَالَ رَسُولُ اللهِ ﷺ الْخِلاَفَةُ فِي أُمَّتِي ثَلاَثُونَ عَاماً ثُمَّ يَكُونُ مُلْكٌ ط وجاء بلفظ الْخِلاَفَةُ فِي أُمَّتِي ثَلاَثُونَ سَنَةً ثُمَّ مُلْكٌ بَعْدَ ذَلِكَ ت قال حديث حسن حم ن في الكبرى ز

[523]Narrated by Ibn ʿAsākir (34:420) cf. *Fayd al-Qadīr* (5:462 §7969).

[524]A sound ḥadīth narrated from Safīna by al-Tirmidhī *(ḥasan)* with a fair chain according to ʿAbd Allāh al-Talīdī who declared the ḥadīth itself *ṣaḥīḥ* because of its corroborative and witness-chains cf. his *Tahdhīb al-Khasāʾis* (p. 293 §375); also narrated by al-Nasāʾī, Abū Dāwūd with a fair chain and al-Bazzār with a fair chain as indicated by al-Haythamī, Aḥmad with two chains; al-Ḥākim; Ibn Ḥibbān with two fair chains as stated by al-Arnaʾūṭ (15:34 §6657, 15:392 §6943); al-Ṭayālisī in his *Musnad* (p. 151, 479); and al-Ṭabarānī in *al-Kabīr* with several chains.

ابن أبي عاصم في السّنّة طب هق في المدخل والإعتقاد والدلائل كر وفي المعجم شرح السّنّة وجاء بلفظ **الْخِلاَفَةُ ثَلاَثُونَ سَنَةً ثُمَّ يَكُونُ بَعْدَ ذَلِكَ مُلْكاً** ابن أبي عاصم في السّنّة والآحاد وبلفظ **ثُمَّ تَكُونُ مُلْكاً** طب مسند ابن الجعد كر في المعجم شرح السنّة وبلفظ **ثَلاثُونَ عَاماً** حم وفي فضائل الصحابة مشكل الآثار ابن راهويه عد الروياني أو **الْخِلاَفَةُ بَعْدِي ثَلاَثُونَ سَنَةً ثُمَّ تَكُونُ مُلْكاً** ز حب أو **ثَلاثُونَ عَاماً** نوادر الأصول ك خط في المتفق والمفترق وبلفظ **خِلافَةُ النُّبُوَّةِ ثَلاثُونَ سَنَةً ثُمَّ يُؤْتِي اللهُ المُلْكَ مَنْ يَشاءُ** د مشكل الآثار طب ك شرح السّنّة هق في الإعتقاد والدلائل وعند أكثرهم زيادة **ثُمَّ قَالَ** أي سَفِينَةُ أو سَعِيدُ بْنُ جُهْمَانَ **أَمْسِكْ عَلَيْكَ خِلاَفَةَ أَبِي بَكْرٍ ثُمَّ قَالَ وَخِلاَفَةَ عُمَرَ وَخِلاَفَةَ عُثْمانَ ثُمَّ قَالَ أَمْسِكْ خِلاَفَةَ عَلِيٍّ قال فَوَجَدْنَاهَا ثَلاَثِينَ سَنَةً** وقال هق في الدلائل خلافة أبي بكر كانت سنتين وأربعة أشهر إلا عشر ليال وخلافة عمر عشر سنين وستة أشهر وأربعة أيام وخلافة عثمان اثنتي عشرة سنة إلا اثني عشر يوما وعلي رضي الله عنه خمس سنين إلا ثلاثة أشهر اه. وأما قول القاضي ابن العربي المالكي في العواصم من القواصم (هذا حديث لا يصح) فلعله قاله تقليدا لابن خلدون في تاريخه فلا يلتفت إليه وقد جاء في (تاريخ أبي زرعة) قال أبو زرعة الدمشقي سألت أحمد بن حنبل عن حديث سفينة الخلافة بعدي ثلاثون سنة يثبت قال نعم وفي (المنتخب من علل الخلال) قال المروذي ذكرت لأبي عبد الله حديث سفينة فصححه وقال هو صحيح وقال أبو عمر ابن عبد البر في (جامع بيان العلم وفضله) قال أحمد بن حنبل حديث سفينة في الخلافة صحيح وإليه أذهب في الخلفاء

[This narration is among the shining proofs of Prophethood *(dalā'il al-nubuwwa)* as the sum of the first five caliphates is exactly thirty years while al-Dhahabī cites the saying by Mu'āwiya: 396 "I am the first of the kings" *(anā awwalu al-mulūk)*.[525] Ibn Rajab in *Jāmi' al-'Ulūm wal-Ḥikam* said that Imam Aḥmad declared Safīna's narration sound and that he adduced it as a proof for the caliphate of the four Imams.[526] This count is attributed to Safīna himself by Imam al-Qurṭubī.[527]

Yet Ibn al-'Arabī al-Mālikī weakened Safīna's hadīth in *al-'Awāsim* to pre-empt the claim that the thirty year-span includes al-Ḥasan's successorship after 'Alī, whereas al-Ḥasan, after 'Alī's murder, pledged fealty *(bay'a)* to Mu'āwiya in the year 41 as stated by al-Suyūṭī in *Tārīkh al-Khulafā'*.[528] Al-Ḥasan's pledge was foretold by the Prophet ﷺ in his hadīth from the pulpit with al-Ḥasan by his side: "Truly, this son of mine – al-Ḥasan – is a leader of men *(sayyid)*, and Allah may put him in a position to reconcile two great factions of the Muslims."[529] Ibn al-'Arabī further rejects the authenticity of the thirty-year hadīth on the basis of the Divine praise of kingship and its synonymity with Prophethood in the verse ❨**And Allah gave him** [Dāwūd ﷺ] **the kingdom and wisdom**❩ (2:251).[530] Another purported proof against the authenticity of the thirty-year hadīth is the stronger hadīth just cited above: "Verily, this matter shall not end until there come to pass among them twelve Caliphs, all from Quraysh."

However, none of these three purported counter-proofs actually contradicts the thirty-year hadīth, as pointed out by Imam al-Nawawī, Ibn Ḥajar and others.[531] The twelve caliphs according to al-Suyūṭī are the Four Rightly-Guided Caliphs, then Mu'āwiya after al-Ḥasan's pledge to him, then his son Yazīd, then 'Abd al-Mālik b. Marwān, then the latter's four sons al-Walīd, Sulaymān, Yazīd, and Hishām, then al-Walīd b. Yazīd b. 'Abd al-Mālik.[532] In strict terms only the Four Rightly-Guided Caliphs and al-Ḥasan represent the *khilāfa nubuwwa* mentioned in the hadith of Safīna,[533] and "the Sunna is not to call Mu'āwiya a caliph but a king."[534]

Safīna ؓ (d. 71) was the Prophet's ﷺ freedman whose name was Mahrān. One day, when the Prophet ﷺ saw him carrying all his comrades' belongings, the Prophet ﷺ said to him: 397 "Today you are none other than a ship *(safīna)*" *(mā kunta al-yawma*

---

[525]Cf. *Tārīkh al-Khulafā'* (p. 22, 198-199); al-Talīdī, *Tahdhīb al-Khaṣā'is* (p. 293 §375); *Siyar* (3:157).

[526]Cf. 'Abd Allāh b. Aḥmad b. Ḥanbal, *al-Sunna* (p. 235-236 §1276-1277) and Ibn Ḥajar, *Fatḥ al-Bārī* (1959 ed. 7:58 §3494).

[527]Cf. al-Qurṭubī in his *Tafsīr* (12:298) and al-'Aẓīm Ābādī in *'Awn al-Ma'būd* (12:260).

[528]Ibn al-'Arabī, *'Awāsim min al-Qawāsim* (p. 201); Suyūṭī, *Tārīkh al-Khulafā'* (p. 199).

[529]See hadīth at note 138 above.

[530]Ibn al-'Arabī, *'Awāṣim* (p. 210)

[531]Nawawī, *Sharḥ Ṣaḥīḥ Muslim* (1972 ed. 12:201); Ibn Ḥajar, *Fatḥ* (13:212); Munāwī as cited in Mubārakfūrī, *Tuḥfat al-Aḥwadhī* (6:396); 'Aẓīmābādī, *'Awn al-Ma'būd* (11:245).

[532]Al-Suyūṭī, *Tārīkh al-Khulafā'* (p. 24). Al-'Aẓīm Ābādī (12:253) recommends in this chapter Shāh Walī Allāh al-Dihlawī's two books *Izālat al-Khafā' 'an Khilāfat al-Khulafā'* and *Qurrat al-'Aynayn fī Tafḍīl al-Shaykhayn*.

[533]Ibn Ḥajar, *Fatḥ* (13:212).

[534]Ibn Kathīr, *Bidāya* (8:144).

illā safīna).[535] When Safīna alighted on a desert island after a shipwreck and saw a lion he said: 398 "Lion! I am Safīna, the freedman of the Messenger of Allah ﷺ," whereupon the lion showed him the way and muttered something. Safīna said: "I believe he meant *salām*."[536]]

Al-Bayhaqī narrated that Abū Bakrah ؓ said, "I heard the Messenger of Allah ﷺ say: 399 'The successorship of Prophethood *(khilāfat al-nubuwwa)* will last for thirty years, after which Allah will give kingship to whomever He will.'"[537] Muʿāwiya said [when Abū Bakrah kept narrating this ḥadīth to him]: a "We are satisfied with kingdom."[538]

عَنْ عَبْدِ الرَّحْمَنِ بْنِ أَبِي بَكْرَةَ عَنْ أَبِيهِ قَالَ سَمِعْتُ رَسُولَ اللهِ
ﷺ يَقُولُ خِلاَفَةُ النُّبُوَّةِ ثَلاَثِينَ عَاماً ثُمَّ يُؤْتِي اللهُ المُلْكَ مَنْ
يَشَاءُ فَقَالَ مُعَاوِيَةُ قَدْ رَضِينَا بِالْمُلْكِ هق في الدلائل وتمام لفظه
وَفَدْنَا إِلَى مُعَاوِيَةَ مَعَ زِيَادٍ وَمَعَنَا أَبُو بَكْرَةَ فَدَخَلْنَا عَلَيْهِ فَقَالَ لَهُ
مُعَاوِيَةُ حَدِّثْنَا حَدِيثًا سَمِعْتَهُ مِنْ رَسُولِ اللهِ ﷺ أَنْ يَنْفَعَنَا بِهِ
قَالَ نَعَمْ كَانَ نَبِيُّ اللهِ ﷺ تُعْجِبُهُ الرُّؤْيَا الصَّالِحَةُ وَيَسْأَلُ عَنْهَا
فَقَالَ رَسُولُ اللهِ ﷺ ذَاتَ يَوْمٍ أَيُّكُم رَأَى رُؤْيَا فَقَالَ رَجُلٌ أنا يَا
رَسُولَ اللهِ إِنِّي رَأَيْتُ رُؤْيَا رَأَيْتُ كَأَنَّ مِيزَانًا دُلِّيَ مِنَ السَّمَاءِ
فَوُزِنْتَ أَنْتَ وَأَبُو بَكْرٍ فَرَجَحْتَ بِأَبِي بَكْرٍ ثُمَّ وُزِنَ أَبُو بَكْرٍ

[535]Narrated from Safīna by Aḥmad in his *Musnad* with a fair chain and others.

[536]Narrated by al-Mizzī in *Tahdhīb al-Kamāl* (7:388) and al-Dhahabī in the *Siyar* (4:324).

[537]Narrated from ʿAbd al-Raḥmān b. Abī Bakrah, from Abū Bakrah by Aḥmad with three chains, Abū Dāwūd in his *Sunan*, al-Ṭayālisī (§866), Ibn Abī Shayba (11:60-61, 12:18-19), Ibn Abī ʿĀṣim in *al-Sunna* (§1131-1136), al-Bazzār (§3652), al-Ṭaḥāwī in *Sharh Mushkil al-Āthār* (§3348), al-Bayhaqī in *Dalā'il al-Nubuwwa* (6:342) and *al-Iʿtiqād* (p. 364).

[538]Narrated from ʿAbd al-Raḥmān b. Abī Bakrah by al-Ṭayālisī and Aḥmad.

بِعُمَرَ فَوَزَنَ أَبُو بَكْرٍ عُمَرَ ثُمَّ وُزِنَ عُمَرُ بِعُثْمَانَ فَرَجَحَ عُمَرُ بِعُثْمَانَ ثُمَّ رُفِعَ الْمِيزَانُ فَاسْتَاءَ لَهَا رَسُولُ اللهِ ﷺ ثُمَّ قَالَ خِلاَفَةُ نُبُوَّةٍ ثُمَّ يُؤْتِي اللهُ الْمُلْكَ مَنْ يَشَاءُ فَغَضِبَ مُعَاوِيَةُ وَزُخَّ فِي أَقْفَائِنَا فَأُخْرِجْنَا فَقَالَ زِيَادٌ لأَبِي بَكْرَةَ مَا وَجَدْتَ مِنْ حَدِيثِ رَسُولِ اللهِ ﷺ حَدِيثًا تُحَدِّثُ بِهِ غَيْرَ هَذَا فَقَالَ وَاللهِ لاَ أُحَدِّثُهُ إِلاَّ بِهِ حَتَّى أُفَارِقَهُ قَالَ فَلَمْ يَزَلْ زِيَادٌ يَطْلُبُ الإِذْنَ حَتَّى أُذِنَ لَنَا فَأُدْخِلْنَا فَقَالَ مُعَاوِيَةُ يَا أَبَا بَكْرَةَ حَدِّثْنَا بِحَدِيثٍ عَنْ رَسُولِ اللهِ ﷺ أَنْ يَنْفَعَنَا بِهِ قَالَ فَحَدَّثَهُ أَيْضًا بِمِثْلِ حَدِيثِهِ الأَوَّلِ فَقَالَ مُعَاوِيَةُ لاَ أَبَاً لَكَ تُخْبِرُنَا أَنْ نَكُونَ مُلُوكًا فَقَدْ رَضِينَا أَنْ نَكُونَ مُلُوكًا ط حم ونحوه عند ش د ز مشكل الآثار ابن أبي عاصم في السنّة كر وعقب ابن كثير في البداية والنهاية على قول معاوية بقوله والسنة أن يقال لمعاوية ملك ولا يقال له خليفة لحديث سفينة

Al-Bayhaqī narrated from Ḥudhayfa ؓ that the Messenger of Allah ﷺ said: [400] "There will be Prophethood among you for as long as Allah wishes. He will lift it up when He wishes. Then [a] there will be caliphate after the pattern *(minhāj)* of Prophethood for as long as Allah wishes. He will lift it up when He wishes. <Then [b] there will be a trying kingship *(mulkan ʿāḍḍan)* for as long as Allah wishes it to be. He will lift it up when He wishes.> Then [c] there will be <a tyrannical kingship *(mulkan jabriyyatan)*> for as long as Allah wishes. He will lift it up when He wishes. Then [d] there will be caliphate after the pattern of Prophethood."[539] When ʿUmar b.

[539]A sound-chained ḥadīth narrated from Ḥudhayfa b. al-Yamān by Aḥmad (al-Zayn ed. 14:163 §18319 *isnād ṣaḥīḥ*=al-Arna'ūṭ 30:355-357 §18406 *isnād ḥasan*), Ṭayālisī in his

al-'Azīz was made ruler, this ḥadīth was mentioned to him and he was told: "We believe and hope that you have come **[529]** after tyranny." He was pleased to hear this.[540]

عَنْ حُذَيْفَةَ رَضِيَ اللهُ عَنْهُ قَالَ رَسُولُ اللهِ ﷺ تَكُونُ فِيكُمْ النُّبُوَّةُ مَا شَاءَ اللهُ أَنْ تَكُونَ ثُمَّ يَرْفَعُهَا إِذَا شَاءَ أَنْ يَرْفَعَهَا ثُمَّ تَكُونُ خِلاَفَةٌ عَلَى مِنْهَاجِ النُّبُوَّةِ ثُمَّ تَكُونُ مَا شَاءَ اللهُ أَنْ تَكُونَ ثُمَّ يَرْفَعُهَا إِذَا شَاءَ أَنْ يَرْفَعَهَا ثُمَّ تَكُونُ مُلْكًا عَاضًّا فَتَكُونُ مَا شَاءَ اللهُ أَنْ تَكُونَ ثُمَّ يَرْفَعُهَا إِذَا شَاءَ أَنْ يَرْفَعَهَا ثُمَّ تَكُونُ مُلْكًا جَبْرِيَّةً فَتَكُونُ مَا شَاءَ اللهُ أَنْ تَكُونَ ثُمَّ يَرْفَعُهَا إِذَا شَاءَ أَنْ يَرْفَعَهَا ثُمَّ تَكُونُ خِلاَفَةٌ عَلَى مِنْهَاجِ نُبُوَّةٍ ثُمَّ سَكَتَ قَالَ حَبِيبٌ يعني حبيب بن سالم الراوي عن حذيفة فَلَمَّا قَامَ عُمَرُ بْنُ عَبْدِ الْعَزِيزِ وَكَانَ يَزِيدُ بْنُ النَّعْمَانِ بْنِ بَشِيرٍ فِي صَحَابَتِهِ فَكَتَبْتُ إِلَيْهِ بِهَذَا الْحَدِيثِ أَذْكُرُه إِيَّاهُ فَقُلْتُ لَهُ إِنِّي أَرْجُو أَنْ يَكُونَ أَمِيرَ الْمُؤْمِنِينَ يَعْنِي عُمَرَ بَعْدَ الْمُلْكِ الْعَاضِّ وَالْجَبْرِيَّةِ فَأُدْخِلَ كِتَابِي

Musnad (p. 58-59 §438), al-Bazzār (7:223-224 §2796), al-Ṭabarānī in part in *al-Awsat* (§6581) cf. Haythamī (5:188-189): "Narrated by Aḥmad, al-Bazzār with a more complete wording, and al-Tabarānī partly, in *al-Awsat*. The narrators in its chain are trustworthy"; Dāraquṭnī in *al-Afrād* (*Aṭrāf* 1:365 §1993), and Ibn al-A'rābī in his *Mu'jam* (2:803-804 §1645). Nabhānī omits the bracketed passage and has "tyranny *(jabriyya)*" instead of "a tyrannical kingship." Cf. Ibn Rajab in *Jāmi' al-'Ulūm wal-Ḥikam* (Arna'ūṭ ed. 2:122 *ḥasan*). Also narrated from Abu 'Ubayda by Ṭabarānī, *al-Kabīr* (1:157) with the wording "There will be kingship and tyranny" after the mention of the first caliphate. Also narrated from 'Umar b. al-Khaṭṭāb by al-Bāghundī in *Musnad 'Umar b. 'Abd al-'Azīz* (p. 99-100). Al-Ba'lī in *al-Arba'ūn min Riyāḍ al-Janna* cites it (§20) and declares it sound.

[540]Ibn Rajab cited something to this effect in his commentary on the ḥadīth in *Jāmi' al-'Ulūm wal-Ḥikam*.

عَلَى عُمَرَ بْنِ عَبْدِ الْعَزِيزِ فَسُرَّ بِهِ وَأَعْجَبَهُ ط حم ز هق في الدلائل
وجاء عنه مرفوعا بلفظ إِنَّكُمْ فِي نُبُوَّةٍ وَرَحْمَةٍ وَسَتَكُونُ خِلاَفَةٌ وَرَحْمَةٌ ثُمَّ
يَكُونُ كَذَا وَكَذَا ثُمَّ يَكُونُ مُلْكاً عَضُوضاً يَشْرَبُونَ الْخُمُورَ
وَيَلْبَسُونَ الْحَرِيرَ وَفِي ذَلِكَ يُنْصَرُونَ إِلَى أَنْ تَقُومَ السَّاعَةُ طس
وبلفظ أَنْتُمُ الْيَوْمَ فِي نُبُوَّةٍ وَرَحْمَةٍ ثُمَّ تَكُونُ خِلاَفَةٌ وَرَحْمَةٌ ثُمَّ يَكُونُ
كَذَا وَكَذَا ثُمَّ يَكُونُ كَذَا وَكَذَا مُلُوكاً عَضُوضاً يَشْرَبُونَ الْخَمْرَ
وَيَلْبَسُونَ الْحَرِيرَ وَفِي ذَلِكَ يُنْصَرُونَ عَلَى مَنْ نَاوَأَهُمْ قط في الأفراد
ابن الأعرابي في المعجم

His ﷺ Foretelling the Status of Banū Umayya After Mu'āwiya

Ibn Manī' [Abū al-Qāsim al-Baghawī's grandfather the ḥadīth Master Abū Ja'far Aḥmad b. Manī' b. 'Abd al-Raḥmān al-Aṣamm al-Baghawī (160-244) in his *Musnad*)], Abū Ya'lā, al-Bayhaqī, and Abū Nu'aym narrated from Abū 'Ubayda b. al-Jarrāḥ ؓ that the Messenger of Allah ﷺ said: 401 "This great matter will continue to be moderate and stand on justice and truth until it is brought down by a man from the Banū Umayya <whose name is Yazīd>."[541]

عَنْ أَبِي عُبَيْدَةَ بْنِ الْجَرَّاحِ رَضِيَ اللهُ عَنْهُ قَالَ قَالَ رَسُولُ اللهِ ﷺ
لاَ يَزَالُ أَمْرُ أُمَّتِي قَائِمًا بِالْقِسْطِ حَتَّى يَكُونَ أَوَّلَ مَنْ يَثْلُمُهُ

[541]Narrated from Abū 'Ubayda b. al-Jarrāḥ (without the bracketed segment) by al-Bazzār (4:109 §1284), Bayhaqī, *Dalā'il* (6:467), Ibn 'Asākir (63:336), Nu'aym b. Ḥammād, *al-Fitan* (1:280 §817 and 1:282 §824); and (with the bracketed segment, broken-chained) by Abū Ya'lā (2:175-176 §870-871), al-Ḥārith, *Musnad* (2:642 §616), Aḥmad b. Manī' in his as stated by al-Būṣīrī in *Itḥāf al-Khiyara*. Cf. *Bidāya* (6:229, 8:231), al-Haythamī (5:241-242), Ibn Ḥajar, *Lisān al-Mīzān* (6:294), and al-Suyūṭī in *Tārīkh al-Khulafā'*.

رَجُلٌ مِنْ بَنِي أُمَيَّةَ ز هق في الدلائل كر وفي رواية بسند منقطع رَجُلٌ مِنْ بَنِي أُمَيَّةَ يُقالُ لَهُ يَزِيدُ ع مسندا الحارث وابن منيع

The Two Masters [al-Bukhārī and Muslim] narrated from Abū Hurayra ﷺ: "I heard the Messenger of Allah ﷺ say: 402 'The destruction of my Community will take place at the hands of boys *(ghilma)* from the Quraysh.' I could name them if I wanted – Banū Fulān and Banū Fulān."[542]

عَنْ أَبِي هُرَيْرَةَ رَضِيَ اللهُ عَنْهُ قَالَ رَسُولُ اللهِ ﷺ هَلَكَةُ أُمَّتِي عَلَى يَدَيْ غِلْمَةٍ مِنْ قُرَيْشٍ فَقَالَ مَرْوَانُ لَعْنَةُ اللهِ عَلَيْهِمْ غِلْمَةً فَقَالَ أَبُو هُرَيْرَةَ لَوْ شِئْتُ أَنْ أَقُولَ بَنِي فُلَانٍ وَبَنِي فُلَانٍ لَفَعَلْتُ فَكُنْتُ أَخْرُجُ مَعَ جَدِّي إِلَى بَنِي مَرْوَانَ حِينَ مُلِّكُوا بِالشَّأْمِ فَإِذَا رَآهُمْ غِلْمَانًا أَحْدَاثًا قَالَ لَنَا عَسَى هَؤُلَاءِ أَنْ يَكُونُوا مِنْهُمْ قُلْنَا أَنْتَ أَعْلَمُ خ وجاء بلفظ أُغَيْلِمَةٍ سُفَهَاءَ مِنْ قُرَيْشٍ خ حم وبلفظ يُهْلِكُ أُمَّتِي هَذَا الحَيُّ مِنْ قُرَيْشٍ ق حم

[Another sound version has "boylings" *(ughaylima)*. In another report Abū Hurayra narrated that the Prophet ﷺ said: 403 "Those who will destroy the people are this particular clan *(hādhā al-ḥayyu)* of the Quraysh." They said, "What do you order us to do, Messenger of Allah?" He replied: a "If only the people stayed away from them *(i'tazalūhum)*!"[543] This is precisely what Abū Dharr did.]

Al-Bayhaqī narrated from Abū Sa'īd al-Khudrī ﷺ, "I heard the Messenger of Allah ﷺ say: 404 'There will be after sixty years, ﴿**a later generation who have ruined worship and have followed lusts. But they will meet deception**﴾ (19:59). Then a there

[542]Narrated by al-Bukhārī and Aḥmad cf. Ibn 'Asākir (46:455-456).

[543]Narrated by al-Bukhārī, Muslim, and Aḥmad. See also ḥadīth at note 81.

will be a later generation who recite the Qur'ān but it will not reach beyond their throats. [b] <Three types will be reciting the Qur'ān [at that time]: the Believer, the hypocrite, and the open rebel.>"[544]

عَنْ أَبِي سَعِيدٍ الْخُدْرِيِّ رَضِيَ اللهُ عَنْهُ سَمِعْتُ رَسُولَ اللهِ ﷺ يَقُولُ يَكُونُ خَلْفٌ بَعْدَ سِتِّينَ سَنَةً ﴿أَضَاعُواْ ٱلصَّلَوٰةَ وَٱتَّبَعُواْ ٱلشَّهَوَٰتِۖ فَسَوْفَ يَلْقَوْنَ غَيًّا﴾ الآية من سورة مريم ثُمَّ يَكُونُ خَلْفٌ يَقْرَءُونَ الْقُرْآنَ لاَ يَعْدُو تَرَاقِيَهُمْ وَيَقْرَأُ الْقُرْآنَ ثَلاَثَةٌ مُؤْمِنٌ وَمُنَافِقٌ وَفَاجِرٌ طس ك وزاد بعضهم قَالَ بَشِيرٌ فَقُلْتُ لِلْوَلِيدِ مَا هَؤُلاَءِ الثَّلاَثَةُ فَقَالَ الْمُنَافِقُ كَافِرٌ بِهِ وَالْفَاجِرُ يَتَأَكَّلُ بِهِ وَالْمُؤْمِنُ يُؤْمِنُ بِهِ حم ورجاله ثقات مج حب ك هب وفي الدلائل الآجري في أخلاق حملة القرآن كر خ في خلق أفعال العباد الأخير دون لفظ بَعْدَ سِتِّينَ سَنَةً

Aḥmad and al-Bazzār narrated with a sound chain from Abū Hurayra ؓ that the Messenger of Allah ﷺ said: [405] "Seek refuge in Allah from the turn of the year 70 and from the rule of young boys" *(imārat al-ṣibyān)*.[545] And he said: [a] "The world will not pass before it first belongs to a mean fool son of a mean fool *(luka' b. luka')*."[546]

[544]Narrated from Abū Sa'īd by Aḥmad, al-Bukhārī in *Khalq Af'āl al-'Ibād* (p. 117), al-Ṭabarānī in *al-Awsat* (9:131), Ibn Hibbān (3:32 §755), al-Ḥākim (1990 ed. 2:406 *sahīh* and 4:590 *isnād ṣaḥīḥ*) and others, all "with a good strong chain meeting the *Sunan* criteria": Ibn Kathīr, *Bidāya* (6:228) cf. al-Haythamī (6:231). Al-Nabhānī omits the bracketed segment.

[545]Al-Nabhānī has the Year 60. Narrated from Abū Ṣāliḥ the *mu'adhdhin*, from Abū Hurayra by Aḥmad, al-Bazzār, Ibn Abī Shayba (7:461 §37235) and others, all with the number 70 with a chain of trustworthy narrators cf. al-Haythamī (7:220) but cited by al-Suyūṭī in *Ziyādat al-Jāmi' al-Saghīr* (§2040) and the *Kanz* (§30854) with the number 60. Also – second sentence only – from Abū Hurayra, Hāni' b. Nyār, and Hudhayfa b. al-Yamān by al-Tirmidhī *(ḥasan)* and Aḥmad with sound chains cf. *Fath* (1:129-131).

[546]In Aḥmad and Ibn 'Adī.

[Some versions have "and the rule of fools" *(imārat al-sufahā')*.[547] Another version adds in the beginning: "A time will come when people will see the truthful one be to be considered a liar and the liar to be trusted; the trustworthy one to be considered a traitor and the treacherous one to be considered trustworthy; a person will bear witness without being called to bear witness and swear an oath without being asked to swear. At that time the happiest person in the world will be a mean fool son of a mean fool; he will not believe in Allah and His Prophet."[548]]

عَنْ أَبِي هُرَيْرَةَ رَضِيَ اللهُ عَنْهُ قَالَ قَالَ رَسُولُ اللهِ ﷺ تَعَوَّذُوا بِاللهِ مِنْ رَأْسِ السَّبْعِينَ وَمِنْ إِمَارَةِ الصِّبْيَانِ حم ورجاله رجال الصحيح غير كامل بن العلاء وهو ثقة مج ز ش مسند أحمد بن منيع وزاد بعضهم وَقَالَ لاَ تَذْهَبُ الدُّنْيَا حَتَّى تَصِيرَ لِلُكَعِ ابْنِ لُكَعٍ حم عد وجاء حديثاً مفرداً مرفوعاً عن عدة صحابة بلفظ حَتَّى يَكُونَ أَسْعَدَ النَّاسِ بِالدُّنْيَا لُكَعُ بْنُ لُكَعٍ حم ت وقال حسن غريب ع ابن أبي عاصم في الزهد طس أبو نعيم في المعرفة هق في الدلائل البغوي في شرح السّنّة وحسّنه وجاء بزيادة ثُمَّ يَصِيرُ إِلَى النَّارِ خت وجاء عَنْ أُمِّ سَلَمَةَ رَضِيَ اللهُ عَنْهَا أَنَّهَا سَمِعَتْ رَسُولَ اللهِ ﷺ يَقُولُ لَيَأْتِيَنَّ عَلَى النَّاسِ زَمَانٌ يُكَذَّبُ فِيهِ الصَّادِقُ وَيُصَدَّقُ فِيهِ الْكَاذِبُ وَيُخَوَّنُ فِيهِ الأَمِينُ وَيُؤْتَمَنُ الْخَؤُونُ وَيَشْهَدُ الْمَرْءُ وَلَمْ يُسْتَشْهَدْ وَيَحْلِفُ وَإِنْ لَمْ يُسْتَحْلَفْ وَيَكُونُ أَسْعَدَ النَّاسِ بِالدُّنْيَا لُكَعُ بن لُكَعٍ لا يُؤْمِنُ بِاللهِ وَرَسُولِهِ خت طب طس

[547]Cf. al-Bukhārī in *al-Adab al-Mufrad* (p. 27 §66), Ibn ʿAbd al-Barr, *al-Tamhīd* (2:303) and al-Shawkānī, *Nayl al-Awṭār* (9:167).

[548]Narrated from Umm Salama by al-Bukhāri in *al-Tārīkh al-Kabīr* and al-Ṭabaranī in *al-Kabīr and* al-Awsaṭ.

Al-Bayhaqī narrated from Abū Hurayra ؓ that he used to walk in the marketplace and say: 406 "O Allah, do not let me live to see the year 60! a Hold on to the two temples of Muʿāwiya! b O Allah, do not let me live to see the rule of the boys!"[549]

عَنْ عُمَيرِ بْنِ هَانِئٍ قَالَ كَانَ أَبُو هُرَيْرَةَ يَمْشِي فِي سُوقِ المَدِينَةِ وَهُوَ يَقُولُ اللهُمَّ لاَ تُدْرِكْنِي سَنَةَ السِّتِّينَ وَيْحَكُمْ تَمَسَّكُوا بِصُدْغَيْ مُعَاوِيَةَ اللهُ لاَ تُدْرِكْنِي إِمَارَةَ الصِّبْيَانِ ابن سعد هق في الدلائل كر وجاء بلفظ تَشَبَّثُوا تاريخ أبي زرعة

Ibn Abī Shayba, Abū Yaʿlā, and al-Bayhaqī narrated from Abū Dharr ؓ, "I heard the Messenger of Allah ﷺ say: 407 "The first to change my Sunna will be a man from the Banū Umayya."[550] Al-Bayhaqī said: "This is most probably Yazīd b. Muʿāwiya."

عَنْ أَبِي ذَرٍّ أَوَّلُ رَضِيَ اللهُ عَنْهُ قَالَ سَمِعْتُ رَسُولَ اللهِ ﷺ يَقُولُ أَوَّلُ مَنْ يُبَدِّلُ سُنَّتِي رَجُلٌ مِنْ بَنِي أُمَيَّةَ ش ع هق في الدلائل وقال يشبه أن يكون يزيد بن معاوية والله أعلم وبعضهم رواه بلفظ إِنَّ أَوَّلَ مَنْ يُبَدِّلُ جميعهم مرسلاً ورواه كر مسنداً

Abū Nuʿaym narrated from Muʿādh ؓ that the Messenger of Allah ﷺ said: 408 "Ahead of you await strifes like amassed layers of the darkest night! Every time a herd goes out, another

[549]Narrated from 'Umayr b. Hāni' al-'Anasī by Ibn Saʿd (4:340-341), al-Bayhaqī, *Dalā'il* (6:466), Ibn ʿAsākir (59:217=*Mukhtasar Tārīkh Dimashq* 29:206), Ibn Ḥajar, *Iṣāba* (7:443), and Ibn Kathīr, *Bidāya* (6:228-229). "Hold on to the two temples of his head" *i.e.* love him while you still can, as those who come after him will not be so lovable.

[550]Narrated by Ibn Abī Shayba (7:260), Abū Yaʿlā and al-Bayhaqī in the *Dalā'il* (6:467) with a broken chain between Abū al-'Āliya and Abū Dharr, and Ibn ʿAsākir (65:250) with an unbroken chain through the narrators of al-Bukhārī and Muslim except for Abū Khālid Muhājir b. Makhlad who is merely "acceptable" *(maqbūl)*. Cf. *Fayḍ* (3:94), *Bidāya* (6:229), *Siyar* (Risāla ed. 1:330), and Ibn ʿAdī, *Kāmil* (3:164).

comes in. [a] Prophethood has been reshuffled *(tanāsakhat)* and has become monarchy. Keep note of this list, Mu'ādh!" [He started mentioning names.] When the list reached five names, he said: "Yazīd? [b] May Allah not bless Yazīd in anything!" Then his eyes brimmed with tears and he said: [c] "The death of Ḥusayn has just been announced to me. I was brought a handful of his burial-ground and I was told of the identity of his killer." When the list reached ten names, he said: [d] "Al-Walīd is the name of Pharaoh. He is the destroyer of the laws of Islam. His blood will be on the head of a man of his house."[551]

عَنْ مُعَاذِ بنِ جَبَلٍ رَضِيَ اللهُ عَنْهُ قَالَ خَرَجَ عَلَيْنَا رَسُولُ اللهِ ﷺ مُتَغَيِّرَ اللَّوْنِ فَقَالَ أَتَتْكُمْ فِتَنٌ كَقِطَعِ اللَّيْلِ الْمُظْلِمِ كُلَّمَا ذَهَبَ رِسْلٌ جَاءَ رِسْلٌ تَنَاسَخَتِ النُّبُوَّةُ فَصَارَتْ مُلْكًا رَحِمَ اللهُ مَنْ أَخَذَهَا بِحَقِّهَا وَخَرَجَ مِنْهَا كَمَا دَخَلَهَا أَمْسِكْ يَا مُعَاذُ وَأَحْصِ قَالَ فَلَمَّا بَلَغْتُ خَمْسَةً قَالَ يَزِيدُ لَا يُبَارِكُ اللهُ فِي يَزِيدَ ثُمَّ ذَرَفَتْ عَيْنَاهُ ﷺ ثُمَّ قَالَ نُعِيَ إِلَيَّ حُسَيْنٌ وَأُتِيتُ بِتُرْبَتِهِ وَأُخْبِرْتُ بِقَاتِلِهِ فَلَمَّا بَلَغْتُ عَشَرَةً قَالَ الْوَلِيدُ اِسْمُ فِرْعَوْنَ هَادِمِ شَرَائِعِ الإِسْلامِ بَيْنَ يَدَيْهِ رَجُلٌ مِنْ أَهْلِ بَيْتٍ وفي نسخة مِنْ أَهْلِ بَيْتِهِ والصواب يَبُوءُ بِدَمِهِ رَجُلٌ مِنْ أَهْلِ بَيْتِهِ يَسُلُّ اللهُ سَيْفَهُ فَلاَ غِمَادَ لَهُ وَاخْتَلَفَ النَّاسُ فَكَانُوا هَكَذَا وَشَبَّكَ بَيْنَ أَصَابِعِهِ ثُمَّ قَالَ بَعْدَ الْعِشْرِينَ وَمِئَةٍ مَوْتٌ سَرِيعٌ وَقَتْلٌ ذَرِيعٌ فَفِيهِ هَلاَكُهُمْ

[551] Part of a longer hadith narrated from Mu'ādh by al-Ṭabarānī in *al-Kabīr* (3:129 §2861, 20:38-39 §56) and through him al-Shajarī in his *Amālī* (1:169) with a chain containing an arch-liar cf. al-Haythamī (9:190) which Ibn Ḥajar said is very weak: *Fath* (10:580) cf. *al-Qawl al-Musaddad* (p. 15-16). See also the hadith naming al-Walīd further down.

وَيَلِي عَلَيْهِمْ رَجُلٌ مِنْ وَلَدِ الْعَبَّاسِ طب أمالي الشجري فيه مجاشع بن عمرو وهو كذاب مج سنده ضعيف جداً فتحومع ذلك استشهد به في القول المسدد

[An authentic version states: 409 "Ahead of you are coming strifes like amassed layers of the darkest night! In that time a a man shall wake up a believer in the morning and reach night a disbeliever. b The one who sits at that time is better than the one who stands, the one who stands is better than the one who walks, and the one who walks is better than the one who runs." They said: "What do you order us to do [then]?" He said: c "Be the saddle-cloths *(aḥlās)* of your houses."[552] The *ḥils* is the blanket one puts under the camel's saddle. *I.e.* "Stay in your houses and do not take any part in it."[553]

This narration is confirmed by the hadith narrated in the *Sunan* from Abū Mūsā: "He said with regard to the *fitna*: 410 'At that time shatter your bows to pieces, cut your bow-strings, and do not move from inside your houses but be like the son of Ādam [*i.e.* do not resist]."[554] Abū Dāwūd has: "and a smash your swords against rocks, and if someone enters to kill one of you, be like the better one of the two sons of Ādam."]

Al-Ḥākim narrated – he declared it sound – that Abū Hurayra ﷺ said: 411 "Woe to the Arabs for a disaster that is fast approaching at the turn of the year 60! a The public trust will become spoils of war, almsgiving will be considered a fine, people will only bear witness for their friends, and lusts will rule."[555]

عَنْ أَبِي هُرَيرة رَضِيَ اللهُ عَنْهُ قَالَ وَيْلٌ لِلْعَرَبِ مِنْ شَرٍّ قَدِ اقْتَرَبَ إِلَى رَأْسِ السِّتِّينَ تَكُونُ الصَّدَقَةُ مَغْرَمًا وَالأَمَانَةُ غَنِيمَةً وَالشَّهَادَةُ بِالمَعْرِفَةِ وَالحُكْمُ بِالهُوِيَّةِ عق في جامع معمر ك قط في العلل وجاء بلفظ عَنْ أَبِي هُرَيْرَةَ أَنَّهُ قَالَ فِي كِيسِي هَذَا حَدِيثٌ لَوْ حَدَّثْتُكُمُوهُ

[552]Narrated from Abū Mūsa al-Ash'arī by Abū Dāwūd and Aḥmad. Its basic wording is in Muslim.

[553]Cf. Ibn al-Athīr, *al-Nihāya*, article "*ḥ-l-s*".

[554]Narrated by al-Tirmidhī *(ḥasan gharīb ṣaḥīḥ)*, Abū Dāwūd, Ibn Mājah, and Aḥmad.

[555]Narrated as a saying of Abū Hurayra by Ma'mar b. Rāshid in his *Jāmi'* (*Musannaf* 11:373), al-Ḥākim (1990 ed. 4:530 *ṣaḥīḥ* per the criterion of al-Bukhārī and Muslim), and Nu'aym b. Hammād in *al-Fitan* (2:703 §1981) cf. al-Dāraquṭnī, *'Ilal* (10:371-372 §2059). Al-Ṭabarānī narrates something similar in *al-Kabīr* (4:300 §400) and *al-Awsaṭ* (2:106) al-Haythamī (4:199).

لَرَجَمْتُمُونِي ثُمَّ قَالَ اللهُمَّ لاَ أَبْلُغَنَّ رَأْسَ السِّتِّينَ قَالُوا وَمَا رَأْسُ السِّتِّينَ قَالَ إِمَارَةُ الصِّبْيَانِ وَبَيْعُ الْحُكْمِ وَكَثْرَةُ الشُّرَطِ وَالشَّهَادَةُ بِالْمَعْرِفَةِ وَيَتَّخِذُونَ الأَمَانَةَ غَنِيمَةً وَالصَّدَقَةَ مَغْرَمًا وَنَشْوٌ يَتَّخِذُونَ الْقُرْآنَ مَزَامِيرَ طب طس قال الحافظ يشير إلى خلافة يزيد بن معاوية لأنها كانت سنة ستين من الهجرة قلت وتوفي أبو هريرة رضي الله عنه سنة ٥٧ وَعَنِ الْحَسَنِ قَالَ أَبُو هُرَيْرَةَ لَوْ حَدَّثْتُكُمْ كُلَّ مَا فِي كِيسِي لَرَمَيْتُمُونِي بِالْبَعْرِ قَالَ الْحَسَنُ صَدَقَ وَاللهِ لَوْ حَدَّثَهُمْ أَنَّ بَيْتَ اللهِ يُهْدَمُ أَوْ يُحْرَقُ مَا صَدَّقَهُ النَّاسُ تاريخ ابن أبي خيثمة الفسوي في المعرفة والتاريخ خط في الفقيه والمتفقه

Al-Bayhaqī narrated that [ʿAbd Allāh] Ibn Mawhib was with Muʿāwiya when Marwān [b. al-Ḥakam] entered and said, "Help me with my need, Commander of the Believers! For, by Allah, my daily expenses are huge because I have ten children, ten nephews and nieces, and ten brothers and sisters!" When Marwān left – Ibn ʿAbbās was sitting on the throne next to Muʿāwiya – the latter said, "Ibn ʿAbbās! Do you not know that the Messenger of Allah ﷺ said the following? 412 'When the Banū al-Ḥakam reach thirty men, they will take the treasury of Allah for their own exclusive need, the servants of Allah as their own servants , and the Book of Allah for the purpose of corruption. When they reach four hundred and ninety nine men, their destruction will be faster than one can chew a date.'" Ibn ʿAbbās said yes.[556] Marwān sent [his

[556]Narrated from Ibn Mawhib by al-Ṭabarānī in *al-Kabīr* (12:236 §12982, 19:382), al-Bayhaqī in the *Dalā'il* (6:508), Ibn Asākir (57:252), and Nuaym b. Ḥammād in *al-Fitan* (1:130-131 §316) cf. al-Haythamī (5:243); from Abū Saīd al-Khudrī by Abū Yalā (2:383 §1152) and al-Ṭabarānī in *al-Awsat* (8:6 §7785); and from Abū Dharr by al-Ḥākim (1990 ed. 4:526 *saḥīh*) cf. *Bidāya* (8:259, 10:48).

son] ʿAbd al-Malik to Muʿāwiya, to speak to him about a personal need. When he left, Muʿāwiya said, "Ibn ʿAbbās! Do you not know that 413 the Messenger of Allah ﷺ mentioned this one [ʿAbd al-Malik], and called him 'the father of the four tyrants'?" Ibn ʿAbbās replied, "O Allah! Yes. *(Allāhumma naʿam)*"[557] **[530]**

عَنِ ابْنِ مَوْهَبٍ أَخْبَرَهُ أَنَّهُ كَانَ عِنْدَ مُعَاوِيَةَ بْنَ أَبِي سُفْيَانَ فَدَخَلَ عَلَيْهِ مَرْوَانُ فَكَلَّمَهُ فِي حَوَائِجِهِ فَقَالَ اِقْضِ حَاجَتِي يَا أَمِيرَ الْمُؤْمِنِينَ فَوَاللهِ إِنَّ مُؤْنَتِي لَعَظِيمَةٌ إِنِّي أَصْبَحْتُ أَبَا عَشَرَةٍ وَأَخَا عَشَرَةٍ وَعَمَّ عَشَرَةٍ فَلَمَّا أَدْبَرَ مَرْوَانُ وَابْنُ عَبَّاسٍ جَالِسٌ مَعَ مُعَاوِيَةَ عَلَى سَرِيرِهِ فَقَالَ مُعَاوِيَةُ أَنْشُدُكَ اللهَ يَا ابْنَ عَبَّاسٍ أَمَا تَعْلَمُ أَنَّ رَسُولَ اللهِ ﷺ قَالَ إِذَا بَلَغَ بَنُو الْحَكَمِ ثَلاثِينَ رَجُلاً اتَّخَذُوا آيَاتِ اللهِ بَيْنَهُمْ دُوَلاً وَعِبَادَهُ خَوَلاً وَكِتَابَهُ دَغَلاً فَإِذَا بَلَغُوا تِسْعَةً وَتِسْعِينَ وَأَرْبَعَمِائَةٍ كَانَ هَلاَكُهُمْ أَسْرَعَ مِنَ الثَّمَرَةِ قَالَ ابْنُ عَبَّاسٍ اللهُمَّ نَعَمْ فَذَكَرَ مَرْوَانُ حَاجَةً لَهُ فَرَدَّ مَرْوَانُ بْنُ عَبْدِ الْمَلِكِ إِلَى مُعَاوِيَةَ فَكَلَّمَهُ فِيهَا فَلَمَّا أَدْبَرَ قَالَ مُعَاوِيَةُ أَنْشُدُكُمُ اللهَ يَا ابْنَ عَبَّاسٍ أَمَا تَعْلَمُ أَنَّ رَسُولَ اللهِ ﷺ ذَكَرَ هَذَا فَقَالَ أَبُو الْجَبَابِرَةِ الأَرْبَعَةِ فَقَالَ ابْنُ عَبَّاسٍ اللهُمَّ نَعَمْ طب هق في الدلائل كر وفي الباب عن أبي سعيد الخدري طس ع هق في الدلائل كر وأبي ذر ك وأبي هريرة ع كر

[557]Narrated from Ibn Mawhib by al-Ṭabarānī, Ibn Asākir, and Nuaym cf. previous note. ʿAbd al-Mālik b. Marwān ruled after Yazīd b. Muʿāwiya, followed by ʿAbd al-Malik's four sons al-Walīd, Sulaymān, Yazīd, and Hishām.

[An identical narration names the Banū Abī al-Āṣ instead of the Banū al-Ḥakam but they are one and the same clan since al-Ḥakam is the son of Abū al-'Āṣ.[558] Another narration states: 414 "When the Banū Umayya reach forty men, they will take the servants of Allah as their own servants, the treasury of Allah for their own exclusive need, and the Book of Allah for the purpose of corruption."[559]]

Abū Ya'lā, al-Ḥākim, and al-Bayhaqī narrated that 'Umar b. Murra al-Juhanī ﷺ – he was a Companion[560] – said al-Ḥakam b. Abī al-'Āṣ came to ask permission from the Prophet ﷺ who said: 415 "Give him permission – a viper son of a viper! The curse of Allah be on him and whoever comes from his loins other than the believers, and they are few. They will preside in this world and will be humiliated in the next. They are people of deceit and treachery. They will be given plenty in the world and have no share in the hereafter."[561]

عَنْ عَمْرِو بْنِ مُرَّةَ الجُهَنِي رَضِيَ اللهُ عَنْهُ قَالَ اسْتَأْذَنَ الحَكَمُ بْنُ أَبِي العَاصِي عَلَى رَسُولِ اللهِ ﷺ فَعَرَفَ صَوْتَهُ فَقَالَ ائْذِنُوا لَهُ حَيَّةٌ أَوْ وَلَدُ حَيَّةٍ عَلَيْهِ لَعْنَةُ اللهِ وَعَلَى كُلِّ مَنْ يَخْرُجُ مِنْ صُلْبِهِ إِلاَّ المؤْمِنَ مِنْهُمْ وَقَلِيلٌ مَا هُمْ يَشْرُفُونَ فِي الدُّنْيَا وَيُوضَعُونَ فِي الآخِرَةِ ذَوُو مَكْرٍ وَخَدِيعَةٍ يُعْطَوْنَ فِي الدُّنْيَا وَمَا لَهُمْ فِي الآخِرَةِ مِنْ خَلاَقٍ ع ك هق في الدلائل كر فيه أبو الحسن الجزرى وهو مستور وبقية رجاله

[558]Narrated from Abū Saīd al-Khudrī by Aḥmad with the wording "Banū Abī Fulān," al-Ṭabarānī in *al-Saghīr* (2:271 §1150), and al-Ḥākim (1990 ed. 4:527); Abū Hurayra by Abū Ya'lā (11:402 §6523); and Abū Dharr by al-Ḥākim (4:526 *sahīh* per Muslim's criterion) cf. al-Haythamī (5:241).

[559]Narrated from Abū Dharr by al-Ḥākim (1990 ed. 4:525-526 *isnād sahīh* but al-Dhahabī said *munqati'*).

[560]As stated in Ibn Ḥajar's *Taqrīb* but with the spelling 'Amr instead of 'Umar.

[561]Narrated from 'Amr b. Murra al-Juhanī by al-Ḥākim (1990 ed. 4:528 *isnād sahīh*), al-Ṭabarānī, *Kabīr*, Ibn 'Asākir and partly Nu'aym, *Fitan* (1:129 §311) cf. Haythamī (5:243), *Bidāya* (6:243), and *Kanz* (§31729). Ibn Ḥajar questioned its authenticity in the *Iṣāba*.

ثقات مج وعزاه للطبراني بلفظ وَيَرْذُلُونَ فِي الآخِرَةِ قلت وهذا الاستثناء إشارة
إلى عمر بن عبد العزيز ومعاوية بن يزيد ويزيد الناقص والصالح منهم

[In Ibn Kathīr: Al-Ḥakam, Marwān's father, was among the greatest of the enemies of the Prophet ﷺ and he entered Islam only after the conquest of Mecca. Al-Ḥakam came to al-Madīna then the Prophet ﷺ expelled him to al-Ṭā'if where he died. Marwān was among the foremost causes for the siege of ʿUthmān ﷺ because he counterfeited his signing of a letter to Egypt commanding for its bearers to be killed. (When they discovered the letter they besieged and killed ʿUthmān.) When Marwān was the governor of al-Madīna under Muʿāwiya he would curse ʿAlī every Jumuʿa from the pulpit. Al-Ḥasan b. ʿAlī said to him: "Allah has cursed your father al-Ḥakam, while you were in his loins, with the tongue of His Prophet ﷺ who said: 'The curse of Allah be on al-Ḥakam and his children!'"[562]

Al-Shaʿbī said, "I heard ʿAbd Allāh b. al-Zubayr say as he was leaning against the Kaʿba: 'By the Lord of this Kaʿba! 416 The Messenger of Allah ﷺ has cursed Fulān and his progeny.'"[563] Al-Ḥakam is named verbatim in al-Bazzār's version.

Muḥammad b. Zyād said that when Muʿāwiya gave the pledge of allegiance to his son Yazīd, Marwān – who governed Madīna – said: "(In conformity to) the Sunna of Abū Bakr and ʿUmar." ʿAbd al-Raḥmān b. Abī Bakr said: "Rather, to the Sunna of Heraclius and Caesar!" Marwān tried in vain to have him arrested then said: "It is about you that Allah revealed ﴿**And whoso says unto his parents: Fie upon you both. Do you threaten me that I shall be brought forth again when generations before me have passed away? And they twain cry unto Allah for help and say: Woe unto you! Believe! Lo! the promise of Allah is true. But he says: This is naught save fables of the men of old**﴾ (46:17). ʿĀ'isha replied from behind the door: "Marwān lies! Nothing was revealed about us [children of Abū Bakr] in the Qur'ān except my exoneration[564] while that verse was revealed about Fulān b. Fulān al-Fulānī. Rather, 417 the Messenger of Allah ﷺ cursed the father of Marwān while Marwān was in his loins! So Marwān got his lot (*qasasun / fadadun / baʿdun*) of the Divine curse."[565]]

[562]In Ibn Kathīr, *Bidāya* (8:259).

[563]Narrated from ʿAbd Allāh b. al-Zubayr by Aḥmad and al-Bazzār (6:159 §2197), both through highly trustworthy narrators cf. *Mukhtāra* (9:311 §270) and al-Haythamī (5:241) who said al-Ṭabarānī narrates something similar.

[564]Narrated to here from Yūsuf b. Māhak by Bukhārī "in overly abridged form" per some of his commentators (*Fatḥ* 8:576-577) without detailing the exchange between Marwān and ʿAbd al-Raḥmān. Ibn Ḥajar said that ʿĀ'isha's denial puts to rest Ṭabarī's narration from Ibn ʿAbbās, al-Suddī's, and Muqātil's, that verse 46:17 was revealed about ʿAbd al-Raḥmān b. Abī Bakr as pointed out by al-Jaṣṣāṣ as well as Ibn Abī Ḥātim's narration from Ibn Jurayj that it was revealed concerning ʿAbd Allāh b. Abī Bakr cf. *Fatḥ* (8:577).

[565]Narrated from Muhammad b. Zyād al-Jumaḥī al-Qurashī by al-Ismāʿīlī and al-Nasā'ī in *al-Sunan al-Kubrā* (6:458 §11491) cf. *Fatḥ* (8:576-577), al-Ḥākim (1990 ed. 4:528 *isnād saḥīḥ*) cf. *Istīʿāb* (1:360), *Iṣāba* (2:105), al-Suyūṭī's *Tatrīf* (p. 72 §107), and Ibn Kathīr, *Tafsīr* (4:160). Al-Dhahabī claimed its chain was broken but Muḥammad b. Zyād al-

The Prophet's ﷺ Knowledge of the Unseen • 403

Al-Fākihī narrated from al-Zuhrī and ʿAṭāʾ al-Khurasānī that the Prophet ﷺ said about al-Ḥakam: 418 "I can almost see his sons climbing up and down my pulpit!"566 [Also narrated with the wording 419 "I saw in my dream the Banū Umayya climbing up and down my pulpit in the shape of apes and pigs."]567

عَنِ الزُّهْرِيِّ وَعَطَاءٍ الْخُرَاسَانِيِّ أَنَّ أَصْحَابَ النَّبِيِّ ﷺ دَخَلُوا عَلَيْهِ وَهُوَ يَلْعَنُ الْحَكَمَ بْنَ أَبِي الْعَاصِ فَقَالُوا يَا رَسُولَ اللهِ مَا لَهُ قَالَ دَخَلَ عَلَى شِقِّ الْجِدَارِ وَأَنَا مَعَ زَوْجَتِي فُلَانَةَ فَكَلَحَ فِي وَجْهِي فَقَالُوا أَفَلَا نَلْعَنُهُ نَحْنُ قَالَ كَأَنِّي أَنْظُرُ إِلَى بَنِيهِ يَصْعَدُونَ مِنْبَرِي وَيَنْزِلُونَهُ الفاكهي في أخبار مكة ذكره الحافظ في الإصابة

Al-Fākihī narrated from Muʿāwiya ؓ that the Prophet ﷺ said concerning al-Ḥakam: 420 "When his children number thirty – or forty – they will control leadership."568

عَنْ مُعَاوِيَةَ رَضِيَ اللهُ عَنْهُ أَنَّ النَّبِيَّ ﷺ قَالَ لِلْحَكَمِ إِذَا بَلَغَ وَلَدُهُ ثَلَاثِينَ أَوْ أَرْبَعِينَ مَلَكُوا الْأَمْرَ البلاذري والأغاني بلا سند في

Qurashī did narrate from ʿĀʾisha cf. *Tahdhīb al-Tahdhīb* (9:149), so al-Nasāʾī's and al-Ḥākim's chains are sound but not per the criterion of the Two Masters. Allah knows best.

566 Narrated from Zuhrī and ʿAṭāʾ from unnamed Ṣaḥāba by Fākihī in *Akhbār Makka* (5:238 cf. *Iṣāba* 2:104) through Abū Sinān ʿĪsā b. Sinān who is *layyin* (somewhat weak).

567 Narrated from Abū Hurayra by Abū Yaʿlā (11:348 §6461) through the narrators of Muslim but for Musʿab b. ʿAbd Allāh al-Zubayrī who is trustworthy *(thiqa)* cf. al-Haythamī (5:243-244) and *Bidāya* (8:259), and with two chains by Ibn al-Jawzī in his *ʿIlal* (2:701-702), one of them through Abū Khālid Muslim b. Khālid al-Zanjī who is weak according to most but he is corroborated by the second chain (Ibn al-Jawzī's weakening of al-ʿAlāʾ b. ʿAbd al-Raḥmān b. Yaʿqūb is rejected in light of the fact that Muslim narrated 168 ḥadīths through him and both al-Dhahabī and Ibn Ḥajar concurred on his truthfulness); and *mursal* from Saʿīd b. al-Musayyib by al-Khaṭīb (9:44) and Ibn al-Jawzī in *al-ʿIlal* cf. *Bidāya* (8:259 *sanad daʿīf*) both with a weak or very chain because of Sulaymān al-Shādhakūnī, Sufyān b. Wakīʿ, and ʿAlī b. Zayd b. Judʿān.

568 Narrated chainless by al-Balādhurī in *Ansāb al-Ashrāf* (5:125).

الأنساب وعزاه في الإصابة والخصائص للفاكهي

Ibn Najīb narrated that Jubayr b. Muṭ'im said: "We were with the Prophet ﷺ when al-Ḥakam b. Abī al-'Āṣ passed. The Prophet ﷺ said: 421 "Woe to my Community because of this man's unborn progeny!"[569]

عَنْ جُبَيْرِ بْنِ مُطْعَمٍ قَالَ كُنْتُ مَعَ النَّبِيِّ ﷺ فِي الْحِجْرِ فَمَرَّ الْحَكَمُ بْنُ أَبِي الْعَاصِ فَقَالَ النَّبِيُّ ﷺ وَيْلٌ لأُمَّتِي مِمَّا فِي صُلْبِ هَذَا طس جزء ابن نجيب كر استنكره أبو حاتم الرازي علل وفيه من لا يُعرف مج

Ibn Abī Usāma narrated from Abū Hurayra that the Messenger of Allah ﷺ said: 422 "A tyrant from the tyrants of the Banū Umayya will certainly bleed from the nose on this pulpit of mine!" The day came when ʿAmr b. Saʿīd b. al-'Āṣ had a nosebleed on the pulpit of the Prophet ﷺ until his blood ran on its steps.[570]

عَنْ أَبِي هُرَيْرَةَ رَضِيَ اللهُ عَنْهُ قَالَ رَسُولُ اللهِ ﷺ لَيَرْعَفَنَّ جَبَّارٌ مِنْ جَبَابِرَةِ بَنِي أُمَيَّةَ عَلَى مِنْبَرِي هَذَا قَالَ فَحَدَّثَنِي مَنْ رَأَى عَمْرَو بْنَ سَعِيدِ ابْنِ الْعَاصِ رَعَفَ عَلَى مِنْبَرِ النَّبِيِّ ﷺ حَتَّى سَالَ الدَّمُ عَلَى دَرَجِ الْمِنْبَرِ حم مسند الحارث كر

[569]Both this and the previous report are cited in *al-Iṣāba* (2:105). The latter is narrated from Jubayr by al-Ṭabarānī in *al-Awsat* (2:144, 6:377) and Ibn ʿAsākir (57:267) through unknowns cf. al-Haythamī (5:241). Abū Ḥātim said it is a disclaimed narration cf. Ibn Abī Ḥātim, *ʿIlal* (2:415 *ḥadīth munkar*).

[570]Narrated from Abū Hurayra with a weak chain by Aḥmad, al-Ḥārith b. Abī Usāma in his *Musnad* (2:643 §617) cf. al-Haythamī (5:240), and Ibn ʿAsākir (46:36). ʿAmr b. Saʿīd was one of Yazīd's generals and accompanied Marwān in the latter's conquest of Egypt. When he maneuvered for the throne Marwān's son ʿAbd al-Malik had him murdered cf. *Bidāya* (8:311).

Al-Bayhaqī and Abū Nu'aym narrated from Sa'īd b. al-Musayyib that a boy was born to Umm Salama's brother whom they called al-Walīd. The Messenger of Allah ﷺ said: [423] "Do you give them the names of your Pharaohs? [a] There will be in this Community a man called al-Walīd who will certainly be worse for my Community than Fir'awn!"[571] Al-Awzā'ī said: "The people thought al-Walīd b. 'Abd al-Malik was meant. Then we realized that it was al-Walīd b. Yazīd <in light of the confusion of the people because of him, until they went and killed him, civil strife ensued in the Community, and massacres took place>."[572] Al-Bayhaqī declared it *mursal hasan*. Al-Ḥākim narrated it in the same wording from Ibn al-Musayyib, from Abū Hurayra, connected [to the Prophet ﷺ], declaring it sound, while Imam Aḥmad narrated it from 'Umar b. al-Khaṭṭāb ﵁. [Al-Ḥākim said: "It is al-Walīd b. Yazīd without the shadow of a doubt."]

عَنْ عُمَرَ بْنِ الْخَطَّابِ رَضِيَ اللهُ عَنْهُ قَالَ وُلِدَ لأَخِي أُمِّ سَلَمَةَ
زَوْجِ النَّبِيِّ ﷺ غُلامٌ فَسَمَّوْهُ الْوَلِيدَ فَقَالَ النَّبِيُّ ﷺ سَمَّيْتُمُوهُ
بِأَسْمَاءِ فَرَاعِنَتِكُمْ لَيَكُونَنَّ فِي هَذِهِ الأُمَّةِ رَجُلٌ يُقَالُ لَهُ الْوَلِيدُ لَهُوَ
شَرٌّ عَلَى هَذِهِ الأُمَّةِ مِنْ فِرْعَوْنَ لِقَوْمِهِ حم وإسناده حسن مج كر وفي

[571]Narrated from [1] 'Umar by Aḥmad with a *mursal* chain of trustworthy narrators cf. *Siyar* (Risāla ed. 5:371); [2] Abū Hurayra by Ḥākim (1990 ed. 4:539 *ṣaḥīḥ 'alā shart al-shaykhayn*), both deemed anomalous by Ibn Ḥajar in *al-Qawl al-Musaddad* (p. 15) and the *Fatḥ* but in the *Nukat 'alā Ibn al-Ṣalāḥ* (1:457) he agrees with al-Bayhaqī's grading of *mursal ḥasan*; [3] Umm Salama by al-Ḥārith in his *Musnad* (2:794-795 §804), Nu'aym b. Ḥammād in the *Fitan* (1:133 §328), Ma'mar b. Rāshid in the 2nd vol. of 'Abd al-Razzāq's *Amālī*, Ibn 'Asākir, Abū Nu'aym, and Bayhaqī in the *Dalā'il* cf. *Fatḥ* (10:580); and [4] Zaynab bint Umm Salama, from her mother by Ibrāhīm al-Harbī in his *Gharīb al-Ḥadīth* with a chain Ibn Ḥajar grades fair in the *Qawl*. Deemed a forgery by Ibn Hibbān (*Du'afā'*), Ibn al-Jawzī (*Mawḍū'āt*), and al-'Irāqī as cited in the beginning of Ibn Ḥajar's *al-Qawl* (p. 6) but the latter brilliantly demonstrates its validity cf. *Qawl* (p. 13-16), *Fatḥ* (10:580-581), and *Nukat* (1:455-459). Cf. also ḥadīth at n. 551. The name of Mūsā's ﵇ Pharaoh is given as al-Walīd b. Muṣ'ab by Ibn Nāṣir al-Dīn al-Dimashqī in *al-Lafẓ al-Mukarram bi-Faḍli 'Āshūrā' al-Muḥarram* in *Majmū'un fīhi Rasā'il Ibn Nāṣir al-Dīn* (p. 83).

[572]Cf. *Bidāya* (6:241-242) and *al-Qawl al-Musaddad* (p. 14). Al-Nabhānī omits the bracketed passage.

الباب عن أبي هريرة ك وابن المسيب مسند الحارث هق في الدلائل كر توضيع ابن حبان وابن الجوزي مردود وجوّده الحافظ في القول المسدد قال الحاكم قال الزهري إن استخلف الوليد بن يزيد فهو هو وإلا فالوليد بن عبد الملك قال الحاكم هو الوليد بن يزيد بلا شك ولا مرية

Al-Bayhaqī and Abū Nuʿaym narrated from Ibn Masʿūd ﷺ that the Messenger of Allah ﷺ said: 424 "Certain leaders will lead you after me who will smother the Sunna, proclaim innovation, and delay the prayer from its times."[573]

عَنْ عَبْدِ اللهِ بْنِ مَسْعُودٍ رَضِيَ اللهُ عَنْهُ أَنَّ النَّبِيَّ ﷺ قَالَ سَيَلي أُمُورَكُمْ بَعْدِي رِجَالٌ يُطْفِئُونَ السُّنَّةَ وَيَعْمَلُونَ بَالْبِدعَةِ ويُؤَخِّرُونَ الصلاةَ عَنْ مَواقِيتها فَقُلْتُ يَا رَسُولَ اللهِ إِنْ أَدْرَكْتُهُمْ كَيْفَ أَفعلُ قَالَ تَسْأَلُنِي يَا ابْنَ أُمِّ عَبْدٍ كَيْفَ تَفْعَلُ لاَ طَاعَةَ لِمَنْ عَصَى اللهَ جه كر وجاء بلفظ وَيُعْلِنُونَ الْبِدعَةَ أبو نعيم في الدلائل وَيُحْدِثُونَ بِدعَةً حم هق وفي الدلائل كر

Ibn Mājah and al-Bayhaqī narrated from Ibn Masʿūd ﷺ that the Messenger of Allah ﷺ said: 425 "You might live to see people who will perform their prayers outside their times. If you live to see them, then do your prayers in your houses and at the time that you know is correct, then pray with them and make the latter prayer supererogatory."[574]

[573]Narrated from Ibn Masʿūd by Aḥmad with a fair to sound chain and Ibn Mājah with a weak chain.

[574]Narrated from Ibn Masʿūd by al-Nasāʾī, Ibn Mājah, Aḥmad and others with a good chain, from Abū Dharr by Muslim and others, and *mawqūf* from Ibn Masʿūd by Muslim, Aḥmad and others among other versions.

عَنِ ابْنِ مَسْعُودٍ رَضِيَ اللهُ عَنْهُ قَالَ رَسُولُ اللهِ ﷺ لَعَلَّكُمْ سَتُدْرِكُونَ أَقْوَامًا يُصَلُّونَ الصَّلاَةَ لِغَيْرِ وَقْتِهَا فَإِنْ أَدْرَكْتُمُوهُمْ فَصَلُّوا الصَّلاَةَ لِوَقْتِهَا وَصَلُّوا مَعَهُمْ وَاجْعَلُوهَا سُبْحَةً ن د جه حم ز خز حب ابن الجارود معجم ابن الأعرابي هق وفي الدلائل وفي الباب عن أنس ع طس وفي إسناده من لا يعرف مج وعن قَبِيصَةَ بنِ وَقّاصٍ د وعن أبي ذر م ن ت د مستخرج أبي عوانة وعبادة بن السامط يأتي وجاء موقوفاً على ابن مسعود م حم طب ش هق وفي الدلائل

Ibn Mājah narrated from 'Ubāda b. al-Ṣāmit ؓ that the Prophet ﷺ said: 426 "There will be leaders who become so busy that they will delay the prayer from its proper time. Therefore, make your prayers with them supererogatory."[575] The ḥadīth Master al-Suyūṭī said: "These leaders were of the Banū Umayya. They were known for delaying the prayer until the day 'Umar b. 'Abd al-'Azīz ruled, at which time he returned the prayer to its proper time."[576]

عَنْ عُبَادَةَ بْنِ الصَّامِتِ رَضِيَ اللهُ عَنْهُ عَنِ النَّبِيِّ ﷺ سَتَكُونُ أُمَرَاءُ تَشْغَلُهُمْ أَشْيَاءُ يُؤَخِّرُونَ الصَّلاَةَ عَنْ وَقْتِهَا فَصَلُّوا الصَّلاَةَ لِوَقْتِهَا وَاجْعَلُوا صَلاَتَكُمْ مَعَهُمْ تَطَوُّعًا جه حم قال في الخصائص كانت هذه الأمراء بني أمية فإنهم معروفون بذلك إلى أن ولي عمر بن عبد العزيز فأعاد الصلاة إلى ميقاتها

[575]Narrated from 'Abd Allāh b. al-Sāmit (not 'Ubāda), from Abū Dharr by Muslim, in the four *Sunan*, Aḥmad, and al-Dārimī.

[576]Al-Suyūṭī, *Khasā'is* (2:242).

His ﷺ Foretelling of the Status of the Banū al-ʿAbbās

Al-Bazzār and others narrated from Abū Hurayra ؓ that the Prophet ﷺ said to al-ʿAbbās: 427 "In you all are Prophethood and Kingdom" *(fīkum al-nubuwwatu wal-mamlaka)*.[577]

عَنْ أَبِي هُرَيْرَةَ رَضِيَ اللهُ عَنْهُ أَنَّ النَّبِيَّ ﷺ قَالَ لِلْعَبَّاسِ بْنِ عَبْدِ الْمُطَّلِبِ فِيكُمُ النُّبُوَّةُ وَالْمَمْلَكَةُ ز عد أمالي ابن بشران هق في الدلائل كر

الداني في الفتن وعزاه الذهبي فى السير لابن ديزيل فى جزئه وقال هو منكر وقال ابن القيم

في المنار كل حديث فيه ذكر الخلافة في ولد العباس فهو كذب

Abū Nuʿaym narrated that Ibn ʿAbbās رضي الله عنهما said: "Umm al-Faḍl [his mother] narrated to me that as she passed by the Prophet ﷺ he said to her: a 'You are pregnant with a boy. When you give birth, bring him to me.' She said that when she gave birth she brought her child to him **[531]** and he raised the call to prayer in his right ear and the start of prayer in his left. Then he blew some moist air into his mouth and named him ʿAbd Allāh. Then he said: b 'Take the Father of Caliphs with you.' She went back and told al-ʿAbbās who came to the Prophet ﷺ, asking for confirmation. The latter said: c 'Just as she said, this is the Father of Caliphs until al-Saffāḥ comes out from them, to the time when al-Mahdī comes out from them.'"[578]

عَنِ ابْنِ عَبَّاسٍ رَضِيَ اللهُ عَنْهُمَا قَالَ حَدَّثَتْنِي أُمُّ الْفَضْلِ بِنْتُ الْحَارِثِ قَالَتْ بَيْنَا أَنَا مَارَّةٌ وَالنَّبِيُّ ﷺ فِي الْحِجْرِ فَقَالَ يَا أُمَّ الْفَضْلِ قُلْتُ لَبَّيْكَ يَا رَسُولَ اللهِ قَالَ إِنَّكِ حَامِلٌ بِغُلَامٍ قَالَتْ

[577]Narrated by al-Bazzār (*Kashf al-Astār* 2:229 §1581), Ibn ʿAdī (4:1574), Ibn Bishrān in his *Amālī* (1:65 §101), al-Bayhaqī in the *Dalāʾil* (6:517), al-Dānī in *al-Sunan al-Wārida fīl-Fitan* (1:488-489 §107), and Ibn ʿAsākir (26:347) all through Muḥammad b. ʿAbd al-Raḥmān al-ʿĀmirī who is weak cf. al-Haythamī (5:192-193), *Lisān* (3:299), Ibn al-Jawzī, *ʿIlal* (1:298), *Mīzān* (*s.v.* ʿAbd Allāh b. Shabīb), and *Siyar* (Risāla ed. 2:93 *munkar*).

[578]See first hadith in section entitled "Umm al-Faḍl the wife of al-ʿAbbās."

كَيْفَ وَقَدْ تَحَالَفَتْ قُرَيْشٌ لاَ تُولِدُونَ النِّسَاءَ قَالَ هُوَ مَا أَقُولُ لَكِ فَإِذَا وَضَعْتِيهِ فَائْتِنِي بِهِ فَلَمَّا وَضَعَتْهُ أَتَتْ بِهِ النَّبِيَّ ﷺ فَسَمَّاهُ عَبْدَ اللهِ وَأَلْبَأَهُ مِنْ رِيقِهِ ثُمَّ قَالَ اذْهَبِي بِهِ فَلَتَجِدِنَّهُ كَيِّسًا قَالَتْ فَأَتَيْتُ الْعَبَّاسَ فَأَخْبَرْتُهُ فَتَلَبَّسَ ثُمَّ أَتَى النَّبِيَّ ﷺ وَكَانَ رَجُلاً جَمِيلاً مَدِيدَ الْقَامَةِ فَلَمَّا رَآهُ رَسُولُ اللهِ ﷺ قَامَ إِلَيْهِ فَقَبَّلَ بَيْنَ عَيْنَيْهِ ثُمَّ أَقْعَدَهُ عَنْ يَمِينِهِ ثُمَّ قَالَ هَذَا عَمِّي فَمَنْ شَاءَ فَلْيُبَاهِ بِعَمِّهِ قَالَ الْعَبَّاسُ بَعْضَ الْقَوْلِ يَا رَسُولَ اللهِ قَالَ وَلِمَ لاَ أَقُولُ وَأَنْتَ عَمِّي وَبَقِيَّةُ آبَائِي وَالْعَمُّ وَالِدٌ طب وورد زيادة فَقَالَ يَا عَبَّاسُ لِمَ لاَ أَقُولُ لَكَ هَذَا وَأَنْتَ عَمِّي وَصِنْوُ أَبِي وَبَقِيَّةُ آبَائِي وَخَيْرُ مَنْ أَخْلَفَ بَعْدِي مِنْ أَهْلِي فَقُلْتُ يَا رَسُولَ اللهِ مَا شَيْءٌ أَخْبَرَتْنِي بِهِ أُمُّ الْفَضْلِ عَنْ مَوْلُودِنَا هَذَا قَالَ نَعَمْ يَا عَبَّاسُ إِذَا كَانَتْ سَنَةُ خَمْسٍ وَثَلاَثِينَ وَمِائَةٍ فَهِيَ لَكَ وَلِوَلَدِكَ مِنْهُمُ السَّفَّاحُ وَمِنْهُمُ الْمَنْصُورُ وَمِنْهُمُ الْمَهْدِيُّ كر وورد زيادة حَتَّى يَكُونَ مِنْهُمْ مَنْ يُصَلِّي بِعِيسَى ابْنِ مَرْيَمَ عَلَيْهِ السَّلاَمُ

طس أبو نعيم في الدلائل خط فيه أحمد بن رشد الهلالي وقد اتهم بهذا الحديث مج ميزان لسان وقد مر عند ذكر أحاديث أم الفضل رضي الله عنها وقال ابن القيم في المنار المنيف كل حديث في ذكر الخلافة في ولد العباس فهو كذب وحديث عدد الخلفاء من ولد العباس كذب اهـ. والله أعلم بالصواب

Ibn ʿAdī, al-Bayhaqī, and Abū Nuʿaym narrated that Ibn ʿAbbās رضي الله عنهما said: "I passed by the Prophet ﷺ as Jibrīl was with him but

I thought it was Diḥyat al-Kalbī. I was wearing white clothes. Jibrīl عليه السلام said to the Prophet ﷺ: a 'What bright clothes he wears! But his children will wear black.' Later, I said to the Prophet ﷺ: 'I passed and saw you with Diḥyat al-Kalbī.'" Then he mentioned the account of his blindness and its removal before his death.[579]

عَنِ ابْنِ عَبَّاسٍ رَضِيَ اللهُ عَنْهُمَا قَالَ مَرَرْتُ بِالنَّبِيِّ ﷺ وَقَدِ انْصَرَفَ مِنْ صَلَاةِ الظُّهْرِ وَعَلَيَّ ثِيَابُ بَيَاضٍ وَهُوَ يُنَاجِي دِحْيَةَ الْكَلْبِيَّ فِيمَا ظَنَنْتُ وَكَانَ جِبْرِيلُ وَلَا أَدْرِي فَقَالَ جِبْرِيلُ لِلنَّبِيِّ ﷺ يَا رَسُولَ اللهِ هَذَا ابْنُ عَبَّاسٍ أَمَا إِنَّهُ لَوْ سَلَّمَ عَلَيْنَا لَرَدَدْنَا عَلَيْهِ أَمَا إِنَّهُ شَدِيدٌ وَضَحُ الثِّيَابِ وَلَيَلْبَسَنَّ ذُرِّيَّتُهُ مِنْ بَعْدِهِ السَّوَادَ الحَدِيثَ كر وقد مر تخريجه ولفظه الصحيح عند ذكر أحاديث ابن عباس رضي الله عنهما

Al-Bayhaqī and Abū Nuʿaym narrated from Abū Hurayra ؓ that the Prophet ﷺ said: 428 "The black flags shall come out of Khurāsān. Nothing will stop them until they are hoisted in Jerusalem (Īlyāʾ)!"[580]

عَنْ أَبِي هُرَيْرَةَ رَضِيَ اللهُ عَنْهُ عَنْ رَسُولِ اللهِ ﷺ قَالَ يَخْرُجُ مِنْ خُرَاسَانَ رَايَاتٌ سُودٌ لَا يَرُدُّهَا شَيْءٌ حَتَّى تُنْصَبَ بِإِيلِيَاءَ حم ت طس هق في الدلائل كر قال ياقوت إيلياء بكسر أوله واللام وياء وألف ممدودة إسم مدينة

---

[579] See second hadith in section entitled "ʿAbd Allāh b. ʿAbbās."
[580] Narrated with weak chains by al-Tirmidhī (gharīb, some mss. adding hasan), Aḥmad, al-Ṭabarānī in al-Awsaṭ (4:31 §3536), all with a weak chain through Rishdīn b. Saʿd cf. Ibn Ḥajar, al-Qawl al-Musaddad (1:42), Bidāya (10:51), al-Suyūṭī, Ziyādat al-Jāmiʿ al-Ṣaghīr (§4326), and Kanz (§38652).

بيت المقدس قيل معناه بيت الله وحكى الحفصي فيه القصر وفيه لغة ثالثة حذف الياء الأولى فيقال إلياء بسكون اللام والمد قال أبو علي وقد سمي البيت المقدس إيلياء

Al-Ḥākim and Abū Nuʿaym narrated from Ibn Masʿūd ﷺ that the Prophet ﷺ said: 429 "For us – the People of the House – Allah has chosen the next world over this world. Truly, a the people of my House will endure trial, alienation, and expulsion after me, until a people come from there – he pointed toward the East – bearing black flags. They will demand their due right without obtaining it. They will fight and gain victory. They will be given the rule until they pass it on to one of my descendants who will fill the world with justice even as it was filled with injustice before. <Whoever lives to see this among you, let him come to him even if he must crawl over ice>."[581] [The black flags are mentioned in other ḥadīths, most specifying they hail from the East.][582]

عَنْ عَبْدِ اللهِ رَضِيَ اللهُ عَنْهُ قَالَ بَيْنَمَا نَحْنُ عِنْدَ رَسُولِ اللهِ ﷺ إِذْ أَقْبَلَ فِتْيَةٌ مِنْ بَنِي هَاشِمٍ فَلَمَّا رَآهُمُ النَّبِيُّ ﷺ اغْرَوْرَقَتْ عَيْنَاهُ وَتَغَيَّرَ لَوْنُهُ قَالَ فَقُلْتُ مَا نَزَالُ نَرَى فِي وَجْهِكَ شَيْئًا نَكْرَهُهُ فَقَالَ إِنَّا أَهْلُ بَيْتٍ اخْتَارَ اللهُ لَنَا الْآخِرَةَ عَلَى الدُّنْيَا وَإِنَّ أَهْلَ بَيْتِي سَيَلْقَوْنَ بَعْدِي بَلَاءً

---

[581]Narrated from Ibn Masʿūd by Ibn Mājah cf. *Misbāḥ al-Zujāja* (4:203) and Ibn al-Qayyim, *al-Manār al-Munīf*, Ibn Abī Shayba (7:527 §37727), al-Ḥākim (1990 ed. 4:511 inauthentic cf. *Mīzān*, ʿAbd Allāh b. Dāhir and Yazīd b. Abī Zyād) cf. *Lisān* (3:282) and Ibn ʿAdī (4:228), al-Shāshī, *Musnad* (1:347 §329, 1:362 §351), al-Ṭabarānī in *al-Awsaṭ* (6:29-30 §5699), Abū Yaʿlā (9:17 §5084 in part), Nuʿaym b. Ḥammād in the *Fitan* (1:310-311 §895), al-Dānī in *al-Sunan al-Wārida fīl-Fitan* (5:1029-1032 §546-547), all through Yazīd b. Abī Zyād who is weak although some graded his chain fair cf. Ibn Kathīr, *Bidāya* (6:246 *isnād ḥasan*) and al-Haythamī (7:316). Yazīd is further corroborated [1] by ʿUmāra b. al-Qaʿqāʿ in al-Khaṭīb's narration in *al-Riḥla fī Ṭalab al-Ḥadīth* ('Iṭr ed. p. 146-147=p. 208-209) although with two very weak chains; and [2] by al-Ḥakam b. ʿUtayba by al-Bazzār (4:310 §1491) with a usable chain. Al-Nabhānī omits the bracketed segment.

[582]Narrated from [1] Thawbān by Aḥmad (al-Mahdī) with a weak chain cf. Ibn Ḥajar, *al-Qawl al-Musaddad* (1:42); [2] ʿAlī by Nuʿaym b. Ḥammād (1:314 §907, 1:349 §1007); and *mursal* from [3] Saʿīd b. al-Musayyib and [4] Kaʿb al-Aḥbār by Nuʿaym b. Ḥammād (1:203 §555, 1:206 §562, 1:209 §570, §572, 1:313 §906, 2:696-697 §1975) cf. *Kanz* (§31037).

وَتَشْرِيدًا وَتَطْرِيدًا حَتَّى يَأْتِيَ قَوْمٌ مِنْ قِبَلِ الْمَشْرِقِ مَعَهُمْ رَايَاتٌ سُودٌ فَيَسْأَلُونَ الْخَيْرَ فَلاَ يُعْطَوْنَهُ فَيُقَاتِلُونَ فَيُنْصَرُونَ فَيُعْطَوْنَ مَا سَأَلُوا فَلاَ يَقْبَلُونَهُ حَتَّى يَدْفَعُوهَا إِلَى رَجُلٍ مِنْ أَهْلِ بَيْتِي فَيَمْلَؤُهَا قِسْطًا كَمَا مَلَئُوهَا جَوْرًا فَمَنْ أَدْرَكَ ذَلِكَ مِنْكُمْ فَلْيَأْتِهِمْ وَلَوْ حَبْوًا عَلَى الثَّلْجِ جه ش

ع ك عد وحسّن إسناده الحافظ ابن كثير في البداية وله توابع ز خط في الرحلة

Aḥmad, al-Bayhaqī, and Abū Nuʿaym narrated from Abū Saʿīd al-Khudrī ﷺ that the Messenger of Allah ﷺ said: 430 "There will appear a man of my House, after a lapse of time and when the dissensions appear, named al-Saffāḥ. He will distribute money and property in abundance."[583]

عَنْ أَبِي سَعِيدٍ الْخُدْرِيِّ رَضِيَ اللهُ عَنْهُ قَالَ قَالَ رَسُولُ اللهِ ﷺ يَخْرُجُ عِنْدَ انْقِطَاعٍ مِنْ الزَّمَانِ وَظُهُورٍ مِنْ الْفِتَنِ رَجُلٌ يُقَالُ لَهُ السَّفَّاحُ فَيَكُونُ إِعْطَاؤُهُ الْمَالَ حَثْيًا حم ش أبو نعيم في أخبار أصبهان

هق في الدلائل كر فيه عطية العوفى وهو ضعيف ووثقه ابن معين وبقية رجاله ثقات مج قلت فيه أيضا عنعنة الأعمش وهو مدلس قال ابن أبي الدنيا: كان السفاح أبيض طويلاً أقنى ذا شعرة جعدة حسن اللحية مات بالجدري

Al-Bayhaqī and Abū Nuʿaym narrated from Ibn ʿAbbās رضي الله عنهما that the Messenger of Allah ﷺ said: 431 "From us will come al-Saffāḥ, al-Manṣūr and al-Mahdī."[584] Al-Bayhaqī narrates something similar with a sound chain.[585]

[583]Narrated from Abū Saʿīd by Aḥmad and al-Khaṭīb (10:48), both with a weak chain because of ʿAṭiyya b. Saʿd al-ʿAwfī cf. al-Haythamī (7:314).

[584]Narrated from Ibn ʿAbbās by al-Khaṭīb (1:62-63, 9:399) but Ibn al-Jawzī in *al-ʿIlal* (1:290-292) and Ibn Kathīr in *al-Bidāya* (6:246) weaken it while al-Dhahabī, *Mīzān* (*s.v.* Muḥammad b. Jābir al-Yamāmī) and Ibn Ḥajar, *Tahdhīb al-Tahdhīb* (9:78) grade it "thoroughly disclaimed" *(munkar jiddan)* cf. al-Aḥdab, *Zawāʾid* (1:164 §26), and rather a

عَنِ ابْنِ عَبَّاسٍ رَضِيَ اللهُ عَنْهُمَا قَالَ مِنَّا ثَلاَثَةٌ مِنَّا السَّفَّاحُ وَمِنَّا الْمَنْصُورُ وَمِنَّا الْمَهْدِيُّ ش وجاء بلفظ مِنَّا أَهْلِ البَيْتِ أَرْبَعَةٌ مِنَّا السَّفَّاحُ وَمِنَّا المُنْذِرُ وَمِنَّا المَنْصُورُ وَمِنَّا المَهْدِيُّ ك صححه وتعقب وروي مرفوعاً خط هق في الدلائل كر قال في الميزان منكر منقطع ثم أثبته في التاريخ موقوفاً وقال ابن كثير في البداية والنهاية قد نطقت هذه الأحاديث التي أوردناها آنفا بالسفاح والمنصور والمهدي ولا شك أن المهدي الذي هو ابن المنصور ثالث خلفاء بني العباس ليس هو المهدي الذي وردت الأحاديث المستفيضة بذكره وأنه يكون في آخر الزمان يملأ الأرض عدلاً وقسطاً كما ملئت جَوراً وظلماً وأما السفاح فقد تقدم أنه يكون في آخر الزمان فيبعد أن يكون هو الذي بويع أول خلفاء بني العباس فقد يكون خليفة آخر وهذا هو الظاهر فإنه قد روى نعيم بن حماد عن ابن وهب عن ابن لهيعة عن يزيد بن عمرو المعافري من قدوم الحميري سمع تُبَيْعَ بن عامر يقول يعيش السفّاح أربعين سنة اسمه في التوراة طائر السماء قلت أي ابن كثير وقد تكون صفة للمهدي الذي يظهر في آخر الزمان لكثرة ما يسفح أي يريق من الدماء لإقامة العدل ونشر القسط وتكون الرايات السود المذكورة في هذه الأحاديث إن صحت هي التي تكون مع المهدي ويكون أول ظهور بيعته بمكة ثم تكون أنصاره من خراسان كما وقع قديما للسفاح والله تعالى أعلم هذا كله تفريع على صحة هذه الأحاديث وإلا فلا يخلو سند منها عن كلام والله سبحانه وتعالى أعلم بالصواب. اهـ.

Al-Zubayr b. Bakkār narrated in the *Muwaffaqiyyāt* from ʿAlī b. Abī Ṭālib ﷺ that he dictated a last will after Ibn Muljam

mawqūf report from Ibn ʿAbbās cf. al-Khaṭīb (10:48), al-Ḥākim (1990 ed. 4:559 *isnād ṣaḥīḥ* but Ismāʿīl b. Ibrāhīm b. Muhājir is weak), and Ibn Ḥajar, *Tahdhīb* (9:354); also from Ibn ʿAbbās and ʿAbd Allāh b. ʿAmr by Nuʿaym in the *Fitan* (1:96 §228, 1:400 §1203-1205, 2:444 §1282) with an odd chain of trustworthy narrators per al-Bukhārī's criterion: al-Walīd b. Muslim, from ʿAbd al-Malik b. Ḥumayd b. Abī Ghaniyya, from al-Minhāl b. ʿAmr, from Saʿīd b. Jubayr, from Ibn ʿAbbās. Al-Dhahabī declares that chain strong in the chapter on the Caliph al-Mansur in his *Siyar*.

[585]*Mawqūf* on Ibn ʿAbbās cf. *Khaṣāʾis* (2:203) with the chain cited in the previous note.

stabbed him. In it he said: 432 "The Messenger of Allah ﷺ informed me of the differences that would arise after him and ordered me to fight traitors, deceivers, and renegades. He told me of this one who struck me. He told me that Mu'āwiya would reign, then his son Yazīd, then the Banū Marwān after them by hereditary succession, then this rule would end up with the Banū Umayya, followed by the Banū al-'Abbās. He showed me the soil from al-Ḥusayn's killing-ground."[586]

قال في الخصائص وأخرج الزبير بن بكار في الموفقيات وليس في المطبوع فيكون في الجزء المفقود منه عَنْ عَلِيِّ بْنِ أَبِي طَالِبٍ رَضِيَ اللهُ عَنْهُ أَنَّهُ أَوْصَى حِينَ ضَرَبَهُ ابْنُ مُلْجَمٍ فَقَالَ فِي وَصِيَّتِهِ إِنَّ رَسُولَ اللهِ ﷺ أَخْبَرَنِي بِمَا يَكُونُ مِنْ إِخْتِلَافٍ بَعْدَهُ وَأَمَرَنِي بِقِتَالِ النَّاكِثِينَ وَالْمَارِقِينَ وَالْقَاسِطِينَ وَأَخْبَرَنِي بِهَذَا الَّذِي أَصَابَنِي وَأَخْبَرَنِي أَنَّهُ يَمْلِكُ مُعَاوِيَةُ وَابْنُهُ يَزِيدُ ثُمَّ يَصِيرُ إِلَى بَنِي مَرْوَانَ يَتَوَارَثُونَهَا وَأَنَّ هَذَا الْأَمْرَ صَائِرٌ إِلَى بَنِي أُمَيَّةَ ثُمَّ إِلَى بَنِي الْعَبَّاسِ وَأَرَانِي التُّرْبَةَ الَّتِي يُقْتَلُ بِهَا الْحُسَيْنُ وقد مر مختصراً في باب سيدنا علي رضي الله عنه وأرضاه

Al-Ḥākim narrated from Abū Sa'īd al-Khudrī ﷺ that the Messenger of Allah ﷺ: 433 "The people of my House will meet with murder and dispossession after my time. a <Those of our people that will hate us the most are the Banū Umayya and the Banū al-Mughīra of the Banū Makhzūm.>"[587]

[586]Narrated in this long version only in the *Khaṣā'iṣ* (see note 117) and not found in the printed edition of the *Muwaffaqiyyāt*, which is only a partial remnant of the much longer original, for the most part lost.

[587]Narrated from Abū Sa'īd by Nu'aym, *Fitan* (1:131 §319) Ḥākim (1990 ed. 4:534) both through Abū Rāfi' Ismā'īl b. Rāfi' who is weak despite al-Ḥākim's claim that the chain is *saḥīḥ*. Nabhānī omits the bracketed segment. Something close is related from Ibn Mas'ūd by Ibn Mājah, Bazzār, Ṭabarānī and others, through very weak or forged chains. See Ibn al-Mulaqqin, *Mukhtaṣar* (7:3322-3324 §1108 and 7:3366-3367 §1122); Ibn Abī Shayba

عَنْ أَبِي سعيدٍ الخُدْرِيِّ رَضِيَ اللهُ عَنْهُ قَالَ قَالَ رَسُولُ اللهِ ﷺ إِنَّ أَهْلَ بَيْتِي سَيَلْقَوْنَ مِنْ بَعْدِي مِنْ أُمَّتِي قَتْلاً وَتَشْرِيداً وَإِنَّ أَشَدَّ قَوْماً لَنَا بُغْضاً بَنُو أُمَيَّةَ وَبَنُو الْمُغِيرَةِ وَبَنُو مَخْزُومٍ رواه نعيم بن حماد في الفتن ومن طريقه ك وقال صحيح الإسناد وتعقبه الذهبي فقال لا والله كيف وإسماعيل متروك ثم لم يصح السند إليه اهـ. أي لعنعنة الوليد بن مسلم ولضعف نعيم وجاء من وجه آخر عَنْ عَبْدِ اللهِ بْنِ مَسْعُودٍ رَضِيَ اللهُ عَنْهُ قَالَ بَيْنَا نَحْنُ عِنْدَ رَسُولِ اللهِ ﷺ إِذْ أَقْبَلَ فِتْيَةٌ مِنْ بَنِي هَاشِمٍ فَلَمَّا رَآهُمَ النَّبِيُّ ﷺ اغْرَوْرَقَتْ عَيْنَاهُ وَتَغَيَّرَ لَوْنُهُ قَالَ فَقُلْتُ لَهُ مَا نَزَالُ نَرَى فِي وَجْهِكَ شَيْئًا نَكْرَهُهُ قَالَ إِنَّا أَهْلَ البَيْتِ اخْتَارَ اللهُ لَنَا الآخِرَةَ عَلَى الدُّنْيَا وَإِنَّ أَهْلَ بَيْتِي سَيَلْقَوْنَ بَعْدِي بَلاَءً وَتَشْرِيدًا وَتَطْرِيدًا حَتَّى يَأْتِيَ قَوْمٌ مِنْ قِبَلِ الْمَشْرِقِ مَعَهُمْ رَايَاتٌ سُودٌ الحديث جه ش طس ع السنة لابن أبي عاصم العقيلي أبو نعيم في أخبار أصبهان وأربعين المهدي الآجري في الشريعة جميعهم من طريق يزيد بن أبي زياد الكوفي الشيعي عن إبراهيم وتابعه عمرو بن قيس الملائي عن الحكم عن إبراهيم به ك قال الذهبي موضوع أي بهذا الإسناد إذ فيه حَنَان (بالحاء المهملة ثم النونين مخففة) بن سَدير الكوفي رافضي غال وابن أبي دارم الرافضي شيخ الحاكم وهو القائل فيه إنه ضال وشيخه وشيخ شيخه مجهولان فلا يبعد أن يكون هذا السند من تركيب أحدهم بعدما سرقه من يزيد وتابعه ابن أبي ليلى عن الحكم عن إبراهيم به طب ز عد من طريق عبد الله بن داهر الرازي وهو أيضاً رافضي وتابعه مغيرة بن مقسم عن عمارة بن القعقاع عن إبراهيم به خط في الرحلة وسنده منقطع وفيه محمد بن إبراهيم بن زياد الطيالسي الرازي قال قط دجال يضع الحديث والله أعلم

(ʿAwwāma ed. 21:336-338 §38882); and Ājurrī, *Sharīʿa* (Sayf al-Naṣr ed. 3:322 §1727).

His ﷺ Foretelling of Other Unseen Matters

Al-Bayhaqī narrated that Umm Kulthūm رضي الله عنها [Umm Salama's daughter] said, "When the Prophet ﷺ married Umm Salama رضي الله عنها, he said: 434 'I gifted a few ounces of musk and a tunic to the Negus but I believe he died and I do not think except the gift will be returned to me.'" Al-Bayhaqī said he meant – Allah knows best – that he died before receiving the gift even though the Prophet ﷺ made this statement before the death of the Negus then, when he did die, he announced his death and led the funeral prayer for him [in absentia]. [The gifts were returned and the Prophet ﷺ gave each of his wives an ounce of perfume and gave the rest and the tunic to Umm Salama.][588]

عَنْ أُمِّ كُلْثُومٍ بِنْتِ أَبِي سَلَمَةَ قَالَتْ لَمَّا تَزَوَّجَ رَسُولُ اللهِ ﷺ أُمَّ سَلَمَةَ قَالَ لَهَا إِنِّي قَدْ أَهْدَيْتُ إِلَى النَّجَاشِيِّ حُلَّةً وَأَوَاقِيَّ مِنْ مِسْكٍ وَلاَ أَرَى النَّجَاشِيَّ إِلاَّ قَدْ مَاتَ وَلاَ أَرَى إِلاَّ هَدِيَّتِي مَرْدُودَةً عَلَيَّ فَإِنْ رُدَّتْ عَلَيَّ فَهِيَ لَكِ قَالَ وَكَانَ كَمَا قَالَ رَسُولُ اللهِ ﷺ وَرُدَّتْ عَلَيْهِ هَدِيَّتُهُ فَأَعْطَى كُلَّ امْرَأَةٍ مِنْ نِسَائِهِ أُوقِيَّةَ مِسْكٍ وَأَعْطَى أُمَّ سَلَمَةَ بَقِيَّةَ الْمِسْكِ وَالْحُلَّةَ حم طب حب ك

هق وفي الدلائل وغيرهم ورواه حب عن أم سلمة متصلاً

The Two Masters [Bukhārī and Muslim] narrated from Jābir رضي الله عنه that the Messenger of Allah ﷺ said: 435 "Today a righteous man died, so pray over Aṣḥama."[589] **[532]**

[588]Narrated from Umm Kulthūm by Aḥmad, Ibn Saʿd (8:95), Saʿīd b. Manṣūr in his *Sunan* (p. 161 §485), Ibn Abī ʿĀṣim in *al-Āḥād wal-Mathānī* (6:226 §3459), al-Ṭaḥāwī in *Sharḥ Mushkil al-Āthār*, al-Ṭabarānī in the *Kabīr*, al-Taymī in *Dalā'il al-Nubuwwa* (p. 150 §162), Ibn Ḥibbān (15:515-516 §5112), al-Ḥākim (1990 ed. *isnād saḥīḥ*), al-Bayhaqī in the *Sunan* (6:26) and *Dalā'il*, Ibn ʿAbd al-Barr in *al-Istīʿāb* (4:1953) and others.

[589]Narrated from Jābir by al-Bukhārī and Muslim, the former with the wording, "your brother Aṣḥama."

عَنْ جَابِرٍ رَضِيَ اللهُ عَنْهُ قَالَ النَّبِيُّ ﷺ حِينَ مَاتَ النَّجَاشِيُّ مَاتَ الْيَوْمَ رَجُلٌ صَالِحٌ فَقُومُوا فَصَلُّوا عَلَى أَخِيكُمْ أَصْحَمَةَ ق

They also narrated from Abū Hurayra ؓ that the [436] Messenger of Allah ﷺ announced the death of the Negus on the day that he died and went out with them to the place of prayer. He had them line up then pronounced *Allāhu akbar* four times.

عَنْ أَبِي هُرَيْرَةَ رَضِيَ اللهُ عَنْهُ نَعَى رَسُولُ اللهِ ﷺ النَّجَاشِيَّ فِي الْيَوْمِ الَّذِي مَاتَ فِيهِ وَخَرَجَ بِهِمْ إِلَى الْمُصَلَّى فَصَفَّ بِهِمْ وَكَبَّرَ عَلَيْهِ أَرْبَعَ تَكْبِيرَاتٍ ق

Al-Ḥākim and al-Bayhaqī narrated that al-Walīd b. ʿUqba ؓ said: "[437] When the Messenger of Allah ﷺ conquered Mecca, the people of Mecca took to bringing him their little boys and he would pat them on the head and pray for them. My mother took me out and went to see him. I had been daubed with saffron-mixed perfume so he did not pat me on the head or touch me." Al-Bayhaqī said [that Aḥmad b. Ḥanbal said]: "This is because of what Allah revealed to him concerning al-Walīd, so the latter was deprived of the blessing of the Messenger of Allah ﷺ."[590] Al-Walīd's notoriety at the time ʿUthmān appointed him is well-known, such as wine-bibbing and delaying the prayer. He was among the reasons ʿUthmān ؓ was criticized.

---

[590] Narrated by Aḥmad, al-Bukhārī in *al-Tārīkh al-Kabīr* (under al-Walīd b. ʿUqba), al-Ṭabarānī in *al-Kabīr* (22:150-151 §405-406), al-Ḥākim (3:100), al-Bayhaqī (9:55) and in the *Dalāʾil*, but Ibn ʿAbd al-Barr and Ibn Ḥajar (cf. *Iṣāba*, under al-Walīd) as well as al-Ṣanʿānī in his discussion of the probity of the Companions in *Tawḍīḥ al-Afkār* doubted the veracity of this report since al-Walīd must have already been older at that time.

عَنِ الْوَلِيدِ بْنِ عُقْبَةَ ﷺ قَالَ لَمَّا فَتَحَ رَسُولُ اللهِ ﷺ مَكَّةَ جَعَلَ أَهْلُ مَكَّةَ يَأْتُونَهُ بِصِبْيَانِهِمْ فَيَمْسَحُ عَلَى رُؤُوسِهِمْ وَيَدْعُو لَهُمْ فَجِيءَ بِي إِلَيْهِ وَإِنِّي مُطَيَّبٌ بِالْخَلُوقِ وَلَمْ يَمْسَحْ عَلَى رَأْسِي وَلَمْ يَمْنَعْهُ مِنْ ذَلِكَ إِلَّا أَنَّ أُمِّي خَلَّقَتْنِي بِالْخَلُوقِ فَلَمْ يَمَسَّنِي مِنْ أَجْلِ الْخَلُوقِ حم وهذا لفظه د خت طب ك هق وفي الدلائل والمعرفة والصغرى قال قَالَ أَحْمَدُ بْنُ حَنْبَلٍ مُنِعَ بَرَكَةَ رَسُولِ اللهِ ﷺ لِسَابِقِ عِلْمِ اللهِ فِيهِ لكن قال الحافظ في الإصابة قال ابن عبد البر قد ذكر الزبير وغيره من أهل العلم بالسير أن أم كلثوم بنت عقبة لما خرجت إلى النبي ﷺ مهاجرة في الهدنة سنة سبع خرج أخواها الوليد وعمارة ليرداها فمن يكون صبيا يوم الفتح كيف يكون ممن خرج ليرد أخته قبل الفتح قلت أي الحافظ ومما يؤيد أنه كان في الفتح رجلاً أنه كان قدم في فداء ابن عم أبيه الحارث بن أبي وجزة بن أبي عمرو بن أمية وكان أُسِر يوم بدر فافتداه بأربعة آلاف حكاه أصحاب المغازي. اهـ.

Al-Khaṭīb narrated from Aslam ﷺ that ʿUmar b. al-Khaṭṭāb ﷺ said to the chieftain of Khaybar: "Do you think I forgot the saying of the Messenger of Allah ﷺ [concerning you]: 438 'What will you do when you and your camel amble on your way to Syro-Palestine, closer and closer day by day?'"[591]

قال في الخصائص الكبرى أخرج الخطيب في رواة مالك عَنْ أَسْلَمَ قَالَ قَالَ عُمَرُ ابْنُ الْخَطَّابِ رَضِيَ اللهُ عَنْهُ لِرَئِيسِ خَيْبَرَ تُرَى ذَهَبَ عَنِّي قَوْلُ رَسُولِ اللهِ ﷺ كَيْفَ بِكَ إِذَا رَفَصَ بِكَ بَعِيرُكَ يَوْماً نَحْوَ الشَّامِ

[591]Narrated by al-Ṭaḥāwī in the *Mushkil* (chapter on the Prophetic command to expel Jews and Christians from the Arabian peninsula) and al-Bayhaqī in the *Sunan* (9:137) and *Dalā'il*. The context of this incident is described in al-Bukhārī (*Shurūṭ, idhā ishtaraṭa fīl muzāraʿa idhā shi'tu akhrajtuk*), hence Ibn Ḥajar also discusses this hadith in the *Fatḥ* (5:328-329) and *Taghlīq al-Taʿlīq* (3:412).

The Prophet's ﷺ Knowledge of the Unseen • 419

ثُمَّ يَوْماً ثُمَّ يَوْماً جاء عند المؤلف بلفظ رَمَضَ ورواه حب بلفظ أَتُرَاهُ سَقَطَ عَنِّي قَوْلُ رَسُولِ اللهِ ﷺ كَيْفَ بِكَ إِذَا أَفْضَتْ بِكَ رَاحِلَتُكَ نَحْوَ الشَّامِ يَوْماً ثُمَّ يَوْماً وجاء بلفظ إِذَا رَقَصَتْ بِكَ مشكل الطحاوي هق وفي دلائل النبوة له إِذَا رَقَصَتْ بِكَ رَاحِلَتُكَ تُخُومَ الشَّامِ والتخوم الحدود والمعالم الفاصلة بين الأرضين وجاء في بداية ابن كثير بلفظ أَتُرَانِي سَقَطَ عَلَيَّ قَوْلُ رَسُولِ اللهِ ﷺ كَيْفَ بِكَ إِذَا وَقَصَتْ بِكَ رَاحِلَتُكَ نَحْوَ الشَّامِ يَوْماً ثُمَّ يَوْماً ثُمَّ يَوْماً

Sayf said in *Kitāb al-Ridda* that al-Mustanīr b. Yazīd narrated to them from ʿUrwa b. Ghaziyya al-Dathanī, from al-Ḍaḥḥāk b. Fayrūz, from Jushaysh al-Daylamī ؓ: "Wabara b. Yuḥannas[592] came to us holding a letter from the Prophet ﷺ in which the latter was ordering us to tend unto our religion and rise to war and act against al-Aswad the Arch-Liar. So we fought him until I killed al-Aswad and I threw his head over to them after waging a major raid.[593] We wrote the Prophet ﷺ to inform him when he was still alive, whereupon revelation called him on that very night and he told his Companions of it. Our messengers arrived after his time, reaching Abū Bakr. He is the one that replied to our letters."[594]

قال سيف في كتاب الردة عَنْ جُشَيْشٍ الدَّيْلَمِيِّ قَالَ قَدِمَ عَلَيْنَا وَبَرَةُ بْنُ يُحَنَّسَ بِكِتَابِ النَّبِيِّ ﷺ يَأْمُرُنَا فِيهِ بِالْقِيَامِ عَلَى دِينِنَا

---

[592]Misspelt حبيس in al-Nabhānī, cf.*Istīʿāb*, *Usd al-Ghāba*, *Iṣāba* (Jushaysh al-Daylamī and Wabara b. Yuḥannas).

[593]Also taking credit for beheading al-Aswad was Fayrūz al-Daylamī cf. Ibn ʿAsākir (49:7), Ibn Ḥajar, *Tahdhīb* (s.v.) and others.

[594]Narrated by al-Dāraquṭnī, *al-Muʾtalif wal-Mukhtalif* (2:894-895); al-Ṭabarī, *Tārīkh* (3:231); Ibn al-Athīr, *Kāmil* (2:338) and the sources mentioned above.

وَالنُّهُوضِ فِي الْحَرْبِ وَالْعَمَلِ عَلَى الْأَسْوَدِ الْكَذَّابِ فَقَاتَلْنَاهُ حَتَّى قَتَلْتُ الْأَسْوَدَ وَأَلْقَيْتُ إِلَيْهِمْ رَأْسَهُ وَشَنَنَّا الْغَارَةَ وَكَتَبْنَا إِلَى النَّبِيِّ ﷺ بِالْخَبَرِ وَهُوَ حَيٌّ فَنَادَاهُ الْوَحْيُ مِنْ لَيْلَتِهِ وَأَخْبَرَ أَصْحَابَهُ بِذَلِكَ وَقَدِمَتْ رُسُلُنَا بَعْدَهُ عَلَى أَبِي بَكْرٍ الصِّدِّيقِ فَهُوَ الَّذِي أَجَابَنَا عَنْ كُتُبِنَا كذا في الخصائص قط في المؤتلف والمختلف الطبري في التاريخ كر الذهبي في التاريخ بألفاظ مختلفة

Al-Daylamī narrated from Ibn ʿUmar رضي الله عنهما that he said: "440 News came to the Prophet ﷺ the night al-Aswad al-ʿAnsī was killed, whereupon he came out to us and said: 'al-Aswad was killed last night! A blessed man from a blessed house killed him.' Someone asked who he was and he replied: 'Fayrūz. 441 Fayrūz has triumphed *(fāza Fayrūz)*!'"[595]

عَنِ ابْنِ عُمَرَ قَالَ أَتَى النَّبِيَّ ﷺ الْخَبَرُ مِنَ السَّمَاءِ فِي اللَّيْلَةِ الَّتِي قُتِلَ فِيهَا الْأَسْوَدُ الْعَنْسِيُّ فَخَرَجَ عَلَيْنَا وَقَالَ قُتِلَ الْأَسْوَدُ الْبَارِحَةَ قَتَلَهُ رَجُلٌ مُبَارَكٌ مِنْ أَهْلِ بَيْتٍ مُبَارَكِينَ قِيلَ وَمَنْ هُوَ قَالَ فَيْرُوزٌ فَازَ فَيْرُوزٌ الطبري في التاريخ من طريق سيف وعزاه السيوطي للديلمي

The two Arch-Masters narrated from Ibn ʿAbbās رضي الله عنهما that the Messenger of Allah ﷺ said: "442 Allah will certainly hamstring Musaylima the Arch-Liar."[596] A sound version has: "Allah will certainly hamstring you." Another sound version has "will certainly kill you."[597] Musaylima claimed to be a prophet toward the end of

[595]Narrated by al-Ṭabarī, *Tārīkh* (3:236).

[596]Narrated by al-Bukhārī, Muslim, and in the books of *Dalā'il*.

[597]Narrated by Muslim.

the Prophet's ﷺ life, after which Abū Bakr al-Ṣiddīq—Allah be well-pleased with him—raised an army against him early in his caliphate, and put Khālid b. al-Walīd in command. They fought Musaylima and his people until Allah killed him at the hand of Waḥshī, Ḥamza's killer, and others who helped.

أخرج الشيخان عَنِ ابْنِ عَبَّاسٍ رَضِيَ اللهُ عَنْهُمَا أَنَّ رَسُولَ اللهِ ﷺ قَالَ إِنَّ مُسَيْلِمَةَ الْكَذَّابَ يَعْقِرُهُ اللهُ وَفِي رِوَايَةٍ يَقْتُلُهُ وَكَانَ ادَّعَى النُّبُوَّةَ فِي آخِرِ حَيَاةِ النَّبِيِّ ﷺ فَجَهَّزَ إِلَيْهِ الصِّدِّيقُ رَضِيَ اللهُ عَنْهُ فِي أَوَّلِ خِلافَتِهِ جَيْشاً وَأَمَّرَ عَلَيهِمْ خَالِدَ بْنَ الْوَلِيدِ فَقَتَلُوا مُسَيْلِمَةَ وَقَوْمَهُ حَتَّى قَتَلَهُ اللهُ عَلَى يَدِ وَحْشِيٍّ قَاتِلِ حَمْزَةَ رَضِيَ اللهُ عَنْهُ وَشَارَكَهُ فِيهِ نَاسٌ كذا في الخصائص والمرفوع في خ م بلفظ لَيَعْقِرَنَّكَ اللهُ وجاء بلفظ لَيَقْتُلَنَّكَ اللهُ م

Al-Shāfiʿī narrated in *al-Umm* from ʿĀ'isha رضي الله عنها that [443] the Messenger of Allah ﷺ designated Dhūl-Ḥulayfa as a pilgrim's initial consecration-point for Medinans and he designated al-Juḥfa for people from Syro-Palestine, Egypt, and the Maghreb. The latter three regions were not conquered, nor did their populations become Muslim, until after he died.[598]

وأخرج الشافعي في الأم عَنْ عَائِشَةَ رضي الله عنها أَنَّ رَسُولَ اللهِ ﷺ وَقَّتَ لِأَهْلِ الْمَدِينَةِ ذَا الْحُلَيْفَةِ وَلِأَهْلِ الشَّامِ وَمِصْرَ وَالْمَغْرِبِ الْجُحْفَةَ كذا في الخصائص وحسن المحاضرة للحافظ السيوطي وجاء معناه في كتاب الأم عن جابر موقوفاً وعن عطاء مرسلاً دون التصريح بلفظ مصر وجاء ذكره عند ن قط هق عن عائشة

[598]Cf. al-Shāfiʿī, *al-Umm* (2:339-344 §1001-1013), and the *Sunan* of Nasā'ī, Dāraquṭnī (2:236 §5), and Bayhaqī (5:26f.).

أَيْ جَعَلَ الْجُحْفَةَ مِيقَاتاً لِإِحْرَامِ أَهْلِ الْبِلادِ الْمَذْكُورَةِ بِالْحَجِّ
وَمَا فُتِحَتْ هَذِهِ الْبِلادُ وَأَسْلَمَ أَهْلُهَا إِلَّا بَعْدَ وَفَاتِهِ

Al-Bayhaqī narrated from ʿAlī ﵁: "When the host approached on the day of Badr and we lined up in rows facing their rows, one of their men began marching among them on top of a red camel. The Messenger of Allah ﷺ said: 444 "Who is the rider on the red camel?" Then he said: "If there is anyone in that host who commands goodness, it may be the rider on the red camel." Later Ḥamza ﵁ came and said: "That is ʿUtba b. Rabīʿa, he is telling them not to battle and to return home instead. He is saying: 'My people, tie it to my head on this day and say ʿUtba was a coward!' and Abū Jahl kept refusing."[599] **[533]** He [al-Bayhaqī] also narrated something similar through Ibn Shihāb and through ʿUrwa, adding after "the red camel": "if they obey him they will be well-guided."

عَنْ عَلِيٍّ رَضِيَ اللهُ عَنْهُ قَالَ لَمَّا دَنَا الْقَوْمُ مِنَّا يومَ بَدْرٍ
وَصَافَفْنَاهُمْ إِذَا رَجُلٌ مِنْهُمْ يَسِيرُ فِي الْقَوْمِ عَلَى جَمَلٍ أَحْمَرَ
فَقَالَ رَسُولُ اللهِ ﷺ مَنْ صَاحِبُ الْجَمَلِ الْأَحْمَرِ ثُمَّ قَالَ إِنْ يَكُ
فِي الْقَوْمِ أَحَدٌ يَأْمُرُ بِخَيْرٍ فَعَسَى أَنْ يَكُونَ صَاحِبَ الْجَمَلِ
الْأَحْمَرِ فَجَاءَ حَمْزَةُ فَقَالَ هُوَ عُتْبَةُ بْنُ رَبِيعَةَ وَهُوَ يَنْهَى عَنِ
الْقِتَالِ وَيَأْمُرُ بِالرُّجُوعِ وَيَقُولُ يَا قَوْمُ اعْصِبُوهَا الْيَوْمَ بِرَأْسِي
وَقُولُوا جَبُنَ عُتْبَةُ وَأَبُو جَهْلٍ يَأْبَى حم ز ش ابن المنذر في الأوسط الطبري
في التاريخ هق في الدلائل وجاء بزيادة وَإِنْ يُطِيعُوهُ يَرْشُدُوا ش هق في الدلائل
كر الطبري في التاريخ وأصحاب المغازي والسير

[599]Narrated by Aḥmad (2:259-261 §948) and others.

Al-Bayhaqī and Abū Nuʿaym narrated through Mūsā b. ʿUqba, from al-Zuhrī, and through ʿUrwa b. al-Zubayr, that both said 445 the Prophet ﷺ went out to Banū al-Naḍīr to assist them with the issue of the blood-price *(ʿaql)* of the Kilābīs. They said to him: "Sit, O Abū al-Qāsim, until you eat and then you go back after you finish what you need to do." He sat together with those of his Companions that were with him in the shade of a wall, waiting for them to mend their affair. But once they were among themselves, the 446 devils conspired to kill the Messenger of Allah ﷺ, saying: "You will never find a better opportunity of him being near at hand." One of their men said: "If you wish I will climb over the roof of the house under which he is presently sitting and I will hurl a rock on him and kill him."[600] Allah then revealed to him ﷺ what they were conspiring to do to him, whereupon he rose and returned together with his Companions. The Qur'ān came down: ﴾**Believers! Remember Allah's favor unto you, how a people were minded to stretch out their hands against you but He withheld their hands from you; and keep your duty to Allah. In Allah let the believers put their trust**﴿ (5:11). When Allah exposed their treachery to the Prophet ﷺ he ordered that they be expelled from their homes and exiled to wherever they chose to go. When the hypocrites heard of what lay in store for their brethren and allies among the People of the Book they sent word to them that "We are with you in life and death, if anyone fights you it is incumbent upon us to aid you to victory and if you are brought out we will not stay behind." Once they trusted in the promise of the hypocrites they stopped thinking and the devil gave them false hopes. They called out to the Prophet ﷺ and his Companions: "By Allah we will never come out, and if you fight us we will fight you back!" The Prophet ﷺ besieged them, destroying their [outer] houses and cutting down and burning their datepalm orchards. Allah voided their action and the action of the hypocrites who lent them no help whatsoever. [On the contrary] Allah cast fear unto the hearts of both parties. When they despaired of the hypocrites' help they

[600] Al-Nabhānī mentions a variant specifying that "they brought a huge millstone to hurl it down on him (*fa-jā'ū ilā riḥan ʿaẓimatin li-yaṭraḥūhā ʿalayh*), whereupon Allah held back their hands until Jibrīl came to him and made him get up and leave thence, after which the verse was revealed." Narrated by al-Ṭabarī, *Tafsīr* (Sūrat al-Mā'ida verse 10).

turned back to the Prophet ﷺ and asked him the same terms he had offered them before. 447 He decided to exile them with whatever their camels could carry except weapons.[601]

عَنِ الزُّهْرِيِّ وَعُرْوَةَ بْنِ الزُّبَيْرِ قَالَا خَرَجَ النَّبِيُّ ﷺ إِلَى بَنِي النَّضِيرِ يَسْتَعِينُهُمْ فِي عَقْلِ الْكِلَابِيَّيْنِ فَقَالُوا اجْلِسْ يَا أَبَا الْقَاسِمِ حَتَّى تَطْعَمَ وَتَرْجِعَ بِحَاجَتِكَ فَجَلَسَ وَمَنْ مَعَهُ مِنْ أَصْحَابِهِ فِي ظِلِّ جِدَارٍ يَنْتَظِرُ أَنْ يُصْلِحُوا أَمْرَهُمْ فَلَمَّا خَلَوْا وَالشَّيْطَانُ مَعَهُمْ لَا يُفَارِقُهُمْ ائْتَمَرُوا بِقَتْلِ رَسُولِ اللهِ ﷺ فَقَالُوا لَنْ تَجِدُوهُ أَقْرَبَ مِنْهُ الْآنَ فَقَالَ رَجُلٌ إِنْ شِئْتُمْ ظَهَرْتُ فَوْقَ الْبَيْتِ وَدَلَّيْتُ عَلَيْهِ حَجَرًا فَقَتَلْتُهُ فَأَوْحَى اللهُ إِلَيْهِ فَأَخْبَرَهُ بِمَا ائْتَمَرُوا مِنْ شَأْنِهِ فَعَصَمَهُ اللهُ فَقَامَ رَسُولُ اللهِ ﷺ ثُمَّ قَامَ أَصْحَابُ رَسُولِ اللهِ ﷺ فَرَجَعُوا وَنَزَلَ الْقُرْآنُ ﴿ يَٰٓأَيُّهَا ٱلَّذِينَ ءَامَنُواْ ٱذْكُرُواْ نِعْمَتَ ٱللَّهِ عَلَيْكُمْ إِذْ هَمَّ قَوْمٌ أَن يَبْسُطُوٓاْ إِلَيْكُمْ أَيْدِيَهُمْ فَكَفَّ أَيْدِيَهُمْ عَنكُمْۖ وَٱتَّقُواْ ٱللَّهَۚ وَعَلَى ٱللَّهِ فَلْيَتَوَكَّلِ ٱلْمُؤْمِنُونَ ١١ ﴾ المائدة فَلَمَّا أَظْهَرَ اللهُ رَسُولَهُ عَلَى خِيَانَتِهِمْ أَمَرَ بِإِجْلَائِهِمْ وَإِخْرَاجِهِمْ مِنْ دِيَارِهِمْ وَأَمَرَهُمْ أَنْ يَسِيرُوا حَيْثُ شَاءُوا هق وجاءت تتمة فَلَمَّا سَمِعَ الْمُنَافِقُونَ مَا يُرَادُ بِإِخْوَانِهِمْ وَأَوْلِيَائِهِمْ مِنْ أَهْلِ

[601]Narrated by al-Bayhaqī, *Sunan* (9:200) and *Dalā'il* (3:181-182); cf. al-Dhahabī, *Tārīkh al-Islām* (Ghazwat Banī al-Naḍīr).

الْكِتَابِ أَرْسَلُوا إِلَيْهِمْ فَقَالُوا لَهُمْ إِنَّا مَعَكُمْ مَحْيَانَا وَمَمَاتَنَا إِنْ قُوتِلْتُمْ فَلَكُمْ عَلَيْنَا النَّصْرُ وَإِنْ أُخْرِجْتُمْ لَمْ نَتَخَلَّفْ عَنْكُمْ فَلَمَّا وَثِقُوا بِأَمَانِي الْمُنَافِقِينَ عَظُمَتْ غِرَّتُهُمْ وَمَنَّاهُمُ الشَّيْطَانُ الظُّهُورَ فَنَادَوْا النَّبِيَّ ﷺ وَأَصْحَابَهُ إِنَّا وَاللهِ لَا نَخْرُجُ وَلَئِنْ قَاتَلْتَنَا لَنُقَاتِلَنَّكَ فَحَاصَرَهُمْ رَسُولُ اللهِ ﷺ وَهَدَمَ دُوْرَهُمْ وَقَطَّعَ نَخْلَهُمْ وَحَرَّقَهَا وَكَفَّ اللهُ تَعَالَى أَيْدِيَهُمْ وَأَيْدِي الْمُنَافِقِينَ فَلَمْ يَنْصُرُوهُمْ وَأَلْقَى اللهُ عَزَّ وَجَلَّ فِي قُلُوبِ الْفَرِيقَيْنِ الرُّعْبَ فَلَمَّا يَئِسُوا مِنَ الْمُنَافِقِينَ سَأَلُوا رَسُولَ اللهِ ﷺ الَّذِي كَانَ عَرَضَ عَلَيْهِمْ قَبْلَ ذَلِكَ فَقَاضَاهُمْ عَلَى أَنْ يُجْلِيَهُمْ وَلَهُمْ مَا أَقَلَّتِ الْإِبِلُ إِلَّا السِّلَاحَ كذا في الخصائص وهو لفظ رواية الذهبي في التاريخ الكبير مختصرا من رواية هق في الدلائل

Al-Wāqidī narrated: "Ibrāhīm b. Ja'far narrated to me from his father who said that when Banū al-Naḍīr went out of Medina 'Amr b. Su'dā went forward and made the rounds of their dwellings and saw their destruction. Then he went over to Banū Qurayẓa and said to them: 'I saw today great lessons. I saw our brethren laid bare after vast power and strength and honor and intelligence. they left behind all their possessions and went out humiliated. I swear by the Torah! Allah never allows this to happen to a people for whom He has any regard. Therefore 448 obey me and come, let us follow Muḥammad. For, by Allah! you certainly do know that he is a Prophet, and that both Ibn al-Haytān Abū 'Amr and Ibn Ḥawwāsh had already given us his tidings and told us of his whole affair; and they are the most knowledgeable of all Jews. They both came from the House of the Holy (Bayt al-Maqdis) waiting for him to come. They both commanded us to follow him, and to give him their salaam. Then they died and we buried them in this town of ours.' Al-Zubayr b. Bāṭā[602] said: 'I did read his description in the Books of the Torah that was revealed to Mūsā, not in the Mishnah which we ourselves devised.' Whereupon Kaʿb b. Asad said to him **[534]** 'and what stops you from following him?' He replied, 'You.' Kaʿb said: 'How is that? I never came between you and him.' Zubayr said, 'You are our leader and decide for us, so if you follow him we follow him and if you refuse we refuse.' ʿAmr b. Suʿdā then went over to Kaʿb and they conferred. The upshot was that Kaʿb said 'I have nothing [to say] concerning him other than what I said [except that] I cannot bring myself to be a follower.'" Al-Bayhaqī and Abū Nuʿaym narrated it.[603]

وأخرج الواقدي قال حدثنا إبراهيم بن جعفر عن أبيه قال لَمَّا خَرَجَتْ بَنُو النَّضِيرِ مِنَ المَدِينَةِ أَقْبَلَ عَمْرُو بْنُ سُعْدَى فَأَطَافَ بِمَنَازِلِهِمْ فَرَأَى خَرَابَهَا ثُمَّ رَجَعَ إِلَى بَنِي قُرَيْظَةَ فَقَالَ لَهُمْ رَأَيْتُ الْيَوْمَ عِبَراً رَأَيْتُ مَنَازِلَ إِخْوانِنَا خَالِيَةً بَعْدَ ذَلِكَ الْعِزِّ وَالجَلَدِ وَالشَّرَفِ الْفَاضِلِ وَالْعَقْلِ الْبَارِعِ قَدْ تَرَكُوا أَمْوَالَهُمْ وَخَرَجُوا خُرُوجَ ذُلٍّ لَا وَالتَّوْرَاةِ مَا سُلِّط هَذَا عَلَى قَوْمٍ قَطُّ لِلَّهِ بِهِمْ حَاجَةٌ فَأَطِيعُونِي وَتَعَالَوْا نَتَّبِعْ مُحَمَّداً فَوَاللهِ إِنَّكُمْ لَتَعْلَمُونَ أَنَّهُ نَبِيٌّ وَقَدْ بَشَّرَنَا بِهِ وَبِأَمْرِهِ ابْنُ الهَيَّبَانِ أَبُو عُمَيْرٍ وابْنُ حِرَاشٍ/جَوّاسٍ/الحَوَّاسِ وَهُمَا أَعْلَمُ يَهُودٍ جَاءَا مِنْ بَيْتِ المَقْدِسِ يَتَوَكَّفَانِ قُدُومَهُ وَأَمَرَانَا بِاتِّبَاعِهِ وَأَمَرَانَا أَنْ نُقْرِئَهُ مِنْهُمَا السَّلَامَ ثُمَّ مَاتَا عَلَى دِينِهِمَا وَدَفَنَّاهُمَا بِحَرَّتِنَا هَذِهِ فَقَالَ

[602]Misspelled Baṭṭa in al-Nabhānī.

[603]In their *Dalā'il al-Nubuwwa* (3:361-362 and p. 496-498 §428 respectively).

الزُّبَيْرُ بْنُ بَاطَا قَدْ وَالتَّوْرَاةِ قَرَأْتُ صِفَتَهُ فِي كِتَابِ التَّوْرَاةِ الَّتِي أُنْزِلَتْ عَلَى مُوسَى لَيْسَ فِي المَثَانِي الَّذِي أَحْدَثْنَا قَالَ فَقَالَ لَهُ كَعْبُ بْنُ أَسَدٍ وَمَا يَمْنَعُكَ مِن اتِّبَاعِهِ قال أَنْتَ قَالَ كَعْبٌ وَلِمَ وَمَا حُلْتُ بَيْنَكَ وَبَيْنَهُ قَطُّ قَالَ الزُّبَيْرُ أَنْتَ صَاحِبُ عَهْدِنَا وَعَقْدِنَا فَإِنِ اتَّبَعْتَهُ اتَّبَعْنَاهُ وإِنْ أَبَيْتَ أَبَيْنَا فَأَقْبَلَ عَمْرُو بْنُ سُعْدَى عَلَى كَعْبٍ فَذَكَرَ مَا تَقَاوَلَا فِي ذَلِكَ إِلَى أَنْ قَالَ كَعْبٌ مَا عِنْدِي فِي أَمْرِهِ إِلَّا مَا قُلْتُ مَا تَطِيبُ نَفْسِي أَنْ أَصِيرَ تَابِعاً

أبو نعيم هق في دلائليهما

Abū Nuʿaym narrated through Abū al-Zubayr from Jābir ﷺ that 449 after the Prophet ﷺ had laid siege to Banū al-Naḍīr—and they took a lot of time—Jibrīl, upon him peace, came to him as he was washing his head and said: "Allah forgive you, O Muḥammad, how quickly you all tired/laid down your gear! By Allah, we [angels] have not removed any of our armors since you first went to face them. 450 Get up and strap on your weapons! By Allah, I swear I will smash them like eggs on a rock." Then we rose to face them [Banū Qurayẓa] and Allah conquered them.[604]

عَنْ جَابِرٍ رَضِيَ اللهُ عَنْهُ قَالَ لَمَّا رَابَطَ النَّبِيُّ ﷺ بَنِي النَّضِيرِ وَطَالَ الْمُكْثُ بِهِمْ أَتَاهُ جِبْرِيلُ عَلَيْهِ السَّلَامُ وَهُوَ يَغْسِلُ رَأْسَهُ فَقَالَ عَفَا اللهُ عَنْكَ يَا مُحَمَّدُ مَا أَسْرَعَ مَا مَلَلْتُمْ/حَلَلْتُم وَاللهِ مَا

[604]Ibn Hishām (2:233-240). This report is missing from the printed edition of Abū Nuʿaym's *Dalāʾil* but it is sourced back to him by al-Zaylaʿī and Ibn Ḥajar in their respective *Takhrij Aḥādīth al-Kashshāf.*

نَزَعْنَا مِنْ لَأْمَتِنَا شَيْئاً مُنْذُ نَزَلْتَ عَلَيْهِمْ قُمْ فَشُدَّ عَلَيْكَ
سِلَاحَكَ وَاللهِ لَأَدُقَّنَّهُمْ كَمَا يُدَقُّ الْبَيْضُ عَلَى الصَّفَا قَالَ
فَنَهَضْنَا إِلَيْهَا فَفَتَحَهَا اللهُ سيرة ابن هشام أبو نعيم في دلائل النبوة

The two arch-masters narrated from Sahl b. Saʿd al-Sāʿidī that the Messenger of Allah ﷺ encountered the pagans in one of his campaigns. They fought, then each side retreated to its camp. Among the Muslims there was a man who did not leave a single pagan alone except he would follow them and strike them with his sword. Someone said, "Messenger of Allah, none met our need today like So-and-so."[605] He replied: "Behold, [451] he is of the people of hellfire." This weighed heavily on people; they said: "How far we are from being people of Paradise if such a one is of the people of hellfire!" But one of them said, "I swear by Allah he is not going to die in that [excellent] state!" Then he started following him everywhere. Wherever he went fast, he went fast after him; wherever he slowed down, he slowed down with him. Then he [the first man] got wounded. His wound worsened so he hastened his own death: he put the grip of his sword down on the ground, held up its point and fell on it, killing himself. After that the man came to the Prophet ﷺ and said: "I bear witness that you are certainly the Messenger of Allah!" The Prophet ﷺ said: "What happened?" He recounted everything to him.[606]

عَنْ سَهْلِ بْنِ سَعْدٍ السَّاعِدِيِّ رَضِيَ اللهُ عَنْهُمَا أَنَّ رَسُولَ اللهِ
ﷺ الْتَقَى هُوَ وَالْمُشْرِكُونَ فِي بَعْضِ مَغَازِيهِ فَاقْتَتَلُوا فَمَالَ كُلُّ

[605] Identified as Quzmān b. al-Ḥārith [al-ʿAbsī: *ʿUyūn al-Athar*] al-Ẓafarī the ally of the Banū Ẓafar, on whose exclusive behalf he admitted fighting before expiring, and the man who decided to follow and observe him was Aktham b. al-Jawn: al-Bulqīnī, *al-Ifhām li-mā fīl-Bukhārī min al-Ibhām* (p. 278-280 §2898) and Ibn Ḥajar, *Iṣāba* (*s.v.* "Quzmān").

[606]Narrated by al-Bukhārī, Muslim and others including al-Bayhaqī in the *Dalā'il* (4:252), also from Abū Hurayra in al-Bukhārī and others.

قَوْمٍ إِلَى عَسْكَرِهِمْ وَفِي الْمُسْلِمِنَ رَجُلٌ لَا يَدَعُ لِلْمُشْرِكِينَ شَاذَّةً وَلَا فَاذَّةً إِلَّا اتَّبَعَهَا يَضْرِبُهَا بِسَيْفِهِ فَقِيلَ يَا رَسُولَ اللهِ مَا أَجْزَأَ أَحَدٌ الْيَوْمَ مَا أَجْزَأَ فُلَانٌ فَقَالَ ﷺ أَمَا إِنَّهُ مِنْ أَهْلِ النَّارِ فَأَعْظَمَ النَّاسُ ذَلِكَ فَقَالُوا أَيُّنَا مِنْ أَهْلِ الْجَنَّةِ إِنْ كَانَ فُلانٌ مِنْ أَهْلِ النَّارِ فَقَالَ رَجُلٌ مِنَ الْقَوْمِ وَاللهِ لَا يَمُوتُ عَلَى هَذِهِ الْحَالَةِ أَبَداً فَاتَّبَعَهُ كُلَّمَا أَسْرَعَ أَسْرَعَ وَإِذَا أَبْطَأَ أَبْطَأَ مَعَهُ حَتَّى جُرِحَ فَاشْتَدَّتْ جِرَاحَتُهُ وَاسْتَعْجَلَ الْمَوْتَ فَوَضَعَ سَيْفَهُ بِالْأَرْضِ وَذُبَابَهُ بَيْنَ ثَدْيَيْهِ ثُمَّ تَحَامَلَ عَلَيْهِ فَقَتَلَ نَفْسَهُ فَجَاءَ الرَجُلُ إِلَى النَّبِيِّ ﷺ فَقَالَ أَشْهَدُ أَنَّكَ لَرَسُولُ اللهِ قَالَ وَمَا ذَاكَ فَأَخْبَرَهُ بِالَّذِي كَانَ مِنْ أَمْرِهِ ق ع طب عبد بن حميد هق في الدلائل وهذا لفظه وقال النبهاني وأخرجه الشيخان عن أبي هريرة رضي الله عنه بلفظ شَهِدْنَا مَعَ رَسُولِ اللهِ ﷺ خَيْبَرَ فَقَالَ رَسُولُ اللهِ ﷺ لِرَجُلٍ مِمَّنْ يَدَّعِي الإِسْلَامَ هَذَا مِنْ أَهْلِ النَّارِ فَلَمَّا حَضَرَ الْقِتَالُ قَاتَلَ الرَّجُلُ أَشَدَّ الْقِتَالِ حَتَّى كَثُرَتْ بِهِ الْجِرَاحُ فَأَثْبَتَتْهُ فَجَاءَ رَجُلٌ مِنْ أَصْحَابِ رَسُولِ اللهِ ﷺ فَقَالَ : يَا رَسُولَ اللهِ أَرَأَيْتَ الرَّجُلَ الَّذِى ذَكَرْتَ أَنَّهُ مِنْ أَهْلِ النَّارِ قَدْ وَاللهِ قَاتَلَ فِي سَبِيلِ اللهِ أَشَدَّ الْقِتَالِ وَكَثُرَتْ بِهِ الْجِرَاحُ فَقَالَ رَسُولُ اللهِ ﷺ أَمَا إِنَّهُ مِنْ أَهْلِ النَّارِ فَكَأَنَّ [نسخة: فَكَادَ] بَعْضَ النَّاسِ يَرْتَابُ فَبَيْنَا هُوَ عَلَى ذَلِكَ وَجَدَ الرَّجُلُ أَلَمَ

الْجِرَاحِ فَأَهْوَى بِيَدِهِ إِلَى كِنَانَتِهِ فَاسْتَخْرَجَ مِنْهَا سَهْمًا فَانْتَحَرَ بِهَا فَاشْتَدَّ رِجَالٌ مِنَ الْمُسْلِمِينَ إِلَى رَسُولِ اللهِ ﷺ فَقَالُوا : يَا رَسُولَ اللهِ قَدْ صَدَّقَ اللهُ حَدِيثَكَ خ طس هق

Al-Bayhaqī narrated from Zayd b. Khālid al-Juhanī that one of the male Companions of the Messenger of Allah ﷺ died during the days of Khaybar so he said: 452 "Pray over your friend [without me]." Upon [hearing] this people's faces changed. When the Prophet saw how it affected them he said: "Truly 453 your friend has acted treacherously in the path of Allah." We searched his possessions and we found some beads like those the Jews make. By Allah, they were not even two dirhams' worth.[607]

عَنْ زَيْدِ بْنَ خَالِدٍ الْجُهَنِيِّ رَضِيَ اللهُ عَنْهُ ذَكَرَ أَنَّ رَجُلا مِنَ الْمُسْلِمِينَ تُوُفِّيَ بِخَيْبَرَ وَأَنَّهُمْ ذَكَرُوهُ لِرَسُولِ اللهِ ﷺ لِيُصَلِّيَ عَلَيْهِ فَقَالَ صَلُّوا عَلَى صَاحِبِكُمْ فَتَغَيَّرَتْ وُجُوهُ النَّاسِ فَلَمَّا رَأَى رَسُولُ اللهِ ﷺ مَا بِهِمْ قَالَ إِنَّ صَاحِبَكُمْ غَلَّ فِي سَبِيلِ اللهِ قَالَ فَفَتَّشْنَا مَتَاعَهُ فَوَجَدْنَا خَرَزًا مِنْ خَرَزِ يَهُودَ وَاللهِ مَا تُسَاوِي دِرْهَمَيْنِ الأربعة حم طأ عبد بن حميد ز ش طب حب ك هق وفي الدلائل والمعرفة منتقى ابن الجارود وهذا لفظه

Al-Bayhaqī and Abū Nuʿaym narrated from [ʿAbd Allāh b.] ʿAmr: "I heard the Messenger of Allah ﷺ say when we went out to al-Ṭāif with him, as we were passing by a grave: 454 'This is the grave of Abū Righāl. He is the progenitor of Thaqīf and originated from Thamūd. He was in this sanctuary and used to

[607]*Sunan*, *Musnad*, *Muwaṭṭa'* and elsewhere.

defend it. When he came out, the Divine punishment that targeted his people hit him in this spot and that is where he was buried. The sign to that effect is that a golden bough was buried with him. If you dig and look for it you will find it. People dug briskly and brought out that bough.[608]

عَنْ عَبْدِ اللهِ بْنِ عَمْرٍو رَضِيَ اللهُ عَنْهُمَا سَمِعْتُ رَسُولَ اللهِ ﷺ يَقُولُ حِينَ خَرَجْنَا مَعَهُ إِلَى الطَّائِفِ فَمَرَرْنَا بِقَبْرٍ فَقَالَ رَسُولُ اللهِ ﷺ هَذَا قَبْرُ أَبِي رِغَالٍ وَكَانَ بِهَذَا الْحَرَمِ يَدْفَعُ عَنْهُ فَلَمَّا خَرَجَ أَصَابَتْهُ النِّقْمَةُ الَّتِي أَصَابَتْ قَوْمَهُ بِهَذَا الْمَكَانِ فَدُفِنَ فِيهِ وَآيَةُ ذَلِكَ أَنَّهُ دُفِنَ مَعَهُ غُصْنٌ مِنْ ذَهَبٍ إِنْ أَنْتُمْ نَبَشْتُمْ عَنْهُ أَصَبْتُمُوهُ مَعَهُ فَابْتَدَرَهُ النَّاسُ فَاسْتَخْرَجُوا الْغُصْنَ د الطحاوي في المشكل طس هق وفي الدلائل قال ابن كثير في التفسير قال شيخنا أبو الحجاج المزي هو حديث حسن عزيز اهـ ورواه عق والطبري في التفسير مرسلا

Al-Bayhaqī narrated from ʿUrwa that the Messenger of Allah ﷺ marched back from Tabūk until, when he reached part of the way, **[535]** some of the hypocrites plotted and conspired to throw him from the top of a cliff on the way. When they reached the cliff they asked to take it together with him. When the Messenger of Allah ﷺ reached them he was informed of their intent and said: [455] "Whoever of you wishes, let them take the valley road for it is wider for you." Then the Messenger of Allah ﷺ took the cliff road and the people took the valley road, except the group that were plotting against him: when they heard what he said, they got ready and cloaked their faces in preparation for their

[608]Narrated by Abū Dāwūd with a fair chain according to Mizzī as related by his student Ibn Kathīr in his *Tafsīr* for verse 7:79. Also narrated thus by Ṭaḥāwī in *Sharḥ Mushkil al-Āthār*, Ṭabarānī in *al-Awsaṭ*; al-Bayhaqī in the *Sunan* and *Dalā'il*, and, *mursal*, by ʿAbd al-Razzāq and al-Ṭabarī in his *Tafsīr* with the additional detail that they used their swords to dig. Al-Nawawī erroneously sources it to the *Ṣaḥīḥ* in *al-Majmūʿ* and *al-Adhkār*.

enormity. The Messenger of Allah ﷺ sent Ḥudhayfa b. al-Yamān to order them back and Ḥudhayfa noticed the anger of the Messenger of Allah ﷺ. He went back carrying a prod until he was facing their mounts head on. He started smacking them with the prod and noticed the riders were cloaked, but he told himself that was only something travellers do. However, Allah Most High terrified them when they saw Ḥudhayfa as they thought their plot had been discovered. So they hurried back and blended into the rest of the people. Ḥudhayfa returned to the Messenger of Allah ﷺ who asked him [and ʿAmmār]: "Did you realize what those riders were about and what they wanted to do?" They said, "No, by Allah, O Messenger of Allah!" He said: [456] "They plotted to ride alongside me until I was on top of the cliff so they would push me off it."[609] In one version from Ibn Isḥāq the Prophet identifies by name twelve men.[610]

عَنْ عُرْوَةَ قَالَ رَجَعَ رَسُولُ اللهِ ﷺ قَافِلًا مِنْ تَبُوكَ إِلَى الْمَدِينَةِ
حَتَّى إِذَا كَانَ بِبَعْضِ الطَّرِيقِ مَكَرَ بِرَسُولِ اللهِ ﷺ نَاسٌ مِنْ
الْمُنَافِقِينَ فَتَآمَرُوا أَنْ يَطْرَحُوهُ مِنْ رَأْسِ عَقَبَةٍ فِي الطَّرِيقِ فَلَمَّا
بَلَغُوا الْعَقَبَةَ أَرَادُوا أَنْ يَسْلُكُوهَا مَعَهُ فَلَمَّا غَشِيَهُمْ رَسُولُ اللهِ
ﷺ أُخْبِرَ خَبَرَهُمْ فَقَالَ مَنْ شَاءَ مِنْكُمْ أَنْ يَأْخُذَ بِبَطْنِ الْوَادِي
فَإِنَّهُ أَوْسَعُ لَكُمْ وَأَخَذَ رَسُولُ اللهِ ﷺ الْعَقَبَةَ وَأَخَذَ النَّاسُ بِبَطْنِ
الْوَادِي إِلَّا النَّفَرَ الَّذِينَ هَمُّوا بِالْمَكْرِ بِرَسُولِ اللهِ ﷺ لَمَّا سَمِعُوا

[609]Narrated *mursal* from ʿUrwa by al-Bayhaqī in his *Sunan* (9:33) and *Dalāʾil* (5:256) citing Ibn Isḥāq; also narrated chainless by al-Wāqidī (3:, and corroborated by similar narrations from Abū al-Ṭufayl and Ḥudhayfa by Muslim, Aḥmad and others. In some versions it is ʿAmmār who faces and smacks the plotters' mounts.

[610]Bayhaqī, *Dalāʾil* (5:257-258). They are named in full by Zubayr b. Bakkār as narrated by al-Ṭabarānī, *Kabīr* (3:166 §3017) and are also known (like the Anṣār who gave the first *bayʿa*) as *Aṣḥāb al-ʿAqaba*, cf. Muslim (*Kitāb ṣifāt al-munāfiqīn wa-aḥkāmihim*).

بِذَلِكَ اسْتَعَدُّوا وَتَلَثَّمُوا وَقَدْ هَمُّوا بِأَمْرٍ عَظِيمٍ وَأَمَرَ رَسُولُ اللهِ ﷺ
حُذَيْفَةَ بْنَ الْيَمَانِ أَنْ يَرُدَّهُمْ وَأَبْصَرَ حُذَيْفَةُ غَضَبَ رَسُولِ اللهِ
ﷺ فَرَجَعَ وَمَعَهُ مِحْجَنٌ وَاسْتَقْبَلَ وُجُوهَ رَوَاحِلِهِمْ فَضَرَبَهَا ضَرْبًا
بِالْمِحْجَنِ وَأَبْصَرَ الْقَوْمَ وَهُمْ مُتَلَثِّمُونَ وَلَا يَشْعُرُ إِلَّا أَنَّ ذَلِكَ
فِعْلُ الْمُسَافِرِ فَأَرْعَبَهُمْ اللهُ سُبْحَانَهُ حِينَ أَبْصَرُوا حُذَيْفَةَ وَظَنُّوا
أَنَّ مَكْرَهُمْ قَدْ ظَهَرَ عَلَيْهِ فَأَسْرَعُوا حَتَّى خَالَطُوا النَّاسَ وَأَقْبَلَ
حُذَيْفَةُ حَتَّى أَدْرَكَ رَسُولَ اللهِ ﷺ فَقَالَ لِحُذَيْفَةَ هَلْ عَلِمْتُمْ مَا
كَانَ شَأْنُ الرَّكْبِ وَمَا أَرَادُوا قَالُوا لَا وَاللهِ يَا رَسُولَ اللهِ قَالَ
فَإِنَّهُمْ مَكَرُوا لِيَسِيرُوا مَعِي حَتَّى إِذَا اطَّلَعْتُ فِي الْعَقَبَةِ طَرَحُونِي
مِنْهَا هق وفي الدلائل عن ابن اسحاق وفي رواية وَقَالَ ابْنُ إِسْحَاقَ فِي هَذِهِ
الْقِصَّةِ إِنَّ اللهَ قَدْ أَخْبَرَنِي بِأَسْمَائِهِمْ وَأَسْمَاءِ آبَائِهِمْ وَسَأُخْبِرُكَ بِهِمْ
إِنْ شَاءَ اللهُ فَسَمَّى لَهُ اِثْنَيْ عَشَرَ رَجُلاً هق في الدلائل

Al-Bayhaqī also narrated with a sound chain from Ḥudhayfa b. al-Yamān—Allah be well-pleased with him and his father: "I was holding the halter of the camel of the Messenger of Allah ﷺ and ʿAmmār was driving it—or vice versa—when lo and behold, twelve men faced us, their faces cloaked. He said: [457] 'These are the hypocrites until the Day of Resurrection.' We said: 'Messenger of Allah, why do you not send [someone] to each of them to kill him?' He replied, [458] 'I hate that people should say Muḥammad kills his Companions. I hope that Allah will suffice them with the *dubayla.*' We asked what that was and he replied: 'a torch of fire placed on the heart's aorta for each of them that will kill him.'"[611]

عَنْ حُذَيْفَةَ بْنِ الْيَمَانِ رَضِيَ اللهُ عَنْهُمَا قَالَ إِنِّي لَآخِذٌ بِزِمَامِ نَاقَةِ رَسُولِ اللهِ ﷺ أَقُودُهُ وَعَمَّارٌ يَسُوقُ بِهِ أَوْ عَمَّارٌ يَقُودُهُ وَأَنَا أَسُوقُ بِهِ إِذْ اِسْتَقْبَلَنَا اِثْنَا عَشَرَ رَجُلاً مُتَلَثِّمِينَ قَالَ هَؤُلَاءِ الْمُنَافِقُونَ إِلَى يَوْمِ الْقِيَامَةِ قُلْنَا يَا رَسُولَ اللهِ أَلَا تَبْعَثُ إِلَى كُلِّ رَجُلٍ مِنْهُمْ فَتَقْتُلُهُ فَقَالَ أَكْرَهُ أَنْ يَتَحَدَّثَ النَّاسُ أَنَّ مُحَمَّداً يَقْتُلُ أَصْحَابَهُ وَعَسى اللهُ أَنْ يَكْفِيَهُمْ بِالدُّبَيْلَةِ قُلْنَا وَمَا الدُّبَيْلَةُ قَالَ شِهَابٌ مِنْ نَارٍ يُوضَعُ عَلَى نِيَاطِ قَلْبِ أَحَدِهِمْ فَتَقْتُلُهُ

طس وقال السيوطي في الجامع الكبير ومن غريب الحديث الدُّبَيْلة هى خُراج ودُمَّلٌ كبير تظهر فى الجوف فتقتل صاحبها غالبا اهـ وانظر الذي بعده

Muslim also narrated from Ḥudhayfa—Allah be well-pleased with him—that the Prophet ﷺ said: [459] "Among my Companions there are twelve hypocrites. They will not enter Paradise until the camel passes through the eye of the needle. For eight of them the *dubayla* will be enough—a flame of fire that will appear between their shoulder-blades until it spreads over their chests."[612]

[611]Narrated by al-Ṭabarānī in *al-Awsaṭ* (8:102 §8100) and al-Bayhaqī in the *Dalā'il* (5:261).

[612]Narrated (i) in this wording by Muslim (*Kitāb ṣifāt al-munāfiqīn wa-aḥkāmihim*), Aḥmad (38:345-346 §23319), Ibn Abī ʿĀṣim in the *Āḥād* (2:465-466 §1270), al-Bayhaqī in the *Sunan* (8:198) and the *Dalā'il* (5:261); and also (ii) with the wording "In my Community" by Muslim in the same chapter, Aḥmad (31:180-181 §18885), Abū Yaʿlā (3:190 §1616), al-Bazzār (1:427 §2788) and al-Bayhaqī in the *Dalā'il* (5:262).

عَنْ حُذَيفَةَ رَضِيَ اللهُ عَنْهُ إِنَّ رَسُولَ اللهِ ﷺ قَالَ فِي أَصْحَابِي
اثْنَا عَشَرَ مُنَافِقًا لاَ يَدْخُلُونَ الْجَنَّةَ وَلاَ يَجِدُونَ رِيحَهَا حَتَّى يَلِجَ
الْجَمَلُ فِي سَمِّ الْخِيَاطِ ثَمَانِيَةٌ مِنْهُمْ تَكْفِيكَهُمُ الدُّبَيْلَةُ سِرَاجٌ مِنَ
النَّارِ يَظْهَرُ فِي أَكْتَافِهِمْ حَتَّى يَنْجُمَ مِنْ صُدُورِهِمْ م ابن أبي عاصم في
الآحاد هق ورواه أيضاً بلفظ فِي أُمَّتِي م ع ز هق في الدلائل

Al-Bayhaqī also narrated from Abū Masʿūd—Allah be well-pleased with him: "The Prophet ﷺ spoke to us from the pulpit and said: 'O people! indeed [460] some of you are hypocrites, so whoever I name, let them stand up [and leave]; get up, So-and-so! Get up, So-and-so!' and he named thirty-six people."[613]

عَنْ أَبِي مَسْعُودٍ رَضِيَ اللهُ عَنْهُ قَالَ خَطَبَنَا رَسُولُ اللهِ ﷺ فَذَكَرَ
فِي خُطْبَتِهِ مَا شَاءَ اللهُ عَزَّ وَجَلَّ ثُمَّ قَالَ أَيُّهَا النَّاسُ إِنَّ مِنْكُمْ
مُنَافِقِينَ فَمَنْ سَمَّيْتُ فَلْيَقُمْ قُمْ يَا فُلاَنُ قُمْ يَا فُلاَنُ حَتَّى عَدَّ
سِتَّةً وَثَلاَثِينَ هق في الدلائل خت طب

Ibn Saʿd narrated from Thābit al-Bunānī: "The hypocrites gathered and talked among themselves, after which the Prophet said, 'Truly [461] some men among you gathered and said such and such. Therefore get up and ask forgiveness of Allah, and I will ask forgiveness for you!' But they did not get up. He said this three times, then he said: 'You will certainly get up, otherwise I will certainly call you out by your names!' And he said: 'Get up, So-

[613]Narrated from Abū Masʿūd by Aḥmad (37:36-37 §22348-22349), al-Bukhārī in his *Tārīkh al-Kabīr* in the entry *ʿIyāḍ*, al-Ṭabarānī in *al-Kabīr* (17: §687) and al-Bayhaqī in the *Dalāʾil* (5:283, 5:286); also from Abū Mūsā by Abū Yaʿlā cf. al-Būṣīrī, *Itḥāf al-Khiyara* (7:377 §7117), all through unknown narrators.

and-so! Get up, So-and-so!' and they got up deeply humiliated, faces masked."[614]

عَنْ ثَابِتٍ يَعْنِي الْبُنَانِيَّ قَالَ اجْتَمَعَ الْمُنَافِقُونَ فَتَكَلَّمُوا بَيْنَهُمْ
فَقَالَ رَسُولُ اللهِ ﷺ إِنَّ رِجَالاً مِنْكُمْ اِجْتَمَعُوا فَقَالُوا كَذَا وَقَالُوا
كَذَا فَقُومُوا وَاسْتَغْفِرُوا اللهَ وَأَسْتَغْفِرُ لَكُمْ فَلَمْ يَقُومُوا فَقَالَ مَا
لَكُمْ قُومُوا فَاسْتَغْفِرُوا اللهَ وَأَسْتَغْفِرُ لَكُمْ ثَلَاثَ مَرَّاتٍ فَقَالَ
لَتَقُومُنَّ أَوْ لَأُسَمِّيَنَّكُمْ بِأَسْمَائِكُمْ فَقَالَ قُمْ يَا فُلَانُ قَالَ فَقَامُوا
خَزَايَا مُتَقَنِّعِينَ ابن سعد

Aḥmad, al-Ḥākim—he declared it sound—and al-Bayhaqī narrated from Ibn ʿAbbās: "The Messenger of Allah ﷺ was sitting in the shade of his room"—Yaḥyā [a sub-narrator] added: "which was at the point of shifting from him"—"when he said to his Companions: [462] 'A man is about to come to you looking at you with the eye of a devil; when you see him, do not talk to him.' A man then came, blue-eyed ['and one-eyed' in al-Ḥākim]; when the Prophet ﷺ saw him he called him over and said: 'What is the reason you and your friends are insulting me?' He said: 'Stay right here until I bring them to you.' He went and brought them, whereupon they started swearing by Allah that they had never said and they had never done. At that time Allah Most Glorious revealed [the verse], *On the day when Allah will raise them all together, then will they swear unto Him as they swear unto you, and they will fancy that they have some standing. Behold! Truly it is they who are the liars* (58:18)."[615]

[614]Narrated *mursal* from Thābit al-Bunānī by Ibn Saʿd (1:176).

[615]Narrated by Aḥmad (4:231-232 §2407; 5:316-317 §3277) and al-Ṭabarānī in *al-Kabīr* (12: 7-8 §12307-12309; 13:16 §12140), both through the narrators of the *Ṣaḥīḥ* according to al-Haythamī (7:260-261); al-Ṭabarī, *Tafsīr* (22:491); al-Ḥākim (2:482, *ṣaḥīḥ ʿalā sharṭ Muslim*) and al-Bayhaqī in the *Dalāʾil* (5:282-283). In an alternate narration in Aḥmad (4:48 §2147) and al-Bazzār (11:236-237 §5010 cf. al-Haythamī, *Kashf al-Astār* 3:74-75

عَنْ ابْنِ عَبَّاسٍ رَضِيَ اللهُ عَنْهُمَا قَالَ كَانَ رَسُولُ اللهِ ﷺ جَالِسًا فِي ظِلِّ حُجْرَتِهِ قَالَ يَحْيَى قَدْ كَادَ يَقْلِصُ عَنْهُ فَقَالَ لِأَصْحَابِهِ يَجِيئُكُمْ رَجُلٌ يَنْظُرُ إِلَيْكُمْ بِعَيْنِ شَيْطَانٍ فَإِذَا رَأَيْتُمُوهُ فَلَا تُكَلِّمُوهُ فَجَاءَ رَجُلٌ أَزْرَقُ [زاد الحاكم في روايته: أَعْوَرُ] فَلَمَّا رَآهُ النَّبِيُّ ﷺ دَعَاهُ فَقَالَ عَلَامَ تَشْتُمُنِي أَنْتَ وَأَصْحَابُكَ [وفي رواية البيهقي عَلَامَ تَسُبُّنِي أَنْتَ وَفُلَانٌ وَفُلَانٌ؟ لِقَوْمٍ دَعَا بِأَسْمَائِهِمْ] قَالَ كَمَا أَنْتَ حَتَّى آتِيَكَ بِهِمْ قَالَ فَذَهَبَ فَجَاءَ بِهِمْ فَجَعَلُوا يَحْلِفُونَ بِاللهِ مَا قَالُوا وَمَا فَعَلُوا وَأَنْزَلَ اللهُ عَزَّ وَجَلَّ ﴿ يَوْمَ يَبْعَثُهُمُ ٱللَّهُ جَمِيعًا فَيَحْلِفُونَ لَهُۥ كَمَا يَحْلِفُونَ لَكُمْ ﴾ إِلَى آخِرِ الْآيَةِ ١٨ من سورة المجادلة حم طب رجالهما رجال الصحيح مج الطبري في التفسير ك هق في الدلائل وفي رواية عنه قَالَ قَالَ رَسُولُ اللهِ ﷺ يَدْخُلُ عَلَيْكُمْ رَجُلٌ يَنْظُرُ بِعَيْنِ شَيْطَانٍ أَوْ بِعَيْنَيْ شَيْطَانٍ قَالَ فَدَخَلَ رَجُلٌ أَزْرَقُ فَقَالَ يَا مُحَمَّدُ عَلَامَ سَبَبْتَنِي أَوْ شَتَمْتَنِي أَوْ نَحْوَ هَذَا قَالَ وَجَعَلَ يَحْلِفُ قَالَ فَنَزَلَتْ هَذِهِ الْآيَةُ فِي الْمُجَادِلَةِ ﴿ وَيَحْلِفُونَ عَلَى ٱلْكَذِبِ وَهُمْ يَعْلَمُونَ ﴾ الآية ١٤ وَالْآيَةُ الْأُخْرَى حم ز

قال الشيخ أحمد شاكر هذا خطأ ينافي السياق أي زيادة **يَا مُحَمَّدُ** والله أعلم

§2270) it is the *munāfiq* himself who says to the Prophet ﷺ, "O Muḥammad, why are you insulting me?"—an erroneous wording cf. Arnā'ūṭ in Aḥmad (4:48 §2147).

Al-Khaṭīb narrated in *Ruwāt Mālik* from Abū Salama b. ʿAbd al-Raḥmān that Qays b. Maṭāṭiya[616] came to a circle **[536]** in which Salmān the Persian, Ṣuhayb the Byzantine and Bilāl the Abyssinian were sitting. He said: "Those Aws and Khazraj rose up in support of that man; but why these?" whereupon Muʿādh got up, grabbed him by the front of his clothes and dragged him to Prophet ﷺ, telling him what he had just said. The Messenger of Allah ﷺ stood up in anger and went into the mosque dragging his garment. The call to prayer was raised, after which he stood up, glorified and praised Allah then said: 463 "O people, the Lord is a single lord, the father is a single father, the faith is a single faith. Truly 464 Arabness is not a matter of who your father and mother are but is only a language. 465 Whoso speaks Arabic is an Arab." Muʿādh said, still holding him: "Messenger of Allah, what do you instruct concerning this hypocrite?" He replied: "Leave him for hellfire." Ultimately he recanted and was killed in the [war of] *ridda*.[617]

عَنْ أَبِي سَلَمَةَ بْنِ عَبْدِ الرَّحْمَنِ قَالَ جَاءَ قَيْسُ بْنُ مَطَاطِيَةَ إِلَى
حَلَقَةٍ فِيهَا سَلْمَانُ الْفَارِسِيُّ وَصُهَيْبٌ الرُّومِيُّ وَبِلَالٌ الْحَبَشِيُّ
رَضِيَ اللهُ عَنْهُمْ فَقَالَ هَؤُلَاءِ الْأَوْسُ وَالْخَزْرَجُ قَامُوا بِنُصْرَةِ هَذَا
الرَّجُلِ فَمَا بَالُ هَؤُلَاءِ فَقَامَ مُعَاذٌ رَضِيَ اللهُ عَنْهُ فَأَخَذَ بِتَلْبِيبِهِ
حَتَّى أَتَى بِهِ النَّبِيَّ ﷺ فَأَخْبَرَهُ بِمَقَالَتِهِ فَقَامَ رَسُولُ اللهِ ﷺ مُغْضَباً
يَجُرُّ رِدَاءَهُ حَتَّى دَخَلَ الْمَسْجِدَ ثُمَّ نُودِيَ الصَّلَاةُ جَامِعَةٌ فَحَمِدَ
اللهَ وَأَثْنَى عَلَيْهِ ثُمَّ قَالَ يَا أَيُّهَا النَّاسُ إِنَّ الرَّبَّ رَبٌّ وَاحِدٌ وَإِنَّ
الْأَبَ أَبٌ وَاحِدٌ وَإِنَّ الدِّينَ دِينٌ وَاحِدٌ أَلَا وَإِنَّ الْعَرَبِيَّةَ لَيْسَتْ

616 Misspelt Maṭāṭa.

617 Narrated through Mālik from Abū Salama by Ibn ʿAsākir (24:224-225) and from Abū Hurayra by al-Silafī, cf. Ibn Taymiyya, *Iqtiḍā' al-Ṣirāt al-Mustaqīm*, ed. Nāṣir al-ʿAql, 2 vols. (Riyadh: Maktabat al-Rushd,) 1:409.

لَكُمْ بِأَبٍ وَلَا أُمٍّ إِنَّمَا هِيَ لِسَانٌ فَمَنْ تَكَلَّمَ بِالْعَرَبِيَّةِ فَهُوَ عَرَبِيٌّ
فَقَالَ مُعَاذٌ وَهُوَ آخِذٌ بِنَفْسِهِ يَا رَسُولَ اللهِ مَا تَقُولُ فِي هَذَا
الْمُنَافِقِ فَقَالَ دَعْهُ إِلَى النَّارِ قَالَ فَكَانَ فِيمَنِ ارْتَدَّ فَقُتِلَ فِي
الرِّدَّةِ كر وفي الباب عن أبي هريرة رواه الحافظ السِّلَفي

Muslim narrated from Jābir that the Prophet ﷺ said, [466] "Whoever climbs up the pass—the *Murār* Pass[618]—then verily it shall remit from him that which was remitted from the Banū Isrā'īl!" Whereupon the first to climb were the horse riders of the Banū al-Khazraj. Then the people followed in succession, so the Messenger of Allah ﷺ said, [a] "And every single one of you is forgiven except the one of the precious red camel."[619] We [went to him and] said to him, "Come so that the Messenger of Allah ﷺ will ask forgiveness for you!" He replied, "By Allah! I swear that for me to find my lost propery is more beloved to me than for your friend to ask forgiveness for me." Behold, he was a desert Arab calling out to people for his lost mount.

عَنْ جَابِرِ بْنِ عَبْدِ اللهِ رَضِيَ اللهُ عَنْهُمَا قَالَ: قَالَ رَسُولُ اللهِ
صَلَّى اللهُ عَلَيْهِ وَسَلَّمَ: مَنْ يَصْعَدُ الثَّنِيَّةَ - ثَنِيَّةَ الْمُرَارِ - فَإِنَّهُ يُحَطُّ
عَنْهُ مَا حُطَّ عَنْ بَنِي إِسْرَائِيلَ قَالَ فَكَانَ أَوَّلَ مَنْ صَعِدَهَا خَيْلُنَا
خَيْلُ بَنِي الْخَزْرَجِ ثُمَّ تَتَامَّ النَّاسُ فَقَالَ رَسُولُ اللهِ صَلَّى اللهُ عَلَيْهِ
وَسَلَّمَ وَكُلُّكُمْ مَغْفُورٌ لَهُ إِلَّا صَاحِبَ الْجَمَلِ الْأَحْمَرِ فَأَتَيْنَاهُ فَقُلْنَا

618 A slope overlooking Ḥudaybiya outside Mecca on the road to al-Madīna. *Murār*—thus vowelized by Nawawī in *Sharḥ Ṣaḥīḥ Muslim*—is a perennial bitter (*murr*) plant of the centaurea family native to Arabia known as starthistle and knapweed.

619 He was a hypocrite who was too busy looking for his camel to care. He was said to have been al-Jadd b. Qays per Abū al-ʿAbbās al-Qurṭubī in his *Sharḥ Ṣaḥīḥ Muslim*.

لَهُ: تَعَالَ يَسْتَغْفِرْ لَكَ رَسُولُ اللهِ صَلَّى اللهُ عَلَيْهِ وَسَلَّمَ فَقَالَ
وَاللهِ لَأَنْ أَجِدَ ضَالَّتِي أَحَبُّ إِلَيَّ مِنْ أَنْ يَسْتَغْفِرَ لِي صَاحِبُكُمْ
قَالَ وَكَانَ رَجُلٌ يَنْشُدُ ضَالَّةً لَهُ م وعنده من طريق آخر قَالَ وَإِذَا هُوَ
أَعْرَابِيٌّ جَاءَ يَنْشُدُ ضَالَّةً لَهُ

Bibliography

ʿAbd al-Razzāq. *Al-Muṣannaf.* 11 vols. Ed. Ḥabīb al-Raḥmān al-Aʿẓamī. Beirut: al-Maktab al-Islāmī, 1983. With al-Azdī's *Kitāb al-Jāmiʿ* as the last two volumes.

Abū Nuʿaym al-Aṣfahānī. [*Al-Muntakhab min*] *Dalāʾil al-Nubuwwa.* Eds. Muḥammad Rawwās Qalʿajī and ʿAbd al-Barr ʿAbbās. Beirut: Dār al-Nafāʾis, 1999[4].

Abū al-Shaykh al-Aṣbahānī, ʿAbd Allāh b. Muḥammad b. Jaʿfar b. Ḥayyān (274-369). *Al-ʿAẓama.* 5 vols. Ed. Rida' Allāh al-Mubārakfūrī. Riyadh: Dār al-ʿĀṣima, 1988.

Aḥmad b. Ḥanbal. *Faḍāʾil al-Ṣaḥāba.* 2 vols. Ed. Waṣī Allāh Muḥammad ʿAbbās. Beirut: Muʾassasat al-Risāla, 1983.

———. *Al-ʿIlal wa Maʿrifat al-Rijāl.* 4 vols. Ed. Waṣī Allāh b. Muḥammad ʿAbbās. Beirut and Ryadh: al-Maktab al-Islāmī, 1988.

———. *Al-Musnad.* 50 vols. Ed. Shuʿayb al-Arnaʾūṭ. Beirut: Muʾassasat al-Risāla, 2000-2001.

———. *Al-Zuhd.* Beirut: Dār al-Kutub al-ʿIlmiyya, 1978.

Al-ʿAskarī.*Taṣḥīfāt al-Muḥaddithīn.* 2 vols. Ed. Maḥmūd Aḥmad Mīra. Cairo: al-Maṭbaʿat al-ʿArabiyya al-Ḥadītha, 1982.

Al-Bājūrī, Ibrāhīm. *Sharh Jawharat al-Tawhīd.* Ed. ʿAbd al-Karīm al-Rifāʿī. Beirut: Muʾassasat Anas b. Mālik, 1391/1971-2.

Al-Bayhaqī. *Dalāʾil al-Nubuwwa wa-Maʿrifat Aḥwāl Ṣāḥib al-Sharīʿa.* Ed. ʿAbd al-Muʿṭī Qalʿajī. 7 vols. Beirut: Dār al-Kutub al-ʿIlmiyya and Dār al-Rayyān lil-Turāth, 1408/1988.

———. *Shuʿab al-Īmān.* 8 vols. Ed. Muḥammad Zaghlūl. Beirut: Dār al-Kutub al-ʿIlmiyya, 1990.

———. *Al-Sunan al-Kubrā.* 10 vols. Ed. Muḥammad ʿAbd al-Qādir ʿAṭā. Mecca: Maktaba Dār al-Bāz, 1994.

Al-Bazzār. *Al-Musnad.* [*Al-Baḥr al-Zakhkhār.*] 9 vols. Ed. Maḥfūẓ al-Raḥmān Zayn Allāh. Beirut and Madīna: Muʾassasat ʿUlūm al-Qurʾān & Maktabat al-ʿUlūm wal-Ḥikam, 1989.

Daḥlān, Sayyid Aḥmad Zaynī. *Al-Sīra al-Nabawiyya.* 2 vols. in 1. Cairo: al-Maṭbaʿa al-*Maymuniyya,* 1310/1892.

Al-Dhahabī, *Mīzān al-Iʿtidāl fī Naqd al-Rijāl.* 4 vols. Ed. ʿAlī Muḥammad al-Bajawī. Beirut: Dār al-Maʿrifa, 1963; 8 vols.

Eds. ʿAlī Muḥammad Muʿawwaḍ and ʿĀdil Aḥmad ʿAbd al-Mawjūd. Beirut: Dār al-Kutub al-ʿIlmiyya, 1995.

———. *Siyar Aʿlām al-Nubalāʾ*. 19 vols. Ed. Muḥibb al-Dīn al-ʿAmrāwī. Beirut: Dār al-Fikr, 1996.

Ḍyāʾ al-Dīn al-Maqdisī. *Al-Aḥādīth al-Mukhtāra*. 10 vols. Ed. ʿAbd al-Mālik b. ʿAbd Allāh b. Duhaysh. Mecca: Maktabat al-Nahḍat al-Ḥadītha, 1990.

Al-Ḥākim. *Al-Mustadrak ʿalā al-Ṣaḥīḥayn*. With al-Dhahabī's *Talkhīṣ al-Mustadrak*. 5 vols. Indexes by Yūsuf ʿAbd al-Raḥmān al-Marʿashlī. Beirut: Dār al-Maʿrifa, 1986. Reprint of the 1334/1916 Hyderabad edition.

———. *Al-Mustadrak ʿAla al-Ṣaḥīḥayn*. With al-Dhahabī's *Talkhīṣ al-Mustadrak*. 4 vols. Annotations by Muṣṭafā ʿAbd al-Qādir ʿAṭāʾ. Beirut: Dār al-Kutub al-ʿIlmiyya, 1990.

Al-Halabī, ʿAlī (d. 1044). *Al-Sīra al-Ḥalabiyya*. [*Insān al-ʿUyūn fī Sīrat al-Amīn al-Maʾmūn*.] 3 vols. Beirut: Dār al-Maʿrifa, 1980.

Al-Ḥalabī, Badr al-Dīn (d. 779). *Al-Muqtafā min Sīrat al-Muṣṭafā*. Ed. Muṣṭafā Muḥammad Ḥusayn al-Dhahabī. Cairo: Dār al-Ḥadīth, 1996.

Al-Haytamī, Aḥmad. *Al-Minah al-Makkiyya fī Sharh al-Hamziyya*. 3 vols. Ed. Bassām Muḥammad Bārūd. Abū Zabī: al-Mujammaʿ al-Thaqāfī, 1998.

Al-Haythamī, Nūr al-Dīn. *Majmaʿ al-Zawāʾid wa Manbaʿ al-Fawāʾid*. 10 vols. in 5. Cairo: Maktabat al-Qudsī, 1932-1934. Repr. Beirut: Dār al-Kitāb al-ʿArabī, 1967, 1982, and 1987.

Ibn ʿAbd al-Barr. *Al-Durar fī Ikhtiṣār al-Maghāzī wal-Siyar*. 2nd ed. Ed. Shawqī Ḍayf. Cairo: Dār al-Maʿārif, 1983.

———. *Al-Istīʿab fī Maʿrifat al-Aṣḥāb*. 8 vols. in 4. Ed. ʿAlī Muḥammad al-Bajawī. Beirut: Dār al-Jil, 1992.

Ibn Abī ʿĀṣim. *Al-Awāʾil*. Ed. Muḥammad b. Nāṣir al-ʿAjamī. Kuwait: Dār al-Khulafāʾ lil-Kitāb al-Islāmī, n.d.

Ibn Abī Shayba. *Al-Muṣannaf*. 7 vols. Ed. Kamāl al-Ḥūt. Ryadh: Maktabat al-Rushd, 1989.

Ibn ʿAdī. *Al-Kāmil fī Ḍuʿafāʾ al-Rijāl*. 7 vols. 3rd ed. Ed. Yaḥyā Mukhtār Ghazawī. Beirut: Dār al-Fikr, 1988.

Ibn al-Athīr al-Jazarī. *Al-Kāmil fī al-Tārīkh*. 10 vols. Ed. Abu al-Fidāʾ ʿAbd Allāh al-Qāḍī. Beirut: Dār al-Kutub all-ʿIlmiyya, 1995.

Ibn Bashkuwāl. *al-Ghawāmiḍ wal-Mubhamāt*. Ed. Maḥmūd Maghrāwī. 2 vols. Jeddah: Dār al-Andalus al-Khaḍrā', 1415/1994.

Ibn Ḥajar al-'Asqalānī. *Fatḥ al-Bārī Sharḥ Ṣaḥīḥ al-Bukhārī*. 13 vols. Ed. Muḥammad Fu'ād ʿAbd al-Bāqī and Muḥibb al-Dīn al-Khaṭīb. Beirut: Dār al-Maʿrifa, 1959-1960.

———. *Al-Iṣāba fī Tamyīz al-Ṣaḥāba*. 8 vols. in 4. Ed. ʿAlī Muḥammad al-Bijāwī. Beirut: Dār al-Jīl, 1992.

———. *Natā'ij al-Afkār fī Takhrīj Aḥādīth al-Adhkār*. 3 vols. Ed. Ḥamdī ʿAbd al-Majīd al-Salafī. Damascus and Beirut: Dār Ibn Kathīr, 2000.

Ibn Ḥibbān. *Ṣaḥīḥ Ibn Ḥibbān bi Tartīb Ibn Balbān*. 18 vols. Ed. Shuʿayb al-Arna'ūṭ. Beirut: Mu'assasat al-Risāla, 1993.

Ibn Hishām. *Al-Sīra al-Nabawiyya*. 6 vols. Ed. Ṭāha ʿAbd al-Ra'ūf Saʿd. Beirut: Dār al-Jīl, 1991.

Ibn Isḥāq. *Sīrat Ibn Isḥāq al-Musammāh bi-Kitāb al-Mubtada' wal-Mab'ath wal-Maghāzī*. Ed. Muḥammad Ḥamīdullāh. Rabāṭ: Ma'had al-Dirāsāt wal-Abḥāth lil-Ta'rīb, 1976.

Ibn al-Jawzī. *Al-ʿIlal al-Mutanāhiya fīl-Aḥādīth al-Wāhiya*. 2 vols. Ed. Shaykh Khalīl al-Mays. Beirut: Dār al-Kutub al-ʿIlmiyya, 1983.

———. *Ṣifat al-Ṣafwa*. 4 vols. Eds. Maḥmūd Fākhūrī and Muḥammad Rawwās Qalʿajī. Beirut: Dār al-Maʿrifa, 1979.

———. *Talqīḥ Fuhūm al-Athara fīl-Tārīkh wal-Sīra*. Ed. Faḍl al-Raḥmān Dīn Muḥammad. Delhi: al-Dār al-ʿIlmiyya, 1988.

Ibn Kathīr. *Tafsīr al-Qur'ān al-'Aẓīm*. 4 vols. Beirut: Dār al-Fikr, 1981.

———. *Al-Bidāya wal-Nihāya*. 14 vols. Beirut: Maktabat al-Ma'ārif, n.d.

Ibn Khuzayma. *Al-Ṣaḥīḥ*. 4 vols. Ed. Muḥammad Muṣṭafā al-A'ẓamī. Beirut: Al-Maktab al-Islāmī, 1970.

Ibn Nāṣir al-Dīn al-Dimashqī. *Majmū'un fīhi Rasā'il Ibn Nāṣir al-Dīn*. Ed. Mish'al Bānī al-Jibrīn al-Muṭayrī. Beirut: Dār Ibn Ḥazm, 2001.

Ibn Qāniʿ. *Mu'jam al-Ṣaḥāba*. 3 vols. Ed. Ṣalāḥ b. Sālim al-Miṣrātī. Madīna: Maktabat al-Ghurabā' al-Athariyya, 1998.

Ibn al-Qayyim. *Zād al-Ma'ād fī Hadī Khayr al-'Ibād*. 6 vols. 30th ed. Eds. ʿAbd al-Qādir al-Arna'ūṭ and Shuʿayb al-Arna'ūṭ. Beirut: Mu'assasat al-Risāla, 1997.

Ibn Saʿd b. Manīʿ al-Hāshimī–*waliyyuhum*–al-Baṣrī al-Baghdādī, Abū ʿAbd Allāh Muḥammad. *Al-Ṭabaqāt al-Kubrā*. 8 vols. Beirut: Dār Ṣādir, n.d.

Al-Ismāʿīlī, Abū Bakr. *Muʿjam al-Shuyūkh*. 3 vols. Ed. Zyād Muḥammad Manṣūr. Madīna: Maktabat al-ʿUlūm wal-Ḥikam, 1990.

Al-Kattānī, Muḥammad ʿAbd al-Ḥayy b. ʿAbd al-Kabīr (d. 1382). *Niẓām al-Ḥukūma al-Nabawiyya*. [*Al-Tarātīb al-Idāriyya*]. 2 vols. Beirut: Dār al-Kitāb al-ʿArabī, n.d.

———. *Ibid.* 2nd ed. Ed. ʿAbd Allāh al-Khālidī. Beirut: Dār al-Arqam, n.d.

Al-Kattānī, Muḥammad b. Jaʿfar (d. 1345). *Naẓm al-Mutanāthir fī al-Ḥadīth al-Mutawātir*. Ed. Sharaf Ḥijāzī. Cairo: Dār al-Kutub al-Salafiyya, n.d. and Beirut: Dār al-Kutub al-ʿIlmiyya, 1980.

Al-Khazrajī. *Khulāṣat Tadhhīb Tahdhīb al-Kamāl*. With al-Kawkabānī's *Itḥāf al-Khāṣṣa bi Taṣḥīḥ al-Khulāṣa*. Ed. ʿAbd al-Fattāḥ Abū Ghudda. Beirut: Dār al-Bashā'ir al-Islāmiyya, 1996[5]. Reprint of the original 1301/1883 Cairo Bulāq edition.

Khaythama b. Sulayman cf. *Min Hadīthi Khaythama*. Ed. ʿUmar ʿAbd al-Salām. Beirut: Dār al-Kitāb al-ʿArabī, 1980.

Al-Khuzāʿī, ʿAlī b. Muḥammad b. Suʿūd. *Takhrīj al-Dilālāt al-Samʿiyya*. Ed. Iḥsān ʿAbbās. Beirut: Dār al-Gharb al-Islāmī, 1405/1985.

Al-Kilāʿī, Abū al-Rabīʿ Sulaymān b. Mūsā (565-634). *Al-Iktifā' bimā Taḍammanahu min Maghāzī Rasūlillāh wal-Thalāthati al-Khulafā'*. 4 vols. Ed. Muḥammad Kamāl al-Dīn ʿIzz al-Dīn ʿAlī. Beirut: ʿĀlam al-Kutub, 1997.

Al-Māwardī, Abū al-Ḥasan ʿAlī b. Muḥammad b. Ḥabīb (370-429). *Aʿlām al-Nubuwwa*. Ed. Muḥammad al-Muʿtaṣim Billāh al-Baghdādī. Beirut: Dār al-Kitāb al-ʿArabī, 1987.

Al-Munāwī. *Fayḍ al-Qadīr Sharḥ al-Jāmiʿ al-Ṣaghīr*. 6 vols. Cairo: al-Maktaba al-Tijāriyya al-Kubrā, 1356/1937. Repr. Beirut: Dār al Maʿrifa, 1972.

Al-Muttaqī al-Hindī, ʿAlāʾ al-Dīn ʿAlī al-Muttaqī b. Ḥusām al-Dīn. *Kanz al-ʿUmmāl fī Sunan al-Aqwāl wal-Afʿāl*. Ed. Bakrī Ḥayyānī & Ṣafwat Saqqā. 5th ed. 18 vols. Beirut: Mu'assasat al-Risāla, 1405/1985

Nuʿaym b. Hammād al-Marwazī. *Kitāb al-Fitan*. 2 vols. Ed. Samīr Amīn al-Zuhrī. Cairo: Maktabat al-Tawhīd, 1992.

Al-Qāḍī ʻIyāḍ. *Al-Shifā' bi-Taʻrīf Ḥuqūq al-Muṣṭafā*. Ed. ʻAbduh ʿAlī Kawshak. Damascus and Beirut: Maktabat al-Ghazzālī and Dār al-Fayḥā', 2000.

Al-Qasṭallānī, Aḥmad b. Muḥammad. *Al-Mawāhib al-Ladunniyya bil-Minaḥ al-Muḥammadiyya*. Ed. Ṣāliḥ Aḥmad al-Shāmī. 2nd ed. 4 vols. Beirut: al-Maktab al-Islāmī, 1425/2004.

Al-Qurṭubī. [*Tafsīr*.] *Al-Jāmiʻ li Aḥkām al-Qur'ān*. 2nd ed. 20 vols. Ed. Aḥmad ʿAbd al-ʿAlīm al-Bardūnī. Cairo: Dār al-Shaʻb; Beirut: Dār Iḥyā' al-Turāth al-ʿArabī, 1952-1953. Reprint.

Saʿīd b. Manṣūr. *Sunan*. 2 vols. Ed. Ḥabīb al-Raḥmān al-Aʻẓamī. India: al-Dār al-Salafiyya, 1982.

Al-Shāfiʻī. *Al-Umm*. 8 vols. Ed. Muḥammad Zahrī al-Najjār. Beirut: Dār al-Maʿrifa, 1973.

Al-Shaʻrānī, ʿAbd al-Wahhāb b. Aḥmad b. ʿAlī (898-973). *Al-Yawāqīt wal-Jawāhir [fī ʻAqā'id al-Akābir*. 2 vols. in 1. Repr. Beirut: Dār Iḥyā' al-Turāth al-ʿArabī, 1997.

Al-Shawkānī. *Nayl al-Awṭār*. 9 vols. Beirut: Dār al-Jīl, 1973.

Shurrāb, Muhammad Hasan. *Al-Maʻālim al-Athīra fī al-Sunna wal-Sīra*. Damascus: Dār al-Qalam; Beirut: al-Dār al-Shāmiyya, 1991.

Al-Suhaylī. *Al-Rawd al-Unuf fī Tafsīr al-Sīra al-Nabawiyya li-Ibn Hishām*. 4 vols. Ed. Majdī Manṣūr al-Shūrā. Beirut: Dār al-Kutub al-ʿIlmiyya, 1997.

Al-Suyūṭī. *Al-Khaṣā'iṣ al-Kubrā aw Kifāyat al-Ṭālib al-Labīb fī Khaṣā'iṣ al-Ḥabīb* ﷺ. 2 vols. Hyderabad al-Dakn: Dā'irat al-Maʻārif al-Niẓāmiyya, 1901-1903. See also below, *Tahdhīb al-Khaṣā'iṣ*.

———. *Tahdhīb al-Khaṣā'iṣ al-Nabawiyya al-Kubrā*. 2nd ed. Ed. ʿAbd Allāh al-Talīdī. Beirut: Dār al-Bashā'ir al-Islāmiyya, 1990.

———. *Tārīkh al-Khulafā'*. Ed. Raḥāb Khiḍr ʻAkkāwī. Beirut: Mu'assasat ʻIzz al-Dīn, 1992.

———. *Al-Taṭrīf fīl-Taṣḥīf*. Ed. ʿAlī Ḥusayn al-Bawwāb. ʿAmmān: Dār al-Fā'iz, 1988-1989.

Al-Ṭabarānī. *Al-Muʻjam al-Awsaṭ*. 10 vols. Eds. Ṭāriq b. ʻAwaḍ Allah and ʿAbd al-Muḥsin b. Ibrāhīm al-Ḥusaynī. Cairo: Dār al-Ḥaramayn, 1995.

———. *Al-Muʻjam al-Kabīr*. 20 vols. Ed. Ḥamdī b. ʿAbd al-Majīd al-Salafī. Mosul: Maktabat al-ʿUlūm wal-Ḥikam, 1983.

———. *Al-Mu'jam al-Saghīr*. 2 vols. Ed. Muḥammad Shakūr Maḥmūd. Beirut and Amman: Al-Maktab al-Islāmī, Dār ʿAmmār, 1985.

Al-Taymī, Ismā'īl b. Muḥammad b. al-Faḍl (457-535). *Dalā'il al-Nubuwwa*. Ed. Muḥammad Muḥammad al-Ḥaddād. Riyadh: Dār Ṭība, 1989.

Al-ʿUqaylī. *Al-Ḍuʿafā' min al-Ruwāt*. 4 vols. Ed. ʿAbd al-Mu'ṭī Amīn Qalʿajī. Beirut: Dār al-Kutub al-ʿIlmiyya, 1984.

Al-Wādyāshī (d. 804). *Tuḥfat al-Muḥtāj*. 2 vols. Ed. ʿAbd Allāh al-Laḥyānī. Mecca: Dār Ḥirā', 1986.

Al-Wāqidī. *Al-Maghāzī*. 3 vols. Ed. Marsden Jones. London: Oxford University Press, 1966. Reprint Beirut: Mu'assasat al-A'lamī, n.d.

Yāqūt al-Ḥamawī. *Mu'jam al-Buldān*. 5 vols. Beirut: Dār al-Fikr, n.d.

Al-Zayla'ī, Jamāl al-Dīn Abū Muḥammad ʿAbd Allāh b. Yūsuf. *Naṣb al-Rāya li-Aḥādīth al-Hidāya*. 4 vols. Ed. Muḥammad Yūsuf al-Binnawrī. Cairo: Dār al-Ḥadīth, 1357/1938.

Hadith Index

'Abbās! Hand me some pebbles, 210
'Abbās! Rally the Emigrants and the Helpers, 210
About to come into your presence is a man from among the best, 224
Abū Bakr al-Ṣiddīq shall not tarry but little after me, 40
Abū Bakr is in *Janna*, 'Umar is in *Janna...*, 37
Abū Dharr! What will you do when you see leaders inclined…, 131
Abū al-Ḥakam, by Allah! You shall laugh little and weep much, 293
Abū Sufyān, did you say such-and-such to Hind?, 197
Abū Sufyān is in al-Arāk. Catch him, 192
Abū Sufyān, neither for Allah nor His Prophet are you angry, 293
Abū Turāb! Shall I not tell you of the two wickedest people, 74
Abū Yaḥyā! Your sale has gained threefold, 127
Adī b. Ḥātim! Surrender and you will be safe, 235
Adī b. Ḥātim, were you not a *Rakūsī*?, 234
Adī b. Ḥātim! What terrifies you about saying *Lā ilāha illa-l-Lāh*?, 233
After Jarīr entered Islam whenever the Prophet ﷺ saw him he ﷺ laughed or smiled, 224
After the Prophet ﷺ did the pilgrimage he sent out Mu'ādh, 149
Ahead of you come strifes like layers of the darkest night, 396, 398
('Alī) shall not die other than murdered, 66
Allah and His Messenger believe you and excuse you, 146
Allah bless Zabīd!, 180
Allah disclosed to His Prophet what had happened to their charter, 313
Allah has brought up the whole world before my eyes, 27
Allah has destroyed your friend!" ﴾**He launches the thunderbolts**, 348
Allah has folded up the earth for me so that I saw it east to west, 377
Allah has given me the glad tidings, at this spot where I am standing, that Yemen, the Romans, and Persia would be conquered, 323
Allah has given me a guarantee concerning Shām and its people, 317
Allah have mercy on Abū Dharr! He walks alone, he shall die alone, 136
Allah looks at those who fought at Badr and says, Do what you like, 140
Allah looks not at your bodies but He looks at your hearts, 248
Allah removed distances for me so that I could see their battle, 101
Allah said: Shām, you are the quintessence of My lands, 318
Allah shall most certainly bring this endeavor to perfection, 235
Allah will certainly hamstring Musaylima the Arch-Liar, 420

Allah would not have Ṭalḥa enter Paradise except firmly, 66
Allāhu akbar! Allah has brought us Ḥimyar as supporters, 329
Allāhu Akbar! Then he struck it a third time shattering it, whereupon a great light glimmered, illuminating al-Madīna, 327
Almsgiving will be considered a fine, 398
ʿAmmār has not died, 123
Among my Companions there are twelve hypocrites, 434
Among us is the Messenger of Allah reciting His Book (Ibn Rawāḥa), 27
Anas, let him in, give him the glad tidings of Paradise, 38
And upon you be peace and the mercy of Allah, 110
The Angel of rain asked permission to visit the Prophet ﷺ, 83
Arabness is not who your father and mother are but only a language, 438
Are you not happy that he should reach your age then go to al-Shām, 152
Are you not a *Rakūsī*? Do you not get a fourth-part annual levy from your people?, 235
Are you the one who said that if the women of Quraysh came out with their claws, 256
As for you, you will take charge of my Community after me, 202
As Yūsuf عليه السلام neared the King's wife, his father Yaʿqūb عليه السلام appeared and slapped him in the chest, 195
Ashajj! If I give you permission to drink this much, 269
Ask Allah forgiveness for me and may Allah forgive you, 34
Ask forgiveness for me, Messenger of Allah! 'Allah forgive you', 208
Ask [for land] wherever you wish, 214
Asmā'! Here is Jaʿfar with Jibrīl, Mīkā'īl, and Isrāfīl, all greeting us, 106
Assembly of the *Anṣār*! You said a man longs to see his own town, 146
At that time shatter your bows to pieces, cut your bow-strings, and do not move from inside your houses, 398
Avoid saying this, 28
ʿAwf <b. Mālik>? The camel-meat man?, 261
A band of Muslims shall conquer the treasures of Chosroes, 369
Be Abū Dharr!", 136
"Be Abū Khaythama!" They said, "It is, by Allah! Abū Khaythama", 164
Be glad! For Allah will grant the upper hand to His Religion, 288
Be like the better one of the two sons of Ādam, 398
Be like the son of Ādam [*i.e.* do not resist], 398
Be the saddle-cloths *(aḥlās)* of your houses, 398
Be still [Ḥirā']! There is none on top of you but, 47
Be true to the pledge made to the Caliphs, 382

Bear with it until you meet me, 131
Before time you were blessed in the shades, 355
Before your time, a man might be raked with iron rakes and skinned alive, 351
The beginning of dissensions is the murder of 'Uthmān (Ḥudhayfa), 55
The best of your dates is the *barnī*. It removes disease and contains nothing harmful, 268
Better shame than the Fire (al-Ḥasan), 78
Beware of newfangled matters, 384
Beware of the world and beware of women!, 375
Bismillāh! He struck it and broke a third. He said: *Allāhu akbar!*, 325
Black flags shall come out of Khurāsān. Nothing will stop them, 410
Bless that face!, 153
Bless that face, Abū Qatāda, Master of horsemen!, 159
A boy shall be born to you after me, 75
Bring me Ja'far's children.' When I brought them he smelled them and his eyes filled with tears, 108
Buy a new waterskin and use it to bring water to people until it wears out, 272
By Allah, you will never stop until His punishment comes to pass, 288
By Him in whose hand is the soul of Muḥammad, you do not hear my words better than they do, 295
Caliphate after me shall last for thirty years. Then there will be kingship, 386
Call your father and brother so I will put something in writing, 36
Certain leaders will lead you after me who will smother the Sunna, 406
Choose one of your camels and take your waterskin then go to people that have hardly any access to drinking water, 270
Chosroes has just torn up his kingdom, 339
"Come near" then he spat into his eyes ('Alī), 72
Come near, Wābiṣa, come near, Wābiṣa!, 247
Come, Shayba! Then he ﷺ placed his hand on my chest, 210
Consult yourself, consult your heart!, 247
The curse of Allah be on al-Ḥakam and his children, 401-402
Dajjāl will wreak havoc towards the East, 360
The day that you turn to blood will be a terrible day, 79
The days and nights will not be long until Mu'āwiya rules, 202
The death of Ḥusayn has just been announced to me. I was brought a handful of his burial-ground, 397

The first time, Allah opened Yemen for me; the second, al-Shām and al-Maghrib; the third time, he opened the East, 324
The first time, the palaces of Ḥīra and Madā'in were illuminated, 327
The first to change my Sunna will be a man from the Banū Umayya, 396
The first to come in through this door is a man from Paradise, 94
The first trial of the Israelites was because of women, 375
For my part I fear other than the hyenas for you. I fear the world pouring down on you like rain, 376
For us – the People of the House – Allah has chosen the next world, 411
Forgive us and may Allah forgive you ('Umar), 33
From this opening a man is going to enter who is of noble ancestry, 245
From us will come al-Saffāḥ, al-Manṣūr, and al-Mahdī, 412
Get up and get your weapons! Then we face the Banū Qurayẓa, 427
Give away one third, and one third is a lot, 95
Give him permission – a viper son of a viper!, 401
Give him permission and give him the glad tidings, 42, 43
Give the tidings of Hellfire to the killer of the son of Ṣafiyya, 93
Glory to Allah Who took them away from Kisrā and adorned Surāqa with them, 241
Glory to Allah! The armlets of Kisrā on the arms of Surāqa, 371-372
Go [and wait] until you hear that I have migrated, 215
Go and live in Bayt al-Maqdis. Perhaps, Allah will give you offspring, 319
Go and see Abū Bakr. You will find him sitting inside his house, 44
Go to Bādhān and tell him that my Lord killed Kisrā last night, 334
Go to your friend and say, 'My Lord killed your Lord last night, 342
Go to your friends. Whoever joins under this banner of yours is safe, 238
Go with him <but do not trust even your own firstborn brother>, 171
Go, Abū Qatāda! May Allah accompany you, 158
Go, and you shall find Ukaydir of Dūma hunting wild beasts, 170
Good things of Byzantium! Good things of Persia!, 329
A group of riders from the East are coming who were not forced to enter Islam, 265
Ḥāṭib has told you the truth, 140
Ḥīra was displayed before me, [shining] like canine teeth!, 359
He [ﷺ] blew on my eyes ('Alī), 73
He decided to exile them with whatever their camels could carry except weapons, 424
He entered Paradise having turned sideways, 104
He entered Paradise marching. After him, Ja'far, 103

He gave me a push or slap on the chest which made me sore, 195
He informed me that I entered Islam alone and would die alone, 132
He joined three fingers together and poked my chest, 196
He killed him and yet shares his high rank – meaning, in Paradise, 205
He placed his hand upon my head and opened my upper button, 195
He put up, in front of me, a blaze of fire like a lightning bolt, 208
He slapped my chest, I broke into a sweat as if looking at Allah, 194
He spat into his eyes and he was cured, 70
He told us about all that would take place from that time to the Rising, 32
He took a handful of dust and threw it in their direction, 292
He will not die until the wart disappears, 219
Hear and obey, even an Abyssinian slave, 134, 384
Hear, O Quraysh! By Allah, I bring you slaughter!, 284
Here is where So-and-so will find his demise, 289, 294
His kingdom has ended, 346
His last drink in the world shall be milk, 122
The Hour will not rise until tribes of my Umma join the pagans, 379
The Hour will not rise until you fight Khūz and Karmān, 315
How can you be the poor man of Quraysh when you own gold, 111
How many a weak, belittled servant wearing two tattered garments, 150
How will you fare, Abū Rayḥāna, when you pass by those who use a live animal as their shooting target, 251
Hush! By Allah, even if there is none among us to tell him, 26
I [Muʿāwiya] am the first of the kings, 388
I also know what is keeping you away from Islam. You are thinking: Only the weaklings follow him, 235
I am giving you glad tidings that Allah gave Jaʿfar two wings, 109
I am the Prophet, this is no fib! I am the son of ʿAbd al-Mut.t.alib!, 162
I am the scout at the Basin, 383
I am the Seal of Prophets: there is no Prophet after me!, 379
I appeal to Muḥammad by the time-honored pact of both our fathers, 173
I begged my Lord that my Community not be destroyed by famine, 377
I call upon You, my Lord, to grant us victory over them, 150
I call you to the witnessing that there is no God but Allah, 352
I can see (al-Ḥakam's) sons climbing up and down my pulpit, 403
I can see you wearing the armlets of Chosroes, 240
I can see you wearing the armlets of Chosroes, his girdle and crown, 371
I can see a spotted dog drooling over the blood of the people of my House, 80

I could tell you about a great number of those who will be in the Fire, 34
I dearly hope that Allah shall place his (ʿAdī's) hand in my hand, 232
I did not abase them but loathed to shed their blood (al-Ḥasan), 78
I did not think that Zayd was below Jaʿfar in rank, 111
I do not allow them at all to corrupt what I have reformed, 148
I do not fear poverty for you but that the world be open for you, 381
I do not know whether my companions forgot or pretended to, 32
I do not think he circumambulated it while we are under siege, 57
I entered Paradise and gazed. There was Jaʿfar flying with the angels, 109
I exhort you to beware of Allah, 384
I fear for my Community misguiding leaders, 379
I gifted musk and a tunic to the Negus but I believe he died, 416
I hate that people should say Muḥammad kills his Companions, 433
I have been given the keys to Persia!, 325
I have been given the keys to *Shām*, 325
I have been given the keys to Yemen, 325
I have heard Muḥammad ﷺ say he will kill you [Umayya b. Khalaf], 297
I have seen the spots where they are going to be killed, 296
I interpreted the black [sheep] to refer to the Arabs and the dirt-white to the non-Arabs, 369
I know better than you about your religion, 235
I know nothing except what my Lord taught me, 25, 276
I never saw any master of his people hoist water better than ʿUmar, 369
I received news that Ibn Nubayḥ al-Hudhalī is mobilizing, 153
I remind you by Allah concerning the Copts of Egypt!, 321
I saw a great flock of black sheep with a white sheep intermingled, 368
I saw in dream black sheep succeeded by dirt-white sheep. Abū Bakr! Interpret it, 368
I saw in my dream the Banū Umayya climbing up and down my pulpit in the shape of apes and pigs, 403
I saw Jaʿfar as an angel flying in Paradise, 110
I saw the Prophet ﷺ raising his hands supplicating, 56
I saw, last night, as if black sheep were following me. Then white sheep succeeded them, 367
I shall kill Ubay, 301
I shall not eat until you bear witness that there is no God but Allah and that I am the Messenger, 299
I shall not mutilate lest Allah mutilate me, even if I am a Prophet, 188

'I shall not spare you until I kill you!' Abū Jahl said: 'Are you able to do that?', 287
I shall show you a better way. Be led wherever they lead you, 132
I shall tell you what happened to your army, 102
I surely fear more for you your having much than your having little, 349
I swear that Abū Qatāda is on their tracks, taunting them with rhymes!, 159
I turned around and noticed that the Messenger of Allah ﷺ had tied up his belly with a stone, 329
I was granted the two treasures, the red and the white, 377
I was not sent to you except to bring you slaughter, 286
If Allah had not wished that you sleep through it [the prayer], you would not have slept, 119
If he [the Prophet] hit me only with his spittle he would kill me!, 304
If only the people stayed away from them *(i'tazalūhum)*!, 393
if someone enters to kill one of you, be like the better one of the two sons of Ādam, 398
If there is anyone in that host who commands goodness, it is the rider on the red camel ['Utba b. Rabī'a], 422
If this soil turns to blood, know that my son has been killed, 79
If this were something I claimed on my own, I would cease, 337
If you have her in your power, treat her gently!, 84
If you hear a ḥadīth reported from me which your hearts recognize, xxiii
If you submit, I shall give you what is under your authority, 337, 342
If you wish, Allah shall return your eye to you in a better state than it used to be, 198
If you wish, I can tell you what you came to ask me, and if you wish, I can wait until you ask, 281
If you wish, tell me the news and, if you wish, I shall tell you, 101
In the Mosque of al-Khayf is the grave of seventy Prophets, 282
In you all [al-'Abbās and his family] are Prophethood and Kingdom, 408
In you are two traits Allah loves: forbearance and equanimity, 266
In your defense, 'Amr b. Sālim!, 173
Invite your maternal uncle to Islam, 264
Is it new or has it been washed already?, 47
Is it poverty you fear when Allah is about to open to you the lands, 365
Īsā ﷺ will descend at the dawn prayer, 360
Israelites were ruled by Prophets. Every time one of them died, another succeeded him, 382
It may be Allah will grant victory at your hands, 96

It may be that you shall not meet me again after this year, 148
It may be that you will live on so that people will benefit from you, 94
It smells of hardship and affliction, 79
It was Jibrīl and lo! your sight shall fade and return to you only at the time of death, 116
It was shown to me the abode of your emigration was a saline land, 126
Its agents shall enter the Fire except those that fear Allah, 330
Ja'far b. Abī Ṭālib went past in a group of angels flying, 101-103, 110
Jews ﴾**earned Divine anger**﴿ (1:7) and Christians are misguided, 233
Jibrīl told me that my son, al-Ḥusayn, would be killed, 78-81
Jibrīl! How was he granted such a rank by Allah?, 260
Jibrīl, why did the sun rise today white, with its full heat and light, 258
Just as she said, this is the Father of Caliphs, Caliphate will be yours, 113
Just so did the angel interpret it [to me] before the dawn, 368
Keep firm, Uḥud!, 41
The killer of 'Ammār and his plunderer are in the Fire, 123
Kisrā! Are you going to accept Islam before I break this staff?, 332
Kisrā! Surrender, or else I shall break your kingdom, 334
Kissing neither annuls ablution nor cancels the fast, 85
"*Labbayka*" –thrice– then "*nuṣirta*", 171
Last night as [I dreamed] I was hoisting up [water from a well], 369
The last of you to die shall be in the fire, 181
'Leave him!' When he approached, the Prophet ﷺ took the spear, 303
Leave me be today and come back tomorrow, then I will inform you, 335
Leave what seems dubious to you for what does not seem dubious, 248
Let it not make anyone quit practicing [archery] with his arrows!, 329
Let whoever oversleeps of my Community do the same, 119
Lion! I am Safīna, the freedman of the Messenger of Allah ﷺ, 389
Little daughter, be still, 291
Little time shall pass before Persian and Romans are conquered, 365
Look for a travel companion, 236
A man came out of a tent nearby and looked at the sky... he stood and prayed, 370
A man from among you shall die in a desert attended by Muslims, 129
A man from Paradise is about to come, 59
A man from the dwellers of Paradise is about to come, 36, 46
A man from the people of Paradise is about to enter, 45
A man is about to come looking at you with the eye of a devil, 436
A man might be given a hundred [dinars] but he will scorn it, 349

A man shall enter from this gate from the dwellers of Paradise, 143
A man shall awake as a believer in the morning and reach night as a disbeliever, 398
Many lands shall be laid open for you. Allah will suffice you, 329
"May Allah bless your mouth!" After this, he never lost a tooth, 165
May Allah forgive you, Messenger of Allah, 34
May Allah not bless Yazīd in anything, 397
May they be disfigured! ﴾**Hā Mīm**﴿. They shall not be victorious!, 211
May they perish the day they kill 'Uthmān, 41
Meccans brought the Prophet their children to pray for them, 417
Messenger of Allah ﷺ announced the Negus' death on its day, 417
Messenger of Allah ﷺ called 'Abd al-Malik 'father of four tyrants', 400
Messenger of Allah ﷺ took pebbles and threw them in their faces, 211
Messenger of Allah ﷺ cursed Marwān's father as he was in his loins, 402
Messenger of Allah ﷺ designated Dhūl-Ḥulayfa as a pilgrim's initial consecration-point for Medinans, 421
Messenger of Allah ﷺ informed us that we would be the victims, 145
Messenger of Allah ﷺ did not omit one instigator of sedition, 32
Messenger of Allah ﷺ endowed me with a land in al-Shām known as "the Valley", 319
Messenger of Allah ﷺ forbade us to put this substance in our bellies, 386
Messenger of Allah ﷺ foretold us our raiding India, 316
Messenger of Allah ﷺ announced my coming to them three days before, 226
Messenger of Allah ﷺ cursed [Ḥakam b. Abī al-'Āṣ] and progeny, 402
Messenger of Allah gave him a young she-camel and said: Allah shall bless you with it, 237
Messenger of Allah ﷺ informed me of the differences after him, 414
Messenger of Allah ﷺ informed me they could not kill me, 131
"Messenger of Allah, none aided us like So-and-so." "He is in hellfire", 428
Messenger of Allah, only recently were we in a time of ignorance, 33
Messenger of Allah ﷺ sighted the clavicle of Ubay b. Khalaf, 301
Messenger of Allah ﷺ slapped him between his shoulder-blades and said: "Then Allah shall disgrace you!", 192
Messenger of Allah ﷺ told me both jinn and human beings shall share responsibility in [shedding] my blood, 252
Messenger of Allah ﷺ told me that I would not die in Mecca, the, 90
Messenger of Allah ﷺ told me that my sight would fade and it did, 117

Messenger of Allah ﷺ took a covenant from me, 52
Messenger of Allah ﷺ walked over and slapped him in the chest, 196
The Messenger of Allah ﷺ walked over to him and slapped him in the chest, saying: "Then Allah shall disgrace you!", The, 193
The molar tooth of one of them in the Fire shall be greater than Uḥud, 186
Money shall flow to the point that no one will accept it from you, 235
The most criminal of all people is he that shall strike you (ʿAlī) here, 64
Muʿāwiya, Allah gave you some responsibility over this Community, 202
Muʿāwiya, when you receive authority over a certain affair, fear Allah and be just!, 200
Muʿāwiya, when you rule, rule well, 199
Muʿāwiya will never lose!, 203
Muslims shall have three chief regions, 360
My beloved, the Messenger of Allah ﷺ, informed me that the rebellious faction shall kill me, 122
My Companions were killed, but later, I saw them ﴾**as brethren, face to face, resting on couches raised**﴿, 106
My eyes were never sore nor inflamed again ('Alī), 73
My faith and authority shall reach all of Chosroes' empire, 337, 342
My father's relatives are not my patrons and friends, 149
My funeral has just been announced, 76
My Lord destroyed Chosroes and there will no longer be a Chosroes, 338
My Lord has promised me Abū al-Dardā' would submit, 139
My Lord killed your Lord [Chosroes] last night, 331, 339
My Lord told me to let grow my beard freely and cut my moustache, 341
My nephew has informed me–he never lied to me!–Allah wants nothing to do with this charter, 307, 311
My only Patron and Friend is Allah with the righteous believers, 149
Never was there Prophethood but Caliphate followed it, 385
News came to the Prophet ﷺ the night al-Aswad al-ʿAnsī was killed, 420
No [*fitna*] as long as Ibn al-Khaṭṭāb is alive (Khālid), 50
No dissension can reach as long as this man is among you, 50
No harm shall come to you from your sickness, 147
No people shall prosper who are ruled by a woman, 338
No two goats will butt heads over her, 156
No, it is the sandal repairman, 59
None shall die with a mustard seed's worth of love (Ḥudhayfa), 55
Now blazes the furnace, 105
Nuḍayr! Is this better, or what you wanted to do at Ḥunayn?, 254

Nuʿmān b. Bashīr supplicated Allah for Ibn al-Zubayr. So the people of Himṣ killed him, 152
O Allah! Count it as a good deed for Abū Sufyān, guide him with it, 199
O Allah! drive away from him its heat and its coolness and its harm, 194
O Allah! Forgive ʿAbd al-Qays, 266
O Allah! Grant him blessing in his transaction, 109
O Allah! Grant him steadfastness and make him a guide of righteousness and a rightly guided one!, 195
O Allah! Guide his heart and make firm his tongue, 195
O Allah! If You wish, let it be ʿAlī, 46
O Allah! Make him more steadfast, 255
O Allah! remove from him hot and cold, 73
O Allah! You have completed for me what You had promised, 290
O Allah, do not let me [Abū Hurayra] live to see the year 60, 396
O Allah, protect him from the devil, 208
O Allah, teach him [Muʿāwiya] writing, make firm his power, 203
O Allah, ward it off from them, 227
O people, the Lord is a single lord, the father is a single father, the faith is a single faith, 438
O So-and-so son of So-and-so! Did you find true what your Lord had promised?, 294
One does not attain true God-wariness until one leaves alone all that troubles the conscience, 248
One of you [women] will come out riding a heavy-maned red camel, 86
One person in this group shall end up in the Fire, 185
The one that is bottom-side is a dead man.' Then the idolater fell, 92
The one who sits at that time is better than the one who stands, 398
Over you looms the shadow of a Prophet who is the last Prophet, 222
Pay the right you owe and ask Allah for the right owed to you, 383
The people of my House believe that they are closest to me, 148
The people of my House will endure trial, alienation, and expulsion, 411
The people of my House will meet with murder and dispossession after my time, 414
People will only bear witness for their friends, 398
People! Do not loathe Muʿāwiya's leadership, 204
People! Truly, your lives and properties are sacred to one another, 124
Perhaps Allah shall let you meet Ukaydir while he is hunting, 168
Perhaps he shall one day take a stand of which you will approve, 188, 190
Perhaps the way will open for you this year, so go back, Ḥabīb, 239

Perhaps you came to ask Fāṭima's hand?, 64
Perish these faces! *(qabuḥat al-wujūh)*, 287, 292
Persia and Byzantium shall be laid open for you, 363
Persia will give one or two head-butts then there will be no more Persia, 372
Pray over your friend [without me], 430
Prophet ﷺ went to Abū Sufyān and slapped his chest, saying: "With Allah he is beating you!", 198
Prophet ﷺ compared the world to some rain water on a mountain plateau, 318
Prophet ﷺ gave command to Zayd b. Ḥāritha over the Mu'ta expedition, 98
Prophet ﷺ gave Khuzayma's testimony the weight of two testimonies, 238
Prophet ﷺ handed me a handful of red earth, 84
Prophet ﷺ informed Chosroes' envoy of the death of Chosroes the same day he died, 340
Prophet ﷺ informed me of all that would happen until the Day of Resurrection, 32
Prophet ﷺ jumped up with a motion that sent us scampering away from him, 303
Prophet ﷺ mentioned that one of the Mothers of the Believers would go to war, 84
Prophet ﷺ never struck anyone in the chest suffering from satanic influence except he was cured, 194
Prophet ﷺ once nicknamed Abū Dharr "Junaydib", 129
Prophet ﷺ ordered that the bodies of the idolaters slain on the Day of Badr be thrown into a well, 295
Prophet ﷺ ordered us to tend unto our religion and act against al-Aswad the Arch-Liar, 419
Prophet ﷺ placed his hand on my chest, 196
Prophet ﷺ prayed *fajr* with us then climbed the pulpit, 30
Prophet ﷺ said, pointing to the heart: Fear of Allah is right here, 248
Prophet ﷺ slapped his chest and said three times: "Off, devil!", The, 194
Prophet ﷺ stood among us [speaking] for a long time, 31
Prophet ﷺ taught him ﴾***al-Ḥamd***﴿ and ﴾***Iqra' bismi Rabbik***﴿, 264
Prophet ﷺ took my pledge that I must fight traitors, 61, 414
Prophet ﷺ went out to Banū al-Naḍīr to assist them with the issue of the blood-price of the Kilābīs, 423
Prophet named Mas'ūd b. al-Ḍaḥḥāk "Obeyed among your people", 238

Prophet put his hand on Faḍāla b. ʿUmayr al-Laythī's chest, 196
Prophet took me by the hand, The, 232
A Prophet who sees around him what others do not (Ḥassān), 28
Prophethood has been reshuffled and has become monarchy, 397
The public trust will become spoils of war, 398
Qabāth! Are you the one who said, the day of the battle of Badr: I never saw anything like this, 257
Qays! Perhaps, if you live long enough, you might serve, after me, under rulers to whom you will be unable to speak the truth, 250
Quit chattering in him, devil!, 212
Quraysh are restless against ʿAmmār, The, 123
Rāfiʿ, if you wish, I shall remove both the arrow and the *qiṭba*, 162
Ransom yourself with your property in Jeddah, 118
The rebellious faction shall kill you, 120
Receive the glad tidings! A day shall come when one of you will have meat and bread for breakfast and dinner, 331
Recite to them ﴾Those who disbelieve among the People of the Scripture and the idolaters﴿, 124
Religion is absolute good faith, 217
Religion will not cease to be strong until <the rising of the Hour of Judgment, 382
Remit them to Abū Bakr, 41
Return with him for he is going to die soon, 240
Ride out until you reach the meadow of Khākh, 139
Riders are about to come into your sight from this direction who are the best of the people of the East, 263
The Rightly-Guided Caliphs counted Khuzayma's word as two men, 238
Romans shall enter into a firm truce with you, 316
Sacrifices of Allah are being slaughtered there as we speak, The, 227
Save those on board the ship!, 179
Say nothing to me as long as I say nothing to you, 34
Say the Name of Allah and go!, 296
Say: 'Muḥammad believes, and I am the first of the believers', 124
The seat of reason is the heart, 248
Seek refuge in Allah from the year 70 and the rule of boys, 394
Send for that force. No harm will come your way this year, 241
Shayba, come here! I went near him and he wiped my breast, 208
"Shayba, come on!" by which Allah jolted his heart with fear, 212

Shayba, what Allah desired for you is better than what you desired for yourself, 208
Should I not weep when I can see you decorating your houses the way you decorate the Ka'ba?, 378
The sign by which you shall know him is that when you see him you will get goose flesh, 153
'Sit on this [cushion].' and he sat on the floor, 234
Sit quietly in your house for Allah shall grant you martyrdom, 246
A small band of Muslims will conquer the house of Chosroes, A, 382
Smash your swords against rocks, 398
Some hypocrite has gloated that the she-camel of the Messenger of Allah had gotten lost, 272
Some men among you gathered and said such and such. Ask forgiveness of Allah!, 435
Some of us would refrain from approaching his wife, 29
Some of you are hypocrites, so whoever I name, let them stand up, 435
Speak justice and give away your surplus, 270
Spray it with water.' They sprayed it then the Prophet ﷺ came, seized the pick, said *'Bismillāh!'* and struck it, 328
Successorship of Prophethood will last for thirty years, 389
The sun shall not set before Allah first brings you some sustenance, 55
Take al-Ḥārith b. Suwayd outside the door of the mosque and strike his neck, 278
Take for your leaders the two that come after me, 37
Take it, [with a right] revered and time-honored, 206
Take it, Banū Ṭalḥa, [with a right] revered, immortal, time-honored, 213
Take the Father of Caliphs with you, 113, 408
Tamīm, you tell me what you discussed or, if you wish, I'll tell you, 214
Tell him he shall be my successor after 'Umar, 38
Tell him he shall be my successor after Abū Bakr, 38
Tell me the truth. What brings you, 'Umayr?, 176
Tell them we have not come to fight but for the Minor Pilgrimage, 57
Tell your friend my Lord killed his lord Chosroes seven hours ago, 335
Then where is the money you and Umm al-Faḍl buried, 112
There are four in Mecca I consider above any suspicion, 187
There are seventy-odd missionaries of hellfire in my Community, 33
There is in you ('Alī) a similarity to 'Īsā ﷺ, 68
There is no leader of one hundred or more except the Prophet ﷺ named him for us, 33

There is no Prophet after me! There will be successors, many 382
There shall be a dissension and strife, 52
There shall be among you twelve caliphs, 40
There shall be dissensions and your people shall argue with you, 63
There shall be, among you, one who shall fight over the interpretation of the Qur'ān, 59
There will appear a man of my House, after a lapse of time, 412
There will be favoritism and things you will find reprehensible, 383
there will be <a tyrannical kingship> for as long as Allah wishes, 390
There will be a conflict between you and ʿĀ'isha, 85
there will be a later generation who recite the Qur'ān but it will not reach beyond their throats, 394
there will be a trying kingship for as long as Allah wishes, 390
There will be arch-liars just before the Hour <so beware of them, 383
there will be caliphate after the pattern of Prophethood, 390
there will be caliphate after the pattern of Prophethood, 390
there will be in my Community thirty arch-liars, all claiming that he or she is a Prophet, 379
There will be in this Community a man called al-Walīd who will be worse than Fir'awn, 405
There will be Prophethood among you for as long as Allah wishes, 390
There will be, after sixty years, a generation who ruined worship, 393
There will not cease to be a group in my Umma that follows truth, 379
There will be leaders who are so busy they will delay the prayer, 407
These are allies, not foes! The tribe of Sulaym b. Manṣūr have come, 242
These are the hypocrites until the Day of Resurrection, 433
These are the ones that shall govern after me, 39
These are the sandals of [Thaʿlaba] Ibn Sa'ya coming to announce to me Rayḥāna's *islām*, 91
These shall be torn asunder but those shall have some remnants, 340
They are Abū Mūsā al-Ash'arī's people [a people whom He loves and who love Him], 181
They [Romans] are a people of rocks and sea, and so on to the end of time, 372
They [Romans] will be with you as long as there is something to be gained from living, 372
They are going to kill you, 220
They have come with a holy man leading them, 179

They plotted to ride alongside me until I was on top of the cliff so they would push me off it, 432
They shall turn my Community away from her Religion, 149
This [light] illumined the cities for me, 323
This [ʿAbd Allāh ibn ʿAbbās] is the father of caliphs until al-Saffāḥ, 408
This (ʿUmar) is the bolt against dissension, 49
This boy shall live for a century, 218
This clan of the Quraysh shall remain safe until, 34
This cloud is initiating the victory of the Banū Kaʿb, 173
This glittering Ḥīra [in Iraq] was brought up before my eyes, 356
This great matter will continue to be moderate and stand on justice, 392
This is from the ground on which he [al-Ḥusayn] shall be killed, 84
This is the grave of Abū Righāl. He is the progenitor of Thaqīf, 430
This is Muḥammad, my nephew, together with his wife Khadīja and his paternal cousin ʿAlī, 370
This is what I say – and you [Abū Jahl] are among the slaughtered, 290
This is what Muḥammad the Messenger of Allah has appropriated for Tamīm al-Dārī, 215
This is a writ in which is stated what Muḥammad the Messenger of Allah granted to the Dāriyyīn, 215
This man (ʿUthmān), at that time [*fitna*], shall follow right guidance, 53
This man was killed by the Messenger of Allah ﷺ. This is Ubay b. Khalaf, 305
This power shall continue to remain with you until Allah opens up the lands of Persia, 349
This son of mine (al-Ḥasan) is a leader of men, xxxvi, 77
This son of mine' (al-Ḥusayn), 81
This staff is a sign between you and me on the Day of Resurrection, 153
This was the poetry champion of the Banū Kaʿb invoking my aid, 171
This wind was sent because of the death of a hypocrite, 272
Those men you see are of those Allah shall slaughter at your hands, 288
Those of our people that will hate us the most are the Banū Umayya and the Banū al-Mughīra, 414
Those who will destroy the people are this clan of the Quraysh, 393
Three types will be reciting the Qur'ān: the Believer, the hypocrite, and the open rebel, 394
time has almost come when wealth shall flow among them to the point no one can be found to take it, 234

time has almost come when you will hear that a woman can travel out of al-Qādisiyya on her camel, 234
time has almost come when you will hear that the white palaces of Babylon have been conquered, 234
time will come when people will see the truthful one be to be considered a liar, 395
Today a beggar came to you and you turned him away, 88
Today a righteous man died, so pray over Aṣḥama, 416
Today you are none other than a ship *(safīna)*, 388
Today you will ask me about nothing except I shall tell you about it, 33
Today, you love one another, but that day, you will hate one another, 379
Tomorrow I'll give the flag to one who loves Allah and His Messenger, 72
Tomorrow I'll give the flag to a man Allah and His Messenger love, 70
Tomorrow shall come a people more sensitive in their hearts than you, 179
Tonight a man of wisdom shall come to you, 178
The treasures of Chosroes shall certainly be conquered, 230
Truly he [Khālid] is one of Your drawn swords, 102
Twelve caliphs first rule over you, all of them from the Quraysh, 382
Two groups in my Community whom Allah has protected from the Fire; one is a group that shall raid India, 316
Two types of people shall perish concerning me ('Alī), 68
A tyrant of the Banū Umayya will bleed from the nose on this pulpit, 404
'Umar b. 'Abd al-'Azīz made everyone rich, 232
'Umar! The Qur'an is all correct as long as you do not turn mercy into punishment, 194
Umm Salama, keep the door closed, 83
'Uqba tried to strangle the Prophet ﷺ with his cloak as the latter was praying at the Ka'ba, 300
'Uthmān! Allah may vest you with a shirt, 41
'Uthmān passed by me while one of the angels was with me, 51
'Uthmān! You will be given the caliphate after me but the hypocrites, 53
'Uthman, you may see this key in my hand one day; then I shall dispose of it in any way I wish, 206
'Uwaymir is the wise man of my Community; Jundub is the fugitive, 133
Victory is yours, and much booty, and many conquests, 376
Virtue consists in good character and vice is that which disquiets you and which you would hate for people to see, 248
Virtue is what sets the soul and heart at rest, 247

Virtue is what sets the soul at rest and brings peace of mind, 248
Virtue is what sets your mind at rest and vice is what pricks your conscience, 247
Wābiṣa! Consult yourself, no matter what people keep saying to you, 247
Wābiṣa! Shall I tell you what you came to ask me about? You came to ask me about virtue and vice, 247
Wait and see! It will not be long until Allah causes you to inherit the land of Chosroes, 353
Walīd is the name of Pharaoh. He is a destroyer of the laws of Islam, 397
We [Muʿāwiya] are satisfied with kingdom, 389
We feel he shall be killed on the shore of the Euphrates, 82
We have found our Lord's promise to be true; have you found your Lord's promise to be true?, 295
We held the Messenger of Allah ﷺ in great awe and reverence, 63
We kept away from conversation with our women, 29
Were it not for fear that you would stop burying one another, 34
What are you but a finger that bled in the way of Allah?, 162
What bright clothes he [ʿAbd Allāh ibn ʿAbbās] wears! But his children will wear black, 410
What brings you?, 63
what is Islam?" He said: "Your bearing witness that there is no God but Allah and that I am the Messenger of Allah, 235
What is stopping you from accepting Islam?, 242
What prevented you from giving salaam?, 116
What will happen to you when Allah vests you (Muʿāwiya) with a certain shirt?, 201
What will one of you women do when the dogs of Ḥaw'ab bark at her?, 86
What will you do when you and your camel amble on your way to Syro-Palestine, 418
What will you do when you wear the armlets of Chosroes?, 371
When al-Dajjāl sees 'Īsā, he will melt like lead. 'Īsā will spear him, 360
When Allah gives one of you material goods, let him begin with himself and his dependents, 383
When Allah opens for us Syro-Palestine, that land is yours, 319
when Caesar perishes there will be no more Caesar after him, 372
When Chosroes perishes there will be no more Chosroes after him, 372
When construction reaches Salʿ, depart from here, 134
When Egypt is conquered, treat the Copts *(al-qibṭ)* well! For they have inviolable rights, 320

When he was wounded he flinched, so he rebuked himself, 104
When his children number thirty they will control leadership, 403
When I find you outside the mountains of Mecca, I will execute you, 299
When my Umma struts in pomp and the children of Persia and Byzantium serve them, 364
When the armies met at Mu'ta the Messenger of Allah ﷺ sat on the *minbar*, 103
When the Banū al-Ḥakam reach thirty men, they will take the treasury of Allah for their own, 399
When the Banū Umayya reach forty men, they will take the servants of Allah as their own servants, 401
When the houses reach Salʿ, exit from here, 128
When the Messenger of Allah ﷺ left us there was not a bird, 30
When the sword is thrust at my Umma it will not be lifted from them, 379
When they resort to jargon, say: 'Translate it!', 125
When you are in a certain land and hear two men quarrelling, 138
When you arrive at the land of his people, beware of him, 236
When you get to their country, do not enter it by night but wait until morning, 124
When you see construction on Mount Salʿ, go and live with the Bedouins, 130
When you see him you will be awed and feel afraid of him, 155
when you see two men fight with one another over the placement of a brick, leave, 320
Where among the lands of Allah is Shukar, 227
Where are the two camels you hid in al-'Aqīq, in such-and-such a woodland?, 229
Where is the remainder of the thousand?, 241
Which of you is ʿAbd Allāh b. ʿAwf al-Ashajj?, 266
Who is the man?' I replied, 'ʿAdī b. Ḥātim.', 234
"Who is your Lord?" She said, "Allah", 194
'Who is your representative?' She said, ʿAdī b. Ḥātim, 233
Who will defend me against the daughter of Marwān?, 156
Who will guard us?' I said, 'I will.' He replied: 'You will fall asleep, 119
Whoever abstains [from illicit things], Allah shall forgive him, 163
Whoever cannot adapt to Shām, let him go to Yemen, 318
Whoever climbs up the the *Murār* Pass—verily it shall remit sins, 439
Whoever does without [his needs], Allah shall enrich him, 163
Whoever Khuzayma witnesses for or against, it is enough for him, 238

Whoever of you lives shall live to see great divisions, 384
Whoever of you wishes, take the valley road, it is wider for you, 431
Whoever speaks Arabic is an Arab, 438
Whoever worshipped Muḥammad, truly, Muḥammad has died, 188-190
Why are you terrified of saying *Lā ilāha illa-l-Lāh*? Do you know of a god other than the One God?, 233
Why is it, 'Ā'ish, that you are out of breath?, 195
Will you kill a man because he says, 'My Sovereign Lord is Allah'?, 300
Will you not be happy that he live as his maternal uncle lived, 151
With this strike Allah shall bring me the people of Yemen as helpers and supporters, 323
With this strike Allah shall lay open for us the treasures of Persia, 323
With this strike Allah shall lay open for us the treasures of the Romans, 323
Woe to my Community because of [al-Ḥakam's] unborn progeny, 404
Woe to the Arabs for a disaster that is fast approaching, 398
Woe to you when I am gone!, 130
Woe to you! Who told you to do such a thing?, 341
Woe to your mother! Many [a horse] turn away from you in war!, 159
world east and west shall be laid open for my Community, The, 330
world is sweet and verdant. Allah will surely make you inherit it, 375
world shall be laid open for you to the point that you will be furnishing your houses, 329
world will certainly glut you three times, 378
world will not pass before it first belongs to a mean fool son of a mean fool, The, 394
Would you not be happy to live a blameless life, die a martyr, and enter Paradise?, 147
Write it, for truly you shall suffer something similar, 67
Yes, this was Jibrīl, and he ['Abd Allāh] shall not die before first losing his sight, 115
You ('Alī) shall be given leadership and caliphate, 69
You ('Alī) shall certainly experience great hardship after me, 61
You are about to see Abū Sufyān coming and saying, 'Renew the treaty, 191
You are Abū Ṣufra. Rid yourself of "Thief" and "Felon.", 244
You are better off today than when a dish for ten is served to you, 365, 378-379
You are lying! You said to them such-and-such, 283

You are pregnant with a boy. When you give birth, bring him to me, 113, 408
You asked Hind, 'Do you consider that this is from Allah?' Yes, it is from Allah!, 196
You came to ask about your late-night prayer, your bowing, your prostrating, 281
You came to ask about your leaving your home to head for the Ancient Mosque and what you should, 281
You did not witness Badr with us. Truly, we did not vanquish through numbers, 100
You do not hear better than they do but they are unable to reply, 294
You have a date that you call such-and-such," and he went on to list all the various types of dates they grew, 267
You have helped Allah and His Prophet, O ʿUmayr, 156
You might live to see people perform prayers outside their times, 406
You might reach a time a dish for ten will be served to each one, 379
You must follow my Sunna and the Sunna of the rightly-guided, upright successors, 384
You must go to Shām, 317
You said many shall renege." He said: "Yes, but not you", 137
You saw a mole on her cheek that made every hair of yours stand!, 87
You shall behold a man bring out his two hands' fill of gold or silver, 230
You shall experience, after I am gone, favoritism, 144
You shall never conquer any city until the Day of Resurrection except Allah ﷻ gave Muḥammad ﷺ its keys beforehand, 322
You shall rebel against him and fight him unjustly, 91
You shall remain steadfast in Islam to your death, 143
You will all be joining [opposite] armies: one army in al-Shām, one in Yemen, and one in Iraq, 317
You will conquer a land where the *qīrāṭ* is mentioned. Treat its people well, 320
You will definitely live on, you will definitely emigrate to the land of Shām, and you will die and be buried in al-Ramla, 253
You will divide into three armies: one in Syro-Palestine, 349
You will find him [Ukaydir] hunting oxen, 167
You will find him hunting oxen, 165
You will own fringed rugs, 380
You will raid the Anti-Christ (al-Dajjāl) and Allah shall defeat him, 367
You will raid the Arabian peninsula and Allah shall lay it open, 366

You will see a legion of their fleshy-rumped white men under the command, 350
Your friend has acted treacherously in the path of Allah, 430
Your land was displayed for me to see from the moment you sat with me, 267
Zayd b. Ḥāritha is in command of the troops; if Zayd is killed, then Ja‘far b. Abī Ṭālib, 99, 102
Zayd carried the flag and was struck down; then Ja‘far seized it and was struck down, 97
Zayd took the flag, whereupon the devil came to him and made him long for life, 103
Zayd will not survive the fever of the town, 225
Zubayr b. Bāṭā said: ‘I did read his description in the Books of the Torah’, 426

Lightning Source UK Ltd.
Milton Keynes UK
UKHW040944211221
396026UK00001B/6

9 781938 058622